Yankees Coming, Yankees Going

ALSO BY LYLE SPATZ

New York Yankee Openers:
An Opening Day History of Baseball's
Most Famous Team, 1903–1996
(McFarland, 1997)

Yankees Coming, Yankees Going

New York Yankee Player Transactions, 1903 Through 1999

by
LYLE SPATZ

McFarland & Company, Inc., Publishers
Jefferson, North Carolina, and London

Library of Congress Cataloguing-in-Publication Data

Spatz, Lyle, 1937–
    Yankees coming, Yankees going : New York Yankee player
transactions, 1903 through 1999 / by Lyle Spatz.
        p.   cm.
    Includes bibliographical references and index.
    ISBN 0-7864-0787-5 (illustrated case binding : 50# alkaline paper)
    1. New York Yankees (Baseball team)—History.
    2. Baseball players—Trading of—United States—History.
    I. Title.
    GV875.N4S65   2000
    796.357'64'097471—dc21   99-57767

British Library Cataloguing-in-Publication data are available

Manufactured in the United States of America

*McFarland & Company, Inc., Publishers
    Box 611, Jefferson, North Carolina 28640
    www.mcfarlandpub.com*

For my grandson,
Kyle Benjamin Spatz,
with love

Contents

Preface

The trading, buying, and selling of players has forever been an indispensable part of the quest to create better baseball teams, while also serving as a major contributor to the game's history and folklore. However, the most important aspect of these deals may be their amazing ability to stir the interest and passion of fans. Whether it is the purchase of a veteran star during the heat of a pennant race, or a multiplayer trade made in the dead of winter, player transactions engender more interest and heated debate among fans than almost any other aspect of the game. In no other sport are the movements of players from one team to another so eagerly anticipated and analyzed as they are in baseball. More than three quarters of a century have now passed since the Boston Red Sox sold Babe Ruth to the New York Yankees. Yet, it remains not only the most important player transaction in sports history, but also the one most discussed and written about. Baseball fans love trade rumors; they love to hear about them, to read about them, and to talk about them. They even love those that are rumored but don't get made. We are still pondering the "what-ifs" of the Joe DiMaggio for Ted Williams deal.

Ostensibly, there is in every trade the assumption that the combination of current players, future players, and or money that a particular team is getting is approximately equal in value to what it is giving up. Red Sox owner Harry Frazee tried to convince the Boston fans that the money he was receiving in exchange for Ruth would allow him to buy the players to keep the Red Sox on top. Of course, it did not work out that way. It often doesn't. Furthermore, some trades that seem one-sided when they are made, often turn out to be so, but not necessarily in favor of the team that appeared to have the advantage initially.

The Yankees, who played their first American League game on April 22, 1903, made their first trade seven weeks later, on June 10. They sent Herman Long, a veteran shortstop, and Ernie Courtney, a second-year infielder, to the Detroit Tigers for Kid Elberfeld, the Tigers' disgruntled shortstop. On learning of the trade, Elberfeld said: "I always wanted to play in a large city like New York. The encouragement a fellow gets from the fans aids his playing, and when I get used to the diamond there I expect to play better than ever."

Since that first deal, the Yankees have been involved in more than six hundred additional transactions, and with very few exceptions, the desire to play for the Yankees, or in New York, has remained constant. For each of those transactions—each trade, sale, purchase, or free agent signing—both the players and the deal are put in historical perspective. Also explained: the reasons why the Yanks and the other club involved made the deal; the expectations the owners, general managers, and managers of the respective teams had for their new players, and, for some, what the players involved thought about their old and new teams.

The primary source for information and quotes relating to these transactions was the newspapers of the day. Primary sources for statistical data were *Total Baseball*, fifth and sixth editions, *The Sporting News Baseball Registers*, and *The Sporting News Baseball Guides*. This book focuses strictly on the baseball aspects of these transactions, and for the most part deliberately excludes discussions of money and length of contracts, including these details only when they were believed essential to the story. Obviously, the business aspects of baseball transactions are important, especially in the age of free agency; however, it is a subject covered adequately elsewhere.

This book does not cover players the Yankees signed or drafted as amateurs, nor does it cover transactions involving players who were signed by or traded to or from the Yankees but never played for their new team. Outfielder Ken Williams, pitcher Robin Roberts, and first baseman Sam Horn are examples of players who were traded to but never played for the Yankees, and first baseman Joe Collins and pitcher Bill Bevens are examples of players the Yanks sold, but who never played for their new teams. Lifelong Yankees, such as Lou Gehrig, Joe DiMaggio, Mickey Mantle, Whitey Ford, and Don Mattingly, appear in the narratives only in their relation to other transactions.

As for the various teams, reference is made to the name that was current at the time of the transaction, with one exception: this book uses the name "Yankees" throughout. There is precedence for this, for although between 1903 and 1912 the team was perhaps better known as the "Highlanders," several New York newspapers had begun calling them the "Yankees" as early as 1904. For minor league teams, the league in which they played will be identified, and often its classification.

Mention of a player as a minor leaguer in the title of a trade means that he has never before appeared in a major league game. And unless specifically noted, a player's career end specifically refers to his *major* league career. Many players, particularly in the days before salaries became so large, would return to the minor leagues when their time in the big leagues ended.

Because this is primarily a reference book, each trade is treated as if the reader is looking at it without necessarily having read what came before. This makes it necessary to repeat certain facts pertaining to individual players and teams, for which your forbearance is begged.

During my research I came across errors in many of the trade dates listed in the encyclopedias and trade registers. Several were off by weeks or even months. For instance, the Yankees traded Gordon Rhodes to the Red Sox for Wilcy Moore on August 1, 1932, not May 1; they sold Russ Van Atta to the St. Louis Browns on May 15, 1935, not July 15; they traded Allie Clark to Cleveland for Red Embree on December 11, 1947, not October 10.

A few transaction dates proved exceptionally difficult to ascertain. For their help in tracking them down, I thank my SABR colleagues Jim Charlton, Joe Dittmar, Jerry Gregory, Bob McConnell, Tony Morante, Lee Sinins, John Phillips, and Joe Simenic. I also thank Jim Charlton and Joe Dittmar for their encouragement and advice when this project was taking shape, with a special thanks to Joe for his generously allowing me to use many of the photos that appear in this book. Other photos are from the National Baseball Library, Transcendental Graphics and from the George Brace collection.

Most of all, I thank my wife Marilyn for her patience, her support, and her love.

Lyle Spatz
Edgewater, Maryland

I. The Early Years

On January 10, 1903, at the St. Nicholas Hotel in Cincinnati, the National and American leagues reached an agreement that ended their two-year war. The two leagues had been battling over the ownership rights to players ever since 1901, when the Americans declared themselves a major league. A crucial feature of the peace agreement settled the question, with a few exceptions, of which players belonged to which teams. The agreement also recognized the relocation of the American League's Baltimore franchise to New York in return for a guarantee that the Americans would stay out of Pittsburgh.

Eighteen players were assigned to the New York club, consisting mainly of two groups: former National League players and those players who had moved with the team from Baltimore. The first roster for the New York American League team, the one that opened the 1903 season at Washington on April 22, included these players:

PITCHERS: Clark Griffith, Jesse Tannehill, Jack Chesbro, Harry Howell, Barney Wolfe, Doc Adkins, and Snake Wiltse

CATCHERS: Jack O'Connor and Monte Beville

INFIELDERS: John Ganzel, Jimmy Williams, Wid Conroy, Herman Long, and Ernie Courtney

OUTFIELDERS: Willie Keeler, Dave Fultz, Lefty Davis, and Herm McFarland

June 10, 1903: Traded Shortstop Herman Long and Infielder Ernie Courtney to the Detroit Tigers for Shortstop Kid Elberfeld

The Yankees were 17-23 and in seventh place when they made their first-ever trade. It was for shortstop Kid Elberfeld, whom the Tigers had recently suspended and had tried unsuccessfully to trade to the Philadelphia Athletics. Although the 28-year-old Elberfeld had been the Tigers' regular shortstop since 1901, and was batting .341 at the time of the trade, he was glad to leave Detroit.

"I always wanted to play in a large city like New York," Elberfeld said. "The encouragement a fellow gets from the fans aids his playing, and when I get used to the diamond there I expect to play better than ever."

Both Tigers president Samuel Angus and manager Ed Barrow appeared pleased to have unloaded Elberfeld. "I am perfectly satisfied with the deal," said Angus. "I am an admirer of [Herman] Long and believe [Ernie] Courtney will make a good third baseman. In Long we have a player of wonderful gameness and inside knowledge of how to play ball at critical stages."

Herman Long had reached the major

June 10, 1903: *Kid Elberfeld*. **The disgruntled Tiger shortstop was the first player the Yankees traded for.**

leagues back in 1889 with Kansas City of the American Association, which then had major league status. From 1890 to 1902 he'd been the star shortstop for the Boston club of the National League, before jumping to the newly created American League franchise in New York this season. Long had been among the nineteenth century's best players, but at 37 he was far past his prime and this would be his final season. He'd played only 22 games for the Yankees and was batting just .188.

Ernie Courtney, playing in his second major league season, had a .266 average in 25 games this year, mostly at shortstop.

July 16, 1903: Traded Infielder Paddy Greene to the Detroit Tigers for Cash and the Rights to Righthanded Pitcher John Deering

When the Yanks needed a fill-in for shortstop Kid Elberfeld earlier this month, they'd traded pitcher Doc Adkins to the Baltimore Orioles of the Eastern League to get Paddy Greene. (Elberfeld was being restrained from

playing because the New York Giants were claiming he belonged to them.)

Now Elberfeld was back, and it was Detroit who was seeking an infield replacement. Having temporarily lost Joe Yeager to an ankle injury, the Tigers needed someone to play third base. They chose to go after the 28-year-old Greene, who had impressed Detroit manager Ed Barrow by getting four hits in 13 at-bats for the Yankees in a recent series against the Tigers.

Actually, the Yankees were not trading Greene to Detroit; they were just "lending" him there. The lending of players was a practice of the time where one team sent a player to another team for part or all of the season. It was usually done, as it was here, when the "receiving" team had a temporary vacancy to fill because of an injury. In this case, however, Greene would not return to New York. After playing in just one game for the Tigers, in which he went hitless in three at-bats, he never again played in the major leagues.

In return for the loan of Greene, the Tigers were sending the Yankees a cash payment and also giving them the opportunity to negotiate with 24-year-old rookie pitcher John Deering. Deering had won three and lost four for the Tigers until Barrow sent him to the Columbus Senators of the American Association on July 13. He refused to report and instead of going to Columbus went home to New Haven, Connecticut. After agreeing to sign with the Yankees on July 18, Deering would pitch in nine games, winning four and losing three, but 1903 would be his lone major league season.

October 6, 1903: Traded Catcher Jack O'Connor to the St. Louis Browns for Outfielder–First Baseman John Anderson

Norwegian-born John Anderson had a .299 career average in nine big league seasons, six in the National League and three in the American. Aside from 1898, which he'd spent mostly with Washington, Anderson had played for Brooklyn from 1894 to 1899, and for the past three seasons with the Milwaukee Brewers/ St. Louis Browns.

Since coming to the American League, Anderson had batted .330 for Milwaukee in 1901, and .284 for each of the past two seasons for St. Louis, after the franchise relocated there in 1902. Primarily an outfielder with Brooklyn, he'd played mostly first with the Brewers/Browns, but figured to return to the outfield in New York to replace the just-released Lefty Davis. The Yanks were satisfied with their first baseman, John Ganzel, though according to the Browns, Ganzel could be in St. Louis in 1904. Should Tom Jones, the rookie they planned to use at first in 1904, fail to live up to expectations, the Browns claimed the Yanks would either return Anderson or send them Ganzel. (Jones would hit only .243 in 1904; nevertheless, he would remain the Browns' first baseman for six seasons.)

Jack O'Connor, who lived in St. Louis, had told the Yankees that if they were to trade him that was his city of preference. At 34, O'Connor was four years older than Anderson and had been a big leaguer since breaking in with the Cincinnati Reds of the American Association in 1887. In 1892, when the Association failed, O'Connor moved to the National League, where he'd played for Cleveland, St. Louis, and Pittsburgh. He jumped to the Yanks in 1903, but batted just .203 in 64 games and his general manner and play failed to impress manager Clark Griffith. When the club was in St. Louis on its final swing through the West, Griffith suspended O'Connor and didn't reinstate him for the rest of the season.

December 20, 1903: Traded Lefthanded Pitcher Jesse Tannehill to the Boston Americans for Righthanded Pitcher Tom Hughes

Yankee owner Frank Farrell returned from the American League meetings in Chicago to announce that he'd traded 29-year-old Jesse Tannehill to the Boston Americans for 25-year-old Tom Hughes. Fans in Boston greeted the news with outrage, distressed at losing a pitcher who'd had a 20-7 record for their world championship team and getting one with a 15-15 mark in return. They were also skeptical at the reasons for the trade, believing that American League President Ban Johnson was

so determined to have a successful team in New York, he was encouraging the league's seven other franchises to do whatever they could to help the Yankees.

Yet before "jumping" to New York in 1903, Tannehill had been among the game's better pitchers. He'd been a three-time 20-game winner with the Pittsburgh Pirates, and including his one win for the 1894 Cincinnati Reds and that 15-15 season for the Yankees, had a very impressive 132-73 lifetime record. Moreover, as Boston manager Jimmy Collins noted, Tannehill was a quality lefthander, something the team had lacked since their inception.

Hughes had made his debut with National League's Chicago team in September 1900, splitting two decisions and then going 10-23 in 1901, but with 225 strikeouts. He jumped to the American League in 1902 and went a combined 10-8 for Baltimore and Boston. But this past season, Hughes had joined with Cy Young and Bill Dinneen to pitch Boston to the pennant and a victory over Pittsburgh in the World Series, although he'd lost to the Pirates in his only Series appearance.

The exact words of Farrell's announcement were, "Jesse Tannehill virtually has been exchanged for pitcher Tom Hughes of Boston." The word "virtually" was key, as there was much negotiating back and forth before this deal finally became official. It eventually did, but would not prove to be a good one for New York. Tannehill would be a 20-game winner for Boston in both 1904 and 1905, while the Yanks would trade Hughes to Washington the following July.

February 21, 1904: Purchased Catcher Deacon McGuire from the Detroit Tigers

Forty-year-old Deacon McGuire had been a major league catcher since breaking in with the American Association Toledo Blue Stockings back in 1884. He'd played for many teams since, but had his best years with the National League Washington Senators of the 1890s. He'd spent the past two seasons with Detroit, splitting the catching duties with Fritz

Buelow. When the 1903 season ended, the Tigers told McGuire that they would sell him to the team of his choice. However, neither they nor any of McGuire's closest friends had expected him to choose New York.

March 6, 1904: Traded Righthanded Pitcher Harry Howell and Cash to the St. Louis Browns for Righthanded Pitcher Jack Powell

Although he'd never played for any of the local teams, Jack Powell was well liked by the fans in New York. He'd won their admiration after hooking up in some memorable pitching duels with the Giants' Christy Mathewson, back in 1901. Powell was pitching for the Cardinals then, in what was his fifth and final season in the National League; he'd joined the Browns in 1902, the year they moved from Milwaukee to St. Louis.

The 29-year-old Powell was a three-time 20-game winner, who'd compiled records of 23-15 for the 1898 Cleveland Spiders, 23-19 for the 1899 Cardinals, and 22-17 for the 1902 Browns. Nevertheless, after he won only 15 games in 1903 and lost an American League-leading 19, the Browns sent him a 1904 contract for $3,250, a cut of $1,250 from the previous season. When he refused to sign, Yankee co-owner Frank Farrell began negotiating with the Browns to bring the portly Powell to New York. Browns owner Robert Hedges asked the Yankees for pitcher Tom Hughes in return, but Farrell declined to part with the man he'd traded Jesse Tannehill to Boston to get two months earlier.

"I told him we needed Hughes right here," Farrell said. Then Hedges asked for Jack Chesbro, and again Farrell balked. At this point, Yankee manager Clark Griffith stepped in and persuaded Hedges to accept Harry Howell and a cash payment of $8,000. After completing the trade, Farrell claimed that getting Hughes and Powell gave the Yankees the best pitching staff in the game.

Howell, a 30-year-old spitballer, had been with the franchise since it originated in Baltimore in 1901. Before that he'd pitched for five seasons in the National League. Howell had a combined 23-36 record for the 1901-02 Orioles, but a solid 13-9 for New York in 1903.

May 8, 1904: Purchased Outfielder Jack Thoney from the Washington Senators

A proposed four-player trade between the two clubs overshadowed the Yanks' purchase of outfielder Jack Thoney from the Senators. Seemingly all but settled, the trade would have brought outfielder Kip Selbach and catcher Mal Kittredge, who had been the Senators' manager, to New York and sent outfielder John Anderson and catcher Monte Beville to Washington. However, Patsy Donovan, who'd replaced Kittridge as manager after the Senators had gotten off to a 1-16 start, canceled the deal.

Thoney was returning to the franchise he'd played three games for in 1902, when it was based in Baltimore. He'd appeared in all of Washington's 17 games this spring and was batting .300. But Thoney would be much less successful with the Yankees, batting a meager .188 in 36 games. He spent the next three seasons in the minors, before returning to the major leagues with the 1908 Red Sox.

June 17, 1904: Traded Infielder Bob Unglaub to the Boston Americans for Outfielder Patsy Dougherty

The Yankees needed an outfielder to replace Dave Fultz whose football-related leg injuries were severely limiting his playing time. Nevertheless, many Boston fans suspected that American League President Ban Johnson was behind this trade, just as they'd suspected he'd been responsible for the December 1903 trade of Long Tom Hughes to New York for Jesse Tannehill. Johnson's desire to strengthen the Yankees in their battle with the well-established National League Giants for the devotion and dollars of New York's fans was well known; however, it meant little to Bostonians who were furious at losing an outstanding young player like Patsy Dougherty and getting an untested rookie like Bob Unglaub in return.

Dougherty, 27, had batted a sparkling .342 as a rookie in 1902 and followed that with a .331 average in 1903. In 49 games this season, he was batting .272. Meanwhile, Unglaub, a 22-year-old rookie who'd been Boston property

June 17, 1904: *Bob Unglaub.* **Red Sox fans were outraged at giving up Patsy Dougherty for Unglaub.**

originally, had played in six games, with four singles in 19 at-bats.

Dougherty would bat a combined .280 for the 1904 season and lead the league with 113 runs scored (33 for Boston, 80 for New York). But the following year, 1905, he played in only 116 games and his average dropped to .263. When manager Clark Griffith wanted to cut his 1906 salary by $600, Dougherty refused to sign. Although he had no contract for 1906, Dougherty did play in 12 games for the Yankees, batting .192, before he quit the team and went home. Later that summer, White Sox manager Fielder Jones saw Dougherty playing in an exhibition game and signed him.

July 20, 1904: Traded Righthanded Pitchers Tom Hughes and Barney Wolfe to the Washington Senators for Righthanded Pitcher Al Orth

Known as the "Curveless Wonder" for obvious reasons, Al Orth had been a successful National League pitcher for Philadelphia between 1895 and 1901, compiling a 100-72 record before jumping to the American League. He won 19 games for Washington in 1902 and was the Senators' opening-day pitcher in 1903, defeating New York 3-1 in the Yanks' first game since moving from Baltimore. Yet overall, 1903 had been a poor season for Orth, as he finished with just ten wins and 22 losses. He was 3-4 this season, and had said several times that he was unhappy pitching for the last-place Senators.

A Washington reporter, knowing Orth's feelings, had broached this deal to Yankee manager Clark Griffith in May. He suggested to Griffith that the 32-year-old Orth could help his club make up their then–3½ game deficit with first-place Boston. However, while the Yanks and Senators were negotiating that deal, they appeared to have also completed a separate one. That trade would have sent outfielder John Anderson and catcher Monte Beville from New York to Washington in exchange for outfielder Kip Selbach and catcher Mal Kittredge. Patsy Donovan, the Senators' new manager, killed the deal, thereby creating a bad feeling between the teams that still existed.

While Orth wanted out of Washington, Yankee pitcher Tom Hughes had expressed a desire to go there, mainly because he was a good friend of manager Donovan. The Yanks had high expectations for Hughes when they traded pitcher Jesse Tannehill to Boston to get him this past winter. He was only 25 years old and was coming off a 20-7 season. But Hughes had not shown any semblance of that form this year, winning only seven games while losing 11 with a high 3.70 earned run average.

The Yanks had signed Barney Wolfe on the recommendations of scouts whom he'd impressed with his fastball while pitching in the New York State League. Wolfe made 20 starts as a 27-year-old rookie in 1903, fourth most on the club. He won only six games, lost nine, and had a 2.97 earned run average. In seven games this season, Wolfe had three decisions, all losses.

Orth won 11 of 17 games after coming to the Yankees; however, it was not enough for the club to overtake Boston. He had several good years in New York and one great one. In 1906, he led the league in wins (27), complete games (36), and innings pitched (338.2). Following a 2-13 season for the last place Yankees of 1908, Orth appeared in one final game in 1909. His overall record as a Yankee was 72-73.

July 27, 1904: Sold Catcher Monte Beville to the Detroit Tigers

After selling Fritz Buelow to Cleveland a few days earlier, the Tigers had installed Bob Wood as their first-string catcher. But Wood had slipped and dislocated an elbow while attempting to field a bunt by Rube Waddell in the previous day's game at Philadelphia. Lew Drill, signed by Detroit after the Buelow sale, finished the game behind the plate, but with Wood out indefinitely, the Tigers were desperate for another catcher. Team secretary Frank Navin wired Yankee manager Clark Griffith to ask if he could borrow the little-used Monte Beville. Borrowing players was a common practice of the time where one team sent a player to another team for all or part of a season. It was usually the result of the "receiving" team's need to fill a vacancy created by an injury, as it was here. While money usually changed hands in these transactions, Griffith agreed to "lend" Beville to the Tigers seemingly for nothing in return.

The Yanks certainly didn't need Beville. A year ago, theirs and his first in the big leagues, Beville batted a meager .194 in 82 games while splitting the catching duties with Jack O'-Connor. But veteran Deacon McGuire and rookie Red Kleinow were doing the catching this season, and Beville had been in only nine games with 22 at-bats.

Beville would bat .207 in 54 games for Detroit, but 1904 would be his final big league season.

September 9, 1904: Purchased Righthanded Pitcher Ned Garvin from the Brooklyn Superbas

Ned Garvin had pitched his last game for Brooklyn on August 22. His manager, Ned Hanlon, had accused Garvin of insubordination and given him the choice of a release or an indefinite suspension. Garvin chose the release. He seemed on the verge of signing with Pittsburgh, but Pirates manager Fred Clarke was unsure of the 30-year-old Garvin's contractual status and passed on him. The Yanks, however, were engaged in a tight pennant race with Boston and were willing to take the gamble.

Garvin, who'd debuted with the Philadelphia Phillies in 1898, had also pitched for the Milwaukee Brewers and both the National and American League Chicago clubs. He joined Brooklyn late in the 1902 season and went 15-18 for the Superbas in 1903, but was only 5-15 this season. Yet, despite that poor won-lost record, Garvin had an excellent 1.68 earned run average, second in the league to the Giants' Joe McGinnity.

Garvin made two starts for the Yankees. He lost his only decision and never again pitched in the major leagues.

May 30, 1905: Sold Outfielder-First Baseman John Anderson to the Washington Nationals

Shortly after purchasing John Anderson's contract, Washington manager Jake Stahl called him long distance to welcome him to the Nationals. Anderson, who was with the Yankees in Philadelphia, replied that he was anxious to join his new team. He assured Stahl that he preferred to play in Washington rather than anywhere else.

Anderson had almost gotten his wish to play in the Nation's Capital one year earlier. In May 1904 the Yanks had agreed to trade him and catcher Monte Beville to Washington for outfielder Kip Selbach and catcher Mal Kittredge, but Washington's new manager, Patsy Donovan, canceled the deal.

Actually, Anderson had played for Washington once before. It was in 1898 when the Brooklyn club "lent" him to Washington for the bulk of the season. The Washington Nationals (again the club's official name this season) were then a member of the 12-team National League.

Anderson, who was now 31, began his big league career with Brooklyn in 1894. He'd also played for the American League's Milwaukee team in 1901, and for the Browns in 1902 and 1903 after the Brewers moved to St. Louis. He'd been primarily a first baseman for Milwaukee/St. Louis, but when the Yankees got him in 1904 they moved him back to the outfield. Anderson batted .278 that season and had a team-leading 82 runs batted in for a club that just missed winning its first pennant.

However, along with the rest of the Yankees, he'd started slowly this season. After 32 games Anderson was batting just .232.

July 12, 1905: Signed First Baseman Jack Doyle as a Free Agent

Jack Doyle's outstanding big league career (a .299 average over 16 years) ostensibly had ended the year before. However, when a series of injuries, including a broken nose suffered by first baseman Hal Chase, left the Yankees desperate for players, manager Clark Griffith induced the 35-year-old Doyle to play again. The following day in Detroit he was at first base in what would be his only appearance as a Yankee. The Yanks lost, 6-3, a loss Doyle helped cause by dropping two throws.

July 13, 1905: Purchased Catcher Mike Powers from the Philadelphia Athletics

While this transaction was officially listed as a sale, the Yankees really just "borrowed" Mike Powers from Philadelphia. Borrowing players was a practice of the time where one team sent a player to another team for all or part of a season. It generally occurred when a team lost a player to an injury and needed someone to temporarily fill the vacancy created by that loss. The Yanks needed Powers to back up Deacon McGuire until their regular catcher, Red Kleinow, recovered from a finger injury he'd suffered in a game against Detroit a day earlier.

The 34-year-old Powers, a licensed physician, began his big league career in 1898. Before joining the A's in 1901, the first year the American League had major league status, he'd played with the now-defunct Louisville and Washington clubs in the National League. Powers, a career .248-batter, was Philadelphia's number one catcher that year, but had shared the role with Ossee Schreckengost ever since.

Although the third place Athletics were in a three-way race for the pennant with Cleveland and Chicago, manager Connie Mack had no qualms about "lending" Powers to New York. Schreckengost had assumed almost full-

July 13, 1905: *Mike Powers.* **Connie Mack just "lent" Powers to the Yankees.**

time duty behind the plate, while Powers had been in just 21 games, with a .167 average. The A's, who were in the middle of an extended road trip, left Powers in Cleveland. He joined the Yanks when they arrived the next day and caught that afternoon's game.

Yankee first baseman Hal Chase had broken his nose in the same game in which Kleinow was hurt, so manager Clark Griffith also used Powers at first base during his brief stay in New York. In all, Powers played 11 games for the Yankees, seven at first and four behind the plate. He had six hits in 33 at-bats, for a .182 average.

At the time of the "sale" Mack said that he "would take Powers back if Griffith didn't need him." On August 7 Powers went back to the Athletics and caught the next day's game.

September 11, 1905: Sold Righthanded Pitcher Jack Powell to the St. Louis Browns

In 1904 Jack Powell won 23 games for the Yankees, and his 390.1 innings pitched were second in the league to teammate Jack Chesbro. The pitching of Chesbro and Powell kept the Yankees in the pennant race all season before they lost out to Boston on the final day. But Powell's second season in New York had been much less successful for both him and for the team. The Yanks were on their way to a sixth-place finish, and Powell had won only eight games, while losing 13.

Only 31, Powell would pitch for another seven years after returning to St. Louis.

April 29, 1906: Acquired Outfielder Danny Hoffman from the Philadelphia Athletics for the Rights to Outfielder Dave Fultz

New York City had suspended its law against Sunday baseball for the day to allow the Yankees and Athletics to play a benefit exhibition game for the victims of the recent San Francisco earthquake. Moreover, while the city had a law forbidding the playing of an official game of baseball on a Sunday, it had no comparable law barring the conducting of baseball business; so the two managers, Clark Griffith of New York and Connie Mack of Philadelphia, took advantage of their meeting to negotiate this transaction. Mack agreed to give up 26-year-old Danny Hoffman, once a most highly

April 29, 1906: *Danny Hoffman.* **Hoffman was never the same after being hit in the eye with a Jesse Tannehill pitch in 1905.**

rated prospect, for a chance to attempt to lure former Yankee Dave Fultz out of retirement.

Before joining the Yankees in 1903, Fultz had played two seasons for the Athletics. In 1902 he batted .302 and scored a league-leading 109 runs, helping to lead Mack's A's to the pennant. But under the terms of his contract, he was free to play anywhere he wanted in 1903, and because the Yanks offered him the most money, Fultz signed with them. Nevertheless, he parted on good terms with Mack, who remained fond of Fultz and considered him among baseball's best outfielders.

Fultz, who'd gotten the Yankees' first-ever base hit, played three seasons for the Yanks, batting .243 in 305 games. Still only 31, he had retired after the 1905 season to practice law, a choice Mack was unable to persuade him from abandoning.

Hoffman had led the American League with 46 stolen bases in 1905, but he'd batted just .261. The year before he'd batted .299 in 52 games; however, Hoffman had never again seemed to be as good a player as he'd been before Boston's Jesse Tannehill hit him in the eye with a pitch in '05.

May 10, 1906: Sold Outfielder Ed Hahn to the Chicago White Sox

Outfielder Ed Hahn was only 19 years old when the Yanks purchased him from New Orleans of the Southern Association in June 1905. He batted .319 in 43 games in a year when the American League batted .241 as a whole, and Cleveland's Elmer Flick's .308 led all qualifiers for the batting title. Hahn had started slowly this season, just two hits in 22 at-bats; yet manager Clark Griffith still thought highly of him and so did the New York fans. Despite his newness to the team, Hahn was among the Yankees' most popular players.

However, the Yanks had recently added outfielder Danny Hoffman from Philadelphia, and Griffith now had more outfielders than he needed. Meanwhile, Fielder Jones, the manager of the White Sox, was short of outfielders. Jones, himself an outfielder, had been temporarily unable to play because of an injury, and he'd been dissatisfied with rookie outfielder Frank Hemphill, who'd had only three hits in 40 at-bats.

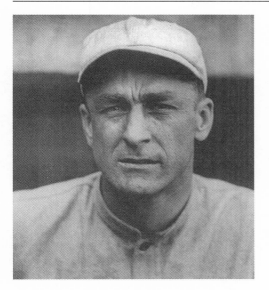

February 27, 1907: *Branch Rickey*. Browns manager Jimmy McAleer felt Rickey lacked team spirit.

February 27, 1907: Traded Infielder Joe Yeager to the St. Louis Browns for Catcher Branch Rickey

After batting .284 in 66 games as a rookie in 1906, Branch Rickey appeared set for a long career in St. Louis. But Browns manager Jimmy McAleer had revealed a key reason for disposing of Rickey a day earlier, after he'd traded for veteran catcher Fritz Buelow. According to McAleer, Rickey would not play on Sundays and Buelow would. McAleer had not forgotten a Sunday afternoon in 1906 when one of his catchers, Tubby Spencer, was hurt, and another, Jack O'Connor, wasn't playing well. McAleer would have liked to use Rickey, but because of his religious principles, Rickey was unavailable. McAleer also felt that Rickey didn't mix well with the other players and therefore had failed to absorb the team spirit.

Joe Yeager had played for Brooklyn and Detroit between 1898 and 1903 and for the Yankees in 1905 and 1906. The Browns needed infield help, and Yeager, though primarily a third baseman, could play the other infield spots also. He'd doubled as a pitcher with Brooklyn and Detroit, compiling a 33-49 record, but Yankee manager Clark Griffith had never used him that way. Yeager batted .267 as the Yanks'

regular third baseman in 1905, and .301 in 57 games as a utility infielder in 1906.

The Yanks had wanted Rickey for the offensive capabilities he'd shown with St. Louis, but he proved to be a flop in New York, batting .184 in just 52 games. Though he was only 26, Rickey would play only two more major league games, and those would be seven years later when he was managing the Browns.

May 16, 1907: Traded Righthanded Pitcher Walter Clarkson and Outfielder Frank Delahanty to the Cleveland Naps for Righthanded Pitcher Earl Moore

Although the Yankees were playing the Naps in Cleveland when they made this trade, Walter Clarkson was not with them. Clarkson was back in New York, where manager Clark Griffith had sent him to heal his injured pitching hand. At 29, Clarkson was the youngest of the three pitching Clarkson brothers and the only one still active. (Dad and future Hall of Famer John were the others.) He'd signed with the Yankees in 1904 after pitching for Harvard, and had his best season in 1906. He was 9-4 with a 2.32 earned run average in '06, and was 1-1 before his injury this season.

Twenty-four-year-old Frank Delahanty was also the youngest member of a famous baseball family. Four brothers had preceded him to the big leagues, two of whom, Joe and Jim, were still active. The most famous of the brothers was future Hall of Famer Ed Delahanty, who had fallen to his death at Niagara Falls in July 1903.

Frank came up to the Yankees in August 1905 and then batted .238 as a semi-regular in 1906. He was sitting out this year while studying medicine at Baldwin Wallace College, near Cleveland; however, upon hearing of the trade, he announced that he would report to manager Nap Lajoie's club when his classes ended in two weeks.

Delahanty would later return to the Yankees. In July 1908 he was playing for the New Orleans Pelicans of the Southern Association when the Yanks bought him to replace outfielder Jake Stahl, whom they'd sold to the Red Sox.

Earl Moore had used a crossfire delivery and an outstanding curveball to win 16 games as a Cleveland rookie in 1901. He had an 80-65 career record, but he'd peaked in 1903 when he won 20 games with just eight losses and led the American League with a 1.74 earned run average. Early in 1906 Moore was injured when a batted ball hit him on the instep in a game against the Yankees. He pitched just five games that season and had split two decisions thus far in 1907.

Nevertheless, the Yanks were woefully short of pitching and made the trade hoping Moore would return to his old form. He hadn't, and after he'd struggled with a 2-6 record, the Yanks sent him to Jersey City in the Eastern League. Moore would return to the big leagues in 1908, with the Philadelphia Phillies.

May 30, 1907: Purchased Righthanded Pitcher Frank Kitson from the Washington Senators

Manager Clark Griffith was looking for pitching help, and Frank Kitson had once been a consistent winner. That was in the National League between 1898 and 1902. But after jumping to the American League in 1903, he'd had four consecutive losing seasons: three with the Tigers, and a 6-14 mark with the Senators in 1906. Kitson was 0-3 in five games this season, but the Yanks added the 35-year-old ten-year veteran to their staff before leaving Washington, where they'd split a morning-afternoon Decoration Day doubleheader. Kitson would win all four of his decisions with the Yankees in what would be his final major league season.

June 7, 1907: Sold Catcher Deacon McGuire to the Boston Red Sox

The Red Sox weren't interested in Deacon McGuire as a player; at age 43, his playing days were about over. They were bringing him to Boston to manage the club and attempt to restore its stability. Jimmy Collins, their star third baseman, had managed the Red Sox (then known as the Americans) from the team's first

year in 1901 until he quit in the last weeks of the 1906 season. Chick Stahl took over and finished out the year, but shortly before the 1907 season got underway, he committed suicide. Since then three men had already served as manager: Cy Young, the great Boston pitcher began the season, but left after going 3-4. George Huff, from the University of Illinois, went 3-5, and first baseman Bob Unglaub was 8-20.

McGuire, who began his big league career in 1884, came to the Yankees in 1904 and for the next three seasons shared the catching duties with Red Kleinow. Including his one hitless at-bat this season, he batted .230 in 225 games as a Yankee. His managerial tenure in Boston would last just over a year. In August 1908 they sold him to Cleveland, where he also managed briefly and continued to play an occasional game behind the plate up through 1912.

October 13, 1907: Traded Second Baseman Frank LaPorte to the Boston Red Sox in a Three-Way Deal and Received First Baseman Jake Stahl from the Chicago White Sox

Jake Stahl reached the majors in 1903 as a part-time player with the Boston Americans. In 1904 Boston traded him to Washington, and he spent the next three seasons as the Senators' full-time first baseman. He was also their manager in 1905 and 1906, but following a series of disagreements with the club's owners, Washington traded him to the White Sox in March 1907. Stahl refused to report and sat out the entire year. But he was only 26, and an excellent first baseman who would give manager Clark Griffith the option of moving the versatile Hal Chase to another position.

In return for Stahl Chicago would get Boston third baseman Freddy Parent, who'd been the best of the three players involved in this deal. Like Stahl, Parent was feuding with his club's management, which is why the Red Sox had made him available. His departure left only pitcher Cy Young, catcher Lou Criger, and second baseman Hobe Ferris remaining from Boston's first American League team in 1901.

The Red Sox planned to replace Parent at third base with Frank LaPorte, their new acquisition. LaPorte had played third for the Yanks in 1906, but split the position with George Moriarty in 1907, while playing half his games in the outfield. Though his defense at third was suspect, LaPorte was a competent batsman, with a .273 average in his 264 games as a Yankee.

November 5, 1907: Traded Second Baseman Jimmy Williams and Outfielder Danny Hoffman to the St. Louis Browns for Righthanded Pitcher Fred Glade, Second Baseman Harry Niles, and Outfielder Charlie Hemphill

Everyone connected with the Yankees believed they had gotten the better of this trade, a rare occurrence when dealing with St. Louis manager Jimmy McAleer. Manager Clark Griffith, whom team secretary Abe Nahon had announced earlier in the day would return in 1908, was especially pleased at getting the speedy Harry Niles. Along with Detroit's Ty Cobb and their own Hal Chase, Niles was considered among the best young players in the game. Niles, of course, couldn't match Cobb's overall speed; still, baseball people judged him the fastest man ever in getting down to first base. After a .229 rookie season in 1906, Niles was leading the American League in batting in 1907, helped greatly by his ability to beat out ground balls. But he had to sit out several weeks after suffering an injury in a collision with Cleveland's Bill Bradley, and ended the season at .289.

Niles had been an outfielder as a rookie, before the Browns moved him to second base in 1907. The Yankees planned to continue playing him at second, where he would replace Jimmy Williams who'd held the position since the team landed in New York in 1903. Before that, Williams had been the team's second baseman for the two years they'd played in Baltimore, and before that, for two years with Pittsburgh. He'd twice led the league's second basemen in fielding and had a .261 average for his five seasons in New York.

Barring other changes, the Yankee batting order for 1908 figured to have Niles leading off, Willie Keeler batting second, and Hal Chase and Charlie Hemphill (or Hemphill and Chase) in the three-four spots. Hemphill, a 31-year-old veteran of seven big league seasons, had also played for St. Louis and Cleveland in the National League and Boston and Cleveland in the American League. He'd had his best season in 1902, batting .308, but declined sharply the next two seasons. McAleer sent him to St. Paul of the American Association in 1905, but Hemphill returned to St. Louis in 1906 and batted .289 in 154 games. Partly because of his disappointment at not getting the contract he thought he deserved, Hemphill slumped to .259 in 1907. He would bounce back to hit .297 for the Yanks in 1908, and though he played three more seasons in New York, his final three as a big leaguer, he never again did so well.

Like Hemphill, Fred Glade also had weathered an up-and-down career with the Browns. He was 18-15 as a rookie in 1904, 6-25 in 1905, and 15-14 and 13-9 the past two seasons. Although he was well off financially and thought likely to soon retire, several teams had tried to get Glade. He would begin the 1908 season with the Yankees, but after appearing in five games, four of which he lost, he did retire. Glade said he was doing so because he had a sore arm, and that his retirement had nothing to do with his financial situation.

For McAleer and the Browns, the key player in the deal was Danny Hoffman. Still only 27 years old, he'd been the Yanks' center fielder since joining them early in the 1906 season. While his batting averages were not particularly high (.256 and .254), he'd led the club with 32 stolen bases in 1906, and with five home runs and 81 runs scored in 1907.

December 12, 1907: Sold Catcher Ira Thomas to the Detroit Tigers

Both the Tigers and the White Sox were after catcher Ira Thomas, but Detroit made Yankee owner Frank Farrell the better offer. While each club was satisfied with its first-string catcher (Billy Sullivan for Chicago and Boss Schmidt for Detroit), each sought Thomas as a reserve, the same role he'd had in New York. Freddie Payne and Jimmy Archer had

June 7, 1907: *Deacon McGuire.* **McGuire was going to Boston as the team's new manager.**

filled that position for the pennant-winning Tigers in 1907, but it now appeared they would have to battle for the number three spot in 1908.

At six-foot two inches and 200 pounds, the 27-year-old Thomas was one of the largest men in the game. He came to the Yankees in 1906 after his heavy-hitting helped lead Providence to the 1905 Eastern League championship. But he'd been a disappointment in New York, batting a combined .195 in 124 games over the next two seasons. Jack Dunn, his manager at Providence, said that for Thomas to be effective he had to play every day. That hadn't happened with the Yankees, where he'd shared the catching duties with Red

Kleinow, and it appeared not likely to happen in Detroit.

July 10, 1908: Sold Outfielder Jake Stahl to the Boston Red Sox

During their 8-2 loss to Detroit, a loss that put the last-place Yanks 17 games behind the league-leading Tigers, rumors arose that the club had sold outfielder Jake Stahl. First came word that he was going to Washington, and then later it was to Cleveland. However, both reports were erroneous. Finally, after the game, in which he had three hits including a home run, the club announced Stahl's sale to Boston.

The 29-year-old Stahl was in his first season in New York, having come in a three-way trade the previous October. He'd been in 75 games and had a .225 batting average with 45 runs batted in. Stahl had been a first baseman in his four season before coming to the Yankees, and he would be a first baseman in his five seasons after leaving the Yankees. But in New York first base belonged to Hal Chase, and Stahl had been playing the outfield.

The Yanks also announced that Frank Delahanty, whom they'd traded to Cleveland in May 1907, had rejoined them and would take Stahl's spot in left field. Delahanty had been playing for the New Orleans Pelicans of the Southern Association.

August 17, 1908: Traded Second Baseman Harry Niles to the Boston Red Sox for Second Baseman Frank LaPorte

Much had been expected of Harry Niles after the Yankees got him in the big November 1907 trade with the St. Louis Browns, but he had failed to live up to those expectations. His 12th-inning sacrifice fly on Opening Day gave Joe Doyle and the Yanks a 1-0 victory over the powerful Philadelphia Athletics, but he was hitless that day and had continued to falter all season. Niles, who'd replaced the popular Jimmy Williams at second base, was batting just .249, and in recent games Yankee manager Kid Elberfeld had been using rookie Queenie O'Rourke (playing in his one major league season) in Niles's place. (With the club foundering, Clark Griffith had resigned on June 24, but Elberfeld, his replacement, was a disaster as a manager and the Yanks would end this dreadful season in last place.)

Frank LaPorte was returning to the Yankees who'd traded him to Boston in a three-way deal in October 1907. He had been a third baseman–outfielder in New York, but Red Sox manager Deacon McGuire had used him mostly as a backup to second baseman Amby McConnell. LaPorte had been in 62 games for Boston and had a .237 batting average.

With O'Rourke playing well, Elberfeld would have to decide what to do with Laporte. He could use him at third base to allow Wid

November 5, 1907: *Charlie Hemphill.* **Hemphill's first year with the Yankees would be his best.**

Conroy to rest his injured ankle, or, as was rumored, he could trade him to Cleveland for outfielder Dave Altizer.

January 14, 1909: Sold Third Baseman George Moriarty to the Detroit Tigers

The Yankees and Tigers had been discussing a deal for George Moriarty for several weeks, but the Yanks wouldn't make it final until they knew whether they would have Hal Chase to play first base in 1909. When Frank Farrell selected Kid Elberfeld to replace deposed manager Clark Griffith during the Yanks' disastrous 1908 season, Chase, thinking the job should have gone to him, left the team late in the year to join the Stockton club of the California State League. Although primarily a

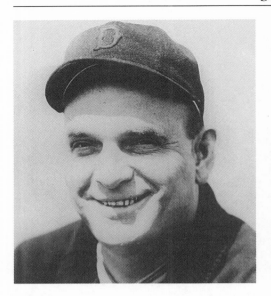

January 14, 1909: *George Moriarty.* **The Yanks waited until they were sure they'd have Hal Chase back before trading Moriarty.**

third baseman, Moriarty had played first in Chase's absence and done an excellent job.

The National Commission had now approved Chase's application for reinstatement, and so the Yanks, with veteran Wid Conroy and rookies Jimmy Austin and Joe Ward to play third base, felt free to part with Moriarty.

Moriarty had gone hitless in 18 at-bats in brief trials with the Cubs in 1903 and 1904, but was having an outstanding season with Toledo in the American Association in 1905. Umpire Tim Hurst, who was also scouting for the Yankees, signed him in August. In 1906 Moriarty backed up third baseman Frank La-Porte, then split the position with LaPorte in 1907. Conroy reclaimed third base in 1908, while Moriarty finished the season as Chase's replacement at first. The speedy Moriarty had stolen 50 bases over the last two seasons, had a .254 average for his three years in New York. He would be a regular in Detroit, replacing third baseman Bill Coughlin whose major league career was now over.

Rather than money, new Yankee manager George Stallings had asked Detroit for rookie catcher Oscar Stanage in return for Moriarty. But because of Stallings' reputation as an excellent judge of young talent, Tiger manager Hughie Jennings decided that Stanage might be worth keeping.

February 17, 1909: Sold Third Baseman Wid Conroy to the Washington Senators

After his rookie season with the American League Milwaukee Brewers in 1901, and a season with Pittsburgh in 1902, Wid Conroy signed with the new Yankee team in 1903. He played third base in the club's first-ever game, and had a .250 average and 184 stolen bases in 797 games with the Yanks. He played mostly at third, but also at shortstop and in the outfield and at various times led the club in games, at-bats, stolen bases, walks, doubles, and triples.

But with Conroy now 32 years old and coming off an ankle injury, new Yankee manager George Stallings decided he wanted a new third baseman. He would choose among a pair of promising youngsters, Jimmy Austin and Joe Ward, and veteran shortstop Kid Elberfeld, who'd managed the team for much of 1908 but played sparingly because of a badly spiked leg. Meanwhile, Senators manager Joe Cantillon admitted that he'd been trying to get his friend Conroy since taking over the Washington club in 1907.

Coincidentally, this same day Elberfeld was reported to have been traded to the Senators for pitcher Bill Burns, but Stallings and Cantillon both denied the report. That disappointed Elberfeld because a trade to Washington would have brought him geographically closer to his family.

Cleveland had also been pursuing a deal for Conroy, and their owner, Charles W. Somers, said that Washington had been very fortunate in buying him. Somers added that he thought buying players would soon replace trading them.

"The time is not far distant when there will be no trading of players. The fact that one manager may foist an undesirable player on another for a first-class man, thereby creating dissatisfaction and hard feelings is surely bringing about the elimination of trades. Hereafter, when a manager has a player to dispose of he will put a price on him and take the money thus secured to purchase another man in his place."

May 18, 1909: Sold Shortstop
Neal Ball to the Cleveland Naps

Manager George Stallings waited until the Yankees had finished their series in Cleveland and were ready to move on to St. Louis before selling shortstop Neal Ball to the Naps. A year earlier, when Clark Griffith was the Yankee manager, he had made Ball his regular shortstop after Kid Elberfeld suffered an early season leg injury. Ball's only previous major league experience had been 15 late-season games in 1907, but he was an immediate sensation both at the bat and in the field.

But after his great start, Ball cooled off and batted just .247 in 1908. And while he made numerous spectacular plays in the field, he made far too many errors, a league-leading 81. This season Stallings had put Elberfeld back at shortstop and moved Ball to second base, where in eight games he was hitting a measly .207.

Having previously expressed dissatisfaction with his treatment in New York, Ball was happy to go to Cleveland where he expected to play shortstop alongside second baseman and manager, Nap Lajoie.

June 7, 1909: Sold Infielder Joe Ward
to the Philadelphia Phillies

In going to the Phillies, infielder Joe Ward was returning to a team he'd played for as a 21 year old back in 1906. He batted .295 that season, while appearing in 35 games, mostly at third base. In 1907 Ward jumped to the outlawed, independent Tri-State League, and the Yanks had to get him reinstated before they could purchase his contract. They'd done so this past winter, and expected Ward to compete with rookie Jimmy Austin to replace traded third baseman Wid Conroy. Austin won the job, but Ward was the Yanks' opening-day first baseman, replacing Hal Chase who'd contracted smallpox during spring training and was recuperating in Augusta, Georgia. Ward got into eight more games, seven of them at second base, but was a disappointment at the plate, getting just five singles in 28 at-bats.

September 11, 1909: *Jack Chesbro.* **The Yanks' first great pitcher had been totally ineffective this season.**

September 11, 1909: Sold
Righthanded Pitcher Jack Chesbro
to the Boston Red Sox

When the sixth-place Yanks returned home following a 24-day road trip in which they'd visited every American League city, they were without Jack Chesbro. The 35-year-old Chesbro, the team's first great pitcher, had been totally ineffective this season, appearing in just nine games, with no wins and four defeats. Chesbro had hinted that this season would likely be his last, so manager George Stallings, anxious to make room for young minor league pitchers Russ Ford, Ray Fisher, and Jim Vaughn, was just hurrying along the process.

After starring for Pittsburgh, Chesbro was New York's starting pitcher in the franchise's first major league game in 1903. He'd won 128 games as a Yankee, including a 20th century major league high of 41 in 1904. After pitching and losing one game for Boston, Chesbro did retire.

December 14, 1909: Sold Shortstop
Kid Elberfeld to the
Washington Senators

The sale of Kid Elberfeld followed the post-season release of Willie Keeler, the last

February 17, 1909: *Wid Conroy*. **Conroy was the Yanks' third baseman in the first league game they played.**

remaining starter from the Yankees first opening-day game in 1903. Elberfeld, now 35, had come to the Yanks in June 1903 from Detroit in the club's first-ever trade. Aside from time lost to injuries, he'd been the Yanks shortstop ever since, batting .268 with 117 stolen bases. Always a fiery player, Elberfeld also had a disastrous 27-71 record as the team's manager after replacing Clark Griffith in June 1908.

The Yanks were really interested in more than just selling Elberfeld. They were trying to talk Washington into a multiplayer trade that would have brought the Senators' sensational young pitcher Walter Johnson, and catcher Gabby Street, to New York. The Senators refused and instead just paid the Yankees $5,000 for Elberfeld.

December 16, 1909: *Traded Righthanded Pitcher Joe Lake and Outfielder Ray Demmitt to the St. Louis Browns for Catcher Lou Criger*

St. Louis had delayed this deal while trying to convince New York manager George Stallings to part with young infielder Jimmy Austin, before finally settling for pitcher Joe Lake and outfielder Ray Demmitt.

Lake, a spitballer, had led the American League with 22 losses as a rookie for the last-place Yanks in 1908. He'd followed that this past season with a team-high 14 wins and a formidable 1.88 earned run average.

A University of Illinois graduate, Demmitt batted .246 in 123 games as a rookie in 1909. He would go on to play six more major league seasons, but only in two would he play more than 100 games.

Lou Criger, now 37, had been a big league catcher since 1896, and a longtime teammate of Cy Young, in both the National and American leagues. He was a weak hitter, but an excellent receiver who'd been behind the plate for most of Young's victories.

In 1910, his one season in New York, Criger would play in just 27 games with a .188 batting average. He'd play a final game with the Browns in 1912.

II. The Teens

January 18, 1910: Purchased Lefthanded Pitcher Harry Wolter from the Boston Red Sox

In 1909, Red Sox manager Fred Lake used Harry Wolter as both a pitcher and as a substitute first baseman when Jake Stahl was injured. For the season, Wolter had a .246 average in 122 at-bats, while splitting eight decisions as a pitcher. Two years earlier, in 1907, he'd played a combined 21 games as a pitcher and outfielder for the Reds, Pirates, and Cardinals, batting .286 and losing two decisions, both with St. Louis.

During the '09 season Boston had added pitchers Ed Karger (5-2 after coming over from Cincinnati in June) and rookie Ray Collins. Projecting big seasons for both in 1910, Patsy Donovan, who'd replaced Lake as manager, felt free to put the 25-year-old Wolter on waivers.

Yankee first baseman Hal Chase, for one, was glad the club paid the $1,500 to get Wolter. Chase had played against him in the outlaw California State League in 1908, where Wolter had gone after rebelling against having been moved around the National League in 1907. Pitching for San Jose, he compiled a 25-2 record, the highest winning percentage in all of baseball that season.

On Opening Day, 1910, Wolter was in right field for the Yankees, replacing Willie Keeler who'd been released following the 1909 season. Wolter would remain an outfielder throughout his four seasons in New York, and none of his managers, George Stallings, Chase, Harry Wolverton, or Frank Chance would ever use him as a pitcher. Wolter was a regular in each of those seasons except 1912 when he was

January 18, 1910: *Harry Wolter.* Wolter replaced Willie Keeler in the Yankee outfield.

injured and played in only 12 games. Overall, he batted .277 in 396 games as a Yankee.

May 10, 1910: Sold Outfielder Clyde Engle to the Boston Red Sox

As a 25-year-old rookie, Clyde Engle was the Yankees' full-time left fielder in 1909. In 135 games, he batted .278, had 20 doubles, 78 runs batted in, and stole 18 bases. The club had undergone many personnel changes since

20

Opening Day, 1909, and Engle was one of only two players who'd started both the 1909 and 1910 openers; the other was center fielder Charlie Hemphill.

Engle had reported to training camp out of shape, and by Opening Day still appeared overweight. He'd played that day only because Birdie Cree had an injured hand. After the opener, Engle played in four more games, getting a total of three hits in 13 at-bats.

With Tris Speaker in center, Harry Hooper in right, and Duffy Lewis in left, Boston had the league's best outfield. However, Engle could also play third base, as he had with Newark of the International League before joining the Yankees. Both Red Sox manager Patsy Donovan and team captain Harry Lord liked Engle's batting ability, particularly against lefthanders, and viewed him as a capable backup for Lord at third.

May 26, 1910: Sold Catcher Red Kleinow to the Boston Red Sox

In February 1904, the Yankees traded Jack Zalusky, who'd caught seven games for them in 1903, to Toledo of the American Association for catcher Red Kleinow. After playing behind Deacon McGuire as a rookie, Kleinow took over as the Yanks' number one catcher in 1905 and remained so through 1909. But third-year man Jeff Sweeney was number one this season, and Fred Mitchell, seeing his only major league action between 1905 and 1913, was Sweeney's primary backup. Kleinow, hampered by a sore arm, had dropped to number three. Although he'd had five hits in 12 at-bats this season, the 30-year-old Kleinow had always been a weak hitter and had just a .219 career average,.

Boston already had three catchers on their roster, including their number one receiver, Bill Carrigan. However, manager Patsy Donovan liked to give Carrigan an occasional day off, and the two reserve catchers, Tom Madden and Pat Donahue, currently had worse arm problems than Kleinow.

May 31, 1910: Sold Righthanded Pitcher Joe Doyle to the Cincinnati Reds

Yankee rookie Joe Doyle made history in August 1906 by becoming the first major league pitcher to throw shutouts in his first two starts. They were the only two games he won that year, and injuries that ranged from elbow problems to blood poisoning had negatively affected his career since. His best seasons had been a modest 11-11 in 1907 and 8-6 in 1909.

Doyle had pitched well in spring training this year, leading manager George Stallings to anticipate his having a big season. But he'd been ineffective in his three 1910 outings and left with an 0-2 record, making him 22-21 for his career.

Clark Griffith, Doyle's first manager in New York and now the manager of the Reds, had claimed him because he was in dire need of pitching. Doyle would pitch in five games for Cincinnati, with no decisions. They were his final major league games.

February 11, 1911: Traded Second Baseman Frank LaPorte and Third Baseman Jimmy Austin to the

May 26, 1910: *Red Kleinow.* A dapper Kleinow at spring training in 1909.

St. Louis Browns for Third Baseman Roy Hartzell and Cash

Manager Hal Chase had first discussed this trade with Browns President Robert Hedges at the American League meetings two months earlier, but had to wait as Hedges was in the middle of negotiating the sale of the club. Now that the sale had fallen through, the Yankees and Browns consummated the deal, the first the Yanks had completed since Chase took over as manager from George Stallings late in the 1910 season. The teams announced the trade in two parts. The Yankees were trading third baseman Jimmy Austin to the Browns in exchange for their third baseman, Roy Hartzell, while second baseman Frank LaPorte was going to St. Louis in exchange for cash.

St. Louis had been after Austin since 1909, his rookie year. In December of '09, they had tried to get him in the trade that brought catcher Lou Criger to New York. Stallings refused, and the Browns accepted pitcher Joe Lake and outfielder Ray Demmitt instead.

The Yanks had secured Austin from Omaha of the Western League, where he'd stolen a league-leading 97 bases in 1908. He'd been very popular in New York for his strong defense and hustling style of play. However, the 31-year-old Austin's batting had been very weak; after hitting just .231 as a rookie in 1909, he'd dropped even below that to .218 in 1910.

Hartzell, who also played shortstop and the outfield, was much the same kind of player as Austin. He too was known for his aggressive style of play, and although he was two years younger than Austin, had been a major leaguer for five seasons. Hartzell had also batted a modest .218 in 1910, but a respectable .265 and .271 in the two preceding years and had a lifetime batting average of 242.

Austin would go on to a fine career in St. Louis, meanwhile, Hartzell would also be a valuable player, although for not as many years. In 1912, his first season as a Yankee, he batted a career-high .296 and broke a club record by driving in 91 runs. Hartzell batted .261 in 697 games with the Yanks before they released him to the minors in 1916.

LaPorte was leaving New York for the second time. Traded to Boston in a three-way deal in October 1907, he'd returned the following summer in a trade for Harry Niles. In the two-plus years since his return, he'd played in 252 games while batting .276, but he'd missed many games with what seemed like minor injuries. Stallings had been his biggest booster, but even he conceded that LaPorte, now 31, one, was not a "gamer."

February 18, 1912: Traded Infielder John Knight to the Washington Senators for Catcher Gabby Street

John Knight first reached the major leagues as a 19-year-old shortstop with the 1905 Philadelphia Athletics. He went to the Red Sox in the summer of 1907, who after the season sold him to the Baltimore Orioles of the Eastern League, where he was rated the league's best shortstop in 1908. The Yankees purchased Knight's contract from Baltimore, and he'd been their number one shortstop for the past three seasons. The best of those seasons came in 1910, when he batted .312; however, it was sandwiched between a .236 average in 1909, and a .268 average in 1911. Additionally, Knight's erratic play in the field had alienated the fans who blamed his sloppy play on what they considered negligence and indifference.

Those traits were the opposite of those attributed to 29-year-old

February 11, 1911: *Roy Hartzell.* **Hartzell was known for his aggressive style of play.**

Gabby Street. Despite a weak bat—he'd hit .222 in 72 games in 1911, and had only a .212 mark lifetime—Street was a hustler and a diligent worker, with an excellent throwing arm. He had also become the favorite receiver of Washington's great pitcher, Walter Johnson.

But Ed Sweeney would do most of the catching for the last-place Yankees in 1912, with Street batting .182 in 29 games. It was the end of Street's major league playing career, except for one at-bat when he was managing the St. Louis Cardinals in 1931.

Knight, meanwhile, would return to the Yankees in 1913. After batting .161 in 32 games for the Senators in 1912, they sent him to the International League Jersey City Skeeters. Knight was having a strong season with the Skeeters in 1913, and so on July 7, Yankee manager Frank Chance brought him to New York to play first base. Although he had been primarily a shortstop when he previously played for the Yankees, Knight could play all the infield positions. He replaced Babe Borton who'd been playing first since coming from the White Sox in a June trade for Hal Chase. Borton had fielded the position well, but Chance was dissatisfied with his .130 batting average and had released him to Jersey City.

Knight got into 80 games for the 1913 Yankees, but batted just .236; the Yanks released him after the season, and although he was only 28, he never again played in the major leagues.

The Yanks also released 21-year-old outfielder Dan Costello (1 for 2 in two games) to Lowell of the New England League. In January 1914, they sold Costello to the Pittsburgh Pirates, with whom he would later play for three seasons.

April 9, 1912: Purchased Catcher Gus Fisher from the Cleveland Naps

With the season-opener just two days away, Harry Wolverton, the Yankees' new manager, did not have a second-string catcher. Wolverton had planned for Gabby Street, whom the Yanks had gotten from Washington during the off-season, to be the backup to first-string catcher Jeff Sweeney. Sweeney had split the catching chores with Walter Blair in 1911, but Blair, after five years with the Yankees, was out of the major leagues, and Sweeney was a holdout. He was demanding $6,000 for 1912, and said if he didn't get it he would remain in the automobile business in Chicago.

The Yanks purchased Gus Fisher, who'd batted .261 in 70 games as a Cleveland rookie in 1911, as an emergency measure. Fisher lasted just ten games with the Yanks; he had one hit

April 9, 1912: *Harry Wolverton*. **New manager Wolverton was desperate for a backup catcher.**

in ten at-bats and never again played in a major league game. Sweeney eventually signed and was the club's first string catcher in 1912.

June 26, 1912: Sold Lefthanded Pitcher Jim Vaughn to the Washington Senators

After pitching two games for the Yankees in 1908, Jim "Hippo" Vaughn came back in 1910 to win 13 games and post a 1.83 earned run average. But in 1911 his record dropped to 8-10, and his ERA jumped all the way to 4.39. The 24-year-old Vaughn had continued to struggle this season. He had a 2-8 mark in 15 games, and manager Harry Wolverton was set to send him to the International League Providence Grays. But Vaughn balked, saying he would go back to the minors only if he were paid $50, plus part of the purchase price. The dispute ended when Clark Griffith of the Senators put in a waiver claim and got Vaughn for Washington.

It was Griffith, then the Yankees' manager, who had originally brought Vaughn to New York from Hot Springs of the Arkansas State League. Griffith also knew that the arms of certain pitchers stiffened up from the cool breezes that constantly blew through New York's Hilltop Park. Vaughn, he suspected, was one of those pitchers. Vaughn won four and lost three for Washington, but the following season he went to the Chicago Cubs where he eventually became a five-time 20-game winner.

June 26, 1912: *Jim Vaughn.* **After moving to the Cubs, Vaughn would be a five-time 20-game winner.**

April 15, 1913: Purchased Infielder Bill McKechnie from the Boston Braves

Finding himself short of roster room, Braves manager George Stallings asked for waivers on utility infielder Bill McKechnie, and Yankee manager Frank Chance claimed him. McKechnie was only 20 years old when he made his major league debut, playing three late-season games for Pittsburgh in 1907. After spending two more seasons in the minors, he returned to Pittsburgh in 1910 and played three seasons for the Pirates. This season, McKechnie was hitless in one game for the Braves, who'd drafted him off the roster of the St. Paul club in the American Association.

McKechnie was a very heady player, but an extremely weak hitter. He played in 45 games as a Yankee, batting a paltry .134, with all of his 15 hits being singles. He left the Yankees in 1914 to play for the Indianapolis club in the Federal League.

May 25, 1913: Traded Outfielder Jack Lelivelt and Infielder Bill Stumpf to the Cleveland Naps for Shortstop Roger Peckinpaugh

Cleveland had rotated three men at shortstop in 1912: one was holdover Ivy Olson, and the other two were a pair of 21-year-old rookies, Roger Peckinpaugh and Ray Chapman. Peckinpaugh played the most, 67 games, but batted just .236. This season Chapman had won the shortstop job; Olson was playing third base, and Peckinpaugh had been relegated to the bench. He'd played in only one of Cleveland's 36 games and had no official at-bats.

Nevertheless, Frank Chance liked Peckinpaugh enough to make him the object of his first trade since becoming the Yankees manager. The club had been seeking a solid everyday shortstop since selling Kid Elberfeld to Washington after the 1909 season, and Chance thought that in Peckinpaugh he'd found one. In fact, Chance had been talking to Indians manager Joe Birmingham about Peckinpaugh since the beginning of the season.

The opportunity to get outfielder Jack Lelivelt, persuaded Birmingham to make the trade. He himself was an outfielder, but one

May 25, 1913: *Roger Peckinpaugh*. **New manager Frank Chance made Peckinpaugh his first acquisition.**

who wouldn't be seeing much action because of a broken ankle. And while Lelivelt was slow-footed and weak defensively, he could hit. A onetime Washington Senator, he'd been sent by Washington to the Rochester Hustlers of the International League in 1912. The Yankees got him from Rochester in August of that year, and he batted .362 in 149 at-bats. This season Lelivelt would hit a combined .294 for New York and Cleveland, while leading the league with 12 pinch hits.

Bill Stumpf was only 20 when he batted .240 as a rookie in 1912. He was at .207 in 12 games this year, but those would be his final big league games.

June 1, 1913: Traded First Baseman Hal Chase to the Chicago White Sox for First Baseman Babe Borton and Second Baseman Rollie Zeider

Hal Chase was the Yankees' senior member in length of service, and the last remaining player from the 1905 team that he'd joined after a successful career in the Pacific Coast League. He was also their former manager, their biggest star, and the most popular player with the New York fans. Yet, despite all that Chase had meant to the franchise, manager Frank Chance had no reservations about trading him. Not only were the Yanks mired in last place with a 9-28 record, but Chance had

begun to suspect, as had many other baseball people, that Chase was "throwing" games. He was batting just .212, and Chance noticed that he seemed to lack "concentration" in the field, which led the manager to accuse Chase of "laying down."

Chase was only 30 years old, a lifetime .284 hitter, and at the time considered the finest defensive first baseman ever. However, Chase's reputation, combined with Chance's remarks, made it difficult to find a taker for him. Only White Sox manager Nixey Callahan was willing to take Chase and to offer something of comparable value in return.

Babe Borton was six years younger than Chase. He came to Chicago late in the 1912 season after playing at St. Joseph, where he led Western League batters with a .364 average. After joining the Sox, Borton batted a sensational .371 in 31 games, and was at .275 this year.

In making the trade, Chance said that he planned to take the first base position and use Borton in the outfield. Instead, Chance remained on the bench while Borton replaced the departed Chase at first. But after Borton batted just .130 in 33 games, Chance sent him to the International League Jersey City Skeeters.

Twenty-nine-year-old Rollie Zeider had played every infield position during his three years with the White Sox. Despite his .350 average in 16 games this season, Zeider wasn't much of a hitter. He did, however, have excellent speed, with stolen base totals of 49 in 1910, 28 in 1911, and 47 in 1912. Chance indicated

June 1, 1913: *Hal Chase*. **Yankee manager Frank Chance accused Chase of "laying down."**

that he would likely play him at second base or third.

Zeider batted .233 in 50 games for the 1913 Yankees, then signed with the Federal League Chicago Whales for 1914.

June 26, 1913: Sold Shortstop Claud Derrick to the Philadelphia Athletics

Between September 1910 and September 1912, Claud Derrick had played a total of 59 games for the Athletics; however, A's manager Connie Mack had too many good infielders to allow him to keep the weak-hitting Derrick. Mack sent him to Baltimore of the International League and in November 1912, the Orioles sold him to the Yankees. Derrick won the Yanks' shortstop job in spring training, but missed some early season games after Brooklyn's Zack Wheat spiked him on his throwing hand three days before the opener.

Now Derrick was going back to the A's, although before selling him to Philadelphia the Yanks had tried to send him to Rochester. That fell through when Orioles manager Jack Dunn protested, claiming that if Derrick were being returned to the International League, Baltimore should have the first chance to get him. Evidently, Mack agreed. After getting Derrick, who'd been in 23 games for the Yankees with a .292 batting average, he sent him back to Baltimore.

May 13, 1914: Purchased Catcher Les Nunamaker from the Boston Red Sox

Yankee manager Frank Chance had first seen Les Nunamaker in 1910. Chance was managing the Chicago Cubs, and Nunamaker, then 21, was trying to make the team. He was unsuccessful, but he did make the Red Sox the following season. Since then, or until Yankee owner Frank Farrell paid Boston owner Joseph Lannin $5,000 to get him, Nunamaker had been the backup to catcher (and now manager) Bill Carrigan. The Yankees expected the six-foot-two, 190-pounder (he was one of the bigger men in the league) to serve in the same ca-

May 13, 1914: *Les Nunamaker*. **The Yanks acquired the six-foot-two Nunamaker to back up first-string catcher Jeff Sweeney.**

pacity in New York, backing up first-string catcher Jeff Sweeney.

May 27, 1914: Sold Righthanded Pitcher Guy Cooper to the Boston Red Sox

Guy Cooper was a 21-year-old rookie who'd pitched in just one game: three innings of relief in a 14-1 loss at Washington on May 2. Yankee President Frank Farrell had asked the Red Sox for a player in return for Cooper, but settled for cash when Boston refused. Farrell had specifically mentioned three players: outfielders Olaf Hendricksen and Wally Rehg, and Clyde Engle, a first baseman and former Yankee.

Cooper pitched in nine games for the Red Sox in 1914 and in one the following year, winning his only decision.

June 13, 1914: Traded Outfielder Jimmy Walsh to the Philadelphia Athletics for Outfielder Tom Daley

Both Jimmy Walsh and Tom Daley had been outfielders on the 1913 world champion Philadelphia Athletics. Walsh, 28, was a semi-regular who'd batted .254 in 97 games, while Daley, 29, batted .255 in just 62 games. After the season, A's manager Connie Mack offered to send one or the other to New York as a favor to Yankee manager Frank Chance. Chance

June 13, 1914: *Jimmy Walsh* was happy to leave the second-division Yanks for the first-place Athletics.

chose Walsh, but after 43 games this season Walsh was batting just .191, and Chance changed his mind. Mack graciously agreed to take Walsh back and send the Yankees Daley, who was at .256 for Philadelphia.

Walsh claimed that his hitting problems were caused by the angle of the sun at the Polo Grounds, which was in its second year as the Yankees' home park. He added that he was glad to be leaving the second-division Yanks to go back to Philadelphia, where he expected to earn another World Series share. He would, although it was the losing share.

Daley would hit .251 for the Yankees in the second half of 1914, and then play his final ten games in 1915. In January 1916, the Yanks released him to Vernon of the Pacific Coast League.

July 6, 1914: Purchased Righthanded Pitcher Boardwalk Brown from the Philadelphia Athletics

In 1913, one year after going 13-11 as a rookie, Boardwalk Brown won 17 games for the world champion Athletics. Brown also led the A's in games started; however, he didn't get to pitch in the World Series as manager Connie Mack used only Eddie Plank, Joe Bush, and Chief Bender in Philadelphia's five-game defeat of the New York Giants. The A's were on their way to another pennant this season, but it was without any help from Brown. He'd

won only one of six decisions, and his earned run average had gone from 2.94 in 1913 to 4.09 this season.

Brown's pitching improved greatly after he went from league-leading Philadelphia to New York, a team that would finish seventh. He won six and lost five, and his ERA in 20 games as a Yankee was only 3.24. But after a 3-6 season in 1915, the Yanks released Brown to Louisville of the American Association, ending his major league career.

Brown's purchase was one segment of manager Frank Chance's two day mini-overhaul of his roster. In other moves, he brought outfielder Birdie Cree back from Baltimore of the International League, where he'd sold him this past winter, and sent second-year man Bill Holden and cash to the Orioles in return. (A month later, Baltimore sold Holden to Cincinnati.) Cree had begun his major league career with the Yankees in 1908, and he would finish it with them in 1915.

In still another move, the Yanks sent two part-time first basemen and cash to the Lincoln Tigers of the Class A Western League in exchange for Lincoln's first baseman. Going to the minors were Harry Williams, a .192-batter in 86 games in 1913-14, and Harry Kingman,

July 6, 1914: *Boardwalk Brown*. Brown's pitching would improve after leaving the league-leading A's to join the lowly Yanks.

hitless in three at-bats this season. Both had played their final major league games.

Coming to New York was 25-year-old Charlie Mullen, who'd played some for the 1910-11 Chicago White Sox. Between 1914 and 1916 Mullen would play in 192 games for the Yanks, with a .263 batting average.

And finally, the club signed Pi Schwert, a 21-year-old catcher whose big league career would consist of two games this season (hitless in five at-bats) and nine games (5 for 18) in 1915.

February 4, 1915: Purchased First Baseman Wally Pipp and Outfielder Hugh High from the Detroit Tigers

A month earlier, when Jacob Ruppert and Til Huston bought the Yankees, American League President Ban Johnson promised them he would help funnel players to New York to make that very important franchise more competitive. On the advice of manager Bill Donovan, the new owners immediately asked to purchase Hugh High, an outfielder, and Wally Pipp, a first baseman, both the property of the Detroit Tigers. Now that the money had changed hands, and Ruppert and Huston officially owned the Yankees, the sale was completed. Tiger owner Frank Navin reportedly received $5,000 for each player.

The 22-year-old Pipp had almost no major league experience, having appeared in just 12 games with the Tigers in 1913. However, he had batted .314 for the Rochester Hustlers in 1914, while hitting an International League–leading 15 home runs.

High, by contrast, was already 27 years old and had played in 171 games for the Tigers in 1913-14, with a combined .247 batting average. That's about what he would hit (actually .250) as a regular in the Yankees' outfield over the next three seasons and a final seven games in 1918.

February 4, 1915: *Jacob Ruppert* and *Bill Donovan.* New Yankee owner Ruppert (left) bought Wally Pipp and Hugh High on the advice of manager Donovan (right).

April 7, 1915: Purchased Lefthanded Pitcher Ensign Cottrell from the Boston Braves

While Ensign Cottrell had spent almost his entire career in the minor leagues, he had managed to pitch at least one game at the major league level in each of the past four seasons, and he did it for four different teams. He'd been in one game for the 1911 Pirates, one for the 1912 Cubs, two for the 1913 Athletics, where he earned his only win, and one for the 1914 Braves, a loss. (He'd spent most of the 1914 season with Baltimore of the International League.)

Cottrell got into seven games for the 1915 Yankees, his fifth and final team, and lost his only decision.

June 28, 1915: Purchased Righthanded Pitcher Bob Shawkey from the Philadelphia Athletics

The fourth-place Yankees had just split a doubleheader with the third-place Red Sox at Fenway Park, when manager Bill Donovan announced that the club had purchased pitcher Bob Shawkey's contract from the Philadelphia Athletics. The Yanks and Athletics had been discussing this deal for several days, but it had to wait until Donovan could persuade Shawkey to come to New York. Estimates of the price Connie Mack got for the 24-year-old Shawkey, who had a 6-6 record this season, ranged from a low of $18,000 to as much as $80,000.

Shawkey had reached the majors with the

June 28, 1915: *Bob Shawkey.* **Eight years later, Shawkey would face Boston's Howard Ehmke in the first regular season game at Yankee Stadium.**

A's in July 1913, and by the next season was one of Mack's top pitchers. He won 16 games in 1914 to help the Athletics to their second consecutive pennant. However, Mack had already begun the dismantling of the Athletics that would lead them from that first place finish in 1914 to last place in 1915. It was only late June, but they were already 19½ games behind the first-place Chicago White Sox.

Except for 1918, most of which he missed while serving in the U.S. Navy, Shawkey would be a fixture on the Yankee pitching staff for the next 13 seasons. He was a 20-game winner four times, and in 1920 led the American League with a 2.45 earned run average. In 1923 manager Miller Huggins gave Shawkey the honor of pitching the first game at the new Yankee Stadium. He was then the senior member of the staff and trailed only first baseman Wally Pipp in length of service on the club.

The Yanks released Shawkey in November 1927, but he stayed on as a coach in 1928 and 1929, and following Huggins's death managed the club in 1930.

Donovan also announced that he'd purchased another pitcher, George Mogridge, a 26-year-old lefthander who had pitched briefly with the White Sox in 1911 and 1912. Mogridge was currently with Des Moines of the Western League, where he had a record of 13-4.

August 19, 1915: Sold Outfielder Ed Barney to the Pittsburgh Pirates

The Yankees had picked up Ed Barney, a 25-year-old outfielder, from the International League Jersey City Skeeters in July. He played in 11 games with the Yanks, getting seven hits—all singles—in 36 at-bats. Claimed on waivers by Pittsburgh, he ended his big league career with the Pirates in 1916.

January 14, 1916: Purchased Outfielder Lee Magee from the Brooklyn Tip-Tops

Lee Magee's sale to the Yankees made him the first player from the collapsed Federal League to return to what the American and National Leagues called "organized baseball."

Yankee co-owner Til Huston negotiated the deal with Feds representative Harry Sinclair, purchasing Magee's contract for what was reported to be between $20,000 and $25,000.

Magee had spent just one season in the Federal League, 1915. He was the manager and second baseman for the Brooklyn Tip-Tops and batted .323, third best in the league. Before "jumping" to the Tip-Tops, Magee had three solid seasons with the St. Louis Cardinals. He'd been an outfielder for the Cardinals, and Yankee manager Bill Donovan said he would likely return him there in 1916.

January 21, 1916: Purchased Lefthanded Pitcher Nick Cullop from the Kansas City Packers

After a 3-7 rookie season with Cleveland in 1913, and a loss in his first 1914 decision, Nick Cullop "jumped" to the Federal League Kansas City Packers. He won 14 for the Packers while losing 19, but had an excellent 2.34 earned run average. The following season Cullop was among the league's better pitchers, going 22-11, with an ERA of 2.44. He also pitched 22 complete games, all of which made Yankee manager Bill Donovan, who'd been extremely short of lefthanded starting pitchers, delighted at his acquisition.

January 21, 1916: Purchased Second Baseman Germany Schaefer from the Newark Peppers

Nearing his 39th birthday, Germany Schaefer's playing days were just about over. He'd begun his career with the Chicago Cubs back in 1901, but had spent most of it as an American Leaguer, first in Detroit and then in Washington. Schaefer had "jumped" to the Federal League Newark Peppers in 1915, and batted .214 in 59 games.

Although Schaefer had a .respectable .257 career-batting average, the fans knew him more for his clowning than for his ability. The Yanks, however, were interested in neither his batting (he would only bat once as a Yankee) nor his clowning; they wanted Schaefer for his ability to coach younger players.

February 15, 1916: Purchased Third Baseman Frank Baker from the Philadelphia Athletics

With a little help from Ban Johnson, the president of the American League, the Yanks made the most significant acquisition in their short history. Johnson helped persuade the A's Connie Mack to sell Frank "Home Run" Baker to the Yankees rather than to Charles Comiskey, who was anxious to have Baker join his Chicago White Sox. Colonel Jacob Ruppert and Captain Til Huston paid the Athletics a reported $37,500 for the 30-year-old Baker who, despite not playing in 1915, was still the game's greatest slugger. In each of the four seasons prior to his sit-out, Baker had won or tied for the league home crown, something no Yankee player had done in the club's 13-year history. But Baker was more than just an outstanding hitter; he was also an excellent base stealer and ranked among the finest defensive third basemen in the game.

The sportswriters had been calling him "Home Run" Baker since the 1911 World Series, when he hit home runs in consecutive games against the Giants' Rube Marquard and Christy Mathewson. He'd led the American League with 11 that year, and followed with league-leading totals of 10 (tied with Tris Speaker), 12, and nine. Baker had also batted better than .300 in five of his six full seasons, including a .347 mark in 1912, and was the league's RBI leader that year and the next.

But after the Boston Braves swept the Athletics in the 1914 World Series, Mack

February 15, 1916: *Frank Baker*. **Yankee fans thought Baker's arrival would bring a pennant in 1916.**

began to disassemble his team. The ongoing breakup of the A's, and what he considered an insufficient contract offer, induced Baker to skip the 1915 season. He spent it at his farm in Trappe, on Maryland's Eastern Shore, while also playing some semi-pro baseball in Pennsylvania.

New Yorkers were excited at the news of Baker's arrival and predicted that he would help lead the club to its first pennant in 1916. But the Yanks finished fourth that year and wouldn't win their first pennant until 1921. Although he sat out again in 1920 to take care of his children following his wife Ottalee's death, Baker remained with the Yankees until he retired following the 1922 season. Never as good a player as he'd been with the A's, he still batted a solid .288 for the Yanks, while hitting 48 home runs, half his lifetime total.

July 13, 1916: Signed Outfielder Rube Oldring as a Free Agent

Rube Oldring was a .273 lifetime hitter who'd had his best season when he batted .308 for the 1910 world champion Athletics. He was also a regular on the Philadelphia teams that won the World Series in 1911 and 1913. But following the A's loss to Boston in the 1914 Series, manager Connie Mack began selling or trading his best players. As a result, for the past two seasons the Athletics had been baseball's worst team.

Oldring had announced his retirement on July 1. But when Yankee business manager Henry Sparrow called, offering him an opportunity to again play on a pennant-contending team, the 32-year-old Oldring chose to end his retirement. Mack, who'd given him his unconditional release, said he would not stand in Oldring's way.

"Oldring is a free agent and can do as he pleases," Mack said. "He has several years of great baseball in him, to my mind. A change of scenery will not do him any harm."

The Yankees had been shorthanded in the outfield since losing Frank Gilhooley, who'd broken an ankle. Roy Hartzell had been playing in Gilhooley's place; however, at 34, Hartzell had slowed considerably and manager Bill Donovan figured Oldring would be an improvement.

Oldring had begun his career with the Yankees, coming to them from Montgomery of the Southern League in late 1905. He played in eight games, getting nine hits in 30 at-bats, but he actually belonged to Philadelphia, and the Athletics were just "lending" him to the Yankees. The Yanks then tried to buy his contract, but the A's refused.

Oldring batted .234 in 43 games for the 1916 Yankees, and although he'd said he would retire again at the end of the season, he came back to play 49 games for Philadelphia in 1918.

July 15, 1917: Traded Outfielder Lee Magee to the St. Louis Browns for Outfielder Armando Marsans

Lee Magee was in the final year of a two-year contract that he'd signed after the Yanks bought him from the Federal League Brooklyn Tip-Tops. His salary was $8,300 per year, which was quite a bit more than St. Louis was paying Armando Marsans. So before they could make this deal, Yankee owners Jacob Ruppert and Til Huston had to agree to pay the Browns the difference in the two players' salaries. They did so gladly. The Yankees were

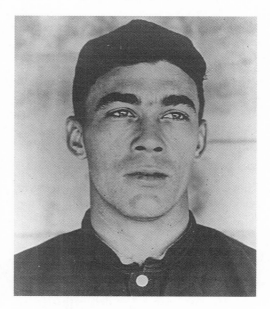

July 15, 1917: *Armando Marsans.* **Manager Bill Donovan said he'd play Marsans as long as the Cuban native hit well.**

eager to get rid of the switch-hitting Magee after he'd hit a disappointing .257 in 1916, and a meager .220 after 51 games this season.

The 30-year-old Marsans, a half-black native of Cuba, was having a similarly unproductive year, with a .230 average in 75 games. Yankee manager Bill Donovan believed that the change of scenery would help Marsans, who despite the falloff with the bat remained an excellent defensive player. With two of his outfielders, Hugh High and Frank Gilhooley, sidelined with injuries, Donovan said he would put Marsans in the starting lineup and keep him there for as long as his hitting would allow.

Because of poor hitting and a broken leg, Marsans didn't remain in the starting lineup for long. He played a final season in 1918, batting .236.

August 21, 1917: Purchased Catcher Muddy Ruel from the St. Louis Browns

Muddy Ruel was only 19 when he went hitless in 14 at-bats for the 1915 St. Louis Browns. Since then he'd been with Memphis, where the Yanks agreed he could stay until the Southern Association season ended.

January 22, 1918: Traded Righthanded Pitcher Urban Shocker, Lefthanded Pitcher Nick Cullop, Infielder Fritz Maisel, Second Baseman Joe Gedeon, and Catcher Les Nunamaker to the St. Louis Browns for Second Baseman Del Pratt, Lefthanded Pitcher Eddie Plank, and Cash

That the Browns were going to trade Del Pratt was a certainty. The only question was to whom, as the Yankees, the Washington Senators, and the Cleveland Indians all eagerly sought the 30-year-old star second baseman. Pratt's exit from St. Louis was assured after Browns owner Phil Ball accused both him and his double play partner, second baseman Doc Lavan, of "laying down" during the 1917 season. The two men responded with slander suits, but the Browns had already traded Lavan to Washington, and now that they'd traded Pratt, both players dropped their suits.

Pratt was generally considered to trail only Chicago's Eddie Collins in a ranking of American League second basemen. His six-year stay in St. Louis had been a mostly successful one, and his abilities were well-known to Miller Huggins, the newly named Yankee manager. Huggins had managed the Browns' St. Louis neighbor, the National League Cardinals, for the past five seasons. He was aware that Pratt had led the American League with 103 RBIs in 1916, but then batted .247 in 1917, his worst season ever. Nevertheless, Huggins was confident that by adding Pratt to an infield that had Wally Pipp at first, Roger Peckinpaugh at short, and Frank Baker at third, the Yanks would greatly improve on their sixth-place finish of 1917. With that in mind, he'd pursued a deal for Pratt all winter, failing to complete one only because he believed the Browns wanted too much in return. Huggins finally accomplished his goal by putting together the right combination of players, plus $15,000 of Colonel Jacob Ruppert's money.

Huggins had been hesitant about parting with Urban Shocker and Nick Cullop, but St. Louis insisted on getting pitching help in return for Pratt. Both pitchers had spent two seasons in New York: Shocker was 12-8, and Cullop was 18-15. Cullop's big league career ended the next season, but Shocker, who'd been the best pitcher in the Canadian League when the Yanks purchased him from Ottawa in 1915,

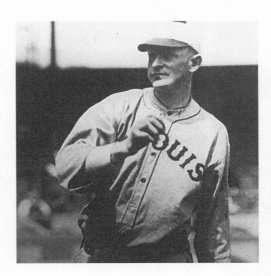

January 22, 1918: *Joe Gedeon.* **Gedeon hit .211 in 1916, his one season as a Yankee regular.**

would become one of baseball's best pitchers, and six years later Huggins would get him back in a trade.

Fritz Maisel, now 29, had been an exciting player in his first three seasons (1913–15), stealing a total of 150 bases including a league-leading 74 in 1914. However, he'd fallen off sharply the last two years, and like Cullop, his one season in St. Louis would be his last.

(Surely, the Yankees bemoaned their mistake of not trading Maisel earlier. In the winter and spring of 1916, they'd turned down even-up offers for him from the White Sox for Joe Jackson and from the Red Sox for Tris Speaker.)

The Yanks purchased Les Nunamaker from Boston in May 1914, and he'd done most of the catching for them since, batting .262 in 369 games. Now that he was gone, Roxy Walters seemed the logical successor, with rookies Truck Hanna and Muddy Ruel competing for the number two spot.

Joe Gedeon, who had played briefly for the 1913-14 Washington Senators, came to the Yankees in 1916 following an outstanding 1915 season with Salt Lake City of the Pacific Coast League. Gedeon batted .317 for the 1915 Bees, with 67 doubles, 11 triples, 19 home runs, and 25 stolen bases, but hadn't come close to duplicating those numbers in New York. Gedeon had a .211 average as the club's regular second baseman in 1916, then lost his job to Maisel the following year.

At 42, Eddie Plank was the game's oldest active player. He'd announced his retirement at the end of the 1917 season, and the trade to the Yankees did not change his plans. "I will not go to New York next season," he said from his Gettysburg, Pennsylvania, farm. "I am through with baseball forever. I have my farm and my home and enough to take care of me, so why should I work and worry any longer?"

March 8, 1918: Purchased First Baseman George Burns from the Detroit Tigers and Traded Him to the Philadelphia Athletics for Outfielder Ping Bodie

A day before he would lead the first group of players from New York's Pennsylvania Station south to Macon, Georgia, for spring training, manager Miller Huggins secured the hard-hitting outfielder he'd been seeking the entire off-season. It wasn't easy. Before they could persuade Philadelphia manager Connie Mack to part with that outfielder, Ping Bodie, the Yanks first had to buy Detroit Tiger first baseman George Burns. Mack had traded his first baseman, Stuffy McInnis, the last remaining member of Philadelphia's famed "$100,000 infield," to the Red Sox in January. Now he needed Burns, who'd been the Tigers' first baseman the past four seasons, to replace McInnis.

Huggins had also been talking to the A's about outfielder Tilly Walker, newly acquired from the Red Sox, but came away with the 30-year-old Bodie instead. Bodie had hit well in his first two years in the league, with the 1913-14 White Sox, but slipped the following two seasons. He ended up back in the Pacific Coast League before Mack brought him to Philadelphia in 1917. Weighing less than he had in previous years, the always colorful Bodie batted a solid .291 with 74 runs batted in for the last-place Athletics.

Born Francesco Pezzolo, Bodie was the first of a progression of San Francisco area players, many of Italian heritage, who would contribute so much to the Yankees' success over the years.

March 8, 1918: *Ping Bodie.* **Miller Huggins would have preferred getting Tilly Walker from the A's.**

March 18, 1918: Traded Outfielder Tim Hendryx to the St. Louis Browns

in a Three-Way Deal and Received a Player to be Named from the Cincinnati Reds

The Yankees were sending Tim Hendryx to the Browns to compensate them for sending former Yankee Lee Magee to Cincinnati. The deal would be completed on April 25 when the Reds sent catcher Tommy Clarke to New York.

Although Magee batted just .170 for St. Louis after the Yanks traded him there in July 1917, Reds manager Christy Mathewson predicted that he would return to his old form now that he was back in the National League.

The Yanks had purchased Hendryx from the Southern Association New Orleans Pelicans in August 1915. After playing 13 games for the Yanks that season, and just 15 games in 1916, Hendryx was a semi-regular outfielder on the 1917 team, batting .249 in 125 games.

The 30-year-old Clarke had been with Cincinnati since 1909 and had a .265 career batting average. He never played for the Yankees, but did play one final game for the Chicago Cubs.

December 9, 1918: Purchased Righthanded Pitcher Pete Schneider from the Cincinnati Reds

Pete Schneider was only 23, but he'd already pitched five seasons for the Reds. He had a 20-19 record with a 2.10 earned run average in 1917, but was only 10-15 with a 3.53 ERA in 1918. In both seasons he led the National League in walks. After Schneider had gone 0-1 in seven games for the Yanks in 1919, they returned him to the minor leagues where he eventually became an outfielder and played until 1926.

December 18, 1918: Signed Outfielder George Halas as a Free Agent

The Yanks signed George Halas, a former star at the University of Illinois, on the recommendation of scout Tom Connery. Halas had appeared in New York the previous fall as a member of the Great Lakes Naval Training

Center football team. He would play in 12 games for the Yanks in 1919, getting two hits in 22 at-bats before going on to football fame with the Chicago Bears.

December 18, 1918: Traded Right-handed Pitcher Ray Caldwell, Lefthanded Pitcher Slim Love, Outfielder Frank Gilhooley, Catcher Roxy Walters, and Cash to the Boston Red Sox for Righthanded Pitcher Ernie Shore, Lefthanded Pitcher Dutch Leonard, and Outfielder Duffy Lewis

Ray Caldwell, a 30-year-old spitballer who'd spent his entire nine-year career with the Yankees, was a fine fielder, a speedy base runner, and among the best hitting-pitchers of his time. Pitching mostly for weak teams, he had a 95-99 record, with his best years coming in 1914 (17-9) and 1915 (19-16). Caldwell hadn't had a winning record since, and because many of his losses had been by one run he'd developed a reputation as a "hard-luck" pitcher.

Six-foot seven-inch Slim Love had been a Yankee since 1916, compiling a three-year record of 21-17. His fastball was among the league's best, but his inability to control it had limited his success. Love was coming off his best season: a 13-12 record with a 3.07 earned-run average. However, he'd led the league in walks, and 12 of his 13 wins came at home at

December 18, 1918: *Ray Caldwell.* **Between 1910 and 1918, Caldwell won 95 games for the Yanks.**

the Polo Grounds. Love's only road win was at Philadelphia against the lowly Athletics.

The St. Louis Cardinals had given Frank Gilhooley brief looks in 1911 and 1912, before releasing him to the International League Montreal Royals. In August 1913, Montreal traded him to the Yankees for righthander George McConnell and cash. Gilhooley played 24 games for the Yanks in 1913 and single games in 1914 and 1915, but spent the major portion of those seasons back in the International League with Buffalo. In 1916, the Yanks brought him back to stay.

In all Gilhooley played a total of 259 games for the Yankees, mainly as a part-time outfielder. He missed a lot of time because of injuries—a broken ankle in 1916 and a broken collar bone in 1917—and the 112 games he played in 1918 was his career high. Gilhooley batted .276 that year, with one home run, one of the two he would hit in more than a thousand career at-bats. A lefthanded batter but a righthanded thrower, he also took part in eight double plays, the most in the league by an outfielder in 1918.

Gilhooley would revert to being a part-timer for Boston in 1919, which, though he was only 27, was his last major league season.

The Yanks purchased Roxy Walters from the Waco Navigators of the Texas League late in July 1915. He was only 22 at the time, nevertheless he was considered the smartest and fastest catcher ever to have played in the Texas League.

Walters, who made his Yankee debut on September 16, playing in two late-season games, had caught between 61 and 66 games in each of the past three seasons as a backup to Les Nunamaker. After hitting in the .260s in 1916 and 1917, his average skidded to a paltry .199 in 1918. However, Walters's chief value was as a receiver, and he was best-known for his outstanding throwing arm.

The Yanks were confident that by adding a steady, clutch-hitting veteran like Duffy Lewis, they had greatly improved their outfield—the team's weakest link in 1918. Between 1910 and 1915 Lewis and his Boston teammates, Tris Speaker and Harry Hooper, had comprised baseball's finest outfield. But the Red Sox traded Speaker to Cleveland in April 1916, and now Lewis was also gone. The 30-year-old Lewis, who'd spent the entire 1918

season in the U.S. Navy, had a .289 batting average for his eight years in Boston, with 500 runs scored and 102 stolen bases.

After pitching one game for the Giants in 1912 and a stint with the minor league Baltimore Orioles, Ernie Shore joined the Red Sox in 1914. He had a 58-33 record over the next four years and had been a major contributor to Boston's world championship teams of 1915 and 1916. However, Shore had also spent the 1918 season in the Navy, and he would not regain his former success. He would win just seven games while losing ten for the 1919-20 Yankees, which would be his final two big league seasons.

Pitcher Dutch Leonard refused to join the Yankees, and early in 1919 the Red Sox sold him to Detroit.

This was the first of what would be several major trades and sales between Boston and New York over the next five years. Those deals would play a major part in reversing the fortunes of the two teams. In December 1918 the Red Sox were the defending world champions and had won four of the last seven World Series. Yet they would fall to sixth place in the coming season and not win another pennant for 28 years.

Meanwhile, Yankee owners Jacob Ruppert and Til Huston, and manager Miller Huggins were determined to bring a championship to New York. Moreover, Ruppert and Huston were willing to spend their money (reportedly $15,000 in this deal) to speed the process. The Yanks would not win the pennant in 1919, nor would they win it in 1920. However, beginning in 1921 they would win three straight flags and then become the dominant team in baseball for the next 45 years.

March 6, 1919: Sold Righthanded Pitcher Ray Keating to the Boston Braves

In September 1912, the Yanks had paid a New England League record $7,000 for Ray Keating, a 21-year-old pitcher who'd won 26 games for the Lawrence Barristers that season. Keating was in manager Frank Chance's starting rotation for the seventh-place Yankee teams of 1913-14, winning a combined 13 games against 23 losses. But because of his failure to live up to the expectations the team had for him, manager Bill Donovan used him much less frequently in 1915 and 1916.

After Keating spent 1917 in the minors, new manager Miller Huggins brought him back to the Yankees in 1918, using him mostly in relief. In all, Keating compiled a 24-40 record in his six years in New York. He would go 7-11 for the Braves in 1919, then return to the minor leagues and pitch for another 13 years.

March 15, 1919: Sold Righthanded Pitcher Ray Fisher to the Cincinnati Reds

Ray Fisher joined Ray Caldwell and Ray Keating as the third longtime Yankee pitcher named Ray that Miller Huggins had disposed of since the end of the 1918 season. Actually, Fisher had missed the 1918 campaign due to military service, which along with his age (he was 31) influenced every American League club to waive on him. He'd been a Yankee stalwart since 1910, with his best year coming in 1915 when he won 18 games for a Yankee team that won only 69. Fisher battled tuberculosis the next two years, but he still managed to win 19 games.

The Yanks had finished second in 1910, Fisher's rookie year, but for the rest of his stay in New York he played for weak teams. Nevertheless, he managed a very respectable 76-78 record. Then, after going 24-16 in his two seasons in Cincinnati, Kenesaw M. Landis, baseball's new commissioner, unfairly suspended Fisher from baseball. It would take more than half a century before that suspension was overturned.

June 13, 1919: Sold Outfielder Bill Lamar to the Boston Red Sox

Bill Lamar was just 20 years old when the Yankees called him up from Baltimore of the International League in late September 1917. He was batting .188 in 11 games this season when the Yanks put him on the waiver list and the Red Sox claimed him. Lamar left with a combined .228 batting average in 50 games as a Yankee.

June 13, 1919: *Bill Lamar.* Lamar was just 20 years old when he joined the Yankees in 1917.

July 29, 1919: Traded Righthanded Pitchers Allan Russell and Bob McGraw and Cash to the Boston Red Sox for Righthanded Pitcher Carl Mays

Carl Mays was unpopular with both teammates and opposing players; nevertheless, he was a quality pitcher. His lifetime record with Boston was 72-51, including 20-win seasons in 1917 (22-9) and 1918 (21-13). But after struggling with a 5-11 mark this season, Mays left the Red Sox in mid–July complaining that the team had failed to give him either batting or fielding support. He said he would never again pitch for Boston and demanded that they trade him. The other Red Sox players may not have liked Mays, but they didn't want to lose him. They said that if the Sox did trade him, they would go on strike.

Owner Charles Comiskey of the Chicago White Sox instructed his manager, Kid Gleason, to offer $40,000 for Mays. Red Sox manager Ed Barrow declined the offer, saying he would have to get pitchers in return before he would part with the 27-year-old Mays. When the Yankees put in their bid for Mays, Barrow specifically asked for pitcher Allan Russell. He also agreed to take pitcher Bob McGraw and some of Jacob Ruppert and Til Huston's money, reportedly upwards of $40,000.

Russell had been with the Yankees since

August 1915. He'd worked as both a starter and a reliever, with an overall record of 26-36. He was 5-5 in 23 games this season.

The 24-year-old McGraw had made brief appearances with the Yanks in 1917 (0-1 in two games) and 1918 (0-1 in one game), and had a 1-0 record in six games this season.

American League President Ban Johnson condemned the trade and demanded that the Yankees not use Mays. But Ruppert and Huston, insisting that they had made a binding deal, defied Johnson and said Mays would pitch for the Yankees. The directors of the American League, and the courts, eventually upheld the legitimacy of the trade.

III. The Twenties

January 3, 1920: Purchased Outfielder Babe Ruth from the Boston Red Sox

Red Sox owner Harry Frazee had agreed to sell Babe Ruth's contract to Jacob Ruppert and Til Huston, co-owners of the Yankees, in late December 1919, but both teams chose to withhold the announcement until after the New Year. When they made it, the news of the sale staggered the baseball world. This past season, Ruth, still a month short of his 25th birthday, had established himself as baseball's greatest-ever power hitter. He'd led the American League in runs batted in (114) and runs scored (103), while setting new major league records in slugging percentage (.657) and home runs (29).

In addition to his batting heroics Ruth also pitched in 17 games in 1919, winning nine and losing five. Of course, before Boston moved him to the outfield on a permanent basis, Ruth had been the game's best left-handed pitcher. Still, it was that transition from pitcher to everyday player that had allowed Ruth to supersede Ty Cobb as the game's greatest attraction. However, in doing so he set in motion the events that made his departure from Boston inevitable. Fans around the league were turning out specifically to see Babe Ruth hit home runs, and Ruth wanted Frazee to pay him accordingly. He had signed a three-year contract in 1919 calling for a salary of $10,000 per year, but after completing his record-breaking season, he was insisting that the Red Sox renegotiate.

Ruth was demanding that Frazee double his yearly salary to $20,000 for the contract's two remaining seasons. Frazee refused and began to look for a buyer. The Red Sox assumed that because they had won pennants in

1916 and 1918 after trading another star player, Tris Speaker, they would win again with the players they would be able to buy with the money from this sale.

The loss of the game's greatest and most popular player enraged the Boston fans. Losing him to a team from New York only deepened their resentment. Frazee, faced with a public relations debacle, attempted to pacify infuriated Bostonians.

"The price was something enormous, but I do not care to name the figures. It was an amount the club could not afford to refuse," he said. "I should have preferred to have taken players in exchange for Ruth, but no club could have given me the equivalent in men without wrecking itself, and so the deal had to be made on a cash basis."

Along with citing instances of Ruth's subordination, Frazee went on to offer other reasons why he thought he'd made a good deal.

"No other club could afford to give the amount the Yankees have paid for him, and I do not mind saying I think they are taking a gamble. With this money the Boston club can now go into the market and buy other players and have a stronger and better team in all respects than we would have had if Ruth had remained with us. I do not wish to detract one iota from Ruth's ability as a ballplayer, nor from his value as an attraction, but there is no getting away from the fact that despite his 29 home runs, the Red Sox finished sixth in the race last season. What the Boston fans want, and what I want because they want it, is a winning team, rather than a one-man team which finishes in sixth place."

The gloom pervading Boston was in direct contrast to the joy felt in New York. Yankee fans recalled that Ruth's 28th home run in

January 3, 1920: *Babe Ruth*. **The Yankees' purchase of Ruth remains the most significant sports transaction ever.**

1919, the one that broke Ned Williamson's long-forgotten 1884 one-season mark, was among the longest ever hit at the Polo Grounds. They couldn't wait to see him hitting those home runs in a Yankee uniform. It was possible, they thought, even probable, that by playing 77 games at the Polo Grounds, with its short distance down the right field line, Ruth could break his own home run record.

Ruppert was so jubilant at having added Ruth to his team that not even a Supreme Court ruling denying his request to have the manufacture and sale of his 2.75 percent beer declared legal could dampen his bliss. He suggested that the Yanks would play Ruth in right field, reminding everyone that besides being a great pitcher and a great hitter, he was also a superior outfielder. Playing left field for Boston in 1919, he'd made only two errors and had thrown out 16 base runners. But however great a pitcher or fielder Ruth might be, it was the offense that he would bring to the Yankees that had everyone excited. Pitcher Bob Shawkey predicted that the addition of Ruth would be enough to elevate the Yanks from their third-place finish in 1919 to a pennant in 1920.

Ruth was in Los Angeles when Johnny Igoe, his business manager, telegraphed him with the news of his sale to New York. He sent a telegram back to Igoe. "Will not play anywhere but Boston. Will leave for the East Monday."

Later, perhaps after learning that Ruppert was glad to meet his salary demands, the Babe changed his mind about playing in New York. "I am not surprised," he said about the sale. "When I made my demand on the Red Sox for $20,000 a year, I had an idea they would choose to sell me rather than pay the increase, and I knew the Yankees were the most probable purchasers in that event."

Because it affected the fortunes of both teams for decades to come, and because of the legends that have grown up around it, Boston's sale of Babe Ruth to the Yankees remains the most significant player transaction in sports history. Ruth attained legendary status in New York, while also leading the Yankees to seven pennants and five World Series titles before they unceremoniously released him following the 1934 season. Meanwhile, the Red Sox did not bounce back after selling Ruth as they had after trading Speaker. Frazee evidently did not use the reported $125,000 sale price, nor the reported $350,000 loan he got from Ruppert and Huston, to bring new and better players to the Red Sox. The club that Ruth helped lead to a world championship in 1918 would not finish in the first division again until 1934, would not win another pennant until 1946, and, to date, has yet to win another World Series.

December 15, 1920: Traded Second Baseman Del Pratt, Catcher Muddy Ruel, Outfielder Sammy Vick, and Lefthanded Pitcher Hank Thormahlen to the Boston Red Sox for Righthanded Pitcher Waite Hoyt, Lefthanded Pitcher Harry Harper, Catcher Wally Schang, and Infielder Mike McNally

When the Yankees fell out of the pennant-race late in the 1920 season, a race they and their fans had expected to win, rumors surfaced that manager Miller Huggins would not be back. Second baseman Del Pratt, who'd had three fine seasons in New York, batting a combined .295, including a .314 average with 97 runs batted in 1920, campaigned actively for the job. However, the Yanks chose to retain Huggins, almost assuring that Pratt would not be a member of the club in 1921. With the Red

Sox coveting Pratt, Ed Barrow, who'd recently replaced the deceased Henry Sparrow as the Yankees' business manager, wasted no time in making a trade with the club he'd managed the past three seasons.

Barrow and Huggins were less anxious to part with 24-year-old Muddy Ruel, who had split the catching duties with Truck Hannah the past two seasons. Huggins suspected that Ruel had a promising future, but he was now under even more pressure to win the club's first pennant. To do so, he felt he needed a more experienced backstop, one who could adequately handle a staff that included veteran pitchers such as Bob Shawkey, Carl Mays, and Jack Quinn. So, just as Pratt was the key player for Boston in this deal, Wally Schang was the key player for New York. Still only 31, Schang had bettered the .300-mark the last two seasons and was also among the best defensive catchers in the league.

In Mike McNally, the Yanks were getting a five-year veteran capable of playing all the infield positions. He'd been a semi-regular for

December 15, 1920: *Waite Hoyt.* **The Yanks had high hopes for the 21-year-old Hoyt.**

the Red Sox this past season, with a .256 average in 312 at-bats. Huggins expected to use McNally as a backup infielder, while Chick Fewster, who had filled that role the past few seasons, would replace Pratt at second base.

Harry Harper had debuted with Washington as an 18 year old in 1913 and pitched for them through the 1919 season—a season in which his 21 losses led the American League. The Senators traded him to Boston a year ago, and he went 5-14 for the fifth-place Red Sox in 1920.

Sammy Vick had spent part or all of his first four major league seasons with the Yankees, yet only in 1919 did he receive much playing time. He batted .248 in 106 games, but in 1920 yielded his position to the newly-acquired Babe Ruth.

Although he'd won 28 games in his three-plus seasons in New York, Hank Thormahlen had never quite developed into the pitcher the Yankees had hoped he'd be. They now had similar hopes for 21-year-old Waite Hoyt. The former Brooklyn schoolboy star had pitched one inning for John McGraw's Giants in 1918, and compiled a 10-12 record in two seasons with the Red Sox.

December 31, 1920: Traded Lefthanded Pitcher George Mogridge and Outfielder Duffy Lewis to the Washington Senators for Outfielder Braggo Roth

Two weeks earlier, the Yanks had traded for veteran catcher Wally Schang as they strove to fashion a team capable of bringing them their first American League pennant. Adding a fine all-around player like Braggo Roth, manager Miller Huggins believed, was another big step toward achieving that goal. Roth, who got the nickname "Braggo" for his habit of promoting himself, reached the majors with the White Sox in 1914. The following season Chicago sent him to Cleveland in the Joe Jackson deal, and Roth with his combined seven home runs finished with the most in the league.

Since then Roth had played for the Athletics, the Red Sox, and in 1920 for Washington, where he batted .291. He had a lifetime

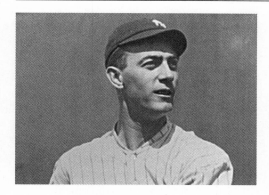

December 31, 1920: *George Mogridge.* **Senators manager Clark Griffith believed that Mogridge was still a first-rate pitcher.**

.284 average, although both Huggins and owner Jacob Ruppert felt Roth would hit .300 or better in New York. He was also a fine fielder, had a strong arm, and his 24 stolen bases in 1920 were third best in the league.

Washington manager Clark Griffith believed that by adding George Mogridge, he too had strengthened his club. Mogridge had been the Yanks' best pitcher in 1918 when he won 16 games and led the league in games pitched with 45. His win total slipped to a ten in 1919, and he had only a 5-9 record in 1920. Nevertheless, Griffith felt that at 31, Mogridge was still a first-rate pitcher, and he would be proven correct. Over the next four seasons, Mogridge won 65 games for Washington.

In 1919, his first season in New York, Duffy Lewis batted .272 and led the club with 89 runs batted in. He virtually duplicated that average in 1920, batting .271, but he missed a month because of an injured knee, played only 107 games, and had just 61 runs batted in. The 32-year-old Lewis would play just 27 games for Washington in 1921 before ending his career.

Nineteen twenty-one would also be Roth's final year in the big leagues. Injured for a good part of the season, he played only 43 games.

December 20, 1921: Traded Righthanded Pitchers Jack Quinn, Bill Piercy, and Rip Collins, and Shortstop Roger Peckinpaugh to the Boston Red Sox for Righthanded

Pitchers Joe Bush and Sam Jones, and Shortstop Everett Scott

Fresh off winning their first American League pennant, the Yanks made their first trade in 12 months—another multiplayer deal with their favorite trading partners, the Boston Red Sox. Although not reported as part of the transaction, a large sum of cash supposedly accompanied the Yankee players to Boston. Adding Sam Jones and Joe Bush, Boston's two best pitchers in 1921, to a Yankee staff that already had Carl Mays, Waite Hoyt, and Bob Shawkey gave manager Miller Huggins the league's best starting rotation.

Jones was briefly with Cleveland before they traded him to Boston in the 1916 Tris Speaker deal. In 1918, his .762 winning percentage (16-5) led the league for the world champion Red Sox, and his 23-16 mark in 1921 raised his lifetime record to 68 wins and 68 losses.

Bush, 16-9 in 1921, had been part of both the Philadelphia A's pennant-winning teams of 1913-14, and the last-place teams that Connie Mack created by selling or trading many of the stars from those championship clubs. His turn to leave came in 1918. Mack traded him to Boston, where Bush went 15-15 in the Red Sox championship season.

That the Yanks would trade Roger Peckinpaugh, their team captain, came as a big surprise to the fans, and as an absolute shock to Peckinpaugh.

December 20, 1921: *Joe Bush.* **Bush pitched for Connie Mack's pennant-winning A's of 1913-14.**

"I am too stunned to make any statement," he said. "The deal is entirely news to me, but it seems that no matter how good a player one is or how loyal service he gives the New York team, his position is never safe. It naturally distresses me to face the prospects of leaving a championship club, and a team which has a great chance to win again next season to play with a second-division club. It will take me some time to decide what I will do. My contract with the Yankees expired last fall, and if I decide to report to Boston I will have to make a new deal with Mr. [Harry] Frazee."

Peckinpaugh's dismay was understandable. He had been the glue of the Yankee infield since coming over from Cleveland in May 1913. He'd led the team in almost every offensive category at one time or another, while on defense he'd led American League short-stops in assists three times. Former Yankee owners Frank Farrell and Bill Devery thought so highly of Peckinpaugh, they made him the manager of the club for the final 17 games of the 1914 season, although he was only 23 at the time. He remains the youngest manager in big league history.

But Peckinpaugh never would play for Boston. Exactly three weeks after this trade, the Red Sox sent him to Washington as part of a three-team deal that also included the Athletics.

At 29 (the same age as Bush and Jones), Everett Scott was a year younger than Peckinpaugh, the man he would replace as the Yankee shortstop. Extremely durable, Scott hadn't missed a game since back in the 1916 season. And while not the equal of Peckinpaugh as a hitter, Scott was the better defensive player, having led the leagues' shortstops in fielding percentage in each of the last six seasons. (He would continue to do so in his first two seasons as a Yankee.)

Two of the pitchers going to Boston, Bill Piercy and Rip Collins, were only 25 years old while the third, Jack Quinn, was 38. Piercy had pitched in one game for the Yankees back in 1917, a loss, then returned to go 5-4 in 1921. Collins, who would pitch in the American League for another nine years, had won 14 games as a rookie in 1920 and 11 in 1921.

Quinn was leaving New York for the second time. He'd broken in with the Yanks back in 1909 and pitched four seasons for them. In 1913, the Yanks sent him to Rochester of the International League, and from there Quinn had gone on to the Boston Braves, to Baltimore of the Federal League, and in 1918 to the Chicago White Sox. He returned to the Yanks in 1919 by decision of the National Commission and over the protests of White Sox owner Charles Comiskey.

Quinn was among those pitchers that baseball still allowed to throw the spitball following the outlawing of the pitch in 1920. However, his 8-7 record in 1921, down from 18-10 the year before, led Huggins to believe that Quinn's career was finished. It wasn't; he would pitch in the big leagues for another 12 years and win 122 more games.

February 24, 1922: Sold Righthanded Pitcher Alex Ferguson to the Boston Red Sox

In 1921, Alex Ferguson, a 25-year-old forkballer, won three and lost one for the Yankees. However, the likelihood of his returning to New York in 1922 had diminished greatly after the Yanks acquired pitchers Joe Bush and Sam Jones from Boston. On the same day Bush ended his holdout and signed his 1922 contract, Hugh Duffy, who'd managed him at Boston, claimed Ferguson for the Red Sox.

April 17, 1922: Purchased Outfielder Whitey Witt from the Philadelphia Athletics

Whitey Witt, Babe Ruth, and Bob Meusel would eventually make up New York's regular outfield this season. Yet, Witt wouldn't play his first game until April 21, and Ruth and Meusel wouldn't make their 1922 debuts until a month after that. Commissioner Kenesaw M. Landis had suspended Ruth and Meusel until May 20 for their "barnstorming" tour following the 1921 season, which violated Landis's edict that World Series participants were not to appear in post-season exhibition games.

Norm McMillan, Elmer Miller, and Chick Fewster constituted the Yankee outfield in most of their early season games, but the

April 17, 1922: *Whitey Witt.* **Witt would be the Yankees' leadoff hitter for the next three seasons.**

club would soon trade all three to the Red Sox: Miller and Fewster in July, and McMillan after the season ended.

Witt was an established outfielder who'd spent five seasons with Philadelphia and had hit better than .300 in each of the last two. Yankee manager Miller Huggins wanted a player of Witt's caliber to stabilize his outfield while Ruth and Meusel were absent, and A's manager Connie Mack was happy to get the $16,000 the Yanks reportedly paid for him.

Huggins planned to use Witt to replace McMillan in right field for the next day's game at Boston. However, Witt failed to show up, and McMillan, a rookie, batted fourth and went three for five. The following day, Witt again failed to report and McMillan had four hits in a doubleheader against the Red Sox. Two days later, when the Yanks played their home opener against Washington, they were still without Witt, and McMillan had three more hits. Witt finally made his Yankee debut the next day, April 21. He led off and played right field, with Huggins shifting the hot-hitting McMillan to center and giving Miller a rest.

The speedy Witt eventually took over in center field and was the Yankees' leadoff batter until they released him in July 1925. In three full seasons, 1922 through 1924, he batted .297, .314, and .297 again. But he started very poorly in 1925, and was struggling with a .200 batting average after 31 games when the Yanks let him go. Witt played a final season

with Brooklyn in 1926, and then retired, though he was only 31.

July 23, 1922: Traded Outfielders Chick Fewster and Elmer Miller, Shortstop Johnny Mitchell, a Pitcher to Be Named, and Cash to the Boston Red Sox for Third Baseman Joe Dugan and Outfielder Elmer Smith

So apparently one-sided was this trade, criticism from around the American League began immediately after Yankee business manager Ed Barrow announced it. The loudest complaints, naturally, came from Boston, where the fans had become fed up with owner Harry Frazee for divesting the team of its best players. Sending them to New York made it that much more galling. An unidentified fan summed up the feeling of Red Sox fans this way: "Looks as if New York can get what it wants in baseball, especially when the Red Sox are involved." Former mayor John Fitzgerald, who himself wanted to buy the Red Sox, said that Frazee appeared "willing to smash the club and get his money in trades rather than at the turnstiles."

Manager Tris Speaker of the Indians was even more exasperated by news of the trade. "It's a crime," Speaker said. "The Yanks got all the best of it, as usual. [Chick] Fewster is the best of the players sent to Boston, but even he doesn't compare with Elmer Smith and [Joe] Dugan. Twice the Cleveland club has tried to get Smith back from Boston, but each time President Frazee has imposed exorbitant terms. The last time he asked for outfielder Joe Evans, pitcher Jim Bagby, and $5,000 cash."

Kid Gleason, the manager of the Chicago White Sox, also sounded bitter when he learned that Joe Dugan was going to New York. "I tried to make a trade with Boston for Dugan," he said, "but was told there was nothing doing." (Some think that it was this deal that led Commissioner Landis to impose the June 15 deadline for making intraleague trades without getting waivers.)

The only person who thought the deal might not be such a good one for the Yankees was American League President Ban Johnson. "New York may secure temporary relief in the deal with Boston," he said. "Personally, I do not regard Dugan an asset to any ballclub. He is temperamental and does not take the game as seriously as he should. Unfortunately, the New York club seems to have too many players of that type."

Johnson's low opinion of the 25-year-old Dugan was based on the problems Connie Mack had with him when Dugan played for the Athletics. He'd come to the A's out of Holy Cross College in 1917 as a shortstop. Mack moved him to third base in 1920, and he'd blossomed the last two seasons, batting .322 in 1920 and .295 in 1921. But Dugan was unhappy with the A's losing ways and left the club several times during the '21 season. Mack suspended him each time and then granted his wish to be traded by sending him to Boston in January 1922. (Actually, it was a three-way-trade, with Dugan going from Philadelphia to Washington, and then to Boston.)

While Dugan was not a better fielder than Mike McNally, the Yanks incumbent third baseman, he was clearly a better hitter. Currently batting .287, Dugan would be in the lineup the following day when the Yanks began a Western swing in St. Louis. The Browns were battling the Yankees for the pennant, so the news that New York had shored up its weakest position disturbed them too.

Like Dugan, Smith was also in his first season with the Red Sox. Before that he'd sandwiched two stints with the Indians around a brief stay with the Senators. He'd batted .316 with 103 RBIs for the world champion Indians in 1920 and followed with a .290 mark in 1921. The Yanks did not expect Smith, who was batting .286 in 73 games for Boston this season, to break into their starting outfield of Bob Meusel, Whitey Witt, and Babe Ruth. In fact, Smith would have only 27 at-bats for the Yanks in 1922, getting just five hits for a .185 average. He did better in 1923, batting .306 in 70 games, but it was his final year with the club.

The Yanks had purchased Elmer Miller from the Mobile Sea Gulls of the Southern Association in July 1915. He spent a total of six seasons with them (1915–18, 1921-22), mostly as a spare outfielder. Only in 1917, when he was the regular right fielder, did Miller play as many as 100 games; he played in 114 that

July 23, 1922: *Elmer Smith*. **Other AL managers protested the one-sidedness of the trade that brought Smith and Joe Dugan to the Yankees.**

season and batted .251. Overall, Miller had a .250 batting average as a Yankee.

The Yanks had gotten Chick Fewster from Baltimore of the International League in 1917. After playing a combined 16 games in 1917-18, he got in 81 games in 1919 and batted .283. In an exhibition game the following spring, Fewster suffered a near fatal beaning by Brooklyn's Jeff Pfeffer. He had only 21 at-bats in 1920, but came back to bat .280 in 1921, and had a .242 average after 44 games this season.

Johnny Mitchell had been an outstanding shortstop with Vernon of the Pacific Coast League before joining the Yankees in 1921. Unfortunately, for him, the Yanks had Roger Peckinpaugh at short then and Everett Scott now, so Mitchell hadn't gotten much playing time. He played in just 13 games in 1921 and had only four at-bats this season.

Besides another $50,000 going from Yankee owner Jacob Ruppert to Red Sox owner Harry Frazee, Boston later received Lefty O'Doul as the pitcher to be named. The future two-time National League batting champion had been in five games in 1919-20 and six this season, but was yet to have a win or a loss.

January 3, 1923: Traded Catcher Al Devormer and Cash to the Boston Red Sox for Minor League Right-

handed Pitcher George Pipgras and Minor League Outfielder Harvey Hendrick

Although Yankee business manager Ed Barrow and Red Sox owner Harry Frazee, the same two men who had been responsible for many of the recent deals between the two clubs, engineered this trade, it was different in several ways from the previous ones. First, there was no money going from Yankee owner Jacob Ruppert to Frazee. Second, two Red Sox players were going to New York and only one Yankee player was going to Boston; Frazee generally received more players than he gave up. And, in perhaps the most unusual aspect of the trade, Al DeVormer, the best-known player and the only one of the three with major league experience, was heading to Boston, not New York.

DeVormer came to the Yankees in 1921 after starring in the Pacific Coast League. He batted .347 in 22 games as a rookie third-string catcher, but fell off to .203 in 24 games in 1922. With Wally Schang catching most of the games, and with a capable reserve in Fred Hofmann, the Yanks felt that retaining the 31-year-old DeVormer was needless. Furthermore, manager Miller Huggins was high on young Benny Bengough, reputed to be the best defensive catcher in the minor leagues.

The two minor leaguers coming to New York were Harvey Hendrick, a 25-year-old lefthanded hitting outfielder who'd played with Galveston of the Texas League in 1922, and George Pipgras, just two weeks past his 23rd birthday, who'd pitched for Charleston of the South Atlantic League in '22. Pipgras was a righthander, and because the Yankees' five starters from 1922—Joe Bush, Bob Shawkey, Waite Hoyt, Carl Mays, and Sam Jones—were also righthanded, he was given little chance of joining the starting rotation.

January 30, 1923: Traded Outfielders Norm McMillan and Camp Skinner, Righthanded Pitcher George Murray, and Cash to the Boston Red Sox for Lefthanded Pitcher Herb Pennock

Having lost the last two World Series to

the New York Giants, the Yankees were determined to fashion a club in 1923 that would bring them a world championship. So while this trade, which sacrificed future prospects for help in the upcoming season, appeared heavily one-sided in favor of the Red Sox, it was part of a wider plan. Manager Miller Huggins wanted a lefthanded starter—even one with a so-so record like Herb Pennock—to offset the all-righthanded rotation of Bob Shawkey, Carl Mays, Waite Hoyt, Joe Bush, and Sam Jones, the Yanks had used in 1922.

Additionally, the Yanks felt that by adding Pennock, they could now afford to trade Hoyt. They were pursuing a deal that would send Hoyt, outfielder Bob Meusel, and second baseman Aaron Ward to the White Sox, in exchange for Chicago's great second baseman Eddie Collins, pitcher Charlie Robertson, and outfielder Bibb Falk. If they could complete this deal, the Yanks believed, they would be a greatly improved team in 1923.

This trade had been designed originally as a one-for-one swap of Pennock for Norm McMillan. But after Red Sox owner Harry Frazee persuaded his Yankee counterpart, Colonel Jacob Ruppert, to throw in pitcher George Murray and outfielder Camp Skinner, it inspired one Yankee official to call it "the worst trade the Yanks ever made." However, Yankee manager Miller Huggins seemed to favor the deal. Ruppert and Frazee had negotiated the swap earlier, but didn't formally

January 30, 1923: *Herb Pennock.* **Miller Huggins wanted the lefthanded Pennock because all his other starters were righthanded.**

announce it until Ruppert had gotten Huggins's approval.

"Murray is a first-rate pitcher," Huggins said, "but he would only sit on the bench next year. I have enough righthanders now—all I need. The staff needed a lefthander of experience." Huggins claimed Pennock was that man and that he should win 15 games for the Yankees in 1923.

Pennock had debuted with the 1912 Philadelphia Athletics when he was just 18 years old. Two years later he went 11-4 for Connie Mack's pennant-winning A's, but in June 1915 Mack sold him to Boston. Known more for his steadiness than for possessing any great ability, Pennock was 10-17 for the last-place Red Sox in 1922, and had a career record of 80-78.

Of the three players leaving the Yankees, they'd had the most hopes for Murray. Signed out of North Carolina State College in 1920, he pitched for the Rochester Colts of the International League before joining the Yanks in May 1922. Murray, now 24, appeared in 22 games, all but two in relief, winning four and losing two.

McMillan, a converted infielder, got off to a great start in 1922, his rookie season, while filling in for the suspended Babe Ruth. But he didn't see much action after Ruth returned, playing in only 33 games, and batting .256.

As it had been for Murray and McMillan, 1922 was also Skinner's rookie season. He batted .182 in 33 at-bats, all but three as a pinch hitter.

Despite the Yankee official who thought this trade was such a bad one, it actually turned out to be one-sided in New York's favor. In their major league careers after leaving the Yankees, Murray won only 16 games, McMillan played in fewer than 400, and Skinner played in only seven. Meanwhile Pennock, benefiting by pitching for five Yankee pennant-winners between 1923 and 1933, won 162 games and lost only 90. He was 40 years old when the Yanks released him in January 1934, but he pitched one final season for the Red Sox.

May 31, 1923: Purchased Shortstop Ernie Johnson from the Chicago White Sox

This routine waiver purchase was the Yankees' first transaction under the sole own-ership of Jacob Ruppert, who earlier in the day had finalized his purchase of Til Huston's half-share in the club. Every team in the American League had to pass on paying the $4,000 waiver price before the first-place Yankees could claim 35-year-old veteran shortstop Ernie Johnson.

The Yankees, of course, had Everett Scott at shortstop, but Miller Huggins had plans for the lefthand hitting Johnson, whose erratic fielding in recent weeks had led White Sox manager Kid Gleason to replace him with Harvey McClellan. Nevertheless, Huggins said he would use Johnson to complement Mike McNally, the club's other utility infielder.

Johnson would play in just 19 games in the second half of 1923, but he hit a spectacular .447, with a .605 slugging average. He continued to hit well in his final two seasons with the Yankees (and in the majors), batting .353 in 64 games in 1924, and .282 in 76 games in 1925.

December 11, 1923: Sold Righthanded Pitcher Carl Mays to the Cincinnati Reds

Rumor had it that after all seven American League clubs waived on him, Carl Mays would be heading across town to John McGraw's Giants. Instead, the Yanks sold the 32-year-old submariner to the Cincinnati Reds. With the Reds likely to be the Giants' chief competitors in 1923, the Yanks were only too happy to make a deal that might adversely affect their bitter intracity rivals.

Actually, Yankee manager Miller Huggins would have rejoiced over ridding the team of Mays no matter where he went. Huggins disliked Mays intensely, as did many of his players, and he had never forgiven Mays for what he felt was a questionable pitching performance in the fourth game of the 1921 World Series. The following season, Mays went 12-14, and in 1923, though he was perfectly healthy, Huggins used him in only 23 games, mostly in relief.

All this after Mays's first two full seasons as a Yankee, in which he'd been sensational, winning 26 games in 1920 and a league-leading 27 in 1921. He would return to that form with Cincinnati in 1924; still, getting rid of

December 11, 1923: *Carl Mays.* **Miller Huggins never forgave Mays for his poor performance in the 1921 World Series.**

Mays was for Huggins the type of transaction that Branch Rickey would later define as "addition by subtraction."

December 10, 1924: Traded Infielder Mike McNally to the Boston Red Sox for Infielder Howard Shanks

Mike McNally came to the Yankees from the Red Sox in the December 1920 deal that also brought Waite Hoyt and Wally Schang. In four seasons with the Yanks, the speedy McNally batted a combined .252 while filling in at all the infield positions, primarily at third base, and was often used as a pinch runner. He played third base in seven of the eight games of the 1921 World Series loss to the New York Giants, batting just .200, but with two stolen bases, including a first game steal of home. One day after being traded back to Boston, the Sox would trade him to Washington for third baseman Doc Prothro.

At 33, Howard Shanks was two years older than McNally. He'd spent 13 years in the American League, the first 11 with the Washington Senators. Although primarily a defensive player, he had his best offensive year in 1921, batting .302 and leading the league with 18 triples. Shanks would bat .258 in 66 games in 1925, his one year with the Yankees, and his final big league season.

December 15, 1924: Purchased Catcher Steve O'Neill from the Boston Red Sox

Before spending 1924 with the Red Sox, Steve O'Neill had been with Cleveland since his big league debut in September 1911. He'd established himself as one of the game's better catchers, and in 1920 he was clearly the best, batting .321 in 149 games for the world champion Indians. But after two more successful seasons, .322 in 1921 and .311 in 1922, O'Neill added a great deal of weight and his average fell to .248 in 1923. He did even worse in 1924 after the Indians traded him to Boston. O'Neill reported out of shape, and after a good start he slumped badly. Eventually Val Picinich replaced him behind the plate, and O'Neill played in only 106 games, catching 92, and batted just .238.

December 15, 1924: *Steve O'Neill.* **O'Neill batted .321 for the world champion Indians in 1920, but had fallen off sharply by 1924.**

The Yanks got O'Neill for the $4,000 waiver price after the six American League clubs that finished below them in 1924 chose to pass. His likely spot for 1925 figured to be as the third-string catcher behind Wally Schang and Benny Bengough. (Veteran receiver Fred Hofmann, a Yankee for the past six seasons, would be let go after appearing in three games in 1925.) Manager Miller Huggins also planned to use the 33-year-old O'Neill as a teacher for his young pitchers, a role he had played for manager Lee Fohl with the Red Sox.

Playing behind Bengough and Schang, O'Neill batted .286 in 91 at-bats for the Yanks in 1925, but after the season ended they sent him to Reading of the International League.

December 17, 1924: Traded Right-handed Pitchers Joe Bush and Milt Gaston, and Lefthanded Pitcher Joe Giard to the St. Louis Browns for Righthanded Pitcher Urban Shocker

Back in 1918, in Miller Huggins's first major move after becoming manager of the Yankees, he traded five players to the St. Louis Browns for second baseman Del Pratt. Among them was pitcher Urban Shocker, a move that Huggins had come to regret. Shocker became a four-time 20-game winner for the Browns (1920–23), before slipping to 16-13 in 1924. When Browns manager George Sisler, who'd had several clashes with Shocker during the preceding season, announced several weeks earlier that the 34-year-old righthander was available, the Yanks went after him. St. Louis insisted that Waite Hoyt be included in the deal and turned down several offers from the New Yorkers before finally agreeing to this package.

Huggins was overjoyed at having Shocker back. "He'll just about make our pitching staff," he said. The Yanks had tried to pry him loose from the Browns a year ago, at the winter meetings in December 1923. But when Browns owner Phil Ball asked for Sam Jones and Bob Meusel in return, an incensed Huggins replied that he would not even trade Jones alone to get Shocker.

One of the last legal spitball pitchers, Shocker had been a favorite target of his new teammate, Babe Ruth. Although the Babe had failed to connect against him this past season, he'd hit more home runs off Shocker (nine) than any other pitcher except George Dauss of the Tigers.

Shocker pitched the Yanks to victory on Opening Day, 1925, and won 49 games over the next three seasons. Following a lengthy holdout in 1928, he pitched in only one game after signing, and then died prematurely on September 9, 1928, of an enlarged heart.

Joe Bush had spent three years in New York, after five in Philadelphia and four in Boston. He had his best season in 1922, his first as a Yankee, when he went 26-7 and led the American League with a .788 winning percentage. Remarkably, Bush's record as a Yankee against his new team, the Browns, was 16-1, with six of the wins (and the one loss) coming in 1922, the year the Yanks edged St. Louis for the pennant. He followed that by beating the Browns six times in 1923 and four times during the 1924 season.

Not nearly as successful against the rest of the league, Bush's record in 1923 was 19-15, and in 1924 it was 17-16. That 17-16 mark for a team that finished two games out of first place was much less impressive than Shocker's 16-13 record for the sub–.500 Browns.

Milt Gaston was already 27 years old when the Yanks purchased him from the semi-pro Doherty Silk Sox of Paterson, New Jersey in the winter of 1923. Considered a promising prospect by Huggins, he had appeared in 29 games in 1924, primarily in relief, winning five and losing three.

To sweeten the deal for St. Louis, the Yanks sent them Joe Giard, a 26-year-old left-hander with no major-league experience, whom they had just purchased from Toledo of the American Association.

December 17, 1924: *Milt Gaston*. In 1924, Gaston won five and lost three as a 28-year-old rookie.

May 5, 1925: Traded Lefthanded Pitcher Ray Francis and Cash to the Boston Red Sox for Outfielder Bobby Veach and Righthanded Pitcher Alex Ferguson

With Babe Ruth still out with the intestinal abscess that had prevented him from playing thus far this season, the Yanks obtained Bobby Veach to help fill the void. Along with pitcher Ray Francis, the Yankees paid Detroit the $4,000 waiver price for both Veach and pitcher Alex Ferguson.

Manager Miller Huggins had given Ben Paschal the first shot at filling Ruth's position, but the righthanded-hitting Paschal had trouble hitting righthanded pitching. Huggins had also given rookie first baseman Lou Gehrig, a lefthanded batter, a brief try in the outfield, but he too had proved ineffective. A five-game losing streak spurred the Yankees to action.

The lefthanded hitting Veach had averaged better than .300 during 12 outstanding years with the Detroit Tigers. He'd teamed with Ty Cobb and Sam Crawford, and later with Cobb and Harry Heilmann, to form two of the all-time great outfields. Veach batted .295 for Boston in 1924, his first year with the Red Sox, but he was approaching his 37th birthday and had been in only one game this season. Nevertheless, Huggins felt Veach could help the Yankees as a part-time right fielder until Ruth returned, and then as a pinch hitter.

Ferguson was returning to the Yankees, for whom he had pitched briefly before they sold him to Boston in February 1922. Winless with two losses this season, his 17 losses in 1924 tied him for the most in the American League.

Francis had pitched for Washington in 1922 and Detroit in 1923, but spent 1924 with the Atlanta Crackers of the Southern Association. The Yanks purchased him from Atlanta along with outfielder Ben Paschal on August 14, 1924. Paschal joined the club later in the '24 season, but Francis didn't become a Yankee until this season. He had appeared in four games in 1925, with no record.

June 17, 1925: Sold Shortstop Everett Scott to the Washington Senators

In May, manager Miller Huggins had ended Everett Scott's record-setting consecutive game streak at 1,307 by replacing him with Pee Wee Wanninger. Scott had begun the streak as a member of the Boston Red Sox and continued it after Boston traded him to the Yankees in December 1921. Now, with Scott batting .212, Huggins was making the change permanent.

Scott batted .254 in his three-plus seasons as a Yankee. He'd also been the American League's best defensive shortstop of his era, having led in fielding for eight consecutive seasons, six with the Red Sox (1916–21) and two with the Yankees (1922-23).

The Senators, the defending world champions, didn't need Scott to play shortstop, since they had the league's best in Roger Peckinpaugh. However, Washington manager Bucky Harris was dissatisfied with his utility infielders, Spencer Adams and Mike McNally, and planned to use Scott in that role.

August 17, 1925: Sold Outfielder Bobby Veach and Righthanded Pitcher

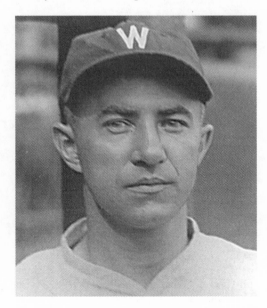

June 17, 1925: *Everett Scott*. **A month after Miller Huggins ended Scott's consecutive game streak, he traded him to Washington.**

Alex Ferguson to the Washington Senators

Just three and a half months after getting Bobby Veach and Alex Ferguson from the Red Sox, the Yankees sold them both to Washington for the same $4,000 waiver price they'd paid Detroit to obtain them. Unlike the Senators, who were looking to strengthen themselves for the stretch-drive, the Yanks were on their way to a disastrous seventh-place finish and had no need for the two veterans.

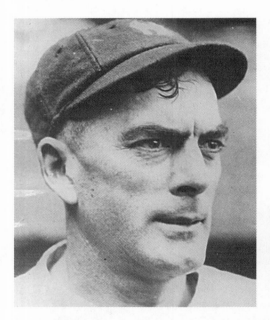

August 17, 1925: *Bobby Veach*. The Yanks acquired the veteran Veach as a fill-in until Babe Ruth recovered from his stomach problems.

Veach had done an excellent job in New York, batting .353 in 56 games. But he would bat just .243 in 18 games with Washington, and though he would play several more years in the minors, this was his last major league season.

Ferguson, who was 4-2 in 21 games in his second stint with the Yankees, won five of six for the pennant-winning Senators, and then split two decisions against Pittsburgh in the World Series.

January 15, 1926: Sold First Baseman Wally Pipp to the Cincinnati Reds

Gentlemanly Wally Pipp was not only one of manager Miller Huggins's favorite players, he was also among the most popular with Yankee fans. He'd come to New York from the Tigers as a 22-year-old rookie in 1915, a time when American League president Ban Johnson was still encouraging league members to help strengthen the New York franchise. Pipp was the Yankees' first baseman from that year through 1924, although he missed part of the 1918 season while serving in the military. He was an outstanding fielder and a reliable clutch hitter who five times in his Yankee career batted in more than 90 runs. Pipp led the league in home runs in 1916 and 1917, and with Babe Ruth and Bob Meusel supplied the power that helped the Yankees win three straight pennants between 1921 and 1923.

A self-imposed benching early in the 1925 season led to Pipp's losing his first base job to Lou Gehrig. After that the Yanks tried to trade him to several different American League

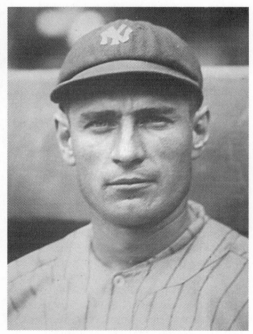

January 15, 1926: *Wally Pipp*. The former two-time home run king had lost his job to Lou Gehrig.

clubs, but couldn't come to terms with any of them. So, after asking and getting waivers on him, they sold Pipp to Cincinnati for what was said to be more than the $7,500 waiver price.

Pipp would play three seasons at first base for the Reds before retiring.

January 20, 1926: Purchased Infielder Spencer Adams from the Washington Senators

Spencer Adams, a left-hand hitting utility infielder, played in only 39 games with Washington in 1925; nevertheless, Senators owner Clark Griffith claimed he hated to lose him. Actually, some observers believed that Griffith was selling him to New York as a gesture of appreciation for the Yanks sending Bobby Veach, Alex Ferguson and Everett Scott to Washington during the 1925 season. All three had helped the Senators repeat as American League champions.

Adams batted .120 in 28 games for the Yanks in 1926 and then finished his major league career with the Cardinals in 1927.

February 6, 1926: Traded Catcher Wally Schang to the St. Louis Browns

February 6, 1926: *Wally Schang.* Schang would outhit his Yankee replacements for each of the next three seasons.

for Lefthanded Pitcher George Mogridge and Cash

With Wally Schang's departure, only Babe Ruth, Bob Meusel, Aaron Ward, and Bob Shawkey remained from the Yankee team that participated in the club's first World Series against the Giants in 1921. Schang was the first-string catcher that year, his first with the Yanks after his trade from Boston. He remained the first-string catcher until 1924, although injuries limited his playing time in 1923, and by 1925 Benny Bengough had replaced him as number one.

Schang batted .297 in his five years in New York, but he was 36 years old and had batted just .240 in 1925, leading manager Miller Huggins to conclude that his best days as a player had passed. But Schang would prove Huggins wrong by outhitting his replacements with the Yankees for each of the next three seasons.

George Mogridge was a former Yankee, but at age 37 he did not fit into Huggins's plans for 1926. As a ten-year man, Mogridge could have vetoed a move to the minor leagues, but he didn't. The Yanks sent him to St. Paul of the American Association, and then in June sold him to the Boston Braves.

In an unrelated move the Yanks announced that 22-year-old lefthanded pitcher Ben Shields had asked to be placed on the "voluntarily retired" list. Doctors had advised Shields, who'd pitched in two games in 1924 and was 3-0 in 1925, that rest was necessary to recover from his illness and to rebuild his health. He wouldn't pitch in the major leagues again until 1930, and then with the Boston Red Sox.

June 15, 1926: Purchased Outfielder Roy Carlyle from the Boston Red Sox

By getting 25-year-old Roy Carlyle, the Yankees concluded their season-long search for a lefthanded pinch hitter. Although Carlyle had batted .325 as a rookie in 1925, and was batting .287 for the wretched Red Sox this year, manager Lee Fohl was willing to part with him because of his defensive liabilities. The Yanks, on the other hand, were not concerned with Carlyle's defense. With an outfield

June 15, 1926: *Earle Combs, Babe Ruth, Bob Meusel*. **Roy Carlyle was not going to break into this outfield.**

of Babe Ruth, Bob Meusel, and Earle Combs, Carlyle's role would be strictly as a pinch hitter.

Carlyle batted a resounding .385 in 35 games for the Yankees, but never again played in the major leagues.

July 22, 1926: Purchased Catcher Hank Severeid from the Washington Senators

After announcing that first-string catcher Pat Collins would likely miss two weeks with a strained elbow, the Yanks paid Washington the waiver price to get Hank Severeid, a durable, good-hitting catcher with a strong throwing arm. Severeid, who'd spent most of his career with the St. Louis Browns, was in his 15th and final major league season. He would bat .255 in 63 games with the Yankees, and then catch all seven World Series games against the Cardinals.

August 27, 1926: Purchased Lefthanded Pitcher Dutch Ruether from the Washington Senators

Dutch Ruether was a 32-year-old veteran with a career record of 122-86, including a solid 12-6 mark for Washington this season. For the other clubs in the league to waive on him and allow Ruether to go to the league-leading Yankees, who were already nine games ahead of the second-place Cleveland Indians, seemed to make no sense. The explanation would come in October when the Yanks shipped lefthanded pitcher Garland Braxton and rookie outfielder Nick Cullop to Washington.

Braxton had pitched for the Braves in 1921-22, but spent the next three seasons in the minor leagues. He was having an outstanding 1925 season with Springfield of the Eastern League when the Yanks purchased him, and manager Miller Huggins made him a relief pitcher. Braxton had a 1-1 record in the last weeks of 1925, and was 5-1 in 1926.

Cullop's Yankee career consisted of a hit in two at-bats this past April, before Huggins returned him to the minors.

To make room on the roster for Ruether, the Yanks sent reserve catcher Bill Skiff to Toronto of the International League. Skiff had been 1 for 11 in six games in what would be his only year with the Yanks. (He'd also played in 16 games with the 1921 Pirates.) On January 13, 1927, they sent him to Newark of the International League, and he never again played in the big leagues.

Ruether was 2-3 for the Yankees in the last month of 1926, and won 13 and lost six in 1927, his final major league season.

January 13, 1927: Traded Second Baseman Aaron Ward to the Chicago White Sox for Catcher Johnny Grabowski and Second Baseman Ray Moreheart

The White Sox had recently released 39-year-old Eddie Collins and now needed a second baseman to replace the future Hall of Famer. The man they wanted was Aaron Ward, who'd been an important member of the Yankees' pennant-winning teams of 1921, 1922, and 1923. Ward had come to New York as a 21 year old in 1917 and spent the next three seasons as a utility player. In 1920 Miller Huggins made him his third baseman after Frank Baker chose to sit out the season following the death of his wife, Ottalee. When Baker returned in 1921, Ward shifted to second and had his best season. He batted .306, with 75 runs-batted-in and 77 runs scored, and remained the Yankee second baseman until he lost the job to rookie Tony Lazzeri in 1926.

Lazzeri's emergence made Ward expendable, and allowed the Yanks to go after Johnny Grabowski. In three years with the Sox, Grabowski had established himself as one of the best-throwing catchers in the game. He would spend three seasons with the Yankees, sharing the catching duties with Benny Bengough and Pat Collins in the first two, but got into only 22 games in 1929 as Bill Dickey took over as the club's full-time catcher.

Ray Morehart, who batted .318 as a fill-in for Collins at Chicago in 1926, would bat .256 as a fill-in for Lazzeri in New York in 1927. It was Morehart's final major league season.

February 8, 1927: Traded Righthanded Pitcher Sam Jones to the St. Louis Browns for Outfielder Cedric Durst and Lefthanded Pitcher Joe Giard

Yankee manager Miller Huggins revealed that he had been after both Cedric Durst, a 30-year-old outfielder, and Joe Giard, a 28-year-old pitcher, for more than a year. Although Durst was merely a .234-hitter in parts of three seasons with the Browns, several major league clubs had tried to get him. Huggins said he would use Durst as a pinch hitter, and as his lefthanded hitting spare outfielder to complement the righthanded hitting Ben Paschal.

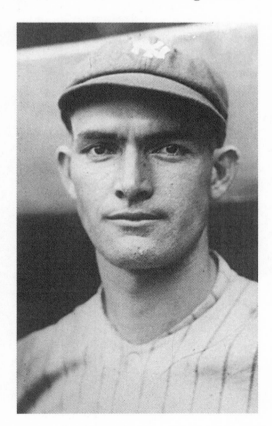

January 13, 1927: *Aaron Ward.* **Chicago needed a replacement at second base for Eddie Collins.**

February 8, 1927: *Urban Shocker*. **Three years earlier, the Yanks had included Joe Giard in a trade for Shocker.**

Giard had been Yankee property before Huggins dealt him to St. Louis in the December 1924 trade for Urban Shocker. Nevertheless, Huggins claimed that "Giard was the man I wanted most. Both my lefthanders are aging," he said, "and you never can tell when they will crack. What I needed was a young southpaw who is coming instead of going. [Sam] Jones had a bad year last season. I had to shake up the pitching staff, and so I decided to take a chance on Giard." (One of the "aging" lefthanders Huggins was referring to was his ace, Herb Pennock, who was in the midst of a holdout battle with general manager Ed Barrow. The other was Dutch Ruether.)

Giard, 13-15 in his two seasons in St. Louis (1925–26), had been hampered by a lack of control, with his walks far exceeding his strikeouts. He would be of little help to the Yankees in 1927, his last big league season. In 16 relief appearances, he neither won nor lost a game, while walking 19 batters in 27 innings.

Manager Dan Howley of the Browns was also pleased with his new acquisition.

"They tell me that Jones was a big disappointment last season," said Howley, "but he couldn't be worse than some of the Browns' pitchers. He still has a world of stuff, is only thirty-five, and might thrive under a change of scene."

As Howley suggested, Jones had been a disappointment in New York. He'd won 21 games for the Yanks in 1923, but two years later he led the league with 21 losses, and in 1926

he won only nine while losing eight. And despite Howley's hopes, Jones did not "thrive under a change of scene." After he went 8-14 for the seventh-place Browns in 1927, they sold him to Washington.

December 21, 1927: Signed Right-handed Pitcher Stan Coveleski as a Free Agent

Stan Coveleski was a four-time 20-game winner for Cleveland, but the Indians had released him following the 1924 season. Washington manager Bucky Harris signed him, and Coveleski won 20 games and lost only five for the pennant-winning Senators of 1925. He was 2-1 in 1927 when Harris released him in mid-season. The Yanks were interested in signing him then, but learned that he had a sore arm. However, Coveleski had written to Ed Barrow during the winter assuring the Yankee GM that his arm was sound, and Barrow had invited him to spring training in 1928.

Coveleski made the team, but the Yanks released him in late August after purchasing lefthander Tom Zachary from the Senators. He'd won five games with only one loss, which seemed to justify the gamble the Yankees had taken on him. Nevertheless, both Barrow and manager Miller Huggins felt that they'd gotten all they could out of Coveleski, who was now 38, and that Zachary would be of more help down the stretch.

August 23, 1928: Purchased Lefthanded Pitcher Tom Zachary from the Washington Senators

The combination of Lefty Grove's 3-1 victory over Cleveland and the rainout of the Yanks-Browns game at the Stadium had cut New York's lead over Philadelphia to five games. So in an attempt to hold off the surging Athletics, the Yanks made a change of pitchers. They added 32-year-old Tom Zachary and released 39-year-old Stan Coveleski, thereby ending Coveleski's 14-year major league career. Every club in the league had waived on Zachary, a pitcher the Yanks wanted because they had no idea how soon lefty Herb

Pennock would recover from his sore arm. (He never really would, sitting out the rest of the 1928 season and never again regaining his former mastery.)

Zachary, who'd yielded Babe Ruth's 60th home run the previous September, had spent eleven years in the American League, nearly all with Washington. At the time of the trade, he was 6–9 for a Senators team that had spent most of the season in the second division.

September 17, 1928: Purchased First Baseman George Burns from the Cleveland Indians

Ten years earlier the Yanks had purchased George Burns from the Detroit Tigers so that they could trade him to the Philadelphia Athletics for Ping Bodie. Since then Burns had moved from the A's to the Indians, to the Red Sox, and then back to the Indians. He was a lifetime .300-hitter, but at age 35, he was obviously nearing the end of his career.

Burns claimed he would refuse to report to the Yanks until they informed him of their plans regarding his status for 1929, although that was something Yankee manager Miller Huggins seemed to have already done. "Burns is still a good ballplayer," Huggins said, "and will be a fine substitute for Gehrig next year."

Burns did report and had two hits in four at-bats in the season's remaining weeks. He went hitless in his first nine at-bats in 1929 and

in June the Yanks again sold him to Connie Mack's Philadelphia Athletics.

December 13, 1928: Sold Catcher Pat Collins to the Boston Braves

Shortly after the Yanks' four-game victory over the St. Louis Cardinals in the 1928 World Series, manager Miller Huggins hinted that he would likely trade or sell up to eight members of his championship club. Thirty-two-year-old Pat Collins, a Yankee for three years, all pennant-winning seasons, was the first to go.

Before joining the Yankees, Collins had played six years with the St. Louis Browns (1919–24). In 1925, the Browns sold him to St. Paul of the American Association, and after he batted .316 for the Saints, the Yankees purchased his contract.

An excellent receiver, Collins served as the Yanks' first-string catcher in 1926 and 1927, batting .286 and .275 respectively. In 1928 he shared the catching duties with Benny Bengough and Johnny Grabowski, and his average fell off to .221. With Huggins extremely high on Bill Dickey, a 21-year-old catcher added late in the '28 season, either Bengough or Grabowski seemed likely to also be leaving.

September 17, 1928: *George Burns*. Burns's Yankee career would consist of 13 at-bats.

December 13, 1928: *Bill Dickey*. Dickey would take over Yankee catching duties in 1929.

December 24, 1928: *Lou Gehrig, Tony Lazzeri, Mark Koenig,* and *Joe Dugan.* **Third baseman Dugan (right) was part of the great Yankee infield that included Gehrig at first, Lazzeri at second, and Koenig at short.**

December 24, 1928: Sold Third Baseman Joe Dugan to the Boston Braves

Though Joe Dugan was still only 31 years old, the Yanks had made it known they were going to move him. Everyone assumed it would be to the Chicago Cubs, where Dugan had expressed a desire to play for manager Joe McCarthy, so it came as a surprise when the Braves claimed him. On the other hand, it may not have been so surprising. Braves owner Judge Emil Fuchs was looking to bring Sunday baseball to Boston in 1929, and some felt there was a behind-the-scenes agreement by the other owners to make his franchise more competitive. A more competitive team meant greater attendance and more money for all the owners. Since the close of the 1928 season, Boston had added catcher Pat Collins, Dugan's former teammate with the Yankees, and shortstop Rabbit Maranville and outfielder George Harper from the Cardinals.

Dugan had been the Yankee third baseman since coming in a controversial July 1922 trade with the Red Sox. A marvelous fielder and a steady hitter, he had a .286 average for his six-plus Yankee seasons. Dugan had batted .276 in 1928, but a knee injury limited him to just 94 games, and he would be only a utility player for the Braves in 1929.

June 15, 1929: Sold Righthanded Pitcher Myles Thomas to the Washington Senators

Myles Thomas had been a Yankee since they purchased him from the International League's Toronto Maple Leafs in 1926. He had a 14-12 record in his three-plus seasons, including an 0-2 mark in five games this season.

The Yanks were selling Thomas to make room for Bots Nekola, a recently-signed left-handed pitcher out of Holy Cross College in Massachusetts. Nekola's Yankee career would consist of nine games in 1929 without a decision.

September 17, 1929: Sold Third Baseman Gene Robertson to the Boston Braves

Gene Robertson became the third member of the Yanks' 1928 championship club that they had sold to the Braves. (Pat Collins and Joe Dugan were the other two.) Nineteen twenty-eight had been Robertson's first year with the Yankees, following five plus seasons with the Browns and one (1927) with St. Paul of the American Association. He took over at third base after Joe Dugan's injury and batted .291 in 83 games. Robertson became the club's regular third baseman again early this season, after Mark Koenig failed to live up to manager Miller Huggins's expectations. But when it became apparent that the Yankees would be unable to overtake the Philadelphia Athletics and win a fourth consecutive pennant, Huggins began playing rookie Lyn Lary in place of Robertson.

Huggins had asked for waivers on Robertson a week earlier, but no American League club put in a claim. The last-place Braves had the first shot at him in the National League and paid the Yanks the $7,500 waiver price. Robertson finished the season with Boston and ended his career with them in 1930.

Huggins said he planned no more deals until after the season, at which time he would trade, sell, or release several other Yankee veterans. But, sadly, this would be Huggins's final player transaction. Exactly one week later he managed his final game, and five days after

October 17, 1929: *Bob Meusel.* **After Meusel's poor 1929 season, all seven American League clubs waived on him.**

that died of erysipelas, a form of blood poisoning.

October 17, 1929: Sold Outfielder Bob Meusel to the Cincinnati Reds

On the same day Jacob Ruppert announced that he had chosen Bob Shawkey as his new manager, the club sold Bob Meusel, Shawkey's longtime teammate, to Cincinnati. All American League teams waived on Meusel, a player who'd been a participant in New York's first six World Series, and an integral part of "Murderers' Row." He'd joined the Yankees in 1920, and in his first nine seasons batted better than .300 seven times, and batted in more than 100 runs five times. During that stretch Meusel never hit lower than .290, and that was in 1925, the year Babe Ruth played in only 98 games because of an intestinal abscess, and Meusel led the league in home runs (33) and runs-batted-in (138).

But Meusel was more than just a splendid hitter. He had an exceptionally strong throwing arm and was speedy enough to lead the Yankees in stolen bases five times. Nineteen twenty-nine had been an off-year for Meusel, as it had been for the Yankees, who finished 18 games behind Philadelphia. He played in only 100 games, and his average slipped to .261. Meusel played just one season for the Reds, batting .289 in 113 games.

IV. The Thirties

February 5, 1930: Sold Shortstop Leo Durocher to the Cincinnati Reds

Leo Durocher first played for the Yankees as a 20 year old in the final two games of the 1925 season. He returned from the minors in 1928 and batted .270 in 102 games, primarily as a backup to second baseman Tony Lazzeri and shortstop Mark Koenig. In 1929, Durocher shared the shortstop job with Koenig, and while he did an outstanding job in the field, he batted just .246.

The Yanks were already preparing rookie Lyn Lary, a much better hitter, to take over at shortstop in 1930, with Durocher moving to the bench. But when the always cocky Durocher acted disrespectfully to general manager Ed Barrow during contract negotiations, Barrow decided to get rid of him. The only surprise was that all American League teams allowed Durocher to pass through waivers when he could have improved several of them, most notably the last-place Boston Red Sox.

May 6, 1930: Traded Outfielder Cedric Durst and Cash to the Boston Red Sox for Righthanded Pitcher Red Ruffing

Shortly after he pinch-ran for Earle Combs in the ninth inning of a 7-6 loss to the Indians, Cedric Durst learned he'd been traded. A Yankee since 1927, mostly as a spare outfielder, he had a .249 batting average in 239 games, with only six home runs. Just 3 for 19 at the time of the trade, Durst got into 102 games for Boston and batted .245, but it was his final season.

Although Red Ruffing had been pitching for the Red Sox since 1924, he still was only 26 years old. He'd led the American League in losses in each of the past two seasons and already had three losses without a win this season. Yet, despite his pitiful 39-96 won-lost record, the Yankees knew that statistic wasn't a true measure of Ruffing's ability. He'd compiled that record while pitching for a team that had finished last in every one of his five full seasons, and would do so again this year. Ruffing was a pitcher of obvious ability, and the Yanks were sure that he would be a worthwhile addition to their staff.

May 6, 1930: *Red Ruffing*. Throughout the 1930s Ruffing would be the Yankees' "money pitcher."

They were, of course, correct, and Ruffing started proving it immediately by going 15-5 over the rest of the 1930 season. He then went on to be the "money pitcher" for the great Yankee teams of the 1930s and early 1940s, winning a total of 231 games for the Yankees, including four consecutive 20-win seasons between 1936 and 1939.

In 1943, the Army drafted Ruffing although he was thirty-eight years old and was missing four toes on his left foot. He returned to the Yankees in 1945 to go 7-3, and then 5-1 in 1946. After the Yanks released him in September 1946, Ruffing signed with the White Sox where he ended his career in 1947. Many years later, Bill Dickey, his catcher during all those Yankee years, said: "If I were asked to choose the best pitcher I ever caught, I would have to say Ruffing."

May 12, 1930: Sold Lefthanded Pitcher Tom Zachary to the Boston Braves

After joining the Yankees in late August 1928, Tom Zachary split six decisions and added a complete game victory in the World Series sweep over St. Louis. He'd followed that with a remarkable 1929 season. Zachary led the Yanks in earned run average (2.48), while compiling a 12-0 mark that set a still-standing major league record for the most wins in a season without a loss.

He was 1-1 in three games this season, but manager Bob Shawkey claimed that the 34-year-old Zachary did not fit into his plans. The addition of rookie lefthander Lefty Gomez and the previous week's trade for Red Ruffing had made Zachary expendable.

May 30, 1930: Traded Righthanded Pitcher Waite Hoyt and Shortstop Mark Koenig to the Detroit Tigers for Righthanded Pitcher Ownie Carroll, Shortstop Yats Wuestling, and Outfielder Harry Rice

With the Yanks struggling along in third place, manager Bob Shawkey made a bold move. He traded away two former teammates, both of whom had been major contributors to the Yankees' successes of the 1920s.

Waite Hoyt's best seasons were in 1927 (22-7) and 1928 (23-7), but he'd tailed off to a mediocre 10-9 in 1929, and was just 2-2 this season. Nevertheless, no one expected the Yanks to trade him. Hoyt had won 157 games since coming from the Red Sox ten years earlier, and despite his many years of service, he was only 30 years old. He would go on to pitch in the big leagues for another eight seasons and win 70 more games.

Mark Koenig joined the Yankees in September 1925 after they bought his contract from St. Paul of the American Association for $35,000. The next year he teamed with another rookie, second baseman Tony Lazzeri, to form the double play combination that helped lead the Yankee to three consecutive pennants. But after registering four solid seasons at the plate, Koenig was batting just a modest .230 at the time of the trade.

May 12, 1930. *Lefty Gomez and Red Ruffing.* With newcomers Gomez and Ruffing, the Yanks no longer needed Tom Zachary.

May 30, 1930: *Mark Koenig.* None of the three players the Yanks got for Koenig and Waite Hoyt were with them the following season.

Leo Durocher, with whom he'd shared the shortstop position in 1929, was also gone, so Shawkey would replace Koenig with second-year man Lyn Lary. Koenig was only 26, and like Hoyt, he would play most of the rest of his career (which lasted until 1936) in the National League. Meanwhile, none of the three players the Yankees obtained in this trade were with them the following season.

Outfielder Harry Rice spent his first five years in the league with the St. Louis Browns and was now in his third season in Detroit. A lifetime .300 hitter, and currently batting .305, he was the major reason the Yanks made the deal. Shawkey was not satisfied with rookie Dusty Cooke as the successor to the departed Bob Meusel and wanted Rice to fill that role.

Following a sensational career at Holy Cross College Ownie Carroll joined the Tigers in 1925. He had a 37-37 record for his first four seasons, but was 0-5 in six games this year.

Yats Wuestling batted .200 in 54 games as a rookie in 1929, but was hitless in nine at-bats for the Tigers this year. He would bat .164 in 29 games with the Yankees, but never again appear in a big-league game.

June 30, 1930: Purchased Righthanded Pitcher Ken Holloway from the Cleveland Indians

Ken Holloway had a 64-52 record for his nine big league seasons, spent mostly with the Tigers. He'd had double-digit win totals in four of those seasons, with a high of 14 in 1924, a league-high nine of which were in relief. To make room for Holloway, the Yanks sent rookie infielder Bill Werber to Albany of the Eastern League.

Holloway, who'd been 1-1 with Cleveland, pitched in 16 games with the Yankees without a decision in what was his final major league season. In November, the Yanks traded him to the International League Baltimore Orioles in a four-player deal that brought them pitcher Jim Weaver. Weaver's Yankee career would consist of two wins and a loss in 1931.

September 13, 1930: Sold Righthanded Pitcher Ownie Carroll to the Cincinnati Reds

Three and a half months after getting him from Detroit in the Waite Hoyt deal, the Yankees sold Ownie Carroll out of the league. He'd been in ten games, nine of them in relief, with an 0-1 record and a 6.54 earned run average. Two years later, in 1932, Carroll would lead the National League in losses, dropping 19 games for the last-place Reds.

December 10, 1930: Purchased Catcher Cy Perkins from the Philadelphia Athletics

Now nearing his 35th birthday, Cy Perkins had been a member of Connie Mack's Athletics for 15 years. He was the A's first-string catcher between 1919 and 1924, but had seen only limited action after rookie Mickey Cochrane took over that role in 1925. The Yanks already had Bill Dickey and Art Jorgens behind the plate, but new manager Joe McCarthy felt that the club would benefit from Perkins's knowledge and experience. Always better known for his defense than his hitting, Perkins batted .255 in 16 games in 1931, his one season in New York.

January 13, 1931: Sold Outfielder Harry Rice to the Washington Senators

The Yanks got Harry Rice in the May 1930 trade that sent Waite Hoyt and Mark Koenig to Detroit. Rice, a good outfielder with a strong throwing arm, batted a solid .298 for manager Bob Shawkey in 1930. However, Joe McCarthy had replaced Shawkey at the end of the 1930 season, and apparently Rice didn't fit into McCarthy's plans.

January 24, 1931: Signed Third Baseman Joe Sewell as a Free Agent

In 1920, Joe Sewell, a former University of Alabama football star, was playing his first year of professional baseball for the New Orleans Pelicans of the Southern Association. But in August, Cleveland shortstop Ray Chapman died after being beaned by the Yanks' Carl Mays, and the Indians purchased Sewell from the Pelicans to take Chapman's place. He then went on to play 11 seasons for Cleveland, and before he sat out on May 20, 1930, Sewell had played in 1,102 consecutive games, the longest consecutive-games streak ever while playing for a single team. (Everett Scott had the longest streak, 1,307 games, but he'd accomplished that while playing for two teams, the Red Sox and the Yankees.)

Overall, the 32-year-old Sewell had a .320 batting average with Cleveland, and amazingly had struck out only 99 times in more than 5,600 at-bats. The Indians had released him after he batted .289 in 1930, the first time he had failed to hit .300 or better in eight years.

Sewell had also slowed defensively, and

January 24, 1931: *Joe Sewell.* **Cleveland released Sewell after his 1930 batting average dropped below .300.**

in 1929, manager Roger Peckinpaugh had moved him from shortstop to third base. Rookie Ben Chapman and Tony Lazzeri, normally a second baseman, had split the third base duties for the Yanks in 1930, but new manager Joe McCarthy would install Sewell as his third baseman in 1931, while moving Chapman to the outfield and Lazzeri back to second.

Sewell would be the Yankee third baseman for his final three seasons, batting .282, and striking out only 15 times.

June 5, 1932: Traded Righthanded Pitchers Ivy Andrews and Hank Johnson, and Cash to the Boston Red Sox for Righthanded Pitcher Danny MacFayden

Manager Joe McCarthy negotiated this trade with his Red Sox counterpart, Shano Collins, shortly before George Pipgras pitched the first-place Yanks to a 12-1 home victory over Boston. While the Yanks had bought and sold players in the past 24 months, this was their first trade with another major league team since sending Waite Hoyt and Mark Koenig to Detroit in May 1930.

Danny MacFayden had been with the Red Sox since reaching the majors late in the 1926 season. For much of that time the Sox were the league's worst team, and MacFayden's 16-12 mark in 1931 had been his first winning season. This year he had one win and ten losses for the last-place Sox, who after today's game had just nine wins and 34 losses. His 1-10 record dropped MacFayden's lifetime mark to 52 wins and 78 losses.

Just 19 when he joined the Yankees in 1925, Hank Johnson pitched in 24 games that season, winning one and losing three. He spent the next two years in the minors, except for one game with the Yanks in 1926. But beginning in 1928, while being used as both a starter and a reliever, Johnson was 46-33 for the Yankees. Perhaps his greatest claim to fame was defeating Philadelphia's Lefty Grove four times without a loss in 1928, which constituted half of Grove's eight losses that season. Johnson had undergone an appendectomy during this year's spring training, and his 2-2 mark in

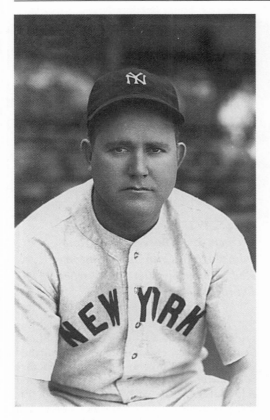

June 5, 1932: *Ivy Andrews.* **Back problems had kept Andrews idle the past three weeks.**

five games for the Yanks would be his only action this season.

Ivy Andrews had also had physical problems in 1932. He'd come to the Yankees from Jersey City of the International League in the summer of 1931 and won two games without a loss. This season Andrews was 2-1 in four games, but he'd missed the last three weeks due to muscle spasms in his back.

August 1, 1932: Traded Righthanded Pitcher Gordon Rhodes to the Boston Red Sox for Righthanded Pitcher Wilcy Moore

Technically, this exchange of two right-handed pitchers, Gordon Rhodes for Wilcy Moore, was not a trade; it was two separate waiver deals. The Yanks claimed Moore, and Boston claimed Rhodes.

Moore was returning to the Yankees after an absence of two years. He'd gone 19-7 as a 30-year-old rookie reliever on Miller Huggins's great Yankee team of 1927, but just 4-4 and 6-4 the next two seasons. In 1930 the Yanks sent him to the American Association St. Paul Saints, where he won a league-leading 22 games. The Red Sox took Moore in the major league draft, and he went 11-13 in 1931, while leading the league with ten saves. He was 4-10 with four saves for the last-place Sox this season.

Although the Yankees had a comfortable lead in the race for the pennant, both general manager Ed Barrow and manager Joe McCarthy wanted Moore. Each felt he would be a valuable man to have should the summer heat began to wear down the rest of the Yankee pitching staff.

Moore would win two games without a loss in the final two months of 1932, then go 5-6 with a team-leading eight saves in 1933. Nevertheless, he was then 37 years old, and the Yanks released him at the end of the 1933 season.

Rhodes had worked his way into the starting rotation this season on the basis of his strong finish in 1931. However, he'd been unimpressive as a starter, and continued to pitch poorly after McCarthy sent him back to the bullpen. Rhodes had a 1-2 record this season, and a 7-9 mark for the parts of the past four seasons he'd spent as a Yankee.

The Yanks made one other move this day. With Bill Dickey's 30-day suspension ending, they returned catcher Eddie Phillips (.290 in nine games) to Newark of the International League.

April 14, 1933: Sold Lefthanded Pitcher Ed Wells to the St. Louis Browns

One day after they'd opened the season with a 4-3 win over the Red Sox, the defending world champion Yankees sold 32-year-old Ed Wells to the woeful St. Louis Browns. Wells had pitched for Detroit from 1923 to 1927, but in 1928 the Tigers sent him to Birmingham of the Southern Association. He went 25-7, to lead the Barons to the league championship, and the Yanks signed him.

Wells was mainly a starter in his first two

seasons in New York, going 13-9 in 1929 and 12-3 in 1930. But when Joe McCarthy became manager in 1931, he began to use Wells mostly out of the bullpen, and his 22 appearances in 1932 were all in relief. His overall record in 107 games as a Yankee was 37-20.

May 12, 1933: Sold Righthanded Pitcher George Pipgras and Third Baseman Bill Werber to the Boston Red Sox

The sale of George Pipgras and Bill Werber, reportedly for $20,000, got the Yankees down to the 23-man player limit three days earlier than necessary. Also, Pipgras's departure allowed manager Joe McCarthy to get his pitching staff down to ten men, the number he planned to carry during the season.

Pipgras, 2-2 this season, was a minor leaguer when manager Miller Huggins brought him to New York in a January 1923 trade with the Red Sox. He didn't become part of the starting rotation until 1927, then had his best season in 1928, leading the American League in wins (24), games started (38), and innings (300.2). He was only 32 and had a 93-64

May 12, 1933: *George Pipgras*. Pipgras was adjudged the 11th pitcher on a ten-man staff.

record as a Yankee, but the emergence of rookie Russ Van Atta had made him the odd man out on the staff. Pipgras won nine games for Boston in 1933, but injured his arm during the season and never won another.

Werber played in four games after signing with the Yankees in 1930 as a 22-year-old graduate of Duke University. He spent the next two years in the minors and was hitless in two at-bats this season.

Three days later, the Yanks made another deal with Boston. They sent the Red Sox outfielder Dusty Cooke, from their Newark team in the International League, for outfielder Johnny Watwood and second baseman Marv Olson.

At one time the Yanks thought Cooke would be the man to replace Bob Meusel, but Cooke had a serious shoulder injury in 1931 and that had hindered his career. Overall, he batted .267 in 122 games for the Yankees.

Both Watwood and Olson went to the minor leagues and never played a game for the Yanks.

July 24, 1933: Signed Righthanded Pitcher George Uhle as a Free Agent

George Uhle, who broke in with the Cleveland Indians back in 1919, pitched ten seasons for them, and then four with Detroit. He was a three-time 20-game winner for Cleveland and had twice led the American League in victories (26 in 1923, and 27 in 1926).

Uhle, now 34, had a lifetime record of 192 wins and 160 losses; however, he was only 6-6 in 1932, and the Yankees would be the third team he'd pitched for in 1933. He began this season with the Tigers, but they released him after one appearance. Uhle then signed with the Giants and was 1-1 in six games until they too released him. That was on July 8, when they let Uhle go to make room for Harry Danning, a rookie catcher whom manager Bill Terry was calling up from Buffalo of the International League.

Despite a shabby 5.16 earned run average, Uhle would win six of seven decisions for the '33 Yankees. He was 2-4 in 1934 when they released him on June 2 to clear a spot for pitcher Johnny Broaca, who was about to graduate from Yale.

May 15, 1934: Traded Shortstop Lyn Lary to the Boston Red Sox for Infielder Freddie Muller and Cash

Lyn Lary had been Yankee property since 1928, when the club paid Oakland of the Pacific Coast League $150,000 for him and his double play partner, Jimmie Reese. Reese made it to New York in 1930, playing behind Tony Lazzeri and batting an impressive .346, though he had only 188 at-bats. But the next year he hit only .241 and the Yanks had him at St. Paul of the American Association for the 1932 season. In early June of that year, the Cardinals purchased Reese off the St. Paul roster to fill in for their injured second baseman, Frankie Frisch.

Lary joined the Yanks in 1929 as a utility infielder, but he became the full-time shortstop after the May 30, 1930, trade of Mark Koenig to Detroit. In 1931, he batted .280 in 155 games while knocking in 107 runs—still the RBI record for a Yankee shortstop. Nevertheless, rookie Frank Crosseti won the job away from him in 1932, and for the next two years Lary was again a utility player. As a way to protest his lack of playing-time Lary had held out this spring, but it hadn't helped. The current season was already a month old, and he'd played in only one game. However, after joining the Red Sox, Lary immediately became their everyday shortstop.

The trade helped get the Yankees down to the required 23-man player limit as they sent Freddie Muller (whose major league career consisted of 17 games played this year and last) to the International League Newark Bears. Also going to Newark were two other would-be Yankees: pitcher Charlie Devens and catcher Norman Kies.

Devens had signed out of Harvard in June 1932 and pitched in one game that year, a complete game 8-2 victory against Boston. He was 3-3 in 1933 and would come back later this season to make his final appearance, a route-going 11-inning victory.

Kies, who had been serving as the club's third string receiver, left without having ever gotten into a major league game. He would never make it back to the big leagues, and neither would Muller.

May 29, 1934: Purchased Righthanded Pitcher Burleigh Grimes from the Pittsburgh Pirates

Burleigh Grimes, the last big league pitcher allowed to throw the spitball legally, had spent his entire 19-year major league career in the National League. He'd pitched for every team in the league (some more than once) except Cincinnati, and had a 269-210 record. Grimes had begun this season with the

May 15, 1934: *Lyn Lary*. With the season a month old, Lary (here with his wife) had been in only one game.

May 29, 1934: *Burleigh Grimes.* **The last legal spitballer, Grimes concluded his Hall of Fame career with the Yankees.**

Cardinals, for whom he won two of three decisions, before moving on to Pittsburgh, where he had lost two of three.

Speaking of his intention to use Grimes as a starter, Yankee manager Joe McCarthy said: "Burleigh is no kid, and you can't expect him to pitch every fourth day like a young fellow. But I think he can still turn in a good game every little while, and I believe he will be a big help to us."

Grimes, now three months short of his 41st birthday, said he was delighted to complete his career with the Yankees, and he was confident of his ability to win some games for them.

He made ten starts for the Yanks, completed none, and had a 1-2 record with a 5.50 earned run average.

May 29, 1934: Sold Lefthanded Pitcher Harry Smythe to the Brooklyn Dodgers

The Yanks cleared a spot for newly-acquired pitcher Burleigh Grimes by selling 29-year-old lefthander Harry Smythe (0-2 in eight games) to the Dodgers for the $7,500 waiver price. Smythe, who had a 4-9 record for the 1929-30 Phillies, split two 1934 decisions with Brooklyn, his final two.

November 22, 1934: Sold Righthanded Pitcher Danny MacFayden to the Cincinnati Reds

In June 1932, the Yanks had sent two young pitchers, Ivy Andrews and Hank Johnson, plus $50,000 to the Boston Red Sox for pitcher Danny MacFayden. But, MacFayden had been a huge disappointment. He won seven and lost five in the second half of '32, after which manager Joe McCarthy had relegated him to mostly relief roles in 1933 and 1934. MacFayden started only 17 of the 47 games he'd appeared in during those two seasons, while going 3-2 and 4-3.

The Yanks and Reds structured the sale to allow Cincinnati until June 1, 1935 to decide whether or not they wanted to keep MacFayden. He'd gone 1-2 in seven games by June 1, when the Reds decided they didn't want to keep him and returned MacFayden to the Yankees. Three days later, on June 4, the Yanks sold him to the Boston Braves.

December 19, 1934: Sold Outfielder Sammy Byrd to the Cincinnati Reds

While Sammy Byrd could never duplicate his outstanding minor league batting feats with the Yankees, he had been an adequate hitter, averaging .281 for his six seasons in New York. But this past year, although he did lead American League outfielders in fielding percentage, Byrd had by far his worst season at the plate, a .246 average in 106 games. Once thought to be Babe Ruth's eventual replacement, Byrd's primary function the past few years had been to serve as a pinch runner or late-inning defensive replacement for Ruth.

Cincinnati, which finished last in 1934, claimed Byrd after the seven other American League clubs had waived on him. Byrd played two years for the Reds before beginning a successful career as a professional golfer.

March 26, 1935: Purchased Right-handed Pitcher Pat Malone from the St. Louis Cardinals

It was Yankee manager Joe McCarthy, then the manager of the Chicago Cubs, who'd

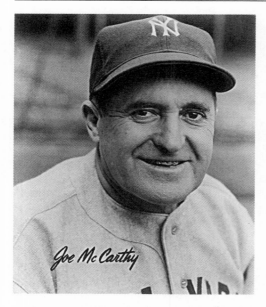

March 26, 1935: *Joe McCarthy*. **Pat Malone had helped lead McCarthy's Cubs to the National League pennant in 1929.**

brought Pat Malone to the big leagues in 1928. Malone won 18 games as a rookie, and the following year led the league in wins (22), shutouts (5), and strikeouts (166), while helping pitch the Cubs to a pennant. He also tied for the league-lead in wins (20) in 1930, McCarthy's last year in Chicago.

In October 1934, the Cubs traded Malone to the world champion St. Louis Cardinals for Ken O'Dea, a minor league catcher. But the Cardinals were having trouble signing him, and the Yanks had asked about his availability as early as January of this year. Eventually St. Louis did sign him; however, following a visit from Cardinals general manager Branch Rickey to Colonel Jacob Ruppert in St. Petersburg, Malone was now a Yankee, while Rickey came away with $15,000.

Malone pitched almost exclusively in relief in his three Yankee seasons—his final three. In 1936, both his eight relief-wins and nine saves were American League highs.

May 15, 1935: Sold Lefthanded Pitcher Russ Van Atta to the St. Louis Browns

In 1933, his rookie year, Russ Van Atta had a 12-4 record and pitched ten complete games. But because of arm troubles in 1934, he made only nine starts and had a 3-5 won-lost record. Although Van Atta seemed to have recovered this spring, he had pitched poorly since the season began. Manager Joe McCarthy had given him a final chance in the previous day's game at Detroit, bringing him in to relieve Johnny Broaca. It didn't go well as Van Atta mishandled two fielding plays and walked two men before McCarthy replaced him with Johnny Murphy.

Needing to subtract one more player to get down to the 23-player limit, the Yanks sent infielder Don Heffner to Newark of the International League.

August 6, 1935: Purchased Shortstop Blondy Ryan from the Philadelphia Phillies

An injury to shortstop Frank Crosetti prompted the Yanks to acquire a temporary replacement and Blondy Ryan of the Phillies was available. Ryan had been the Giants' shortstop in 1933-34, but a weak bat led to his inclusion in a November 1934 trade to Philadelphia, a trade that brought the Giants their current shortstop, Dick Bartell.

Ryan was batting .264 for the Phillies, when manager Jimmie Wilson sent him to Baltimore of the International League and replaced him with Mickey Haslin. The feisty Ryan, who had threatened to quit baseball to study law rather than return to the minor leagues, played in 30 games for the Yanks and batted .238. In December, the Yanks sold him to the Minneapolis Millers of the American Association.

December 11, 1935: Traded Righthanded Pitcher Johnny Allen to the Cleveland Indians for Righthanded Pitchers Monte Pearson and Steve Sundra

The pitcher the Yankees really wanted from Cleveland was the Indians' ace, Mel Harder. They'd offered pitcher Johnny Allen, second baseman Tony Lazzeri, outfielder Dixie Walker, and catcher Joe Glenn for Harder and

December 11, 1935: *Johnny Allen*. Despite Allen's four-year 50-19 record, Joe McCarthy thought him too temperamental.

infielder Odell Hale, but Indians owner Alva Bradley turned down the offer, saying he would neither trade nor sell Harder. He did, however, agree to part with two other pitchers, Monte Pearson and minor-leaguer Steve Sundra.

The 30-year-old Allen had a spectacular 50-19 record in his four years as a Yankee, including a 13-6 mark in 1935. He had his best season in 1932, as a rookie, when he went 17-4 with a league-leading .810 winning-percentage. In his first three seasons in Cleveland (1936–38), Allen would go 49-19, duplicating almost exactly his won-lost record of the past four seasons in New York.

Pearson had also had a strong rookie season. His was in 1933; he won ten games while losing five, with an excellent 2.33 earned-run-average. The following year Pearson went 18-13, but in 1935 he won ten fewer games with the same number of losses. Furthermore, like Allen, Pearson was very temperamental, a factor that managers Joe McCarthy of the Yankees and Steve O'Neill of the Indians cited as contributing to the trade.

Sundra had split the 1935 season between Minneapolis of the American Association and the Yanks' Newark farm club of the International League. He was 5-6 with the Millers and 5-1 with the Bears.

January 17, 1936: *Traded Righthanded Pitcher Jimmie Deshong and Outfielder Jesse Hill to the Washington Senators for Righthanded Pitcher Bump Hadley and Outfielder Roy Johnson*

In Roy Johnson, 33, and Bump Hadley, 32, the Yanks were getting two established veterans. Johnson had spent seven years as a regular in Detroit and Boston and had in different seasons led the league in doubles (1929) and triples (1931). He had a .300 lifetime batting average, including a .315 mark for the Red Sox in 1935. In December, Boston had traded Johnson and outfielder Carl Reynolds to Washington for outfielder Heinie Manush, but, of course, Johnson had never gotten to play for the Senators.

Hadley, on the other hand, had broken in with Washington in 1926 and pitched for them until they traded him to the Chicago White Sox in December 1931. He pitched just three games for Chicago in April 1932, before they

January 17, 1936: *Bump Hadley*. After a career with mostly bad teams, Hadley would play on pennant winners for the next four seasons.

traded him to the Browns. Hadley spent the next three seasons in St. Louis, in two of which he was a 20-game loser. In January 1935, St. Louis traded him back to Washington, and he won 10 and lost 15 for the Senators, bringing his lifetime record to 107-128.

Jimmie DeShong had pitched in six games for the Athletics in 1932, without a decision. Having failed to sufficiently impress his manager, Connie Mack, he spent the 1933 season with the Sacramento Senators of the Pacific Coast League. The Yanks bought him from Sacramento, and DeShong spent two seasons in New York, winning ten and losing eight, while pitching mostly in relief.

Jesse Hill, a 28-year-old rookie, had served as an outfield replacement for the injured Earle Combs in 1935, batting .293 in 107 games.

May 1, 1936: Sold Outfielder Dixie Walker to the Chicago White Sox

This was 25-year-old Dixie Walker's fifth season with the Yankees, but only in 1933 had

he seen much playing time. He got into 98 games in '33, batting .274 with 15 home runs. The Yanks sold him to make room for rookie outfielder Joe DiMaggio, who would be making his long-awaited big league debut in two days. Walker would go from Chicago to Detroit, and then in 1939 to stardom and immense popularity in Brooklyn.

June 14, 1936: Traded Outfielder Ben Chapman to the Washington Senators for Outfielder Jake Powell

Because of their recent history of ill feelings toward each other, the Yanks and Senators had brawled on the field several times in the past few years. Now they were exchanging players, discarding one 27-year-old racist, anti–Semite for another, although that was not the reason for the trade.

Ben Chapman had been a Yankee regular since 1930, as an infielder his rookie season, and as an outfielder since 1931. But he'd fallen out of favor with the club during spring

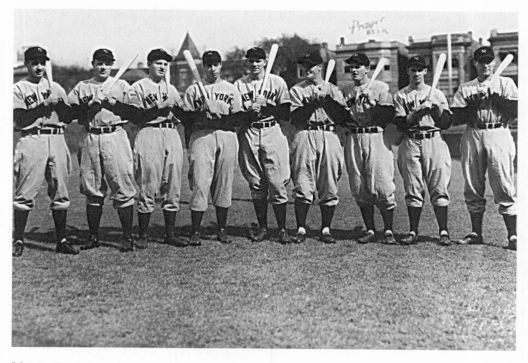

May 1, 1936: *The 1938 Yankees.* **Dixie Walker was sold to make room for rookie Joe DiMaggio, who by 1938, was the Yanks' cleanup hitter and best player.**

June 14, 1936: *Ben Chapman*. **The outspoken Yankee falls out of favor with the club.**

struggling to do so; he was batting just .266 and had only one stolen base. Those marks were far below average for Chapman, who was a career .305 batter and who'd led the American League in stolen bases in 1931, 1932, and 1933. Moreover, the Yanks had a center fielder to replace Chapman, rookie Joe DiMaggio, who'd played extremely well since debuting in May.

Jake Powell batted .361 for the Albany Senators in 1934, and then hit .312 as a Washington rookie in 1935. His average this year was .295, and he'd stolen ten bases, but his new manager, Joe McCarthy, said he expected Powell to do even better when he joined the Yankees.

February 17, 1937: Purchased First Baseman Babe Dahlgren from the Boston Red Sox

training. First, he staged a holdout, and then he asked the Yanks to trade him, preferably to the Red Sox. He eventually signed, but missed some early-season games while working his way into playing shape. Chapman was still

After rookie Babe Dahlgren batted .263 as Boston's regular first baseman in 1935, the Red Sox traded for Jimmie Foxx. So, while Foxx played first base for Boston in 1936, Dahlgren played it for Syracuse of the International League. After batting .318 for the

February 17, 1937: *Joe McCarthy and six of his Yankee stalwarts*. **If the Yanks couldn't sign Lou Gehrig (second from left), McCarthy (left) would have to use Babe Dahlgren at first base.**

Chiefs, he asked for a raise for 1937, but Boston offered the same salary he'd earned in 1936. An unhappy Dahlgren returned two contracts unsigned. "I had a swell season at Syracuse, but the Red Sox wanted me to sign up at the same salary as last year," he said. "I think I deserve some recognition for good work."

Coincidentally, owner Jacob Ruppert purchased him for the Yankees to head off a first base holdout problem of his own. The club was having trouble signing Lou Gehrig, and the purchase of the 24-year-old Dahlgren was ostensibly to have a successor to Gehrig in case they couldn't sign him. Dahlgren said he expected to receive a better offer from the Yankees than he had from the Red Sox.

May 11, 1937: Sold Outfielder Roy Johnson to the Boston Bees

The Yanks had called up rookie outfielder Tommy Henrich from Newark of the International League two weeks earlier, and he was playing extremely well. That was all the reason manager Joe McCarthy needed to get rid of Roy Johnson, who'd batted .265 in 1936, his first Yankee season, and was at .294 after 51 at-bats this year. Johnson had led the club in batting during spring training, but, despite his good batting average had performed in a lackluster manner since the regular season began.

May 11, 1937: *Tommy Heinrich*. Rookie Heinrich's fine play made Roy Johnson expendable.

August 14, 1937: Purchased Righthanded Pitcher Ivy Andrews from the Cleveland Indians

A little more than five years after the Yanks traded Ivy Andrews to the Red Sox, they paid Cleveland the $7,500 waiver price to get him back. They did so because manager Joe McCarthy felt he needed a pitcher like Andrews to help the Yanks maintain their lead over the second-place Detroit Tigers.

Andrews had pitched for Boston for a season and a half, before they traded him to the Browns in December 1933. His 13-7 record with the 1935 Browns, a seventh-place team, would be his best major league season. Cleveland had gotten him in a six-player deal this past January, and he had a 3-4 record with them, while being used mostly in relief.

August 14, 1937: *Spud Chandler*. The Yanks' purchase of Ivy Andrews sent Chandler to Newark for the second time in 1937.

To make room for Andrews, the Yanks returned rookie Spud Chandler to Newark. It was the second time this season they'd sent Chandler to their International League affiliate.

Andrews got into 11 games, winning three, losing two and saving one. The next season his last, he went 1-3 in 19 games.

February 15, 1938: Traded Second Baseman Don Heffner and Cash to the St. Louis Browns for Shortstop Bill Knickerbocker

This was the Yankees' first trade since June 1936, when they'd sent Ben Chapman to Washington for Jake Powell, and it was hardly a blockbuster. In fact, general manager Ed Barrow was forced to deny that the primary reason for getting Knickerbocker was for him to function as an advertisement for a beer of the same name that came from Yankee owner Jacob Ruppert's brewery. Barrow also denied that the Yanks sent $25,000 to St. Louis as part of the deal. "Oh no, much less than that," he said. (It was probably $10,000.)

Knickerbocker had been the Cleveland Indians' regular shortstop from 1934 to 1936, and in those three seasons never batted below .294. In 1934 he was among the league's batting leaders for most of the year before tailing off and finishing at .317. Traded to the Browns in a six-player deal a year ago, he replaced former Yankee shortstop Lyn Lary, but batted just .261. However, that didn't deter Barrow. "Knickerbocker is an aggressive player and a far better hitter than his batting average of .261 in 1937 indicates," Barrow maintained. "He will be insurance for us at second and short and is a great fellow to have around a club."

Despite having won their second consecutive World Series, the Yanks felt a bit vulnerable at those two positions. Five days after their victory over the Giants, they'd released veteran second baseman Tony Lazzeri, the Series' leading hitter. And Lazzeri's double-play partner, shortstop Frank Crosetti had batted just .234 in 1937, while leading the league in strikeouts.

Lazzeri had been the Yankee second baseman since 1926. He had a lifetime batting average of .293, hit better than .300 five times, and knocked in more than 100 runs seven times. But he was now 34 years old, and the Yanks had to make room for Joe Gordon, their "can't-miss" second base prospect. Knickerbocker would serve as insurance should Crosetti fail to hit again, or should Gordon fail to live up to expectations.

At 26, Heffner, was a year older than Knickerbocker, but had been strictly a reserve since the Yanks paid the International League

February 15, 1938: *Don Heffner*. In St. Louis Heffner would get a chance to play regularly.

Baltimore Orioles $25,000 for him in 1934. A fine fielder but a so-so hitter (the reverse of Knickerbocker), he'd batted a combined .257 in 161 games. Heffner figured to get much more playing time in St. Louis, which he did.

August 14, 1938: Signed Righthanded Pitcher Wes Ferrell as a Free Agent

The Yanks signed 30-year-old Wes Ferrell two days after the Washington Senators

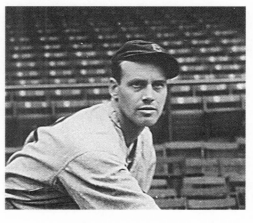

August 14, 1938: *Wes Ferrell*. The Senators had released Ferrell, a six-time 20-game winner, two days earlier.

released him, and one day after righthander Joe Vance, whom they'd recently recalled from Kansas City of the American Association, underwent a season-ending appendectomy.

While Ferrell was often temperamental and difficult to handle, he had been a top pitcher in the American League since 1929, his first full season. He went 21-10 for Cleveland that year and followed with three more 20-win seasons. But after an arm injury in 1933 caused Ferrell to lose some speed off his fastball, Cleveland traded him to the Boston Red Sox. He bounced back with a league-leading 25 wins in 1934, and then had a sixth 20-win season in 1935. Traded to Washington in June 1937, Ferrell had a combined 14-19 record for the year and was 13-8 with a 5.92 ERA for the Senators this season.

Ferrell would split four decisions in the last weeks of the 1938 season and was 1-2 in 1939 when the Yanks released him on May 28.

October 26, 1938: Traded Outfielder Myril Hoag and Catcher Joe Glenn to the St. Louis Browns for Righthanded Pitcher Oral Hildebrand and Outfielder Buster Mills

It was unlikely that come the 1939 season Yankee manager Joe McCarthy would miss

October 26, 1938: *Charlie Keller*. With Keller coming up from Newark, the Yanks didn't expect to miss Myril Hoag.

either outfielder Myril Hoag or catcher Joe Glenn. The club's Newark team in the International League had been among the greatest minor league teams ever, and two of its stars were set to join the Yanks in 1939: Charlie Keller (.365 with 22 home runs) would likely win a spot in the outfield, and catcher Buddy Rosar (.387 with 15 home runs) would replace Glenn as the number two man behind Bill Dickey.

The Yanks had purchased Hoag from the Sacramento Senators, and he'd been an outfield semi-regular since coming up in 1931. He missed much of the 1936 season with a head injury sustained in a collision with rookie Joe DiMaggio, but bounced back to have his best season in 1937, batting .301 in 106 games. Sharing an outfield spot with George Selkirk in 1938, he had a .277 average in 267 at-bats, but no home runs. While Hoag was a decent hitter and had an outstanding throwing arm, he lacked power. In seven seasons, he had just 11 home runs in 1,228 at-bats, although he would hit a career-high ten with the Browns in 1939.

Like Hoag, Glenn had spent his entire major league career with the Yankees. His began in 1932, but it wasn't until 1936 that he replaced Art Jorgens as the club's number two catcher. In his six Yankee seasons, Glenn played in 138 games with a .252 batting average.

After failing to hit in trials with the 1934 Cardinals and the 1935 Dodgers, Buster Mills spent 1936 in the minors. He returned in 1937 to bat .295 for the Red Sox, then, following his trade to St. Louis, .285 for the 1938 Browns. But because there would be no room for Mills on the 1939 Yankees, he spent the season in Newark. Mills did get to play briefly for the Yanks in 1940, batting .397 in 34 games.

At 31, Oral Hildebrand was one year older than the other three men in this deal. He'd pitched six seasons for Cleveland before going to St. Louis in 1937. Hildebrand's best season was 1933; he had a 16-11 record, led the American League with six shutouts, and was chosen for the AL team in the major leagues' first All Star Game. His overall record with Cleveland was 56-46, but in his two seasons with the hapless Browns, he'd won only 16 while losing 27.

After a fine first year with the Yankees, in which he went 10-4, Hildebrand finished his career with a 1-1 mark in 1940.

November 19, 1938: Sold Righthanded Pitcher Johnny Broaca to the Cleveland Indians

Johnny Broaca joined the Yankees in 1934 following an excellent collegiate career at Yale.

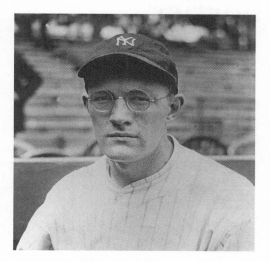

November 19, 1938: *Johnny Broaca.* **Suspended for the entire 1938 season, Broca was reinstated by the Yanks so they could trade him.**

He won 12 and lost nine as a rookie, and then had a 15-7 record in 1935. Broaca was 12-7 in 1936, when in September he chose to leave the Yankees to take up a career in boxing, thereby foregoing a World Series check. He returned in 1937, but in July, Broaca, who had appeared in just seven games and had a 1-4 record, again left the club. Upset at his un–Yankee-like behavior, the Yanks suspended him for the remainder of the '37 season and all of 1938. They'd reinstated him earlier this month, but it was solely for the purpose of trading him.

June 13, 1939: Traded Outfielder Joe Gallagher to the St. Louis Browns for Second Baseman Roy Hughes and Cash

The Browns had started the season with nine consecutive wins, but were now back in their accustomed place in the American League cellar. Beau Bell's departure in a ten-man trade with Detroit a month earlier had left them without much power in their outfield, a shortcoming they hoped Joe Gallagher would rectify. Gallagher was currently on the roster of the International League Newark Bears, where the Yanks had sent him 11 days earlier.

A one-time Manhattan College football star, Gallagher had made the club during spring training, following an outstanding year with the Yankees' American Association team in Kansas City. His .343 average with the Blues was second only to Minneapolis's Ted Williams in the American Association's 1938 batting race. Coincidentally, when the Yanks opened the 1939 season at home with Boston, Gallagher and Williams were the opposing right fielders.

Gallagher went hitless that day and was batting just .244 in 14 games when the club sent him to Newark on June 2. Going the other way was pitcher Marius Russo, whom manager Joe McCarthy called up from the Bears to replace the recently released Wes Ferrell.

Roy Hughes was a lifetime .277-hitter who'd come to the Browns in 1938, following three seasons in Cleveland. He had his best year in 1936 when he batted .295 as the Indians' everyday second baseman. Hughes played in only 58 games for the Browns in '38, and was batting a pathetic .087 in 17 games at the time of the trade. The Yanks sent him to Newark, and then in July to the Phillies in a minor league deal for pitcher Al Hollingsworth.

V. The Forties

January 4, 1940: Traded Righthanded Pitcher Joe Beggs to the Cincinnati Reds for Lefthanded Pitcher Lee Grissom

At the December 1939 baseball meetings in Cincinnati, the owners of the seven other American League teams pushed through a measure that would bar their league's defending champion from making a player transaction with any other club in the league. They clearly aimed this bizarre ruling at the Yankees, who were not only the defending champions, but winners of the last four World Series. However, because the National League voted not to impose a similar restriction, the Yanks were free to deal with any club in that league. So, after getting waivers on pitcher Joe Beggs from all seven American League clubs, they sent him to the Cincinnati Reds, their victims in last October's four-game Series sweep.

For all the other American League clubs to have waived on Beggs was startling, when so many seemed in need of a good young pitcher. Beggs was only 26 and had excellent minor league credentials, including 20-win seasons at Norfolk of the Piedmont League in 1936 and Newark of the International League in 1937. He'd spent part of 1938 with the Yanks, going 3-2 in 14 games, but was back with Newark in 1939.

It seems likely that had the other American League clubs known the Yanks were going to use Beggs to make an interleague deal, one of them would have claimed him. Beggs would go 12-3 to help the Reds repeat as pennant-winners in 1940, and he would continue to pitch in the National League until 1948.

Despite Beggs's impressive minor league statistics, Yankee manager Joe McCarthy felt he had enough good young righthanders on his staff. So despite Lee Grissom's age (33), and his previous arm injury, he threw lefthanded and McCarthy wanted him.

Grissom had developed arm trouble during his 12-17 season for the last-place Reds in 1937. His arm continued to bother him in 1938; however, unlike all the National League teams that passed on him, the Yanks were encouraged by Grissom's 9-7 mark for the pennant-winning Reds in 1939.

May 15, 1940: Sold Lefthanded Pitcher Lee Grissom to the Brooklyn Dodgers

On cut-down day, while the Yanks were rained out in St. Louis, manager Joe McCarthy got the roster down to the prescribed 25 players by selling Lee Grissom to the Dodgers' Montreal team of the International League. Grissom had made five relief appearances for the Yankees, pitching five scoreless innings.

December 30, 1940: Traded Righthanded Pitcher Monte Pearson to the Cincinnati Reds for Outfielder Don Lang and Cash

In 1936, Monte Pearson's first year with the Yankees, he was 19-7 and led the American League with a .731 winning percentage. The Yanks were world champions that year, as they were the next three years. Pearson won 37 and lost 15 between 1937 and 1939, giving him

December 30, 1940: *Monte Pearson*. **Pearson assured the Reds his shoulder was sound, but it wasn't.**

21 games played for Cincinnati in 1938. The Yanks kept him in the minors, and Lang wouldn't return to the majors until 1948, and then it would be with the St. Louis Cardinals.

December 31, 1940: Sold Righthanded Pitcher Bump Hadley to the New York Giants

Bump Hadley was the third veteran, and second pitcher, to leave the Yankees in two days. Accompanying the 36-year-old Hadley out of New York were pitcher Monte Pearson, whom the Yanks had traded to Cincinnati the day before, and infielder Bill Knickerbocker, whom they traded to the White Sox in another deal today. Hadley went for the $7,500 waiver price, becoming the first player ever to move in a direct deal between the Yankees and their intracity rivals, the Giants.

Like Pearson, Hadley had played on World Series winners in each of his first four years in New York (1936–39). He was 46-26 during that four-year run, but won only three games 1940, while pitching mostly in relief. Unfortunately, Hadley is best remembered for the May 25, 1937, pitch that beaned Tigers manager/catcher Mickey Cochrane and ended his playing career.

an outstanding 56-22 record for his four years with the Yankees. He'd also had a victory in each of the four World Series wins, including a two-hit, 4-0 shutout in game two of the 1939 Series against his new team, the Reds.

But in 1940, Pearson won only seven and lost five, and didn't pitch at all after the Browns knocked him out in the first inning at St. Louis on July 24. As he often did, Pearson complained of a sore shoulder, and manager Joe McCarthy responded by just letting him sit the rest of the season. Reds GM Warren Giles said that Pearson assured him that he could have pitched late in the season and that he expected to be at full strength in 1941. However, though he was only 31, Pearson's career was just about over. He pitched in just seven games for the Reds in 1941, winning one and losing three, and it was his final season.

Don Lang was a 25-year-old career minor-leaguer whose only big league experience was

December 31, 1940: Traded Infielder Bill Knickerbocker to the Chicago White Sox for Catcher Ken Silvestri

After winning four consecutive world championships, finishing third pleased neither Yankee GM Ed Barrow nor his manager, Joe McCarthy. The trade of Bill Knickerbocker, along with today's sale of Bump Hadley to the Giants, increased the number of players from the 1940 club that would not be back in 1941 to five. Knickerbocker, a 29-year-old utility infielder batted .242 as a Yankee, playing a total of 97 games that spread over the past three seasons.

Barrow claimed that he "hated" to see both Hadley and Knickerbocker go. "They have always been two of my favorite ballplayers," he said. "However with so many youngsters coming up for whom we must make room, something had to be done." Among those youngsters "coming up" were shortstop Phil Rizzuto and second baseman Jerry Priddy, both of whom had starred in the Yankee farm system for the past four seasons.

Ken Silvestri, a 24-year-old switch hitter, had caught McCarthy's eye the previous June when on successive afternoons he pinch hit a home run and a single to contribute to two Yankee defeats. He'd played in only 50 games in his two seasons in Chicago, and with Bill Dickey and Buddy Rosar ahead of him got into just 17 for the 1941 Yankees. Silvestri spent the next four seasons in the military, before returning to play 13 games in 1946 and three in 1947.

February 25, 1941: Sold First Baseman Babe Dahlgren to the Boston Bees

The Yanks bought Babe Dahlgren in February 1937 in what they claimed was an emergency measure in case they were unable to sign holdout Lou Gehrig. After token appearances in 1937 and 1938, Dahlgren did become the Yankees first baseman, taking over after Gehrig stepped down on May 2, 1939. He was an outstanding fielder, but batting averages of .235 and .264 and a two-year total of 27 home runs convinced manager Joe McCarthy that Dahlgren was too weak a hitter to play that position for the Yankees.

February 25, 1941: *Babe Dahlgren.* Dahlgren didn't hit enough to play first base for the Yankees.

Moving Dahlgen was a part of McCarthy's plan to revamp the Yankee infield to make room for the rookie double play combination of shortstop Phil Rizzuto and second baseman Jerry Priddy. He would stay with Red Rolfe at third, but Joe Gordon, voted the major leagues' best second baseman in each of the last two years, would move to first. If Priddy proved unready for the big leagues, Gordon would move back to second, with rookie Johnny Sturm or outfielder Tommy Henrich taking over at first.

A month into the 1941 season, when Priddy failed to hit, McCarthy moved Gordon back to second and Sturm became the full-time first baseman. However, Sturm was an even weaker hitter than Dahlgren. After batting .239 with three home runs, he spent the next four years in the U.S. Army and never returned to the major leagues.

March 27, 1941: Sold Righthanded Pitcher Steve Sundra to the Washington Senators

After pitching in one game for the Yanks in 1936, Steve Sundra was 6-4 as a rookie in 1938 and then had a sensational season in 1939. Sundra won his first 11 decisions, and finished 11-1, with a 2.26 earned run average. But he was nowhere the same pitcher in 1940, with four wins and six losses, and a 5.53 earned run average. Manager Joe McCarthy seemed to have lost confidence in him, making Sundra's departure from the Yankees a surprise to no one.

February 5, 1942: Traded Minor League Outfielder Tommy Holmes to the Boston Braves for First Baseman Buddy Hassett and Outfielder Gene Moore

The Yanks and Braves had negotiated the Tommy Holmes–for–Buddy Hassett portion of this deal a few weeks earlier, but had not settled on the additional player that would go from Boston to New York. They finally settled on Gene Moore, a 32-year-old veteran who'd spent ten years in the National League. While

Moore was a decent hitter and a fine outfielder, no one expected him to be a member of the 1942 Yankees. He seemed destined for one of the Yanks' top farm teams, either Newark of the International League or Kansas City of the American Association. But on February 24, 19 days after getting him, the Yanks sold Moore to the Montreal Royals, Brooklyn's affiliate in the International League.

First baseman Hassett, on the other hand, was very much in the Yankees' plans for 1942. Johnny Sturm, their first baseman in 1941, was now in the Army, and a potential shift of Tommy Henrich from the outfield to first base remained dependent on Henrich's draft status.

Hassett was a native New Yorker who'd once had three excellent seasons in the Yankee farm system. Unfortunately for him, they came between 1933 and 1935, a time when Lou Gehrig was at the peak of his career. The Yanks sold Hassett to Brooklyn, and three years later the Dodgers traded him to the Braves (coincidentally, for Gene Moore). Hassett would bat a respectable .284 for the pennant-winning Yankees in 1942, but he entered the Navy after the season and never again played in the big leagues.

Holmes, like Hassett, was a native New Yorker who'd been stuck in the Yankees' farm system. He'd been there five years and had been a .300-hitter in each one. He'd failed to advance because Yankee manager Joe McCarthy liked his outfielders to hit with power, something the 25-year-old Holmes did not do.

It appeared that general manager Ed Barrow and farm director George Weiss had made an excellent deal for the Yankees. They'd added a full time first baseman for an outfielder who most likely wouldn't make their club. However, it would be among the worst trades the club ever made as Holmes went on to have a first-rate major league career, batting above .300 five times and twice leading the National League in hits.

March 23, 1942: Sold Outfielder Frenchy Bordagaray to the Brooklyn Dodgers

Colorful Stan Bordagaray, better known as Frenchy, was returning to Brooklyn where he'd batted .282 and .315 as a Dodger regular

in 1935 and 1936. He'd followed with two decent seasons as a part-timer with the Cardinals, but then batted a paltry .197 for the National League champion Cincinnati Reds in 1939. Sent back to the minor leagues, Bordagaray had a strong 1940 season for the Kansas City Blues of the American Association, and made it to the Yankees in 1941.

Bordagaray batted .260 in 36 games for the '41 Yanks, but although at age 32, he was not likely to be drafted, manager Joe McCarthy had no place for him on the 1942 club.

May 10, 1942: Sold Outfielder Mike Chartak to the Washington Senators

Mike Chartak had been in the Yankee farm system for six years, including two excellent seasons with the Newark Bears of the International League. Chartak batted .317 for the Bears in 1938 and then .326 in 1939. The Yanks brought him to spring training in 1940 and 1941, but in both years returned him to their Kansas City team in the American Association. He did get into 11 games for the Yanks in September 1940, but got just two hits in 15 at-bats.

The Yankees brought Chartak north this season, after he'd batted .293 for Kansas City in 1941. However, with an outfield of Joe DiMaggio, Tommy Henrich, and Charlie Keller, and with George Selkirk in reserve, there was no room for Chartak. He'd been in only five games, all as a pinch hitter, and had failed to get a base hit. Nevertheless, manager Joe McCarthy seemed reluctant to part with the 26-year-old power hitter.

McCarthy called him "a real good ballplayer who I wouldn't sell except that I am two players over the limit of 25 and had to cut down." He went on to say that "Chartak may be even a better ballplayer than I think he is. He's never had a chance to play regularly for us, and I admit I may be making a mistake in letting him go."

Senators manager Bucky Harris had lost George Case to an injury and was playing backup outfielder Roberto Ortiz in right field. Harris said he would immediately replace Ortiz with Chartak, even though that would give him an all–lefthanded hitting outfield. (His other two starting outfielders were Stan

Spence and Bruce Campbell.) Because Chartak had also played some first base in the minor leagues, Harris indicated that he might use him there too should anything happen to Mickey Vernon.

Chartak would hit .217 in 24 games for Washington, and less than a month after getting him, they traded him to the St. Louis Browns.

July 16, 1942: Traded Minor League Outfielder Frank Kelleher to the Cincinnati Reds for Righthanded Pitcher Jim Turner and Minor League Righthanded Pitcher Joe Abreau

Although Frank Kelleher led the International League in home runs (37) and runs batted in (125) at Newark in 1941, the Yanks had returned him to the Bears again this season. However, the Reds put him on their roster and two days after this trade he would make his major league debut. Kelleher would get into 47 games for Cincinnati in 1942-43, batting .167, with three home runs.

Jim Turner had won 20 games as a 33-year-old Boston Braves rookie in 1937. Since then he'd moved from Boston to Cincinnati and had been in three games for the Reds this year, with no record. The Yanks assigned both him and minor league pitcher Joe Abreau to Newark, but while Abreau never rose any higher, Turner did. On August 30, in time for him to be eligible for the World Series, manager Joe McCarthy brought Turner to New York and sent righthander Norm Branch, 5-1 in 1941 and 0-1 this season, to Newark.

Turner won a game and lost a game down the stretch and continued with the Yankees for the next three wartime seasons. In 1945, his final campaign, Turner then 41, saved ten games for the Yankees, the most in the American League.

July 19, 1942: Signed Catcher Rollie Hemsley as a Free Agent

Having been released two days earlier by the Cincinnati Reds, Rollie Hemsley was shocked to get a phone call from Yankee man-

ager Joe McCarthy. "The Reds let me go Friday," said the 35-year-old Hemsley, a veteran of 15 major league seasons. "My trunks were all packed ready to go back home. You can imagine how I felt when I realized that phone call wasn't a joke, that Joe McCarthy actually wanted me to join the Yanks, the greatest team in baseball. I was so happy tears almost came to my eyes. Within four hours after the phone rang I was on a plane from Cincinnati, bound for New York."

The Reds had purchased Hemsley from Cleveland this past winter to replace Ernie Lombardi, whom they'd sold to the Boston Braves. But Hemsley batted just .113 in 36 games, most of which were in the season's first month, and had since been replaced by rookie Ray Lamanno.

Hemsley got to New York in time to catch both games of a Sunday doubleheader against the White Sox. The Yanks won both games and Hemsley had five hits in seven at-bats. That surprised the Yankee Stadium crowd almost as much as the fact that the journeyman Hemsley was now the Yankees' catcher.

McCarthy had signed Hemsley following a dispute with Buddy Rosar, who had been doing the catching while Bill Dickey recovered from a shoulder injury. Against McCarthy's wishes, Rosar had left the team for the weekend to take a police examination in Buffalo, leaving rookie Eddie Kearse as the Yanks' only catcher. (For Kearse, who batted .192 in 11 games, this would be his one big league season.)

Rosar explained his leaving the club to take the test this way. "This is a sane desire for protection. Baseball is my meat and drink right now but no one can say when I'll go out there and meet with an accident that will end my baseball days."

When Rosar told McCarthy he was going even without permission, McCarthy said: "That's entirely up to you." But when Rosar asked what would happen to him if he did, the manager responded: "That's up to me." When the season ended, the Yankees, who'd won their second consecutive pennant, traded Rosar to Cleveland.

August 31, 1942: Purchased Outfielder Roy Cullenbine from the Washington Senators

The previous day's departure of Tommy Henrich for the Coast Guard left the Yankees with only four outfielders and forced them to act quickly. For while they had a comfortable eight-game lead over Boston, the roster deadline for World Series eligibility was only hours away. The hurried addition of Roy Cullenbine meant that manager Joe McCarthy could use the 28-year-old switch hitter against the National League pennant-winner (either St. Louis or Brooklyn) in the Series.

August 31, 1942: *Roy Cullenbine.* **Cullenbine joined the Yanks just in time to be eligible for the 1942 World Series.**

Cullenbine, a big-leaguer since 1938, would be joining his third team this season: he'd begun 1942 with the St. Louis Browns, but they'd traded him to Washington on June 7. He had a combined .257 average for the Browns and Senators, with four home runs and 49 runs batted in. Cullenbine's best season had come a year earlier, in 1941, when he batted .317 with 98 RBIs for the Browns. That led McCarthy to call him "the most improved outfielder in the league."

December 17, 1942: Traded Outfielder Roy Cullenbine and Catcher Buddy Rosar to the Cleveland Indians for Outfielder Roy Weatherly and Infielder Oscar Grimes

As the loss of personnel to the military began to significantly affect all major league teams, a player's draft status had now become an important consideration of any deal. In this one, each of the four involved players was married with at least one child, giving each a draft classification of 3-A.

After starring with the great International League Newark Bears teams of the late 1930s, Buddy Rosar had been Bill Dickey's backup since coming to New York in 1939. The Yankees regarded him as Dickey's eventual successor, but this past July, the 28-year-old Rosar had committed an unpardonable sin in the eyes of manager Joe McCarthy. He'd left the team

December 17, 1942: *Buddy Rosar.* **Rosar had upset manager Joe McCarthy by leaving the team without permission.**

at a crucial time, returning home to Buffalo to take a civil service police examination. That and a .230 batting average in 69 games made him expendable.

The Yanks had purchased switch-hitting Roy Cullenbine from Washington for the $7,500 waiver price on August 31, 1942, following Tommy Henrich's enlistment in the Coast Guard. Cullenbine batted .364 in 21 games down the stretch, and played right field in each of the five World Series games against the Cardinals.

Roy Weatherly, a .258-hitter in 1942, was coming to New York after seven years in Cleveland. His best season had been in 1940, when he batted .303 with 12 home runs in 135 games. The 27-year-old Weatherly, who was a better outfielder than Cullenbine, played his first game as a Yankee at Yankee Stadium on Opening Day, 1943. As Joe DiMaggio's replacement in center field (DiMaggio was in the Army), he hit a ninth-inning double that drove in the tying and winning runs in a 5-4 victory over Washington. In all, Weatherly played in 77 games in 1943, batting .263 with seven home runs and 28 runs batted in. After serving two years in the military, he returned in 1946, but after getting one hit in two at-bats, the Yankees, loaded with returning outfielders, released him.

Like Weatherly, Oscar Grimes was 27 years old and had spent his entire big league career (five years) with the Indians. A right-hand hitter, he had been mainly a utility player filling in at all the infield positions. Grimes had hoped to be the Indians' full-time first baseman in 1942, following the retirement of Hal Trosky; however, rookie Les Fleming won the job, and Grimes remained a utility infielder. He played in only 51 games in '42, batting a feeble .179. However, with the Yanks expecting to lose first baseman Buddy Hassett to the military, they viewed Grimes as a possible replacement.

The Yanks would later get Nick Etten to play first base in 1943, and because they were set at the other infield positions, Grimes played in only nine games in 1943. Third baseman Billy Johnson, who'd had a great rookie year in '43, went into the service in 1944, and Grimes was the Yankee third baseman that season and the next.

January 22, 1943: Traded First Baseman Ed Levy, Minor League Right-handed Pitcher Al Gettel, and Cash to the Philadelphia Phillies for First Baseman Nick Etten

In the four years since Lou Gehrig ended his streak of consecutive games played, several different men had played first base for the Yankees. Besides Babe Dahlgren, the original replacement, the Yanks had used Johnny Sturm, Ed Levy, Buddy Hassett, and even Joe Gordon, normally a second baseman and Tommy Henrich, normally an outfielder.

The 26-year-old Levy had been in the Yankee farm system for six years, although the Phillies had him for one at-bat in 1940 before returning him to the International League Newark Bears. He was the Yanks' opening-day first baseman in 1942, winning the job in spring training by outhitting Hassett. But after 13 games, Levy was batting just .122, and Hassett reclaimed the position.

Later, the Yankees sent Levy to Kansas City in the American Association, where he regained his touch, batting .306 in 139 games. With Hassett set to leave for Navy service, he had hoped to win back the first base job in 1943.

Al Gettel had also been at Kansas City in 1942, where he'd won 12 and lost 11 for the Blues, with a 3.62 earned run average. The 24-year-old Gettel had come to spring training with the Yankees twice, but each time had failed to make the team.

After brief trials with the Athletics in 1938 and 1939, Nick Etten won the first base job with the Phillies in 1941. He batted .311, with 14 home runs and 79 runs batted in, but fell off to .264, eight home runs, and 41 RBIs in 1942. Still, Etten was only 29, batted left-handed, played well defensively, and had a 3A draft status (as did Levy and Gettel). His draft status (married with at least one child) made him especially attractive at a time when the Yanks and every other team were losing many of their best players to the military.

Etten had the typical reaction when he heard he'd been traded to the Yankees. "Christmas comes early this year," he said about leaving the woeful Phillies to join the pennant-winning New Yorkers.

A month after the trade, William D. Cox purchased the Phillies from Gerry Nugent and asked to have the deal restructured. Philadelphia returned Levy and Gettel to the Yankees, and in return received veteran catcher Tom Padden and Al Gerheauser a young lefthanded pitcher. Padden was a one-time major leaguer who was on the Kansas City roster, while Gerheauser was with the Newark Bears.

January 25, 1943: Sold Lefthanded Pitcher Lefty Gomez to the Boston Braves

Lefty Gomez was only 21 years old when the Yankees purchased him from the Pacific Coast League San Francisco Seals in 1929. He struggled as a rookie in 1930 (Bob Shawkey's one season as manager), and even spent the second half of the season in the minors. But beginning in 1931 under Joe McCarthy, Gomez became one of the game's best pitchers and one of the most popular Yankees ever. He was a four-time 20-game winner with a 189-101 record for his 13 seasons in New York. Particularly effective in big games, Gomez was 3-1 in All-Star Games and unbeatable in World Series play, winning six times without a loss.

A sore arm limited Gomez to just three

January 25, 1943: *Lefty Gomez*. **"Of course it's a surprise; these things always are."**

victories in 1940, but he bounced back the next year to go 15-5. He saw little action in 1942, making only 13 starts, with a 6-4 record, and his sale to the Braves came after all seven American League clubs had waived on him.

Gomez, who was working in a war production plant in Lynn, Massachusetts, said that "he was tickled to death at the chance to play ball somewhere. Of course it's a surprise, these things always are. But I'll sure do my best and I hope my new bosses will be as nice to me as the old ones were." About pitching in Braves Field, a park with a reputation for favoring pitchers, Gomez said "I'm beginning to feel like a kid again."

The Braves released Gomez in May without him ever pitching a game for them. He did make one final start (a losing one) for the Washington Senators who signed him a few days after the Braves released him.

January 29, 1943: Traded Second Baseman Gerry Priddy and Minor League Righthanded Pitcher Milo Candini to the Washington Senators for Righthanded Pitcher Bill Zuber and Cash

In 1941, manager Joe McCarthy had visions of second baseman Jerry Priddy and his minor league teammate, shortstop Phil Rizzuto, being the Yankees' double play combination for years to come. But Priddy, now 23, had never hit enough to win a full-time job (.248 in 115 games), although he had been a valuable utility player at all the infield positions these last two seasons.

Bill Zuber was 29, married, and had two children. That gave him a 3-A draft classification, which probably more than his undistinguished pitching record made him attractive to Yankee president Ed Barrow. After spending parts of four seasons with Cleveland, Zuber had been 6-4 and 9-9 for Washington the past two seasons. Eight of his wins in 1942 (and five of his losses) had come in relief. McCarthy called Zuber the "sleeper" in the deal, predicting he would win more games in 1943 than the 14 that Red Ruffing had won in 1942. (Ruffing was now in the Army.)

Despite Milo Candini's youth (he was 25), and several good minor league seasons, the

January 29, 1943: *Gerry Priddy* and *Phil Rizzuto*. Both Priddy and Rizzuto were expected to be Yankee stars, but only Rizzuto would be.

Yanks had given up on him. Hampered by a sore arm, Candini had just a 4-7 mark for the International League Newark Bears in 1942, and the Yanks doubted he could come back from that injury.

Candini would begin his big league career in spectacular fashion by winning his first seven decisions for Washington, before finishing the 1943 season at 11-7.

June 17, 1944: Signed Outfielder Johnny Cooney as a Free Agent

Despite his three hits in four at-bats this season, Brooklyn had released Johnny Cooney two days earlier. Cooney, now 43 years old, had spent 20 years in the National League, most of them with Boston, and had a .287 lifetime batting average. He would get one hit in eight at-bats for the Yankees before they released him on August 4.

June 20, 1944: Traded Outfielder Ed Levy to the Milwaukee Brewers of the American Association for Outfielder Hersh Martin

Two years earlier, in 1942, Ed Levy was the Yankees' opening-day first baseman. Johnny Sturm, who'd occupied that position in 1941, was in the Army, and Levy won the job in spring training by outhitting Buddy Hassett. But Hassett quickly regained the position, and the Yankees sent Levy to Kansas City of the American Association after he'd played in only 13 games. In 1943, he was at Newark, where he batted .322—second in the International League to Rochester's Red Schoendienst—and the Yanks brought him back in 1944, this time as an outfielder. The 27-year-old Levy had been in 40 games this season, and had a .242 average with four home runs.

Hersh Martin was having an outstanding season in the American Association, batting .358 in 58 games for the league-leading Brewers, a non-affiliated team. Martin did have previous major league experience, having played 405 games for the 1937-40 Phillies.

A week and a half after getting Martin, the Yankees sent veteran outfielder Larry Rosenthal to Newark of the International League and then on July 6 sold him to the Philadelphia Athletics. Out of the major leagues since 1941, Rosenthal had batted just .198 in 36 games for the Yanks this season. His failure to hit, combined with the fine play of Martin and the return of Tuck Stainback from an injury and Russ Derry from the voluntarily retired list, had made Rosenthal superfluous.

The 34-year-old Martin proved to be a more than adequate wartime player for the Yankees. Serving as the regular left fielder, he batted .302 in 85 games for the remainder of 1944, and .267 in 117 games in 1945.

September 1, 1944: Signed Outfielder Paul Waner as a Free Agent

Now 41, Paul Waner was a lifetime .333-hitter and a three-time National League bat-ting champion. After spending his most productive years with Pittsburgh, from 1926 to 1941, he had since played with the Boston Braves and the Brooklyn Dodgers,

Waner was batting .287 in 83 games for the Dodgers when they released him. However, because the Yanks didn't sign Waner until September 1, they would not have been allowed to use him in the World Series had they won the 1944 pennant.

Waner reported to Yankee Stadium where he was put to work immediately, delivering a pinch hit run-scoring single in a 10-7 loss to Washington. It was his 3,152nd and final major league hit, and his high point as a Yankee. He went hitless in eight subsequent at-bats that September, and in one final major league plate appearance in 1945, before the Yanks released him on May 3.

December 15, 1944: Traded Lefthanded Pitcher Johnny Johnson to the Chicago White Sox for Lefthanded Pitcher Jake Wade

Johnny Johnson was 0-2 as a 29-year-old rookie in 1944. He pitched a total of 26.2 innings in 22 games, all but one in relief, and earned three saves. He would save four more and have a 3-0 record for the White Sox in 1945, his final season.

Jake Wade was only two years older than Johnson, but he'd made his major league debut with the Tigers back in 1936. Out of the majors in 1940 and 1941, he returned with the White Sox in 1942. Wade carried a career record of 25-39 into the 1945 season, which he would spend in the Navy.

July 27, 1945: Sold Righthanded Pitcher Hank Borowy to the Chicago Cubs

Any of the seven other American League clubs could have had Hank Borowy for the $7,500 waiver price, but all chose not to claim him. Perhaps they thought the Yankees weren't really serious about parting with their ace and would have withdrawn his name had another team claimed him. Nevertheless, Borowy's sale to the National League–leading Cubs outraged many club owners, particularly Washington's Clark Griffith, who said of the Yankees: "it's just one of those things they put over on you." The Yanks "have been asking waivers on everybody on their ballclub trying to get somebody out of the league," said Griffith, whose Senators trailed the league-leading Tigers by three games. "I'm going to fight for a return to the old waiver rule which said in effect that you may put a player up for waiver once, but if you put him up a second time he has to go." Griffith called the 27-year-old Borowy "a real attraction, a great pitcher, and one of the best ball players in the league."

Borowy had signed with the Yankees out of Fordham University, and in three full seasons since reaching the majors in 1942 had won 56 games with only 30 losses. He was 10-5 this season, but was currently nursing a sore arm, an injury that Yankee President Larry MacPhail had used as part of his rationalization for the sale.

"He has pitched three complete games since April," MacPhail explained. "He has not pitched a complete game since June 24, when he won his ninth and had a record of nine and three. Last year he won only five and lost eight after July 15."

July 27, 1945: *Hank Borowy*. Borowy, whose sale to the Cubs baffled Yankee fans, finished his career with the Tigers.

MacPhail said that he'd discussed the deal with manager Joe McCarthy, who was recuperating in Buffalo after having collapsed, and McCarthy had approved. With prewar ace Red Ruffing having returned from military service, the Yanks felt their pitching was strong, but that they had to strengthen other parts of the club.

"This deal can be regarded as the first step in a general plan worked out by Joe McCarthy and myself to improve the Yankees," MacPhail said, while suggesting that the Cubs would be sending several players to New York.

Borowy had mixed emotions about his sale to the Cubs. "I hate to leave the Yankees and the American League where I have spent my major league career," he said. "But that's baseball. Of course, in a sense it may be a break for me. I'm going to a club that is leading the pennant fight and I may get into a World Series. I'll give them my best as I have given it to the Yankees. I hope I can."

By going 11-2 after joining the Cubs, Borowy did help them win that National League pennant. In return, Chicago would send no players to New York, and all the Yanks would ever get from the deal was money, reportedly about $100,000.

Several years later a possible explanation surfaced for the Yankees' seemingly inexplicable sale of Borowy to the Cubs. It was, the theory went, MacPhail's repayment to Chicago general manager Jim Gallagher for selling him Billy Herman back in 1941, a deal which helped MacPhail's Dodgers win their first pennant in 21 years.

March 25, 1946: Sold Catcher Rollie Hemsley to the Philadelphia Phillies

An emergency pickup in July 1942, Rollie Hemsley had served admirably (.262 in 174 games) as a reserve catcher on the Yankees' 1942 and 1943 pennant-winning teams. He also played in 81 games in 1944 before entering the Navy, where he served through the 1945 season. With Aaron Robinson and Bill Dickey set to do the catching in 1946, the Yankees had no place for Hemsley, who was now almost 39 years old and coming off that long layoff.

April 29, 1946: Sold Outfielder Russ Derry to the Philadelphia Athletics

Although Russ Derry had an excellent minor league career, he had to wait until Joe DiMaggio, Tommy Henrich, and Charlie Keller went into the military before getting his chance with the Yankees. That came in 1944, and Derry played 116 games over the next two seasons, batting a combined .234, but with 17 home runs.

Now, with everybody back from the service, the Yanks tried to send Derry to the International League Newark Bears, but he refused to report. Philadelphia's Connie Mack, who thought the 29-year-old Derry could help the A's, contacted Yankee farm director George Weiss and arranged for the sale.

Besides cutting their ties with Derry, the Yankees released Tuck Stainback, another of their wartime outfielders. The Yanks had called Stainback up from Newark in August 1942 to help fill the spot being vacated by Tommy Henrich who was entering the Coast Guard. Used mostly as a reserve by manager Joe McCarthy, Stainback batted .252 for the Yanks between 1942 and 1945. Four days after the Yanks released him, Mack's woeful A's would also sign Stainback.

May 3, 1946: Sold Righthanded Pitcher Steve Roser to the Boston Braves

The postwar rosters of all major league teams were bulging in the spring of 1946. Returning servicemen who had missed from one to four years while serving in the military were trying to win their old jobs back from those who had replaced them during the war. Also competing for jobs was a larger than usual group of rookies. The Yankees were no different, and manager Joe McCarthy had to part with many of the men who had reported to spring training.

Twenty-eight-year-old pitcher Steve Roser was typical of those who'd "filled in" during the war. Roser went 4-3 with a save as a rookie in 1944 and had no decisions in 1945. He had pitched only 3.1 innings this season, yet had both won a game and lost one.

Between Opening Day and mid–May, the Yankees were forced to make many roster decisions. They would send righthander Ken Holcombe (3-3 as a rookie in 1945) to Kansas City of the American Association and three other pitchers to Newark of the International League. Going to the Bears were righthander Steve Peek (4-2 in 1941), rookie lefthander Herb Karpel (0-0 in two games this season), and righthander Monk Dubiel. After a 16-9 season for the Bears in 1943, Dubiel joined the Yankees' starting rotation as a rookie in 1944 and went 23-22 over the next two seasons. Both he and Holcombe would return to the major leagues in 1948: Dubiel with the Phillies, and Holcombe with the Reds.

On April 29, the Yanks had lopped wartime outfielders Russ Derry and Tuck Stainback from their bloated roster. Now it was Bud Metheny's turn. Derry and Stainback would play this season with the Philadelphia A's, but Metheny's major league career, spent entirely with the Yankees, was over. After coming up from Newark, he'd batted a combined .248 as the team's right fielder from 1943 through 1945, and had gone hitless in three at-bats in 1946.

June 5, 1946: Sold Righthanded Pitcher Charley Stanceu to the Philadelphia Phillies

After going 3-3 as a 25-year-old rookie in 1941, Charley Stanceu spent the next four years in the Army. He'd been in three games this season with no decisions, but would win two and lose four with the Phillies.

The Yanks also exchanged catchers with their American Association team at Kansas City. They sent Bill Drescher (.266 in 57 games as a wartime fill-in) to the Blues and brought up rookie Gus Niarhos.

June 14, 1946: Sold Third Baseman Hank Majeski to the Philadelphia Athletics

Baseball's ruling body had attempted to accommodate the returning war veterans by increasing the post–June 15 roster limit to 30. Nevertheless, each team still would have a

"31st" man to get rid of, and new manager Bill Dickey determined that for the Yankees that man was Hank Majeski. (Actually, two men had to go: the other was rookie righthander Frank Hiller who went to Newark of the International League.)

Joe Gordon was back from the Army to play second base, which meant that George Stirnweiss, the team's second baseman in 1945, would compete with another returning serviceman, Billy Johnson, for the third base slot. Majeski, 29, had been Yankee property since September 1942, although he'd spent the next three years in the Coast Guard. Before going to the Athletics for the $7,500 waiver price, he'd gotten into eight games, with one hit (a triple) in eight at-bats.

Majeski immediately became Philadelphia's third baseman, replacing future Hall of Famer George Kell whom Connie Mack had traded to Detroit for outfielder Barney McCoskey a month earlier.

June 17, 1946: Purchased Outfielder Frank Colman from the Pittsburgh Pirates

Pittsburgh brought Frank Colman to the big leagues in September 1942, and he continued to play for the Pirates through the war years. He had his best season in 1944, when he batted .270 in 99 games. A 28-year-old lefthanded hitter, Colman had been in 26 games this season, mostly as a pinch hitter, and was currently batting .170.

Colman had four hits in 15 at-bats for the 1946 Yankees, but spent most of the season with Newark in the International League. He had a solid season for the Bears and was back in New York in 1947. But after just three hits in 28 at-bats, he went back to Newark and never again played in the majors.

June 18, 1946: Sold Righthanded Pitcher Bill Zuber to the Boston Red Sox

Boston had a seven-game lead on the second-place Yankees when they added pitcher Bill Zuber. The 33-year-old Zuber had lost his

only decision this season and was 18-23 since coming to the Yanks in 1943. He would go 5-1 as a spot starter for the pennant-winning Red Sox, which was mainly the role the 4-F Zuber had occupied on the Yankee pitching staff.

July 11, 1946: Sold Infielder Oscar Grimes to the Philadelphia Athletics

Throughout this season, the Yanks had been selling and releasing many of their prewar and wartime players. Today, it was Oscar Grimes's turn. After playing in only nine games in 1942, Grimes was the Yankees' regular third baseman in 1944 and 1945. However, the Yanks no longer needed him. Along with the return from the military of second baseman Joe Gordon, shortstop Phil Rizzuto, and third baseman Billy Johnson, the Yanks still had George Stirnweiss, the league's defending batting champion whom they were using in a utility role.

Grimes, now 31, had batted .205 in 14 games this season and had an overall .266 average in 282 games as a Yankee.

August 5, 1946: Sold Lefthanded Pitcher Jake Wade to the Washington Senators

Jake Wade had turned in a solid relief effort against Washington earlier this season that had impressed Senators manager Ossie Bluege. So, when the Yanks asked waivers on the 34-year-old Wade, Bluege was quick to claim him, although his club's six losses in their last seven games were due more to a lack of hitting than pitching. Nevertheless, Bluege also claimed second-year lefthander Joe Page, who the Yanks had also put on the waiver list, but whom they then quickly removed.

Wade, who spent 1945 in the Navy, had a 2-1 record with a 2.29 earned run average this season. He'd been in 13 games, but only one as a starter. Wade would make six relief appearances for Washington, but this would be his final big league season.

It would also be the final season for Marius Russo, sent by the Yankees to Kansas City of the American Association in the day's other roster reduction. Russo had compiled a 45-32 record for the Yankees between 1939 and 1943, including back-to-back 14-win seasons in 1940 and 1941. He spent the next two seasons in the Army, and then this past winter underwent arm surgery. Mostly ineffective this year, Russo had an 0-2 record and a 4.34 ERA in eight appearances.

October 11, 1946: Traded Second Baseman Joe Gordon to the Cleveland Indians for Righthanded Pitcher Allie Reynolds

Because of the Yankees' surplus of infielders, rumors that they'd be sending one or more of them to Cleveland had surfaced throughout

October 11, 1946: *Ed Lopat* and *Allie Reynolds*. The Yanks asked for Red Embree in return for Joe Gordon, but Reynolds (right) would go on to be one of their greatest pitchers ever.

the 1946 season. Conversely, Indians president Bill Veeck was satisfied with his club's pitching, but he was looking for offensive help; Cleveland's team batting average of .245 in '46 was the lowest in the American League. The Indians, who had one of the game's best shortstops in their manager, Lou Boudreau, were particularly weak at second base. Veterans Dutch Meyer and Ray Mack had shared the position this past season, but Meyer batted just .232, and Mack did even worse at .205.

Actually, Joe Gordon, their new second baseman, hadn't done any better. Gordon batted just .210 in 112 games; moreover, for someone who'd always been a standout defensively, he'd played uncharacteristically poorly in the field. Veeck's hope was that the 31-year-old Gordon had needed a season to readjust after two years in the military and would return to his prewar form in 1947. He'd been baseball's best second baseman for most of the years between 1938, his rookie season, and 1942, but had since surrendered that honor to Bobby Doerr of the Red Sox. Gordon had his greatest season in 1942, when he batted a career-high .322 and won the American League's Most Valuable Player Award. In all, he'd played exactly 1,000 games as a Yankee and had a .271 batting average, 153 home runs, and 617 runs batted in.

While Allie Reynolds was the same age as Gordon (although at the time he was thought to be only 28), he'd never had the same kind of success. He'd been an 18-game winner in 1945 but had just a 51-47 lifetime record, far below what the Indians had expected. Reynolds had gotten off to a 2-10 start in 1946, before winning six straight and eventually finishing with an 11-15 mark. Nevertheless, the Yanks asked Cleveland for Red Embree, who had an 8-12 record in '46, in return for Gordon. Veeck said no and countered with Steve Gromek (5-15). Reynolds was the eventual compromise choice.

Gordon did return to form with the Indians in 1947, and in 1948 he helped lead them to a world championship. However, after falling off the next two years, he retired after the 1950 season. Meanwhile, Reynolds became one of the greatest of Yankee pitchers, one who was especially effective in big games. Between 1947 and 1954, first as a starter and later as a reliever, Reynolds won 131 and lost 60 and added seven more victories in the World Series.

October 12, 1946: Traded Third Baseman Eddie Bockman to the Cleveland Indians for Cash and Two Players to Be Named

A day after the Yanks traded Joe Gordon, their former All Star second baseman to Cleveland for pitcher Allie Reynolds, they sent the Indians Eddie Bockman, a promising young infielder. In 1946, Bockman batted .303, with 29 stolen bases for Kansas City, which led his manager, Billy Meyer, to call the 26-year-old Navy veteran one of the three best players in the American Association. The Yanks brought Bockman to New York in September, but he managed just one hit in 12 at-bats.

On December 5, Cleveland sent the Yankees second baseman Dutch Meyer, who'd batted .232 in 72 games in 1946. Meyer had shared the second base position with Ray Mack, but with the acquisition of Gordon was no longer needed. Neither was Mack, who would go to New York one day later (December 6) in a five player trade, which seemed to fulfill the second "player to be named" segment of this trade. The 31-year-old Meyer went to the International League Newark Bears and never returned to the major leagues.

October 24, 1946: Traded Righthanded Pitcher Ernie Bonham to the Pittsburgh Pirates for Lefthanded Pitcher Cookie Cuccurullo

Ernie Bonham was one of the few major leaguers who played a significant role on his team before, during, and after World War II. Since coming up from Kansas City of the American Association in August 1940, he'd compiled a very impressive 79-50 record with the Yankees. In 1942, Bonham was the Yanks' best pitcher. He went 21-5, had a 2.27 earned run average, and led the American League in winning percentage (.808) and shutouts (6). He also tied Boston's Tex Hughson for the most complete games in the league with 22.

Hindered by physical problems in 1946, Bonham won only five games, lost eight, and had a 3.70 earned run average. He came back to win 24 games for the Pirates over the next three seasons, before dying prematurely at age 35 from appendicitis surgery complications on September 15, 1949.

Cookie Cuccurullo had pitched one game for Pittsburgh at the end of 1943 and then remained with the Pirates the next two years. He had a combined 3-5 record in 62 games, all but nine in relief. In 1946, Pittsburgh sent Cuccurullo to Hollywood of the Pacific Coast League where he went 8-6, but he never again came back to the major leagues.

December 6, 1946: Traded Outfielder Hal Peck, Righthanded Pitcher Al Gettel, and Minor League Lefthanded Pitcher Gene Bearden to the Cleveland Indians for Second Baseman Ray Mack and Catcher Sherm Lollar

Of the three players going to Cleveland, Al Gettel was the only one who'd ever actually played for the Yankees. He'd spent nine years in their farm system, before going 9-8 as a 27-year-old rookie in 1945 and 6-7 (but with a 2.97 ERA) in 1946.

Gene Bearden, 26, had been a promising minor league pitcher before the war. He'd missed the 1943 and 1944 seasons, but had gone 15-5 for Binghamton of the Eastern League in 1945 and 15-4 with Oakland of the Pacific Coast League in 1946. Cleveland would keep Bearden in the minors in 1947, but the following year he would help pitch them to the world championship.

The Yanks had purchased Hal Peck from the Athletics in June 1946, but he'd had a nervous breakdown and never reported. He joined the Indians in 1947 and was a valuable member of the team for the next three seasons.

While Ray Mack had never been much of a hitter, he had, nevertheless, been the Indians' second baseman throughout the early 1940s. He missed the 1945 season because of military service and then played only part-time in 1946, batting just .205. Still only 30, he remained a fine fielder, and the Yanks figured to use him as a backup to second baseman George Stirnweiss. But Mack's Yankee career would be short-lived, consisting of just one 1947 pinch running appearance before he moved on to the Cubs.

In 1945 Sherman Lollar, then 21, batted an International League-leading .364 for the Baltimore Orioles. The following year he had a .242 mark in 28 games for the Indians, but because of injuries, spent a good part of the season back in Baltimore. Lollar figured to join veteran Ken Silvestri and the Yankees' other young catchers, Ralph Houk, Yogi Berra, and Gus Niarhos, in a battle for the additional spots behind returning first-stringer Aaron Robinson.

January 25, 1947: Signed First Baseman George McQuinn as a Free Agent

First base had been a weak spot in 1946, and Yankee president Larry MacPhail was

January 25, 1947: *Bucky Harris.* **The Yanks' new manager promised McQuinn he'd have a chance to win the first base job in 1947.**

offering to spend up to $150,000 to bring a new first baseman to New York. Signing veteran George McQuinn would not affect MacPhail's pursuit. During spring training, he would offer Washington that amount of money for Mickey Vernon, the league's 1946 batting champion. But Senators owner Clark Griffith, upset at MacPhail for his recent negative remarks about him, turned down the offer.

McQuinn had actually come up through the Yankee farm system, but after playing briefly for Cincinnati in 1936, went to the St. Louis Browns in 1938 and was their full time first baseman through 1945. An outstanding defensive player, McQuinn led American League first basemen in fielding in 1939, 1940, 1941, and 1944. He was the AL's All-Star first baseman in '44 and hit .435 for the Browns in their World Series loss to the Cardinals that fall.

The Browns traded McQuinn to the A's in October 1945 for first baseman Dick Siebert, who never reported to St. Louis; meanwhile, McQuinn played 136 games for the A's in 1946. A lifetime .275 hitter, his average slipped to .225 for the A's, and manager Connie Mack released him after the season.

Before signing him, the Yankees had McQuinn examined by Dr. Mal Stevens, the team physician. Stevens pronounced him fit, whereupon Bucky Harris, recently named to manage the club in 1947, told McQuinn that he would be given a chance to win a job during spring training.

The 37-year-old McQuinn took advantage of that offer. Following an excellent exhibition game season, McQuinn would play 144 games for the world champion Yankees in 1947. He batted .304 (the first time he'd topped .300 since 1939), with 13 home runs and 80 RBIs. He would play a final season in 1948, batting .248 in 94 games.

March 1, 1947: Purchased Infielder Johnny Lucadello from the St. Louis Browns

Johnny Lucadello was the only member of the St. Louis Browns who hadn't signed his 1947 contract. Lucadello, a 28-year-old switch hitter, had reached the majors with the Browns in 1938, but played in only 33 games for St.

Louis over the next three years. Then, after batting .279 in 107 games in 1941, he spent four years in the Navy. Lucadello returned to bat .248 in 87 games in 1946, and he would end his career by batting .083 in 12 games for the 1947 Yankees.

April 14, 1947: Sold First Baseman Nick Etten to the Philadelphia Phillies

The Yankees had signed veteran first baseman George McQuinn as a free agent during the offseason, promising him a chance to compete for a job in 1947. McQuinn did so well during spring training that he'd won the first base position outright and was scheduled to play first base in the Yanks' opener at Washington. Rain canceled the game, but later in the day, the Yanks announced that they'd sold 33-year-old Nick Etten, their World War II first baseman, to the Phillies.

April 14, 1947: *Nick Etten.* **Etten was hoping to play for the White Sox.**

Etten had played in more than 150 games in each season from 1943 to 1945, while batting .271, .293, and .285. He led the American League in home runs (22), and walks (97) in 1944, and in runs batted in (111) in 1945. But in 1946, under Joe McCarthy and his two successors as manager, Bill Dickey and Johnny Neun, Etten appeared in only 108 games, with just 84 at first base. His average dropped to .232, and he had only nine home runs. While aware that he didn't fit into new manager Bucky Harris's plans for 1947, Etten had hoped to make his own deal with the White Sox, one that would allow him to play closer to home.

The Yankees also announced that right-hander Johnny Murphy, their longtime bullpen ace whom they'd released three days earlier, had signed with the Boston Red Sox. Murphy, 4-2 in 1946, had pitched 12 seasons for the Yanks (1932, 1934-43, and 1946), compiling a 93-53 record with 107 saves.

June 3, 1947: Purchased Infielder-Outfielder Ted Sepkowski from the Cleveland Indians

Ted Sepkowski had played in five games for the Indians as an 18 year old in 1942, and then two more games in 1946 after returning from the service. He'd spent most of the '46 season with Oklahoma City of the Texas League, where he batted an even .300 in 136 games. Used this season mostly as a pinch hitter by manager Lou Boudreau, he'd been in ten games but had just eight at-bats and only one hit (.125.)

Yankee manager Bucky Harris used Sepkowski twice, both times as a pinch runner, before sending him to Newark of the International League. He never returned to the majors.

June 25, 1947: Purchased Second Baseman Lonny Frey from the Chicago Cubs

Other than two years out for service in World War II, Lonny Frey had been in the National League since 1933. He'd been a shortstop in his first five seasons, with the Dodgers and Cubs, but switched to second base after going to Cincinnati in 1938. Frey was the Reds' regular second baseman through 1943, then spent 1944 and 1945 in the Army. The Cubs reacquired him in 1946, playing him at second base and the outfield, where he batted .209 in 24 games.

The 36-year-old Frey took the roster spot of Ted Sepkowski, whom the Yanks had dropped after he appeared in just two games as a pinch runner. Frey batted .179 in 24 games in 1947, and even played a game in 1948 before the Yanks released him. He finished the '48 season, and his career, with the Giants.

July 10, 1947: Sold Righthanded Pitcher Mel Queen to the Pittsburgh Pirates

Mel Queen spent parts of four seasons with the Yanks (1942, 1944, 1946, and 1947), going 8-4 in 33 games. He'd been in only five games this season, with no record. To replace Queen, the Yankees recalled 28-year-old Vic Raschi, who was 7-2 with Portland of the Pacific Coast League. In 1946, Raschi had impressed the Yanks by going 2-0 after they called him up from the International League Newark Bears in September.

July 11, 1947: Purchased Righthanded Pitcher Bobo Newsom from the Washington Senators

The Yankees had just won their 11th consecutive game and had a nine-game lead over Detroit and Boston. (They would eventually tie a major league record by winning 19 straight games.) Nevertheless, manager Bucky Harris, who'd managed Bobo Newsom at Washington, felt that the boisterous veteran could help the club down the stretch. Not surprisingly, Newsom, who was a few weeks short of his 40th birthday and had been a big league pitcher for eight different teams (some more than once) since 1929, agreed.

"It's wonderful to be with the Yankees," he said. "I don't know how it will go, but I think I can help them. Not that they're not a cinch already without me."

Harris put Newsom into the starting rotation, where he made 15 starts over the last

July 11, 1947: *Bobo Newsom.* **The Yanks were Newsom's eighth different big league team.**

two months of the season, winning seven and losing five.

August 3, 1947: Sold Righthanded Pitcher Al Lyons to the Pittsburgh Pirates

Before entering the Navy, Al Lyons pitched in 11 games (0-0) with the 1944 Yankees. He returned in 1946 to go 7-12 with Kansas City of the American Association and 0-1 in two games with the Yanks. Lyons had been in just six games this season, with one decision, a win.

December 11, 1947: Traded Outfielder Allie Clark to the Cleveland Indians for Righthanded Pitcher Red Embree

Allie Clark had been in the Yankee farm system before spending all of the 1944 and 1945 seasons in the military. In 1946, the Yanks sent him to Newark of the International League, where he batted .344. He followed that with a .334 mark in 1947 with 23 home runs and 86 runs batted in. That earned him a call-up by the Yankees, and the 24-year-old Clark made the most of it. In 24 games, he had 25 hits in 67 at-bats for a .373 average.

Despite that impressive showing, the Yankee outfield was a tough one to break into, and many others in their farm system had numbers similar to Clark's.

Red Embree had been a favorite of Yankee manager Bucky Harris since 1944, when Embree pitched for Baltimore of the International League and Harris was the general manager at Buffalo. Still, the 30-year-old Embree had not been a particularly successful major league pitcher. In parts of six seasons with Cleveland he had a 23-32 record, and had won just eight games in each of the past two seasons: 8-12 in 1946 and 8-10 in 1947.

Adding Embree to the pitching staff seemed a tepid response to the rival Boston Red Sox. Since the 1947 season ended, the Sox, and their new manager, former longtime Yankee skipper Joe McCarthy, had added shortstop Vern Stephens and pitchers Ellis Kinder and Jack Kramer from the St. Louis Browns, and outfielder Stan Spence from the Washington Senators. Still, Harris insisted that this deal would put his club in the running for the pennant in 1948.

February 24, 1948: Traded Catcher Aaron Robinson, Lefthanded Pitcher Bill Wight, and Minor League Righthanded Pitcher Fred Bradley to the Chicago White Sox for Lefthanded Pitcher Ed Lopat

By acquiring Ed Lopat the Yanks were getting their first dependable lefthanded starter since the prewar days of Lefty Gomez. A 29-year-old native New Yorker, Lopat was generally considered the second best lefthander in the league, behind only Detroit's Hal Newhouser. (Yankee manger Bucky Harris and general manager George Weiss both thought Lopat was the best.) Of his conversations with the White Sox, Weiss said, "They mentioned other players, but Lopat was the fellow we wanted."

In his four-year major league career, all spent with the second-division White Sox, Lopat had won 50 games and lost 49. He was, however, coming off a 1947 season that had been his best: a 16-13 record, a 2.81 earned run average (tied for third best in the league), and

22 complete games (tied for second best). Lopat's greatest career success had come against Cleveland—13 wins and only two losses—while against his new club, the Yankees, he'd split 12 decisions.

Aaron Robinson got into one game for the Yanks in May 1943 before leaving for military service with the Coast Guard, returning in mid–1945. In 1946, Robinson hit .297 with 16 home runs in 100 games to earn a place on *The Sporting News* combined major league All-Star team. He fell off to .270 with only five home runs in 1947, and he caught just 74 games as rookie Yogi Berra became the club's first-string catcher. Yet despite Berra's fine season, Weiss felt that Gus Niarhos would be the Yankees' catcher in 1948. Niarhos had batted .321 with the American Association Kansas City Blues in 1947, and he was also a much better receiver than Berra.

Getting Lopat for Robinson would turn out to be among the best trades the Yankees ever made. Robinson played one year for Chicago before the Sox, ironically in one of the best trades they ever made, dealt him to Detroit for rookie pitcher Billy Pierce.

Fred Bradley, who had a 13-4 record with the American Association Kansas City Blues in 1947, would have a very brief big league career. He pitched in eight games for Chicago in 1948 and one in 1949 without ever being involved in a decision.

Bill Wight had won two and lost two as a Yankee rookie in 1946. He was 16-9 with Kansas City in 1947 and pitched a complete-game victory in his one appearance with the Yankees.

April 12, 1948: Sold Righthanded Pitcher Butch Wensloff to the Cleveland Indians

This was the second time this spring that the Yanks had sold Butch Wensloff. The Philadelphia Phillies negated the earlier sale after they failed to agree with Wensloff on salary and had returned him to the Yankees two days earlier. When Indians President Bill Veeck said he would not allow Wensloff to pass through waivers again, Yankee GM George Weiss suggested that Cleveland buy him.

Wensloff had been a 27-year-old rookie in

1943 when he took Red Ruffing's place in the Yankee rotation after Ruffing left for the Army. He went 13-11 and had an excellent 2.54 earned run average, but lost the next two years working in a war plant and serving in the Army. In 1946, he had arm problems, but returned to go 3-1 for the Yanks in 1947. Wensloff would pitch only one game for the Indians, a start, in which he lasted just 1.2 innings and took the loss.

May 13, 1948: Traded Outfielder Bud Stewart to the Washington Senators for Outfielder Leon Culberson and Cash

Bud Stewart had been playing professionally since 1937, with two years out for military service in 1943 and 1944. He was just short of his 32nd birthday, but his only major league experience until this season had been with the 1941-42 Pittsburgh Pirates. Stewart had enjoyed a sensational year with the Yanks' American Association team at Kansas City in 1947: a .358 batting average and 102 runs batted in. He'd made only six pinch-hitting appearances this season with one hit, a double.

Although he was four years younger than Stewart, Leon Culberson had more major league experience. He'd spent five years with the Boston Red Sox before coming to Washington with Al Kozar in a December 1947 trade for Stan Spence. Culberson had begun what would be his final big league season by stroking four singles against the Yanks on Opening Day at Griffith Stadium, but had been just 1 for 24 since. With the May 15 cutdown date approaching, the club had no room on their roster for Culberson and sent him to Kansas City.

July 25, 1948: Sold Righthanded Pitcher Randy Gumpert to the Chicago White Sox

Only 18 when he broke in with the Philadelphia Athletics in 1936, Randy Gumpert also pitched part of the 1937 and 1938 seasons with the A's, before spending several years in the minors and three years in the wartime Coast Guard. Gumpert returned to the big leagues with the Yanks in 1946, compiling an

11-3 record as the club's fifth starter. He was mostly a relief pitcher under manager Bucky Harris in 1947, winning four and losing one, and was 1-0 in 15 relief appearances this season.

Besides selling Gumpert, the Yanks also optioned sore-armed Bill Bevens, a member of the club since 1944, to Newark of the International League. Bevens had made only one mound appearance since his near-miss no-hitter in last fall's World Series, a brief outing in a spring training game against the Cardinals.

Bevens would pitch only eight innings for Newark, and on January 7, 1949, the Yanks would sell him to the White Sox on a conditional basis. The Sox, who had until Opening Day to decide whether to keep Bevens, returned him on March 28, and he never pitched again.

August 9, 1948: Sold Righthanded Pitcher Karl Drews to the St. Louis Browns

Karl Drews made his big league debut in September 1946. He got into three games and lost his only decision, but was 6-6 in 30 games in 1947, and 2-3 in 19 games this season. Drews's sale left the Yanks one man shy of the 25-player limit, but despite being in a fierce four-way pennant fight, manager Bucky Harris wouldn't fill that roster spot for 12 days. And when he did, his choice surprised everyone. Instead of calling up Kansas City Blues outfielder Hank Bauer, as everyone expected, Harris recalled Ralph Houk, Bauer's teammate and the American Association's All-Star catcher. (Harris would call Bauer up in September.)

Harris had a logical reason for his selection of Houk. A few days earlier, he had shifted Yogi Berra to right field and wanted another catcher besides Sherm Lollar to back up new first-stringer Gus Niarhos.

December 13, 1948: Trade Righthanded Pitchers Red Embree and Dick Starr, Catcher Sherman Lollar, and Cash to the St. Louis Browns for Righthanded

Pitcher Fred Sanford and Catcher Roy Partee

Disagreement as to whether Dick Starr would or would not be a part of this trade delayed its completion for two days. St. Louis insisted that the Yanks include him, while Yankee GM George Weiss wanted the Browns to take pitcher Frank Hiller instead. Weiss was hesitant to part with Starr because he was planning to send him to the Washington Senators in a separate trade. Starr would go to Washington in exchange for one of the Senators' pitchers, either Early Wynn or Walt Masterson. "That knocks one of our deals in the head," said Senators owner Clark Griffith when he heard that Starr was going to St. Louis.

The Yanks were reluctant to give up the 27-year-old Starr because they believed he was one of the most promising pitchers in their system. He'd won his only big league decision (in 1947), and had gone 14-9 with 158 strikeouts

December 13, 1948: *Fred Sanford*. Despite the Yankees' hopes, Sanford would not be another Red Ruffing.

for Newark of the International League in 1948.

On the other hand, the Yanks had no regrets in giving up Red Embree, who'd been a major disappointment to manager Bucky Harris in 1948. Expected to be a member of the starting rotation, Embree appeared in only 20 games, mostly in relief, winning five and losing three.

And while the Yanks thought highly of 24-year-old Sherman Lollar, he was, nevertheless, a third-string catcher who had Yogi Berra and Gus Niarhos ahead of him. Lollar had spent the entire 1948 season with the Yanks, but he caught in only ten games and had a combined two-year average of .214 in 33 games.

With enough catching talent to allow them to trade a prospect like Lollar, there was little chance that a run-of-the-mill receiver like Roy Partee would stick with the Yankees. Partee was a five-year veteran with a .250 batting average, but his major league career was now over.

The Yankees fully expected that Fred Sanford would follow the path of Red Ruffing and other pitchers whom they'd rescued from poor teams and who'd become successful pitchers for them. They knew that despite his unimpressive record while pitching for the forlorn Browns—he had lost a league-high 21 games in 1948—the 29-year-old Sanford was a fine pitcher. The Yanks had another incentive for adding Sanford. It prevented him from going to Detroit or Cleveland, both of whom had been trying to trade for him. The Tigers and the Indians were two of the three teams (the other was the Red Sox) the Yanks saw as their chief rivals for the 1949 pennant.

The Browns had more good news for the Yankees. After St. Louis's GM Bill DeWitt concluded this deal, he announced that his club would be making "no more major transactions." That meant that neither pitcher Cliff Fannin nor third baseman Bob Dillinger, the Browns' best remaining players, would find their way to Boston, Detroit or Cleveland.

December 14, 1948: Traded First Baseman Steve Souchock to the Chicago White Sox for Outfielder Jim Delsing

Steve Souchock began working his way through the Yankee farm system in 1939. After spending 1943–1945 in the Army, he was with the Yanks in 1946, batting .302 in 47 games. Nevertheless, Souchock was back at Kansas City of the American Association in 1947. A .294 average and 17 home runs earned him another trip to New York in 1948, but he hit just .203 in 44 games with only three home runs.

Jim Delsing had begun his career during the war, as a 16 year old in 1942, and he'd also spent time in the military (1944–45). Following a .316 season for the Pacific Coast League Hollywood Stars in 1947, Delsing began the 1948 season with the White Sox. However, he got off to a slow start, and Chicago sent him back to Hollywood, where he had another outstanding year. Delsing batted .333 for the '48 Stars, obviously impressing Casey Stengel, then the manager of the PCL Oakland Oaks, but now the newly appointed manager of the Yankees.

August 6, 1949: Sold First Baseman Jack Phillips to the Pittsburgh Pirates

The Yanks were selling first baseman Jack Phillips to make room for the return of pitcher Bob Porterfield from Newark of the International League. Facing a crucial series at Boston later in the week, manager Casey Stengel wanted to start Porterfield in one of those games. Porterfield had suffered arm injuries twice this season, but he appeared to have recovered fully after pitching 16 innings in five games for the Bears. Stengel planned to find out quickly by starting him in one game of this afternoon's doubleheader with St. Louis.

The 27-year-old Phillips had been Yankee property since 1943 and had appeared in 16 games in 1947 and one in 1948. Earlier this season he'd alternated at first base with the left-handed hitting Dick Kryhoski, batting .308 in 45 games. But bursitis in his throwing arm had kept him out of action for much of the summer, and Stengel had moved Tommy Henrich in from the outfield to play first base. Now, with Phillips's departure, and with Kryhoski at Oakland of the Pacific Coast League, Henrich remained the only first baseman on the roster.

August 22, 1949: Purchased First Baseman Johnny Mize from the New York Giants

Johnny Mize had been in the National League since 1936, with three years (1943–45) out for service in the United States Navy. He was with St. Louis for six seasons, and had been with the Giants since 1942. In that time Mize had established himself as one of the game's great hitters, with a .320 lifetime batting average, 315 home runs, and 1,158 runs batted in. He'd won the batting title with a .349 average in 1939, and four times he'd led the league in home runs, including 1947 and 1948 when he'd tied for the lead with Ralph Kiner. But Mize was hitting just .263 this season, with only 18 home runs, and Giants manager Leo Durocher had benched him several times. Actually, with his team in fifth place and trailing the league-leading Cardinals by 13 games, Durocher was looking for reasons to get rid of his older, slower players and was glad to "dump" Mize.

Giants secretary Eddie Brannick announced the crosstown sale, which came after a meeting between Yankee co-owners Dan Topping and Del Webb and Giants owner Horace Stoneham. The Yanks had an open roster

August 22, 1949: *Johnny Mize.* **Giants manager Leo Durocher was getting rid of his older, slower players.**

spot after sending injured pitcher Bob Porter-field back to Newark of the International League, although they would have preferred to fill it with a pitcher.

"Had a worthwhile pitcher been available, I certainly would have grabbed him," said Yankee manager Casey Stengel. "But there weren't any, so with the chance at hand to add possibly a little extra punch, we took Mize."

Stengel, also a former National Leaguer, added that he hadn't seen much of Mize recently and didn't know "just how much of his old form he retained." He also hadn't yet decided how he would use him. If he was satisfied that Mize could still play first base, Stengel had the option of moving Tommy Henrich back to the outfield; if not, Mize would be a pinch hitter.

The 36-year-old slugger was surprised at the move, and also surprised that he'd cleared waivers. "Since I've played in the National League all my life," Mize said, "I never thought I'd ever land in the American League. It's too hard to get waived out. It looks like the Yanks are headed for the pennant, and I'm going to do all I can to help." (The Yanks had a 2½ game lead over the Red Sox.)

Over the next four plus years, until he retired following the 1953 season, Mize proved to be a steal for the reported $40,000 the Yankees paid for him. He played some first base and was also the league's best pinch hitter in 1951, 1952, and 1953. In all, Mize played 375 games as a Yankee, batting .264, with 44 home runs and 179 runs batted in.

September 4, 1949: Signed Righthanded Pitcher Hugh Casey as a Free Agent

After Dodger manager Leo Durocher converted him from a starter to a reliever in the early 1940s, Hugh Casey became the best relief pitcher in the National League. He led the league in saves in 1942 (13) and 1947 (18) and had a career total of 55 to go with his 74-42 won-lost record. But Casey, who was now 36 years old, hadn't thrown a pitch since Pittsburgh released him at the beginning of August and was presently on a fishing trip in Wisconsin. (Coincidentally, the Pirates released Casey to make room for first baseman Jack Phillips, whom they had just purchased from the Yankees.)

Apart from three years out for Navy service in World War II, Casey had been a Dodger mainstay from 1939 through 1947. The Yanks were familiar with him, having faced him three times in the 1941 World Series and six times in the 1947 Series.

Brooklyn had released Casey after a sub-par 1948. He won all three of his decisions that year, but injured his back in an off-the-field brawl and appeared in only 22 games. The Pirates picked him up this spring, and he'd pitched in 33 games for them, winning four, losing one, and saving five.

The Yanks already had the best relief pitcher in the game in Joe Page. Nevertheless, they were leading Boston by just 1½ games, and Cleveland by only 4½, and manager Casey Stengel thought that Casey had the potential to be a valuable addition down the stretch. Casey did manage to get a win for the Yankees, but when the season ended, so did his career.

December 17, 1949: Traded First Baseman Dick Kryhoski to the Detroit Tigers for Outfielder Dick Wakefield

Although the Yanks had veteran first baseman Johnny Mize and rookies Fenton Mole and Joe Collins on the roster, manager Casey Stengel wanted to make a change at the position for 1950. Stengel's plan was to make Tommy Henrich his full time first baseman, thus opening a spot in the outfield. Actually, there would be two open spots, as the Yanks had recently released Charlie Keller. (Keller, a Yankee since 1939, except for wartime service, would sign with Detroit, then return to play two games for the Yanks in 1952.) The acquisition of Dick Wakefield would add him to a group that included Hank Bauer, Gene Woodling, Cliff Mapes, Johnny Lindell, and rookies Jim Delsing and Jackie Jensen, all of whom were battling for the two outfield spots flanking Joe DiMaggio.

Back in 1941, the Tigers had given the 20-year-old Wakefield a $52,000 bonus to sign with them. Two years later, as a rookie, he batted .316—second in the American League to Luke Appling's .328—and led the league in hits (200) and doubles (38). In 1944, Wakefield was batting .355 after 78 games when he left to enter the Navy. But he never hit that well again after returning from the war, and worse, he had developed a reputation for being lazy and temperamental.

In his brief stay in New York Wakefield gave Stengel no reason to dispute that reputation, and the Yankees released him after just three early pinch-hitting appearances.

Dick Kryhoski, a 24-year-old lefthanded hitter, had split his 1949 rookie season between Oakland of the Pacific Coast League and the Yankees. He began and ended the year in New York, batting .294 in 51 games, while posting a .324 average in 66 games with the Oaks.

VI. The Fifties

February 10, 1950: Sold Righthanded Pitcher Frank Hiller to the Chicago Cubs

Frank Hiller appeared briefly with the Yanks in 1946 (0-2), then had an outstanding 15-5 season with the Kansas City Blues of the American Association in 1947. He spent all of 1948 in New York, going 5-2 in 22 games, but was back at Kansas City in 1949. Hiller won 11 and lost eight for the '49 Blues, while getting into four games for the Yanks and losing his only two decisions. At 29, he was unhappy at the prospect of again returning to Kansas City and informed Yankee general manager George Weiss that if they tried to return him to the minors in 1950, he would quit the game. Now that the Cubs would be giving him an opportunity to again pitch at the major league level, Hiller was delighted.

"I am confident I've got enough stuff to hold down a job in the majors," he said, "and I'm going all out to show the Cubs my appreciation for having given me the chance. I spent a lot of time perfecting a forkball last summer and I'm certain it will add to my effectiveness this year."

May 15, 1950: Sold Outfielder Johnny Lindell to the St. Louis Cardinals

Besides selling 33-year-old Johnny Lindell, general manager George Weiss dispatched four other players to pare the Yankee roster down to the required 25 men. He sold righthander Clarence "Cuddles" Marshall to the St. Louis Browns and sent second baseman Billy Martin, righthander Duane Pillette,

and first baseman Johnny Mize to the Kansas City Blues of the American Association. For Mize, it was his first trip to the minors since 1935, when he spent the year at Rochester before joining the Cardinals.

May 15, 1950: *Johnny Lindell.* **The Dodgers were not happy that the rival Cardinals were able to obtain Lindell.**

Originally a pitcher, Lindell was 2-1 in 23 games in 1942. The next year manager Joe McCarthy moved him to the outfield, and Lindell tied Chicago's Wally Moses for the league lead in triples (12). He had his best season in 1944, batting .300 with 18 home runs and 103 runs batted in, while again tying for the league lead in triples. (Lindell and teammate George Stirnweiss both had 16.) With four hits in 21 at-bats this season, Lindell ended his Yankee career with a .275 batting average in 742 games.

98

The Cardinals were hoping that Lindell would supply the righthanded power they were lacking and would find the smaller dimensions of Sportsman's Park to his liking. That possibility did not go unnoticed by the Cards' bitter rivals, the Dodgers, who expressed wonderment that he had been waived out of the American League. It turned out that their fears were unfounded. Lindell batted just .186 and hit only five home runs in 36 games for St. Louis. He was back in the minors in 1951, but returned in 1953 as a pitcher for the Phillies and Pirates.

May 15, 1950: Sold Righthanded Pitcher Clarence Marshall to the St. Louis Browns

Clarence Marshall had flown with the Yankees to St. Louis a day earlier, but he would be in a Browns uniform when the teams played this evening. After going 3–4 as a 21-year-old rookie for the 1946 Yankees, Marshall was in the minors in 1947 and 1948. Returning in 1949, he was in 21 games with a 3–0 record and three saves. Unused so far this season, Marshall went 1–3 for the Browns, but despite being just 25 years old it was his final big league season.

June 15, 1950: Traded Second Baseman George Stirnweiss, Righthanded Pitchers Duane Pillette and Don Johnson, Outfielder Jim Delsing, and Cash to the St. Louis Browns for Righthanded Pitchers Tom Ferrick and Sid Schacht, Lefthanded Pitcher Joe Ostrowski, and Third Baseman Leo Thomas

Youngsters Ned Garver and Cliff Fannin were the Browns pitchers Yankee GM George Weiss coveted, but he was forced to settle for two aging veterans, Joe Ostrowski and Tom Ferrick. In return the Yanks gave up four players that manager Casey Stengel had hardly used, nor planned to use in the future.

Ostrowski was 4–6 as a Browns rookie in 1948 and 8–8 in 1949. After winning his first

two starts this season, he'd lost his next four and hadn't pitched since injuring his back sliding into third base on June 1. Supposedly 30 years old, but really 33, Ostrowski would end his days as a major leaguer with the Yankees. Used by Stengel mostly in relief and as an emergency starter, he pitched through the 1952 season and was 9–7 in 75 games.

The Yanks expected immediate help from Ferrick, a career relief pitcher whom Stengel hoped would ease the burden of his bullpen ace, lefty Joe Page. The 35-year-old Ferrick had been a major leaguer since 1941, except for military service from 1943 to 1945, and had pitched for the Athletics, Indians, and Senators in addition to his two stints with the Browns. In 1949, he'd made 50 relief appearances, winning six and losing four, and was 1–3 in 16 games this season.

George Stirnweiss, who was 4-F because of ulcers, had been arguably the best player in the American League during the war years of 1944 and 1945. (In 1945 he was the best.) Stirnweiss had come up in 1943, after setting an International League record by stealing 73 bases for Newark in 1942. In mid–1943, he replaced Frank Crosetti at shortstop, but in 1944, after Joe Gordon went into the Army, manager Joe McCarthy moved him to second base. Stirnweiss batted .319 in 1944, fourth-best in the league. He led all major leaguers in hits, runs scored, singles, and stolen bases, and finished a strong fourth in the voting for the Most Valuable Player Award.

Stirnweiss was even better in 1945, winning the batting championship and leading the American League in seven major offensive departments. He continued as the Yankee second baseman under manager Bucky Harris, but lost the job to rookie Jerry Coleman in 1949, Casey Stengel's first year as manager. This season, Stirnweiss had been in only seven games with two at-bats. A month earlier, the Yanks had sold outfielder Johnny Lindell to the Cardinals. Stirnweiss, like Lindell, had been with the Joe McCarthy Yankees, and Stengel was obviously working to put his own stamp on the team.

But if Stengel didn't want Stirnweiss, St. Louis did. "He will settle our infield," Browns general manager Bill DeWitt said. "As you know we are building for the future. We hated to part with Ostrowski," DeWitt added, "but

June 15, 1950: *George Stirnweiss.* Stirnweiss (far left) with Yankee teammates in 1945, was the American League's best player that year.

the Yankees were desperate in their desire to get him and we made the deal when we got the players we thought would help our ballclub."

One of those players was Jim Delsing, who'd played nine games for the Yanks in 1949 and 12 this season but figured to get a lot more playing time in St. Louis. So too did the two young pitchers, 23-year-old Don Johnson, and 27-year-old Duane Pillette.

Johnson was 4-3 as a rookie in 1947, but spent the next two seasons in the minors. He'd been in eight games this season with one decision, a win in the Yanks 15-10 victory at Boston on Opening Day.

Pillette came up from Newark of the International League in July 1949 and pitched in 12 games, winning two and losing four. He began this season in New York, but the Yanks sent him to Kansas City of the American Association at cut-down time on May 15, only to call him up again to replace the oft-injured Bob Porterfield. Pillette had been in four games in 1950 without a decision.

The Yankees assigned both Leo Thomas, who was batting .198 in 35 games for St. Louis, and Sid Schacht, who had no decisions in eight appearances, to Kansas City.

June 27, 1950: Sold Catcher Gus Niarhos to the Chicago White Sox

Like so many of his generation, Gus Niarhos's career was interrupted by World War II. Niarhos spent three years in the military and was already 25 when he joined the Yankees in June 1946. In 1947, the Yanks sent him back to Kansas City of the American Association, but he returned the next year and platooned behind the plate with Yogi Berra. Niarhos batted .268, but exhibited no power; zero home runs and just 19 RBIs in 83 games. (While he was an excellent receiver, Niarhos would play nine major league seasons and hit only one home run.)

When Casey Stengel replaced Bucky

June 27, 1950: *Yogi Berra* and *Whitey Ford*. Berra (left) made Gus Niarhos superfluous, which allowed the Yanks to call up Ford.

American League's first place team, the Yankees, each of the other 14 major league clubs had to pass on him. That included the Tigers, Red Sox, and Indians who trailed the Yanks by 1½, 3½, and 4½ games respectively. What made this waiver deal even more baffling was that with a batting average of .340, Hopp was the National League's second leading hitter, trailing only Stan Musial. The fact that he was 34, had a high salary ($20,000), and undoubtedly cost the Yankees far more than the $10,000 waiver price, may have caused some teams to pass on him.

Hopp made his big league debut with the Cardinals back in September 1939 and played with them through 1945. He'd also played for the Braves, briefly for the Dodgers, and was in his second stint with the Pirates. A line-drive hitter with excellent speed, he had a .299 lifetime batting average and was an excellent first baseman. Hopp was also a fine defensive outfielder, which gave manager Casey Stengel several ways to use him. On learning of his new acquisition Stengel said, "I'm enthusiastic about it. Hopp always has been a fine ballplayer and I'm sure he'll help us."

Hopp was clearly elated at going from the last-place Pirates to the league-leading Yankees. "I've been out of the Pittsburgh lineup because of a kidney ailment, but I'm sound as a dollar and ready to go," he said. "I'm glad to be with a team that has a chance for the pennant, and I'm certainly proud to be a Yankee. They have prestige and spirit. I know I'll be right at home with them."

While the parallels between this deal and the one for Johnny Mize a year earlier were obvious, there was one major difference. The Yanks had purchased Mize in August (1949), which made him eligible for the World Series. Hopp's purchase came after the September 1 deadline for World Series eligibility; so while Hopp might help the Yanks get to the World Series, he would be ineligible to participate in it if they did.

Harris as manager in 1949, he made rookie Charlie Silvera Berra's primary backup and moved Niarhos to third-string. But this season Berra was catching just about every game, making Niarhos superfluous; so much so that with the season two and a half months old, he'd been in just one game and had not yet had an at-bat.

Now one man shy of the 25-player limit and in need of pitching, Stengel would fill Niarhos's spot on the roster with lefthander Whitey Ford. Currently at Kansas City, where he was 6-3, the 21-year-old Ford would win nine of ten decisions and help lead the Yanks to the 1950 pennant.

September 5, 1950: Purchased First Baseman Johnny Hopp from the Pittsburgh Pirates

For Johnny Hopp to go from the National League's eighth-place team, the Pirates, to the

With nine hits in 27 at-bats, many of which were key pinch hits, Hopp did help the Yanks win the 1950 pennant. But he dropped to .206 as a reserve first baseman and pinch hitter in 1951, and the Yankees released him in 1952 after he'd batted .160 in 15 games. After releasing Hopp, the Yanks recalled lefthander Bill Miller from Kansas City of the American Association to take his spot on the roster.

Hopp had been playing first base before his release because of injuries to Mize and Joe Collins. A week earlier, when he himself had to sit out with a pulled muscle, Stengel brought center fielder Irv Noren in to play first base and began using rookies Bob Cerv and Mickey Mantle in center field.

May 14, 1951: Traded Third Baseman Billy Johnson to the St. Louis Cardinals for First Baseman Don Bollweg and Cash

Rookie Gil McDougald had so impressed Casey Stengel during spring training, the Yankee manager considered making McDougald his opening-day third baseman. Stengel eventually decided to go with veteran Billy Johnson, but since then he'd used the 32-year-old Johnson sparingly. Johnson had played in just 15 games and had 12 hits in 40 at-bats, which brought his lifetime average to .275.

Johnson had spent his entire career with the Yankees, beginning with his splendid rookie season of 1943 when he led the American League champions in batting (.280), hits (166), and had 94 runs batted in, second to Nick Etten's 107. After spending the next two years in the Navy, Johnson returned in 1946 and had been the club's full-time or part-time third baseman ever since, while playing on three World Series winners.

Don Bollweg, with ten games of major league experience, was a lefthanded-hitting first baseman who was joining a club that had Johnny Mize, Joe Collins, and Johnny Hopp, all similarly lefthanded-hitting first basemen. Stengel sent Bollweg to Kansas City in the American Association, where he remained until 1953.

June 15, 1951: Traded Righthanded Pitchers Bob Porterfield, Tom Ferrick, and Fred Sanford to the Washington Senators for Lefthanded Pitcher Bob Kuzava

Over the season's first two months, Yankee manager Casey Stengel had been going mainly with four starters: Allie Reynolds, Vic Raschi, Ed Lopat, and Frank Shea. Nevertheless, while general manager George Weiss saw Bob Kuzava primarily as a long reliever, he also could envision him as an occasional fifth starter and made this deal for him on the day of the trading deadline.

The 28-year-old Kuzava had brief stays with Cleveland in 1946 and 1947, then went 10-6 as a rookie with the Chicago White Sox in 1949. He was a combined 9-10 for Chicago and Washington in 1950, and had split six decisions for the Senators this season. Kuzava had made nine starts for Washington, but had been impressive in only two: one against the Red Sox, and one in a losing effort against the Yanks.

Back in December 1948, when the Yanks got Fred Sanford from the woeful St. Louis Browns, Weiss and Stengel had great expectations for him. They'd hoped he'd be like Red Ruffing and others who had poor records while pitching for bad teams, but became stars after joining the Yankees. It hadn't worked out that way. Sanford won only 12 games as a Yankee while losing ten, including all three of his decisions this season.

Tom Ferrick had also come to New York

June 15, 1951: *Tom Ferrick.* Ferrick's relief work helped the Yankees win the 1950 pennant.

in a multiplayer trade with the Browns. He'd arrived exactly one year ago, but unlike Sanford, Ferrick had been a valuable addition. He made 30 relief appearances, winning eight (8-4) and saving nine to help the club win the 1950 pennant. In nine games this season, the 36-year-old Ferrick had a win, a loss, and a save.

The Yankees had once considered Bob Porterfield, currently with Kansas City of the American Association, their most promising pitcher. However, injuries had hampered his career, and while he'd pitched for the Yankees in parts of each season since 1948, he left with a combined record of just eight wins and nine losses. (Washington sent lefthander Bob Ross to Kansas City to replace Porterfield, but they continued to retain the rights to Ross.)

June 15, 1951: Traded Lefthanded Pitcher Tommy Byrne and Cash to the St. Louis Browns for Lefthanded Pitcher Stubby Overmire

Earlier in the day the Yanks had traded righthanders Fred Sanford, Tom Ferrick, and

June 15, 1951: *Tommy Byrne.* **Byrne would return to the Yanks in 1955.**

Bob Porterfield to Washington for lefthander Bob Kuzava. Then, minutes before the midnight trading deadline, they swapped Tommy Byrne, one of their veteran lefthanders, and got another veteran lefthander in return.

Byrne, now 31, first appeared with the Yankees back in 1943, following a sensational 1942 season in which he'd gone 17-4 for Newark of the International League. He was 2-1 in '43, then returned after the war, making brief appearances in 1946 and 1947 and then going 8-5 in 1948. Byrne had been a mainstay of the Yankee staff for each of the last two seasons, winning 15 games in each. He was 15-7 in 1949 and 15-9 in 1950 and at one point had won 17 of 19 decisions. Yet, he'd always had control problems, and this season manager Casey Stengel had dropped him from the rotation. In nine games, six in relief, Byrne had two wins and a loss, but had walked 36 batters in 21 innings.

After pitching for the Browns through 1952, Byrne was with the White Sox and Senators in 1953. But in 1954 he was back in the minors with Seattle of the Pacific Coast League. A 20-10 record with the Rainiers persuaded the Yanks to purchase his contract that September. Byrne then had his best season ever, winning 16 and losing five in 1955, and leading the American League with a .762 winning percentage. In all, he would go 30-16 in his second stint with the Yankees before retiring after the 1957 season.

Like Byrne, Overmire, who was seven months older, reached the big leagues in 1943. He'd won 47 and lost 45 during seven seasons with Detroit, was 9-12 for the seventh-place Browns in 1950, and was struggling at 1-6 this season.

July 31, 1951: Sold Outfielder Cliff Mapes to the St. Louis Browns

Cliff Mapes had batted .245 with 22 home runs in 317 games for the Yankees since his debut in 1948. He had an excellent throwing arm, and both his managers, Bucky Harris and Casey Stengel, had often used him as a defensive replacement.

Besides selling Mapes, the Yanks sent second-year outfielder Jackie Jensen to their Kansas City team in the American Association.

The departures of Mapes and Jensen allowed general manager George Weiss to bring up from Kansas City two of the Yankees' brightest prospects: outfielder Bob Cerv and left-handed pitcher Bob Wiesler.

Cerv was leading the American Association in batting (.349), home runs (26), triples (20), and runs batted in (101), while Wiesler (9-6) led in strikeouts (142) and had the Yankee brass calling him "another Whitey Ford."

The Yanks were in first place but Cleveland, Boston, and even Chicago were continuing to challenge them. Both Weiss and Stengel believed the two newcomers would be of more help than Mapes and Jensen in the stretch drive. Stengel said that with the club playing three doubleheaders in the next five days, both would see immediate action.

In a separate transaction, Weiss also obtained four other Brownies: infielders Kermit Wahl and Tom Upton, and pitchers Bob Hogue and Lou Sleater. All four went to Kansas City, and only Hogue would ever play for the Yankees.

Under manager Billy Southworth, Sain was a 20-game winner in each of his first three years back from the service, including his best season, 1948, when he went 24-15 with a 2.60 earned run average. He led the league in wins and innings pitched that year, and teamed with southpaw Warren Spahn to lead the Braves to their first pennant since 1914. After slumping to 10-17 in 1949, Sain bounced back to win 20 again in 1950. But he was only 5-13 this season, and all seven National League clubs had waived on him.

The Yanks made room on the roster for Sain by giving Jack Kramer, another 33-year-old righthander, his unconditional release ending his 12-year career. Signed earlier in the season, Kramer, had been in 19 games with a win and three losses.

In one of those baseball coincidences, after the Braves moved to Milwaukee in 1953, Burdette would succeed Sain as the right-handed ace of the staff, and in 1957 he would beat the Yankees three times to lead Milwaukee to its first and only world championship.

August 29, 1951: Traded Righthanded Pitcher Lew Burdette and Cash to the Boston Braves for Righthanded Pitcher Johnny Sain

For the third consecutive year the Yanks made a late-season acquisition of a one-time National League star. They'd purchased Johnny Mize from the New York Giants in August 1949 and Johnny Hopp from the Pittsburgh Pirates in September 1950. Yet, while money was involved (reportedly $50,000), this deal, unlike the previous two, cost the Yankees a player. That player was Lew Burdette, a 24-year-old pitcher who'd been a Yankee farmhand since 1947 and had pitched in one game for the Yanks in 1950. Burdette was with San Francisco of the Pacific Coast League this season, where he'd won 14 and lost 12.

Now 33, Johnny Sain first appeared with the Braves in 1942, as a relief pitcher. His manager at Boston (and now with the Yankees) was Casey Stengel, who predicted that "this fellow is going to develop into a mighty fine pitcher." Stengel was right, as Sain had been the ace of the Braves pitching staff since coming out of the Navy in 1946.

November 23, 1951: Traded Catcher Clint Courtney to the St. Louis Browns for Righthanded Pitcher Jim McDonald

Clint Courtney was batting .294 for the Kansas City Blues of the American Association when the Yankees called him up in September 1951. Although he'd been a member of their farm system since 1947, Courtney caught his one and only game for the Yanks on September 29, the next to last day of the season. However, in doing so he became the first major league catcher ever to play while wearing glasses during a regular-season game. Despite Courtney's impressive minor league statistics, the Yanks simply had no room on their roster for another catcher. They already had Yogi Berra, the league's Most Valuable Player, and two capable backups in Charlie Silvera and Ralph Houk.

Fortunately for Courtney the Browns had just hired Rogers Hornsby to replace their deposed manager, Zack Taylor. According to Yankee GM George Weiss, Hornsby had managed Courtney at Beaumont in the Texas League in 1950 and was "highly impressed" with him. A third of the way into the 1952 season, the Browns would fire Hornsby and replace him with Marty Marion. Courtney, meanwhile, would stick around the American League for another ten years.

Jim McDonald was 24, the same age as Courtney, and had appeared briefly with the Red Sox in 1950, winning his only decision. He was with Louisville of the American Association to start the 1951 season and was 10-7 when Boston traded him to St. Louis. McDonald won four and lost seven for the last-place Browns in '51, but he'd made a positive impression on the Yankees. He defeated the pennant-winning New Yorkers twice, and his two other victories were against second-place Cleveland and third place Boston.

April 7, 1952: Sold Righthanded Pitcher Dave Madison to the St. Louis Browns

Dave Madison was now 31 years old, yet his only big league appearance was three innings of relief back on September 26, 1950. Madison had spent all of 1951 in the minor leagues, and because he was not expected to make the Yankee team in 1952, his sale to St. Louis kept him from going back to the minors again.

May 3, 1952: Traded Outfielders Jackie Jensen and Archie Wilson, Righthanded

May 3, 1952: *Jackie Jensen.* **Casey Stengel said he just couldn't wait any longer for Jensen to hit.**

Pitcher Frank Shea, and Second Baseman Jerry Snyder to the Washington Senators for Outfielder Irv Noren and Shortstop Tom Upton

With Joe DiMaggio now retired, manager Casey Stengel had opened this season with Jackie Jensen playing center field. But after Jensen got off to a poor start, Stengel benched him and had been playing either veteran Gene Woodling or rookie Bob Cerv in center. Now, two and a half weeks into the season, with the 25-year-old Jensen's batting average at a pathetic .105 (two hits in 19 at-bats), the Yanks finally gave up on him. Jensen, a former football star at the University of California, had batted just .171 in 45 games for the Yanks as a rookie in 1950, but had improved to .298 in 56 games in 1951.

"I tried to give Jensen the job, but he couldn't hit for me," Stengel said. "I couldn't wait any longer. Perhaps we gave up a lot, but we had to in order to get what we wanted. We wanted [Irv] Noren. We need a center fielder who can, hit, run, field and throw."

Stengel's description of what he wanted well fit the 27-year-old Noren, who'd been a Dodger farmhand before they sold him to Washington. In two seasons with the Senators, Noren had batted .295 (1950) and .278 (1951). DiMaggio, now a television broadcaster for the Yankees, thought the trade was a good one. "While Washington, on numbers alone, got the better of it," he said, "I am certain Noren will help the club; he can do everything."

Frank Shea had been an outstanding pitcher for the Yanks in 1947, his rookie season. He won 14 games, lost only five, and then won two more in the World Series. But since then he'd had arm troubles, spent the 1950 season in the minors, and had won only 15 and lost 16. Shea, now 31, had yet to appear in a game this season, but Stengel said "he's in good shape and should help Washington."

Tom Upton had been a Yankee minor leaguer twice before, and the Yanks quickly made him one again. Upton went to the Kansas City Blues of the American Association, where he would take Jerry Snyder's spot. The Yanks had recalled Snyder from Kansas City to include him in this deal.

Snyder, who had no previous major league experience, would spend seven seasons with

Washington. However, Archie Wilson, who'd played in a total of seven games for the Yanks in 1951 and 1952, would move to the Red Sox later this season and then out of the big leagues.

Shortly after trading Jensen, Stengel moved right fielder Mickey Mantle to center field where Mantle would remain for the next 15 seasons.

May 12, 1952: Sold Lefthanded Pitcher Stubby Overmire to the St. Louis Browns

Although technically he was still a Yankee, 33-year-old Stubby Overmire wasn't with the club when they boarded the train for Cleveland to begin their first western swing. General manager George Weiss had instructed Overmire to remain behind while he worked on a deal to move him. That deal turned out to be a straight waiver sale to the Browns, the same team that had traded Overmire to New York (for pitcher Tommy Byrne) eleven months earlier.

Overmire pitched in 15 games for the Yanks in 1951, four as a starter, splitting two decisions. Unused by manager Casey Stengel this season, he went 0-3 with St. Louis to end his major league career.

August 1, 1952: Purchased Lefthanded Pitcher Johnny Schmitz from the Brooklyn Dodgers

For the fourth consecutive year, Casey Stengel fortified his club for the stretch drive by adding a veteran waived out of the National League. In 1949, it was first baseman Johnny Mize from the Giants; in 1950, outfielder–first baseman Johnny Hopp from Pittsburgh, and in 1951, pitcher Johnny Sain from the Braves. This year it was veteran lefthander Johnny Schmitz.

Schmitz broke in with the Chicago Cubs as a 20 year old in 1941 and was with them (minus three years in the Navy) until his trade to Brooklyn in June 1951. He had his best season in 1948, when he was 18-13 with a 2.64 ERA for a team that won only 64 games and

finished in last place. The Cubs traded Schmitz to Brooklyn with Andy Pafko in the trade that was supposed to assure the Dodgers of the pennant. But Schmitz won only one game the rest of the season while losing four, and the Dodgers didn't win the pennant. His record with the Dodgers this season was one win and one loss.

In addition to sending Brooklyn the $10,000 waiver price, the Yanks transferred 26-year-old righthander Wally Hood from their American Association team at Kansas City to the Dodgers' American Association team at St. Paul. Hood had pitched in two games for the Yanks in 1949, which would be his only major league action.

August 4, 1952: Sold Righthanded Pitcher Bob Hogue to the St. Louis Browns

The Yankees cleared a roster spot for Johnny Schmitz, purchased three days earlier from Brooklyn, by selling pitcher Bob Hogue back to the St. Louis Browns. They also got back the $10,000 they'd sent the Dodgers three days earlier to get Schmitz.

Hogue had appeared in seven games with the Yanks in 1951 after coming from the Browns on July 31. He was 1-0 and pitched 2.2 scoreless innings in two World Series relief appearances against the Giants. Hogue, who had a 3-5 record in 27 games this season, learned of the sale after he'd flown back to New York with the Yankees following a series in St. Louis and left immediately to fly back to St. Louis.

August 22, 1952: Purchased Right-handed Pitcher Ray Scarborough from the Boston Red Sox

The Yankees announced that they'd purchased Ray Scarborough (for the $10,000 waiver price) shortly before a game in which the Indians' Bob Lemon beat Allie Reynolds, 6-4. The loss allowed Cleveland to jump over the Yanks into first place by a percentage point.

General manager George Weiss had been after Scarborough for a long time. He'd tried to buy or trade for him several times in the late

1940s when Scarborough was among the league's best pitchers. Scarborough, who broke in with Washington in 1942, had a lifetime record of 73-80, with a career-best 15-8 for the Senators in 1948. Since leaving Washington, he'd also been with Chicago and was 1-5 for the Red Sox this year.

Because the Yanks were in such a fierce pennant battle with Cleveland, manager Casey Stengel was concerned with the depth of his pitching staff. Scarborough was no longer as highly rated as before, nevertheless, Stengel determined that the 35-year-old veteran was the best man available. To make room for Scarborough, the Yanks sent rookie lefthander Harry Schaeffer (0-1) to the Oakland Oaks of the Pacific Coast League.

Scarborough appeared in nine games in the remaining weeks of the 1952 season, winning five and losing one. The Yanks released him the following summer after he'd split four decisions while appearing in 25 games, all but one in relief.

August 28, 1952: *Ewell Blackwell.* **When the Yanks got Blackwell, he was no longer the intimidating pitcher he'd been with Cincinnati.**

August 28, 1952: Traded Lefthanded Pitcher Johnny Schmitz, Righthanded Pitcher Ernie Nevel, and Minor League Outfielders Jim Greengrass and Bob Marquis to the Cincinnati Reds for Righthanded Pitcher Ewell Blackwell

Just four weeks after they acquired him from Brooklyn, the Yankees sent Johnny Schmitz back to the National League. Schmitz had pitched in just five games for New York, winning one (a complete game against Washington) and losing one.

Although the Yanks had now jumped two games ahead of the Indians, they knew they were in a pennant race that likely would not be decided until very late in the season. Yankee manager Casey Stengel thought that despite his 3-12 record with the Reds, Ewell Blackwell would be of greater help in that race

than Schmitz. Once one of baseball's most feared pitchers, the 29-year-old six-foot-six side-armer had, like Schmitz, made his debut in 1942 and then missed the next three years while serving in the military.

A five-time All-Star, Blackwell was the National League's best pitcher in 1947, leading in wins (22), complete games (23), and strikeouts (193). He also compiled a 16-game winning streak, the longest ever by a twentieth century National League righthander. But, due in large part to health problems and an arm injury, Blackwell won only 12 games over the next two seasons. He bounced back to win 17 in 1950 and 16 in 1951 for Cincinnati teams that finished in sixth place both years.

Of the other three players going to the Reds, only pitcher Ernie Nevel had big league experience—a total of four games with the Yanks (0-1) in 1950-51. He was currently with Kansas City of the American Association, as was Bob Marquis, while Jim Greengrass was with the Yanks' Texas League club at Beaumont.

February 16, 1953: Purchased Lefthanded Pitcher Johnny Schmitz from the Cincinnati Reds

The Yanks had traded Johnny Schmitz to Cincinnati the previous August in the Ewell Blackwell deal. Now they were bringing him back to fill the role of lefthanded middle-relief man that Joe Ostrowski had occupied in 1952. (Ostrowski would be pitching for Los Angeles of the Pacific Coast League.) After leaving the Yankees, Schmitz had pitched in three games for the Reds last September, all in relief, and won his only decision.

April 26, 1953: Sold Third Baseman Loren Babe to the Philadelphia Athletics

Despite the Yankees' excellent 12-3 start this season, they had not been hitting well. Only Loren Babe, at .333 (6 for 18), and Gene Woodling, the league's leading batter, had averages above the .300 mark. Nevertheless, manager Casey Stengel had never thought particularly highly of Babe, a 25-year-old rookie, and felt no qualms about disposing of him.

The Yanks negotiated this deal during a Sunday afternoon game with Washington. It was to take effect when the game ended, so Stengel could use Babe in this game. It appeared he might in the eighth inning; the Yanks trailed, 4-2, but had the bases loaded with two out against righthander Connie Marrero. Billy Martin, hitless in four at-bats was the due batter. It seemed a perfect spot for the lefthand hitting Babe, whose two home runs had helped win previous games, to pinch hit. However, Stengel stayed with his pet, Martin, who hit into an inning-ending force out and the Yanks eventually lost to end a five-game winning streak.

With Philadelphia, Babe would platoon at third base with the righthand hitting Pete Suder and bat just .224 with no home runs in 103 games. In December, he would return to the Yankees in the trade that sent first base-

man Vic Power to Philadelphia. Actually, Babe didn't return to the Yankees. He went directly to the club's American Association team at Kansas City and never returned to the major leagues.

May 12, 1953: Sold Lefthanded Pitcher Johnny Schmitz to the Washington Senators

For the second consecutive season, the Yanks were sending veteran lefthander Johnny Schmitz to a second-division team. Schmitz, who had pitched in three games this season for a total of four innings, would later pitch for the Red Sox and the Orioles before his career ended in 1956.

June 12, 1953: Purchased Shortstop Willie Miranda from the St. Louis Browns

With Phil Rizzuto nearing his 36th birthday, the Yanks wanted someone on the bench who could play shortstop if needed. Willie Miranda could do that very well, although as a rookie in 1952, and thus far in 1953, he hadn't shown he could hit major league pitching. In 101 big league games, for the Senators, White Sox, and Browns, he had just 39 hits in 176 at-bats for a .222 average.

December 16, 1953: Traded First Baseman Don Bollweg, Outfielder Bill Renna, Minor League Third Baseman Jim Finigan, Minor League Outfielder–First Baseman Vic Power, Minor League Righthanded Pitcher John Gray, and Minor League Catcher Jim Robertson to the Philadelphia Athletics for Righthanded Pitcher Harry Byrd, First Baseman Eddie Robinson, Third Baseman Loren Babe, and Outfielders Carmen Mauro and Tom Hamilton

No one doubted that Vic Power, a 22-year-old dark-skinned Puerto Rican, was the best prospect in the Yankee system. Playing for the Kansas City Blues the past two seasons, Power had led the American Association in doubles (40) and triples (17) in 1952, while batting .331. Then, in 1953, he won the batting title (.349) and also led in total hits (217). Besides being a fine hitter, Power was also an excellent defensive first baseman and seemingly a sure major leaguer. However, because he played with a flamboyant style that many saw as "showboating," and because he had a reputation as a "troublemaker," Power had become an unlikely candidate to be the Yankees' first black player. Yankee general manager George Weiss denied that Power's race had anything to do with the trade, although he did suggest that it was among the main reasons Philadelphia wanted him.

"Power was the key player," Weiss said. "The Athletics mentioned his name and then wouldn't hear of anybody else. Apparently they are going make a bid for Negro fans and figure Power will help them at the gate."

Weiss continued to reject any criticism of the deal based on race. "Power was the first name they mentioned," he said, "and I don't think you can do business if you're afraid to deal a colored player because of censure."

The Yanks still had one black player on their roster, outfielder Elston Howard. They would send Howard to Toronto of the International League this season so he could make the conversion from an outfielder to a catcher.

Power was not the only top prospect the Yanks were losing. Twenty-five-year-old Jim Finigan, who'd spent the 1951 and 1952 seasons in the military, had batted .303 for Binghamton in 1953 while leading the Eastern League with 38 doubles.

The Yanks were willing to part with Power and Finigan if that's what it took to get 28-year-old Harry Byrd, a pitcher they saw as the eventual replacement for one of their two aging righthanders, Vic Raschi or Allie Reynolds. Byrd had won Rookie of the Year honors in 1952 by winning 15 games for the fifth place A's; however, he'd followed with a terrible sophomore season, winning 11 and losing 20. His earned run average, which was 3.31 in 1952, soared to 5.51 in 1953. Yet, Casey Stengel, who would now be his manager, dismissed the drop-off.

"Byrd is a good strong pitcher," Stengel said. "He wasn't in the best of physical shape last year but did not have a sore arm. He's experienced and strong and should be a top-flight pitcher."

Stengel added that the addition of Eddie Robinson, a lefthanded power hitter with 145 lifetime home runs, greatly strengthened the Yankee bench. A 33-year-old veteran of nine American League seasons, Robinson played for Cleveland, Washington, and Chicago before joining the Athletics in 1953.

Outfielder Bill Renna and first baseman Don Bollweg, both rookies, had done well in 1953, their only seasons as Yankees. Renna batted .314 in 61 games, while the 32-year-old Bollweg batted .297 in 70 games. Their problem was that the Yankees were well set at both first base and the outfield and did not need them.

After getting Loren Babe back from Philadelphia, where they'd sold him this past spring, the Yanks sent him to Kansas City. Babe, who'd batted .224 with no home runs in 103 games for the Athletics in 1953, never returned to the major leagues.

Also going to the Blues and never returning to the majors were outfielder Tom Hamilton (.196 in 58 games for the A's in 1953), and Carmen Mauro (.255 in 81 games for the A's, Senators, and Dodgers in '53). Mauro threatened to quit baseball when he learned he was headed back to the minor leagues, but later reconsidered.

Pitcher John Gray and catcher Jim Robertson moved from the Yanks' minor league system to the big leagues with Philadelphia, although both their major league careers would be brief.

February 23, 1954: Sold Righthanded Pitcher Vic Raschi to the St. Louis Cardinals

Since coming up from the International League Newark Bears in September 1946, Vic Raschi had been a major contributor to the Yankees' post-war success. He'd won 120 games while losing only 50 for a winning-percentage of .706; that was second only to Spud Chandler among Yankee pitchers with at least 100 wins. However, after winning 21 games for three consecutive seasons (1949–51), Raschi

February 23, 1954: *Allie Reynolds, Vic Raschi, Ed Lopat,* and *Tom Ferrick.* **Raschi (second from left) was holding out in protest of a salary cut.**

won only 16 in 1952 and 13 in 1953. The drop-off led general manager George Weiss to offer him a 1954 contract at something less than the $40,000 he'd made in 1953, which then was the highest salary ever for a Yankee pitcher.

The 35-year-old Raschi decided to hold out, joining several other Yankee veterans who were also unhappy at their 1954 contract offers. Raschi's sale to St. Louis served as a warning to the others from Weiss, who conveniently had added righthanded starter Harry Byrd from the Athletics during the winter.

After getting waivers on Raschi from all the American League clubs (getting them from National League clubs before May 15 wasn't necessary), Weiss had to look no further than his St. Petersburg spring training neighbors, the Cardinals, to find a willing buyer.

"We went direct to the Cardinals," Weiss said, "because training right here in St. Pete with us, they were practically next door." Cardinals owner August A. Busch, Jr., paid

$85,000 for Raschi and immediately signed him to a $40,000 contract.

"I am in good shape now and I'm certainly going to give the Cards my best," Raschi said after hearing of his sale. His departure left only seven men who had played on the Yankees' five straight world championship teams of 1949–53: Phil Rizzuto, Allie Reynolds, Yogi Berra, Jerry Coleman, Eddie Lopat, Gene Woodling, and Charlie Silvera.

April 11, 1954: Traded Minor League Righthanded Pitcher Mel Wright, and Minor League Outfielders Bill Virdon and Emil Tellinger to the St. Louis Cardinals for Outfielder Enos Slaughter

For many baseball people the trade of Enos Slaughter to the Yankees was merely the second part of the Yanks' sale of Vic Raschi to

April 11, 1954: *Enos Slaughter.* **The Cardinals were clearing a spot for rookie outfielder Wally Moon.**

the Cardinals seven weeks earlier. The news that the Cardinals had traded him, coming just two days before the season-opener, stunned the 38-year-old Slaughter. He'd come up through the St. Louis farm system, and except for the war years of 1943–45, had been a star with the Cardinals since 1938. He had a .305 lifetime batting average, and among active players only Stan Musial had more hits, and only Ted Williams had more runs batted in.

"This is the biggest shock of my life," Slaughter said tearfully. "Something I never expected to happen. I've given my life to this organization and they let you go when they think you are getting old." (The main reason the Cardinals were trading Slaughter was to make room for outfielder Wally Moon, who would go on to win the National League's 1954 Rookie of the Year Award.)

With Mickey Mantle in center field, Gene Woodling in left, and Hank Bauer in right, the Yankees seemed to have a set outfield. Slaughter figured to join Irv Noren and Bob Cerv in the role of reserve outfielder and pinch hitter. He was also an insurance policy against a breakdown by Mantle. Although Mantle was just 22 years old, he had undergone two knee operations over the winter and the Yanks wanted to be ready in case he reinjured the knee.

Pitcher Mel Wright, 11-2 with the American Association Kansas City Blues in 1953, was the only one of the three minor leaguers

going to St. Louis who was on the Yankee roster. He was also the only one to play with the Cardinals in 1954. Emil Tellinger never did reach the majors, but Bill Virdon did. After a season at Rochester, in which he led the International League in batting, Virdon would win National League Rookie of the Year honors in 1955.

May 11, 1954: Sold Infielder Jim Brideweser to the Baltimore Orioles

The Yanks had signed Jim Brideweser out of the University of Southern California. He'd played parts of the last three years in New York (.327 in 51 games), but spent the major part of those seasons in the minors. Brideweser was currently on suspension for refusing to report to Kansas City after the Yanks sent him to their American Association affiliate this spring.

July 4, 1954: Purchased Righthanded Pitcher Marlin Stuart from the Baltimore Orioles

An injury to pitcher Jim McDonald led the Yankees to purchase Marlin Stuart, a 35-year-old journeyman with a 1-2 record for the Orioles. Stuart would go 3-0 with a save in ten relief appearances for the Yanks, but they released him after purchasing Jim Konstanty, and Stuart never again pitched in the major leagues.

July 22, 1954: Signed Righthanded Pitcher Ralph Branca as a Free Agent

Ralph Branca had never lived up to the promise he'd shown when at age 21, he was a 21-game winner for the 1947 Brooklyn Dodgers. He'd had his last good season in 1951, a season that ended with his pitch that Bobby Thomson hit for a home run to win the pennant for the New York Giants. The next year Branca had arm trouble and pitched in just 16 games, winning four and losing two.

The Dodgers finally gave up on him, but

the Detroit Tigers signed him early in the 1953 season, after he'd been waived out of the National League. Branca won four and lost seven for the Tigers in 1953, and was 3-3 with a 5.76 earned run average this season when they released him on July 15.

After putting him through a workout, the Yanks decided Branca still could pitch and signed him. "I'm happy," he said on joining the Yanks. "It took me 11 years to get here."

Branca would pitch in five games, making three starts and winning his only decision. The Yankees released him in October.

August 7, 1954: Sold Lefthanded Pitcher Bob Kuzava to the Baltimore Orioles

The Yanks had sent three pitchers (Bob Porterfield, Fred Sanford, and Tom Ferrick) to Washington to get Bob Kuzava at the June 15, 1951 trading deadline. Kuzava, 1-3 this season, had been a spot starter and long reliever under manager Casey Stengel, compiling a 23-20 record. He'd also made key contributions to Yankee victories in World Series appearances in 1951 and 1952. The Orioles would be Kuzava's fifth American League team, and he would later pitch for three more in the National League.

August 22, 1954: Purchased Righthanded Pitcher Jim Konstanty from the Philadelphia Phillies

Dreams of a sixth consecutive pennant were beginning to fade. The Yanks had just been swept in a three game series at Fenway Park, which, combined with Cleveland's sweep of Baltimore, left them half 5½ games behind the Indians with just 22 games to play. Nevertheless, they were still in the race, and the purchase of veteran reliever Jim Konstanty was designed to bolster a faltering pitching staff. All seven National League clubs and the six American League clubs beneath the Yankees in the standings had to waive on the 37-year-old Konstanty before the Yanks could buy him.

Konstanty had been the National League's Most Valuable Player in 1950, the first relief pitcher ever to win the MVP Award. He'd earned it by going 16-7 and saving a league-leading 22 games, while pitching in a major league record 74 games for the pennant-winning Philadelphia Phillies. All of Konstanty's 74 appearances were in relief, although he did start the opening game of the World Series, losing 1-0 to the Yanks' Vic Raschi. But although he won 14 games in 1953, Konstanty was never again as effective as he'd been in 1950, and this year had a record of 2-3 in 33 games.

Konstanty would split a pair of decisions and earn two saves for the Yanks in the last month of the 1954 season. He appeared in 45 games in 1955, with a 7-2 record and 11 saves, despite spending part of the season with Richmond in the International League.

Troubled with back problems in 1956, Konstanty pitched in just eight games and had two saves, but his ERA was 4.91, and in mid–May the Yanks asked waivers on him. The St. Louis Cardinals eventually signed Konstanty, and he finished his career with them that year.

November 17, 1954: Traded Righthanded Pitchers Harry Byrd and Jim McDonald, Outfielder Gene Woodling, Shortstop Willie Miranda, Catcher–First Baseman Gus Triandos, and Minor League Catcher Hal Smith to the Baltimore Orioles for Righthanded Pitchers Bob Turley and Don Larsen, and Shortstop Billy Hunter

In announcing this nine-player trade, George Weiss of the Yankees and Paul Richards of the Orioles revealed that it was only the first part of what would emerge as the biggest baseball trade ever. The two general managers said that part two was dependent on the results of the major league draft scheduled for the following week. However, both suggested that it would likely bring three more players to Baltimore and four more to New York.

Weiss and Richards had begun their negotiations during the World Series and had discussed many players before settling on the final deal. The Yankees, who'd finished second in 1954 after five straight championships, had targeted pitching as their major shortcoming vis-à-vis the pennant-winning Cleveland Indians. The need for pitching had intensified when longtime ace Allie Reynolds indicated he would not be back in 1955.

With starting pitching his major priority, Weiss offered general manger Frank Lane of the White Sox a group of players for Chicago lefthander Billy Pierce. The rumor was that if Weiss would include third baseman Andy Carey in his offer, there might be a deal. But while no deal for Pierce, an excellent young pitcher, was ever made, in Bob Turley and Don Larsen the Yanks were getting two other excellent young pitchers.

"When we got Turley and Larsen, we plugged the major weakness of the Yankee club—pitching," Weiss said. "They are two of the finest and fastest young righthanders in the game. Both figure to get better and they are young. Turley is only twenty-four, Larsen twenty-five."

Turley had impressed everyone with his fastball, which had been labeled the best since Bob Feller came up to Cleveland almost 20 years earlier. He'd appeared briefly with the St. Louis Browns in 1951 and 1953, then stuck with the Orioles in 1954, the club's first year in Baltimore. Pitching for a seventh-place team, Turley was 14-15 with a 3.46 ERA and a league-leading 185 strikeouts.

Larsen had gone 7-12 as a Browns rookie in 1953, and then had a horrible season for the Orioles in 1954. He won only three games while losing a league-high 21; yet despite that horrendous '54 won-lost record, many baseball people believed that Larsen had fully as much potential for stardom as did Turley.

Along with pitching, Weiss had also been seeking a shortstop, knowing that Phil Rizzuto's .195 batting average in 1954 was an indication that his long career was nearing its end. Acknowledging that he'd been unsuccessful in attempts to get the White Sox to part with Chico Carrasquel, Weiss said that "[Billy] Hunter was the best available shortstop for whom we could deal."

The 26-year-old Hunter, a former Dodger farmhand, had been the Browns/Orioles shortstop the past two seasons. He'd shown he could handle the job defensively, but with batting averages of .219 in 1953 and .243 in 1954, he had yet to prove he could hit major league pitching.

The same was true of Willie Miranda, whom the Yankees had purchased from the Browns in June 1953. Miranda, perhaps the best defensive shortstop in the league, was a notoriously weak hitter, although he'd improved some in 1954. He had a .250 average in 92 games in '54, serving most often as a late-inning replacement after Rizzuto had been removed for a pinch hitter.

Reaction in Baltimore to Richards's first trade as general manager of the Orioles was overwhelmingly adverse. While claiming the deal was generally one-sided in favor of New York, Baltimoreans were especially upset that the Orioles had traded Turley. However, Yankee manager Casey Stengel disagreed. "This deal is tremendous for Baltimore," Stengel said. "I regret losing the players who helped me win championships. I'm speaking of [Gene] Woodling and [Jim] McDonald."

That description certainly fit the 32-year-old Woodling, a Yankee since 1949 and a member of each of Stengel's teams that won five consecutive World Series. Woodling had a .285 average for his six seasons in New York and a .318 mark in 26 World Series games. But an injured hand had limited him to only 97 games in 1954, and he'd batted just .250.

As he had done in McDonald's previous two seasons with the Yankees, Stengel had used the 27-year-old former Brownie as both a starter and a reliever in 1954. But, as with Woodling, injuries limited McDonald's usefulness. He pitched in just 16 games, winning four and losing one and bringing his three-season record with the Yankees to 16-12.

The Yanks had acquired Harry Byrd 11 months earlier in an 11-player trade with the Philadelphia Athletics. At the time they envisioned him as a likely replacement for either of their aging righthanded aces, Reynolds or Vic Raschi. But Byrd didn't have that kind of success; he won only nine games, lost seven, and had a 3.99 earned run average.

Gus Triandos batted .296 with 18 home runs for the Yanks' American Association team at Kansas City in 1954. He'd gotten into 18 games as a Yankee in 1953 and two in 1954, but hit just .154, with only one home run.

Hal Smith was also in the American Association in 1954. He was with the Columbus

November 17, 1954: *Gene Woodling*. Woodling (third from left) with fellow outfielders Archie Wilson, Bob Cerv, Mickey Mantle, Jackie Jensen, Hank Bauer, and manager Casey Stengel in 1951.

Red Birds where his .350 batting average led the league. However, both Triandos and Smith faced the same dilemma. They were young catchers (both were 24) on a team that already had Yogi Berra, the league's best catcher, and Elston Howard, whom they were preparing to be the number two man behind Berra. The Yanks had sent Howard, originally an outfielder, to the Toronto Maple Leafs in 1954 so he could make the conversion to catching. While learning his new position, Howard batted .330 and won the International League's Most Valuable Player Award. Now, he was set to join the Yankees in 1955 as their first Black player.

December 1, 1954: Traded Lefthanded Pitcher Bill Miller, Third Baseman Kal Segrist, and Minor League Second Baseman Don Leppert to the Baltimore Orioles for First Baseman Dick Kryhoski, Righthanded Pitcher Mike Blyzka, Catcher Darrell Johnson, Outfielder Jim Fridley, Minor League Outfielder Ted Del Guercio, and a Player to Be Named

The Yankees received five players while the Orioles got three as the two teams completed part two of the trade they'd begun on November 17. It brought the total number of players in the two trades to a record-setting 17, nine new faces for Baltimore and eight for New York. (Although announced to include an 18th player, rumored to be Orioles pitcher Lou Kretlow who would go to the Yankees as "a player to be named," Kretlow remained with Baltimore.)

Unlike part one, the players in this deal were primarily minor leaguers, although several had big league experience. Former Yankee

Dick Kryhoski, a .260-batter for the Orioles in 1954, had the most. He'd come up with the Yankees in 1949 and gone on to play for the Tigers and the Browns/Orioles. (The Yanks had no place for Kryhoski, who was now 29, and would sell him to the new Kansas City Athletics just prior to the 1955 season.)

Mike Blyzka and Jim Fridley were with the Orioles in 1954: Blyzka went 1-5 in 37 relief appearances, and Fridley batted .246 in 85 games. Darrell Johnson, who had big league experience with the Browns and White Sox in 1952, was at Richmond of the International League in 1954, where he batted .261.

The recent move of the American League's Philadelphia franchise to Kansas City had forced the Yankees to move their American Association team in that city elsewhere. They eventually chose Denver, which would be the 1955 destination for Blyzka, Fridley, and Johnson. (Of the three, only Johnson would ever play for the Yankees, batting a combined .226 in 26 games in 1957 and 1958.)

Ted Del Guercio was with the Wichita Indians in 1954, where he batted .321 and was the Class A Western League's All-Star center fielder. The Yanks moved Del Guercio up to Class AA, sending him to the Southern Association's Birmingham Barons.

Although Don Leppert was only 24 and had batted .313 at Birmingham in 1954, he did not figure in the Yankees' future plans. Neither did 27-year-old Bill Miller, who had a 6-8 record with the Yankees in 36 appearances spread over the last three seasons; nor did Kal Segrist, a career minor league who batted .291 for the Kansas City Blues in 1954. Segrist's only big league experience had been as a 21 year old in 1952, when he had one hit in 23 at-bats for the Yankees.

Ewell Blackwell had not pitched at all in 1954. In fact, his arm problems had prevented him from pitching since winning his first two decisions early in 1953. Blackwell had asked the Yanks to reinstate him this spring, which they did. He pitched seven and one-third innings in Florida, winning two games, but he was wild and clearly nowhere near the intimidating pitcher he'd once been. Blackwell would get into two games with the Athletics (0-1) before retiring at the relatively young age of 32.

Tom Gorman had been in the Yankees' farm system since 1946, including three years with the American Association Kansas City Blues before he finally reached the majors in 1952. In his three years in New York (1952–54), Gorman had a 10-7 record in 75 games, all but seven in relief. He appeared in 23 games with no decisions for the Yanks in 1954, while also spending part of the season with the Blues, where he went 3-2. Gorman would save 18 games for the sixth-place Athletics s in 1955, one behind the American League leader Ray Narleski of Cleveland.

Since December 1949, when the Yanks traded him to the Tigers, Dick Kryhoski had moved on to St. Louis and then to Baltimore when the Browns moved there in 1954. The Yanks had reacquired him in December '54 in their 17-player trade with the Orioles.

Rumors had it that this deal was the precursor of one that would bring A's righthander Arnie Portocarrero to New York. The 23-year-old native New Yorker won only nine games while losing 18 as a rookie in 1954, but that was enough to make him the leading winner for last-place Philadelphia. Portocarrero likely would have done much better in New York, but the Yanks never did make a deal for him.

March 30, 1955: Sold Righthanded Pitchers Ewell Blackwell and Tom Gorman, and First Baseman Dick Kryhoski to the Kansas City Athletics

This was the first of the many deals the Yankees would make with the Kansas City A's, newly relocated from Philadelphia. Made the day before they broke camp in Florida, the Yanks received $50,000 for the three players, none of whom figured to make their club in 1955.

May 11, 1955: Traded Outfielder Enos Slaughter and Righthanded Pitcher Johnny Sain to the Kansas City Athletics for Righthanded Pitcher Sonny Dixon and Cash

The Yankees sent their two aging former National League stars (Johnny Sain was 37 and Enos Slaughter was 39) to the Athletics as part of a series of moves designed to get

May 11, 1955: *Johnny Sain.* **Just a year earlier, Sain had led the American League in saves.**

down to the 25-man player limit. In others, they sold pitcher Art Schallock to the Baltimore Orioles and optioned pitcher Don Larsen to Denver of the American Association.

The Yanks had gotten Sain from the Boston Braves in late August 1951 to help them win the pennant that season. Sain had been a starter with the Braves and was an occasional spot starter with the Yankees; however, his greatest value to the team had been as a reliever. He had an overall 33-20 record as a Yankee, with 40 saves, including a league-leading 22 just one year ago.

After Slaughter's long, successful career with the Cardinals, they'd traded him to the Yankees just days before the 1954 opener. Slaughter batted .248 in 69 games as a reserve outfielder, and he had one hit in nine at-bats in ten games this season.

Sonny Dixon, a 30-year-old relief specialist, led the American League in games-pitched in 1954, a season he split between the Washington Senators and the Athletics (then in Philadelphia). In 1956 Dixon would pitch in three games for the Yanks, losing his only decision. They were the final games of his career.

May 11, 1955: Sold Lefthanded Pitcher Art Schallock to the Baltimore Orioles

Selling 31-year-old pitcher Art Schallock was one of several moves the Yanks made this day to get their roster down to the required 25 players. In others, they sold Enos Slaughter and Johnny Sain to the Kansas City Athletics and optioned pitcher Don Larsen to Denver of

the American Association. (Larsen would go 9-1 at Denver before the Yanks recalled him in late July.)

Schallock was 11-5 with Hollywood of the Pacific Coast League when the Yanks bought his contract in July 1951. He'd spent at least part the last five seasons in New York, although all three of his big league wins (he was 3-2) had come in 1951. Schallock, who had no record in two games this season, would go 3-5 for Baltimore.

June 30, 1955: Signed Lefthanded Pitcher Ted Gray as a Free Agent

Between 1949 and 1953, Ted Gray had been a regular member of Detroit's starting rotation. In 1954, he injured his arm and pitched only 72 innings, winning three and losing five, with a 5.38 ERA. Traded to Chicago in December '54, Gray pitched two games for the White Sox and two for Cleveland before the Indians had released him the previous week. He'd pitched a combined five innings for the two teams with no record.

The Yanks had just put Bob Grim, the American League's Rookie of the Year in 1954, on the 30-day disabled list and were looking to add another pitcher. They had Gray pitch batting practice at Yankee Stadium, where he impressed manager Casey Stengel enough for the Yanks to sign him. Gray made one start, pitching three innings, before the Yanks released him on July 26. Gray then signed with Baltimore, where he won one and lost two. He was just 30 years old, but he never again pitched in the majors.

July 30, 1955: Traded Lefthanded Pitcher Ed Lopat to the Baltimore Orioles for Righthanded Pitcher Jim McDonald and Cash

Ironically, the Yankees said good-bye to Ed Lopat on Oldtimers Day at Yankee Stadium, a day for honoring their former stars. Lopat had spent eight years in New York and was the last remaining member of the Ed Lopat–Allie Reynolds–Vic Raschi trio that combined to pitch the Yankees to five consecutive

July 30, 1955: *Ed Lopat*. Lopat was 113-59 as a Yankee, but only 4-8 this season.

world championships between 1949 and 1953. (The Yanks had sold Raschi to the Cardinals before the 1954 season and Reynolds retired after that season.)

Since coming from the White Sox in February 1948, Lopat won 113 games and lost only 59. He was a 20-game winner in 1951 and led the American League in earned run average (2.42) and winning percentage (16-4, .800) in 1953. He followed with another fine season in 1954, winning 12 and losing four, but had struggled this year at 4-8. So when the Yanks had to make room for Don Larsen, who'd been rehabilitating a sore arm at Denver in the American Association, the 37-year-old Lopat was the logical choice to go. He would win three and lose four for the Orioles in this his final season.

Bringing back Larsen proved to be an excellent move by the Yankees. He won eight of nine starts down the stretch, helping the club to win the pennant by two games over Cleveland.

Jim McDonald was a former Yankee who'd been traded to Baltimore in the 17-player deal that brought Larsen to New York. Now that he was back, the Yanks sent him to Denver to take Larsen's place with the Bears.

September 14, 1955: Purchased Righthanded Pitcher Gerry Staley from the Cincinnati Reds

With less than two weeks remaining in the season, the Yanks were struggling to main-

tain their slim lead over the second-place Cleveland Indians. So even though Staley was 35 and seemingly near the end of his career, manager Casey Stengel viewed him as "pennant insurance."

In the early 1950s, Staley had been the ace of the St. Louis Cardinals pitching staff. He'd won 54 games for the Cardinals between 1951 and 1953, but fell off to 7-13 in 1954. St. Louis traded him to Cincinnati where his record this season was 5-8 with a 4.66 earned run average.

February 8, 1956: Traded Lefthanded Pitcher Bob Wiesler, Catcher Lou Berberet, Outfielder Dick Tettelbach, Minor League Second Baseman Herb Plews, and a Player to Be Named to the Washington Senators for Lefthanded Pitcher Mickey McDermott and Shortstop Bobby Kline

Mickey McDermott was the only legitimate major leaguer in this five-for-two deal engineered by Calvin Griffith, the president of the Senators, and Bill DeWitt, the Yankees' assistant general manager. (DeWitt had gotten prior approval from general manager George Weiss and manager Casey Stengel.)

The 27-year-old McDermott now joined Whitey Ford and Tommy Byrne to give the Yankees three established lefthanded starters, something no other big league team had. Furthermore, McDermott had another quality that made him attractive to the Yankees. Although he had just a 10-10 record for the last-place Senators in 1955, half his ten wins had come against first division teams: he'd defeated the Cleveland Indians three times and the Boston Red Sox twice.

The Red Sox had been McDermott's first team. He came up with Boston in 1948 and won 48 and lost 34 in six seasons there. Traded to Washington for Jackie Jensen in December 1953, he won only seven games in 1954, while losing 15. Yet, for his career McDermott had allowed an average of just 7.67 hits per nine innings. Among active pitchers, only Ford, Byrne, and Bob Turley of the Yanks, Cleveland's Bob Feller, and the Giants' Hoyt Wilhelm had done better.

February 8, 1955: *Mickey McDermott.* **Half of McDermott's ten wins in 1955 were against Cleveland and Boston.**

McDermott was also an excellent hitter, and both the Red Sox and the Senators had frequently used him as a pinch hitter. He'd batted .263 in 1955, which was 42 points better than his Senators teammate, shortstop Bobby Kline, who'd played 77 games in his rookie year. Kline went to the Yanks' Denver club in the American Association and never returned to the majors.

Of those going to Washington, pitcher Bob Wiesler had the most big league experience. When the Yanks first called him up in the summer of 1951, Wiesler was just 21 years old and reputed to be "another Whitey Ford." But, of course, he wasn't. He lost his only two decisions in '51 and then spent 1952 in the military. Upon returning from the service, Wiesler had spent parts of the last two seasons with the Yankees, going 3-2 in 1954 and 0-2 in 1955.

Dick Tettelbach, a 26-year-old Yale graduate, was at Denver in 1955, where he hit .309, with 16 home runs and 95 runs batted in. The Yanks brought him up at the end of the season, and he went hitless in five at-bats.

Lou Berberet, also 26, had five at-bats for the Yankees in both 1954 and 1955 and had gotten two hits in each season. He'd also batted a solid .265 for the International League Toronto Maple Leafs in '55, and was an excellent receiver. Nevertheless, Berberet had

nowhere to go on a Yankee team that had Yogi Berra behind the plate and Elston Howard in reserve.

Herb Plews was a 27-year-old University of Illinois graduate who'd batted .302 for Denver in 1955.

The Yanks completed the deal on April 2 by sending Washington another player from that 1955 Denver club; he was 24-year-old outfielder Whitey Herzog, who'd batted .289 for the Bears.

May 28, 1956: Sold Righthanded Pitcher Gerry Staley to the Chicago White Sox

Picked up by the Yanks late in the 1955 season, Gerry Staley pitched two innings in two September games. He'd made only one appearance this season, giving up four runs in a third of an inning against Baltimore. The White Sox would convert Staley to a full-time reliever, and before he retired in 1961, he would win 40 more games and save an additional 43.

June 14, 1956: Traded First Baseman Eddie Robinson and Outfielder Lou Skizas to the Kansas City Athletics for Outfielder Bill Renna, Righthanded Pitcher Moe Burtschy, and Cash

Eddie Robinson, now 35, was returning to the team (then still in Philadelphia) that had sent him to New York as part of a multiplayer trade in December 1953. The Yankees had gotten Robinson to serve as a lefthanded pinch hitter and part-time first baseman, and he had filled those roles satisfactorily. He'd been particularly useful in 1954, his first season in New York. Appearing in 85 games, Robinson batted .261, while leading the American League with 15 pinch hits.

Bill Renna had also been part of that December 1953 trade. He'd gone from New York to Philadelphia and had been a semi-regular in the A's outfield since. The Yanks sent Renna to Richmond of the International League, along with pitcher Moe Burtschy who had a 10-6 record in five seasons with the A's franchise, and neither one ever returned to New York.

Rookie Lou Skizas batted .167 in six games for the Yanks this season before they sent him to Richmond. The A's brought Skizas to Kansas City, where he would hit .316 in 83 games, but he never again approached that level in his remaining three big league seasons.

With Renna going to Richmond, the Yankees recalled rookie outfielder Norm Siebern from the Virginians. Siebern had been very impressive in spring training, winning the James P. Dawson Award, given to the top newcomer in camp. However, on March 22, he ran into an outfield wall and sustained a knee injury that had delayed his Yankee debut. It would take place the following day.

August 22, 1956: Purchased Outfielder George Wilson from the New York Giants

The Yanks were cruising along with an 8½ game lead over Cleveland, with just 34 games left to play. Nevertheless, manager Casey Stengel was concerned about his outfield reserves. Bob Cerv was nursing an injured right knee, and first baseman Joe Collins, who was also a reserve outfielder, was ill with a virus. Even center fielder Mickey Mantle, who was having an extraordinary season, was slumping. After getting just three singles in his last 28 at-bats, Mantle's batting average was down to .358.

Stengel created a roster spot by sending rookie righthander Ralph Terry back to the Denver Bears of the American Association. He then filled it with George Wilson, a veteran outfielder who figured to see action only as a pinch hitter or as an outfield replacement in case of a dire emergency. Wilson, a 30-year-old lefthanded hitter, had played briefly with the White Sox and Giants in 1952 and 1953. He was back with the Giants this year, almost exclusively as a pinch hitter, and had been batting a measly .132 in 68 at-bats.

Wilson would end his big league career by getting two hits in 12 at-bats with the Yankees, along with an unsuccessful pinch-hitting appearance in the World Series.

August 25, 1956: Purchased Outfielder Enos Slaughter from the Kansas City Athletics

Back in April 1954, the first time he learned he was going to the Yankees, Enos Slaughter had broken down in tears. This time the future Hall of Famer kept from crying, but greeted the news by saying that he was "sick all over." Slaughter, traded to the Athletics by the Yankees in May 1955, had played well for Kansas City whose fans voted him the team's most popular player that year. Nevertheless, he was able to pass through waivers from every other American League club before leaving the feeble Athletics to join the first-place Yankees. In fact, a chance to play for a team that was pennant-bound was the reason that A's owner Arnold Johnson gave for sending the 40-year-old veteran to New York.

"We never would have parted with him except to give him a chance to play in the World Series," said Johnson. The more likely reason is the considerable amount of cash above the waiver price that the Yanks were rumored to have sent to Kansas City.

To make room for Slaughter, the Yanks unceremoniously released 38-year-old Phil Rizzuto, who except for his wartime service (1943 to 1945) had been the Yankees shortstop since 1941. Always dependable, he'd had his greatest year in 1950, when he batted .324 and won the American League's Most Valuable Player Award. Rizzuto, a future Hall of Famer, had been a sure-handed fielder, a great bunter, and had a lifetime batting average of .273. However, he'd been fading the last few years and had played in just 31 games this season, with a .231 batting average.

The Yankees assured Rizzuto that there was a place for him in the organization if he wanted it, but supposedly he was considering other options. Among them were managerial possibilities, a post-game interview show from the Polo Grounds, and a job as a play-by-play announcer with the Baltimore Orioles.

October 15, 1956: Sold Outfielder Bob Cerv to the Kansas City Athletics

The Yankees' sale of Bob Cerv to Kansas City was very likely the second part of the transaction of the previous August in which the A's sold Enos Slaughter to New York. Cerv was popular in Kansas City, where he'd starred as a minor leaguer when the American Association Blues were the Yankees' top farm team. But beginning in 1951, Cerv had been a Yankee for parts or all of the last six seasons. And while he'd never been able to establish himself as a regular, he'd been among Casey Stengel's most valuable reserves. Things figured to be different in Kansas City. The 30-year-old Cerv was coming off two productive seasons, in which he'd batted .341 and .304, and seemed likely to win a starting position with the last place Athletics.

December 11, 1956: Sold Catcher Charlie Silvera to the Chicago Cubs

The Cubs paid a reported $25,000 for Charlie Silvera, but he would play just one season for them. Silvera had been a Yankee since coming up from Portland of the Pacific Coast League at the very end of the 1948 season. In 1949, he hit .315 in 58 games, but 58 games would be the most Silvera would ever play in one season. He'd spent most of his Yankee career warming up pitchers in the bullpen, playing in only 201 games, with a .291 average. And though he'd been a member of six world championship teams, Silvera played in just one World Series game.

February 19, 1957: Traded Outfielder Irv Noren, Righthanded Pitcher Tom Morgan, Lefthanded Pitchers Rip Coleman and Mickey McDermott, Shortstop Billy Hunter, Minor League Second Baseman Milt Graff, and a Player to Be Named to the Kansas City Athletics for Third Baseman Clete Boyer, Righthanded Pitcher Art Ditmar, Lefthanded Pitchers Bobby Shantz and Jack McMahan, First Baseman Wayne Belardi, and a Player to Be Named

This 13-player transaction, which had both a major league and a minor league component, was the majors' largest since the Yanks

and Orioles swapped 17 players in 1954. It also had some controversy. Commissioner Ford Frick ruled that because Clete Boyer was a "bonus baby," the Athletics couldn't trade him; they had to keep him until May 31, 1957, when he would complete the terms of his bonus arrangement. The A's then agreed to send the Yanks another player before June 15, but that player turned out to be Boyer, whom they sent to New York on June 4.

Boyer had signed with Kansas City out of high school and was only 18 when he reached the majors in 1955. He batted .241 in 47 games that year, and .217 in 67 games in 1956. When the Yanks got him in June '57, he'd been in ten games without an at-bat, and was immediately shipped to Binghamton of the Eastern League. It would be 1959 before Boyer would play for the Yankees.

Of more immediate use to manager Casey Stengel were pitchers Art Ditmar and Bobby Shantz, especially Ditmar, whom Yankee general manager George Weiss called "the ace in the deal." Ditmar had broken in with the Athletics in 1954, their final season in Philadelphia, going 1-4 and then 12-12 in 1955. In 1956, while pitching for a Kansas City team that finished last, 45 games behind the Yankees, Ditmar again won 12, but he lost 22, the most losses in the American League.

Shantz had won a Most Valuable Player Award in 1952, the year he led the American League in wins (24) and winning percentage (.774). Since then he'd been bothered by arm trouble and over the past four seasons had won only 13 and lost 26. Shantz was 2-7 for the A's in 1956, pitching almost exclusively in relief, which is where the Yanks planned to use him. "We figure him as a relief man," Weiss said, "and he should do well in the Stadium."

Irv Noren had been a solid, dependable player for the Yankees since coming from Washington early in the 1952 season. He was the club's regular left fielder in 1954, his best season, and in 1955. In 1954 Noren batted .319, with 12 home runs and 66 runs batted in. But by 1956, knee problems (he'd had surgery on both) limited him to just 29 games.

In all, Noren played 488 games as a Yankee, with a .272 batting average. Though he was only 32, Noren said he might retire if Kansas City planned to make a significant cut in his 1956 salary. They didn't, and Noren did

February 19, 1957: *Irv Noren.* **Noren threatened to retire if the A's tried to cut his salary.**

play for the A's in 1957, at least until August 31 when they sold him to the Cardinals. He finished his career in 1960, having also played for the Cubs and Dodgers.

Like Noren, Mickey McDermott had also come to New York from Washington. He arrived in a February 1956 trade, but had failed to live up to the expectations the Yanks had for him. Used mostly in relief, McDermott won two and lost six in '56, with a 4.24 earned run average.

Pitchers Rip Coleman and Tom Morgan both had come up through the Yankee farm system. Coleman reached New York in August 1955, and then spent all of 1956 with the Yanks, winning five and losing six. Morgan had arrived in 1951 and went 9-3 as a 20-year-old rookie. Then after a 5-4 season in 1952, he spent a year in the military. Returning to the Yanks in 1954, Morgan had an 11-5 record and a 3.34 earned run average. Yet, despite his success as a starter, the next season manager Casey Stengel made him a full time reliever. Morgan went 7-3 in 1955, and then 6-7 in 1956, his first losing season. Suggesting that the departing Morgan "could be a sleeper" for the A's, Weiss said, "I hope that this deal will help us, and I know it gives them a nucleus of major league players."

In 1955, Billy Hunter's first year as a Yankee, he played 98 games at shortstop, more games than fading longtime incumbent Phil Rizzuto, who played 79. Although a fine fielder, Hunter was hitting only .227, and late that summer the Yanks sent him to Denver of the American Association. While playing with the Bears, Hunter broke his ankle, but recovered and spent all of 1956 in New York. His average improved to .280, but he played in only 39 games.

Although he was just 26, Wayne Belardi had been a major leaguer for at least part of each of the last six seasons, three with Brooklyn and three with Detroit. He'd batted .279 for the Tigers in 1956, but that December they traded him to the Athletics. Following this trade, Belardi would never take part in another major league game. Neither would pitcher Jack McMahan, who'd gone 0-5 with the A's in 1956.

It was the reverse for Milt Graff, who'd batted .317 with Birmingham of the Southern Association in 1956. The 25-year-old Graff, who had never before played at the big league level, would play with Kansas City in 1957 and 1958.

The two players to be named were revealed in early April 1957. They were second baseman Curt Roberts and pitcher Jack Urban. Roberts, who'd played for Pittsburgh from 1954 to 1956, but whose big league career was now over, came to the Yanks on April 4. A day earlier, the Yanks had sent Urban, a minor league righthander, to Kansas City. Like Graff, the 27-year-old Urban made the A's squad in 1957.

June 15, 1957: Traded Second Baseman Billy Martin, Righthanded Pitcher Ralph Terry, Outfielder Woodie Held, and Minor League Outfielder Bob Martyn to the Kansas City Athletics for Outfielders Harry Simpson and Jim Pisoni, and Righthanded Pitcher Ryne Duren

Billy Martin was Casey Stengel's favorite player. Stengel had been his manager in 1948 when Martin played for Oakland in the Pacific Coast League, and beginning in 1950, for seven years with the Yankees. Martin, who missed all of 1954 and most of 1955 serving in the military, had played in five World Series with the Yankees. He was 33 for 99 in Series play (.333),

June 15, 1957: *Mickey Mantle* and *Casey Stengel*. **Billy Martin was a Stengel favorite but GM George Weiss found him a negative influence on Mantle.**

while batting .262 in 527 regular-season games. After 43 games this season, he was at .241.

While Stengel had loved Martin's aggressive style of play, general manager George Weiss had become increasingly unhappy with his brawling, un–Yankee-like behavior. Martin had been involved in on-field fights with Jim Piersall of the Red Sox and Clint Courtney of the Browns, and just two days earlier had been a major participant in a multiplayer fracas with the Chicago White Sox.

However, the Yankees wanted Martin gone for a reason even more compelling than his fighting. They believed he exerted a highly negative influence on Mickey Mantle, Martin's good friend, and the Yankees' (and the American League's) best player. Their displeasure had come to a head on May 16 after Martin, Mantle, and several other Yankee players got into a fight with some patrons at New York's Copacabana nightclub. The players, all of whom were later fined for their parts in the

melee, were there celebrating Martin's 29th birthday. After the Copacabana incident, Martin's departure seem assured. It came just one hour before the trading deadline, as the Yanks were playing in Kansas City against their favorite trading partners, the Athletics.

Along with Martin, the Yanks were sending the Athletics three excellent prospects, chiefly Ralph Terry, a 21-year-old pitcher. In August 1956, Terry had come up from Denver of the American Association, where he was 13-4, and made three starts for the Yankees, winning one and losing two. In seven games this season, two of which he started, Terry was 1-1, with the one win being a shutout.

The other two prospects were both outfielders: 25-year-old Woodie Held and 26-year-old Bob Martyn. Held had been in the Yankee farm system since 1951 and was currently at Denver, where he was batting .279. His major league experience consisted of four hitless at-bats, three in 1954 and one earlier this season. Held would play in the majors until 1969 and hit 179 home runs.

Martyn had been at Richmond, the Yanks' Triple-A farm team in the International League. However, the A's had immediate use for him, and he would make his big league debut three days later.

The Yanks were willing to part with these young players in order to get Harry Simpson, an outfielder who'd begun his big league career with Cleveland in 1951. Always an excellent defensive player, Simpson had enjoyed his finest season in 1956, the best he would ever have as a major leaguer. He batted .293, with 21 home runs and 105 runs batted in, and his 11 triples tied him with Boston's Jackie Jensen, Washington's Jim Lemon, and Chicago's Minnie Minoso for the American League lead.

Simpson, who was batting .296 with six home runs and six triples this season, was expected to play for the Yankees in their Sunday afternoon game against the A's, just as Martin figured to be in Kansas City's lineup.

That, however, would not be the case for either pitcher Ryne Duren or outfielder Jim Pisoni. Duren had pitched for the A's in Saturday's 9-2 Yankee win and Pisoni had homered in the game, but both were on their way to Denver. Duren would reach New York in 1958, while Pisoni didn't get there until 1959, and then only after playing briefly for the Milwaukee Braves earlier in the season. He would appear in 17 games as a Yankee in '59 and 20 in 1960, batting a combined .154.

Milt Graff, whom the Yanks sent to Kansas City in the 13-player deal between the two clubs in February, took Martyn's roster spot at Richmond, but remained Kansas City property.

September 1, 1957: Purchased Right-handed Pitcher Sal Maglie from the Brooklyn Dodgers

Despite their being in third place, 7½ behind the league-leading Milwaukee Braves, the Dodgers postponed the sale of Sal Maglie until the August 31 deadline for World Series eligibility had passed. They didn't want to be confronted by their former longtime nemesis if they managed to overtake the Braves and faced the Yankees in the World Series.

Maglie had just arrived at Ebbets Field for the Dodgers' Sunday afternoon game against the Giants when the club informed him of his sale to the Yankees. He left quickly and was on the Yankee bench in time for the game against Washington. When Yankee Stadium public address announcer Bob Sheppard informed the crowd of Maglie's presence, they greeted him with a rousing ovation.

Casey Stengel, his new manager, welcomed Maglie to the Yankees. "We're very happy to have you—and that goes for me, the coaches, the players and the front office." Maglie responded that he "was certainly glad to be here."

Acquired by the Dodgers from Cleveland in May 1956, Maglie went 13-5 and was a key factor in Brooklyn's edging Milwaukee by one game for the '56 National League flag. He was 6-6 for the Dodgers this year, with an impressive 2.93 ERA.

The Yanks had to wait until Maglie got waivers from every team in both leagues, a task made easier because of his age (40) and his relatively high salary ($27,500). Then they reportedly paid Brooklyn $37,500, while also agreeing to send two minor leaguers to the Dodgers in 1958.

Maglie had begun his big league career and first reached stardom with the Giants. By becoming a Yankee, he joined a select group of men who had played for all three New York teams. The group included Willie Keeler, Jack Doyle, Fred Merkle, Waite Hoyt, Lefty O'Doul, Burleigh Grimes, Tony Lazzeri and Bobo Newsom, but, sadly, Maglie would be the last.

September 10, 1957: Purchased Outfielder Bobby Del Greco from the Chicago Cubs

Bobby Del Greco was only 19 when he made his major league debut with the woeful 1952 Pittsburgh Pirates. His next major league season was in 1956, which he split between the Pirates and the St. Louis Cardinals. The Cubs traded for Del Greco in April 1957, but after batting .200 in 20 games, they sent him to Montreal of the International League. He was hitting .278 for the Royals when the Cubs recalled him, a day before selling him to the Yankees who wanted him mainly as a late-inning defensive replacement.

Del Greco would play in eight games for the Yanks, getting three hits in seven at-bats. The following spring he impressed manager Casey Stengel enough for Stengel to predict that Del Greco would stay with the Yankees for the whole season. But on May 15, 1958, cut-down day to the 25-man limit, Stengel sent Del Greco back to Richmond of the International League, ending his Yankee career.

May 14, 1958: Sold Righthanded Pitcher Al Cicotte to the Washington Senators

After nine years in the minors, a 15-12 record with Richmond of the International League in 1956 earned Al Cicotte a chance with the Yankees. He pitched in 20 games in 1957, with a 2-2 record and a 3.03 ERA, but had not been in a game this season.

"I couldn't use Cicotte enough," explained manager Casey Stengel, "and maybe it's my fault I didn't pitch him enough last year." Cicotte would pitch four more years in the majors, but with five different teams.

June 14, 1958: Traded Righthanded Pitcher Sal Maglie to the St. Louis Cardinals for Minor League Right-handed Pitcher Joe McClain and Cash

At 41, Sal Maglie was in the final year of his career. The Yanks had picked him up from Brooklyn the previous September in the last deal the Dodgers made before absconding to California. Maglie won two games for the Yanks down the stretch, but was ineligible to participate in the World Series loss to the Milwaukee Braves. After an unimpressive spring training, he'd appeared in only seven games in 1958, splitting two decisions, with a 4.63 earned run average. Maglie went 2-6 with the Cardinals before announcing his retirement.

A day after the trade the Yanks brought up rookie Zack Monroe from Denver of the American Association. Monroe, the Bears' best pitcher at 10-2, took Maglie's spot on the roster, while Joe McClain, 6-4 with the Cardi-

nals' Rochester team in the International League, replaced Monroe at Denver.

June 15, 1958: Traded Righthanded Pitcher Bob Grim and Outfielder–First Baseman Harry Simpson to the Kansas City Athletics for Righthanded Pitchers Virgil Trucks and Duke Maas

Shutouts by Frank Lary and Jim Bunning in both ends of a Sunday doubleheader had just given the Tigers a four-game series sweep at Yankee Stadium. Nevertheless, the Yanks reacted by making a trading-deadline deal to improve their pitching. Manager Casey Stengel had wanted Duke Maas ever since the 29-year-old curveballer, then with Detroit, had three-hit the Yankees early in the 1957 season. Even after the Tigers included him in their 13-player trade with Kansas City last November, many baseball people thought Maas would eventually be pitching in New York. Yesterday, in his final appearance with the A's, he'd defeated the Red Sox, raising his won-lost record to 4-5.

Both the Tigers and Athletics had used Maas as a starter and a reliever, and Stengel planned to do the same. His plans were different for Virgil Trucks, the veteran pitcher the Yanks had tried to get from Kansas City last summer. A rash of injuries to the A's pitching staff kept that deal from going through and led the Yanks to acquiring Sal Maglie instead. Trucks was a former two-time All Star and the author of two no-hit games in 1952. However, he was now 41 years old and his role in New York would be limited to helping ease the load on rookie Ryne Duren in the bullpen. Trucks did his job. He went 2-1 in 25 games, all in relief, and then retired after the season.

The inability of Bob Grim to be successful out of the bullpen had been the reason for Duren's ascension. It was also the reason for Grim's inclusion in this trade. In 1954, when Grim went 20-6 for the second-place Yankees and was the American League's Rookie of the Year, eight of his wins had been in relief. And he'd been primarily a relief pitcher since suffering an arm injury the following season. All of his 46 appearances in 1957 were in relief, and his 12 relief wins and 19 saves were tops in the league. However, this season,

June 15, 1958: *Bob Grim.* **After leading the league in saves in 1957, Grim was having a sub-par 1958.**

Grim's pitching had been sub-par. He was 0-1 in 11 games and had an awful 5.51 earned run average.

Harry Simpson, allegedly 32, was going back to Kansas City exactly one year after the A's sent him to New York in the Billy Martin trade. That deal, touched off by the famed brawl at the Copacabana night club, had also brought Duren to the Yankees. The lefthanded hitting Simpson, playing outfield and first base, batted just .250 in 75 games for the Yanks in 1957. He did, however, hit three triples as a Yankee, which, combined with the six he'd hit for the Athletics, allowed Simpson to tie for the league lead in triples for the second consecutive year.

Bill Skowron's strained back gave Simpson the chance to play first base in four games of the 1957 World Series. He also appeared as a pinch hitter in one, but managed only one hit in 12 at-bats. In 24 games this season, he was batting .216.

August 22, 1958: Traded a Player to Be Named and Cash to the Kansas City Athletics for Righthanded Pitcher Murry Dickson

When sore-armed pitcher Tom Sturdivant went on the disabled list, the Yanks got veteran Murry Dickson to replace him. Dick-

son, who'd turned 42 the day before the trade, pitched his first major league game for the St. Louis Cardinals back in 1939. Sent to the minors in 1940, he returned in 1941 and had been a big leaguer with the Cards, Pirates, and Phillies ever since, except for two years out for Army service in World War II. Dickson was 9-5 for the woeful Athletics this season, his first in the American League.

On September 29, the Yanks sent Kansas City 28-year-old outfielder Zeke Bella from their Denver team in the American Association. Bella had appeared in five games for the Yanks in 1957, going 1 for 10. He played one year for the Athletics (1959), batting .207.

April 8, 1959: Traded Righthanded Pitcher Mark Freeman to the Kansas City Athletics for Righthanded Pitcher Jack Urban

Mark Freeman had spent eight seasons in the Yankee farm system, the last three at Triple-A Denver of the American Association. He'd never appeared in a major league game and wouldn't have been likely to do so this season if the Yanks hadn't traded him. However, Freeman would get into three games with the Athletics before they sold him back to New York on May 8, whereupon the Yanks promptly sent him to Seattle of the Pacific Coast League.

Jack Urban, a one-time Yankee farmhand, had a 15-15 record in his two big league seasons with Kansas City. The Yanks sent him to Richmond of the International League, but St. Louis picked him up later in the year, and he would pitch his final eight major league games for the Cardinals.

April 12, 1959: Traded Shortstop Tommy Carroll and Minor League Outfielder Russ Snyder to the Kansas City Athletics for Infielder Mike Baxes and Outfielder Bob Martyn

Thwarted in his efforts to make a major trade, Yankee general manager George Weiss made this minor one on the day the Yanks played their twice-postponed opener. Bob

Martyn, a one-time Yankee farmhand, and Jim Baxes had each played two seasons for the A's. The Yanks sent them both to the International League Richmond Virginians and neither one ever returned to the major leagues.

Russ Snyder had a strong minor league season in 1958, but the Yanks, having no room for him on their opening day roster, had optioned him to Richmond a few days earlier. Going to the A's would give the 24-year-old Snyder his chance to play at the major league level, and he would take advantage of it. Snyder would bat .271 while playing for five American League teams over the next 12 seasons.

Yankee scout Paul Krichell, the same scout who'd signed Lou Gehrig, Tony Lazzeri, and Whitey Ford, discovered Tommy Carroll in 1954. The Yanks paid Carroll a large bonus; however, the "bonus baby" rules of the time actually worked against him. The "law" required that the Yanks keep Carroll on the major league roster for all of the 1955 and 1956 seasons, which prevented him from developing his skills in the minor leagues. During those two seasons, Carroll played a total of just 50 games, batting only 23 times with eight hits. His career would end after 14 games with the Athletics.

May 9, 1959: Sold Righthanded Pitcher Murry Dickson to the Kansas City Athletics

Murry Dickson had a 1-2 record with a save for the Yanks in the last five weeks of the 1958 season. Dickson, who had yet to pitch this season, would finish his 18-year major league career by going 2-1 in 38 games for the '59 Athletics.

Selling Dickson left the Yanks still two players over the 25-man limit, which they remedied by sending pitcher Zack Monroe, 4-2 as a rookie in 1958, and catcher Darrell Johnson to their International League team in Richmond. Johnson, who played in 27 games with the Yanks in 1957-58, was sold to Richmond outright and then drafted by the St. Louis Cardinals in November 1959.

May 26, 1959: Traded Righthanded Pitchers Johnny Kucks and Tom Sturdivant, and Second Baseman Jerry Lumpe to the Kansas City Athletics for Righthanded Pitcher Ralph Terry and Infielder Hector Lopez

Trailing the first-place Chicago White Sox by 9½ games, the Yanks turned for help to their favorite trading partner, the Kansas City Athletics. This deal was the 14th between the two clubs in the four years since the A's moved from Philadelphia to Kansas City. It would also prove to be one of the best for New York. The two players they got, Ralph Terry and Hector Lopez, would be key members of the Yankee teams that would win five consecutive pennants between 1960 and 1964.

It was so obvious that the two players coming to New York were better than the three that were leaving, complaints from the league's two leading Yankee-baiters: Chicago's Frank Lane and Cleveland's Bill Veeck, arose immediately.

In reacquiring the 23-year-old Terry, the Yanks were getting a pitcher who had once been one of their most prized farmhands. They'd traded him, somewhat reluctantly, to Kansas City in June 1957 as part of the deal in which they'd unloaded Billy Martin. Terry was still only 23, and some cynics claimed that the Yanks had sent him to KC just to give him more seasoning. He'd been mainly a starter for the A's, although his manager, Harry Craft, had made it clear he didn't think highly of him. Terry's combined record for Kansas City was 17-28, including a 2-4 mark this season.

Manager Casey Stengel was pleased to have Terry back in a Yankee uniform. "He looked like a fine prospect with us a few years ago," Stengel said, "but I understand that after we traded him to the A's, Harry Craft was never quite satisfied with him. Maybe with a fresh start in New York, he'll do better. At least I hope so."

Stengel thought the change of scenery would also be beneficial to the two pitchers he was trading, Johnny Kucks and Tom Sturdivant. The Yanks had come close to trading Sturdivant once before, to Washington in 1956 for Camilo Pascual. They'd changed their minds at the last moment and Sturdivant went on to win 16 games that year and again in 1957. But in 1958 he had a sore arm and went just 3-6 and was 0-2 at the time of the trade.

Kucks had gone 18-9 in 1956, his second season with the Yankees, but since then Stengel had used him both as a starter and reliever, and he'd won a total of only 16 games while losing 19.

Lopez, reportedly 26 years old but actually 29, was in his fifth big league season. Through the first four, the native Panamanian batted .278 with 61 home runs, while never appearing in fewer than 120 games. He played mostly third base, but the Athletics had also used him at second, in the outfield, and even occasionally at shortstop. Thus far this season, playing strictly at second base, Lopez was batting .281 with six home runs and 24 runs batted in.

While Jerry Lumpe was also a very versatile infielder, he was not as consistent a hitter as Lopez. A member of the Yankees since 1956 when he'd been the opening-day shortstop, his best year had been in 1957 when he batted .340 in 103 plate appearances. Lumpe was hitting just .222 with no extra-base hits this season. He would be the A's second baseman through 1963 and then hold that same job for several years in Detroit.

The Yankees moved Lopez to the outfield, and he remained with the club for the final eight seasons of his career. He batted .262, with 69 home runs as a Yankee, and .286 in 15 World Series games.

July 26, 1959: Purchased Righthanded Pitcher Gary Blaylock from the St. Louis Cardinals

This would be the only big league season for Gary Blaylock, a 27-year-old rookie who was 4-5 with St. Louis as a reliever and spot starter. He would make one start and 14 relief appearances after joining the Yankees, and lose his only decision.

To make room on the roster for Blaylock, the Yanks optioned pitcher Jim Bronstad to Richmond of the International League. Bronstad, a rookie, had an 0-3 record in what would be his only season with the Yankees.

September 11, 1959: Sold Outfielder Enos Slaughter to the Milwaukee Braves

Milwaukee was locked in a very exciting three-team battle with Los Angeles and San Francisco for the National League pennant. Currently in third place, but only one game behind the first-place Giants, the Braves were using a tactic employed often in recent years by the Yankees. To help them win a pennant, they were making a mid or late season pickup of a veteran player, in this case, 43-year-old Enos Slaughter.

The list of Yankees added in this manner included Johnny Mize, Johnny Hopp, Johnny Sain, and even Slaughter himself. (The Yanks had purchased Slaughter from the Kansas City A's in August 1956, a year after they'd traded him there.) And while the Yanks usually added only one veteran player, Slaughter was the Braves' third such addition in the past few weeks. Trying to win a third consecutive pennant, they'd earlier acquired second baseman Bobby Avila from the Red Sox and first baseman Ray Boone from the Athletics.

The Yankees, meanwhile, were out of the American League pennant race, which had come down to a battle between Chicago and Cleveland, and had no need for Slaughter. Although he'd hit well in 1958—.304 in 77 games—he was just 17 for 99 with six home runs this season. Nor would Slaughter be of much help to Milwaukee, going 3 for 18 as the Braves finished tied with the Dodgers but lost the pennant in a playoff.

December 11, 1959: Traded Righthanded Pitcher Don Larsen, Outfielders Hank Bauer and Norm Siebern, and First Baseman Marv Throneberry to the Kansas City Athletics for Outfielder Roger Maris, First Baseman Kent Hadley, and Shortstop Joe Demaestri

This seven-player swap brought the total number of players traded between New York and Kansas City to 59 in the 15 deals between the two clubs since 1955. "I know we'll take a lot more ribbing," said Yankee GM George

Weiss, "but it simply got down to where we couldn't close a deal with any other club. We were fairly close to making two with National League clubs, but these still are stalled." (Weiss reportedly had offered veteran infielder Gil McDougald to both the San Francisco Giants and Milwaukee Braves.)

The "ribbing" Weiss expected was because he knew that in 25-year-old Roger Maris, the Yankees were getting one of the best young hitters in the game. Maris had reached the majors with Cleveland in 1957, hitting 14 home runs in 358 at-bats. The Indians traded him to Kansas City in June 1958, and Maris had a combined 28 home runs and 80 runs batted in that year. This past season, Maris was leading the league with a .344 batting average just prior to the first All-Star Game. But after undergoing an appendectomy, he finished the season with a .273 average, 16 home runs, and 72 RBIs. A lefthanded hitter with a batting stroke seemingly made for Yankee Stadium, the Yanks were expecting Maris to reach stardom in New York.

Weiss explained that the opportunity to obtain Maris was the reason the Yanks were willing to part with veteran Yankees Hank Bauer and Don Larsen, and with two 26-year-old potential stars like Norm Siebern and Marv Throneberry.

"I hated to see so fine a competitor as Bauer go," Weiss said, "and we'll always feel indebted to Larsen for his perfect game performance. However, in Maris we have a young outfielder who should develop into a fine player at the Stadium."

In reality, the Yanks had finished a disappointing third in 1959, and Weiss considered all four players he was sending to Kansas City expendable.

The Yanks had once expected the same kind of future for Siebern that they now were predicting for Maris. He'd had an excellent minor league career, then missed two seasons in the military, before returning in 1956. That spring Siebern won the James P. Dawson Award, given to the top newcomer in training camp. But he'd run into an outfield wall and injured his knee on March 22, and the Yanks sent him to Denver of the American Association. He split the season between New York and Denver, then spent all of 1957 with the Bears. Siebern led the American Association

with a .349 average in '57, and also led in hits, runs, doubles, and triples, and won the Minor League Player of the Year Award. Back with the Yankees in 1958, he batted .300 in 134 games, but had a difficult World Series in the field. Siebern's problems with the Autumn sun and shadows in Yankee Stadium's left field made him the target of caustic criticism, much of it coming from his manager, Casey Stengel. Adversely affected by Stengel's disapproval, an unhappy Siebern hit only .271 in 1959.

Just as Siebern had been the Minor League Player of the Year with Denver in 1957, Throneberry had won the same honor with the same team the year before. Blocked at first base by Bill Skowron, Throneberry had been in one game as a Yankee in 1955 (he went 2 for 2) and a combined 140 games in 1958-59 with a .238 batting average.

Larsen had an excellent 45-24 won-lost record in his five seasons as a Yankee, and that included a sub-par a 6-7 mark in 1959, his only losing season in New York. As Weiss suggested, Larsen had secured his place in history with a perfect game against Brooklyn in the 1956 World Series. But though he was still just 30 years old, Larsen had been bothered by arm problems in recent seasons and had no substantive place in the team's plans.

Bauer was a Marine veteran of World War II, who'd come up to the Yankees in September 1948. He'd played on all of Casey Stengel's nine pennant-winning teams, and his departure left Yogi Berra as the only player on the Yankees' current roster who'd preceded Stengel to New York. Throughout his 12 seasons and 1,406 games as a Yankee, Bauer had displayed character and competence. Still, he was 37 years old and was obviously nearing the end of his playing days. A lifetime .277 hitter, he'd had his worst season ever in 1959, suffering career-lows in batting (.238), home runs (9), and runs batted in (39).

Bauer, who lived near Kansas City, said that if he had to be traded, he was glad it was close to home. "Of course, I'm sorry to leave the Yankees," he said. "They're a great organization. But I'm very happy to join the Athletics."

Joe DeMaestri was a veteran of nine big league seasons. He'd come up with the White Sox in 1951, gone to the Browns in 1952, and had been with A's, both in Philadelphia and

December 11, 1959: *Hank Bauer.* **Bauer (third from right) had to break into an outfield of Joe DiMaggio, Charlie Keller, and Tommy Henrich.**

Kansas City, since 1953. The Yanks expected DeMaestri, a lifetime .237-batter to make the team as a utility infielder. He did, and played his final two big league seasons with the Yanks, batting .184 in 79 games.

Kent Hadley was, like Maris, a 25-year-old lefthanded hitter with a home run stroke. He'd hit a Southern Association–leading 34 homers for Little Rock in 1958, and ten for Kansas City in 288 at-bats in 1959.

December 11, 1959: Signed Outfielder Elmer Valo as a Free Agent

The Yanks had made another move this day, a seven-player trade with Kansas City that brought them Roger Maris and far overshadowed their signing of Elmer Valo.

After spending the first 15 of his 18 major league seasons with the Philadelphia/Kansas City Athletics, Valo had played briefly with the Phillies, Dodgers, and Indians. He had a .284 lifetime batting average, and though he would be 39 when the 1960 pennant race got underway, Valo seemingly still could hit. He'd split the 1959 season between the Pacific Coast League Seattle Rainiers and the Indians, batting .324 in 60 games for Seattle and .292 in 34 games for Cleveland.

Valo would play in eight games for the Yanks in 1960. He was hitless in five at-bats when the club released him on May 18. The following week, Valo signed to play with the Washington Senators.

VII. The Sixties

April 5, 1960: Traded Outfielder Gordon Windhorn and Minor League Third Baseman–Outfielder Dick Sanders to the Los Angeles Dodgers for Lefthanded Pitcher Fred Kipp

Both Gordon Windhorn, whose Yankee career consisted of 11 hitless at-bats in 1959, and Dick Sanders, who had never played (or would ever play) in the major leagues, had been with Richmond of the International League in 1959. The Dodgers kept them in the International League, assigning both to the Montreal Royals.

Fred Kipp had pitched a game for the Dodgers in September 1957, the team's last month in Brooklyn. He was 6-6 as a rookie with Los Angeles in 1958, then spent most of 1959 at St. Paul in the American Association, where he had a 14-11 record. Kipp had never been, nor would he ever be, a successful major league pitcher. Nevertheless, the Dodgers thought highly of his baseball knowledge and had offered him a job in their organization after his playing days were over.

Kipp started four games for the 1960 Yankees, his final four major league appearances, losing his only decision.

May 19, 1960: Traded Righthanded Pitcher Mark Freeman to the Chicago Cubs for Lefthanded Pitcher Art Ceccarelli

The Yankees had traded Mark Freeman to Kansas City in April 1959, but after three games with the A's, they sold him back to New York on May 8. The Yanks then sent him to Seattle of the Pacific Coast League, although he later got into one game with the Yanks, a start with no decision.

Art Ceccarelli had a 9-18 record in five years with the Athletics, Orioles, and the Cubs. He went to Richmond of the International League and never again pitched in the majors.

May 19, 1960: Traded Third Baseman Andy Carey to the Kansas City Athletics for Outfielder Bob Cerv

Injury and illness had severely curtailed Andy Carey's playing time in 1959 and had limited him to only three at-bats this season. So, while he regretted leaving many of his longtime teammates, the 28-year-old Carey welcomed the trade. "I was not doing myself or anyone else any good sitting around," he said. "With the Athletics, I'll be able to play regularly."

Casey Stengel, now his ex-manager, felt that while the Yanks had no need for him, Carey would "improve Kansas City two notches." Stengel explained his infield situation this way: "Gil McDougald, who can play three positions in the infield got off to a good start," he said. "And Tony Kubek and Bobby Richardson give me fine protection in the other places. Besides, I still have Cletis Boyer and Joe DeMaestri for infield emergencies."

Carey had debuted with the Yankees in 1952, a year after they signed him out of St. Mary's College in California for a reported $60,000 bonus. He had been the Yankees' number one third baseman since 1954, although

May 19, 1960: *Bob Cerv.* **The Cerv-Carey deal was the 16th between the Yanks and Kansas City in five years.**

he never again hit as well as he did that year (.302 with 65 runs batted in).

Bob Cerv was returning to New York after three plus seasons in Kansas City, the best of which was 1958, when he batted .305, with 38 home runs and 104 runs batted in. In 23 games this season, he had six home runs, 12 runs batted in, and a .256 average. Cerv's return delighted Stengel, who felt that the Yankees were now stronger in left field, catching, and pinch hitting.

"I'm happy to get that player back," Stengel said. "It means that I can put Cerv out there if I want to do that and let Yogi Berra concentrate on catching. Don't think for a minute that I'm dissatisfied with Berra as an outfielder," he added. "He's done an amazing job out there. But with doubleheaders coming up, I'll be able to give Elston Howard a rest, and I can always count on a good pinch hitter with those fellows around. Furthermore, getting Cerv back adds a lot of punch to my ballclub."

Cerv would hit eight home runs in 87 games for the Yanks and then go to the new Los Angeles Angels in the December expansion draft.

The Cerv-Carey deal was the 16th transaction between the Yankees and Athletics since the Philadelphia franchise relocated to Kansas City in 1955. Stengel was aware that other teams suspected that despite its major league status, Kansas City continued to be a Yankee farm team.

"I don't care what anyone might say," Stengel said. "We tried to get a pitcher from five different clubs, but no one would give me the pitcher I wanted."

August 21, 1960: Purchased First Baseman Dale Long from the San Francisco Giants

Yankee manager Casey Stengel was looking for a lefthanded pinch hitter with power. And though Dale Long was batting a paltry .167 for the Giants, he was a power hitter. Between 1955 and 1959 Long had hit 98 home runs.

The Yanks already had a lefthanded hitting first baseman whom they used mostly as a pinch hitter. That was Kent Hadley, acquired with Roger Maris in the December 1959 trade with Kansas City. However, Hadley's .203 batting average induced the club to send him to Richmond of the International League to make room for Long, and he never returned.

Long, serving as a pinch hitter and as a fill-in for the injured Bill Skowron, batted a lusty .366 in 26 games for the Yankees. Nevertheless, he would be 35 by the start of the 1961 season. The Yanks made him available in the December expansion draft, and the new Washington Senators selected him.

December 16, 1960: Purchased Lefthanded Pitcher Danny McDevitt from the Los Angeles Dodgers

The Yanks had lost three second-line pitchers in the expansion draft, held a week earlier to stock the American League's new Los Angeles and Washington franchises. Los Angeles took Eli Grba and Duke Maas, and Washington took Bobby Shantz, whom they then traded to Pittsburgh. Grba was 8-9 in two seasons, Shantz 30-18 in four seasons, and Maas 26-12 in two and a half seasons. The Yanks would get Maas back in a trade just before the 1961 season opened.

To fill one of those spots on the staff, the Yanks added Danny McDevitt, a 28-year-old native New Yorker and boyhood Yankee fan. In four years with the Dodgers, one in Brooklyn and three in Los Angeles, McDevitt had a record of 19-22, including an 0-4 mark in 1960.

April 4, 1961: Traded Infielder Fritz Brickell to the Los Angeles Angels for Righthanded Pitcher Duke Maas

The Angels had paid the Yankees $75,000 for Duke Maas in the December 1960 expansion draft, a draft held to stock both them and the American League's other expansion team, the Washington Senators. Now Roy Hamey, in his first trade since succeeding George Weiss as general manager, was bringing Maas back to New York.

New manager Ralph Houk, who'd succeeded Casey Stengel, was pleased to have the 32-year-old Maas back with the club. "We had to put names on that list for selection last winter," Houk said, "and Maas is one of two or three I hated to make available to the other clubs. He's a pretty fair pitcher."

Maas had been a "pretty fair pitcher," winning 14 games in 1959. He'd both started and relieved that year, but in 1960 arm troubles made him almost exclusively a reliever. He had a 5-1 record in 35 games, all but one in relief.

Maas's arm problem would end his big league career after he pitched just a third of an inning in his only appearance of 1961.

Fritz Brickell batted .256 with nine home runs for Richmond of the International League in 1960, but appeared in only 96 games because of a bad knee. Yet, because Brickell had played a total of 20 games with the Yanks in 1958 and 1959, mostly at shortstop, the Angels believed he'd be a viable candidate for their shortstop job. However, after batting just .122 in 21 games, Brickell was gone from the Angels and the major leagues.

May 8, 1961: Traded Righthanded Pitchers Ryne Duren and Johnny James, and Outfielder Lee Thomas to the Los Angeles Angels for Outfielder

Bob Cerv and Righthanded Pitcher Tex Clevenger

After the Yankees had dropped two out of three in their first ever visit to Los Angeles's Wrigley Field, Roy Hamey and Fred Haney, the teams' respective general managers, concluded the deal they'd been discussing for two weeks.

Bob Cerv, whom the Angels had selected in the December 1960 expansion draft, was joining the Yankees for the third time. Cerv, who was now 35, had started slowly this season, a .158 average in 18 games, still, Ralph Houk, in his first season as the Yankee manager, was glad to have him back.

"I don't think it's a secret anywhere that I hated to make Cerv available in that player pool last winter," Houk said. "We definitely need another righthanded hitter on the bench and Bob will play some games for me too."

Of Tex Clevenger, his new pitcher, Houk said, "I've always liked Clevenger and under the circumstances I must believe that he will help us more than Duren in the bullpen for immediate purposes. He certainly has stopped us a number of times."

Clevenger, who'd pitched for non-contending clubs throughout his career, came up with the Red Sox in 1954 and was with Washington from 1956 to 1960. The Senators moved to Minnesota after the 1960 season, and it was from the Twins roster that the Angels had drafted him. The 29-year-old Clevenger had a lifetime record of 33-36, and was 2-1 this season. He had already been in 12 games for the Angels, the most of any pitcher in either league.

Clevenger would get into 21 games for the Yanks in both 1961 and 1962, splitting two decisions in '61 and winning both in '62.

Ryne Duren had been the ace of the Yankee bullpen in 1958, his first year with the club. He won six and lost four, but had a league-leading 20 saves. Duren hadn't been as effective since; his saves total fell to 14 in 1959 and nine in 1960, and this season, he was 0-1 with no saves.

Houk and Duren had clashed in the past, including a widely-reported scuffle on a train after the Yanks clinched the 1958 pennant when Houk was a coach under Casey Stengel. They'd already had one confrontation this spring, when Houk accused Duren of violating training rules and fined him $200. Nevertheless, Houk denied that either incident had anything to do with the trade.

"Whatever has happened in the past had nothing much to do with this deal," he said. "There is nothing wrong with Ryne's arm but he needs more work then we can give him. I think he will help the Angels."

Houk also spoke briefly about Johnny James and Lee Thomas, the other two now ex–Yankees. He said, "James is a real prospect who also needs work. Thomas is a prospect also."

James had pitched in one game for the Yankees in September 1958. He'd come back in 1960 to go 5-1, before spending the second half of the season with Richmond in the International League. Thomas had one hit in two at-bats this season, his first in the majors after seven seasons in the minors.

June 14, 1961: Traded Lefthanded Pitcher Danny McDevitt to the Minnesota Twins for Infielder Billy Gardner

Billy Gardner reached the majors with the 1954 New York Giants. He'd been the regular second baseman for the Orioles for four years (1956–59), and for the 1960 Washington Senators (now relocated to Minnesota). Gardner was batting .234 for the Twins, a figure very representative of his career average.

Danny McDevitt, whom the Yanks had purchased from the Dodgers in December 1960, was 1-2 in eight games this year. McDevitt won his only decision for the Twins and then ended his career with Kansas City in 1962.

June 14, 1961: Traded Righthanded Pitcher Art Ditmar and Outfielder– Third Baseman Deron Johnson to the Kansas City Athletics for Lefthanded Pitcher Bud Daley

Art Ditmar won a team-high 15 games in 1960, but he'd struggled this season with just

two wins and three losses, and a 4.64 earned run average. A Yankee since 1957, Ditmar left with a 47-32 record. He would pitch in 26 games for Kansas City over the next two seasons and lose all seven of his decisions.

At 28, Bud Daley was three years younger than Ditmar and had won 16 games in each of the past two seasons for the wretched A's. However, like Ditmar, he too had started slowly this season with a 4-8 record and a 4.95 ERA.

Rookie Deron Johnson had shown good home run power in the minors, although he'd yet to hit one in his 23 at-bats with the Yankees over the past two seasons. However, after leaving the Yankees, Johnson would go on to hit 245 home runs in his career. Until Seattle's Jay Buhner hit his 246th in 1997, Johnson had hit the most home runs by any player after being traded away by the Yankees.

June 17, 1961: Signed First Baseman Earl Torgeson as a Free Agent

The Yankees would eventually win 109 games this season, but they were currently in

June 17, 1961: *Earl Torgeson.* **The Yanks signed Torgeson a few days after the White Sox released him.**

third place, two games behind Detroit and looking for offensive help. So, a few days after the Chicago White Sox gave 37-year-old Earl Torgeson his unconditional release, the Yanks signed the 15-year veteran first baseman.

Torgeson, who had a .265 career average, batted .111 in 22 games before the Yanks released him as a player on September 2 and then signed him as a coach.

July 28, 1961: Purchased First Baseman Bob Hale from the Cleveland Indians

Bob Turley had gone on the disabled list with a sore elbow, but rather than add a pitcher to replace him, the Yanks picked up another lefthanded hitter, first baseman Bob Hale. Hale, whom they planned to use primarily as a pinch hitter, was currently batting a measly .167; however, a year ago he'd led the league in both pinch hitting appearances (63) and pinch hits (19).

Along with his pinch hitting, Hale played five games at first for the Yanks, and had two hits in his final 13 major league at-bats.

December 14, 1961: Traded Catcher Jesse Gonder to the Cincinnati Reds for Lefthanded Pitcher Marshall Bridges

Once, Jesse Gonder had been a highly-rated prospect; now he was a month short of his 26th birthday and had never lived up to his early promise. Playing briefly for the Yankees in each of the last two seasons, he was 6 for 19, with all of his 1961 appearances coming as a pinch hitter. The Reds sent Gonder to San Diego, where in 1962 he would hit .342 and win the Pacific Coast League batting title.

Marshall Bridges, a 30-year-old reliever, was 6-3 as a rookie with the 1959 Cardinals and 6-2 with the Cards and Reds in 1960. He had one decision with Cincinnati in 1961, a loss, while spending most of the season with Rochester of the International League where he won six and lost eight.

June 12, 1962: Traded Infielder Billy Gardner to the Boston Red Sox for Outfielder Tom Umphlett and Cash

After a rookie season with the Red Sox in 1953, Tom Umphlett spent the next two years with the Senators. He'd been in the minor leagues ever since and would remain there. The Yanks shipped Umphlett from Seattle of the Pacific Coast League, where he was batting .265, to Richmond of the International League.

The trade ended Billy Gardner's stay with the Yankees two days short of a year. After serving as a reserve infielder in 41 games in 1961, he had been almost invisible for the first two months of this season—four games and one at-bat.

Hal Reniff, a 23-year-old relief pitcher recently reinstated from the National Defense list, took Gardner's place on the roster. Reniff, 2-0 in 25 games as a rookie in 1961, had recently ended his military commitment.

June 26, 1962: Sold Outfielder Bob Cerv to the Houston Colt 45's

Bob Cerv's sale to Houston ended his third tour of duty with the Yankees, this last one beginning when he came from the Angels in May 1961. Cerv batted .271 in 57 games after joining the Yanks, but he was now 36, had undergone off-season knee surgery, and this season was batting just .118 in 14 games. He did a little better with the new club in Houston— .226 in 19 games, the final games of his career.

July 11, 1962: Traded Minor League Outfielder Don Lock to the Washington Senators for First Baseman Dale Long

Although Dale Long had been a valuable addition after the Yanks picked him up in August 1960, they'd let him go to the new Washington Senators in that winter's expansion draft. Long batted .249 with 17 home runs for Washington in 1961, but was criticized, along with teammates Gene Green and Willie Tasby, for not hustling by club president Pete Quesada. (The Senators had since traded Green and Tasby to Cleveland.)

Long had gotten off to a good start this season, but had recently been slumping. After 67 games, he had a .241 average and just four home runs. The 36-year-old Long would bat .298 for the Yankees in the second half of 1962 and play his final 14 games for them in 1963.

Despite a meager .194 average with Richmond of the International League, Don Lock had hit 13 home runs. The Senators, sorely in need of a power hitter, brought Lock to Washington, and he made his major league debut five days later.

September 7, 1962: Purchased Right-handed Pitcher Hal Brown from the Baltimore Orioles

With only a three-game lead on Minnesota and still 19 games to play, the Yanks added Hal Brown to give them the luxury of another veteran pitcher. Brown had been in the American League since 1951, with Chicago, Boston, and since 1956, Baltimore. He was 6-4 for the Orioles this season and became available when all the other clubs in the league waived on him. Manager Ralph Houk was pleased to have the 37-year-old Brown for the stretch drive.

"I feel Brown will definitely help us," he said. "He's a pitcher who, when I send him out on the mound in a tight spot, will know how to pitch to the batters he'll have to face. Because he's been around and has excellent control, I plan to use him either as a spot starter or the long relief man."

October 29, 1962: Sold Righthanded Pitcher Bob Turley to the Los Angeles Angels

Bob Turley had a solid 82-52 record in his eight years in New York, but he'd been slipping steadily since his peak season of 1958. Turley was 21-7 that year, while leading the American League in wins, winning percentage (.750), and complete games (19). His 1958 honors included the Cy Young Award, *The Sporting News* Player of the Year Award, and the Hickok Belt, given to the Top Professional Athlete of the Year. However, Turley had just

October 29, 1962: *Bob Turley.* **After leaving the Yankees, Turley would win just three more games.**

a 3-5 record in 1961 when elbow problems limited him to 15 games, and though he had surgery on the elbow in the off-season, 1962 wasn't much better. He was 3-3 in '62, with all three wins coming in relief.

Turley, the American League's player representative, learned of the deal in Puerto Rico, where he was pitching winter ball for the San Juan team. Despite the change of scenery, he wouldn't show much improvement. He would split the 1963 season, his final one, between the Angels, where he was 2-7, and the Red Sox, where he was 1-4.

November 26, 1962: Traded First Baseman Bill Skowron to the Los Angeles Dodgers for Righthanded Pitcher Stan Williams

Signed out of Purdue University, Bill Skowron was voted Minor League Player of the Year in 1952 as a member of the American Association Kansas City Blues. Despite the honor, the Yanks believed he needed a little more seasoning and returned him to Kansas City in 1953.

Skowron finally made it to New York in 1954 and for one season split the first base duties with veteran Joe Collins. Then, beginning in 1955, he had been the club's full-time first baseman, except for 1959 when a bad back limited him to 74 games, and he was forced to share first base with rookie Marv Throneberry.

Skowron batted better than .300 in each of his first four seasons with the Yankees and five times overall. Always a long-ball threat, he had a .294 lifetime batting average, with 165 home runs and 672 runs batted in. But he was now 32, and Joe Pepitone, ten years younger, was waiting to take over. And while manager Ralph Houk talked about a competition at first between Pepitone, 37-year-old Dale Long, and the inept-fielding Hector Lopez, the job appeared to be Pepitone's. For the Dodgers, however, Skowron's righthanded power would be an asset, although they had no thought of him replacing Ron Fairly, their current first baseman.

Stan Williams, 26, had a 57-46 won-lost record, with 43 of those wins having come in the last three seasons: 14 in both 1960 and 1962, and 15 in 1961. Williams's reaction to being traded was typical, especially for a player being traded to the Yankees. "Naturally I was disappointed to discover I was expendable. But name me a better team to wind up with than the Yankees. I know Ralph Houk and like him very much."

Houk was equally complimentary about his new acquisition: "I know enough about him to know that batters do not like to hit against him."

General manager Roy Hamey of the Yankees summed up the trade this way. "We have been looking for a starting pitcher ever since the season ended. Now we have one and have just about withdrawn from the trading market."

Hamey also added another 26-year-old righthanded pitcher by selecting Bill Kunkel from the International League Toronto Maple Leafs in the draft of minor league players. Kunkel was the first player the Yanks had chosen in this manner since they'd taken Gene Mauch back in 1951. (They'd returned Mauch the next year during spring training.) Kunkel,

3-4 for the Kansas City A's in 1961, spent most of 1962 at Toronto where he won six and lost one. He would go 3-2 for the Yanks in 1963, his final season.

April 21, 1963: Traded Righthanded Pitcher Jim Coates to the Washington Senators for Lefthanded Pitcher Steve Hamilton

A former basketball player with the then Minneapolis Lakers, six-foot seven-inch Steve Hamilton reached the majors for a two-game stay with Cleveland in 1961. The Indians traded him to Washington early in the 1962 season, and he went 3-8 for the last-place Senators, mostly in relief. Hamilton had been in three games this season, all in relief, and had lost his only decision.

Jim Coates, who at 30 was three years older than Hamilton, had never been popular with his teammates, and none seemed sorry to see him go. He'd pitched in two games for the Yanks in September 1956, and then returned to spend four full seasons with the pennant-winning clubs of 1959 through 1962, but had not yet pitched in 1963. Working as both a starter and reliever, Coates compiled an outstanding 37-15 won-lost record. Much of his success, however, could be attributed less to his ability than to his good fortune at being a member of those four pennant-winners.

Coates would split the 1963 season between Washington and Cincinnati, before spending his final three major league seasons (1965–67) with the California Angels.

April 21, 1963: Purchased First Baseman Harry Bright from the Cincinnati Reds

With the trade of Bill Skowron to the Dodgers, the Yanks had turned full-time first base duties over to second-year man Joe Pepitone. They'd acquired Harry Bright, a 33-year-old journeyman, strictly as a backup. He would serve as a righthanded pinch hitter and substitute for Pepitone against tough lefthanded pitchers.

Bright was coming off his best big league

season, a .273 batting average with 17 home runs for the 1962 Washington Senators. Traded to Cincinnati for first baseman Rogelio Alvarez in November '62, he'd played in only one game for the Reds this season.

Bright hit .236 in 60 games with New York in 1963 and would play in four games in 1964 before the Yanks released him.

April 21, 1963: Sold Righthanded Pitcher Hal Brown to the Houston Colt 45's

The sale of 38-year-old pitcher Hal Brown was the Yankees' third transaction of this busy day. They'd previously traded pitcher Jim Coates to Washington for pitcher Steve Hamilton and purchased first baseman Harry Bright from the Cincinnati Reds. Acquired in September 1962, Brown pitched in two games. He lost his only decision and had not yet been in a game this season.

November 30, 1963: Sold Lefthanded Pitcher Marshall Bridges to the Washington Senators

Yogi Berra, the Yankees' newly-named manager, had no regrets about selling Marshall Bridges, saying he planned to build his 1964 bullpen around younger men.

"Bridges did a good job for us in 1962, but he got in only 23 games last year." Berra said. "In selling him to the Senators, we made room for some younger guys and we may have him in this kid [Tom] Metcalf." (Metcalf had debuted in August 1963 and was 1-0 in eight games, but never again pitched in the major leagues.)

As Berra noted, Bridges, now 32, did do a good job in 1962, going 8-4 in 52 games and compiling a team-leading 18 saves. But he missed most of spring training in 1963, after being shot in the leg by a woman, and as Berra said, appeared in only 23 games, with just two wins and one save. Nevertheless, the two-year-old Washington franchise looked on Bridges as a welcome addition.

"I think it's a dandy deal for us," said Senators general manager George Selkirk. "Bridges

strengthens our bullpen, which lacked a good southpaw reliever. He's a willing worker and has the know-how to help us. He could be the stopper we didn't have last year."

June 12, 1964: Sold Lefthanded Pitcher Bob Meyer to the Los Angeles Angels

Rookie pitcher Bob Meyer was 0-3 with a 4.91 earned run average in seven games this season. After selling him, the Yanks recalled Rollie Sheldon, who was 4-2 with a 1.81 ERA for the International League Syracuse Chiefs, to take Meyer's spot on the roster.

September 5, 1964: Traded Two Players to Be Named and Cash to the Cleveland Indians for Righthanded Pitcher Pedro Ramos

With less than a month left in the season, the Yankees were in a three-way race for the pennant with the Chicago White Sox and the Baltimore Orioles. They were currently in third place, but trailed the league-leading White Sox by only three games. Attempting to strengthen themselves for the stretch drive, the Yanks planned to use newly-acquired Pedro Ramos in short relief, even though Ramos had been mostly a starter and long reliever during his big league career.

Pitching for mostly second-division teams, Ramos had a less-than-impressive 104-142 won-lost record for ten seasons, seven with the Washington Senators/Minnesota Twins and the last three with Cleveland. Yet, he'd been a workhorse throughout his career and had once led the American League in losses for four consecutive seasons (1958–61). He'd been in 36 games for the Indians this season, 19 of them as a starter, and had a 7-10 record and a 5.14 earned run average.

Because this was a waiver deal, the three clubs between Cleveland and New York had to pass on Ramos, something that neither first-place Chicago nor second-place Baltimore would likely have done had the Yanks been ahead of them.

Yankee GM Ralph Houk would not answer questions about the identity of the two

September 5, 1964: *Pedro Ramos.* **Ramos's eight saves in September would help the Yanks win the 1964 pennant.**

players the Indians would get for Ramos, nor when they would get them. "I can just say that the players to be delivered are an important part of the deal," Houk said. "It may be after the season, but not necessarily."

It would be after the season, and the players were important. Righthander Ralph Terry went to Cleveland on October 12, and lefthander Bud Daley went on November 27. Since returning to the Yankees in 1959, Terry had become one of the league's best pitchers. He'd put together 16-3, 23-12, and 17-15 seasons in 1961–63, leading the league in wins in 1962 and in complete games (18) in 1963. But Terry had been much less effective in 1964, winning just seven times and posting a 4.54 earned run average.

Daley was 18-16 in four seasons with the Yankees; however, because of arm troubles he'd been in only 14 games over the past two seasons and would never pitch again.

March 30, 1965: Sold Righthanded Pitcher Stan Williams to the Cleveland Indians

The Yanks denied suggestions that they'd sent Stan Williams to Cleveland as extra payment for their getting Pedro Ramos from the Indians in September 1964. They said that only Ralph Terry, who went to the Indians in October, and Bud Daley, who went in November, were the agreed upon "players to be named" in that deal.

Williams was 9-8 as the Yanks' fifth starter in 1963, his first season in New York, but tailed off badly in 1964, going 1-5 and spending much of the season in the bullpen. After a few seasons in Cleveland, Williams would go to Minnesota, where his ten relief wins helped the 1970 Twins capture the Western Division title.

May 3, 1965: Traded Catcher John Blanchard and Righthanded Pitcher Roland Sheldon to the Kansas City Athletics for Catcher Doc Edwards

Shortly after GM Ralph Houk announced that catcher Elston Howard was undergoing surgery on his right elbow, he turned to the Yankees' favorite trading partner for a replacement. (Actually, it was the first deal between the Yanks and Kansas City since June 14, 1961.) Howard, who injured the elbow in a spring training game against the Senators in Puerto Rico, had not caught since Opening Day, and the Yanks expected he would be unable to play for another month and a half.

"The deal had been discussed earlier," Houk said, "but when I got the word on Ellie, I started pushing it."

The Yanks were aware that Doc Edwards was a weak hitter (.224 in 1964), but it was his defensive ability they coveted. He was a much better receiver than John Blanchard, who after his terrific .305 batting average, 21 home run season in 1961 hadn't been a very productive hitter either. In 12 games this season, the 32-year old Blanchard was batting .147. He didn't hit for the Athletics either, or for the Braves, for whom he played his final ten games later in the season.

Rollie Sheldon was 11-5 as a 24-year-old rookie in 1961, and 23-15 overall with the Yankees, but Yankee manager Johnny Keane had used him in just three games this season, all as a mop-up man.

May 10, 1965: Traded Infielder Pedro Gonzalez to the Cleveland Indians for First Baseman Ray Barker

Just as an injury to catcher Elston Howard had prompted a trade for Doc Edwards a week earlier, an injury to right fielder Roger Maris prompted this one for Ray Barker. Manager Johnny Keane said that Barker, a 29-year-old lefthanded hitter, would take over at first base against righthanded pitchers, allowing first baseman Joe Pepitone to move to right field.

Barker had shown early promise when he hit 23 home runs for Portland of the Pacific Coast League in 1960. And as Keane, who'd seen him play in winter ball, said, "He's got good power." Nevertheless, Barker was a ten-year minor leaguer who was hitless in 12 major league at-bats, six with the 1960 Orioles and six with the Indians this year. He arrived during the Yankees' 3-2 loss at Fenway Park and was issued Pedro Gonzalez's old uniform number, 42.

Back in 1963, Gonzalez had won the James P. Dawson Award as the club's outstanding rookie in training camp, but played only 14 games that year. He did much better in 1964, playing 80 games at first, second, third, and the outfield, and batting .277. Gonzalez had two hits in five at-bats this season.

November 29, 1965: Traded Infielder Phil Linz to the Philadelphia Phillies for Infielder Ruben Amaro

While both Phil Linz and Reuben Amaro were weak hitters, each was valued for his abil-

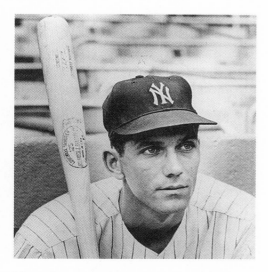

November 29, 1965: *Phil Linz.* **Linz's batting average had declined in each of his four seasons with the Yankees.**

ity to play several positions. For the Yanks, however, there was one critical difference: of the two, Amaro was the better shortstop. That was important because of the uncertain status of Tony Kubek, the Yankees' regular shortstop for the last seven years. Back and neck injuries had slowed Kubek the last two seasons, and the Mayo Clinic had advised rest saying they would re-evaluate his condition in February 1966. Yankee general manager Ralph Houk and manager Johnny Keane were taking no chances. They wanted a shortstop "in place" if Kubek were unable to play and planned to use Amaro there until 19-year-old Bobby Murcer was ready to take over the position. Keane was familiar with Amaro, having been a manager in the St. Louis organization when Amaro broke in with the Cardinals in 1958.

"Amaro has one of the finer gloves in the game," Keane said. "We think highly of Linz," he added, "but we just don't think he could fill the shortstop position for a full season."

Meanwhile, Philadelphia manager Gene Mauch said that he was set at shortstop with Dick Groat and Bobby Wine and didn't need Amaro. As for Linz, Mauch said that he'd never seen him "play anything but fine baseball."

Linz had spent four seasons with the Yankees and had seen his batting average decline each year. It had gone from a .287 as a rookie in 1962, to .269 in 1963, to 250 in 1964, and to a meager .207 in 1965.

Although Kubek was only 29, on the advice of his doctors he retired from playing. Amaro was the Yankees' opening-day shortstop in 1966, but was injured in a collision with outfielder Tom Tresh in the season's first week. He played only 14 games in '66, while Clete Boyer and Horace Clarke split the shortstop duties.

December 10, 1965: Traded Right-handed Pitcher Pete Mikkelsen and Cash to the Pittsburgh Pirates for Righthanded Pitcher Bob Friend

Bob Friend, a former National League player representative, had been a steady, solid pitcher for many years and also one of the most respected players in the game. Friend had spent his entire major league career with the Pittsburgh Pirates; nevertheless, he was overjoyed at the news he was going to the Yankees.

"After 16 years in the major leagues, it's a thrill to become associated with a name like the Yankees, and all it means. I've always kept in good shape, and I believe I have at least two or three good years left as a starter." In discussing his 8-12 record in 1965, Friend said, "But I pitched a lot better than my record. I developed a new pitch, a slider, and I feel I have command of it now."

Yankee GM Ralph Houk was glad to have a pitcher like Friend on the club. "We feel this is a distinct plus for us," Houk said. "We've acquired an experienced starter who can give us insurance for the uncertainties concerning some of our other pitchers, like Jim Bouton. He's never had a sore arm, and all our reports on him have been excellent."

Manager Johnny Keane was also delighted at the news of the trade. "I think of him strictly as a starter, and a good one," said Keane, whose tenure would last only 20 games into the 1966 season.

At 26, Pete Mikkelsen was nine years younger than Friend, but he was a relief pitcher and the Yankees were looking to bolster their starting staff. As a rookie in 1964, Mikkelsen relieved in 50 games, with a 7-4 record and 12 saves. He slipped to 4-9 in 1965, with only one save; he also made three starts and lost them all.

Mikkelsen would pitch in the National League for the next seven years and finish with a lifetime 45-40 record, but he would never make another start.

January 14, 1966: Traded Catcher Doc Edwards to the Cleveland Indians for Outfielder Lu Clinton

The Yankees had spent the entire off-season looking for a righthanded power hitter to add to their lineup. They had talked to Cincinnati about Frank Robinson (since traded to Baltimore) and to San Francisco about Orlando Cepeda, but couldn't consummate either deal.

They finally snagged Lu Clinton, who had shown flashes of power in the past, hitting 18 home runs for the Red Sox in 1962 and 22

in 1963. His production had dropped considerably the past two seasons, while playing for the Angels, the Royals (one game), and the Indians. He played for all three of those teams in 1965, batting .233 with just two home runs. Clearly not the equal of either Robinson or Cepeda, he figured to be strictly a pinch hitter and spot starter.

Clinton would bat .220 in 80 games for the 1966 Yankees, and then have his final four at-bats in 1967.

Edwards's stay in New York had been a short one. The Yanks got him in May 1965 to fill in for Elston Howard after Howard's elbow surgery. In 45 games he batted .190 with one home run. Edwards would play only one more season in the majors, and that wouldn't be until 1970 with the Phillies.

May 3, 1966: Purchased Lefthanded Pitcher Alan Closter from the Washington Senators

The Cleveland Indians paid $8,000 to draft Closter from the Yankee organization in November 1965. Then, just before the start of the 1966 season, they sold him on waivers to Washington. He'd pitched one game for the Senators, working one-third of an inning. Now Closter was returning to the Yankees who promptly shipped him off to Greensboro of the Carolina League.

May 11, 1966: Purchased Shortstop Dick Schofield from the San Francisco Giants

For a reported $25,000, the Yanks got Dick Schofield, a switch-hitting veteran who could play capably at second, short, and third. Schofield, who reached the majors with the St. Louis Cardinals as an 18-year-old bonus boy in 1953, had been a utility player for the first ten years of his career. However, he did eventually become the regular shortstop for the Pittsburgh Pirates in 1963 and 1964, and also for the San Francisco Giants after being traded there early in the 1965 season.

To make room for Schofield, manager Ralph Houk optioned rookie righthander Jack Cullen to the Toledo Mud Hens of the International League. Cullen was in two games with no record in 1962, 3-4 in 1965, and 1-0 in five games this season. Houk said of him, "He wasn't bad and he wasn't great, but I'm sure he has a major league future." He didn't. In April 1967, the Yanks traded him to the Dodgers, but Cullen never again pitched in the major leagues.

June 10, 1966: Traded Righthanded Pitcher Bill Stafford, Lefthanded Pitcher Gil Blanco, and Outfielder Roger Repoz to the Kansas City Athletics for Righthanded Pitcher Fred Talbot and Catcher Billy Bryan

The Yankees had gotten off to a terrible start under manager Johnny Keane, winning only four of their first 24 games. On May 7, Ralph Houk fired Keane and stepped down

from his general manager's role to return to the dugout. Since then the team had compiled a 16-12 record and jumped three places in the standings, from tenth place to seventh. This was Houk's first trade since beginning his second tour as manager, and he accomplished it via a telephone conversation with A's owner Charles Finley.

With longtime Yankee ace Whitey Ford on the disabled list with elbow problems, and with Jim Bouton having a sore arm, the Yanks were short of pitching and Fred Talbot was a needed addition. Talbot, a ten-game winner for Kansas City in 1965, and a pitcher who Houk claimed "everyone's been after," was 4-4 for the Athletics this season.

"He gives us a pretty good pitching staff," Houk added. "Mel Stottlemyre is twenty-four, Al Downing is twenty-four, Fritz Peterson is twenty-four, and Talbot is twenty-four. And if Ford and Bouton come back, as we expect, we've got a solid staff."

June 10, 1966: *Whitey Ford, Luis Arroyo, Ralph Terry,* and *Bill Stafford.* **Bill Stafford (right) in 1962, the second consecutive year he'd won 14 games.**

The Yanks expected Talbot to join the club in time to pitch one game of the next day's doubleheader against Detroit, replacing Bill Stafford. Houk had originally scheduled Stafford to pitch after recalling him from Toledo of the International League, where he had a 5-2 record. Always injury-prone, Stafford had been a Yankee since 1960, reaching his peak with back-to-back 14-9 seasons in 1961 and 1962.

Houk acknowledged that the club "hated to lose a promising young pitcher like [Gil] Blanco," who'd split a pair of decisions as a 19 year old with the Yanks in 1965. This season he was 3-1 with Columbus of the Southern League, but after going 2-4 with the A's never returned to the majors.

Some in the Yankee organization thought the bigger loss was outfielder Roger Repoz, whom they expected to be the successor to Mickey Mantle. The 25-year-old slugger had hit 12 home runs in 79 games in 1965 and was batting .349 in 43 at-bats this season. Repoz would hit just .216 in 101 games for the Athletics, and though he would show occasional power in his nine-year career (mostly with the Angels) he would finish with a lifetime batting average of just .224.

Billy Bryan had been with the A's since 1961. He had his best season in 1965, when he hit .252 with 14 home runs, but was at .132 after 32 games this season. Bryan would bat .210 in 81 at-bats for the Yankees in 1966 and 1967 while serving as a backup catcher and first baseman, and as a lefthanded pinch hitter.

June 15, 1966: Sold Righthanded Pitcher Bob Friend to the New York Mets

The New York Mets had been around since 1962, but their $20,000 waiver purchase of Bob Friend from the Yankees constituted the first deal ever between the two clubs. In going to the Mets, Friend was joining the club against whom he had enjoyed his greatest success during his years with Pittsburgh. In the Mets' first four years of existence, between 1962 and 1965, he'd compiled a 14-2 record against them.

Friend, who had failed to live up to expectations with the Yanks, winning just one

game while losing four, would go 5-8 for the Mets to end his career with 197 wins and 230 losses.

September 10, 1966: Traded Shortstop Dick Schofield to the Los Angeles Dodgers for Minor League Right-handed Pitcher Thad Tillotson and Cash

The Yanks had purchased veteran Dick Schofield from the Giants in May, but now that they were on their way to a tenth-place finish, they had no use for a .155-hitting utility infielder. Meanwhile, Schofield's new team, the Dodgers, were in a fight for the National League pennant with those same Giants and wanted Schofield as insurance should shortstop Maury Wills's troublesome right knee keep him from playing.

Dodger manager Walter Alston would use Schofield mostly at third base in the season's remaining weeks. Schofield batted .257 for the pennant-winning Dodgers and then stayed around the major leagues with various teams for another five years.

Pitcher Thad Tillotson went from the Spokane Indians, the Dodgers club in the Pacific Coast League, to the Toledo Mud Hens, the Yankees club in the International League. He reached New York in 1967, going 3-9 that year and 1-0 the next.

November 29, 1966: Traded Third Baseman Clete Boyer to the Atlanta Braves for Outfielder Bill Robinson and Righthanded Pitcher Chi Chi Olivo

In 1966 the Yankees finished in last place for the first time since 1912. Now, they had a new owner, the Columbia Broadcasting System, a new president, Michael Burke, and a new general manager, Lee MacPhail. The club obviously needed help at many positions, but MacPhail's top priority was finding a right-handed power hitter. He'd been unsuccessful in getting an established major leaguer and so opted for 23-year-old Bill Robinson, a player whom both the Yanks and Braves agreed was an outstanding prospect. Playing for the Richmond Braves this past season, he'd hit .312, with 20 home runs and 79 runs batted in, and finished second to Rochester's Mike Epstein in voting for the International League's Most Valuable Player Award. The addition of Robinson, primarily a right fielder, heightened speculation that the Yankees would trade Roger Maris, who had talked of retiring.

The Yanks were also actively pursuing a shortstop, a position that Clete Boyer, normally a third baseman, and Horace Clarke had shared in 1966. Now, with Boyer traded, the Yanks had holes at both short and third. They were hoping that rookie Bobby Murcer could fill one of those positions, more likely third, although outfielder Tom Tresh had been Boyer's replacement there in '66. For a shortstop, MacPhail was actively pursuing Los Angeles's Maury Wills, even though the Dodgers had said that they wouldn't trade Wills unless they got a shortstop in return. However, with the retirement of Sandy Koufax, the Dodgers would also need pitching, so MacPhail was reportedly offering Jim Bouton or Al Downing for Wills.

Boyer had been a Yankee since 1959, but didn't become the team's regular third baseman until Ralph Houk replaced Casey Stengel as manager in 1961. A so-so hitter with occasional power, Boyer batted .241 with 95 home runs in more than 1,000 games as a Yankee. More noted for his glove than his bat, he was among the finest fielding third basemen ever. Boyer would had several fine seasons in Atlanta before ending his big league career in 1971.

As a result of the trade, Chi Chi Olivo, 5-4 for the Braves in 1966, went from Atlanta's International League team at Richmond, to New York's at Syracuse. But he was at least 39 years old, and his four-year major league career was over.

December 8, 1966: Traded Outfielder Roger Maris to the St. Louis Cardinals for Third Baseman Charley Smith

Five years after he broke Babe Ruth's single-season home run record, the Yanks traded Roger Maris for a journeyman infielder. The

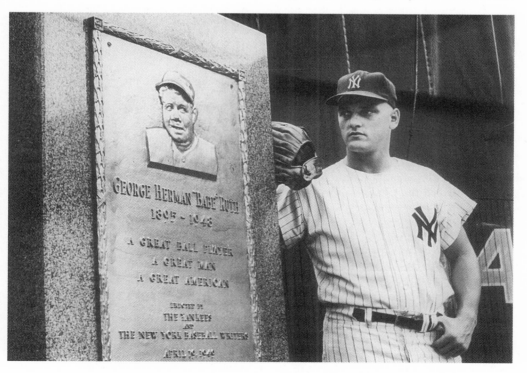

December 8, 1966: *Roger Maris.* **Maris in happier days.**

recent trade of Clete Boyer to Atlanta had left a hole at third base, a hole that Yankee general manager Lee MacPhail used to justify the trade. Charley Smith, a .266-hitter for St. Louis in 1966, had played for five different clubs in his six major league seasons. He was three years younger than Maris, made only $20,000 a year, and would be tried at Boyer's old job.

"We are committed to making a fresh start with young players," said MacPhail. "I think Maris can have three or four more good years, and we hope he does. There doesn't seem to be anything wrong with him physically. But if our new men are going to play, we've got to make room for them. Smith gives us an experienced third baseman. He'll still have to beat out the kids [rookies Bobby Murcer and Mike Ferraro] to get the job, but at least we know he can do it."

In his first two seasons with the Yankees, 1960 and 1961, Maris won back-to-back Most Valuable Player Awards. He had 39 home runs and a league-leading 112 RBIs in '60, and the record-breaking 61 home runs and a league-leading 142 RBIs in '61. Nevertheless, after sportswriters and fans compared him unfavorably both to Ruth and to his more popular teammate, Mickey Mantle, Maris grew increasingly unhappy in New York. Furthermore, because of injuries, he'd started fewer than half the team's games the last two years. For these reasons, the Yanks had been anxious to trade Maris, but his age (32), high salary ($72,000), and recent history of injuries made other clubs reluctant to give up much for him.

MacPhail would prove almost prophetic when he said, "I think Maris can have three or four more good years." Maris would have had two good seasons in St. Louis, seasons in which he helped the Cardinals win consecutive National League pennants.

December 10, 1966: Traded Right-handed Pitcher Pedro Ramos to the Philadelphia Phillies for Righthanded Pitcher Joe Verbanic and Cash

Attempting to rebound from their first last-place finish since 1912, the Yankees, under new GM Lee MacPhail, made their third trade in 11 days. Like the others, Clete Boyer to Atlanta and Roger Maris to St. Louis, the trade

of 31-year-old Pedro Ramos involved giving up age for youth.

"Things are going to be different around here next year, even if I have to go with kids," said manager Ralph Houk. "I'm tired of the attitude of some of the veterans, and changes will be made," he added, "I want a hustling, hungry club next year and will make changes to get it."

Ramos came to the Yanks from Cleveland in September 1964, with the club in a fierce three-way scramble with Baltimore and Chicago for the American League pennant. He'd been primarily a starter during his ten-year big league career, but manager Yogi Berra turned him into a reliever, with excellent results. In 13 games, Ramos had a win, eight saves, and a 1.25 earned run average. After Johnny Keane replaced Berra in 1965, he too used Ramos strictly out of the bullpen, again with great success. Ramos appeared in 65 games, splitting ten decisions, but leading the club with 19 saves.

When Houk stepped down from his role as general manager to replace Keane in May 1966, he continued to use Ramos in relief. But Ramos's effectiveness declined in '66; his record was 3-9, his saves dropped to 13, and his ERA, 2.92 the year before, was up to 3.61. More important, Houk felt that Ramos was overweight and had lost his competitive desire, and he wanted him gone.

The Yanks had offered Ramos to other clubs, but those clubs had offered even less in return than what they were getting from the Phillies. Joe Verbanic had at least pitched in the big leagues. The Phillies had called him up in July 1966, after he had gone 8-1 with a 2.67 earned run average with San Diego of the Pacific Coast League. He got into 17 games, winning one and losing one. A relief pitcher for most of his career, Verbanic was expected to join Hal Reniff and Dooley Womack as Yankee relievers in 1967.

Verbanic would begin the 1967 season with Syracuse of the International League, but the Yanks brought him up on May 30 to replace Whitey Ford, whose circulation problems had forced him to retire. Ford, with a magnificent 236-106 won-lost record, was the Yankees' all-time winningest pitcher. Over the course of his 16 seasons, beginning in 1950 (he was in the military in 1951-52), he'd led the

American League in wins and winning percentage three times, and in earned run average twice.

Verbanic would pitch three seasons for the Yankees (1967, 1968, and 1970), mostly in relief. In 92 games, he won 11, lost 10, and had six saves.

December 20, 1966: Traded Minor League Righthanded Pitcher Gil Downs and Cash to the Cleveland Indians for Shortstop Dick Howser

In getting Dick Howser, general manager Lee MacPhail completed his fourth trade in three weeks. Howser, who was now 30, had never duplicated the success he'd had as a rookie for the 1960 Kansas City Athletics, when he batted .280 and stole 37 bases. He not only made the American League All-Star team that year, the Athletics named him captain, a rare honor for a rookie. Injuries limited his playing time in 1961 and 1962, and in May 1963 the A's traded him to Cleveland.

Howser was the Indians' regular shortstop in 1964, but had been primarily a utility player the last two seasons. The Yanks expected him to fill a similar role in 1967, playing behind Horace Clarke and Ruben Amaro. Clarke was the likely replacement at second base for the retired Bobby Richardson, and Amaro the likely shortstop. That's how it turned out, with Howser serving as an auxiliary at second, short, and third in both 1967 and in his final year, 1968.

Gil Downs had been a Yankee farmhand since they drafted him out of the White Sox organization in 1963. Cleveland assigned him to their Portland club in the Pacific Coast League, but Downs would never reach the major leagues.

April 3, 1967: Traded Righthanded Pitcher Jack Cullen and Outfielder John Miller to the Los Angeles Dodgers for Infielder John Kennedy

With the exhibition season nearing its end, manager Ralph Houk had been disappointed with the mobility afield of both his shortstops, Ruben Amaro and Dick Howser. Houk felt that Amaro did not have the range he'd had before his 1966 knee operation, and that Howser, the backup, just lacked the physical skills to play the position. So although 25-year-old John Kennedy had played mostly at third base in his five-year career with the Senators and the Dodgers, Houk planned to use him at shortstop.

"We need a glove at shortstop," Houk said. "He's not supposed to be much of a hitter, but if he can field, he'll help us."

General manager Lee MacPhail acknowledged that Kennedy was indeed a weak hitter—.201 in 1966 and .171 the year before for Los Angeles—but said: "We felt that we had to do something."

Pitcher Jack Cullen and outfielder John Miller were Yankee farmhands, each of whom had made brief appearances with the club. Cullen had a 4-4 record in 19 games spread over three years (1962, 1965, and 1966), while Miller batted .087 in six games in 1966. The Dodgers sent them both to their Pacific Coast League team at Spokane.

The Yanks also sent outfielder–second baseman Roy White to the Dodgers' Spokane club, but that was on option. White had a disappointing rookie season in 1966 after he'd batted .333 in 14 late-season games in 1965. He would return to the Yanks later in the 1967 season.

May 31, 1967: Signed Righthanded Pitcher Bill Monbouquette as a Free Agent

The Yanks signed Bill Monbouquette to replace Jim Bouton, whom they'd sent to Syracuse of the International League. Bouton had been ineffective and manager Ralph Houk thought the stay in Syracuse would help. "Bouton needs a chance to work regularly," he said.

A 20-game winner for Boston in 1963, Monbouquette spent eight years with the Red Sox before they traded him to the Tigers in October 1965. He went 7-8 for Detroit in 1966 and had been decisionless in two games this season when they released him on May 15.

June 28, 1967: Sold Righthanded Pitcher Hal Reniff to the New York Mets

Hal Reniff was in his seventh, and final, major league season. He'd appeared in 247 games as a Yankee, all in relief, winning 18, losing 20, and saving 41. Twice he'd led the club in games pitched, and in 1963, when the pennant-winning Yanks totaled 31 saves, Reniff had 18 of them.

To make room for Reniff, the Mets returned rookie righthander Bill Denehy (1-7) to the Jacksonville Suns of the International League.

July 4, 1967: Traded First Baseman Ray Barker, Cash, and Two Players to Be Named to the Baltimore Orioles for Lefthanded Pitcher Steve Barber

Steve Barber had been a big league pitcher, and a good one, since 1960. Still only 28 years old, he had a lifetime record of 95-65, including a 20-win season in 1963. His record against the Yankees was 15-10, and Mickey Mantle said that Barber and Herb Score were the two lefthanders he had least liked batting against.

However, Barber had elbow problems, which had forced him to go on the disabled list twice in 1966 and to miss taking part in the Orioles' first World Series appearance. He was 4-9 this season, but had combined with Stu Miller to pitch a no-hitter against the Tigers in May, a game the Orioles lost.

Barber said, "I'm really happy to be with the Yankees." He also assured everyone that his "arm feels better than it has in four or five years."

Barber would go 6-9 for the Yanks in the remaining months of 1967 and then 6-5 in 1968. The club made him available for the expansion draft following the '68 season, and the Seattle Pilots selected him.

Ray Barker came from Cleveland in May 1965 and played in 159 games over the next two seasons. He was currently with Syracuse of the International League, after batting .077 in 17 games for the Yanks earlier in the season. Baltimore transferred Barker from Syracuse to their Rochester club in the same league.

On December 15, 1967, the Orioles got the two players to be named—minor league infielders Chet Trail and Joe Brady.

August 3, 1967: Traded Catcher Elston Howard to the Boston Red Sox for Cash and Two Players to Be Named

Elston Howard admitted that he was "shocked" when manager Ralph Houk called him at home with the news that the Yankees had traded him to Boston. His immediate reaction, he said, was one of betrayal, and he seriously considered retiring. "I've been here all my life and I always felt I would finish my career as a Yankee," he said.

Howard decided not to retire after speaking with Red Sox owner Tom Yawkey and manager Dick Williams, both of whom called to make their case for his joining the Boston club. The Red Sox were two games behind Chicago in a furious scramble for the American League pennant, and both Yawkey and

August 3, 1967: *Elston Howard.* **Red Sox owner Tom Yawkey and manager Dick Williams convinced Howard not to retire.**

Williams told Howard how much they wanted and needed his experience and leadership.

Additionally, many of Howard's friends and teammates reminded him of how fortunate he was in going from the feeble Yankees to a pennant contender. Broadcaster Phil Rizzuto, referring to his own abrupt dismissal 11 years earlier, said: "I know how bad you feel Ellie, but you're much better off than I was. You're going to a contender, and they really want you. I was just dropped."

The Yankees tried to ease the blow by suggesting that they would like Howard back with them after his playing career ended. Having been their first black player, he was a strong candidate to be their first black coach, and some thought baseball's first black manager.

"Ellie has been through the pennant battles before and his experience should prove invaluable to Boston," said Yankee president Michael Burke. "We hope he will talk with us about his future when his playing career is over."

General manager Lee MacPhail felt the same. "Although it's not proper to discuss it while he's in another club's employ," MacPhail said, "we'll be most happy to talk to Ellie at the end of his playing career about his own future if he decides to stay in baseball."

It was MacPhail who had instructed Houk to make the call to Howard to inform him that he was no longer a Yankee. "It was as tough a thing as I've ever had to do," Houk said. "When we got to the ball park later, we had another long talk, but I could see how bad he felt. And I feel bad."

Along with the retirement two months earlier of Whitey Ford, his longtime batterymate, Howard's departure was a further indication that the great New York dynasty of the 1950s and early 1960s was over. Only Mickey Mantle remained from the Yankee team that Howard joined in 1955, and he would retire following the 1968 season.

A nine-time All Star, Howard left with a .279 career batting average, 161 home runs and 733 runs batted in. He was the American League's Most Valuable Player in 1963, although his most productive season may have come two years earlier. Howard batted a career-high .348, but he was overshadowed by teammates Mantle and Roger Maris on that great 1961 Yankee team.

Howard was now 38 and had been slowed by injuries in recent seasons. He'd batted only 199 times in 1967, with a .196 average and just three home runs. Nevertheless, in making this deal the Red Sox were doing what contending teams have always done. They were picking up a veteran from a non-contending team late in the season in exchange for money or prospects. The Yankees had done it successfully for years, but now they were on the other end.

The two players the Yanks received were both righthanded pitchers: 23-year-old Ron Klimkowski and 25-year-old Pete Magrini. Klimkowski, who had no big league experience, was 7-4 with Pittsfield of the Eastern League, while Magrini, currently with Toronto of the International League, had one decision, a loss, for the 1966 Red Sox. Klimkowski would reach the Yankees in 1969, while Magrini never made it back to the big leagues.

Howard would bat just .147 in 42 games for Boston down the stretch, although his steady play behind the plate helped the Red Sox win the pennant. He retired after batting .241 in 71 games in 1968, and then returned to the Yankees as a coach in 1969. Howard remained with the Yanks as a coach and executive until his premature death on December 14, 1980.

August 8, 1967: Purchased Catcher Bob Tillman from the Boston Red Sox

Having traded Elston Howard to the Red Sox five days earlier, the Yanks were left without a backup to catcher Jake Gibbs. They filled the vacancy by buying Boston's Bob Tillman for the $20,000 waiver price. The Yanks denied that the Tillman purchase was part of the Howard deal, claiming that his acquisition was "a result, but not part of" that deal.

Tillman had been with Boston since 1962 and had been their number one receiver between 1963 and 1965. However, he'd been in only 30 games this season, with a .188 batting average.

September 18, 1967: Traded Lefthanded Pitcher Bill Henry to the Cincinnati Reds for Second Baseman Len Boehmer

This "trade" actually consisted of two separate purchases. Syracuse, the Yankees' affiliate in the International League, sold pitcher Bill Henry to the Reds and bought second baseman Len Boehmer from them. Henry who was 8-7 for Syracuse in 1967, had pitched in two games without a decision for the Yanks in 1966. Those two games would be his only big league appearances.

Boehmer got into two games for Cincinnati in 1967, but spent most of the season with Buffalo of the International League, where he hit only .238. He would play a total of 48 games for the Yankees (45 in 1969 and three in 1971), batting a combined .168.

November 30, 1967: Purchased Shortstop Gene Michael from the Los Angeles Dodgers

Baltimore's Luis Aparicio was the shortstop the Yankees wanted, but Aparicio's original team, the White Sox, outbid them. Instead, for a reported $30,000, they settled for Gene Michael, a 29-year-old journeyman with two years of major league experience. After part-time service with Pittsburgh in 1966, the Pirates traded Michael to Los Angeles in the deal that brought Maury Wills to Pittsburgh. Along with Dick Schofield, Michael served as Wills's replacement in 1967, batting a measly .202 with no home runs in 98 games for the Dodgers.

Although never much of a hitter—his lifetime average was just .229—Michael would spend seven years with the Yankees, five of them (1969-1973) as the club's regular shortstop. The Yanks released him in January 1975, and he spent his last active season with the Tigers.

December 7, 1967: Traded Catcher Bob Tillman and Lefthanded Pitcher Dale Roberts to the Atlanta Braves for Minor League Third Baseman Bobby Cox

Unhappy with the 1967 performance of Charley Smith (.224 in 135 games), the Yanks were looking for a new third baseman for 1968. After trying unsuccessfully to trade for a major leaguer to fill the position, they went after the best minor league third baseman available. He,

they determined, was 26-year-old Bobby Cox, who had spent seven years in the minors, mostly in the Dodger organization.

Cox was coming off an excellent 1967 season with the Richmond Braves of the International League. He'd batted .297, with 14 home runs, yet was unlikely to win the job in Atlanta. The Braves had Clete Boyer at third, and the former Yankee had pounded out 26 home runs in his first National League season.

Cox would be the Yanks' regular third baseman in 1968, but his batting was almost identical to Smith's (.229 in 135 games). After serving as a utility player in 1969, the Yanks sent him back to the minors and released him in September 1970.

Bob Tillman caught and pinch hit in 22 games for the Yanks, with a .254 average, after coming from Boston in August 1967. He would spend three seasons sharing the catching duties in Atlanta.

The two innings (in two games) that Dale Roberts worked for the Yanks in September 1967 (after going 9-4 at Syracuse) would be his only big league action.

May 17, 1968: Purchased Righthanded Pitcher John Wyatt from the Boston Red Sox

John Wyatt was a 33-year-old career relief pitcher who broke into the big leagues with the 1961 Kansas City Athletics. In 1964, he led the major leagues with 81 games pitched, but in June 1966, Kansas City traded him to Boston.

Wyatt had a career record of 41-41, including a win and two losses this season; the win had come against the Yankees a few nights earlier. By adding Wyatt, the Yanks went one man over the player limit, which they rectified by putting sore-shouldered pitcher Al Downing on the 21-day disabled list.

June 14, 1968: Sold First Baseman Mike Hegan to the Seattle Pilots

The American League had granted Seattle and Kansas City expansion franchises, but they wouldn't begin play until 1969. So Mike

Hegan, who was currently with Syracuse of the International League, would remain there the entire 1968 season. Hegan had played parts of three seasons with the Yanks (1964, 1966, and 1967), batting .148 in 86 games.

June 15, 1968: Sold Righthanded Pitcher John Wyatt to the Detroit Tigers

A month earlier, when the Yanks bought John Wyatt from Boston, they made room for him by placing Al Downing on the 21-day disabled list. Now with Downing scheduled to come off the DL, they no longer had any need for Wyatt, who'd gone 0-2 in seven games as a Yankee.

Wyatt would do much better in Detroit. Coming out of the bullpen in 22 games, he won his only decision and had a 2.40 earned run average for the pennant-winning Tigers.

The Yanks further reduced their pitching staff by selling Jim Bouton to the newly-born Seattle Pilots. The Pilots, who wouldn't begin play until 1969, sent Bouton to the Seattle Angels of the Pacific Coast League. The Angels were a farm team of the California Angels, but they also included some players the Pilots had signed for the future.

The sale to Seattle ended the 29-year-old Bouton's often controversial eight-year Yankee career. After winning 21 games in 1963 and 18 in 1964, Bouton fell to 4-15 in 1965 and had a total of just five victories since. In 12 games this season, Bouton was 1-1 with a 3.68 ERA.

Not surprisingly, Bouton did not agree with the Yankees' decision to let him go. "If we had a staff of Koosmans and Seavers," he said referring to Mets aces Jerry Koosman and Tom Seaver, "I might see how Bouton would be expendable. But we don't. If I were the low man on the totem pole, I still might see it," he continued. "But I'm not. I felt I was ahead of two or three other guys on the staff and if they were 22-year-old phenoms I still might see it. But they're not."

July 12, 1968: Traded Righthanded Pitcher Bill Monbouquette to the

San Francisco Giants for Righthanded Pitcher Lindy McDaniel

With his team trying to catch the first-place Cardinals, Giants manager Herman Franks was seeking a pitcher he could use both as a starter and a long reliever. That was precisely the role Yankee manager Ralph Houk had been using Bill Monbouquette in since signing him as a free agent in May 1967. Over the two partial seasons he'd been a Yankee, the 31-year-old Monbouquette had pitched in 50 games (21 as starter), winning 11 and losing 12.

At one time, Lindy McDaniel, now 32, had been among the game's best late-inning relievers. McDaniel was the National League saves leader with the Cardinals in 1959 and 1960 and with the Cubs in 1963. But he had only two in 1965, his last year in Chicago, and a total of just nine since coming to St. Louis in 1966. This season, McDaniel had been largely ineffective, with an earned run average of 7.45 in 12 games.

July 15, 1968: Signed Outfielder Rocky Colavito as a Free Agent

Now in the last months of what had been a glorious 14-year career, Bronx-born Rocky Colavito finally fulfilled his boyhood wish to play for the Yankees. The Yanks signed the soon-to-be 35-year-old slugger a few days after the Los Angeles Dodgers released him. A pinch hitter and part time outfielder, Colavito was batting .204 with three home runs for the Dodgers.

As an American Leaguer between 1955 and 1967, mostly for Cleveland and Detroit, Colavito had smashed a total of 366 home runs. He'd also been involved in one of the most controversial trades of recent times. Just prior to the start of the 1960 season, after he'd hit a league-leading 42 home runs for the Indians in 1959, Cleveland sent him to the Tigers for 1959 batting champion Harvey Kuenn. Colavito had also played for the Kansas City A's, the Indians again, and the White Sox. To make room for him, the Yanks sent sore-armed pitcher Al Downing to Binghamton of the Eastern league.

Ralph Houk said he planned to use his new acquisition in much the same way the

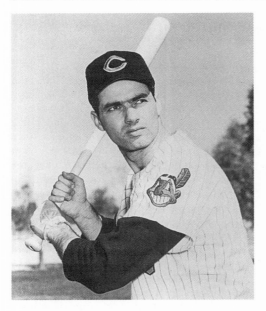

July 15, 1968: *Rocky Colavito*. **Colavito hit the last five of his 374 career home runs in a Yankee uniform.**

Dodgers had. "He gives us another right-handed bat," the Yankee manager said. "We still have a good shot at the first division, and Rocky can hit one out for us occasionally. He also told me he can pitch in relief if I need him."

As it turned out, Colavito not only pitched in a game for the Yankees against the Tigers on August 25, he was the winning pitcher. As a batter, he hit .220 in 39 games, with five home runs.

The Yanks had agreed to make Colavito a free agent at the end of the season, which they did. He said he'd had "a very happy" association with the Yankees, and he was uncertain whether to retire or try to hook on with one of the four expansion teams that would begin play in 1969.

Colavito chose to retire. His 374 career home runs were then 15th on the all-time list.

October 21, 1968: Purchased Right-handed Pitcher Don Nottebart from the Cincinnati Reds

Don Nottebart had compiled a 35-50 record while pitching eight seasons for Mil-

waukee, Houston, and Cincinnati. He'd been a reliever with the Braves, became a starter in his three years in Houston, and then returned to the bullpen with the Reds. In 1968, Cincinnati sent him to Hawaii of the Pacific Coast League, where he won five and lost two in 50 games.

The Yanks' purchase of Nottebart, who was on the roster of the Reds Indianapolis Indians team in the American Association, was on a conditional basis. They had 30 days into the 1969 season to decide whether they wanted to keep him.

The 32-year-old Nottebart had pitched six innings in four games, with no record, when the Yanks returned him to Indianapolis on April 26. The Indians then sold him to the Chicago Cubs.

November 6, 1968: Sold Infielder Ruben Amaro to the California Angels

Although the Yanks had made Ruben Amaro available for the recent expansion draft, neither Seattle nor Kansas City selected him. Amaro had been New York's opening-day shortstop in 1966, but then injured his knee in an early season collision with outfielder Tom Tresh and played in only 14 games that season. He reclaimed his role as the regular shortstop in 1967; however after he batted just .223, manager Ralph Houk replaced him in 1968 by moving Tresh from the outfield to shortstop. Amaro became a utility player, appearing in just 47 games and making only 41 plate appearances. His average fell to a minuscule .122, and he failed to drive home a single run.

November 13, 1968: Sold Infielder John Kennedy to the Seattle Pilots

The creation of the four expansion teams for 1969 allowed many of the established clubs to rid themselves of marginal players. Weak-hitting John Kennedy was just such a player. Kennedy spent 1967 with the Yankees, but not as their full-time shortstop, the position general manager Lee MacPhail and manager Ralph Houk had envisioned him filling when they'd traded for him that spring. Instead,

Kennedy played in just 78 games, both at short and third, and batted a disappointing .196. He then spent the entire 1968 season in the International League, where he hit a combined .268 while playing for both the Syracuse Chiefs and the Columbus Jets.

December 4, 1968: Traded Righthanded Pitcher Dooley Womack to the Houston Astros for Outfielder Dick Simpson

Dooley Womack had 18 of the Yankees' 27 saves in 1967, but only two in 1968. His teammate Lindy McDaniel was mainly responsible for the sharp drop-off in Womack's save total. After McDaniel joined the club in July '68, he replaced Womack as the righthander manager Ralph Houk called on in save situations. In all, the 29-year-old Womack spent three seasons in New York (1966–68), pitching in 152 games, all but one in relief, winning 15 and losing 16, with 24 saves.

Dick Simpson was only 25, but he had already played parts of six seasons in the big leagues, although he'd done so for five different teams. In 1968, he'd split the season between St. Louis and Houston, batting a combined .197 in 85 games. Simpson had spent his career as a spare outfielder, and Houk said he would give him a similar opportunity in New York.

December 4, 1968: Traded Outfielder Andy Kosco to the Los Angeles Dodgers for Lefthanded Pitcher Mike Kekich

On the same day they traded pitcher Dooley Womack to Houston for Dick Simpson, a spare outfielder, the Yanks traded Andy Kosco, who had been their best spare outfielder, to the Los Angeles Dodgers for a pitcher. But in place of Womack, an expendable righthanded reliever, the Yanks were getting Mike Kekich, a lefthanded starter. Kekich had gone 2-10 as a Dodger rookie in 1968, but he was young, just 23, and had made a favorable impression on several Yankee scouts.

Conversely, Simpson seemed a potentially poor replacement for the 27-year-old Kosco. In 1968, Kosco's one season in New York, he'd batted .240, with 15 home runs and 59 runs batted in. While those weren't spectacular numbers, he had, nevertheless, played exceptionally well at times, and manager Ralph Houk was sorry to see him go. "Andy gave us a real good year and we hate to lose him," Houk said.

Kosco would have his best season ever for the Dodgers in 1969, hitting 19 home runs and driving in 74 runs.

December 6, 1968: Traded Third Baseman Charley Smith to the San Francisco Giants for Infielder Nate Oliver

Charley Smith and Nate Oliver had at least two things in common. Both had started their careers as shortstops in the Dodger organization and both had missed much of the 1968 season because of injuries. An off-season knee operation limited Smith to 46 games, mostly as a pinch hitter, while Oliver, who had a stomach ailment, played in just 36 games for the Giants and batted .178.

Before his one season in San Francisco, Oliver had spent the previous five years (1963–67) as a part-time player with the Dodgers, primarily as a second baseman. In all, he'd been in 365 games, with a .230 average.

Smith had come to the Yanks from St. Louis in the December 1966 trade for Roger Maris. He batted .224 as the team's regular third baseman in 1967, but, as previously noted, missed much of his second season in New York. Smith would never get to play for the Giants, who sold him to the Chicago Cubs during spring training of 1969. He would make two pinch-hitting appearances for Chicago before his big league career ended.

April 14, 1969: Purchased Outfielder Jimmie Hall from the Cleveland Indians

One week into the new season, when it became obvious to Yankee management that the club lacked lefthanded-hitting bench strength, they purchased Jimmie Hall to rectify that shortcoming. Hall had hit 114 home runs in his first five seasons, four with the Twins and one with the Angels, and though he hit only two with the Angels and Indians in 1968, the Yankees felt he still possessed a home run stroke that was perfect for Yankee Stadium.

April 19, 1969: Sold Infielder Nate Oliver to the Chicago Cubs

Injuries had prevented Nate Oliver from playing much for San Francisco in 1968, and his Yankee career had consisted of one unsuccessful pinch-hitting appearance. Nevertheless, the Cubs, who'd gotten off to a good start, and were leading the National League's Eastern Division, were in need of an experienced utility infielder. Oliver, they felt, would be an adequate backup to shortstop Don Kessinger and give manager Leo Durocher greater maneuverability on defense.

Perhaps as part of this deal, the Cubs "lent" infielder Lee Elia to the Yanks' International League team at Syracuse. Elia played 17 games for the Chiefs, then went on the disabled list on May 24 and was returned to the Cubs' organization the next day.

May 19, 1969: Traded Outfielder Dick Simpson to the Seattle Pilots for Outfielder Jose Vidal

When the Yanks traded for Dick Simpson in December 1968, manager Ralph Houk said that he would give Simpson a chance to make the club as a spare outfielder. But after he'd appeared in just six games and gone 3 for 11, the Yanks sent him to Syracuse of the International League. Now, he would be going to the new Seattle Pilots. The Pilots would be Simpson's seventh and final team big league team in his seventh and final season.

Jose Vidal, who had played parts of the previous three seasons with Cleveland, was batting .192 in 18 games. He took Simpson's roster spot at Syracuse and never returned to the big leagues.

May 20, 1969: Traded Righthanded Pitcher Fred Talbot to the Seattle Pilots for Righthanded Pitcher Jack Aker

Since reaching the majors with the Kansas City Athletics in 1964, Jack Aker had pitched in 235 games, all in relief. His best season came in 1966, when he won eight and lost four and led the American League with 32 saves. The A's (now in Oakland) made him available in the expansion draft of October 1968, and the Pilots selected him. He was 0-2 in 15 games for Seattle, but did have three saves.

Fred Talbot had been part of the Yankees' starting rotation in 1966 and 1967, but was used as both a starter and a reliever in 1968. Overall, he had a 14-24 record, including a 1-9 mark in '68. He'd appeared in eight games this season, all in relief and with no decisions. Before the summer was over, Seattle would trade Talbot to Oakland where he ended his career the following season.

June 10, 1969: Purchased Righthanded Pitcher Ken Johnson from the Atlanta Braves

Thirty-six-year-old Ken Johnson had been a big league pitcher for the Athletics, Reds, Astros and Braves since 1958. Used as both a starter and reliever, he had a lifetime record of 89-102 and was 0-1 with one save in nine games for Atlanta this season.

June 14, 1969: Traded Outfielder-Shortstop Tom Tresh to the Detroit Tigers for Outfielder Ron Woods

Tom Tresh was the last remaining member of the Yankees to have played on a Yankee team that won a World Series. As a rookie on the 1962 team that defeated the San Francisco Giants in seven games, Tresh batted .286, with 20 home runs and 93 runs batted in, and won the American League's Rookie of the Year Award. (Joe Pepitone and Al Downing also played some for the '62 Yankees, but neither one was eligible for that year's Series.)

Tresh had also proved his versatility in

1962, starting the season at shortstop and then moving to left field in August when Tony Kubek returned from the Army. Tresh remained an outfielder through the 1967 season, before manager Ralph Houk returned him to shortstop in 1968.

A switch hitter with power, Tresh hit 140 home runs as a Yankee, but he had never again hit for as high an average as he had as a rookie. He had his last good year in 1965, when he batted .279 with 26 home runs. And while Tresh hit 27 homers the following year, his batting average fell to .233. The past two seasons were even worse: .219 in 1967, and .195 in 1968. This season, he'd dropped even below that, a feeble .182 mark in 45 games. After Tresh strained his back in late May, Gene Michael replaced him at shortstop, and he'd been in only two games since, both as a pinch hitter.

In saying good-bye to the 32-year-old Tresh, Houk said, "It is always tough to see a veteran go, but we felt we needed help in the outfield and [Ron] Woods seems to fit the bill. He is five years younger than Tommy, was impressive this spring in Florida and could help a lot. Tresh has been a fine, hustling player since he joined us in 1962, and we wish him well." (Tresh had actually made his debut in September 1961.)

As Houk said, Woods, who batted .292 with 16 home runs with Toledo of the International League in 1968, had looked good in spring training. However, he'd been unable to win a starting job in a Tiger outfield that had Al Kaline, Willie Horton, and Jim Northrup, and had batted only 15 times (with four hits) this season.

But while the Tigers were well-stocked in the outfield (Mickey Stanley, who'd played shortstop in the 1968 World Series and earlier this season, had also returned to the outfield) they were without an everyday shortstop.

Going to Detroit would reunite Tresh with Wally Moses, who'd helped him a lot when Moses was the Yankees' batting coach. He'd also be going home.

"No one likes to leave the Yankees," Tresh said, "but if I have to leave I'm glad it's for Detroit. I am a native of Detroit and still reside in Michigan, so I'll be among friends."

Tresh took over as the Tigers' shortstop and batted .224 for the rest of the season, which turned out to be his final one.

Fortunately for Woods, the outfield competition in New York wouldn't be so daunting, and he was expected to become the Yanks' number one righthanded hitting outfielder. Bill Robinson and Billy Cowan had shared that spot so far this season, but both were hitting below .200.

July 26, 1969: Sold Outfielder Billy Cowan to the California Angels

The Yanks had drafted Billy Cowan from the Phillies Pacific Coast League team in San Diego in December 1968. He was 30 years old and had played previously for the Cubs, Mets, Braves and Phillies. In 32 games as a Yankee, he'd batted .167 with one home run. Despite that poor output, California acquired him because they needed an outfielder to step in for Lou Johnson, who'd been placed on the disabled list.

Cowan would be a worthy addition for the Angels; he hit .304 in 28 games and continued to play for California until 1972.

August 11, 1969: Sold Righthanded Pitcher Ken Johnson to the Chicago Cubs

Chicago was leading the National League's Eastern Division, but the Mets were challenging and Cubs manager Leo Durocher always liked to have veteran pitchers in a pennant race. Ken Johnson, who went for the $20,000 waiver price, had been a Yankee for two months. He was 1-2 in 12 games, with the one victory coming in a 6.1-inning relief effort against the Seattle Pilots.

September 11, 1969: Traded Outfielder Jimmie Hall to the Chicago Cubs for Minor League Righthanded Pitcher Terry Bongiovanni and Cash

Jimmie Hall had played in 80 games for the Yankees following his purchase from Cleveland in April. However, he'd not supplied the batting punch the Yanks had hoped for, hitting only three home runs to go along with a .236 batting average. That mattered little to the Cubs, who one day earlier had surrendered their season-long Eastern Division lead to the surging New York Mets and were now desperate for help.

After failing to help the Cubs overtake the Mets, Hall played a final year in 1970, both with Chicago and Atlanta.

Twenty-year-old Terry Bongiovanni had a 3-7 record for the Cubs' San Antonio team in the Texas League. The Yankees assigned him to Triple-A Syracuse of the International League, the highest level Bongiovanni would ever attain. As an addendum to this trade, the Yankees purchased outfielder Rick Bladt from the Cubs on January 6, 1970.

December 4, 1969: Traded First Baseman Joe Pepitone to the Houston Astros for Outfielder–First Baseman Curt Blefary

Efforts to trade Joe Pepitone had begun in August, after he disappeared twice, missing seven games. The Yanks had responded by suspending him and fining him $500. Often the center of controversy, the 29-year-old Pepitone was the senior Yankee regular in length of service, having joined the club back in 1962. He came up as a first baseman, but switched to center field in 1967 when the Yanks tried to ease the pain in Mickey Mantle's ailing legs by moving him to first base. When Mantle retired following the 1968 season, Pepitone moved back to first base. His career totals for his eight Yankee seasons included a .252 batting average, 166 home runs, and 541 runs batted in. Still, many felt that by being such a "free spirit" Pepitone had never gotten the most out of his ability.

Lee MacPhail, the Yankees' general manager, was not sorry to see Pepitone leave. "In a sense, I feel relieved of a problem," he said. "But it'll be hard to imagine the Yankees without him. He's been a real good player, but not as good as everyone hoped he'd be. He was colorful, and he had the spirit of youth, and some of the problems that go with it." Manager Ralph Houk agreed that it was best for Pepitone to go. "I have nothing against Pepi," Houk

said, "but I think a change of scenery might help both players."

Pepitone said the trade was not unexpected, but still he regretted leaving the Yankees, although he admitted that it was probably "the best thing to get away from New York."

Houston manager Harry Walker claimed that Pepitone's reputation for difficulty didn't worry him. "I'm not worried about the personality problem," Walker said. "Joe might do a few things that antagonize people, but he's a ballplayer, and the change may help him." (Walker would put up with Pepitone for 75 games before selling him to the Chicago Cubs.)

Curt Blefary, three years younger than Pepitone, was especially pleased to be leaving Houston and its Astrodome. A three-time 20–home run hitter for Baltimore, he hit only 12 in his one year with the Astros. Blefary had been Yankee property originally, but they'd failed to protect him. The Orioles drafted him in 1963, and two years later he was the American League's Rookie of the Year.

Blefary was very excited about playing for the Yankees. "I know it sounds corny, but I always wanted to play for New York," he said. "It's my home and the pinstripes do something to me. I stand in the same batter's box where Babe Ruth stood."

Although Blefary had been Houston's full-time first baseman, he wasn't a very good fielder and Houk had no intention of using him as Peptone's replacement. His plan, he hinted, was to use Blefary in right field, and if he couldn't trade for a first baseman, he'd try rookie catcher John Ellis there.

December 5, 1969: Traded Lefthanded Pitcher Al Downing and Catcher Frank Fernandez to the Oakland Athletics for First Baseman–Third Baseman Danny Cater and Infielder Ossie Chavarria

One day after trading Joe Pepitone, who'd been a Yankee longer than anyone but Al Downing, the Yanks traded Downing. While the 28-year-old lefthander had not been the perpetual problem to management that Pepitone had, he had staged a long holdout in the spring. He then upset the club even further by hiring an agent, before finally signing for $30,000.

Downing first appeared with the Yankees for five games in 1961 and one in 1962. He came back to stay in 1963 and was a part of the starting rotation for the next five years, compiling a 62-48 record. But he had arm troubles in 1968 and won only three games, then pitched only 130.2 innings with a 7-5 record in 1969.

After coming up to the Yanks in mid–September 1967, Frank Fernandez played behind Jake Gibbs in 1968, and then split the catching duties with Gibbs in 1969. He played in a total of 149 games as a Yankee, batting .204, but his best-remembered game was Opening Day, 1968. Fernandez, a 25-year-old rookie, caught Mel Stottlemyre's 1-0 shutout of the California Angels and hit a second-inning home run to give the Yankees the game's only run. That followed a gesture that had endeared him to the crowd even before the game started. After catching the first ball thrown out by poet Marianne Moore, Fernandez spontaneously leaned over and kissed the 81-year-old Miss Moore on the cheek.

Fernandez had become extraneous because manager Ralph Houk decided that

rookie Thurman Munson would be his catcher in 1970, with Gibbs serving as the number two man. Houk also said he preferred that one of his rookies, John Ellis or Frank Tepedino, win the first base job. However, if they didn't, he would feel secure in using Danny Cater there. "I've always liked Cater as a hitter," Houk said. "With the addition of Blefary [acquired the day before] and Cater, we're 40 runs batted in better than last year."

The 29-year-old Cater had played first, third, and the outfield while batting .275 in his six big league seasons with the Phillies, White Sox, and Athletics. His reaction to being traded once again was brief. "When I was a kid in Texas, the Yankees were the only team," he said.

Infielder Ossie Chavarria had spent time with the A's in 1966 and 1967, when the team was based in Kansas City. The Yanks assigned him to the International League Syracuse Chiefs.

December 18, 1969: Traded Minor League Lefthanded Pitcher Mickey Scott and Cash to the Chicago White Sox for First Baseman–Third Baseman Pete Ward

Twenty-one-year-old Mickey Scott had been in the Yankee farm system since 1965. Pitching for Binghamton in 1966, he'd led the New York–Pennsylvania League in wins (15) and strikeouts (170). But after spending the 1967 season in the military, Scott was back with Binghamton in 1968, and then Syracuse of the International League in 1969. He would eventually reach the majors in 1972, with Baltimore.

The best of Pete Ward's seven seasons with the White Sox were his first two: 1963 (.295 with 22 home runs) and 1964 (.282 with 23 home runs). Neck and back injuries had prevented him from reaching those heights again; nevertheless, his ability to play first base, third base, and the outfield made the 30-year-old Ward a valuable addition for the Yankees. He was also a fine pinch hitter, having led the American League in that department with 17 in 1969.

General manager Lee MacPhail and

December 5, 1969: *Danny Cater.* **"When I was a kid in Texas, the Yankees were the only team."**

manager Ralph Houk agreed that Ward and two other newly-acquired players, Danny Cater and Curt Blefary, greatly increased the club's versatility. Blefary would probably play right field, Cater first base or third base, and Ward would be an alternate at all three positions.

Recently returned from visiting military bases and hospitals in Vietnam, Ward joked that he was relieved he would no longer have to bat against Yankee lefthander Steve Hamilton, a pitcher he'd had great difficult in hitting. "It gives me a chance to prove myself again," he added.

Ward would bat .260 in 77 at-bats for New York in 1970, mostly as a pinch hitter. Only 13 of his 66 games were in the field, and all of those were at first base. Just prior to the opening of the 1971 season, the Yanks released him, ending his career.

VIII. The Seventies

February 28, 1970: Purchased Shortstop Ron Hansen from the Chicago White Sox

Ron Hansen, the American League's Rookie of the Year with Baltimore in 1960, had spent most of his career as the regular shortstop for both the Orioles and the Chicago White Sox. However, the 32-year-old Hansen had recurrent back problems that had now reduced him to a part-time player. In 1969, he batted .259 playing in 85 games for Chicago, primarily as a backup at all four infield positions. Hansen also hit two home runs in '69, raising his major league total to 100.

Hansen would fill in at second, short, and third for two years in New York, and his .297 batting average in 1970 (in 59 games) was the highest of his career. He dropped to .207 in 61 games the next season, and after the Yanks released him in February 1972, he played a final season with the Kansas City Royals.

May 15, 1970: Traded First Baseman Dave McDonald to the Montreal Expos for Righthanded Pitcher Gary Waslewski

The arrival of Gary Waslewski ended the major league career of Joe Verbanic, whom the Yanks optioned to Syracuse of the International League to make room. Waslewski had a 9-20 record in four seasons with Boston, St. Louis, and Montreal and was winless with two losses for the Expos so far in 1970.

Waslewski would split four decisions while pitching in 26 games for New York, then

make 24 relief appearances in 1971 (0-1), while spending almost two months on the disabled list. The Yankees released him in 1972.

Dave McDonald was at Syracuse of the International League in 1969, but did make his major league debut, batting .217 in nine September games for the Yanks. Montreal sent him back to the International League, to their affiliate at Winnipeg.

July 20, 1970: Traded Lefthanded Pitcher John Cumberland to the San Francisco Giants for Lefthanded Pitcher Mike McCormick

The Giants were still in New York when Mike McCormick, then a 17-year-old "bonus baby," reached the major leagues in 1956. The San Francisco Giants traded him to Baltimore in 1963, but after two seasons with the Orioles and two with the Washington Senators, he was traded back to the Giants in December 1966. The next year McCormick had his finest season. He had a 22-10 record and a 2.85 earned run average, and won both the National League's Cy Young Award and its Comeback Player of the Year Award. Now, in his 15th big league season, he'd won three and lost four for the Giants, with a bloated 6.20 ERA.

McCormick would also be unimpressive in nine games as a Yankee, although he won his only two decisions. Released in March 1971, he signed with Kansas City, but pitched only four games for the Royals.

John Cumberland, 23, was up with the Yankees for one game in 1968 and two in 1969 without a decision. Pitching as both a starter and long reliever, he was 3-4 in 15 games this season. Cumberland would pitch for the Giants, Cardinals and Angels before injuries ended his career in 1974.

September 9, 1970: Sold Lefthanded Pitcher Steve Hamilton to the Chicago White Sox

Steve Hamilton, who went to the White Sox for the $20,000 waiver price, came to New York in 1963 and was the last player left from the pennant-winning teams of that year and 1964. In 311 games as a Yankee, all but seven in relief, he had a 34-20 won-lost record with 36 saves. Hamilton was having another solid season this year, a 4-3 record and a 2.78 ERA.

Yankee manager Ralph Houk cited Hamilton's age (he was 36) as the reason for his sale. "We really regret to see Steve leave us," Houk said. "But there's a need to make room for younger players from our Syracuse club in the International League."

September 9, 1970: *Steve Hamilton.* **The Yanks sold 36-year-old Hamilton because manager Ralph Houk wanted to make room for younger players.**

December 3, 1970: Traded Outfielder Bill Robinson to the Chicago White Sox for Lefthanded Pitcher Barry Moore

Bill Robinson was a "can't-miss" prospect for Atlanta when the Yankees traded Clete Boyer to get him in November 1966. But in three seasons in New York, Robinson had never fulfilled that promise. His combined totals for 1967 through 1969 were 310 games played, a .206 batting average, and just 16 home runs. Disappointed with his performance, the Yanks sent him back to the minors in 1970, where he batted .258 with 13 home runs for Syracuse of the International League.

The White Sox assigned Robinson, who was already 27 years old, to Tucson of the Pacific Coast League. He would return to the majors with Philadelphia in 1972, and then go on to have a long and productive career with the Phillies and the Pirates.

Barry Moore, also 27, had won 26 and lost 37 in his big league career. He'd spent five years with Washington before splitting the 1970 season between Cleveland and Chicago. Like Robinson, he received a minor league assignment (to Syracuse), but unlike Robinson, Moore never returned to the major leagues.

April 9, 1971: Traded Righthanded Pitcher Ron Klimkowski and Lefthanded Pitcher Rob Gardner to the Oakland Athletics for Outfielder–First Baseman Felipe Alou

Felipe Alou had been a major leaguer since joining the Giants in 1958, the team's first year in San Francisco. He'd also played for the Braves, in Milwaukee and Atlanta, before they traded him to Oakland in December 1969. Felipe, the only one of the three Alou brothers with any power, had 187 home runs to go with a fine .289 lifetime batting average. He'd hit .271 for the A's in 1970 as an outfielder–first baseman, the same role he was expected to have with the Yankees.

After coming to New York in the 1967 deal that sent Elston Howard to Boston, Ron Klimkowski reached the majors for three games in 1969. In 1970, he pitched in 45 games for the Yankees (all but three in relief) winning six and losing seven.

Rob Gardner was a former Met, Cub, and Indian, who made one start for the Yankees in 1970, and won it. He spent the rest of the '70 season at Syracuse, where he led the International League in wins (16) innings pitched (192), and earned run average (2.53). Gardner had appeared in two games this season, while Klimkowski had yet to make his 1971 debut.

In 1972 Oakland transferred Klimkowski back to the Yankees, and he went 0-3 in 16 games.

May 26, 1971: Traded Outfielder–First Baseman Curt Blefary to the Oakland Athletics for Lefthanded Pitcher Rob Gardner and Righthanded Pitcher Darrell Osteen

Manager Ralph Houk had expected a lot more from Curt Blefary in 1970. Blefary's poor fielding didn't surprise Houk, or the Yankees, but his weak hitting did. In 99 games, Blefary produced a .212 batting average, nine home runs, and just 37 runs batted in, and he'd started poorly this season, with a .194 average, one home run, and two RBIs.

Blefary was only 27 years old, but in his remaining two seasons, with the Athletics and the Padres, he was never again the hitter he'd been as a youngster with the Baltimore Orioles.

Rob Gardner (0-0 in four games for the A's) was returning to New York, one month after the Yanks traded him to Oakland in the Felipe Alou deal.

Darrell Osteen was a minor leaguer who'd seen brief big league action with the Reds and A's. The Yanks assigned both pitchers to the International League Syracuse Chiefs.

May 28, 1971: Traded Righthanded Pitcher Bill Burbach and Cash to the Baltimore Orioles for Righthanded Pitcher Jim Hardin

Bill Burbach had been the co-winner with Jerry Kenney of the 1969 James P. Dawson Award, the first time the vote to honor the Yankees' outstanding rookie in spring training had ended in a tie. Burbach won six and lost eight for the Yanks that year, but had spent most of 1970 and 1971 in the minors. He appeared in a total of just six major league games in those two seasons, with three decisions, all losses.

Because the Yankees were out of options on the 23-year-old Burbach, if they tried to return him to the minors they would lose him. The Orioles had no such restrictions and sent Burbach to Rochester of the International League. He never returned to the major leagues.

Jim Hardin had his best season as an Orioles sophomore in 1968. He was 18-13 with a 2.51 ERA, but won only six in each of the next two seasons and had no record this year. Hardin would pitch in 12 games for the Yankees (0-2), while spending most of August on the disabled list. Sent to Richmond in the International League in April 1972, he was later picked up by Atlanta and went 5-2 for the Braves in what was his last season.

June 7, 1971: Traded Outfielder–First Baseman Frank Tepedino and Outfielder Bobby Mitchell to the Milwaukee Brewers for Outfielder Danny Walton

Frank Tepedino and Bobby Mitchell were both 23, and both, the Yanks thought, were major league prospects. Tepedino, drafted out of the Baltimore organization, made brief appearances in New York in 1967, 1969, and 1970. Recalled from the International League Syracuse Chiefs a week earlier, he was hitless in six at-bats.

After Tepedino batted .198 in 53 games for the Brewers, they released him to their American Association team at Evansville. Later, Syracuse picked him up again, and Tepedino was back with the Yankees in 1972.

Mitchell had played in ten games with the Yanks in 1970, but was currently at Syracuse. Although he was now Milwaukee property, the Brewers kept Mitchell at Syracuse, but he was now under option to them. He would join the Brewers later in the season and play with them on and off through 1975.

Danny Walton, just short of his 24th birthday, was *The Sporting News* Minor League Player of the Year in 1969. Although he tended to strike out a lot, Walton was a power hitter who'd left a lasting impression on the Yankees one day during the 1970 season. Batting against Mel Stottlemyre, Walton homered into the left field bleachers at Yankee Stadium, a spot that only 19 other batters had reached.

A knee injury limited him to 117 games in 1970, but Walton still hit 17 home runs, although he also struck out 126 times. In 30 games this season, he was batting .203 with two home runs and had already fanned 22 times.

The Yanks planned to use Walton to augment their righthanded pinch hitting corps of Thurman Munson, Felipe Alou, and Ron Hansen, all of whom filled that role on days they weren't in the starting lineup.

June 25, 1971: Traded Outfielder Ron Woods to the Montreal Expos for Outfielder Ron Swoboda

Although Ron Swoboda had been a local hero in his six seasons with the Mets, manager Gil Hodges had sharply reduced his playing time in 1970. When Swoboda demanded that the Mets play him or trade him, they complied. On March 31, 1971, they traded Swoboda to Montreal for outfielder Don Hahn. But Expos manager Gene Mauch hadn't used him much either; Swoboda had batted just 75 times this season and was hitting .253 with no home runs.

Actually, at Swoboda's urging, the Yanks had discussed a deal for him back during the 1970 World Series, offering the Mets catcher Jake Gibbs in return. Now that they'd made this deal for him, and he was coming back to New York, Swoboda was ecstatic.

"It feels like being brought up from the minor leagues," he said. "I'm still in a fog. I'm so happy. I've always wanted to play for the Yankees, I made no bones about that, and I said so last winter. In Montreal, I don't think they used me very wisely. They never gave me a real chance to show what I could do."

Swoboda rushed out of Montreal, not even stopping to say good-bye to his teammates, or to his former teammates, the Mets, who were in town to play the Expos. He got to New York in time to start in left field against the Washington Senators and contribute a run-scoring single in his first at-bat.

The Yanks had wanted Swoboda for more than just his playing ability. They really didn't

expect that he would break into the starting outfield of Roy White, Bobby Murcer, and Felipe Alou, but they did hope that his popularity would help them close the attendance gap with the Mets. Yankee attendance so far this season had been a mere 40 percent of that of their intracity rivals.

Swoboda would not help the Yankees much at the plate, or at the gate. Over the next three seasons, he batted .235 in 152 games, with just four home runs and 34 runs batted in. With no great improvement in the attendance battle with the Mets, the Yanks released Swoboda after the 1973 season.

Ron Woods batted .208 in 192 games as a Yankee after they acquired him from Detroit in the June 1969 trade for Tom Tresh. The Expos assigned Woods to their International League team at Winnipeg, but after five games with the Whips, they brought him to Montreal.

October 13, 1971: Traded Outfielder Jim Lyttle to the Chicago White Sox for Lefthanded Pitcher Rich Hinton

Jim Lyttle batted .181 in 83 at-bats as a Yankee rookie in 1969. Then after a .310-season (126 at-bats) in 1970, he dropped back to .189 (86 at-bats) in 1971.

Rich Hinton was 8-6 at Tucson of the Pacific Coast League in 1971 when the White Sox called him up in July. He pitched in 18 games for Chicago, winning three and losing four.

December 2, 1971: Traded Righthanded Pitcher Stan Bahnsen to the Chicago White Sox for Infielder Rich McKinney

The Yanks had tried to talk the California Angels out of third baseman Jim Fregosi, but were unsuccessful. (Eight days later, the Mets would be successful in obtaining Fregosi for four players, one of whom was future Hall of Famer Nolan Ryan.) So, while veteran big-name sluggers like Fregosi, Frank Robinson, and Dick Allen had all recently switched teams, the Yanks had to settle for Rich McKinney, an unproven 25-year-old infielder.

December 2, 1971: *Stan Bahnsen*. **Bahnsen was the AL Rookie of the Year in 1968, but never lived up to expectations.**

McKinney had been a shortstop in the minors, but played both second base and right field in 1971, his first full season with the White Sox. He hit .271 in 114 games and his success against the Yankees was well-remembered by Yankee manager Ralph Houk. The Yanks planned to try McKinney at third base, a position filled these past three seasons by the weak-hitting Jerry Kenney. "Our scouts are sure he can play third," Houk said. "I think he's gonna be one helluva hitter. He hurt us. We couldn't get him out."

Aware that they would have to lose one of their starters in any trade they made, the Yanks chose to sacrifice 27-year-old Stan Bahnsen, a pitcher who had never fully lived up to the club's expectations for him. Signed out of the University of Nebraska, Bahnsen had been up briefly in 1966, then returned in 1968 to go 17-12 and win the American League's Rookie of the Year Award. Since then he'd had records of 9-16, 14-11, and 14-12.

In 1972, his first season in Chicago, Bahnsen rewarded his new manager, Chuck Tanner, by winning 21 games.

December 2, 1971: Traded Lefthanded Pitchers Terry Ley and Gary Jones to the Texas Rangers for Infielder Bernie Allen

Bernie Allen was an excellent defensive player who the Yanks planned to use as a backup to both Horace Clarke at second and to newly acquired Rich McKinney at third. Allen had played his first five big league seasons with the Minnesota Twins and the last five with expansion Washington Senators. (The Senators had recently relocated and would be playing in 1972 as the Texas Rangers.) Allen's best season was as a rookie second baseman with the Twins in 1969, when he batted .269 in 159 games.

The two young pitchers leaving the Yanks had each pitched briefly for them. Terry Ley had been in six games in 1971, while Gary Jones had been in 14 games over the past two seasons. Neither one had a decision. The Rangers immediately traded them both to the Cleveland Indians, but their games pitched for the Yankees would be their only ones in the big leagues.

January 20, 1972: Traded a Player to Be Named to the Chicago Cubs for Outfielder Johnny Callison

The Yanks had acquired Johnny Callison conditionally; they had until May 1 to decide whether to keep him or to send him back to the Cubs. Were they to keep him, they visualized

January 20, 1972: *Johnny Callison*. **Callison as a White Sox rookie in 1959.**

the 32-year-old Callison as a lefthanded pinch hitter and reserve outfielder. Callison was a 14-year-veteran who'd spent two seasons with the White Sox, ten with the Phillies, and the last two with the Cubs. He had a career .266 average with 216 home runs, but was coming off his worst season since becoming a regular. Because Cubs manager Leo Durocher seemed to have lost confidence in him, Callison had only 290 at-bats in 1971, with a .210 batting average, eight home runs, and 38 RBIs.

The Yanks would choose to keep Callison, and he would play 74 games in the outfield (92 total) and bat a solid .258. They would release him in August 1973 (he was batting .176 in 136 at-bats) to make room for first baseman Mike Hegan, whom they'd purchased from Oakland.

By keeping Callison beyond the May 1, 1972 deadline, the Yanks had to send a player to Chicago. On May 17, they sent the Cubs Jack Aker, a righthanded relief pitcher. Since joining the club in May 1969, Aker had compiled a 16-10 record with 31 saves, including 16 in 1970.

February 2, 1972: Purchased Shortstop Hal Lanier from the San Francisco Giants

Hal Lanier came up to the Giants in June 1964 and had been an infield regular, first at second and in recent years at shortstop, until this past season. Rookie Chris Speier won the shortstop job in 1971, while Lanier became a backup at all four infield positions. He still played in 109 games in '71, batting .233, which was four points higher than his lifetime average.

Lanier would bat .212 in 95 games over the next two seasons, before the Yankees released him in December 1973.

March 22, 1972: Traded First Baseman Danny Cater to the Boston Red Sox for Lefthanded Pitcher Sparky Lyle

A few hours after being shut out by the Mets, the sixth time they'd been shut out this training season, the Yanks traded away one of their best hitters. However incongruous that may have seemed because of their weak hitting this spring, the club's main goal for 1972 was to strengthen their bullpen. Yankee relievers had registered a ridiculously meager 12 saves in 1971, by far the lowest in the American League. Back in October they'd traded for White Sox rookie Rich Hinton, and they'd also drafted Jim Magnuson out of that same organization. But neither of those lefthanders was of the quality of Sparky Lyle, about whom general manager Lee MacPhail said: "We've been trying to get him for two years."

The 27-year-old Lyle had been in 260 games in his five seasons with the Red Sox, all in relief. He had a 22-17 record and a 2.85 ERA, but what was most important, Lyle had saved 69 games. In 1971, he had 16, four more than the entire Yankee staff.

The Red Sox were sorry to lose Lyle, but they had traded their first baseman, George Scott, to Milwaukee. They would use Danny Cater to fill that spot, while counting on young lefthander Bill Lee to replace Lyle.

Cater had done what the Yankees expected of him these past two years: play first base, third base, and add punch to the lineup. He hit a combined .290 as the Yanks' full-time first baseman in 1970, and part-time first baseman/third baseman in 1971.

The official exchange of teams by Cater and Lyle would take place in Florida the next day when the Yanks went to Winter Haven to play the Red Sox.

April 28, 1972: Purchased Lefthanded Pitcher Jim Roland from the Oakland Athletics

Oakland manager Dick Williams was hoping to get a player in return for Jim Roland, but this would be strictly a cash deal. The 29-year-old Roland was in his tenth big league season, with a lifetime record of 19-16. He was primarily a reliever, who before coming to Oakland had spent six years with the Minnesota Twins. To make room for Roland, the Yanks sent lefthander Alan Closter to Syracuse of the International League.

June 7, 1972: Purchased Lefthanded Pitcher Wade Blasingame from the Houston Astros

The addition of Wade Blasingame raised the current number of lefthanded pitchers on the Yankee staff to seven. Signed originally by the Milwaukee Braves for a $100,000 bonus, Blasingame had never lived up to his early promise. A 16-game winner for the Braves in 1965, he had won only 21 games since, with 35 losses.

Blasingame had no record with Houston this year, and he would lose his only decision with the Yanks—his final major league decision.

August 30, 1972: Traded Lefthanded Pitcher Jim Roland to the Texas Rangers for Righthanded Pitcher Casey Cox

In his four months with the Yanks, Jim Roland was 0-1 in 16 relief appearances. His five games for Texas (0-0) would be his final ones in the major leagues.

Casey Cox's best season was 1969, when he went 12-7 with a 2.78 earned run average for the Washington Senators. Now 31, he'd begun his career with Washington in 1966 and moved with them to Texas this season, where he was currently 3-5 for the Rangers.

Cox would get into five games (0-1) for the Yanks in 1972, and one more in April 1973, but, like Roland, he was at the end of his career. The Yanks let him go after purchasing Jim Ray Hart on April 17, 1973.

September 7, 1972: Sold Lefthanded Pitcher Rich Hinton to the Texas Rangers

The Yanks' sale of Rich Hinton to Texas may have been part of the deal a week earlier in which pitcher Jim Roland went to the Rangers for pitcher Casey Cox. Hinton had split this season between New York, where he was 1-0 in seven games, and the International League Syracuse Chiefs, where he was 3-9 in 19 games.

September 16, 1972: Purchased Right-handed Pitcher Steve Blateric from the Cincinnati Reds

Although Steve Blateric was 28 years old, his only major league experience was two games with the Reds in 1971. A relief specialist, he was 8-9 with Indianapolis of the American Association this season, with a sparkling 1.58 ERA. The deal was structured so that if the Yanks retained Blateric for 30 days into the 1973 season, they would send a player to Cincinnati. However, Blateric appeared in only one game for the Yanks, in October '72, and was not retained.

October 24, 1972: Traded Minor League Catcher George Pena to the San Diego Padres for Shortstop Fred Stanley

Despite already having a good-fielding, weak-hitting shortstop in Gene Michael, the Yanks traded for another in Fred Stanley. In his 128-game career for the Seattle Pilots/Milwaukee Brewers, the Cleveland Indians, and the San Diego Padres, the 25-year-old Stanley had a .223 average, with two home runs in 269 at-bats.

Officially, it was Syracuse, the Yanks affiliate in the International League, that made the trade, and where Stanley would begin the 1973 season.

George Pena had a .250 batting average and 11 home runs in the International League in 1972. He played 34 games for Toledo and 63 for Syracuse, but Triple-A was as high as he would get.

October 27, 1972: Traded Outfielder Danny Walton to the Minnesota Twins for Catcher Rick Dempsey

In June 1971, just two weeks after they got him from Milwaukee, the Yanks sent Danny Walton to the Syracuse Chiefs of the International League. He returned in September, but played in only five games for the Yanks, getting two hits in 14 at-bats. Walton then spent the entire 1972 season with the Chiefs, batting .271 with 23 home runs.

Syracuse was also where the Yanks assigned their new catcher, 23-year-old Rick Dempsey. While Dempsey had made token appearances for the Twins in each of the last four seasons, the 25 games he played in 1972 were by far the most he'd played in any one season. Dempsey's major league totals read 41 games played, with 15 hits in 66 at-bats for a .227 average.

November 24, 1972: Traded Lefthanded Pitcher Rob Gardner and a Player to Be Named to the Oakland Athletics for Outfielder Matty Alou

The Yanks had tried to get Matty Alou from St. Louis this past summer, but the Cardinals traded him to Oakland, where he helped the A's win the World Series. The 36-year-old Alou was a former National League batting champion (.342 for the 1966 Pirates), but the Yanks would be his fourth club in the past four seasons. He was a mediocre outfielder but an excellent hitter, with a .310 lifetime average for 13 major league seasons.

"Basically, we wanted hitting," said Yankee executive vice president Lee MacPhail. "Matty's not the traditional Yankee Stadium hitter—not a power man. But he gets on base a lot and he will help us score runs."

Manager Ralph Houk speculated on what role Alou would play with the 1973 Yankees. "He has a young body for his age. He should play several years more. I'm planning to play him in right field, with Ron Swoboda and Rusty Torres behind him," Houk said. "He'll be a regular, so I'd have to say we'll finally have a set outfield." (The rest of the outfield figured to be Bobby Murcer in center and Roy White in left.)

In contemplating his 1973 lineup, Houk theorized that "our first six hitters would probably be Horace Clarke, Matty Alou, Bobby Murcer, Roy White, Felipe Alou or Ron Blomberg and then Thurman Munson. They can hit and they can run."

Coincidentally, Matty's brother Felipe had also come to New York in a trade that sent Rob Gardner to Oakland. That was in April 1971, and seven weeks later they got Gardner back from the A's in a trade for Curt Blefary.

This past season, as an occasional fifth starter, he'd won eight and lost five.

A week after making the trade, the Yanks completed it by sending third baseman Rich McKinney to the Athletics. In his one season in New York, McKinney had been a major disappointment. He played in just 37 games and batted .215 with one home run.

November 27, 1972: Traded Catcher John Ellis, Outfielders Charlie Spikes and Rusty Torres, and Infielder Jerry Kenney to the Cleveland Indians for Third Baseman Graig Nettles and Catcher Jerry Moses

Indians general manager Gabe Paul proclaimed that 11 clubs had shown interest in Graig Nettles. However, Paul added, "We refused to give him up until we got this kind of deal. They [the Yankees] resisted a long time."

The Yanks had resisted because while they were willing to trade some of their other younger players, they didn't want to part with Charlie Spikes, their most promising prospect. Spikes had yet to reach his 22nd birthday, but he had slugged 22 home runs for Kinston of the Carolina League in 1971, and 26 while batting .309 for West Haven of the Eastern League in 1972. Called up by the Yanks in September, he had five hits in 34 at-bats.

Yankee general manger Lee MacPhail said he had begun pursuing a deal for Nettles during the 1972 season, but that Cleveland had resisted unless the Yanks included Spikes. "We offered pitching," MacPhail said, "but they insisted on Spikes. We finally decided that there was no way to get Nettles without giving him up, even though he was the best prospect we've had in years."

Nettles, 28, had begun his career with the Twins in 1967, but had been with Cleveland since 1970. A lefthanded power hitter, his home run totals for the past three seasons were 26, 28, and 17. The Yanks felt those numbers would get even better with him playing half his games at Yankee Stadium. They envisioned Nettles batting fifth behind newly-acquired Matty Alou and Bobby Murcer.

MacPhail predicted that the addition of Alou and Nettles made the Yanks contenders

November 27, 1972: *Graig Nettles.* **The Yanks expected that playing half his games at the Stadium would improve Nettles's home run totals.**

for the Eastern Division title in 1973. "Now we feel we have as good a club as anybody in baseball," he said. "Our fans have been waiting long enough. We traded tomorrow for today."

Manager Ralph Houk concurred with MacPhail's "tomorrow for today" sentiment. "I'm not worrying about youth," he said. "It's time to go out and win it. Our offensive lineup now should be the best since our winning teams of ten years ago."

Jerry Kenney and John Ellis made their Yankee debuts in 1967 and 1969 respectively. Kenney was in the military in 1968 but was the Yankee third baseman from 1969 to 1971. He played behind shortstop Gene Michael in 1972, as Celerino Sanchez, Bernie Allen, and Rich McKinney shared the third base position, a spot that Nettles seemed sure to take over in 1973. In 460 games as a Yankee, Kenney had a .237 batting average and just 12 home runs.

In 1970, Ellis batted .368 with 18 runs batted in during spring training to beat out

Thurman Munson for the James P. Dawson Award, given to the best rookie in camp. Both Ellis and Munson had come up through the organization as catchers, both played briefly for the Yanks in 1969, and both were in the opening-day lineup in 1970. However, because Munson was the much better receiver, Ellis was at first base for the opener, even though he had never before played the position in his professional career.

Ellis had both caught and played first base in his brief Yankee career, batting .260 with 16 home runs in 235 games. In 1972, he batted .294 in 52 games while serving primarily as Munson's backup, the role that Jerry Moses would likely inherit. The 26-year-old Moses was a lifetime .256 hitter who had previously played for the Red Sox and Angels.

Rusty Torres hit a spectacular .385 in nine games for the Yankees in September 1971. He split the 1972 season between Syracuse of the International League and New York, and though he batted just .211 in 80 games with the Yanks, Indians manager Ken Aspromonte said that he expected both the switch-hitting Torres and Spikes to be in his 1973 lineup.

April 5, 1973: Traded Shortstop Frank Baker to the Baltimore Orioles for Infielder Tommy Matchick

Except for brief stints in New York in 1970-71, Frank Baker had been the shortstop for the International League Syracuse Chiefs for the past four seasons. In his two partial seasons with the Yanks, Baker batted .194 in 78 games as a fill-in for Gene Michael. He was back at Syracuse in 1972, spending the entire season there and batting .254.

Matchick had a .215 batting average in 292 games for Detroit, Boston, Kansas City, Milwaukee, and three games for the 1972 Orioles. The Yanks sent him to Syracuse, while the Orioles assigned Baker to Rochester, their affiliate in the International League. Baker would play for Baltimore in 1973 and 1974, but Matchick's big league career was over.

April 17, 1973: Purchased Outfielder–Third Baseman Jim Ray Hart from the San Francisco Giants

Between 1964 and 1968, Jim Ray Hart had been a San Francisco regular, playing both third base and the outfield. But beginning in 1969, a series of injuries, many the result of being hit by pitched balls, had diminished his productivity, and Hart had spent the past few seasons shuttling between the Giants and their Pacific Coast League team in Phoenix. He'd had an excellent season at Phoenix in 1972, but then had to undergo knee surgery in the off-season.

The Yanks, who asked waivers on pitcher Casey Cox to make room for the 31-year-old Hart, saw him as their righthanded designated hitter, a position that Ron Swoboda and Celerino Sanchez had shared in the season's first week. Because of his frequent injuries, Hart had little mobility, but he still could hit, which seemed the job description for the American League's newly-created designated hitter position.

Hart would become the team's primary designated hitter in 1973, filling that role in 106 games. Overall, he played in 114, batting .254 with 13 home runs. Hart played his final ten big league games as a Yankee in 1974, but was batting just .053 when the club released him on June 7.

June 7, 1973: Traded Outfielder–First Baseman Frank Tepedino, Minor League Outfielder Wayne Nordhagen, and Two Players to Be Named to the Atlanta Braves for Righthanded Pitcher Pat Dobson

Pat Dobson was an established veteran, who over the past two seasons had won 36 games (20 in 1971 and 16 1972) for the Baltimore Orioles. The Orioles had traded him during the off-season to Atlanta, where Dobson had struggled with a 3-7 record and a 4.99 earned run average. Braves manager Eddie Mathews eventually dropped him from the starting rotation, and since May 22 Dobson had pitched just two innings in relief.

But the problems in Atlanta did not discourage Ralph Houk. The Yankee manager knew that the 31-year-old Dobson always started slowly and counted on his return to the American League bringing a return to form.

"He's the type of pitcher who will be hurt by Astroturf because he's a ground-ball pitcher," Houk claimed, "and in the National League he's been pitching on a lot of those infields."

Both Frank Tepedino and Wayne Nordhagen had been playing for Syracuse of the International League, and neither one figured in the Yankee plans this season. Nordhagen reported to the Braves International League team at Richmond. He would not reach the major leagues until 1976, and then with the Chicago White Sox. However, Tepedino, who'd been in eight games for the Yanks as a pinch hitter in 1972, went directly to Atlanta.

To complete the deal, the Yanks would later send the Braves two lefthanded pitchers who had spent the season in the minor leagues—Alan Closter on September 5, and Dave Cheadle on September 10. Closter, briefly a Yankee in 1971 and 1972, would pitch his final four big league games for Atlanta that fall, and Cheadle would pitch in his only two.

June 7, 1973: Purchased Lefthanded Pitcher Sam McDowell from the San Francisco Giants

The Yanks felt they had the necessary offense to win the Eastern Division race (they currently trailed the Detroit Tigers by only half a game), but knew they had to improve their pitching. So in addition to trading for right-hander Pat Dobson earlier in the day, general manager Lee MacPhail purchased lefthander Sam McDowell for a price reported to be in excess of $100,000.

Manager Ralph Houk was delighted to have these two experienced pitchers. "You can't have too much pitching," he said. "I'll just have to sit down and talk to them and work things out. We were trying to get all the pitching we could get. Now we have the bodies; it's up to them to pitch. It puts us in the best position we've been in for quite a while."

Once considered the fastest pitcher in the game, McDowell had recorded an amazing 2,316 strikeouts in 2,314 innings and ranked 13th on the all-time career strikeout list. As a member of the Cleveland Indians, he'd led the American League in strikeouts five times, although he'd also led in walks five times. He topped the AL in innings pitched (305) in 1970 and had the league's lowest earned run average (2.18) in 1965. In all, McDowell pitched 11 seasons for Cleveland (1961-71) compiling a 122-109 record, including a 20-12 mark in 1970, his only 20-win season.

Traded to San Francisco for Gaylord Perry, he went 10-8 in 1972, while missing several weeks on the disabled list. This season Giants manager Charlie Fox has used him mostly in relief, with McDowell starting only three of the 18 games he'd been in. His record was 1-2, but his 35 strikeouts in 40 innings were an indication to the Yankees that at age 30, McDowell still had his fastball.

McDowell, who later admitted he'd had a drinking problem during much of his career, won five and lost eight for the Yankees in 1973. In December 1974, following a 1-6 season in which he appeared in only 13 games, the club released him, and he finished his career with Pittsburgh in 1975.

June 12, 1973: Traded Lefthanded Pitcher Mike Kekich to the Cleveland Indians for Righthanded Pitcher Lowell Palmer and a Player to Be Named

Needing to dispose of two players after the addition of pitchers Sam McDowell and Pat Dobson five days earlier, the Yankees did so by removing two other pitchers. Besides sending Mike Kekich to the Indians, they sent another lefthander, Jim Magnuson, back to Syracuse of the International League. Magnuson, drafted out of the Chicago White Sox organization in November 1971, had pitched for the Chiefs in 1972, going 9-7. He was 0-1 in eight games for the Yanks this year.

Meanwhile, Lowell Palmer, the 25-year-old pitcher they received for Kekich, remained with Cleveland's Triple-A team at Oklahoma City. He was currently 6-3 with the 89ers and led the American Association with 78 strikeouts in 77 innings.

Through his first four seasons in New York, Kekich had been a fairly nondescript pitcher, compiling a 30-31 record as a starter and long reliever. However, he'd received national headlines this spring after he revealed details of his family-swapping with teammate Fritz Peterson. Deluged with condemnation, Kekich didn't pitch until the sixth week of the season, and then not very effectively. He was 1-1 in five games but had a bloated 9.20 earned run average. Nevertheless, the Indians were anxious to get Kekich, even putting in a waiver claim for him before making the trade.

"I'm very happy to obtain him, and I have definite plans for him," said manager Ken Aspromonte. "I'll probably work him into the starting rotation this weekend. He's one of the better lefthanders in our league, and I'm looking forward to him helping our club tremendously."

Despite Aspromonte's enthusiasm, Kekich would go just 1-4 with the Indians and was never again a productive pitcher.

The teams were supposed to decide after the season which player Cleveland would send to New York. But when they couldn't agree on whom it should be, the Indians settled it with a cash payment to the Yankees.

August 7, 1973: Traded Two Players to Be Named to the St. Louis Cardinals for Righthanded Pitcher Wayne Granger

Wayne Granger came up with St. Louis in 1968, but after the season, the Cardinals traded him to Cincinnati. He had three excellent years with the Reds, twice leading the National League in games (1969 and 1971), and compiling a league-leading 35 saves in 1970. At the time that was a National League record, as was Granger's 90 games-pitched in 1969. In both 1969 and 1970, *The Sporting News* named Granger the National League Fireman of the Year.

In December 1971, the Reds traded Granger to Minnesota, but after he recorded 19 saves for the Twins in 1972, they traded him back to his original team, the Cardinals. This season, Granger was 2-4 with five saves for St. Louis.

According to general manager Bing Devine, St. Louis was letting him go because "Granger is good in short relief. We need somebody who can go longer." That somebody, they hoped, would be Mike Nagy, whom they brought up from Tulsa of the American Association.

The Yanks had both Lindy McDaniel and Sparky Lyle in the bullpen, so they figured to use the side-arming Granger to pitch in spot situations against specific righthanded hitters. He would pitch in seven games for the Yanks in 1973 (0-1, 1.76 ERA, no saves), and was released in March 1974.

Righthander pitcher Ken Crosby, 7-8 at Syracuse of the International League, was one of the "players to be named." On September 12, 1973, the Yanks sent Crosby to the Cardinals, who in turn assigned him to Tulsa of the American Association. No other player went from New York to St. Louis, but there was a cash settlement.

August 13, 1973: Sold Second Baseman Bernie Allen to the Montreal Expos

The Montreal Expos, involved in a pennant race for the first time in their five-year existence, needed a second baseman to replace the recently disabled Ron Hunt. They settled on veteran Bernie Allen, who'd been in just 17 games this season with a .228 batting average. Allen closed out his career by batting .180 in 16 games for the Expos.

August 18, 1973: Purchased First Baseman Mike Hegan from the Oakland Athletics

After the Yankees traded Mike Hegan to the expansion Seattle Pilots organization in 1968, Hegan had moved with the franchise to Milwaukee and then was sold to Oakland. While never much of a hitter, he was an outstanding defensive player who, while playing for the 1970 Brewers, had led American League first basemen with 113 assists.

Defense was especially appealing to the Yankees after having made 30 errors in their previous 21 games. So, despite Hegan's weak bat (he was hitting .183 in 75 games for the Athletics), manager Ralph Houk said the 31-year-old lefthanded hitter would be the team's first baseman when they faced righthanded pitching. Houk had been using Matty Alou to fill that role, but Alou had committed seven errors in 26 games.

Hegan's arrival put the Yanks one player over the limit, which they fixed by releasing veteran Johnny Callison, ending Callison's 16-year major league career.

September 6, 1973: Sold First Baseman–Outfielder Felipe Alou to the Montreal Expos

The Expos purchased Felipe Alou with hopes he would help them in their pursuit of the St. Louis Cardinals, whom they trailed by three games in the National League East. (On this same day, the Yanks sold Felipe's brother, Matty, to the Cardinals.) Meanwhile, the Yanks, battling Milwaukee for fourth place in the American League East, were already looking ahead to 1974. Alou had led the American League with ten pinch hits in 1972, and had batted .271 in his almost three full seasons with the Yanks, but he was now 38 years old and did not figure in their future plans.

Alou hit .204 for the Expos, who finished in fourth place.

September 6, 1973: Sold Outfielder Matty Alou to the St. Louis Cardinals

On the same day the Yanks sold Felipe Alou to Montreal, they sent his brother Matty to the division-leading Cardinals, the team that the Expos were chasing. They'd acquired Matty this past winter for his hitting, and he'd done fine average-wise, a .296 mark in 123 games. But, he had driven in only 28 runs and had often failed to move runners along in clutch situations. As was the case with Felipe, Matty had no place in the team's 1974 plans.

By removing the two Alous from the roster, the Yanks freed about $150,000 in salary. Matty Alou would bat only 11 times for the Cards, who finished second to the New York Mets.

September 24, 1973: Purchased Catcher Duke Sims from the Detroit Tigers

Duke Sims was a 32-year-old, ten-year veteran, who'd spent most of his career with the Cleveland Indians. He had 96 home runs to go with his .241 lifetime average, and besides catching could also play first base and the outfield. Sims had hit well above his lifetime average after the Tigers got him from the Los Angeles Dodgers in August 1972 (.316 in 38 games), but he was back at .242 in 80 games this season.

December 6, 1973: Purchased Shortstop Jim Mason from the Texas Rangers

The Yankees didn't yet have a manager to replace Ralph Houk who'd resigned at the end of the 1973 season. The man they wanted to manage the club in 1974 was Dick Williams; however, the Oakland Athletics, Williams's former team, were still using legalities to prevent him from signing with the Yanks. Nor had the club been successful in getting one of the two shortstops they were pursuing. Having failed to land either the Phillies' Larry Bowa or the Cubs' Don Kessinger, they took a chance on 23-year-old Jim Mason.

"This is a gamble on this guy," Yankee president Gabe Paul conceded, "but we're only

gambling money (an estimated $100,000). Hell, we've looked at every infielder who's breathing."

If the Yanks' goal was to replace the incumbent shortstop, the weak-hitting Gene Michael, with a stronger bat, Mason hardly seemed the one to achieve that goal. As a utility infielder with Texas in 1973, his first full season in the majors, he'd batted .206 with three home runs in 92 games. But Mason would prove a pleasant surprise in 1974, playing in 152 games and batting .250. He was a part time player the next two seasons, in both of which he batted below .200. The Toronto Blue Jays selected Mason in the November 1976 expansion draft. He played three more seasons, but never again hit as high as .200.

December 7, 1973: Purchased Infielder Bill Sudakis from the Texas Rangers

Since batting .234 as the Dodgers' regular third baseman in 1969, his rookie season, Bill Sudakis had been a part-time infielder and catcher for the Dodgers, the Mets, and the Rangers. He hit .255 as a Ranger in 1973, with a career-high 15 home runs.

The American League had introduced the "designated hitter" in 1973, and Sudakis had occasionally occupied that spot in the Texas lineup. Today's vote by the American League to make what was supposed to be a "three-year experiment" a permanent one, meant he would probably be doing the same in New York.

December 7, 1973: Traded Righthanded Pitcher Lindy McDaniel to the Kansas City Royals for Outfielder Lou Piniella and Righthanded Pitcher Ken Wright

Over the last five seasons, Lou Piniella, the American League's Rookie of the Year in 1969, had established a reputation as a solid, dependable hitter. He'd finished second to Rod Carew in the 1972 American League batting race with a .312 average (Carew batted .318), but fell to .250 in 1973. Yet, despite his poor '73 season, Piniella was only 30 years old and no one had expected the Royals would trade him.

December 7, 1973: *Lindy McDaniel.* Trading Lou Piniella for McDaniel would be among the worst deals the Royals ever made.

Kansas City manager Jack McKeon explained the trade of Piniella this way: "We had to move him to make room for our young guys. We've picked up three good pitchers here [at the winter meetings]—[Lindy] McDaniel, Marty Pattin [in a trade with the Boston Red Sox], and Nelson Briles [in a trade with the Pittsburgh Pirates]. We scored only three runs less than Oakland all season," he noted of the World Champions, "and if we had more pitching depth we could have won the Western title."

McDaniel had resuscitated his career after coming to New York in July 1968. An indispensable member of the Yankee bullpen, he had a 38-29 won-lost record and more importantly, contributed 58 saves. But, as McDaniel told the Yankees, at age 38 he preferred to play for a team nearer his home in Houston, where he could be closer to his family and his church activities.

The Yankees accommodated him. "In both Houston and Kansas City, Lindy can continue his church work," said Yankee president Gabe Paul. "He's been separated from his family too long, he says, and he didn't want to start another season in New York with them back in Texas."

Ken Wright was 11-15 in four big league seasons, all with the Royals. During that time

he'd battled both his control and his weight; still, Paul suggested that Wright would either replace McDaniel in the bullpen or might even become a starting pitcher. Paul also predicted that Piniella "will either play right field or designated hitter. He's one of the best hitters in the league."

The Royals would come to consider this trade one of the worst in their history. McDaniel lasted just two more seasons, winning six and losing five with two saves. Meanwhile, Piniella, whom they'd traded, they said, to make room for younger players, batted .295 over the next 11 years in New York. When he announced his retirement in June 1984, he had played more than 1,000 games as a Yankee.

March 19, 1974: Traded Catcher Jerry Moses to the Detroit Tigers in a Three-Way Deal and Received Righthanded Pitcher Ed Farmer from the Tigers, and Righthanded Pitcher Rick Sawyer and Outfielder Walt Williams from the Cleveland Indians

While the Yankees had five catchers in training camp, Detroit was seeking an established catcher to share the backstopping duties with aging Bill Freehan. Jerry Moses had served as the number two catcher to Thurman Munson in 1973, but he'd caught in only 17 games, batting .254 in 59 at-bats. The Yanks still had veteran catchers Bill Sudakis and Duke Sims; however, because of his superior defensive abilities, 24-year-old Rick Dempsey was now likely to replace Moses as the number two man behind Munson.

Getting Walt Williams, a .273-hitter in eight big league seasons (mostly with the White Sox), gave new Yankee manager Bill Virdon another solid-hitting veteran outfielder. Williams, who'd batted .289 for the Indians in 1973, seemed likely to be a designated hitter, although Virdon was unimpressed with Roy White's throwing arm, so playing Williams in right field and moving Lou Piniella to left remained a possibility.

Williams said he was surprised that Cleveland had traded him. "I was shocked at first. I thought I was the best hitter over there." On the other hand, he was happy to be going to New York. "I'm really kind of excited now," he said. "If I had to guess, the Yankees would be the last club I would have believed I'd be traded to, a team with a long tradition and a name. This is a dream come true."

Williams would bat .244 in 125 games (55 in the outfield) over the 1974 and 1975 seasons before the Yankees released him in January 1976.

Rick Sawyer had no major league experience, but he was coming off an excellent 1973 season with Class AA San Antonio. He led the Texas League in wins with 18 and had an outstanding 2.81 earned run average. The Yanks assigned Sawyer to Syracuse of the International League, along with Ed Farmer. But Farmer, who had pitched for the Indians and Tigers the last three seasons, refused to report. Several days later the Yanks sold him to the Philadelphia Phillies.

As Cleveland's compensation for losing Williams, they received Detroit pitcher Jim Perry, who would be joining his brother Gaylord on the Indians staff.

March 23, 1974: Purchased Outfielder Elliott Maddox from the Texas Rangers

The Yankees paid $40,000 for Elliott Maddox, a 25-year-old New Jersey native who said he was "delighted" to be going to New York. In four seasons, with the Tigers, Senators, and Rangers, Maddox was just a .239-hitter with five home runs, but had earned a reputation as an excellent defensive outfielder. The problem facing Bill Virdon, the Yankees' new manager, was to decide between making Maddox his regular center fielder or using him as a defensive replacement.

Maddox tried to dispel the rumors that he sometimes failed to hustle, saying it was "only a matter of style." He added that he'd heard gossip about a trade to the Yankees for the last two weeks but didn't believe them. "They were too good to be true," he said. "I've always been a Yankee fan."

April 26, 1974: Traded Lefthanded Pitcher Fritz Peterson and Righthanded Pitchers Steve Kline, Tom

Buskey, and Fred Beene to the Cleveland Indians for First Baseman Chris Chambliss and Righthanded Pitchers Dick Tidrow and Cecil Upshaw

Team president Gabe Paul announced the trade to a stunned Yankee team in the Shea Stadium clubhouse shortly after Mel Stottlemyre had beaten the Texas Rangers, 4-3. Though six of the seven players included in the deal were pitchers, it was Chris Chambliss, a 25-year-old first baseman, who was the key figure. Paul had always had high regard for Chambliss, a player he'd first drafted when he was the Indians general manager.

Afterwards, Paul disclosed that he and current Cleveland GM, Phil Seghi, had been discussing this trade for some time. It had hinged on the Indians' insistence that any deal for Chambliss would have to include their receiving 26-year-old pitcher Steve Kline. Paul readily agreed to give up Kline, and then revealed just how much he thought of his new first baseman.

April 26, 1974: *Chris Chambliss.* "I think Chris has the potential to become one of our league's leading hitters."

"I think Chris has the potential to become one of our league's leading hitters," Paul said. "He's been promising ever since he broke into organized baseball. Why as a rookie [with Wichita] he won the 1970 American Association batting title with an average of .342."

Chambliss was back at Wichita to start the 1971 season, but Cleveland soon recalled him, and he batted .275 and won the American League's Rookie of the Year Award. He followed with a .292 mark in 1972 and a .273 in 1973, both team highs for Indians regulars, and was at .328 after 17 games this season.

Yankee manager Bill Virdon had been playing Mike Hegan at first, but while Hegan was a fine fielder, he wasn't much of a hitter. Virdon replaced him with Chambliss, and on May 13 the Yanks sold Hegan to the Milwaukee Brewers.

Kline, a Yankee since 1970, had records of 12-13 and 16-7 in 1971 and 1972, with earned averages below 3.00 each season. An elbow injury limited him to just 14 games and a 4-7 record in 1973; however, he had seemingly recovered and had two wins and two losses this season.

Kline, who'd entered the season with a lifetime 40-37 record, said he was just happy that he would still be in the majors. He would go 3-8 with Cleveland, but his career was effectively over. He was out of the majors in 1976, then returned for a final 16 games with the 1977 Atlanta Braves.

Since coming up in 1966, Fritz Peterson had taken his regular turn in the Yankee rotation. He'd won at least 12 games in six of the past seven years, including a high of 20 in 1970. Peterson had shocked the baseball community during the 1973 spring training season when he and fellow pitcher Mike Kekich announced that they had traded families. Perhaps because of the negative publicity that followed, Peterson had his worst season, an 8-15 record and a 3.95 earned run average. Virdon had used him in only three games this season, and Peterson, unhappy with his lack of playing time, asked the Yanks to trade him. (They'd traded Kekich to Cleveland in June 1973, but he had since moved on to play in Japan.)

Twenty-seven-year-old Tom Buskey had been in the Yankee system since 1969, reaching the majors in August 1973. He pitched in eight games, losing his only decision, and had also lost his only decision this season.

Of the four Yankees involved in this trade, only Fred Beene, 0-0 in six games this season, expressed disappointment at leaving. The 31-year-old journeyman had been pitching professionally since 1961, but had been in just seven big league games, all with Baltimore between 1968 and 1970. Beene came to the Yankees in a 1972 minor league deal and won one and lost three in 29 games, 28 of which were in relief. The following year he was in 19 games, four as a starter, and had a perfect 6-0 record.

While Chambliss was the reason the Yankees made the trade, Paul said they also were pleased at getting righthander Dick Tidrow, 1-3 this season, but a 14-game winner in each of his first two years in the big leagues. Pitching for Cleveland teams that finished fifth in the Eastern Division in 1972 and sixth in 1973, the 27-year-old Tidrow went 14-15 and 14-16. While Paul said Virdon would make the final decision, he believed that decision would be to immediately insert Tidrow into the club's starting rotation.

No such speculation existed concerning the role of Cecil Upshaw, who before this season had spent his entire career in the National League, seven years with the Braves and one with Houston. Upshaw was headed to the Yankee bullpen. In a career that began with Atlanta in 1966, he had pitched in 283 major league games, including seven this season, without ever having made a start.

May 3, 1974: Traded Righthanded Pitcher Ken Wright to the Philadelphia Phillies for Lefthanded Pitcher Mike Wallace

Ken Wright, a throw-in in the December 1973 Lindy McDaniel for Lou Piniella trade, had been in three games this season without a decision. Mike Wallace was 1-0 with the Phillies after splitting two decisions in 1973, his rookie year.

Their new teams sent both men to the International League: Wallace to Syracuse, and Wright to Toledo. Wallace came up to the Yanks later in the season, but Wright's big league career was over.

May 4, 1974: Traded Minor League Lefthanded Pitcher Mike Pazik and Cash to the Minnesota Twins for Righthanded Pitcher Dick Woodson

Dick Woodson was happy to leave Minnesota, especially after the events of the past February when he'd become the first player to use the new arbitration procedure to settle contract disputes. Mostly a reliever in his first two seasons with the Twins (1969 and 1970), he'd been a starter with Portland of the Pacific Coast League in 1971, and for the Twins in 1972 and '73. Woodson had a 33-30 lifetime record, including his 1-1 mark this season.

Yankee manager Bill Virdon said he planned to use Woodson as the club's fifth starter, behind Mel Stottlemyre, Doc Medich, Pat Dobson, and Dick Tidrow. When asked about a rotation that had five righthanded starters, Virdon replied, "That has never bothered me. If they're capable pitchers, it doesn't matter whether they're lefty or righty."

Virdon also said, somewhat defensively, that because Woodson was the Yanks' fifth new pitcher in a season that was just a month old, it didn't mean that the staff that began the season had been a disappointment. "It's all right now and it was all right before," he said. "It wasn't so turned over so much because we were unhappy, but because we wanted to acquire somebody."

The "acquired" player Virdon was referring to was first baseman Chris Chambliss. The Yanks had gotten Chambliss, along with two pitchers, a week earlier in a seven-player trade with Cleveland in which four pitchers went to the Indians.

Mike Pazik, a 24-year-old minor leaguer, went from the Yanks' International League team in Syracuse to Minnesota's Pacific Coast League club in Tacoma. Pazik would pitch for the Twins in parts of each of the next three seasons, compiling a 1-4 record.

To clear a place on the roster for Woodson, the Yanks sent rookie pitcher Rick Sawyer, whom they'd called up from Syracuse the week before, back to the Chiefs.

Woodson was 1-2 in eight games for the Yanks, but 1974 was his last major league season.

May 5, 1974: Purchased Infielder Fernando Gonzalez from the Kansas City Royals

"Don't get caught in the revolving door," Bobby Murcer cautioned his teammates after the Yanks announced that they'd purchased 24-year-old infielder Fernando Gonzalez, their third deal in three days. Gonzalez, added shortly before the Yanks lost to the Royals, became the sixth player added to the roster since Opening Day. The turnover was becoming so rapid that even the players were getting confused. Ron Blomberg thought the Gonzalez the Yankees were getting was former Oakland outfielder Gonzalo Marquez, now with the Cubs.

Fernando Gonzalez had played under current Yankee manager Bill Virdon at Pittsburgh in 1973, batting .224 in 37 games. Traded to Kansas City with three other players for pitcher Nelson Briles, he was hitting .143 when the Royals sent him to Omaha of the American Association two days earlier. But before Gonzalez had a chance to leave, the Royals sold him to New York and replaced him by recalling Omaha third baseman George Brett.

Gonzalez would bat .215 in 51 games at second, short, and third for the 1974 Yankees. They released him to the Mexican League in the spring of 1975, but he later came back to play in the National League.

May 7, 1974: Traded Catcher Duke Sims to the Texas Rangers for Lefthanded Pitcher Larry Gura and Cash

The Yanks had designated 33-year-old catcher Duke Sims for assignment two days earlier to make room for Fernando Gonzalez, whom they'd purchased from Kansas City. They'd gotten Sims from the Tigers in the last week of the 1973 season, and he'd gone 3 for 9 in four games.

Sims, who'd batted just 15 times this year, with two hits, said he'd been trying to get away from the Yankees for a long time because "the writing was on the wall.

"When they traded for [Chris] Chambliss, I knew it was all over for sure then. They were too deep at both catcher and first, and I asked them to be traded or turned loose or something."

Texas had tried to get Sims during the winter and then again when they were in New York in late April. "Sims is a good catcher and hitter both," said Rangers manager Billy Martin. "He performs capably either way and he can also play first."

Larry Gura had gone 3-7 in parts of four seasons with the Chicago Cubs, and was in his first season in the Texas organization. Gura was at Spokane of the Pacific Coast League, where he'd won one and lost one. The Yanks transferred him to Syracuse of the International League.

May 13, 1974: Sold First Baseman Mike Hegan to the Milwaukee Brewers

Mike Hegan had been sharing the first base job with Bill Sudakis until April 27, when the Yanks made the trade with Cleveland for Chris Chambliss. Since Chambliss's arrival, Hegan had appeared in only one of the club's 16 games, and that as a pinch hitter. In all, he'd played 18 games, batting .226 with two home runs and nine runs batted in.

The 32-year-old Hegan, who was the team's player representative, knew immediately that the arrival of Chambliss would end his days as even a semi-regular in New York. He immediately began asking the Yankees to trade him, preferably to the Brewers, Tigers, or Red Sox.

"I envisioned this year as one where I would go to the plate 400 times and see if I could do the job or not," Hegan said. "If I couldn't, I'd at least have had the satisfaction of having one last shot to see if I could do it."

In going to Milwaukee, Hegan expected he would likely be playing behind George Scott. Although Scott had started slowly, he was a much bigger offensive threat than Hegan and figured to retain his position.

May 31, 1974: Sold Second Baseman Horace Clarke to the San Diego Padres

Horace Clarke was the tenth player to leave the club since the season began, leaving

May 31, 1974: *Mel Stottlemyre.* Only Stottlemyre had been with the Yanks longer than Horace Clarke.

just nine players remaining from the Yankee team that finished the 1973 season. Clarke, soon to be 34, had been in the Yankee organization since 1958 and was the senior non-pitcher in length of service. Only pitcher Mel Stottlemyre, who joined the club in June 1964, had been a Yankee longer than Clarke, whose rookie season was 1965. That was the year after the Yankees won their last pennant, and when the popular Bobby Richardson retired following the 1966 season, Clarke became the club's full-time second baseman.

In more than 1,200 games for the Yankees, mostly from the leadoff position, Clarke hit .257 (with not many walks) and stole 151 bases. Despite problems in making the double play, he led American League second basemen in assists for six consecutive seasons (1967–72) and in putouts for four (1968–71). But, perhaps unfairly, for many Yankee fans Clarke had come to symbolize the franchise's decline. After being named the Yankees' manager, Bill Virdon had spent the whole winter searching for a new second baseman. When the search proved futile, Virdon moved Gene Michael, the Yankees' shortstop for the last five seasons, to second, and installed Jim Mason, purchased from the Rangers last December, at shortstop.

When asked how Clarke took the news of his trade, Virdon said, "Horace is pretty good about anything, but I think he was a little disappointed about leaving New York." Clarke, meanwhile, left immediately for St. Louis, where the Padres were playing the Cardinals. He finished out the year, and his career, with San Diego.

In a separate deal, the Yanks also sold Lowell Palmer, a righthanded pitcher on their Syracuse team in the International League, to the Padres. And finally, with Thurman Mun-

son's sore hand expected to keep him from catching for another week, the club brought up Jim Deidel, a 25-year-old catcher, from Syracuse. Deidel's big league career would consist of two games, with two at-bats and no hits.

June 15, 1974: Purchased Lefthanded Pitcher Rudy May from the California Angels

The purchase of 29-year-old lefthander Rudy May was the Yanks' 12th roster change since the season began. May, in his seventh

June 15, 1974: *Roy White.* **The Angels wanted the Yanks to include White in the deal for Rudy May.**

season, all with the Angels, had a 51-76 career record, including a 7-17 mark in 1973. In 18 games this season, he had a 7.00 earned run average and had lost his only decision. The deal, made just prior to the trading deadline, was for cash although the Angels had wanted to expand it. They were trying to get Yankee outfielder Roy White, but the clubs were unable to work out the details.

May had been primarily a starting pitcher until this season, when all but three of his appearances had come in relief. Yankee manager Bill Virdon said he would keep May in the bullpen at first, but then had plans for him to be his fifth starter.

Jim Deidel's major league career (two games with two at-bats and no hits) ended when the Yanks returned him to Syracuse of the International League to make room for May.

July 8, 1974: Purchased Infielder Sandy Alomar from the California Angels

In 1967, after little success in brief stays with the Atlanta Braves and New York Mets, Alomar was traded to the Chicago White Sox where he became a switch hitter and in 1968 was Chicago's everyday second baseman. The Sox traded him to California in 1969, and he continued as the Angels' regular second baseman until this season, when he lost his job to Denny Doyle. Alomar's streak of 648 consecutive games played for the Angels between 1969 and 1973, was at the time the seventh longest such streak in American League history.

Alomar had a lifetime average of .255 for his 11 big league seasons, and was hitting .222 in 54 at-bats this year. Yankee manager Bill Virdon said he would give him the opportunity to win the second base job from weak-hitting Gene Michael, whom he had been using at that position.

September 9, 1974: Purchased Outfielder Alex Johnson from the Texas Rangers

New York would be the seventh major league stop for Alex Johnson since his debut

with the 1964 Philadelphia Phillies. A former American League batting champion with the 1970 California Angels, he'd batted .291 for the Rangers this season, which matched exactly his lifetime average.

The Yanks, clinging to a one game lead over Baltimore, and sorely in need of right-handed hitting, paid the $20,000 waiver price for Johnson. Despite a well-deserved reputation for sullenness and lack of hustle, no one questioned Johnson's ability as a hitter.

Johnson finished the season with the Yankees, and was batting .261 after 52 games in 1975 when they released him on September 4.

October 22, 1974: Traded Outfielder Bobby Murcer to the San Francisco Giants for Outfielder Bobby Bonds

Early in their careers, many baseball people saw Bobby Bonds as the new Willie Mays and Bobby Murcer as the new Mickey Mantle. While neither had reached that level of greatness, Bonds and Murcer, both of whom were now 28, were, nevertheless, among the game's biggest stars. One-for-one trades of players of this magnitude were rare, although Yankee president Gabe Paul claimed that Giants owner Horace Stoneham had originally asked for pitcher Doc Medich before settling for Murcer.

Originally an infielder when he first came up in 1965, Murcer spent the 1967 and 1968 seasons in the Army. When he returned the Yankees made him their center fielder, where he had played until this past season when manager Bill Virdon moved him to right field and put Elliot Maddox in center.

Murcer hit his stride in 1971, batting .331 with 25 home runs and 94 runs batted in. He followed with a .292 average, 33 home run, 96 RBI season in 1972, and a .304 average, 22 HR, and 95 RBI season in 1973. But after the Yanks moved to Shea Stadium in 1974, Murcer's average fell to .274 and he hit just ten home runs. Only two of the home runs were at Shea, where the Yanks would again be playing in 1975. When asked what Bonds could do that Murcer couldn't, Virdon responded: "Steal 30 bases and produce home runs that Murcer won't produce in our ball park."

Murcer was both shocked and surprised

to hear that he'd been traded. "George Steinbrenner and I talked during the summer," he said, "and he told me that as long as he was with the Yankees, I would be the property of the Yankees. So I didn't have any indication that I would be traded. I'm sorry that whoever made the trade didn't feel I could help the ballclub anymore. It's a blow to me because I had helped build the club up and now that the team is a pennant contender I'm no longer a part of it."

Paul believed the Yankees would gain an overall benefit in adding a powerful righthanded hitter to a mostly lefthanded hitting lineup, a lineup that had struggled against lefthanders in 1974. The addition of Bonds would also work to give lefthanded slugger Ron Blomberg more playing time. "This should give us the opportunity to use Blomberg more," Paul said. "His bat is too good to be dormant on the bench."

Virdon's expectation that Bonds would provide speed and power was well founded; he was the only player besides Mays to hit 30 home runs and steal 30 bases in a season (each had done it twice). Bonds was a .273 career hitter in seven seasons with the Giants, with 263 stolen bases and 186 home runs. His best home run year was 1973 when he hit 39, with the 21 he hit in 1974 the fewest he'd had in any one full season.

According to Virdon, who'd managed against him in the National League, Bonds's tendency to strike out (he'd averaged 156 whiffs a season) was "his only fault." As for Bonds's alleged problems off the field, Paul dismissed

October 22, 1974: *Bobby Bonds.* The Yanks were sure that Bonds would hit more home runs and steal more bases than Bobby Murcer.

them saying, "You don't make these kinds of things blind. We're not concerned about it."

December 1, 1974: Purchased Infielder-Outfielder Bob Oliver from the Baltimore Orioles

In 1974 Bob Oliver batted a combined .243 with eight home runs for California and Baltimore. The Yankees saw several ways to use the versatile Oliver, possessor of a .257 batting average over seven seasons. He could be a righthanded fill-in for Chris Chambliss at first and Graig Nettles at third, or he could serve as a spare outfielder.

There was an added twist to this deal. Back on September 11, the Orioles, engaged in a tight race for the Eastern Division title with the Yankees, had acquired Oliver from the Angels for lefthanded pitcher Mickey Scott and cash. However, Baltimore had also agreed to send the Angels another player. Now that Oliver belonged to the Yankees so too did the obligation to send California that additional player. On December 5, the Yanks sent them minor league outfielder Mike Krizmanich.

Oliver would play only 18 games for the Yanks in 1975: his final 18, getting five hits in 38 at-bats.

December 3, 1974: Traded Infielder Bill Sudakis to the California Angels for Righthanded Pitcher Skip Lockwood

Serving mostly as a designated hitter and substitute first baseman, Bill Sudakis batted .232 in 89 games in 1974, his one year in New York. He would split the 1975 season, his final one in the major leagues, between California and Cleveland.

Skip Lockwood, 2-5 in 1974, would never pitch in a regular-season game for the Yankees. They released him in early April of 1975 and he then caught on with the Mets.

December 5, 1974: Traded Righthanded Pitcher Cecil Upshaw to the Chicago White Sox for Infielder Eddie Leon

Cecil Upshaw came to the Yankees with Chris Chambliss and Dick Tidrow in the big trade with Cleveland in April 1974. But while Chambliss and Tidrow had performed as expected, Upshaw had been a disappointment. Once an outstanding reliever with Atlanta, the 32-year-old, side-arming righthander appeared in 36 games for New York, posting a 1-5 record and only six saves.

The Yanks were planning to convert Tidrow from a starter and use him and the newly-acquired Skip Lockwood as their righthanded relievers to balance lefthander Sparky Lyle. That made Upshaw expendable. (The Yanks released Lockwood before he ever pitched in a regular-season game for them, leaving Tidrow the number one righthander out of the bullpen.)

Eddie Leon had been an outstanding hitter at the University of Arizona, but could never do much with big league pitching. He'd spent seven years as a utility infielder with the Indians and White Sox and had a lifetime batting average of just .236. The Yanks hoped to use him in the same capacity in 1975; however, Leon would play in only one game at short, which would be his last big league appearance.

December 31, 1974: *Catfish Hunter*. Hunter's signing as a free agent changed the game forever.

December 31, 1974: Signed Free-Agent Righthanded Pitcher Catfish Hunter from the Oakland Athletics

Arbitrator Peter Seitz had shocked the baseball world by declaring Oakland pitcher Catfish Hunter a free agent for the 1975 season. Seitz had based his decision on an administrative error that A's owner Charles Finley made regarding an insurance clause in Hunter's contract.

Hunter was coming off a league-leading 25-win season, the fourth consecutive year he'd won more than 20 games. He'd also led the American League with a 2.49 earned run average and captured the league's Cy Young Award. Only 19 when he broke in with the then–Kansas City Athletics in 1965, Hunter's overall record was 161-113. However, over the past four seasons it was an awesome 88-35, and his 4-0 record in World Series play had helped Oakland win the last three Series.

Not surprisingly, Hunter's availability engendered a precedent-setting bidding war for his services. It got down to the Yankees and the San Diego Padres, with Hunter choosing the

Yankees because he believed they were more likely to be a winning team. He also alluded to Yankee tradition and to his closeness to Yankee scout Clyde Kluttz, who'd signed Hunter to his first professional contract. "Clyde never lied to me then and he never lied to me now," he said. "If it hadn't been for him, the Yankees would have had a little more trouble signing me."

Hunter's five-year contract, estimated to be for $3.75 million, was by far the most lucrative ever given to a baseball player. Immediately, questions arose about his high salary creating a morale problem with other Yankee players.

Club president Gabe Paul didn't think so. "The morale of the club is helped when you add a man of Hunter's status," he said. "It increases the club's chances of winning the pennant."

Paul also said that while he believed Hunter was now legally Yankee property, he knew that Finley would challenge the signing in court. "The courts take precedence over everything," Paul said. "We can't go against the decision of the courts." Finley, of course, believed the courts would side with him. "It is my opinion, " he said, "that Hunter still belongs to the A's."

The courts decided in favor of the Yankees, and Hunter went 23-14 in 1975 giving him five straight 20-win seasons. Only two American League pitchers had done that previously, Walter Johnson and Lefty Grove. But 1975 would be the only outstanding year Hunter would have with the Yankees. Troubled by recurring arm injuries, he won only 40 games and lost 39 over the next four years and retired following a 2-9 season in 1979.

April 1, 1975: Traded Minor League Outfielder Ken Bennett, Minor League Catcher Terry Quinn, Minor League Lefthanded Pitcher Fred Anyzeski, Minor League First Baseman–Outfielder John Narron, and Cash to the Chicago White Sox for Catcher Ed Herrmann

Ed Herrmann had asked the Chicago White Sox to raise his 1974 salary of $42,000 to $52,000 for 1975. He based his request on his 1974 output—a .259 average, ten home runs and 39 runs batted in. But when the White Sox offered him only $48,000, Herrmann decided to play without a contract, while asking that Chicago trade him. After the Yanks agreed to pay him $50,000, Herrmann signed a contract with Chicago who then transferred it to New York.

Herrmann had been the White Sox catcher against righthanded pitchers since 1969. He had a reputation as a good hitter and a good receiver, but was a slow runner with an average throwing arm.

The Yanks already had two catchers, Thurman Munson and Rick Dempsey, but both hit righthanded, while the 28-year-old Herrmann swung from the left side. Manager Bill Virdon acknowledged that he would not have gone after Herrmann if he were a right-handed hitter. "Herrmann will be our third catcher," he said. "I don't mean in rating, but he's the third catcher we'll carry. He makes you a better club," Virdon continued. "He gives you another chance to win."

None of the four minor leaguers going to Chicago seemed likely to reach the major leagues, and none did.

June 13, 1975: Sold Lefthanded Pitcher Mike Wallace to the St. Louis Cardinals

After beginning the 1974 season at Syracuse in the International League, Mike Wallace pitched in 23 games for the Yankees, with a perfect 6-0 record and a splendid 2.41 earned run average. He'd been in three games this year with no record, but had not been impressive. The sale of Wallace cleared a spot for Ron Blomberg, who was returning from the disabled list.

June 13, 1975: Purchased Shortstop Ed Brinkman from the Texas Rangers

This was 33-year-old Ed Brinkman's 15th and final major league season. Never much of a hitter—he had a .225 career batting average—Brinkman had been a defensive standout for ten years in Washington and for four in Detroit. The Yanks would be his third team in 1975, a season he began as a member of the St. Louis Cardinals.

Yankee general manager Gabe Paul confessed he'd been trying to get Brinkman "since the season began," but didn't have the lefthanded hitter St. Louis wanted in return. After the Cardinals traded Brinkman to Texas for Willie Davis, Paul said that he "figured we had a better chance to land Brinkman from the Rangers."

Brinkman took the roster spot of outfielder Larry Murray, returned to West Haven of the Eastern League. He served as a utility infielder, getting into 44 games, but had only 63 at-bats and a .174 average. The Yankees released him in late March 1976.

June 20, 1975: Purchased Outfielder Rich Coggins from the Montreal Expos

The Yanks actually purchased Rich Coggins from the Memphis Blues, Montreal's Triple-A team in the International League. The Expos had sent Coggins to Memphis a few days earlier, although he had not yet played in a game for the Blues.

Coggins had batted .319 in 110 games as a Baltimore Orioles rookie in 1973, but when he followed with a .243-mark in 1974, the Orioles traded him. Coggins was included in the deal that sent pitcher Dave McNally to Montreal and brought outfielder Ken Singleton and pitcher Mike Torrez to Baltimore.

Coggins was batting .270 for the Expos this season, but had played in only 13 games because of a thyroid condition that kept him on the disabled list from Opening Day until May 22. A day after getting Coggins, the Yanks made room for him by sending rookie Kerry Dineen to their Syracuse team in the International League.

November 22, 1975: Traded Right-handed Pitcher Pat Dobson to the Cleveland Indians for Outfielder Oscar Gamble

After winning 19 games with a 3.07 ERA in 1974, his first full season with the Yankees, Pat Dobson was 11-14 in 1975, and his ERA went up a full run. Dobson blamed his poor performance on manager Bill Virdon, claiming that Virdon was removing him from games too quickly. Following a confrontation between the two men in Detroit, Dobson asked to be traded. Then, in August, Billy Martin replaced Virdon as manager and Dobson thought his situation would improve. But rather than getting better, it got worse as Martin removed him from the rotation.

Oscar Gamble was a 25-year-old left-handed hitter who seemed to possess a "Yankee Stadium swing." He'd hit 54 home runs the past three seasons with the Indians, and the Yanks were counting on him doing even better in New York.

December 11, 1975: Traded Outfielder Bobby Bonds to the California Angels for Outfielder Mickey Rivers and Righthanded Pitcher Ed Figueroa

By trading Bobby Bonds, and then later in the day Doc Medich, the Yanks clearly were

November 22, 1975: *Oscar Gamble*. **Gamble had a "Yankee Stadium swing."**

setting the club in a new direction. "The pattern of the club now is changing," said team president Gabe Paul. "We will now have outstanding speed and defense. And when we go back to Yankee Stadium next season [the Yanks had played at Shea Stadium in 1974 and 1975], where all that outfield space cuts into your power, we'll score more runs than we did in 1975."

Yankee manager Billy Martin seemed less enthusiastic about the change in direction. "Did I ever think I'd get away from here [the winter meetings] without Bobby Bonds and Doc Medich?" he asked. "No—we gave up a lot," he answered. "Only time will tell."

Paul, however, insisted that a change was needed because the Yanks hadn't won in 1975, although he emphasized that Bonds was not to blame. "He did a hell of a job," Paul said. "I resisted the idea of including him in the deal, and last week we told the Angels that he wasn't available. But we had to do something. You have to shoot craps a little and you're always taking a risk."

Bonds, acquired from the Giants for Bobby Murcer in October 1974, spent only one year with the Yankees. He batted .270 with 32 home runs and 85 runs batted in, and despite a knee injury in June, stole 30 bases. He also struck out 137 times.

"Bonds was carrying the club when he got hurt," said Houston Astros manager Bill Virdon, who was the Yankee manager until Martin replaced him in August. Bonds said that he had "enjoyed playing in New York," and he was "very surprised" that the Yanks had traded him.

At 27, Mickey Rivers was two years younger than Bonds, and while he lacked Bonds's power, he did have great speed. Generally thought to be the fastest man in the game, Rivers led the American League with 70 stolen bases in 1975. He'd also led in triples for each of the last two seasons. And though he didn't draw many walks, Rivers was an excellent lead-off man who'd batted .285 in 1974, and .284 in 1975.

Righthander Ed Figueroa, also 27, had a 2-8 record as a rookie in 1974, but blossomed in 1975, winning 16 games with a 2.91 earned run average for the last-place Angels. Paul happily noted that Figueroa had beaten the defending American League champion Boston Red Sox three times without a loss. Still, he confessed that Figueroa had not been his first choice. Paul revealed that he had tried to talk Angels GM Harry Dalton into trading his ace, lefthander Frank Tanana, before agreeing to take Figueroa.

December 11, 1975: Traded Right-handed Pitcher Doc Medich to the Pittsburgh Pirates for Second Baseman Willie Randolph, Righthanded Pitcher Dock Ellis, and Lefthanded Pitcher Ken Brett

Even Gabe Paul, a veteran baseball executive, admitted that it had been a most unusual day. "No, I don't remember ever trading two like that in one day," the Yankee president said. "This is the jackpot."

Two hours after trading Bobby Bonds, the Yanks' best power hitter, to the California Angels, Paul concluded another major deal by sending Doc Medich, a 16-game winner in 1975, to Pittsburgh. And, he was ready for more. "We're still looking for a shortstop," Paul said. "If we find one we'll jump in with both feet."

The 27-year-old Medich, a fourth-year medical student at the University of Pittsburgh, departed after three fine seasons as a Yankee. He was 14-9 as a rookie in 1973, 19-15 in 1974, and 16-16 in '75.

While Dock Ellis had a very different lifestyle than Medich, he'd been an equally effective pitcher. Ellis had pitched for five division winners in his eight seasons in Pittsburgh, amassing a 96-80 record, including a career-best 19-9 in 1971. However, Ellis won only eight, while losing nine this past season, and he'd missed four weeks after Pirates manager Danny Murtaugh suspended him following a locker room confrontation. The poor season and the suspension made his departure from Pittsburgh appear inevitable.

"He lets his emotions over-rule his intellect," said Pirates general manager Joe Brown. "But Dock never hurt the morale of the team, though the recent unpleasantness did result as much as anything in his being traded."

While Ellis figured to take his place in the Yankee rotation, Ken Brett's future remained questionable. He'd had back-to-back 13-9 seasons for the Phillies in 1973 and the Pirates in 1974, but then underwent surgery on his left elbow. Brett came back to go 9-5 for Pittsburgh in 1975; nevertheless, the Pirates twice had to put the 27-year-old left-hander on the disabled list.

Yankee manager Billy Martin said he would take a wait-and-see approach to his two new pitchers. Speaking of the explosive Ellis, Martin said, "The Hall of Fame is filled with tough cases. I think Ellis will be a starting pitcher for the Yankees. As for Brett, we'll look at him in spring training and see how sound his arm is."

But it was neither Ellis nor Brett that had induced the Yankees to part with Medich; that distinction belonged to 21-year-old Willie Randolph. The Pirates had called Randolph up in late July 1975 from Charleston of the International League, where he was batting .339. And although he batted just .164 in 30 games, Brown said that "Randolph was more in demand by more clubs than any player on the Pittsburgh club." The Pirates were satisfied with Rennie Stennett at second base and thus were willing to let the rookie leave.

Randolph would become one of the Yankees' greatest second basemen, playing the

December 11, 1975: *Willie Randolph*. **Pittsburgh traded Randolph, a rookie, because they were satisfied with Rennie Stennett at second base.**

position for the next 13 years. In almost 1,700 games, he batted .275, stole 251 bases, and scored more than a thousand runs. When the Yanks signed Steve Sax as a free agent following the 1988 season, Randolph left to sign with the Dodgers.

January 8, 1976: Purchased Right-handed Pitcher Jim York from the Houston Astros

Journeyman reliever Jim York had a career 15-17 record with ten saves in six big league seasons, two with Kansas City and the last four with the Astros. He'd been in 174 games, but the four he'd started for Houston this past season were the only games he'd started as a big leaguer. York's record for the Astros in 1976 was 4-4, and it was 2-2 in 31 games with Iowa of the American Association.

Immediately after purchasing him, the Yanks assigned York to their Triple-A Syracuse club in the International League. In 22

games for Syracuse in 1976, he had a 6-1 record, but with no saves and a 5.34 ERA. He appeared in three games for the Yankees, his final three, winning his only decision.

February 20, 1976: Sold Catcher Ed Herrmann to the California Angels

In 1975, his one season with the Yankees, Ed Herrmann hit .255 in 80 games as a catcher and designated hitter. Herrmann's 35 games at DH was the most on the club, as managers Bill Virdon and Billy Martin used many different people at the position. Coincidentally, the Yanks had recently signed veteran Tommy Davis to share the DH role with Ron Blomberg in 1976, but they would release Davis before the season started.

May 16, 1976: Traded Lefthanded Pitcher Larry Gura to the Kansas City Royals for Catcher Fran Healy

With the 1976 season now in its sixth week, Yankee pitcher Larry Gura remained the only major leaguer who'd been on his team's roster all season and had not played in a game. The reason was simple: Billy Martin, his manager, didn't like him. Martin had traded Gura to the Yankees when he managed the Texas Rangers, and so Gura, who was also the team's player representative, wasn't surprised to hear that Martin had traded him again. Gura had gone 5-1 in his brief stay with the Yanks in 1974, and then 7-8 in 1975, the year in which Martin replaced Bill Virdon as manager.

"I had a feeling something was going to happen," he said, adding that he wished the Yanks had dealt him at the beginning of the season. "I'm bitter that they got my spirits up during the winter by telling me I would get a chance to start and then not doing what they said."

Martin said that it came down to a choice between Gura and Dock Ellis and that he and his coaches felt "Ellis has better stuff." Meanwhile, Gura said he was just glad to go to a team that would give him an opportunity to pitch. He would spend the next ten years with the Royals and have double-digit win totals in seven of them.

Catcher Fran Healy was 29, the same age as Gura. He was a seven-year veteran of the Giants and Royals, but had played in more than 100 games in only one season. That was in 1974, when he batted .252 while catching 138 games for Kansas City. Healy also stole 16 bases in '74, but a shoulder injury the next year had hurt his progress. This season, he'd been in just eight games and was batting .125.

Healy's stay in New York, many believed, would be brief. With the Yanks looking to trade for a lefthanded hitter, either Healy or Rick Dempsey, the team's other reserve catcher, figured to be part of that deal. It would turn out to be Dempsey, who a month later went to Baltimore as part of a multiplayer trade. Healy remained in New York, where he served as a backup to Thurman Munson through the 1977 season, ending his career with a final game in 1978.

May 18, 1976: Traded Lefthanded Pitcher Ken Brett and Outfielder Rich Coggins to the Chicago White Sox for Outfielder Carlos May

Before he'd even reported to the Yankees, Carlos May managed to anger Billy Martin, his new manager. Martin was upset because May learned he'd been traded at 9:00 A.M., but didn't get from Chicago to join the Yankees in time for that night's game in Cleveland.

"I tell you I wish he'd been here. I hope he doesn't stay away much longer. I'd appreciate his presence," Martin said after the game, won by the Yankees 11-6 in 16 innings.

May had been *The Sporting News* American League Rookie of the Year in 1969, the year he lost part of his thumb while on duty with the Marine reserve. He'd come back from that injury and had been a Chicago regular ever since, but was batting just .175 in 20 games this season.

The Yanks got Rich Coggins from Montreal in June 1975. He batted .224 in 51 games, but had seen very little action this season, batting four times with one hit.

Ken Brett came to New York with Dock Ellis and Willie Randolph in the big December 1975 trade that sent Doc Medich to Pittsburgh. He'd been in only two games as a Yankee, pitching 2.1 innings and earning a save.

June 15, 1976: Traded Lefthanded Pitchers Rudy May and Tippy Martinez, Righthanded Pitcher Dave Pagan, Catcher Rick Dempsey, and Minor League Lefthanded Pitcher Scott McGregor to the Baltimore Orioles for Lefthanded Pitchers Ken Holtzman, Grant Jackson, and Jimmy Freeman, Righthanded Pitcher Doyle Alexander, and Catcher Elrod Hendricks

A perfect symmetry characterized this ten-player trade, the largest for either team since their 17-player deal back in 1954. Each club gained and lost three lefthanded pitchers, one righthanded pitcher, and one catcher.

"We think it's a deal that will complement both clubs," said Hank Peters, the Orioles general manager. Peters and his Yankee counterpart Gabe Paul had worked out all the particulars, completing the deal just before the trading deadline which came at midnight. Peters hinted that the trade might have been even bigger.

"If I showed you all the combinations that were written down in the last few days, you wouldn't believe it," he said. "It's primarily a pitchers deal but at times it went beyond that into other areas."

From Paul's standpoint, the deal revolved around the Yanks getting Ken Holtzman. "The key man naturally was Holtzman," he said. "That didn't change throughout our talks."

Both Holtzman, 31, and Doyle Alexander, 25, were unsigned, although the deal was structured to stand even if the Yanks failed to sign them. Peters considered each of them to be a bad influence on his team and wanted them gone. He had tried to trade Holtzman to Kansas City three days earlier, but the deal fell through when the Royals and Holtzman's agent, Jerry Kapstein, who also represented Alexander, couldn't agree on terms.

The Orioles had acquired Holtzman from Oakland along with Reggie Jackson just before the beginning of the 1976 season. Signed originally by the Cubs, Holtzman had spent four years with the Athletics and entered this season with a lifetime 151-124 record. He'd had only one 20-win season (21-13 in 1973), but he'd also won 19 twice and 18 once for Oakland, and 17 twice for the Cubs. His record for

Baltimore this season was 5-4, with a 2.86 earned run average.

After Alexander went 6-6 as a Dodger rookie in 1971, they traded him to Baltimore in the Frank Robinson deal. His 3-4 record this season brought his career mark with the Orioles to 35-37. Alexander would win ten and lose five for the Yankees, but they too would be unable to sign him and in 1977 he would leave to play with Texas.

Grant Jackson, 1-1 in 1976, had a 47-55 record in 12 seasons with the Phillies and Orioles. He would go 6-0 for the Yankees, who nevertheless made him available in the expansion draft that fall. The Seattle Mariners selected Jackson, but a month later traded him to Pittsburgh.

Tippy Martinez had spent part of 1974 and 1975 in New York, winning one and losing two with eight saves. He was 2-0 with two saves this season.

Dave Pagan had been back and forth between the Yankees and Syracuse of the International League since 1973. He was 1-3 with the Yanks in 1974 and 1-1 this year.

Scott McGregor was just 22 years old, four years younger than Martinez and Pagan. Unlike them, he had yet to pitch in the big leagues, yet he'd shown exceptional promise. The Orioles, after moving him from Syracuse to their International League team at Rochester, would bring him to Baltimore in September.

Jimmy Freeman was also in the minors, although he had pitched briefly for Atlanta in 1972-73. He swapped places with McGregor, going from Rochester to Syracuse.

The only veteran pitcher the Yanks were losing was 31-year-old Rudy May. They'd bought him from the Angels exactly two years earlier, and May had pitched extremely well in the second half of the '74 season: 8-4, with a 2.28 ERA. His overall record as a Yankee was 26-19, including four wins and three losses in 1976.

"From an experience point," Peters said, "they picked up a good pitcher in Holtzman. But we are very happy. We like May and feel that Martinez is an outstanding relief pitcher. We also like Pagan and have very good reports on McGregor."

At the same time, the Yanks were excited at having what they felt was now the league's best pitching staff. Besides Catfish Hunter, Ed Figueroa, and Dock Ellis, they'd added Alexander and two of the top lefthanders in the league, Holtzman and Vida Blue. They had purchased Blue from Oakland for $1.5 million; however, Commissioner Bowie Kuhn vetoed the deal and Blue never did pitch for the Yankees.

The Yanks added ten years of age in the swap of catchers, losing 26-year-old Rick Dempsey and adding 36-year-old Elrod Hendricks. Except for 17 games with the Cubs in 1972, Hendricks had been with the Orioles since 1968. Clearly nearing the end of his career, he'd been in just 28 games this season and had a .139 batting average. Hendricks would hit .226 in 26 games for the Yanks in 1976, and was 3 for 11 in 1977 when they released him.

Dempsey had filled several roles in the 141 games he'd played with the Yankees since 1973. He'd been a backup to Thurman Munson, a part-time outfielder, and a part-time designated hitter. Like Hendricks, Dempsey hadn't done much this season, batting a measly .119 in 21 games.

July 10, 1976: Traded a Player to Be Named to the San Diego Padres for Outfielder Gene Locklear

In 1975, which was his third big league season, Gene Locklear batted .321 in 100 games for the Padres. But after 43 games this season, he was struggling with a batting average of just .224. The Yanks sent Locklear to the International League Syracuse Chiefs and then later in the year brought him to New York. He had a .219 average in 13 games and played his final major league game in 1977, getting three hits in five at-bats.

On July 31, 1976, the Yanks sent 29-year-old righthander Rick Sawyer (9-4 at Syracuse) to the Padres, who kept him on their major league roster. Sawyer had pitched a total of five games for New York in 1974 and 1975, with no decisions. He would go 12-9 in two seasons in San Diego.

September 1, 1976: Signed Infielder-Outfielder Cesar Tovar as a Free Agent

The Yanks signed Cesar Tovar the same day the A's released him, but it was one day too late for Tovar to be eligible for the playoffs and World Series. Nevertheless, manager Billy Martin was glad to have Tovar, a player he'd managed at both Minnesota and Texas, although he would have rather added a powerful hitting DH. "He's an excellent offensive player and can do a lot of things and help out at a lot of positions," Martin said.

The 36-year-old Tovar had spent the best of his 12 seasons in Minnesota, where he led the league in doubles and triples in 1970 and in hits in 1971. He'd since played for the Phillies, Rangers, and Athletics, compiling a .278 lifetime batting average. Hurt for much of this season, which would be his final one, he'd played in just 29 games, batted only 45 times, and had a .178 batting average.

Tovar batted .154 in 13 September games for the Yanks, who released him in December.

November 18, 1976: Signed Free-Agent Lefthanded Pitcher Don Gullett from the Cincinnati Reds

Pitcher Don Gullett was the first player the Yankees signed under the newly designated free-agent system. They gave him a six-year contract, believed to be longer than that of any current player. Gullett and Gary Matthews, the former San Francisco Giant who was signed today by the Atlanta Braves, brought the number of players who had switched teams to eight under the new arrangement. Oddly, in contrast to what the pundits had predicted, all went to teams that had a lower 1976 winning percentage than the teams they were leaving. That was true even for Gullett, who was joining the Yankees, the American League pennant-winners, but was leaving the Cincinnati Reds, the reigning world champions. It was Gullett who had beaten the Yanks in the first game of the 1976 series, 5-1, starting Cincinnati on its way to a four-game sweep.

Gullet had won 11 and lost three in 1976, raising his career totals for seven years, all with the Reds, to a most impressive 91 wins and 44 defeats. His .674 winning percentage was the highest among active pitchers with at least 100 decisions. The 25-year-old Gullett had not had many injury-free seasons, but Yankee president Gabe Paul dismissed that history.

"We feel Gullett is a modern day Whitey Ford," Paul said, adding that the Yankees weren't through trying to improve their club. "We have been active, and we will be active," he said. "We have the wherewithal. Mr. Steinbrenner's pockets haven't been depleted."

While Gullett's leaving seemed to offend some people in the Cincinnati organization, he showed no remorse. "I don't feel the bad guy," he said. "I feel I made a good selection in playing for the Yankees. I don't feel terrible about leaving the Reds. They're a great organization, but I have no regrets. I can't really look back. I have to look to the future."

Unfortunately, because of a rotator cuff injury, Gullett's baseball future would last only two seasons. He was 14-4 in 1977, as the Yanks won the World Series, but just 4-2 in 1978 when he pitched in just eight games, the last one on July 9. The Yanks eventually gave up on Gullett and released him on October 24, 1980.

November 29, 1976: Signed Free-Agent Outfielder Reggie Jackson from the Baltimore Orioles

By signing Reggie Jackson, 11 days after signing former Cincinnati pitcher Don Gullett, the Yanks had secured two of the three most sought-after free agents. (The third, Baltimore second baseman Bobby Grich would sign with the California Angels.) Several clubs pursuing Jackson had supposedly offered him more money, presumably an even more lucrative deal than the five-year $2.9 million one he got in New York. An executive for the Montreal Expos said: "We were prepared to give him what he wanted." But the 30-year-old Jackson cited owner George Steinbrenner as the reason he signed with the Yankees.

"This was the biggest decision I ever had to make in my life," he said. "Some clubs offered several hundred thousand dollars more, possibly seven figures more, but the reason I'm a Yankee is that George Steinbrenner outhustled everybody else. I got the feeling I was his personal project to go with the Yankees."

Jackson dismissed charges that the Yankees

November 29, 1976: *Reggie Jackson*. "The reason I'm a Yankee is that George Steinbrenner out-hustled everybody else."

were attempting to buy a pennant. "There are other teams that had an opportunity to pick up players," he answered. "No one said the Green Bay Packers bought a championship when they signed Jim Grabowski and Donny Anderson. No one said the Jets bought an entire league when they signed Joe Namath."

Steinbrenner had even talked to Thurman Munson, the Yankee captain, about the ramifications of adding the flamboyant Jackson, who was sometimes thought to be a divisive influence. Munson replied, "Go get the big man. He's the only guy in baseball who can carry a club for a month. And the hell with what you hear. He hustles every minute he's on the field."

Pitcher Catfish Hunter, Jackson's teammate when they were with the Athletics, was overjoyed at the news. "He can be lots of things," Hunter said, "but he can help a club a lot more than he can ever hurt it. You know he's going to talk a lot, but you know he's going to produce a lot along with that talking."

Jackson certainly had produced a lot in his American League career. Since coming up with A's in 1967 (their last year in Kansas City), through eight years in Oakland and one in Baltimore, he'd hit 281 home runs and batted in 824 runs. As an Oriole in 1976, he'd batted .277, with 27 home runs and 91 RBIs.

And Jackson would continue to produce in his five seasons in New York, helping the Yanks to four Eastern Division championships, three American League pennants, and two World Series titles. Jackson batted .281 as a Yankee, with 144 home runs (including a third American League home run title in 1980), and 461 runs batted in. He also continued to talk a lot, getting into scrapes with Munson, manager Billy Martin, and Steinbrenner.

Jackson fell out of favor with Steinbrenner in 1981 and knew he was no longer wanted when the owner said he would emphasize speed over power in 1982. On January 22, 1982, Jackson, a free agent, signed with the California Angels.

November 30, 1976: Purchased Outfielder Jim Wynn from the Atlanta Braves

Jim Wynn had even more lifetime home runs (290 to 281) than Reggie Jackson, whom

the Yanks had signed the day before. But Wynn would be 35 by Opening Day, 1977, and was coming off one of the least productive power seasons of his 14-year career. Wynn, who'd spent 11 seasons with Houston and two with Los Angeles before joining the Braves in 1976, hit just .207 with only 17 home runs. (He did, however, lead the NL with 127 walks.)

Despite his off year, the Yank felt Wynn could help fill their need for a righthanded power hitter. Bill Lucas, Atlanta's director of player personnel, blamed Wynn's sub-par 1976 season on his trying too hard. "I think he recognized the fact that we needed a leader and he took it on himself to be that leader," Lucas said.

Wynn had become expendable when Atlanta signed San Francisco's free-agent outfielder Gary Matthews. Wynn knew the Braves were after Matthews and, expecting to be traded, asked owner Ted Turner to send him to the Yankees. Turner obliged, making Wynn happy enough so that unlike many former National Leaguers, he said he had no problem even if the Yanks wanted to use him as the designated hitter. And, they did.

Wynn was the designated hitter on Opening Day, 1977, and made his first Yankee at-bat a memorable one by hitting a mammoth home run against Milwaukee's Bill Travers. It was the 291st home run of his career, and the last. Wynn was batting .143 when the Yanks released him in July, and although the Brewers signed him, 1977 would be his final big-league season.

January 20, 1977: Traded Outfielders Elliot Maddox and Rick Bladt to the Baltimore Orioles for Outfielder Paul Blair

In 1974, his first season with the Yankees, Elliot Maddox batted .303 and was the team's center fielder. The following year, he was batting .307 when he suffered a knee injury in June that sidelined him for the rest of the season. Maddox had the knee operated on in September 1975 and remained on the disabled list for much of 1976, playing in just 18 games. By then Mickey Rivers was the Yankees center fielder, and Billy Martin, whom Maddox had problems with when he played for him in Texas, was the manager.

Maddox had also clashed with general manager Gabe Paul over a possible second surgery to his knee. Paul didn't think it was necessary, but Maddox did. He had it done in November 1976 and said afterward that his knee now felt more stable without a brace than it did during the '76 season with a brace.

Still, given his disagreements with Paul and Martin, the Yanks trading him did not surprise Maddox. "When I heard Gabe on the phone," he said, "I knew I was traded because I hadn't talked to him since November 1 when he told me I didn't need another operation."

Since joining the Orioles back in 1964, Paul Blair had established himself as one of baseball's finest defensive outfielders. An integral part of the outstanding Baltimore teams of the late 1960s and early 1970s, he was a career .254-batter, with his best season coming in 1968. Blair batted .285 with 26 home runs in '68, but he was now 33 years old and had not been an effective hitter since California's Ken Tatum beaned him in 1970. Blair's batting averages for the last two seasons were .218 and .197.

The Yankees would use Blair primarily as a defensive replacement in 1977, although he did have 164 at-bats and batted a respectable .262. He fell off to .176 in 1978, and in April 1979 the Yanks released him after he'd played just two games. Blair signed with Cincinnati and then came back to the Yankees for a final 12 games in 1980.

Rick Bladt had been with Syracuse in the International League for most of the past two seasons, although he did play in 52 games with the Yankees in 1975. (He batted .222, with one home run.) Baltimore assigned Bladt to their International League affiliate at Rochester.

February 17, 1977: Traded Second Baseman Sandy Alomar to the Texas Rangers for Infielder Greg Pryor, Minor League Infielder Brian Doyle, and Cash

Sandy Alomar was the Yankees' full-time second baseman from the time he joined them early in July 1974 through the 1975 season. But

after batting just .239 in '75, he lost his job to Willie Randolph, the rookie acquired from Pittsburgh. Alomar played only 38 games at second base in 1976 (67 games overall), while again batting .239.

Both 23-year-old Brian Doyle and 27-year-old Greg Pryor were with Sacramento of the Pacific Coast League in 1976. Doyle, whose brother Denny had won the Angels' second base job from Alomar in 1974, batted .290 in 96 games for Sacramento. He also had a .349 average in 25 games with San Antonio of the Texas League. Pryor batted .275 in 122 games for the Solons in '76, and had three hits in eight at-bats with the Rangers.

The Yanks assigned Doyle and Pryor to Syracuse of the International League for 1977. Both would spend the entire season at Syracuse, after which, the Yanks made Pryor a free agent and he signed with the White Sox.

March 14, 1977: Traded Outfielder Terry Whitfield to the San Francisco Giants for Infielder Marty Perez

While continuing to pursue a trade for White Sox shortstop Bucky Dent, the Yanks added Marty Perez to serve as an infield reserve. Originally a California Angel, Perez was with Atlanta from 1971 until they traded him to the Giants in June 1976. He had a .249 career batting average and since 1971 had never played in fewer than 120 games.

The Yanks were expecting a lot from Terry Whitfield after he'd been named Player of the Year in the Appalachian League in 1971, and in the Carolina League in 1973. Yet, over the past three seasons he'd played in just 31 games for the Yankees, with a .267 batting average. The club was loaded with outfielders this spring, 14 in all, and the 24-year-old Whitfield had used up his three options. Because the Yanks couldn't send him back to the minors, they either had to keep him or trade him. They chose to trade him.

April 5, 1977: Traded Outfielder Oscar Gamble and Minor League Righthanded Pitchers LaMarr Hoyt

and Bob Polinsky to the Chicago White Sox for Shortstop Bucky Dent

Fred Stanley had been the Yankee shortstop for most of the 1976 season. However, Stanley was a weak hitter, and manager Billy Martin was not content to start the new season with him as an everyday player. When spring training began, Martin hoped that rookie Mickey Klutts, who'd had a terrific year with Syracuse of the International League in 1976, would play well enough during the exhibition season to win the job. But Klutts broke a finger on the first day of camp, and the club had spent the entire spring trying to trade for a shortstop. They'd specifically targeted Bucky Dent of the White Sox, who had compiled batting averages of .274, .264, and .246 the past three seasons as Chicago's everyday shortstop. Two days before the opener, the Yanks finally got him, which elated club president Gabe Paul. "In obtaining Dent," Paul said, "we feel we've got one of the best young shortstops in baseball."

The addition of two expansion teams in 1977—the Seattle Mariners and the Toronto Blue Jays—had thinned the talent in the American League even further. Therefore, the addition of the 25-year-old Dent, which now gave the Yankees an established player at every position, made them the overwhelming favorites to repeat as pennant-winners.

With their surplus of outfielders, the Yanks felt Oscar Gamble was expendable. He'd batted .232 in 1976, his one season in New York, although he did have 17 home runs and 51 runs batted in. "In particular I was sorry to see Gamble go," said Yankee owner George Steinbrenner. "But we felt we needed more strength in the infield."

Neither Bob Polinsky (4-8, 3.30 with Syracuse), nor 22-year-old LaMarr Hoyt (15-8, 2.50 ERA with West Haven of the Eastern League) figured to pitch for the Yankees in 1977. Polinsky would eventually return to the Yanks in a trade, and then be dealt away again without ever pitching in a big league game. Hoyt, on the other hand, would eventually reach the White Sox, win a Cy Young Award in 1983, and twice (1982 and 1983) lead the American League in wins.

April 27, 1977: Traded Righthanded Pitcher Dock Ellis, Infielder Marty Perez, and Outfielder Larry Murray to the Oakland Athletics for Righthanded Pitcher Mike Torrez

The Yanks had been unable to sign Dock Ellis, a bombastic man who'd hastened his departure from New York by criticizing owner George Steinbrenner during the negotiations.

"I have no animosity toward George Steinbrenner," Ellis said after learning of the trade. "It's his money. He can give it to anyone he wants. He just didn't give it to me. He didn't deal in good faith." Ellis also had nothing but good things to say about his now-former teammates. "It's hard to find a bunch of guys like this to play with," he said. "But me liking the guys here has nothing to do with me being traded. If you gotta go, you gotta go."

Ellis's first year with the Yankees following his trade from Pittsburgh had been 1976. He won 17 and lost eight for a Yankee team that won its first pennant in 12 years. And,

April 5, 1977: Bucky Dent. The Yankees had been after Dent all spring.

despite his contractual problems, Ellis had started well this season, a 1-1 record in three starts with an earned run average of just 1.83.

Because of his effective pitching, and despite his controversial reputation, manager Billy Martin was sorry to see Ellis go; nevertheless, he was glad to have a proven winner like Mike Torrez. After winning 20 games for Baltimore in 1975, the Orioles traded Torrez and Don Baylor to Oakland for Reggie Jackson and Ken Holtzman. (Both Jackson and Holtzman were now with the Yankees.) He'd gone 16-12 for the '76 A's and was 3-1 so far this season. The 30-year-old Torrez had also pitched for St. Louis and Montreal and had a lifetime record of 100-72.

Although the Athletics had signed him for the 1977 season, Torrez was eligible for free agency in 1978. That, no doubt, was the main reason A's owner Charlie Finley was anxious to trade him. Finley and Yankee president Gabe Paul had been discussing an Ellis for Torrez deal for several weeks. The deal had been held up because Finley was asking the Yanks to include pitchers Ron Guidry and Gil Patterson, and shortstop Mickey Klutts. When the Yankees refused to part with any of those three promising rookies, Finley settled instead for Marty Perez and Larry Murray.

The Yanks had gotten Perez, a veteran infielder, from the Giants in the Terry Whitfield trade a month earlier. Also unsigned, he'd been in one game, going 2 for 4.

The 24-year-old Murray, who'd played in 20 games for the Yanks from 1974 to 1976 (one hit in 12 at-bats), was currently batting .310 for Syracuse of the International League.

Torrez won 14 and lost 12 after joining the Yankees, and then won two games in the World Series win over Los Angeles. Still, after it was all over he signed as a free agent to play for the Boston Red Sox in 1978.

June 15, 1977: Traded Minor League Shortstop Mike Fischlin, Minor League Lefthanded Pitcher Randy Niemann, and a Player to Be Named to the Houston Astros for Catcher–First Baseman Cliff Johnson

The Yankees had strained to beat the trading deadline and make this deal because they wanted Cliff Johnson's righthanded bat in their lineup. The team was 25-10 against righthanders this season, but only 11-16 against lefties. Johnson's acquisition was designed to address that imbalance. He'd hit 40 home runs for the Astros between 1974 and 1976 and was off to his best start ever in 1977. Johnson left Houston with a .299 average in 144 at-bats, ten home runs, and 23 RBIs. (He'd also struck out 30 times.)

Now that he was in the American League, the 29-year-old slugger figured to see most of his action as the designated hitter; but the Yanks could also use him as a backup first baseman behind Chris Chambliss, or even as an emergency catcher. Johnson took the roster spot of veteran catcher Elrod Hendricks, whom the Yanks had acquired in the big June 1976 trade with Baltimore, and who would be a free agent after the season.

Both the 21-year-old players going to Houston were in the low minors. Randy Niemann was at West Haven of the Eastern League, where he was 4-4 with a 5.52 ERA, while Mike Fischlin was batting .294 with Fort Lauderdale of the Florida State League. The Astros assigned them both to their Columbus team in the Southern League.

On November 23, the Yanks sent Dave Bergman, one of their best minor league prospects, to Houston as the player to be named. Bergman, an outfielder–first baseman, had played a total of 12 games for the Yankees in 1975 and 1977, with one hit in 21 at-bats.

August 2, 1977: Purchased Righthanded Pitcher Stan Thomas from the Seattle Mariners

After Stan Thomas went 4-4 with a 2.30 earned run average for Cleveland in 1976, Seattle selected him in the expansion draft that November. Pitching for the Mariners in their first year of existence this season, Thomas was 2-6 with a 6.02 ERA. The Yanks sent him to their Class AAA Syracuse team in the International League.

September 15, 1977: Purchased Outfielder–First Baseman Dave Kingman from the California Angels

While Dave Kingman would not be eligible to play in the World Series, the Yankees were hoping he would at least help get them there. With a little more than two weeks left in the season, they were clinging to a 2½ game Eastern Division lead over the Red Sox and Orioles.

The Yanks would be the fourth club the 30-year-old slugger had played for in 1977. He'd started the season with the Mets, who traded him to San Diego in June. Then on September 6, just nine days ago, the Padres sold him to California.

Kingman, who'd entered the season with 150 home runs, would hit four in 24 at-bats for the Yankees to give him a season total of 26. At the time, that was the most home runs ever by a player who had split his season between the two leagues and had at least one home run in each league. Kingman hit 20 in the National League (nine with the Mets and 11 with the Padres), and six in the American League (two with the Angels, four with the Yankees), breaking Deron Johnson's record of 20 (one for the Phillies and 19 for the Oakland A's) set in 1973.

As a free agent, Kingman signed to play in 1978 with the Chicago Cubs.

September 16, 1977: Sold Outfielder– Designated Hitter Carlos May to the California Angels

Carlos May came from the White Sox in May 1976 and batted .278 in 87 games, mostly as the lefthanded designated hitter. He filled that same role this season, but in 181 at-bats his average was a disappointing .227. Though he was just 29, this was May's final season.

November 22, 1977: Signed Free-Agent Righthanded Pitcher Goose Gossage from the Pittsburgh Pirates

Goose Gossage's reported compensation for signing this six-year deal was $3.6 million.

It was, at the time, the largest total package ever for a free agent, surpassing the $3.2 million the Milwaukee Brewers had given outfielder Larry Hisle a week earlier.

Gossage joined Sparky Lyle, the American League's 1977 Cy Young Award winner, to give the Yankees baseball's most dominating bullpen and made them the favorites to repeat as world champions. Even the usually modest Gossage agreed. "I think maybe this is the thing they needed to make a dynasty," he said.

For the first four seasons of Gossage's big league career, the Chicago White Sox had used him almost exclusively as a reliever. In 1975, the last of those four seasons, he compiled a league-leading 26 saves and won the American League's Fireman of the Year Award. But in 1976, Paul Richards replaced Chuck Tanner as manager and put Gossage into the starting rotation. He went 9-17 as a starter, and that winter Chicago traded him to Pittsburgh, now managed by Tanner. Back in the bullpen, Gossage pitched in 72 games for the '77 Pirates, won 11 and lost nine, and had 26 saves.

Gossage was a favorite of both fans and management in Pittsburgh. "I can't say enough good things about this man," said Harding Peterson, Pittsburgh's general manager. "He's very mature for a ballplayer that age, very dedicated to his work. He's got it all together, I guess you could say." Peterson also noted that Gossage was "certainly not a troublemaker."

November 22, 1977: *Goose Gossage.* "I think maybe this is the thing they needed to make a dynasty."

Picked by the maximum 14 teams in the draft, Gossage explained why he chose the Yankees. "The great teams the Yankees are and the class organization they are had something to do with it, but I can't cite any particular reason for being here. I left everything up to Jerry." (Jerry was Jerry Kapstein, Gossage's agent.)

George Steinbrenner dismissed speculation that Lyle would not be pleased at having to share the bullpen load, and glory, with a newcomer. "I think Sparky will tell you he's satisfied," the Yankee owner said. "Sparky's thirty-three and Rich is twenty-six. I think Sparky's happy and feels he's been treated fairly."

Despite Steinbrenner's words, Lyle was not happy with the new arrangement. In 1978, the only season in which Lyle and Gossage were teammates, it was Gossage who was the number one man in the bullpen. Lyle was 9-3 but had only nine saves, while Gossage (10-11) had a league-leading 27.

After the season, the Yanks traded Lyle, and Gossage reigned as their stopper until he signed as a free agent with San Diego in January 1984. He left with a 41-28 record and 150 saves.

December 7, 1977: Purchased Right-handed Pitcher Andy Messersmith from the Atlanta Braves

Andy Messersmith had helped launch a baseball revolution. He and Expos pitcher Dave McNally had played the 1975 season without contracts and then declared themselves free agents. The courts upheld their challenge to baseball's reserve clause, bringing the game into the era of free agency. Messersmith was 30 years old at the time and had an excellent 112-77 career won-lost record in eight years with the Angels and Dodgers. He'd twice won 20, once for each team, and also won 19 for the Dodgers in 1975, the year he'd played without a contract.

After getting his freedom, Messersmith was signed to a lucrative contract by Braves owner Ted Turner, but he'd been a disappointment in Atlanta, going 11-11 in 1976 and 5-4 in 1977. Furthermore, he'd broken his elbow in '77, which led to an extended stay on the disabled list, and then surgery.

The Yanks were willing to take a chance on Messersmith because they needed a righthanded starter to replace Mike Torrez, signed as a free agent by the Boston Red Sox. They reportedly paid the Braves $100,000 for Messersmith, a relatively inexpensive price, although some felt they were taking an expensive gamble on "damaged goods."

"We're taking him as he is," said Yankee president Gabe Paul, who would soon leave the Yankees to become the president of the Cleveland Indians. "If his arm comes around, we feel he is a very good pitcher who will help us tremendously."

Messersmith had to agree to the sale, something that Turner expected him to do. "Andy said he wanted to go to a contender," said Turner, "and we are sending him to the world champions. You can't do any better than that, can you?"

After a strong effort in spring training, Messersmith hurt his shoulder just before the 1978 opener and pitched in only six games, losing all three of his decisions. The Yanks released him, and in 1979 he went back to the Dodgers for a final season.

December 9, 1977: Signed Free-Agent Righthanded Pitcher Rawley Eastwick from the St. Louis Cardinals

Rawley Eastwick became the third pitcher the Yanks had added since winning the World Series two months earlier. He joined Goose Gossage, who also came via free agency from Pittsburgh, and Andy Messersmith, purchased from Atlanta. The Expos, Phillies, and Rangers had also sought Eastwick, and according to Cedric Tallis, the Yankees' new GM, may even have offered him more money. "We were not the highest bidders, " Tallis said, "but he obviously wants to pitch for a winner."

Before being traded to St. Louis the previous June, the 27-year-old Eastwick had pitched for a winner. He was the bullpen ace of the world champion Cincinnati Reds of 1975 and 1976, leading the National League in saves both years. (He tied the Cardinals' Al Hrabosky with 22 in 1975 and had 26 in 1976.) Contract difficulties led to his trade to

St. Louis, and his combined save total for the Reds and Cards fell to 11 in 1977.

Tallis maintained that Eastwick's poor season was due to his mental outlook. "There is nothing wrong with him," he said. "He's A-OK. We've done a lot of checking. His trouble was his mental outlook, and we feel sure that will now improve."

December 9, 1977: Traded Shortstop Sergio Ferrer to the New York Mets for Third Baseman Roy Staiger

Both Sergio Ferrer and Roy Staiger were on their respective team's minor league rosters and both would remain minor leaguers in 1978. Ferrer, a .281-batter with Syracuse of the International League in 1977, went to Tidewater, the Mets club in that league. The Yanks had gotten him from Oklahoma City of the American Association in a March 1977 trade with the Phillies. Philadelphia received Syracuse outfielder Kerry Dineen, who'd played 11 games for the Yanks in 1975–76.

Staiger had gone back and forth between the Mets and Tidewater for the past three seasons. The Yankees sent him to Tacoma, their new farm team in the Pacific Coast League. In 1979, Staiger, played in four games for the Yankees, his final four as a major leaguer.

December 12, 1977: Traded Right-handed Pitcher Stan Thomas and Cash to the Chicago White Sox for First Baseman Jim Spencer

The emergence in 1976 of rookie first baseman Lamar Johnson, along with the previous month's signing of free-agent Ron Blomberg had given Chicago more first basemen than they needed. "There's no question but that it was a difficult decision for us because Jim's [Spencer] a very fine fielder," said White Sox president Bill Veeck. But, Veeck explained, "We figure it's going to be an added incentive to Lamar to feel that he is going to play regularly."

The 30-year-old Spencer had played for the Angels and Rangers before going to Chicago in 1976. He was a lifetime .255 hit-

ter in more than 1,100 games, and also one of the finest defensive first basemen in the league. Spencer batted .247 for the 1977 White Sox while his 18 home runs matched the career high he'd set with California in 1971. The Yanks planned to use him at first base when Chris Chambliss needed a rest and as a part-time designated hitter.

The Yankees bought Stan Thomas from the expansion Seattle Mariners in August 1977, and he went 1–0 in three games. "We're not counting on him, although we're not discounting him either," Veeck said of his new pitcher. "That is not the pivotal point of the transaction by any stretch of the imagination. The pivotal thing is we had more first basemen than we needed. I find absolutely nothing distasteful about accepting money."

Thomas never again played in the big leagues, nor did the three other minor league players involved in a side deal between the two clubs. In that trade the Yanks sent righthander Ed Ricks to Chicago in return for righthander Bob Polinsky and outfielder Tommy Cruz, the only one with previous major league playing time. The White Sox assigned Ricks to Iowa of the American Association, while the Yanks sent Polinsky and Cruz to Tacoma of the Pacific Coast League.

June 10, 1978: Traded Lefthanded Pitcher Ken Holtzman to the Chicago Cubs for a Player to Be Named

Although Ken Holtzman spent the equivalent of two full seasons as a Yankee, he appeared in only 44 games, winning 12 and losing ten. Never very happy in New York, or with the way manager Billy Martin used him, Holtzman had often expressed a desire to go elsewhere. In having his wish granted, he became the sixth consecutive player representative that the Yankees had traded. Holtzman was currently on the 21-day disabled list, despite his claim that his bad back—the reason the Yanks had placed him on the DL—had been better for several days.

He was glad to be going back to the Cubs, Holtzman said, not only because he lived in the Chicago area, or that the Cubs were leading the National League's Eastern Division, but because he hoped that Cubs manager

Herman Franks would give him a chance to pitch. "I think Franks understands it is probably going to require patience on their part before I can help them," he said.

Martin said of the pitcher he'd used in just five games this season, "He may do well over there. He's the kind of pitcher who has to work very regularly to be good. Over here we couldn't do that because we had other pitchers we thought were better. He might have done well here if he could have worked regularly, but that's something we'll never know."

Holtzman would pitch in 23 games for the Cubs (who didn't hold their division lead), mostly in relief, losing his only three decisions.

Two days after the trade, the Cubs sent the Yankees Ron Davis, a 22-year-old righthander who was 3-3 with Midland of the Texas League. Davis went to West Haven, the Yanks affiliate in the Eastern League, but was called up in late July. He pitched in two games for the Yanks, but when they got Paul Lindblad from Oakland on August 1, Davis went back to West Haven.

June 14, 1978: Traded Righthanded Pitcher Rawley Eastwick to the Philadelphia Phillies for Outfielder Jay Johnstone and Minor League Outfielder Bobby Brown

When general manager Cedric Tallis signed Eastwick as a free agent in December 1977, he dismissed questions about the Yankees having an overcrowded bullpen. (Eastwick was joining the recently-signed Goose Gossage and holdovers Sparky Lyle and Dick Tidrow as Yankee relievers.) Tallis said, "If we have surplus pitching, we will be in a position to trade a pitcher in order to shore up a very important position. Left Field? Possibly."

The Yanks did turn out to have a surplus of pitching, and Eastwick was the pitcher they were trading to bring outfield help. Eastwick, with a 2-1 record and no saves, had never been a favorite of manager Billy Martin, who'd used him in just eight games. Al Rosen, who'd succeeded Gabe Paul as team president, chose to put a positive spin on Eastwick's departure.

"Eastwick is an outstanding young man who unfortunately did not get the chance to

do much pitching for us principally because of the staff we have," Rosen said. "Giving up Rawley at this time should provide no problem."

Rosen added that the Yanks were "pretty well set in our bullpen with good middle-distance pitchers in Dick Tidrow and [Ken] Clay, and short relievers in Rich Gossage and [Sparky] Lyle."

Adding Jay Johnstone gave the Yankees a veteran, lefthanded hitting outfielder. Johnstone had been a major leaguer since 1966, playing with California, Oakland, the White Sox, and, since 1974, with Philadelphia. He'd batted .308 for the Phillies over the past four seasons, but was struggling along at .179 this year.

Bobby Brown, a 23-year-old switch hitter with great speed, was batting .287 for Oklahoma City of the American Association. The Yanks sent him to their Tacoma club in the Pacific Coast League.

June 15, 1978: Traded Outfielder Dell Alston, Infielder Mickey Klutts, and Cash to the Oakland Athletics for Outfielder Gary Thomasson

Like the previous day's trade for Jay Johnstone, getting Gary Thomasson, who could also fill in at first base, gave the Yankees another veteran, lefthanded hitting outfielder. The 26-year-old Thomasson had spent five-plus seasons with San Francisco, with 1977 having been his overall best—a .256 average in 145 games and a career-high 17 home runs. But after the season (actually March 1978) the Giants traded him to Oakland in the deal for Vida Blue, and he'd been struggling with the A's, batting just .201.

Both Dell Alston and Mickey Klutts had come up through the Yankee organization, and both had some big league experience. Alston, 25, batted .325 in 22 games as a Yankee in 1977, and was hitless in three at-bats this season.

Klutts, 23, had a terrific 1976 season for the International League Syracuse Chiefs, batting .319, with 24 home runs and 80 RBIs. He played in two games for the Yanks, and came to training camp in 1977 with hopes of winning the regular shortstop job. But on the first day of camp, Klutts broke a finger and again spent the year at Syracuse, playing in just five games for the Yankees. He was 2 for 2 in his only game this season.

Yankee president Al Rosen also announced that the club was exchanging infielders with their Tacoma farm team in the Pacific Coast League. Coming to New York was Brian Doyle and going to Tacoma was George Zeber. In 1977, as a rookie, Zeber hit .323 in 25 games but was hitless in six at-bats (his final six) this season.

August 1, 1978: Purchased Lefthanded Pitcher Paul Lindblad from the Texas Rangers

Having moved to within 6½ games of the first-place Boston Red Sox, the Yanks were ready to narrow the gap even further when they opened a two-game series against Boston at Yankee Stadium. To do so, according to manager Bob Lemon (Lemon had replaced Billy Martin who'd resigned a week earlier) the club had to have another lefthanded reliever.

"We've really got only one lefthander in the bull pen, and that's Sparky [Lyle]," he said. "Once, Lyle pitched 5.2 innings in a game, and you can't do that. [Paul] Lindblad's been to the races. He's been on a winner."

That was true. The 37-year-old Lindblad, who cost the Yankees an estimated $100,000, had been a valuable reliever for the 1973–74 world champion Oakland Athletics. So far in 1978, his 14th (and last) season in the American League, he was 1–1 in 18 games for Texas.

The Yanks made roster space for Lindblad by sending recently-acquired rookie pitcher Ron Davis (0–0 in two games) to West Haven of the Eastern League.

Lindblad's sale to New York reunited him with Catfish Hunter, his close friend and former teammate with the Kansas City and Oakland Athletics. He would pitch in seven games for the Yanks, including one start, without being involved in a decision.

November 10, 1978: Traded Lefthanded Pitchers Sparky Lyle and Dave Rajsich, Righthanded Pitcher Larry McCall,

Catcher Mike Heath, Shortstop Domingo Ramos, and Cash to the Texas Rangers for Lefthanded Pitchers Dave Righetti and Paul Mirabella, Outfielder Juan Beniquez, Minor League Righthanded Pitcher Mike Griffin, and Minor League Outfielder Greg Jemison

According to Yankee GM Cedric Tallis, the two clubs had been negotiating this deal for several weeks. They'd already agreed on nine of the ten players and how much money (said to be $400,000) that would go from Yankee owner George Steinbrenner to Rangers owner Brad Corbett. The holdup was in resolving the identity of the fifth player who would be going from Texas to New York. Rangers general manager Eddie Robinson finally "upgraded" that man to be Greg Jemison, a player that Yankee team president Al Rosen said "has great speed," and the deal was completed. Evidently Jemison did have great speed. He'd stolen 82 bases for Asheville of the Western Carolinas League in 1977, and 65 for Tulsa of the Texas League in 1978 (while batting .263).

Sparky Lyle had been the Yankees' "stopper" from 1972, when he came from Boston, until 1978, when Goose Gossage claimed that role. Lyle saved 132 games in his first six seasons in New York, including league-leading totals of 35 in 1972 and 23 in 1976. He had 26 more saves in 1977, but only nine this past season. Unhappy in his new role, Lyle had given the Yankees permission to trade him and told Rosen he was delighted to be going to Texas. "I hope they pitch my butt off," he said. "I think they will."

The other four players leaving the Yankees were all young, with limited experience. Larry McCall made his Yankee debut in 1977 and had a two-year record of 1–2 in seven games. The other three all reached the big leagues in 1978. Catcher Mike Heath saw the most action, 92 at-bats and a .228 average in 33 games. Shortstop Domingo Ramos appeared in one game, but never batted, and lefthander Dave Rajsich was in four games without a decision.

Rosen said he doubted that Dave Righetti, who was only 20 years old, would be pitching in the big leagues in 1979. Nevertheless,

Righetti was such an outstanding prospect that everyone connected with the Yankees was excited about getting him. In two minor league seasons, Righetti was 16-8 with 228 strikeouts in 200 innings. "This is the kind of deal you have to wait a year or two before you assess it," Rosen said.

Rosen also gave Mike Griffin little chance of sticking with the Yankees in 1979; however, he thought that Paul Mirabella had a good shot at succeeding Lyle in the bullpen. "Don't rule out Mirabella," said Rosen of the 24-year-old lefthander who'd gone 3-2 in ten games as a Rangers rookie in 1978. "He's done some relief pitching and he's a young stud—a cocky kid," Rosen added. "Harry Craft, one of our scouts, believes he can pitch in the big leagues right now."

No one on the Yankees was questioning the major league credentials of Juan Beniquez, a 28-year-old veteran of seven seasons with the Red Sox and Rangers. What was in doubt was whether Beniquez would be happy being a backup to center fielder Mickey Rivers. However, Rosen appeared unconcerned with the amount of playing time Beniquez or anyone else would get.

"Every winter you talk about how many games a guy will or won't play, and then the season starts and it doesn't work out that way," Rosen said. "Paul Blair played a lot more this year than anyone thought he would." And, Rosen asked, "Who says he has to play center field? There are other outfield positions too."

All the players in this deal would see at least some major league action in 1979, except Ramos and Jemison. Ramos would return to the Yankees a year later, but Jemison would never reach the big leagues.

Righetti would pitch 11 seasons for the Yankees, before signing as a free agent with the San Francisco Giants on December 4, 1990. Along with his 74 wins (74-61), he saved 224 games, the most in club history.

November 13, 1978: Signed Free-Agent Righthanded Pitcher Luis Tiant from the Boston Red Sox

The Yankees didn't believe that Luis Tiant was only 38 years old, as he claimed; nevertheless, they hoped he could do as well for them in 1979 as he had for the Red Sox in 1978. Tiant had gone 13-8 in '78, bringing his lifetime record to 204-148. The Yanks were also hoping he could repeat the success he'd had against their Eastern Division rivals: 3-0 against Detroit, and 2-1 with low ERAs against Baltimore and Milwaukee.

Tiant had joined the Red Sox in 1971 after both Cleveland and Minnesota, thinking his career was over, had given up on him. He was a three-time 20-game–winner for Boston, but became a free agent after the Sox offered him just a one-year contract for 1979. The Yanks eagerly signed him because despite winning the World Series, they felt their pitching staff contained several question marks. Chief among them were how well Catfish Hunter would pitch after his shoulder injury in 1978, and whether Don Gullett would ever pitch again after his.

While puffing on a cigar, Tiant discounted the suggestion that he was too old to be effective. "Too much of a problem is made about my age. I know I can throw the ball to home plate. I can do my job. That's what's important, not my age. Nobody cares how old Gaylord Perry is. He's older than me and he won the Cy Young Award."

In 1979, Tiant would exactly match his 13-8 record of 1978, then go 8-9 the following year, after which the Yankees made him a free agent.

November 21, 1978: Signed Free-Agent Lefthanded Pitcher Tommy John from the Los Angeles Dodgers

The defending world champion Yankees, unsure of how effective injured pitchers Catfish Hunter and Don Gullett would be in 1979, signed their second free-agent veteran pitcher in eight days. Last week it was Luis Tiant, allegedly 38, and today it was 35-year-old Tommy John. John said that playing for a winning team, one that had beaten his Dodgers in the last two World Series, was what made him sign with the Yankees rather than the Reds or Royals, the two other teams who'd tried to sign him.

"Having been beaten by the Yankees two years in a row, I like playing for a winner," said John, adding that because his best pitch was a

November 21, 1978: *Tommy John.* **Early in his career, John had seven fine seasons with the White Sox.**

sinkerball, the Yanks' strong inner defense particularly appealed to him.

"When you look at the Yankee infield, you're talking about the best in baseball," he said. "That makes Tommy John a better pitcher. When you're throwing 19 or 20 ground balls a game, you need guys shagging them down. My infielders get a lot of work."

John began his career with Cleveland back in 1963, but in 1965 they traded him to the Chicago White Sox. After seven fine seasons in Chicago, the White Sox sent him to the Dodgers in 1972. It was with the Dodgers that John overcame revolutionary arm surgery, and after missing a season and a half, came back to win 20 games in 1977. But after a 17-10 season in 1978, he asked the Dodgers for a three-year contract and when they refused, John declared his free agency.

George Steinbrenner, who'd made John the Yanks' first choice in the free-agent draft, said, "He's important to us. If he's sitting there, that'll give me time to let Righetti and Mirabella develop." Steinbrenner was referring to Dave Righetti and Paul Mirabella, the two young southpaws acquired from Texas in the Sparky Lyle trade earlier in the month.

February 3, 1979: Purchased Catcher Bruce Robinson from the Oakland Athletics

In addition to paying Charles Finley $400,000 for catcher Bruce Robinson, the Yanks sent him another $100,000 for minor league pitcher Greg Cochran. However, as he had with previous Finley sales, Commissioner Bowie Kuhn held up the deal for further study. When Kuhn realized that Robinson and Cochran were not quite the caliber of Vida Blue or Joe Rudi, he allowed the sales to go through. Kuhn's questioning of this minor transaction surprised both Finley and Yankee owner George Steinbrenner.

"They're just a couple of minor league ballplayers that Steinbrenner was interested in," Finley said. "He offered me $500,000, and I accepted it before he had a chance to change his mind."

Steinbrenner pointed out that he was "buying players who aren't frontline players," and that he was "helping a franchise that was weak."

Robinson, 24, batted .299 with ten home runs for Vancouver of the Pacific Coast League in 1978. He also batted .250 in 28 games for Oakland.

Robinson would play in ten games for the Yankees over the 1979 and 1980 seasons, getting two hits in 17 at-bats. He was on the disabled list for almost all of 1981 and never again played in the major leagues. Cochran would never pitch in a big league game.

February 15, 1979: Traded Outfielder Gary Thomasson to the Los Angeles Dodgers for Catcher Brad Gulden

Yankee general manager Cedric Tallis thought that both clubs had made a sensible deal. "The Dodgers needed an extra outfielder, we didn't," Tallis said. "We were worried about our catching. We liked (Brad) Gulden very much."

The worry Tallis spoke of was finding a capable backup, better defensively than Cliff Johnson, to ease part of the load from Thurman Munson. Tallis also felt a need to upgrade the catching position in the high minors. Jerry Narron, the club's top minor league catcher in 1978 (.278 and 15 home runs for Tacoma) was almost certain to be with the Yanks in 1979. Like Narron, the 22-year-old Gulden had also been in the Pacific Coast League in 1978. He was with the Dodgers team at Albuquerque, where he batted .294, and led all PCL catchers in assists, putouts, and double plays.

Although Gary Thomasson batted .276 and played well in his half season with the Yankees, he was just one of many surplus outfielders on the roster and easily expendable.

May 11, 1979: Purchased Lefthanded Pitcher Jim Kaat from the Philadelphia Phillies

When Ron Guidry read that his new teammate Jim Kaat had pitched in 678 major league games, he was duly impressed. "That's a lot of pitching," said the Yankee ace, who had recently volunteered to also pitch in relief to help make up for the loss of Goose Gossage. (Gossage had injured a thumb in a scuffle with teammate Cliff Johnson.)

Among active pitchers, only San Diego's Gaylord Perry had won more games than the 262 victories Kaat had amassed in a career that began in 1959 with the original Washington Senators. Kaat, now 40, was a three-time 20-game winner, once with the Twins and twice with the White Sox. He'd been with the Phillies since 1976, but manager Danny Ozark had used him only three times this season.

When asked if Kaat would take over from Guidry in the Yankee bull pen, Yankee manager Bob Lemon said, "Not as yet he won't. But he can help in a lot of ways: short relief, long relief, spot starting, even pinch hitting. We didn't buy him to get Guidry out of the bull pen. That'll be up to Ron, and he hasn't said anything to me about it."

May 23, 1979: Traded Righthanded Pitcher Dick Tidrow to the Chicago Cubs for Righthanded Pitcher Ray Burris

Neither Dick Tidrow nor Ray Burris was having a very good season. Tidrow was 2-1 with a 7.94 earned run average in 14 games, while Burris, also in 14 games, had no decisions, but at 6.23, had a similarly poor ERA. It was a trade made with the hope that each player would benefit by coming to a new team.

Tidrow had been a starter in 1974, his first year in New York, and then again in 1978, but mostly he'd pitched out of the bullpen. He was

an 11-game winner in both 1974 and 1977 and had an overall Yankee record of 41-33. He also had 23 saves, with a high of ten in 1976. Tidrow said he was disappointed, but not surprised, that the Yanks had traded him. He said the two things he would miss most were "winning," and his "relationships with the players."

Burris, who was in New York where the Cubs were playing the Mets, was philosophical about being traded. "It's a change-of-scenery trade, I understand," he said. "Tidrow needs a change. I need a change. I've never even seen Yankee Stadium. I don't even know where it's at."

Burris had been mostly a starter since debuting with the Cubs in 1973 and had a lifetime record of 55-58. But with Goose Gossage hurt, Burris assumed his role would be as a reliever, although he said he "hadn't talked to Bob Lemon yet." Lemon, the Yankee manager, wasn't sure how he'd use Burris. "I haven't seen his stats," he said. "I don't know anything about him."

Lemon did, however, know about Tidrow, and like his players, he was sorry to see the popular pitcher leave. "Dick is a good friend of mine," Lemon said. "I hate to see him go, but that's baseball. He took the ball every time I handed it to him—long and short relief, it didn't matter."

June 15, 1979: Traded Catcher–Designated Hitter Cliff Johnson to the Cleveland Indians for Lefthanded Pitcher Don Hood

With George Steinbrenner having witnessed the Yankees' last two losses, which dropped them 7½ games behind the first-place Orioles, the players suspected that some of them would soon be gone. The most commonly discussed deal was one that would have sent pitcher Ed Figueroa, who was anxious to leave, and outfielder Mickey Rivers, who seemed indifferent, to the Texas Rangers for pitcher Jon Matlack and outfielder Al Oliver.

Instead the Yanks made two minor deals, getting rid of outfielder Jay Johnstone and Cliff Johnson, who'd been a part-time player in his first two seasons in New York, mostly as a designated hitter. Johnson batted .296 in 1977, but dropped all the way to a paltry .184

in 1978. He was at .266 this season, but more important, it was Johnson who'd fought with Goose Gossage in the Yankee clubhouse in April, a fight in which Gossage injured his thumb. Causing them to lose the league's best relief pitcher for an extended period had not endeared Johnson to the Yankee brass.

The addition of Don Hood gave manager Bob Lemon another lefthander to back up Jim Kaat in the bullpen. Hood had been both a starter and reliever in his career with Baltimore and Cleveland and had a lifetime 21-25 record. Used strictly in relief this season, he'd won his only decision and had a 3.68 earned run average.

Hood would go 3-1 with the Yanks in 27 games in 1979 (six as a starter), but after the season would sign as a free agent with St. Louis.

June 15, 1979: Traded Outfielder Jay Johnstone to the San Diego Padres for Righthanded Pitcher Dave Wehrmeister

Jay Johnstone's stay with the Yankees ended a year and a day after it began. Traded from Philadelphia on June 14, 1978, he'd batted .262 in 36 games and was at .208 after 23 games this season. Because he hadn't gotten much playing time in New York, Johnstone was not sorry to leave. "I'm going to a place where I can play. Right now that means a lot to me," he said.

Dave Wehrmeister had pitched on and off for the Padres between 1976 and 1978, but was currently with Hawaii of the Pacific Coast League. He was 8-5 for the Islanders, with a sensational 1.88 earned run average, and was leading the league in innings pitched and complete games.

Wehrmeister would spend the next five seasons with Columbus of the International League, getting a brief five-game shot with the Yanks in 1981.

June 26, 1979: Traded Minor League Righthanded Pitcher Paul Semall and Cash to the Chicago Cubs for Outfielder Bobby Murcer

Back in October 1974, when the Yanks traded him to the Giants for Bobby Bonds,

Bobby Murcer expressed both shock and disappointment. His emotions on returning were quite different. "I feel like a new man," he said. "I've never been so happy in my life."

After two seasons in San Francisco, the Giants traded Murcer to the Cubs, who now felt they no longer could afford him. Cubs GM Bob Kennedy said that eliminating Murcer's salary, along with the cash they received for him from the Yankees, amounted to "a financial windfall" for his club. In four-plus seasons in the National League, Murcer batted .274, with 77 home runs and 356 runs batted in. But 1978 had been his poorest season; he had just nine homers and 64 RBIs.

Now 33, and batting .258, Murcer easily cleared waivers. After taking batting practice that afternoon at Wrigley Field in Chicago, he arrived at Toronto's Exhibition Stadium just 20 minutes before the Yankees' game with the Blue Jays. Billy Martin, newly returned as manager, put him in the starting lineup, and Murcer, batting third and playing right field, showed his appreciation by contributing two singles and two walks in the Yanks' 11-2 victory.

Despite Murcer's excellent performance that evening, right field on the Yankees belonged to Reggie Jackson, currently out with a leg injury. Jackson had asked for a trade when he learned that Martin was replacing Bob Lemon, and the new challenge from Murcer was unlikely to please him.

Nevertheless, Martin speculated on how he would handle things when Jackson returned. "I'll use Reggie as the designated hitter for a while until his leg is sound and put Murcer in right and Lou [Piniella] in left," Martin said. "After that we'll have to see. Maybe I'll alternate them, maybe I'll work Murcer out in left field. It's a nice problem to have."

Yankee GM Cedric Tallis, who'd made the trade for Murcer, said, "We feel that coming back to New York and playing for Billy Martin will be good for him." Murcer, who had to agree to the trade, said he was just happy to be a Yankee again.

"My place is in New York," he said. "That's why I came back. It's home to me. It's where I grew up and learned how to play baseball."

Murcer would stay with the Yankees until

his retirement in June 1983. His combined batting average for his two tours as a Yankee, encompassing 13 years, was .278, with a total of 175 home runs.

Twenty-three-year-old Paul Semall, who would never advance beyond the Triple-A level, went from Columbus in the International League, where he was 6-3, to the Cubs Wichita team in the American Association.

August 1, 1979: Traded Outfielder Mickey Rivers and Three Players to Be Named to the Texas Rangers for Outfielder Oscar Gamble, Minor League Third Baseman Amos Lewis, and Two Players to Be Named

It took almost two months and involved five "players to be named," but the Yanks finally got Mickey Rivers traded to Texas. They'd tried to send him to the Rangers back in June, along with pitcher Ed Figueroa in a deal that would have brought outfielder Al Oliver and pitcher Jon Matlack to New York. That fell through, as did various other combinations of this trade before it finally met with Commissioner Bowie Kuhn's approval.

Rivers had been ready to go in June. "You go where you have to go, where you have to be," he said at the time. One of the fastest men in the game, he'd been the Yankee center fielder since 1976, leading the club in hits and stolen bases in each of his first two seasons. In 490 games as a Yankee, the 30-year-old Rivers batted .299 with 26 triples and 93 stolen bases.

Billy Martin, who'd replaced Bob Lemon as manager in midseason, had liked Oscar Gamble when he'd managed him as a Yankee the first time, in 1976. Since then, the 29-year-old Gamble had continued his moving around, playing for the White and San Diego before being traded to Texas in October 1978. He'd now played for seven different teams in eleven seasons, although the Yanks were the only one he'd played for twice.

Gamble, who'd missed a few weeks earlier this season with an injured foot, had played in 64 games and was batting .335. Rangers owner Brad Corbett really didn't want to trade him, but Kuhn had vetoed a deal for Rivers in which the Yanks would be getting only minor

leaguers. Rangers GM Eddie Robinson, suspecting that Gamble might sign as a free agent with the Yanks after the season anyway, agreed to his inclusion in the deal.

Gamble would bat .389 over the final two months of 1979 and remain a Yankee until the White Sox signed him as a free agent following the 1984 season. In his seven seasons in New York (including 1976), he batted .259 with 87 home runs.

Texas had selected Amos Lewis with their first pick in the June 1978 amateur draft. Still two weeks short of his 19th birthday, he was playing with Asheville of the Class A Western Carolina League. The Yanks sent him to their Class A team at Fort Lauderdale in the Florida State League, but in November traded him back to Texas in the deal for Eric Soderholm. Despite his initial promise, Lewis never reached the major leagues.

Neither did Bob Polinsky, Neil Mersch, nor Mark Softy, the three minor league pitchers the Rangers received on October 8 as the players to be named. However the two pitchers the Yanks received, both of whom were in the low minors in 1979, did get to the big leagues and specifically to the Yankees. Gene Nelson, who was 13-5 at Asheville, came in 1981, and Ray Fontenot, who was 3-1 with Sarasota of the Gulf Coast League, arrived in 1983.

August 3, 1979: Purchased Infielder Lenny Randle from the Pittsburgh Pirates

Lenny Randle had spent six years in the Texas organization and the 1977 and 1978 seasons with the New York Mets. Following the '78 season, the Mets released him and he signed with the Giants. Randle had opened this season with Phoenix, the Giants team in the Pacific Coast League; however, he was currently with Portland of the PCL, sent there after San Francisco traded him to Pittsburgh.

Randle's purchase was one of several roster moves the Yanks made in the aftermath of Thurman Munson's tragic death the day before. They added a catcher by recalling Brad Gulden from the International League Columbus Clippers, where he was batting .248. Gulden would share the catching duties for the

August 3, 1979: *Thurman Munson.* **Getting Lenny Randle was one of several moves the Yanks made in the wake of Munson's death.**

rest of the season with rookie Jerry Narron. Also coming up from Columbus, was out-fielder Bobby Brown, a .348 batter with the Clippers whom the Yanks had purchased ear-lier this season from the Toronto Blue Jays.

Randle batted .179 in 20 games for the Yankees in the remaining weeks of 1979, mostly in the outfield, and left as a free agent after the season.

August 20, 1979: Sold Righthanded Pitcher Ray Burris to the New York Mets

Two weeks earlier, the Yanks had an-nounced that pitcher Ed Figueroa would un-dergo surgery to remove bone spurs on his right elbow. They also said that after deciding how to dispose of Ray Burris, they would re-call Jim Beattie from Columbus of the International League to take Figueroa's place in the rotation. When the Yanks still hadn't moved Burris by August 17, they designated him for assignment and made the call for Beattie.

Now they had a taker for Burris, which would end his unimpressive three month stay with the Yankees. In that time, he'd relieved in 15 games, won one, lost three, and had a 6.18 earned run average.

August 26, 1979: Signed First Baseman George Scott as a Free Agent

The Kansas City Royals had released George Scott on August 17, two months after trading outfielder Tom Poquette to the Red Sox to get him. At 35, Scott was no longer the feared slugger he had been in two stints with the Boston Red Sox, broken by a five-year stay in Milwaukee from 1972 to 1976. A highly productive hitter since entering the league in 1966, he had his best year in 1975. Playing for the Brewers, Scott led the league in RBIs (109) and tied Oakland's Reggie Jackson for the home run crown (36). As recently as 1977 Scott had 33 home runs and 95 RBIs for the Red Sox, but he hit only 12 home runs in 1978, and just five for Boston and Kansas City this season.

Still, the Yanks were short of righthanded power and were willing to take a chance on Scott, who, of course, was glad for the opportunity.

"I just want to help the Yankees for the rest of this season," he said. "I hope I can help them win many games. I want to make an impression on the Yankees because I think I can play baseball for another three or four years."

Scott would bat .318 in 16 games for the Yanks, but evidently didn't make an "impression." Neither the Yankees nor any other major league club signed him for the 1980 season.

The Yanks made room for Scott by returning outfielder Bobby Brown to Columbus, where, under manager Gene Michael, the Clippers had just clinched the International League pennant. This was Brown's third trip to Columbus this season, and he was clearly disappointed. "It's obvious they don't want me," he said. "How much can a guy take of this treatment?"

November 1, 1979: Traded Righthanded Pitchers Jim Beattie and Rick Anderson, Outfielder Juan Beniquez, and Catcher Jerry Narron to the Seattle Mariners for Outfielder Ruppert Jones and Righthanded Pitcher Jim Lewis

In 1968, utility infielders Dick Howser and Gene Michael had been Yankee teammates. Now they were the team's new manager and general manager. Howser had left his job as coach at Florida State to replace the newly fired Billy Martin, and the Yanks had just announced that Michael would replace GM Cedric Tallis, who would now be serving as a super-scout. This was Howser's and Michael's first deal as a team; it brought them a center fielder they felt was capable of replacing Mickey Rivers, whom the Yanks had traded to Texas the previous summer.

"We feel that he can play center field with anybody in the league, the way he runs down the ball," said Michael of the 24-year-old Ruppert Jones.

The Mariners had gotten Jones from Kansas City in the 1977 expansion draft. He made the '77 All-Star team as a rookie and had a .255 average, with 52 home runs and 68 stolen bases, in three-plus big league seasons. Playing in 162 games in 1979, Jones batted .267, with 21 home runs, 78 runs batted in, and 109 runs scored.

Jim Lewis got into two games for the Mariners in 1979 after going 13-11 for Spokane of the Pacific Coast League. Three years later, in 1982, he would pitch two-thirds of an inning in his only Yankee appearance.

Of the four players leaving the Yankees, 24-year-old Jim Beattie had been the most promising. Beattie was 6-9 as a rookie in 1978 and then won two important games in the postseason. But in 1979, he missed a month on the disabled list, spent part of the season with Columbus in the International League, and won only three games for the Yankees.

Injuries had also disrupted Juan Beniquez's 1979 season, his only one as a Yankee. With his availability limited by two trips to the disabled list, Beniquez played in only 62 games and batted .254.

Jerry Narron was a 23-year-old rookie in 1979. He batted a lowly .171 in 61 games, most of them in the season's second half following Thurman Munson's death.

Rick Anderson, a relief pitcher was 13-3 with 21 saves at Columbus in 1979. He was in one game as a Yankee and would be in five in 1980 as a Mariner, but never had a major league decision.

November 1, 1979: Traded First Baseman Chris Chambliss, Second Baseman Damaso Garcia, and Lefthanded Pitcher Paul Mirabella to the Toronto Blue Jays for Catcher Rick Cerone, Lefthanded Pitcher Tom Underwood, and Outfielder Ted Wilborn

Gene Michael had just completed his second six-player trade in five hours, still, the new general manager of the Yankees denied that he was "shaking up" the club. "It's not a shakeup," he said. "We're just plugging some holes."

The biggest hole Michael was attempting to plug was behind the plate, where the Yanks needed a first-string catcher to replace the deceased Thurman Munson. Rick Cerone, whose batting average after 269 major league games was only .228, with just 11 home runs, was obviously no Munson. But he was a good receiver, and being only 25, the hope was that his hitting would improve. In 1979, his first full season, Cerone had batted .239 with seven homers and 61 runs batted in.

Tom Underwood had pitched in the National League for the Phillies and Cardinals before coming to Toronto in 1978. He had a 34-29 record in the NL, but was 15-30 for the woeful Blue Jays. Underwood lost his first nine decisions in 1979, but finished 9-16 and led the team in wins, games started, and strikeouts.

The quietly consistent Chris Chambliss had just finished another fine season as the Yankee first baseman. He had a .280 average with a career-high 18 home runs, and 63 runs batted in. Chambliss's RBI total was down from previous years, but his 155 hits tied him with Willie Randolph for the team lead. Not yet 31, he'd been the club's first baseman ever since joining them from Cleveland early in the 1974 season. Responsible for much of the team's recent success, Chambliss batted .282 with 79 homers and 454 runs batted in as a Yankee.

On hearing the Yanks had traded him, Chambliss said, "I'm not going to make any statements at this time, until I talk to my agent and the Blue Jays. I have some things to straighten out."

A month after this trade, the Blue Jays traded Chambliss to the Atlanta Braves. He would play eight seasons for Atlanta before coming back to the Yankees as their hitting coach in 1988. Then, when Jose Cruz went on the disabled list on May 7, the club activated Chambliss, only to release him three days later. He appeared once, as a pinch hitter, and struck out.

Both 25-year-old Paul Mirabella and 22-year-old Damaso Garcia had played briefly in New York, and both would go on to successful major league careers. Mirabella was 11-7 with the International League Columbus Clippers in 1979, but 0-4 with a 8.79 earned run average in ten games with the Yanks, while Garcia had batted .228 in 29 big league games over the past two seasons.

Ted Wilborn batted .247 with Syracuse of

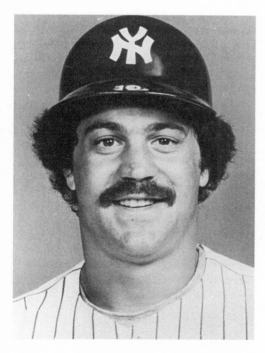

November 1, 1979: *Rick Cerone.* **Cerone was obtained to replace the deceased Thurmon Munson.**

the International League in 1979. He got into 22 games for the Blue Jays, batting 12 times without a hit. Wilborn would play in eight games for the 1980 Yankees, getting two hits in eight at-bats.

November 8, 1979: Signed Free-Agent First Baseman Bob Watson from the Boston Red Sox

One week after completing two six-player trades, the Yanks added two valuable free agents, first baseman Bob Watson and left-hander Rudy May.

"We've solved four problems in ten days," said elated owner George Steinbrenner. "We got a center fielder [Ruppert Jones], a catcher [Rick Cerone], a righthanded hitter [Watson] and a pitcher [May]. It's probably never been done before in baseball so fast and that doesn't count getting a new manager [Dick Howser] and a new general manager [Gene Michael]. We took a team with holes and made a strong contender again."

Having traded first baseman Chris Chambliss to Toronto in one of last week's deals, the Yanks now had his successor. (They'd also re-signed first baseman Jim Spencer for four years.) The 33-year-old Watson had de-buted with the Astros back in 1966 and gone on to play in almost 1,400 games for Houston. In that time, he'd compiled a .297 batting average, 139 home runs, and 782 runs batted in. Houston traded him to the Red Sox in June 1979, and in his first look at American League pitching, Watson batted .337, with 13 home runs and 53 RBIs.

He was leaving Boston, Watson claimed, because of their original salary offer, which he found too low. "The Red Sox made an offer in September," he said, "then they came back after I was drafted by eight or nine clubs and made a significantly better offer. If that had been their original offer, I think I would have signed."

Watson also hypothesized about what his new club expected of him. "My role with the Yankees is to provide some righthanded power and play some first base."

November 8, 1979: Signed Free-Agent Lefthanded Pitcher Rudy May from the Montreal Expos

Rudy May was one of two free agents the Yanks had signed today. The other was first baseman Bob Watson, formerly of the Red Sox. May, now 35, was returning to the Yan-kees three and a half seasons after they'd traded him to Baltimore. That was in June 1976, and he'd won 11 games for the Orioles in the sec-ond half of that season and 18 more in 1977. But in 1978 Baltimore traded him to Montreal, where he spent six weeks on the disabled list and his win total dropped to eight.

This past season, the Expos had used May as a reliever, and he'd done very well in that role—a 10-3 won-lost record and a 2.31 earned run average. Still, he was unhappy with the way Montreal had used him and was glad to leave, although he chose to underplay his prob-lems with the Expos.

"Everybody's concerned about my beef in Montreal," May said. "But I was only con-cerned that my arm couldn't take it, pitching out of the bullpen—in my option year."

Reporters asked May if he had considered signing with some other club, the Mets for in-stance. "Did I come close to signing with any other clubs? No," he said. "The Mets? Well if I've got to play in New York, why should I play with the Mets?"

Despite a brief stay on the disabled list, May would have an outstanding 1980 season. Used as both a starter and reliever by manager Dick Howser, May won 15 and lost five, with three saves and a league-leading a 2.46 earned run average. He was 13-22 over the his final three seasons (1981–83), which also included other stays on the DL and a few trips to the minor leagues.

November 14, 1979: Traded Two Players to Be Named and Cash to the Texas Rangers for Third Baseman Eric Soderholm

Both clubs had actually announced the trade a day earlier, but then had to restructure it. The Yanks had reported they were acquir-ing Eric Soderholm from Texas for "players to be named"; however, the Rangers had disclosed the actual names of the players. Texas said the Yanks had agreed to give them three minor leaguers: lefthanded pitcher Ricky Burdette (on the roster of West Haven of the Eastern League), righthanded pitcher Roger Slagle (on the roster of Columbus of the International League), and third baseman Amos Lewis (on the roster of Ft. Lauderdale of the Florida State League).

Because all three were on minor league rosters, which supposedly were frozen until the minor league draft in December, the deal was canceled. After the restructuring, which was completed on December 13, Slagle, who'd pitched his only big league game for the Yanks in 1979, was no longer part of it.

Soderholm had played for the Minnesota Twins from 1971 to 1975, but missed the entire 1976 season with a knee injury. He then signed as a free agent with the White Sox, where his .280 batting average, 25 home runs, and 67 RBIs earned him the 1977 American League's Comeback Player of the Year Award. Traded by Chicago to Texas in June 1979, he became the backup to Rangers third baseman Buddy Bell.

Soderholm was unhappy with his reserve status, and under the revised rules a player could demand a trade three years after he'd chosen free agency. Soderholm did so, thus becoming the first player to take advantage of the new rule.

However, the rule did not require that the Rangers trade him to a team of his choice. When he learned he was going to New York, Soderholm reacted with mixed emotions, recognizing that he might be going from playing behind Buddy Bell to playing behind Graig Nettles.

"The pros far outweigh the cons," Soderholm said. "I feel I'm in the prime of my career, and I want to play. But I have a feeling things will work out for the good. I'll sit down and talk with Mr. Steinbrenner."

Soderholm would hit .287 in 95 games as a third baseman and designated hitter for the 1980 Yankees. But it would be his final season. An illness made him miss the entire 1981 season and the club released him that October.

IX. The Eighties

April 4, 1980: Signed Catcher Johnny Oates as a Free Agent

Brad Gulden had assumed that newly acquired Rick Cerone would be the Yankees' number one catcher in 1980, and that because he'd been the number two man in 1979, he would fill that same role again. Therefore Gulden was extremely upset when the club signed 34-year-old Johnny Oates, a nine-year veteran who'd played for four different major league teams, mostly as a second-stringer or a platoon player. Oates, who had a lifetime batting average of .254, had spent the last two seasons with the Dodgers, but they'd released him a week earlier.

Gulden said he was "not worried, just confused," about the addition of Oates. When he asked manager Dick Howser about the team's catching plans, Howser responded that he hadn't yet decided, but that he expected Oates would be on the opening-day roster. Howser also informed Gulden that "because he [Gulden] was a younger guy, he might be better off somewhere else."

Oates ended his playing career with the Yankees, remaining with them through the 1981 season and batting .189 in 49 games. The Yanks released him in October 1981.

April 29, 1980: Signed Righthanded Pitcher Doug Bird as a Free Agent

In April 1979, after Doug Bird had spent six seasons with Kansas City, the Royals traded him to the Phillies for shortstop Todd Cruz. The 30-year-old Bird had been primarily a relief pitcher in both places, the one exception being 1976 when he was a member of the Western Division–winning Royals' starting rotation. Bird was 12-10 that year, the most games he'd ever won in a season, although he did go 11-4 in 1977, when he was again primarily a reliever.

Bird was 2-0 in 32 games for the '79 Phillies, while missing three weeks on the disabled list. The Yanks sent him to their International League club at Columbus, but would recall him later that season.

April 30, 1980: Sold Lefthanded Pitcher Jim Kaat to the St. Louis Cardinals

When lefthander Rudy May came off the disabled list on April 22, manager Dick Howser designated Jim Kaat, 0-1 in four relief appearances this season, for assignment. Although he'd been a starting pitcher for most of his 22-year big league career, Kaat had served as a reliever for Yankee managers Bob Lemon and Billy Martin in 1979, going 2-3 in 40 games, all but one in relief.

July 28, 1980: Sold Righthanded Pitcher Ed Figueroa to the Texas Rangers

Having already designated Ed Figueroa for assignment, the Yanks were glad to find a buyer for him, even if it probably was for just the $25,000 waiver price. Had they not sold or traded Figueroa in the next three days, they would have been forced to release him and receive nothing.

It was an unfortunate ending for Figueroa, a one-time top pitcher who'd never fully recovered from a 1979 elbow injury. He'd joined the Yankees in 1976, and over the next three years, each a pennant-winning season, led the club in total wins with 55. But after records of 19-10, 16-11, and 20-9, Figueroa injured the elbow and twice had to go on the disabled list in '79, the second time after surgery on August 17. He missed the rest of the season and finished with just four wins and six losses. In 15 games this season, Figueroa had a 3-3 mark, but he'd been mostly ineffective, as reflected by his 6.98 earned run average.

Figueroa was pleased to hear that the Rangers, who had their own pitching problems, planned to use him as a starter. "All I want is a chance to pitch in the regular rotation," he said. "I like Texas. I like the manager [Pat Corrales]. I think I can help them."

However, Figueroa did not help the Rangers. He lost all seven of his decisions and ended his career after two games with Oakland in 1981.

August 4, 1980: Purchased Third Baseman Aurelio Rodriguez from the San Diego Padres

After hepatitis put Graig Nettles on the disabled list, Eric Soderholm had been playing third base and was not pleased to hear that the Yanks had added Aurelio Rodriguez. Before that day's victory over Texas, a game in which he would hit a home run, Soderholm voiced his concern.

"When I originally negotiated my contract with the Yankees, they said the reason they were getting me was an insurance policy for Nettles. Then the minute something happens to Nettles they run out and get another third baseman."

Soderholm was batting .322, and Yankee manager Dick Howser tried to head off a potential problem by praising him.

"I know he can do the job, but it's not a bad idea to have someone like Rodriguez in the wings," Howser said. "Who's better than Rodriguez in this league defensively besides Nettles? The reports on him are still good defensively. We've seen enough of him to know he can catch the ball and throw."

The 32-year-old Rodriguez had spent 13 years in the American League, mostly with Detroit. But over the winter, the Tigers sold him to San Diego, and in 89 games for the Padres, he was batting just .200.

August 14, 1980: Traded Righthanded Pitcher Ken Clay and a Player to Be Named to the Texas Rangers for Righthanded Pitcher Gaylord Perry

With 285 victories in his 19-year career, Gaylord Perry was the major leagues' winningest active pitcher. A month short of his 42nd birthday, he had a 6-9 record and a 3.43 earned run average with the Rangers this season. Perry, who was in his second stint with Texas, having been traded there by San Diego in February, had also pitched for the Giants for ten years and the Indians for four years. However, he'd never been in a World Series and so was pleased to be joining the first-place Yankees.

"I'm happy to be going to a team that's a contender, and I feel I can help them," he said. "I'm going to pitch as long as I can help teams win ball games."

Cedric Tallis, the Yanks executive vice president said: "We are pleased to be able to acquire a pitcher with Gaylord's ability and experience." General manager Gene Michael agreed, adding that Perry "will definitely help us during the pennant stretch drive. He has been around and has the kind of mental toughness that will stand up to the pennant race."

Manager Dick Howser planned to give Perry his first Yankee start in the middle game of the upcoming five-game series with the second-place Orioles in Baltimore. Mike Griffin, called up a few days earlier from Columbus of the International League, went back to the Clippers to make room for Perry.

Ken Clay had also been at Columbus, where he was 9-4 with a league-leading 1.98 ERA. Clay had come up from Syracuse in June 1977 and spent all of 1978 and 1979 in New York, compiling a 6-14 won-lost record.

Outfielder Marvin Thompson, also from Columbus, went to Texas on October 1, 1980, to complete the deal.

Perry would split eight decisions for the Yankees in the last month and a half of 1980. After the season he was a free agent and signed to pitch for the Atlanta Braves in 1981.

October 24, 1980: Traded Second Baseman Roger Holt to the Texas Rangers for a Player to Be Named

Roger Holt batted .280 at Columbus of the International League in 1979, but only .213 for the Clippers in 1980. He played second base for the Yanks in their final two games of the 1980 season against Detroit, getting a single and an RBI in six at-bats. That would be his only major league action.

On December 8, Texas sent the Yankees 26-year-old third baseman Tucker Ashford as the player to be named. Ashford, who'd played for the Padres between 1976 and 1978, had spent most of the past two seasons in the minors. In 1980, he batted .279 for the Charleston Charlies of the International League, but only .125 in 15 games for the Rangers.

November 3, 1980: Traded Shortstop Fred Stanley and a Player to Be Named to the Oakland Athletics for Right-handed Pitcher Mike Morgan

A week earlier, the Yanks had tried to send Fred Stanley down to Columbus of the International League, but he had refused to report. That meant the club had ten days to either trade, sell, or release him. They found a taker in Billy Martin, now managing in Oakland but for several years Stanley's manager in New York. Martin believed that the 33-year-old Stanley could possibly win a starting middle infield job with the A's, whose 1980 double play combination had been Dave McKay at second and Mario Guerrero at short.

Stanley had spent eight years with the Yankees, batting .222 in 521 games, with his 260 at-bats in 1976 the most he'd ever had in one season. Nevertheless, Stanley was a decent shortstop and had been a valuable member of the team since coming from San Diego in an October 1972 trade for minor league catcher George Pena.

Mike Morgan first came to public attention during the 1978 amateur draft when Oakland's Charles Finley made him the A's number one choice, and the fourth choice overall. Finley brought Morgan directly to Oakland, even though he was only 18 years old and had

just finished high school. Morgan was impressive in his first start, a complete game loss to the Orioles, but then lost his next two starts before being sent to Vancouver of the Pacific Coast League. He split 1979 between Ogden of the PCL and the A's, where he went 2-10, but spent all of 1980 at Ogden.

Two weeks after the trade, on November 17, the Yanks sent second baseman Brian Doyle to the Athletics as the player to be named. Doyle had spent parts of the last three seasons with the Yankees, batting .170 in 93 games.

November 18, 1980: Traded Catcher Brad Gulden and Cash to the Seattle Mariners for Infielder Larry Milbourne and a Player to Be Named

Having sent shortstop Fred Stanley and second baseman Brian Doyle to the Oakland Athletics for pitcher Mike Morgan, the Yanks were left with no middle infielders to back up second baseman Willie Randolph and shortstop Bucky Dent.

Thus the trade for Larry Milbourne, who could play both those positions (also third base) and had done so for three seasons with Houston and four with Seattle. After struggling at the plate early in his career, the 29-year-old Milbourne had batted .278 and .264 for the Mariners the past two seasons.

Though he was still only 24, Brad Gulden had so far failed to live up to his early promise. After he hit only .163 in 40 games for the Yankees in 1979, they sent him to Columbus of the International League to start the 1980 season. After Gulden batted .157 in 14 games, the Yanks sent him down to Class AA Nashville, but he didn't do much better against Southern League pitching, just .237 in 85 games.

Oddly, the player to be named in this deal turned out to be Gulden himself. Seattle would send him back to the Yankees on May 18, 1981.

December 15, 1980: Signed Free-Agent Outfielder Dave Winfield from the San Diego Padres

George Steinbrenner had paid lots of money to free agents before. Catfish Hunter,

December 15, 1980: *Dave Winfield.* **George Steinbrenner made Winfield the highest paid player in baseball history.**

Don Gullett, Reggie Jackson, and Goose Gossage had all signed very lucrative free-agent deals with the Yankees; however, the reportedly $25 million, ten-year contract Steinbrenner gave Dave Winfield set a new standard. It made the multi-talented 29-year-old slugger the highest paid player in baseball history, although given the prevailing pay scales for athletes, no one doubted that he was worth it. In eight years at San Diego, Winfield, with a .284 batting average and 154 home runs, had established himself as one of baseball's most productive players. His best season was in 1979, when he batted .308, hit 34 home runs, and led the National League with 118 runs batted in. He fell off sharply in 1980 (.276, 20 HRs, 87 RBIs) but was still this year's most sought after free agent. The Yankees received serious competition for Winfield's services from both the New York Mets and the Cleveland Indians.

Winfield was an excellent outfielder, but he had played mostly in right field with the Padres, the same position Jackson occupied in New York. Yet, neither man envisioned a problem. When asked about the position he would play with the Yankees, Winfield said, "It's up in the air, but I'm not worried about it. You have a fine outfielder there already."

That fine outfielder, Jackson, seemed confident that the Yankees would find a solution. "I hit 40 home runs (actually a league-leading 41) and I think the manager can find a spot for me. And when you have a guy making the numbers Dave is and putting the numbers on the board that Dave is, they'll work it out."

The manager who would have the task of working it out was Gene Michael, recently named to replace Dick Howser, who'd resigned. Speaking of Winfield, Michael said, "We have some ideas where he'll play. We'll discuss them. I understand he can play center field. I'm sure he's not adverse to moving over there if there's an injury. I also understand he can play first base."

After playing in the relative obscurity of San Diego for eight years, Winfield looked forward to coming to New York. Responding to a reporter who asked if he thought he was the best player in baseball, Winfield said: "I'm a very good ballplayer, a very substantial ballplayer—without a doubt. But we'll see how good I am now. Before this, I've never been able to see what kind of ballplayer I am."

The Yankees weren't through attempting to boost their outfield strength. Steinbrenner was talking to Red Sox general manager Haywood Sullivan about a trade for center fielder Fred Lynn. Steinbrenner said of the negotiations, in which the Red Sox were asking for Ron Guidry, the Yanks' best pitcher, "It's serious, but not close. Certain things have to be right. It would be a fabulous outfield. If Sully is interested in talking to me in earnest, I'm interested in talking to him in earnest."

Sullivan seemed amenable. "If he wants Lynn a deal can be worked out," he said, but it never was.

February 16, 1981: Traded Minor League Shortstop Rafael Santana to the St. Louis Cardinals for a Player to Be Named

The Yankees had signed Rafael Santana as an 18 year old in 1976, but he had progressed very slowly. Santana spent the past four seasons in the Yanks' minor league system, finally reaching the Class AA level in 1980, with the Nashville Sounds of the Southern League.

On June 7, St. Louis sent pitcher George Frazier to New York as the player to be named. Frazier, a 26-year-old relief pitcher, had split each of the past three seasons between St. Louis and Springfield of the American Association. In 61 games with the Cardinals, all in relief, he was 3-11 with three saves. Frazier was back at Springfield this season, where he had a 1-2 record in 21 games. The Yanks assigned him to Columbus of the International League, but would bring him up later in the season.

February 17, 1981: Signed Free-Agent Righthanded Pitcher Bill Castro from the Milwaukee Brewers

The Yanks, having lost Luis Tiant to free agency, were without a proven righthanded starter, although the acquisition of 27-year-old Bill Castro, a career relief pitcher, was obviously not the answer to the problem. Castro had made only five starts (all in 1975) in his seven seasons with the Brewers. Appearing in a total of 253 games, he had a 25-23 record and a solid 2.96 earned run average.

"He's put up pretty good numbers over the years," Yankee manager Gene Michael said, "and getting him afforded the club a chance to do some other things. There's always a possibility of (Ron) Davis being a starter."

The Yanks would also take a serious look at a group of young righthanders they had in training camp, all vying for spots on the roster. Michael and club vice president Cedric Tallis were hoping that one or two from among Gene Nelson, Mike Morgan, Andy McGaffi-

February 17, 1981: *Ron Guidry*. **The Yanks also wanted one of Oakland's righthanded starters but refused to give up Guidry in return.**

gan, Brian Ryder, and Greg Cochran would be impressive enough to win a starting role. Yet, while they were hopeful, they expected that they were more likely to get their righthanded starter in a trade. The club had already spoken with Billy Martin, who was both manager and general manager at Oakland, concerning the A's four righthanded starters: Mike Norris, Matt Keough, Brian Kingman, and Rick Langford. But those talks had ended quickly when Martin asked for Ron Guidry in return.

March 31, 1981: Traded Outfielders Ruppert Jones and Joe Lefebvre, Left-handed Pitcher Tim Lollar, and Minor League Lefthanded Pitcher Chris Welsh to the San Diego Padres for Outfielder Jerry Mumphrey and Righthanded Pitcher John Pacella

Ruppert Jones had spent much of 1980, his one season in New York, on the disabled list, playing in only 83 games and batting a disappointing .223. Bobby Brown had replaced him while he was on the DL, but Jones had looked fully recovered this spring and seemed to have won back his starting job. A week earlier, the Yanks had sent Brown to Columbus of the International League and seemed committed to using Jones in center field this season.

"It's ironic in this game," a dejected Jones said. "One year you're a pretty good center fielder. Then you get hurt and you have to build all over again. The most hurting thing about it," he continued, "is that the people in

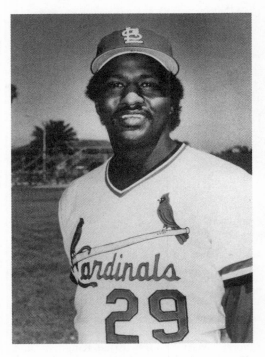

March 31, 1981: *Jerry Mumphrey.* After six years with the Cardinals, Mumphrey had his best season with the 1980 Padres.

New York didn't get to see me play on a consistent day-to-day level."

If Jones was disappointed at leaving, Jerry Mumphrey was thrilled at becoming a Yankee. "It's a great opportunity, " he said. "I'm very happy. I've never been on a winner before. It will be a great experience for me." Mumphrey had committed 11 errors in 1980, still, he was the Yankees' likely new center fielder, playing between Reggie Jackson and his former San Diego teammate, Dave Winfield.

After playing for the Cardinals since 1974, the switch-hitting Mumphrey went to San Diego in 1980 and had his best season, a.298 batting average and 52 stolen bases.

"I like to think I'm a pretty good player," he told reporters, "but you'll have to wait and see for yourself. I'm really confident in myself, but people will have to form their own opinions."

One who already had was Yankee scout Bob Lemon, who'd watched Mumphrey this spring in Arizona. Lemon's reports were so glowing that the Yanks were willing to part with three fine prospects like Joe Lefebvre, Chris Welsh, and Tim Lollar to get him.

"No doubt we're giving up a lot," said Bill Bergesch, vice president for baseball operations. "Sometimes when you're the Yankees you have to, but I think we're getting an outstanding player. We have to feel we are doing something for the overall good of the club." Manager Gene Michael concurred. "Ruppert did all right, but our scouts said Mumphrey's a heck of a complete player."

Although the three youngsters each had a chance of sticking with the Yankees in 1981, all agreed that they would have a greater opportunity to play in San Diego. (All three did play for the Padres in 1981.) Both Lefebvre and Lollar were 25, and both had spent time with the Yankees in 1980. Lefebvre batted .227 with eight home runs in 150 at-bats, while Lollar was 1-0 with a 3.34 ERA in 14 games. The 26-year-old Welsh had spent the entire 1980 season at Columbus, winning nine and losing 12, but with a splendid 2.73 earned run average.

John Pacella, 3-6 in parts of three seasons with the Mets, had been traded to San Diego in the October 1980 deal for Randy Jones. The Yanks assigned Pacella to their minor league camp, and he would spend the 1981 season at Columbus.

April 6, 1981: Traded Minor League Righthanded Pitcher Byron Ballard to the San Diego Padres for a Player to Be Named

Byron Ballard was 17-6 with Greensboro in 1980, leading the Class A South Atlantic League in wins and also in complete games (15). The Padres moved him up to the Class AA level for 1981, assigning him to Amarillo of the Texas League.

On April 30, San Diego sent 27-year-old outfielder Dave Stegman to the Yankees as the player to be named. Stegman had major league experience (85 games with Detroit between 1978 and 1980), but the Yanks shipped him to Columbus of the International League, where he spent the next two seasons. In 1982, Stegman would get into two games for the Yanks as a pinch runner, and after the season sign as a free agent with the Chicago White Sox.

April 17, 1981: Signed Lefthanded Pitcher Dave LaRoche as a Free Agent

Since coming to the big leagues in 1970, Dave LaRoche had pitched in 595 games for four different teams. He had two stints with the California Angels, the team with which he began his career, and the team that had released him just before the start of this season. In that time, LaRoche, a month shy of turning 33, had accumulated 126 saves while making only 14 starts, nine of which came for the Angels in 1980. But, of course, the Yanks hadn't gotten him to be a starter. Adding LaRoche would allow lefty Tom Underwood, who had been pitching in relief, to join the starting rotation, a rotation that already included three lefthanders: Ron Guidry, Tommy John, and Rudy May.

Before signing LaRoche, bullpen coach Jeff Torborg and pitching coach Stan Williams watched him throw for 45 minutes in the bullpen. Torborg, who was a coach with Cleveland when LaRoche pitched for the Indians, said: "I'm happy with what I saw. Our major interest was to see whether Dave had lost any of the life in his arm. But he came through with fine velocity."

LaRoche would finish his career with the

Yankees. He would go 4-1 in 1981 and 4-2 in 1982, and then pitch in one game in 1983.

April 27, 1981: Traded Minor League Righthanded Pitcher Tom Filer and Cash to the Chicago Cubs for Catcher Barry Foote

The Yanks had gone looking for catching help after poor play by backstops Johnny Oates and Dennis Werth contributed to the previous day's loss to Toronto. (A week earlier, first-string catcher Rick Cerone had gone on the disabled list with a broken hand.) "We felt we had a weakness," Yankee manager Gene Michael said. "Most clubs have three catchers."

Barry Foote had compiled a .233 batting average in 630 games with the Expos, Phillies, and Cubs. He'd spent a good part of the 1980 season on the disabled list, and was hitless in 22 at-bats in 1981. On hearing of Foote's hitless string, Bobby Murcer said "He'll fit right in," no doubt referring to the Yanks' own struggles at the plate.

Foote would end his big league career as a Yankee playing in a total of 57 games in 1981 and 1982 and batting .191.

The Oakland Athletics had drafted Tom Filer out of the Yankee farm system in December 1980, but he failed to make the A's roster and they'd returned him this spring. He was currently with Columbus of the International League, but the Cubs assigned him to Iowa of the American Association.

May 20, 1981: Traded Lefthanded Pitcher Tom Underwood and First Baseman Jim Spencer to the Oakland Athletics for First Baseman Dave Revering, Outfielder Mike Patterson, and Minor League Lefthanded Pitcher Chuck Dougherty

The Yankees had completed a deal with the Pirates late in spring training that would have sent first baseman Jim Spencer, two minor leaguers, and $850,000 to Pittsburgh for Pirates first baseman, Jason Thompson. However, because the cash involved was beyond the limit Commissioner Bowie Kuhn had established for such transactions, he vetoed the deal.

Spencer had been with the Yankees since 1978 as a designated hitter and part-time first baseman. His best season was 1979, when he batted .288 and had 23 home runs. But his average dropped to .236 (with 13 home runs) in 1980, and was a feeble .143 in 25 games this season. Manager Gene Michael suggested that Spencer's decline had forced the trade.

"If Spencer would have performed the way he did two years ago," Michael said, "we might not be making this move." He added that Dave Revering would be platooned at first base with Bob Watson, when Watson came off the disabled list, and until then with Dennis Werth.

Revering had been Oakland's first baseman the past three seasons, during which time he batted .282 and hit 50 home runs. In 31 games this season, he had a .230 average and two home runs. However, like so many players before him (and after him), Revering had fallen out of favor with manager Billy Martin. He had been platooning at first base with Jeff Newman, but in the last week Martin had used him only sparingly. When he got the news, Revering hurried down from Boston, where the A's were playing, and got to New York in the eighth inning of the Yankees' 11th-inning 5-4 win over Kansas City. Michael spotted him in the tenth inning and said: "I haven't met you yet, but you're hitting." (Royals pitcher Dan Quisenberry walked Revering intentionally.)

Tom Underwood had a fine 13-9 season in 1980, his first with the Yankees, but he'd been much less effective this season. In nine games, six as a starter, he'd won just one of five decisions and had a 4.41 earned run average. The Yanks recalled lefthander Dave Righetti (5-0, with a 1.00 ERA) from the International League Columbus Clippers to take Underwood's place.

Going to Columbus was rookie Mike Patterson, who'd batted .348 in 23 at-bats with the Athletics. Patterson would play in four games for the Yankees later in the season and 11 more in 1982.

Lefthander Chuck Dougherty went to Fort Lauderdale of the Florida State League and never reached the majors.

June 12, 1981: Traded Righthanded Pitcher Doug Bird, a Player to Be Named, and Cash to the Chicago Cubs for Righthanded Pitcher Rick Reuschel

The Yanks and Cubs completed this trade just as the major league players went on strike. The Yankees (34-22) were in first place, two games ahead of Baltimore, but wanted a pitcher of Rick Reuschel's caliber to offset the injuries suffered by various members of the rotation. They realized, of course, they couldn't use Reuschel until the strike was settled, but didn't suspect it would take seven weeks. When it was finally settled, the Yanks were declared the winners of the "first half" of what had now become a split-season. That automatically put them into postseason play, something that had eluded Reuschel in his ten seasons in Chicago. In that time, the 32-year-old veteran had been a 20-game winner once (in 1977), and had never failed to win fewer than ten games in any season. His 4-7 mark before the strike gave him an aggregate record of 129-121, with a 3.45 earned run average.

Reuschel's reputation as a quality pitcher preceded him. Yankee scout Birdie Tebbets said, "He's a very experienced Catfish Hunter–type pitcher. Rick is a superb athlete who brings to the Yankees a reliability from the right side we've been looking for."

When play resumed, Reuschel won four and lost four in the remaining weeks of 1981, but missed the entire 1982 season with a torn rotator cuff. In 1983, the Yanks sent him to Columbus of the International League and then released him on June 9. His old team, the Cubs signed him, and Reuschel would pitch in the major leagues (also for Pittsburgh and San Francisco) until 1991, winning an additional 81 games.

Doug Bird signed with the Yankees as a free agent in April 1980 and began the season with Columbus. He was later called up and went 3-0 with a 2.66 ERA. Bird had also won his first five decisions this season, giving him eight straight wins before he'd lost to the White Sox, 3-2, in his last appearance. The Yankees had used Bird almost exclusively in long relief, although manager Gene Michael had given him a few emergency starts in recent weeks.

On August 5, the Yanks sent righthanded

pitcher Mike Griffin to the Cubs as the player to be named. Griffin had been back and forth between New York and Columbus the past three seasons and had a career 2-4 record in 18 games as a Yankee.

August 19, 1981: Traded Minor League Third Baseman Pat Tabler to the Chicago Cubs for a Player to Be Named or Cash

Two months earlier, the Yankees had gotten Rick Reuschel from the Cubs for Doug Bird and a player to be named. As part of the deal, the Yanks sent Pat Tabler, then with Columbus of the International League, "on loan" to the Cubs' Iowa team in the American Association. At the time, it was assumed that the "loan" of Tabler fulfilled the "player to be named" portion of the deal. Instead, the Yanks sent pitcher Mike Griffin to the Cubs on August 5.

Now, after Tabler had batted .306 in 63 games for Iowa, the Cubs acquired him officially. Although the announced price was a player to be named or cash, the Yanks would actually get two players, both righthanded pitchers. They received Bill Caudill on April 1, 1982 (and immediately traded him to Seattle) and Jay Howell on August 2, 1982.

November 4, 1981: Traded Minor League Righthanded Pitcher Bryan Ryder and a Player to Be Named to the Cincinnati Reds for Outfielder Ken Griffey

By trading for Ken Griffey, Yankee owner George Steinbrenner accomplished two things. He was getting an excellent ballplayer, while sending a message to Reggie Jackson, who was a free agent, that he wasn't terribly interested in having Jackson return to New York in 1982.

Jackson got the message. "Wow, that's unreal," he said. "You want me to call the Mayflower moving man? George asked me to come and see him. I don't know if it'll be a waste of time now. It doesn't look good for the home team here, does it? I don't think it looks good for me."

Steinbrenner had previously announced that the Yankees would emphasize the speed game in 1982, and the acquisition of Griffey appeared to be his first step in that direction. Coincidentally, two weeks earlier, the club had traded away a youngster who would develop into the type of player Steinbrenner seemed to have in mind. In a little noted deal, the Yanks sent minor-league outfielder Willie McGee to the St. Louis Cardinals for lefthanded pitcher Bob Sykes. McGee, a speedy 23 year old, had batted .322 with 63 RBIs and 24 steals at Class AA Nashville of the Southern League in 1981. He would go on to win two batting championships and a Most Valuable Player Award with the Cardinals, while Sykes never again pitched in the major leagues.

If the Yanks chose not to re-sign Jackson, Griffey, who'd been an important part of Cincinnati's "Big Red Machine," seemed his logical successor in right field. He was a five-time .300-hitter, with a lifetime .307 batting average. He'd also stolen 150 bases, but had hit just 60 home runs.

Whether or not the Yankees signed Jackson, Griffey was determined to win a starting position in the outfield. He had spent his entire 11-year career in Cincinnati and, as a lifetime National Leaguer, had little use for the designated hitter. "Myself, I never really liked the DH," he said. "I'm not planning on sitting around and doing just that."

Although he could have declared himself a free agent, Griffey said he was happy the way things worked out. "I'm more pleased with it this way than if I had gone into the free-agent market," he said. "It was better than traveling all around the country." He admitted that he would have preferred to stay in the National League; however, he no longer wanted to play on the artificial turf of Cincinnati's Riverfront Stadium and was glad that most fields in the American League had real grass.

The Yanks didn't give up much to get Griffey, just two young minor league pitchers. Bryan Ryder was a 21-year-old righthander who was 8-7 at Columbus in 1981 and would never reach the majors. And Fred Toliver, the player to be named, was a 20-year-old righthander who'd gone 5-3 with Greensboro of the South Atlantic League in 1981. Toliver was officially assigned to the Reds on December 10.

November 17, 1981: Traded Third Baseman Aurelio Rodriguez to the Toronto Blue Jays for a Player to Be Named

The "dumping" of Aurelio Rodriguez was unexpected. He'd batted .346 (although in just 52 at-bats) as Graig Nettles's backup in strike-shortened 1981, and had five hits in 12 at-bats (.417) in the Yanks' six-game World Series loss to the Dodgers.

Bill Bergesch, vice president for baseball operations, gave two reasons for the deal: (1) that Rodriguez deserved a chance to play regularly somewhere, and (2) that rookie Tucker Ashford had done so well with the International League Columbus Clippers in 1981, he deserved a chance to play in the majors.

Bergesch further explained that because all teams had to set their 40-man rosters in the next few days, getting rid of Rodriguez "gives us a chance to add a younger player to the roster." The Yanks were thinking not only of Ashford, they were also trying to open some spots for the possible signing of free agents.

Toronto appeared a good place for Rodriguez to go. Danny Ainge, whom they'd hoped would be their third baseman of the future, had recently announced that he was through playing baseball and would concentrate his talents on basketball. However, Rodriguez's stay in Toronto would be brief. Late in spring training the Blue Jays acquired third baseman Rance Mulliniks from Kansas City, and a week later, before he ever played a game for them, they traded Rodriguez to the Chicago White Sox for Wayne Nordhagen.

The player to be named was catcher Mike Lebo, a .232-hitter with Kinston of the Class A Carolina League, whom the Yanks received on December 9, 1981.

December 23, 1981: Signed Free-Agent Outfielder Dave Collins from the Cincinnati Reds

Signing Dave Collins fit well with owner George Steinbrenner's plan to add speed to the Yankee attack. The 29-year-old Collins was just a .277-hitter in seven seasons with Seattle, California, and Cincinnati, but he had a total of 209 stolen bases, including 79 in 1980.

Because of his great speed, vice president Bill Bergesch suggested that manager Bob Lemon might drop Willie Randolph down in the order and use Collins in the leadoff spot.

At first, Collins had been reluctant to sign with the Yankees for fear that he wouldn't get much playing time. But Steinbrenner and Bergesch assured him that while he wouldn't play at any one position, he would "play as much as a regular." Collins said he preferred first base, a position the Yanks were worried about because Bob Watson had been injured for part of the 1981 season and Dave Revering hadn't hit much. Lemon agreed to try Collins at first base, but added that he likely would also use him in the outfield and as the designated hitter. Collins's agent, Rich Bry, said of his client: "He doesn't mind DH-ing once a week, but I can promise you if it's four or five days a week, they'll have their hands full with him being unhappy."

While his contract didn't specifically mention how much playing time he would get, Collins felt that the Yankees would be true to their promises. About playing for George Steinbrenner, he said, "I know Mr. Steinbrenner believes in mental toughness. If you don't play well, he'll call you in and tell you to your face, but if you do, he'll praise you and I like that. It will be exciting to play for Mr. Steinbrenner, but if we lose eight or nine in a row I don't think I'll jump in an elevator with him."

February 22, 1982: Purchased Third Baseman Barry Evans from the San Diego Padres

Barry Evans had a .251 batting average for his four seasons and 207 games with San Diego. He'd batted .323 in 54 games for the Padres in 1981, but spent more than two months on the suspended list in midseason for his refusal to report to San Diego's Texas League club at Amarillo.

Nevertheless, Evans reported when the Yankees assigned him to Columbus of the International League for the 1982 season. He batted .276 with 39 RBIs in 69 games for the Clippers and also .258 in 17 games for the Yanks. Sent back to Columbus in 1983, he was eventually drafted by the Twins organization, but never returned to the major leagues.

March 24, 1982: Traded Righthanded Pitcher Bill Castro to the California Angels for Third Baseman Butch Hobson

Both Butch Hobson and Bill Castro were pleased to be going elsewhere. Hobson, who began his career with the Red Sox, had his best season in 1977, when he hit 30 home runs and drove in 112 runs for Boston. He was the Angels' third baseman in 1981, his first year with the club, but in January 1982 California got Doug DeCinces in a trade with Baltimore. They gave DeCinces the third base job, while Hobson had played in only three games during the current exhibition season.

After he learned he was going to New York, Hobson said, "I should be appreciated there, and I've never felt appreciated here. I'm excited about being around Graig Nettles. A third baseman as good as he is should make me a better player."

Hobson would play in only 30 games for the Yanks in 1982, none of them at third base. Instead, he played first base and served as a designated hitter, batting .172 with no home runs. He spent part of the season in the International League, with Columbus, and then returned to the Clippers and stayed through 1985 without ever returning to the major leagues.

Castro, who at 28 was one year younger than Hobson, also spoke of appreciation. He'd gone 8-1 at Columbus, and 1-1 in 11 games for the Yanks in strike-shortened 1981. Still, he realized that the club had more righthanded relievers than they needed for 1982. "I appreciate what they did for me," he said, "because no relief pitcher is going to have a chance with the Yankees."

Manager Bob Lemon agreed. "It's good for both sides," he said. "Castro wasn't going to pitch here and Hobson wasn't going to play out there. Hobson gives us a righthanded bat and in some parks on the road that'll be real valuable to us with all our lefthanded hitting. As for Castro, he might be the only pitcher out there [California] without a sore arm. He may get a chance to do it every day."

Actually, the Yanks really had no other choice with Castro than to trade him. A clause in his contract said that if they didn't, they would either have to keep him on the 25-man roster or release him and pay his salary. The Yanks would also have been responsible for Castro's salary in 1983 if no other team had picked him up.

This seemingly routine trade of Hobson to New York aroused the ire of Donald Fehr, the lawyer for the Major League Baseball Players Association. Fehr was upset over a quote attributed to Buzzy Bavasi, the Angels' executive vice president. Before signing former Yankee Reggie Jackson as a free agent, Bavasi had said that he would "compensate" the Yankees. Fehr said that constituted collusion, but Bavasi denied the charge saying, "There's no significance to Reggie. Butch was third in line on our club at third base behind Doug DeCinces and Tim Foli, and he was in the first year of a big money three-year contract. We were looking to move him and we wanted to be fair to him."

Yankee owner George Steinbrenner also denied that the deal involved any kind of compensation. "Don't be ridiculous," he said. "The Players Association can say anything it wants and it goes in one ear and out the other."

Lemon agreed. "This is a straight-up trade. You're not getting compensation when you give somebody what they need."

March 24, 1982: Traded First Baseman Dennis Werth to the Kansas City Royals for Minor League Righthanded Pitcher Scott Behan

Besides playing first base in his three seasons with the Yankees, the versatile Dennis Werth had also caught, played third base and the outfield, and served as the designated hitter. He'd spent a part of each of those years with the International League Columbus Clippers, including a rehabilitation assignment there in 1981. In all, Werth played in 76 games with the Yankees and had a .218 batting average, with three home runs, and 13 RBIs. Kansas City assigned him to their Omaha team in the American Association, but they later called him up, and he would play his final 41 games for the Royals.

Twenty-year-old Scott Behan, who would never reach the big leagues, had a 3-3 record at Sarasota of the Gulf Coast League in 1981. The Yanks assigned him to Greensboro of the Class A South Atlantic League.

March 30, 1982: Traded Righthanded Pitcher Andy McGaffigan and Outfielder Ted Wilborn to the San Francisco Giants for Righthanded Pitcher Doyle Alexander

Because he'd been unable to reach a salary agreement with the Giants, Doyle Alexander had not yet reported to the club's training camp at Phoenix. "It was a disagreement on values and I was convinced there was no way it would be resolved," he said. "I had to do what I could to force the issue." Nevertheless, Opening Day was a week away, and Alexander hadn't thrown a pitch in a game all spring.

This would be Alexander's second tour with the Yankees. He'd been there in the second half of 1976, but left after the season to sign as a free agent with the Texas Rangers. Alexander spent three years in Texas, and then one each with Atlanta and San Francisco. His record these past five seasons was 56-46, including a 14-11 mark with the 1981 Giants.

Alexander, who was now 31, said he'd been throwing at home each day to get ready for the season. That caused Yankee outfielder Lou Piniella to remark, half in jest, "If he wins 20 games, nobody will come to spring training next year."

Unfortunately for the Yanks, Alexander didn't come anywhere near 20 wins. After sending him to their Class A Fort Lauderdale club in the Florida State League to get in shape, they activated him on April 24. But he had an awful season—a 1-7 record, with a 6.08 earned run average, and two months on the disabled list.

In 1983, Alexander was 0-2 in eight games when the Yanks released him on May 16. Toronto signed him, and Alexander won seven games for them that season, 17 games in each of the next two seasons, and a total of 86 games before his career ended in 1989.

After going 8-6 at Columbus of the International League in 1981, Andy McGaffigan got into two late September games with the Yankees, with no decisions. He'd had four outings this exhibition season and had been hit hard in each. The Giants would call him up during the '82 season, and he would pitch with them, the Expos, the Reds, and the A's, on and off for the next ten years.

Ted Wilborn appeared in eight games for the Yanks in 1980, going 2 for 8. Sent to Nashville of the Southern League in 1981, he batted .297 with 86 runs batted in and 43 stolen bases. Like McGaffigan, he was 23 years old, but unlike McGaffigan, he never again played in the major leagues.

April 1, 1982: Traded Righthanded Pitchers Gene Nelson and Bill Caudill, and a Player to Be Named to the Seattle Mariners for Lefthanded Pitcher Shane Rawley

The Yanks had been pursuing Shane Rawley since the end of the 1980 season, admitted Bill Bergesch, a team vice president. "We've been talking on and off with Seattle for some time, but this got heated up in the last day or so. We had a chance to get Rawley and we felt we couldn't pass it up because it might not come along again."

While Rawley had been almost exclusively a relief pitcher in his four major league seasons, he hadn't had many "save" opportunities with the expansion Mariners. Nevertheless, he'd chalked up 36 of them to go along with a 20-31 won-lost record. Now that he was joining a Yankee bullpen that already had Goose Gossage and Ron Davis, talk began immediately that the club would trade Davis, which they did nine days later.

Rawley couldn't hide his happiness about going to a winning club like the Yankees. "I heard during the winter that they were interested in me, and I hoped it would happen," he said. "But once spring training starts, you have to put that out of your mind."

If Rawley's career seemed to be taking an upswing, Gene Nelson's appeared to be going in the opposite direction. He'd gone 3-1 as a 21-year-old Yankee rookie in 1981, while also winning all four of his decisions with Columbus during a stay in the International League. During spring training, manager Bob Lemon had indicated that Nelson would be his number four starter this season. However, Seattle already had set their season-opening rotation and sent Nelson to their Salt Lake City team in the Pacific Coast League.

Bill Caudill's Yankee career had lasted a matter of minutes. The Yanks had just gotten him from the Cubs, for whom he'd pitched the past three seasons, as one of the players to be named in the August 1981 trade that sent Pat Tabler to Chicago. (The other player in the Tabler deal would be Jay Howell, who came to the Yanks on August 2, 1982).

The player to be named in this deal would be outfielder Bobby Brown, whom the Yanks would send to Seattle five days later. In three seasons as a Yankee, Brown batted .255 in 198 games, with 14 home runs (all in 1980) and 33 stolen bases.

Brown was unhappy about leaving. "It's a bad situation where you drain a player of everything he's got, bounce him around back and forth," he said. "Seattle's a great place to play, but I got to get there to play."

As they had with Nelson, Seattle also sent Brown to Salt Lake City, but both would return to spend most of the season with the Mariners.

April 6, 1982: Traded Catcher Brad Gulden to the Montreal Expos for Catcher Bobby Ramos

The foot of snow that fell on New York, wiping out the season opener against Texas, did not prevent the Yankees from a last minute roster shuffle. To get down to the necessary 25 players, they put third baseman Butch Hobson on the disabled list, sent outfielder Bobby Brown to Seattle as the player to be named in the previous week's trade for Shane Rawley, sent shortstop Andre Robertson to Columbus of the International League, and traded catcher Brad Gulden to Montreal for catcher Bobby Ramos.

Ramos, who also went to Columbus, was just 13 for 77 in 41 games for the Expos, spread over three seasons. Still, the Yanks liked the fact that he had some major league experience and would be the only catcher at Columbus who had played in the big leagues. Nevertheless, when the season ended, they sold him back to Montreal. Ramos played in four games for the 1982 Yankees, getting one hit in 11 at-bats.

Gulden had spent 1981 on the move, playing with three different teams in three different leagues. He was with the Seattle Mariners, their Spokane team in the Pacific Coast League, and, after he was traded back to the Yankees, with Columbus. (Seattle had traded

him to the Yanks as the player to be named in the November 18, 1980, deal, the deal in which the Yanks had originally traded him to the Mariners.) He'd lost out to Barry Foote in this spring's battle for the number two catching slot behind Rick Cerone, and now that he was with a new team, he could be sent to the minors without consequence. The Expos, who had Gary Carter and had recently signed free-agent Tim Blackwell, sent Gulden to Wichita of the American Association.

Gulden voiced his displeasure with the Yankees. "Why didn't they trade me some place where I can play," he asked? "I don't mind being traded, but why couldn't they have done it earlier? Instead, they bring me to New York and then trade me. They didn't make it right for me," he continued. "I have nothing to prove in Triple-A anymore, nothing. I'm not going to go no place there unless someone breaks a leg."

On October 26, 1982, the Yanks bought Gulden back from the Expos, but he spent the 1983 season back in Columbus. He hit .316 for the Clippers and then signed as a free agent with Cincinnati.

April 10, 1982: Traded Righthanded Pitcher Ron Davis, Minor League Righthanded Pitcher Paul Boris, and Minor League Shortstop Greg Gagne to the Minnesota Twins for Shortstop Roy Smalley

When the Yanks made the trade for reliever Shane Rawley earlier in the month, it made Ron Davis expendable. Bill Bergesch, a Yankee vice president, gave Davis the news that he'd been traded following a workout as the club prepared for the next day's season-opening game against Chicago. Opening Day had been postponed since April 6 because of a snowstorm, and the Yanks and White Sox were the only major league teams yet to play this season.

Davis said he'd been expecting a trade ever since his poor showing in last fall's World Series loss to the Dodgers. "I knew they were going to get rid of me," he said. "I just knew they didn't want me here. No matter what you do, if you don't do it right, they get rid of you. You mess up and they don't want you."

In 1979, the Yanks had recalled Davis

from Columbus of the International League after an injury to Goose Gossage. He had a spectacular rookie year, winning 14 games, losing just two, with nine saves and a 2.85 earned run average. Over the next two seasons, Davis functioned mainly as Gossage's setup man, going a combined 13-8 with 13 saves.

The careers of the two minor leaguers leaving the Yankees would be dramatically different. Paul Boris's big league stay would consist of just 23 games and a 1-2 record with the 1982 Twins. However, after spending the '82 season with Orlando of the Southern League, Greg Gagne would become Minnesota's shortstop in 1985 and go on to a lengthy major league stay.

The addition of Roy Smalley raised to ten the number of players on the Yanks' opening-day roster that had not been there on Opening Day the year before. Smalley, who'd already played four games for the Twins in 1982, had a lifetime .259 average for his seven seasons with Texas and Minnesota. Back problems had limited his playing time in 1981, but the Yanks had him checked by their orthopedist and were satisfied that he was healthy.

"We can use him at shortstop and third base," said manager Bob Lemon. "It gives us more depth than we had. We were short infielders. This gives us a chance to rest players."

Although he was primarily a shortstop, Smalley could also play third base. Bucky Dent and the aging Graig Nettles currently occupied those positions on the Yankees. The Yanks had gotten Butch Hobson to play behind Nettles, but Hobson was beginning the season on the disabled list. Meanwhile, Dent wondered what effect the arrival of Smalley would have on him.

"Maybe they're going to trade me too," he said. "I don't know anything anymore. I just show up." (In August, the Yanks *would* trade Dent to Texas.)

April 23, 1982: Traded First Baseman Bob Watson to the Atlanta Braves for Minor League Righthanded Pitcher Scott Patterson

Bob Watson got the word he was being traded early. As he put it, the Yanks informed him that the trade, which had been rumored for several days, "was no rumor." They were delaying announcing it, they told him, only because "some things had to be worked out." Watson admitted that he was sorry to leave New York; however, he wasn't at all upset that the Yankees had gotten so little for him.

"It could have been for two broken bats and a water bucket for all I care, just so it comes from the hip twice a month," he said, referring to the generous salary he would continue to make.

Watson's new team, the Braves, had gotten off to a great start. "Yeah, they're the best right now, record-wise, and that's a good feeling," he said. Then, speaking of the Yankees: "But this club is not too shabby, and when they get their act together they are definitely going to hurt some people. I'd have liked to finish my career here, but sometimes what you want you don't get."

Watson joined the Yanks as a free agent in 1980, replacing the traded Chris Chambliss at first base. He had a fine season, batting .307 with 13 home runs, but in 1981 a groin injury limited him to just 59 games and a .212 mark. This season, he'd been to bat only 17 times.

Scott Patterson remained in the International League, going from the Braves' team at Richmond to the Yanks' team at Columbus. It would be the highest level he would attain.

May 5, 1982: Traded First Baseman Dave Revering, Minor League Outfielder Tom Dodd, and Minor League Third Baseman Jeff Reynolds to the Toronto Blue Jays for First Baseman John Mayberry

With just ten home runs in their first 22 games (of which they'd won only nine), the Yanks might have been reconsidering George Steinbrenner's commitment to emphasize speed in 1982. And with Graig Nettles, one of their few remaining power hitters, on the disabled list, they may have also been reconsidering their decision not to re-sign slugger Reggie Jackson. Steinbrenner denied that trading for John Mayberry was an admission that he'd made a mistake in letting Jackson go. And in another move, ostensibly to add some more power to the lineup, the club called power-hitting Steve Balboni up from Columbus of the

International League and sent the Clippers lefthanded pitcher Dave LaRoche.

"This doesn't have anything really to do with Reggie," Steinbrenner said, referring to the Mayberry trade. "He [Mayberry] gives us the punch Oscar Gamble has not given us. Mayberry was the guy we've been after for two and a half years. He's given us the most trouble of any lefthanded hitter, and that was with really nothing around him."

The 33-year-old Mayberry had 247 home runs in his 15 seasons with Houston, Kansas City, and Toronto, with his best years coming with the Royals. He'd hit more than 20 home runs in eight different seasons, and had topped the 100 RBI mark in three. Yankee vice president Cedric Tallis was the Royals general manager during part of the time Mayberry was in Kansas City.

"He's a fine pull hitter and a dangerous cleanup man," Tallis said. "He's also an excellent defensive first baseman. He has soft hands, and he comes up with the low throws."

As Steinbrenner noted, Mayberry was a very productive hitter against the Yankees, especially at Yankee Stadium. In 71 at-bats there, he had a .324 average, with nine home runs and 20 runs batted in.

"I plan on hitting him fourth, and he'll play first base every day," said manager Gene Michael, who'd replaced Bob Lemon ten days earlier. "I've had him in my lineup before," Michaels continued. "Not specifically, but in my mind. He's always had power. I never liked to see him coming up to the plate when he was playing against us. You know you can get him out, but you also know he can get a home run."

Despite all the praise, Mayberry's abilities clearly were in decline. In 17 games this year, he had just two home runs and three RBIs, and the Blue Jays had replaced him at first base with Willie Upshaw. He would play his final 69 games for the Yankees, batting .209 with eight home runs and 27 RBIs.

Dave Revering won the first base job in spring training, but after a poor start with the bat, both Lemon and Michael had opted to sit him down against lefthanders. "I'm happy to go," Revering said. "Now I'll get some playing time." Later in the season, Revering went from Toronto to Seattle. He hit a combined .202 for the season, which would be his final one.

Third baseman Jeff Reynolds, who never reached the majors, and outfielder Tom Dodd, who would, briefly with the 1986 Orioles, went from New York's Nashville team in the Southern League to Toronto's Knoxville team in that league.

May 12, 1982: Traded Infielder Larry Milbourne, Righthanded Pitcher John Pacella, and Minor League Lefthanded Pitcher Pete Filson to the Minnesota Twins for Catcher Butch Wynegar and Righthanded Pitcher Roger Erickson

Within hours of first-string catcher Rick Cerone's going on the disabled list, the Yanks replaced him with Minnesota's Butch Wynegar. Despite being a seven-year veteran, Wynegar was just 26 years and had won *The Sporting News'* American League Rookie of the Year Award in 1976 and been an All Star in his first two seasons. He was an excellent receiver, with a .254 lifetime batting average, but he'd had elbow surgery in 1981 and was batting just .209 this season.

"We made this deal because we needed a catcher," said manager Gene Michael. "But we don't even know yet whether we'll carry two or three catchers [Barry Foote was currently the other catcher], or how we'll set up the pitching now. Wynegar's a switch hitter, and he'll catch if he gets hot with the bat."

Roger Erickson's role was more clearly defined. His role would be to help fill the gap created a week earlier when Doyle Alexander joined fellow pitcher Rick Reuschel on the disabled list. Erickson had gone 14-13 as a Twins rookie in 1978, but hadn't had a winning season since, although he was 4-3 thus far in 1982.

Larry Milbourne, a .289-hitter in 75 games since joining the club in 1981, spoke bluntly about his reaction to the trade. "Going from an organization like the Yankees to one like the Twins is like night and day," he said. (Milbourne would return to the Yankees in 1983.)

John Pacella and Pete Filson, both of whom were at Columbus in the International League, reported directly to the Twins. Pacella had been in three games for the Yanks earlier in the season, losing his only decision, but for Filson it was his first chance at the big leagues.

August 8, 1982: Traded Shortstop Bucky Dent to the Texas Rangers for First Baseman–Outfielder Lee Mazzilli

From the time just before Opening Day when the Yanks traded for shortstop Roy Smalley, Bucky Dent had suspected his days in New York were coming to an end. Dent said he was "kind of relieved" that it had finally happened, but was "a little disappointed in some of the circumstances," and that he didn't "understand some things." Then speaking of his five-plus years with the Yankees, he said: "It's been an honor. I had some great moments, a lot of fun."

Dent, now 30, had been sharing the shortstop duties with Smalley, but was batting just .169. Overall, Dent batted .239 in his six-plus years as a Yankee; however, he would be best remembered for his dramatic home run at Fenway Park that won the 1978 Eastern Division playoff game for the Yankees. Dent's leaving reduced the number of players who had been with the Yanks in the World Series that year to five: Goose Gossage, Ron Guidry, Graig Nettles, Lou Piniella, and Willie Randolph. "I guess there's a new start for me," he said. "I'm going to a new club that wants me. I'll go there and do the best I can."

For Lee Mazzilli, a native New Yorker, the trade meant a return to the city just four months after the Mets traded him to the Rangers. The best of Mazzilli's five full seasons with the Mets was in 1979 when he hit .303 with 15 home runs and 79 RBIs. Never really happy in Texas, he'd been in 58 games this season and was batting .241.

Mazzilli called his trade to the Yankees "a dream come true," adding that he'd "always wanted to play for a winner, and this team in the past seven or eight years has been the most consistent team."

August 31, 1982: Traded Lefthanded Pitcher Tommy John to the California Angels for Three Minor League Players to Be Named

California was leading the Western Division, but their pitching had been faltering. By beating the August 31 midnight deadline, the Angels not only had Tommy John for the stretch drive, he would also be eligible for post-season play. For that same reason, California had picked up two other veteran pitchers: free agent Luis Tiant earlier, and John Curtis, purchased from San Diego today.

John had asked the Yankees to trade him back in late July, but was not surprised that it took this long for it to happen. "I knew it would come down to the last day," he said. "It's like playing poker. Everybody makes their bids. Yesterday all the cards were dealt and it came down to today."

To beat the deadline, John had to actually be with the Angels before midnight, so he hurriedly left Minneapolis, where the Yanks were playing, to fly to Detroit, where the Angels were playing the Tigers.

A 20-game winner in 1979 and 1980, his first two seasons in New York, John slipped to 9-8 in strike-shortened 1981, and was 10-10 this season. He started asking for a trade after the Yanks removed him from the starting rotation, and his relations with the team grew worse after a loan dispute with owner George Steinbrenner and vice president for baseball operations Bill Bergesch. But although he was ending his Yankee career on a sour note, John hoped the fans would remember him in a positive way.

"Any time it comes down to this, you're in a position of being a bad guy," he said. "I hope the people don't think of me as a bad guy. I hope they think of Tommy John as an athlete who tried to do his best every time out, which I did."

John would go 4-2 for the Angels, who won the division title by three games over Kansas City. The Yanks called up Jay Howell from Columbus of the International League to take John's place.

Howell was the pitcher they'd gotten earlier in the month to complete the Pat Tabler trade.

Instead of getting three minor leaguers for John, the Yankee got one. On November 24 they received lefthander Dennis Rasmussen who'd won 11 and lost eight with Spokane of the Pacific Coast League.

December 1, 1982: Signed Free-Agent Outfielder Don Baylor from the California Angels

George Steinbrenner had tried to get Don Baylor twice before: in 1976 when he first became a free agent, and this past August as part of the deal in which the Yanks traded Tommy John to the Angels. When the Angels chose not to re-sign Baylor, despite a year in which he hit 24 home runs and drove in 93 runs, Steinbrenner finally got him. "He is the take-charge hitter I've been looking for," said the Yankee owner.

"Mr. Steinbrenner is a very aggressive person," Baylor noted. "He had a ballclub last year that finished fifth. He's like myself; he likes to win." Then, speaking of his departure from California, which he attributed to Angels GM Buzzy Bavasi's dislike of him, Baylor said: "I was forced to leave. I never had a choice."

The 33-year-old Baylor had spent six years in Baltimore and one in Oakland, before signing with California in 1977. During his career, he'd accumulated 213 home runs, 820 runs batted in, and one Most Valuable Player Award. That came in 1979 when he led the Angels to the Western Division title with a .296 average and 36 home runs, while leading the league in runs scored (120) and runs batted in (139).

Primarily a designated hitter the past few seasons, Baylor figured to continue in that role in New York. However, he did say he would be glad to play first base if the club needed him there.

"Just pencil my name in the lineup every day, that's all a manager has to do," he said. "I just don't like to take days off." (Who the Yankee manager would be in 1983 was still uncertain. Clyde King had been the last of three managers in 1982, but many expected Billy Martin to return for the '83 season.)

Along with being one of the most consistent run producers in the American League, Baylor had long had a reputation for leadership, something the Yanks felt they lacked in 1981. "I want to try and help point the club in the right direction with my attitude and by driving in runs," Baylor said. "I cherish the opportunity to stand up there with a man on second or third and drive him in." (He'd led the league in game-winning RBIs in 1981.)

Aware of the difficulties righthanded power hitters often had at Yankee Stadium, and the pressure of playing in New York, Baylor assured everyone he could handle both situations. He said he'd always tried to hit the ball down the line, staying away from Death Valley in left center field, and that "for all the negative things about playing in New York, the mystique is still there."

December 1, 1982: *Don Baylor.* "Just pencil my name in the lineup every day, that's all a manager has to do."

December 9, 1982: Traded Outfielder Dave Collins, Righthanded Pitcher Mike Morgan, Minor League First Baseman Fred McGriff, and Cash to the Toronto Blue Jays for Righthanded Pitcher Dale Murray and Minor League Outfielder Tom Dodd

When Dave Collins signed to play with the Yankees in December 1981, he said, "It will be exciting to play for Mr. Steinbrenner." It may have been exciting, but Collins was never happy in his one year with the Yankees and was glad to be leaving. The Yanks had signed the fleet-footed Collins as part of

George Steinbrenner's plan to add speed to the lineup, but he stole only 13 bases, while batting .253.

Mike Morgan pitched in 30 games, 23 of them as a starter, in 1982, which was his only year as a Yankee. He started well, but pitched poorly in the second half of the season to finish 7-11, with a 4.37 earned run average. Morgan was still only 23 and would have a long career (with numerous teams) ahead of him.

The Yanks saw Dale Murray as a set-up man for Goose Gossage, or, as Clyde King said, "We have been looking for what we call a pre–Gossage guy. We'd like to make Gossage an eighth and ninth inning guy. Sometimes we've had to bring him in earlier, and as a manager, I don't like to do that." King, the incumbent manager, added, "Murray can fill that spot. He's a real experienced pitcher and he made a good comeback this year." (King would be replaced as manager by Billy Martin a month later, in January 1983.)

Murray debuted with the Montreal Expos in 1974 and had several excellent years in the National League with the Expos, Reds, and Mets. He was back with Montreal in 1979-80, but the Expos released him, and after Toronto signed him, he spent most of 1981 with their Syracuse club in the International League. Murray made a strong comeback in 1982, winning eight and saving 11 for the Blue Jays.

Toronto manager Bobby Cox attributed Murray's strong '82 season to a newly developed forkball. "He has no problems with left-handers because of the forkball," said Cox. "He's like a lefthander."

Tom Dodd was originally Yankee property, but they'd included him in the Dave Revering to Toronto for John Mayberry deal in May 1982. He hit a combined .235 playing for the Yanks' Nashville and Blue Jays' Knoxville teams in the Southern League, and would be back in Nashville in 1983.

Nineteen-year-old Fred McGriff had played at Bradenton in the rookie Gulf Coast League in 1981-82. In '82, he'd led the league with nine home runs (in 62 games) and 41 runs batted in. He wouldn't reach the major leagues to stay until 1987, but then would become an outstanding star for many years.

Murray would win three and lose six, with just one save for the Yanks before they released him in late April 1985. Critics would use Murray's disappointing showing and McGriff's and Morgan's eventual success to point out retroactively what a poor trade this was for the Yankees.

December 9, 1982: Signed Free-Agent Outfielder Steve Kemp from the Chicago White Sox

Steve Kemp became the 19th free agent signed by George Steinbrenner since he'd signed his first one, Catfish Hunter in 1975. Kemp was also the 14th he'd made a millionaire.

"People are going to say there goes George again. He's signing as many free agents as he can," Kemp said. "I just hope that some years from now George can look back and say Steve Kemp was one of the best acquisitions I made."

The 28-year-old Kemp spent his first five big league seasons in Detroit, where twice he'd hit more than 20 home runs and knocked in more than 100 runs. Traded to the White Sox for Chet Lemon in November 1981, he batted .286 for Chicago, with 19 home runs and 98 runs batted in. But, perhaps even more than his offensive abilities, Steinbrenner was attracted by Kemp's combative playing style. "I'm a discipline guy. I like hustle," Steinbrenner said. "Steve is the supreme hustler, he'll turn New York on."

Kemp knew it wouldn't be that easy, and that the New York fans and the New York press could be hard on players who didn't live up to their reputations. He said he'd thought about that as he decided between the Yanks, the Orioles, and the Phillies.

"I saw what happened to Ken Griffey last year and I felt really bad for him," Kemp said. "I don't even know him, but I felt bad because of all the abuse he got. I took that into consideration. It's possible that it could happen to me. But the only thing I can promise George and the people of New York is I'll go out and play hard. I'm not saying that can't happen, but I sure hope it won't."

Coincidentally, the Yanks signed Kemp on the same day they traded unhappy outfielder Dave Collins, whom they'd signed as a free agent the year before, and who'd also come to New York with high hopes.

December 15, 1982: Signed Free-Agent Lefthanded Pitcher Bob Shirley from the Cincinnati Reds

By officially signing Bob Shirley, and having already signed Don Baylor and Steve Kemp, the Yanks had now reached the limit of three free agents that any one club could sign. Therefore, they could no longer pursue some of the bigger-name free agents that were still out there, like Los Angeles first baseman Steve Garvey and Pittsburgh center fielder Omar Moreno.

Shirley was a 28-year-old lefthander who was comfortable pitching as either a starter or reliever. In his six seasons—four with San Diego and one each with St. Louis and Cincinnati—Shirley had started 123 games and relieved in 143 others. He held the distinction of being the only pitcher over that span who'd both started more than 100 games, and relieved in more than 100 games. Shirley's career record was 53 wins and 74 losses, and his career earned run average was 3.62.

The Yanks already had three lefthanders in their rotation (Ron Guidry, Dave Righetti, and Shane Rawley); nevertheless, vice president Bill Bergesch said the club viewed Shirley as a starting pitcher. However, he was quick to point out that Shirley's role would be "up to the manager."

Bergesch failed to mention that no one knew who that manager would be. Clyde King had finished the 1982 season, but the possibility loomed that George Steinbrenner would bring back Billy Martin for a third try.

Shirley seemed not to care who would manage the club in 1983; he was just happy to be a Yankee. "I've always dreamed of playing for the Yankees," he said. "But when I was drafted by them, I thought Mr. Steinbrenner was more interested in signing Floyd Bannister. I thought the Yankees were the last team who'd sign me."

Actually, the Yanks would have preferred getting Bannister, but he'd signed as a free agent with the White Sox two days earlier.

Beginning with the 1983 season, Shirley would pitch in 165 games for the Yankees before they released him in June 1987. Used mostly in long relief, he had a 14-20 record.

December 22, 1982: Traded First Baseman–Outfielder Lee Mazzilli to the Pittsburgh Pirates for Minor League Righthanded Pitcher Tim Burke, Minor League Catcher John Holland, Minor League Shortstop Jose Rivera, and Minor League Outfielder Don Aubin

Pittsburgh had a vacancy in center field created by Omar Moreno's departure via free agency to Houston, and they wanted Lee Mazzilli to fill that vacancy. Not coincidentally, Mazilli would be the Pirates' first white starting outfielder since Richie Zisk in 1976. Attendance in Pittsburgh was among the lowest in the National League, and Pirates scout Howie Haak, among others, had said the team needed more white players to bring the fans back to Three Rivers Stadium. Mazzilli, who came to the Yankees in the August 1981 trade for Bucky Dent, spent just two months with the club, batting .266 in 37 games.

Bill Bergesch, the Yankees' vice president for baseball operations, noted that the recent signing of free-agent designated hitter Don Baylor meant Mazzilli would have had little playing time with the Yankees in 1983. "Our outfield picture is pretty complete. We didn't see where he fits in. And he's too young [27] to sit around much."

Mazzilli understood. "It's a tough thing leaving New York," he said. "But it's nice to go somewhere that I'm wanted and needed."

In explaining why the club had sought minor leaguers in return for Mazzilli, Bergesch said, "We feel we've given away some of our fine young talent in other trades, and we're trying to replenish the farm system."

Of the four players the Yankees got, 19-year-old shortstop Jose Rivera was thought to be the only one with major league potential. In his first year as a professional, he'd batted .292 for Bradenton of the rookie Gulf Coast League. Rivera wouldn't become a major leaguer, nor would Don Aubin or John Holland, but Tim Burke would, debuting with Montreal in 1985.

April 18, 1983: Traded Third Baseman Tucker Ashford to the New York Mets

*for Minor League Lefthanded Pitcher
Steve Ray and a Player to Be Named*

In November 1981 the Yanks had traded reserve third baseman Aurelio Rodriguez to the Toronto Blue Jays supposedly to open a spot for Tucker Ashford in 1982. But Ashford's Yankee career consisted of just the three games he'd played in 1981, with no at-bats. He had, however, put together excellent back-to-back seasons with Columbus in the International League, batting .300 in 1981 and .331 in 1982. The Yanks had sold him to the Blue Jays in October 1982, but the sale was on a conditional basis, and the Jays returned him on Opening Day 1983.

The Mets would keep Ashford in the International League, assigning him to their affiliate at Tidewater.

Neither pitcher Steve Ray, who was sent to Class A Greensboro of the South Atlantic League, nor infielder Felix Perdomo, who came from the Mets on May 3, would reach the major leagues.

June 15, 1983: Traded First Baseman Marshall Brant, Minor League Righthanded Pitcher Ben Callahan, and Cash to the Oakland Athletics for Righthanded Pitcher Matt Keough

Matt Keough had been a particular favorite of Yankee manager Billy Martin and Martin's pitching coach Art Fowler when they'd had him at Oakland. In 1980, Martin's first year as manager of the Athletics, Keough's record improved from 2-17 to 16-13, earning him the American League's Comeback Player of the Year Award. Under Martin and Fowler's tutelage, Keough had records of 10-6 in 1981 and 11-18 (tied for the most losses in the AL) in 1982. Keough was 2-3 this season, with most of his appearances under new A's manager Steve Boros coming in relief. Martin, however, planned to return him to a starting role.

"I'm going to put Matt in the rotation," he said. "He pitched great for me. They didn't use him much this year. I noticed when I saw him he wasn't throwing his fastball. He was throwing a lot of off-speed stuff."

Martin was true to his word. Keough ap-peared in 12 games with the Yanks in 1983, all starts, winning three and losing four. But George Steinbrenner had fired Fowler in July, and in December he fired Martin and named Yogi Berra to manage the club in 1984. Keough, who'd lost his biggest boosters, spent that part of the 1984 season when he wasn't on the disabled list with the Yankees' Nashville club in the Southern League. He went 2-4 in seven games for the Sounds, and the Yanks released him after the season.

The Yankees had purchased Marshall Brant from the New York Mets organization on April 1, 1980. Brant, once a highly rated prospect, had spent the previous two seasons at Tidewater of the International League. The Yanks kept him in that league, sending him to Columbus, where he won the league's Most Valuable Player Award. Brant's only major league experience to date had come that same year (1980)—three games with six hitless at-bats for the Yankees. Oakland sent him from Columbus to their Pacific Coast League team at Tacoma.

Pitcher Ben Callahan, who'd been at Nashville, made his big league debut with the A's one week after the trade. He won one and lost two for the Athletics in what would be his only big league action.

July 16, 1983: Purchased Infielder Larry Milbourne from the Philadelphia Phillies

Larry Milbourne had been on the move ever since the Yankees sent him to Minnesota in the May 1982 trade for Butch Wynegar. Two months after getting him, the Twins sold Milbourne to Cleveland, and then this past winter the Indians sold him to Philadelphia. Milbourne had played in 41 games for the Phillies, including 13 starts at second base, and was batting .242. The Yanks were bringing him back to fill in for Willie Randolph, who had just gone on the 15-day disabled list with a pulled hamstring in his right leg.

Earlier in the day the club had called up infielder Bobby Meacham from their International League team in Columbus. But after getting Milbourne they informed Meacham that he would be returning to the Clippers.

Meacham didn't appear to be too upset about the quick turnaround.

"I'll be happy to go back to Columbus so I can play, rather than sitting here," he said. "I just want to play ball, no matter where it is."

August 10, 1983: Traded Outfielder Jerry Mumphrey to the Houston Astros for Outfielder Omar Moreno

Jerry Mumphrey had done well in his first two seasons for the Yankees, batting .307 in 1981 and .300 in 1982. Still he'd requested a trade, preferably to the National League and if possible to Houston, which was near his home in Tyler, Texas. When he learned that the Yankees had fulfilled his request, Mumphrey, batting .262 this season, expressed his relief at getting away.

"I think I can relax a little more. Now I can play the way I can. I'm ready to go," he said. "I feel like I played well here, although the first part of the year I was up and down. I don't think I have anything to be ashamed about."

With the Yanks having won six of their last eight games, manager Billy Martin made no comment about the trade but appeared to disapprove of it. General manager Murray Cook saw both its positive and negative aspects. "It's always a little bit testy when you make a move while the club is going well," Cook agreed. "You hate to upset the balance and you hate to upset a good thing. But on the other hand, we have a deal here we felt would help our club."

Cook added that "the deal should help both clubs. Mumphrey will provide Houston with a little more bat strength," he said, "and we feel Omar Moreno will give us added defensive play plus added speed. That's his forte, naturally."

Moreno, who would replace Mumphrey in center field, was, as Cook suggested, the better defensive player and also one of baseball's best base stealers. He'd stolen as many as 96 (in 1980), and was twice the National League leader, with 71 in 1978 and 77 in 1979. Moreno had accomplished all that for Pittsburgh, for whom he'd played from 1976 until signing with Houston as a free agent following the 1982 season. The 29-year-old Moreno (13 months younger than Mumphrey), who had a lifetime .254 batting average, was at .242 for the Astros, with 30 stolen bases.

Moreno would be the Yankee center fielder until 1985 when the club traded for Rickey Henderson. "It had become obvious," said George Steinbrenner, "that Omar, because of the great job that Rickey Henderson has been doing, was not going to get much playing time." When the Yanks released him on August 16, 1985, he'd played in a total of 199 games for them, batted .250, and stolen 28 bases. He finished out the year, and his career, with Kansas City.

August 26, 1983: Traded Two Players to Be Named and Cash to the San Diego Padres for Righthanded Pitcher John Montefusco

In their attempt to catch the first-place Orioles, the Yanks felt they had to have a fifth starter. They'd been seeking one all season, and among those that manager Billy Martin had tried in that role were Doyle Alexander, Matt Keough, Jay Howell, and Bob Shirley. The four had a combined won-lost record of 7-16, so now they were going to give veteran John Montefusco a try. The 33-year-old Montefusco had an 80-80 record in ten National League seasons, seven of them with the Giants. This season with the Padres, who were using him more as a long reliever than as a starter, he was 9-4, with a 3.30 earned run average, and he'd even saved four games.

Despite his success in San Diego, Montefusco was excited about coming to New York. "I'm from New Jersey," he said, "and the Yankees are the team I followed all my life. It's like a boyhood dream."

Montefusco would go 5-0 (in six starts) down the stretch, as the Yankees finished third. He was 5-3 in 1984, but injuries kept him out for much of that season and almost all of 1985 and 1986. In those two seasons, his final two, he pitched in a total of just seven games.

On September 12, 1983, the Yanks completed this trade by sending lefthanded pitcher Dennis Rasmussen, obtained from the Angels in the Tommy John trade, and second baseman Edwin Rodriguez to San Diego. Both were on the roster of the International League Columbus Clippers, and while Rasmussen had yet to make his big league debut (he would make it four days later), Rodriguez had been in three games for the Yankees in September 1982.

December 7, 1983: Signed Free-Agent Catcher Mike O'Berry from the California Angels

The California Angels had granted Mike O'Berry free agency a week earlier, after he'd refused a minor league assignment. O'Berry, who'd played for the Red Sox, Cubs and Reds before joining the Angels, had a career batting average of .186 in 164 games.

The Yanks sent O'Berry to their Columbus team in the International League so that he'd be available should anything happen to either Butch Wynegar or Rick Cerone. If one of them were to get hurt, O'Berry "is able to step in right now and be a better-than-adequate catcher at the major league level," said Yankee farm director Dave Hersh.

O'Berry would get to play in 13 games with the Yanks in 1984, going 8 for 32, but was back at Columbus in 1985. The club released him on May 25, and he signed with Montreal.

December 8, 1983: Traded Righthanded Pitcher Curt Kaufman and Cash to the California Angels for Shortstop Tim Foli

Tim Foli got the news he'd been traded as he was celebrating his 33rd birthday. Since reaching the majors as a 19 year old with the 1970 New York Mets, Foli had played for the Expos, the Giants, the Mets again, the Pirates, and for the last two seasons, the Angels. He had appeared in more than 1,600 major league games, almost all of them at shortstop, and had a .251 lifetime batting average. Foli's best season was in 1979. Traded from the Mets to Pittsburgh in April of that year, he reached career highs in batting (.288) and runs batted in (65).

Foli was available because the Angels were gambling that Rick Burleson, who'd spent most of the last two seasons on the disabled list, would make a successful comeback. (He wouldn't and Dick Schofield would be the Angels shortstop in 1984.) The Yanks wanted Foli as insurance in case Andre Robertson, their young shortstop injured in an August 1983 automobile crash, could no longer play the way he had before the crash.

In trading Curt Kaufman, the Yankees conceded that they were giving up an excellent pitching prospect, one who had 430 strikeouts in 406 minor league innings. Kaufman had been with Columbus of the International League in 1982 and 1983, along with brief stays in New York in each season. He'd appeared in 11 games with the Yankees and had one decision, a win.

December 8, 1983: Traded First Baseman Steve Balboni and Righthanded Pitcher Roger Erickson to the Kansas City Royals for Righthanded Pitcher Mike Armstrong and Minor League Catcher Duane Dewey

"The legend of Steve Balboni now goes to Kansas City," said Yankee general manager Murray Cook. Balboni had earned his legendary status by leading three different minor leagues in home runs over four consecutive seasons. He led the Florida State League in 1979 (26 with Fort Lauderdale), the Southern League in 1980 (34 with Nashville), and the International League in 1981 and 1982 (33 and 32 with Columbus). However, Balboni had yet to display that power in the majors. In trials with the Yanks in 1981, '82, and '83, he'd hit only seven home runs in 200 at-bats.

"It was a very difficult decision," Cook said about parting with the 26-year-old slugger. "We would have liked to see his power work in New York. But we have three other people who can play first base, and we were never sure he could reproduce those minor league statistics."

The Royals had already indicated that they planned to trade Willie Aikens, their first baseman the past four seasons who'd recently been sentenced to prison in a drug related case. So it was no surprise when Kansas City GM John Schuerholz said of Balboni: "He'll be our everyday first baseman."

In two seasons with the Royals, strictly as a reliever, Mike Armstrong had been in 110 games with a 15-12 record and nine saves. Although the Yanks were unsure if free-agent relief ace Goose Gossage would return (he wouldn't) they didn't get Armstrong to be their closer. He'd been Dan Quisenberry's set-up man in Kansas City, and they planned on him filling the same role in New York.

Armstrong would begin the 1984 season on the disabled list and move back and forth between the Yankees and the minors until the Yanks released him following the 1986 season. His three-year log in New York, mostly compiled in his first season, was 52 games, with three wins, three losses, and one save.

Roger Erickson was 4-5 with the Yanks in 1982, after coming from Minnesota in May. He spent most of 1983 with Columbus, where he was 9-7, but had a high 6.04 ERA. He lost his only decision with the Yanks in '83, in what was his final major league season.

Duane Dewey, a sub–.200 batter in the minors in 1983, never reached the majors.

December 19, 1983: Traded Minor League Righthanded Pitcher Mike Browning to the California Angels for Righthanded Pitcher Curt Brown

After beginning the 1983 season with Edmonston of the Pacific Coast League, 23-year-old Curt Brown joined the Angels in June. In ten relief appearances for California, he had a win and a loss, with an unimpressive 7.31 earned run average.

In 1984, his only season with the Yankees, Brown appeared in 13 games, while spending most of the year with the International League Columbus Clippers. He again split two decisions, but had a much improved 2.70 ERA.

Mike Browning had been working his way through the Yankee farm system. He'd made two stops in 1983, going 5-7 for Double-A Nashville of the Southern League and 5-1 with Triple-A Columbus, but the Triple-A level would be his high point.

January 5, 1984: Signed Free-Agent Righthanded Pitcher Phil Niekro from the Atlanta Braves

Phil Niekro's 45th birthday would come two days before the start of the 1984 season, but evidently that didn't bother the Yankees who signed him to a two-year contract. Pittsburgh and Oakland had also been pursuing Niekro, who was the major league's oldest player, but neither of them was willing to go beyond a one-year offer.

"His age doesn't bother me. And, I'm counting on him to be one of our starters," said Yogi Berra, who was beginning his second term as manager of the Yankees. Niekro's signing "goes a long way toward solidifying our staff and expanding its versatility," added general manager Murray Cook.

Versatility had become important to the Yankees now that bullpen ace Goose Gossage had signed as a free agent with the San Diego Padres. Barring a trade, Berra would have to convert one of his starting pitchers into a reliever to replace Gossage, probably choosing from among John Montefusco, Ray Fontenot, or Dave Righetti. (Berra would choose Righetti, one of the best moves he would ever make.)

Meanwhile, Niekro was set to take his place in the starting rotation. The Braves had released him after he'd spent twenty years with them, dating from 1964 when they were still in Milwaukee. A three-time 20-game winner, he had a 268-230 career record, including an 11-10 mark in 1983.

Niekro would not have any 20-win seasons with the Yankees, but he would have two 16-win seasons: 16-8 in 1984 and 16-12 in 1985. His 8-0 shutout against Toronto on the last day of the 1985 season was the 300th win of his career and also his last appearance as a Yankee. The club would release him on March 28, 1986. Coming so late in spring training, the release angered Niekro.

"All a person looks for is truth," he said. "You hate to be taken advantage of and sucked in like that. Maybe I wasn't, but I can't help feeling like that. It makes you lose faith in front-office people. They knew all along I wasn't going to make it with them. It would have been easier if they had told me in the first place."

Joe Niekro, Phil's brother and now his former teammate, was also very upset at Phil's release. "I am bitter. If that's the way they treat winners here, should I want to be here?" he asked. "I don't understand it. I signed a contract to pitch for this organization and I want to win for Winfield and Randolph and Mattingly, but I don't have to do it with a smile on my face, and I won't."

Phil wasn't through. He pitched two more seasons, winning 18 more games.

February 5, 1984: Traded Outfielder Otis Nixon, Righthanded Pitcher George Frazier, and a Player to Be Named to the Cleveland Indians for Third Baseman Toby Harrah and a Player to Be Named

When asked during the 1983 season which righthanded pitchers the club could least afford to lose, Yankee executives and players rated bullpen stopper Goose Gossage number one and long-and-short reliever George Frazier number two. Now both were gone (Gossage had signed as a free agent with San Diego a month earlier), and the club knew getting replacements for them would be difficult.

"Top-flight relief pitchers aren't available and if they were, the asking price is too high," said Murray Cook, the Yankee GM. "We realize that trading George creates some sort of hole," he added, "and we've lost a lot of saves from last year. But we feel the slack we've created will be made up by Mike Armstrong." (The Yanks had traded for Armstrong the month before.)

Frazier had led the pitching staff in games the past two seasons, appearing in more than 60 in both 1982 and 1983. He had the ability to pitch well no matter what the situation, and manager Billy Martin had taken advantage of that by calling on him no matter the score or the inning. In 1983, the first batters Frazier faced in his 61 appearances hit a combined .180 against him, sixty-five points lower than they hit against Gossage. In all, Frazier appeared in 140 games in his two-plus seasons in New York. He won eight, lost nine, and had 12 saves. He also was a three-time loser to the Dodgers in the 1981 World Series.

Obviously, the Yanks felt that getting a strong righthanded hitter like Toby Harrah was worth giving up a relief pitcher, even one as valuable as Frazier. The club had been vulnerable against lefthanders in 1983, and the 35-year-old Harrah was noted for his ability to hit lefthanded pitchers. He'd broken into the big leagues in 1969 as a shortstop with the Washington Senators and in 1972 moved with the franchise to Texas. In 1977, the Rangers moved him from shortstop to third base and then two years later traded him to Cleveland.

Harrah was a lifetime .267-batter, with 170 major league home runs, but with his age, and with young third basemen Brook Jacoby and Pat Tabler ready for the big leagues, the Indians considered him expendable. Having the right to approve the trade, Harrah negotiated a higher salary with the Yankees, foregoing the specific financial arrangements he'd had with the Indians. Nevertheless, he was still a bit stunned by the deal.

"I'm in shock," Harrah said. "After playing against the Yankees all my career, it's a complete turnaround. All of a sudden I have to change my thinking about the Yankees."

Harrah had been a starter for all his career, but seemed resigned to sharing third base with Graig Nettles in New York. "To me, Graig Nettles is the best," he said. "I'm just going to play as hard as I can and help the Yankees as best I can. The Yankees expressed a desire to have me. That's quite a compliment. This is the biggest challenge of my career."

Cleveland manager Pat Corrales had announced that he wanted to build his 1984 team around speed, so for him, 25-year-old Otis Nixon was an excellent addition. Along with a .291 average for Columbus in 1983, Nixon had stolen a league-high 94 bases. Nixon was also the International League leader in at-bats (557), runs (129) and hits (162). The Yanks had called him up in September, and he went 2 for 14 in 13 games.

Three days later, in an exchange of minor league pitchers, the Yanks sent Guy Elston to Cleveland for Rick Browne to complete the deal.

February 14, 1984: Traded Second Baseman Larry Milbourne to the Seattle Mariners for Minor League

Righthanded Pitchers Scott Nielsen and Eric Parent

The Yanks had reacquired Larry Milbourne in July 1983, after second baseman Willie Randolph went on the disabled list. But with the off-season addition of infielders Tim Foli and Toby Harrah, they no longer needed Milbourne, who'd batted just .200 in 31 games.

Both Eric Parent, who would never pitch in the majors, and Scott Nielsen, who would, had started 1983 with Class A teams in the Mariners farm system. Parent spent the entire season with Wasau of the Midwest League, where he won six and lost nine. However Nielsen, after going 2-0 with Bellingham of the Northwest League, was promoted to Chattanooga of the Southern League, where he won two and lost four.

March 30, 1984: Traded Third Baseman Graig Nettles to the San Diego Padres for Lefthanded Pitcher Dennis Rasmussen and a Player to Be Named

Graig Nettles had been unhappy since the Yanks announced plans to platoon him at third base with Toby Harrah, whom they'd gotten in February in a trade with Cleveland. Nettles, who even at 39 was unwilling to be a platoon player, informed manager Yogi Berra on the first day of training camp that he wanted to be traded. Three days before the opener Nettles got his wish when the Yanks traded him to San Diego, his city of choice. (He may have speeded his exit when George Steinbrenner saw an advance copy of *Balls*, a book Nettles had written that was highly critical of the Yankee owner.)

Berra reacted favorably to the deal, noting that he and his coaches had urged Steinbrenner to trade the disgruntled Nettles. "He wanted to be traded," Berra said. "Why keep an unhappy player to create problems and everything. He's the team captain and he reported late. The team captain should be here on time. This is good for the club." (Nettles had reported for spring training on the last day allowable.)

The Yanks had tried to trade Nettles to San Diego once before, following the 1982 season. The deal collapsed when the Padres refused to give up their best prospect, outfielder Kevin McReynolds, in return.

In his final season as a Yankee, Nettles batted .266 with 20 home runs. During his 11 years in New York, he had established himself as the team's best all-around third baseman ever. His total of 250 home runs as a Yankee put him sixth on the club's all-time list, trailing only Babe Ruth, Mickey Mantle, Lou Gehrig, Joe DiMaggio, and Berra.

Lefthander Dennis Rasmussen had been one of the Yankee minor leaguers (Edwin Rodriguez was the other) who'd gone to San Diego in September 1983 as the players to be named in the trade for John Montefusco. The Padres used him in four games, without a decision, in the season's final weeks.

The player to be named in this trade would be minor league righthander Darin Cloninger, 0-3 with Spokane of the rookie Northwest League in 1983, whom the Yanks received on April 26. Cloninger was at Miami of the Florida State League, and the Yanks kept him in that league, sending him up Interstate 95 to Fort Lauderdale.

March 31, 1984: Sold Catcher Juan Espino to the Cleveland Indians

Signed out of the Dominican Republic in December 1974, Juan Espino had been in the Yankee system ever since 1975. He finally reached the majors in 1982, playing three games and then ten more in 1983, getting a total of six hits in 25 at-bats. The Yanks moved the 28-year-old Espino because Butch Wynegar and Rick Cerone figured to do most of the catching in 1984. If one or the other faltered, they had Mike O'Berry, signed as a free agent, waiting to move up from the International League Columbus Clippers.

June 30, 1984: Traded Lefthanded Pitcher Shane Rawley to the Philadelphia Phillies for Righthanded Pitcher Marty Bystrom and Outfielder Keith Hughes

Shane Rawley had been a short-reliever in Seattle, but midway through the 1982 season, his first in New York, the Yanks made him a starter. He was 11-10 in '82 and then 14-14 in 1983. This season, Rawley had started ten games, without completing any, and he had a bloated 6.21 earned run average to go with a 2-3 won-lost record.

Rawley was not surprised to hear he'd been traded. "For the last two years I've been hearing this and that," he said. "It was always on my mind. It got to the point where it was bound to happen." Yankee manager Yogi Berra used Rawley's being a lefthander to explain the trade. "I wish Shane had done what he did last year," said Berra, "but we need a righthanded pitcher badly."

That righthander was Marty Bystrom. He'd come up to the Phillies at the end of the 1980 season, won five games without losing and had a sparkling 1.50 ERA. He was only 22 at the time, and the Phillies were predicting great things for him. However, as often happens, Bystrom had never lived up to those expectations. Bothered by arm problems, he was 19-22 since, with several trips to both the minors and the disabled list. Bystrom was 4-4 for the Phillies this season, but had a 5.08 earned run average. He would go 5-4 in 15 games for the Yanks over the next two years, but recurring arm problems ended his career after the 1985 season.

Keith Hughes, batting .261 for the Reading Phillies of the Eastern League, went to the Nashville Sounds, the Yankees' team in the Southern League.

July 18, 1984: Traded Shortstop Roy Smalley to the Chicago White Sox for Two Players to Be Named

Roy Smalley batted .257 for the Yanks in 1982 and .275 in 1983, while playing both shortstop and third base. After the '83 season, he asked the Yanks to trade him, but instead they gave him a five-year contract extension and told him he would be their first baseman in 1984. Eventually they changed their minds. Second year man Don Mattingly was now the full-time first baseman, and the 31-year-old Smalley was platooning at third base with Toby Harrah.

Batting just .239 in 67 games, Smalley said he was glad the trade had been made. "It

had become a dead end for me here," he said. "I have five or six years left to play and it looked like it was going to be five or six years of not playing every day."

To take Smalley's roster spot, the Yanks called up outfielder Vic Mata from Columbus of the International League. Mata would hit .329 in 70 at-bats the rest of the season and also play in six games in 1985, but that was the extent of his major league career.

The players to be named were to be selected later in the season from a list of White Sox minor leaguers. On August 13, the Yanks took two pitchers: lefthander Kevin Hickey and righthander Doug Drabek. Hickey had spent the last three seasons with Chicago, but was currently 2-2 with the American Association Denver Bears. The 22-year-old Drabek, who had no big league experience, was 12-5 with Glens Falls of the Eastern League. The Yankees assigned Hickey to Columbus and Drabek to Nashville of the Southern League.

December 4, 1984: Traded Lefthanded Pitcher Ray Fontenot and Outfielder Brian Dayett to the Chicago Cubs for Outfielder Henry Cotto, Catcher Ron Hassey, and Righthanded Pitchers Rich Bordi and Porfi Altimirano

Of the four players the Yankees were getting in this trade, they were most excited about Henry Cotto, a good defensive outfielder with excellent speed. Not yet 24, he'd batted .274 in 146 at-bats in 1984, his just concluded rookie season. The Yanks thought he would do even better with them.

"Our guys all think he could improve as a hitter," said general manager Clyde King. Yankee scout Eddie Robinson believed that Cotto would improve just by being around Yankee veterans like Roy White and Lou Piniella.

For Ron Hassey, coming to the Yankees was a return to the American League. Hassey had come to the Cubs the previous June after having been with Cleveland since 1978. He spent two months on the disabled list after arthroscopic surgery on his knee and got into just 19 games with Chicago. But he was now fully recovered, and because his contract allowed him to demand a trade, he did, asking the Cubs to trade him to a team that needed a catcher. That didn't necessarily describe the Yankees, who already had three catchers on their roster: Butch Wynegar, Rick Cerone, and International League MVP Scott Bradley.

Still, Hassey said he "was not disappointed" at being traded to New York, and was "looking for the Yankees to make another trade." So was everyone else. Hassey's acquisition fueled speculation that the Yanks were about to trade Cerone, and also that they would include Bradley in the deal they were trying to make with Oakland for Rickey Henderson.

Rich Bordi had made brief appearances with Oakland and Seattle before joining the Cubs in 1983. In 1984, he was 5-2 in 31 games, mostly in relief.

Thirty-two-year-old Porfi Altimirano had a 7-4 record in three seasons, the first two with the Phillies. He spent most of 1984 pitching in relief for Iowa of the American Association, and after this trade would never return to the majors.

Ray Fontenot, then 25, came up to the Yanks from the International League Columbus Clippers in June 1983 and had an excellent rookie season. He made 15 starts for manager Billy Martin, winning eight with just two losses. Used as both a starter and reliever in 1984 by Martin's replacement, Yogi Berra, Fontenot was inconsistent and his record slipped to 8-9. So although the Yankees were themselves looking for pitching help, they chose to trade Fontenot now, while there was still a market for him. They felt that if he had another poor season, there wouldn't be one.

Cubs manager Jim Frey said that he planned to use his new lefthander as a relief pitcher. However, Frey hinted that if the team couldn't re-sign lefty starter Steve Trout, then Fontenot would take Trout's place in the rotation. The Cubs did sign Trout, and Fontenot, working as a starter and reliever, had another inconsistent season (6-10, with a 4.36 ERA.)

Brian Dayett, a Yankee farmhand since 1978, had split the last two seasons between New York and Columbus. He'd appeared in a combined 75 games for the Yankees with a .237 batting average and four home runs.

December 5, 1984: Traded Outfielder Stan Javier, Righthanded Pitchers Jay Howell and Jose Rijo, Minor League Righthanded Pitcher Eric Plunk, and Minor League Lefthanded Pitcher Tim Birtsas to the Oakland Athletics for Outfielder Rickey Henderson, Righthanded Pitcher Bert Bradley, and Cash

Even after they'd worked out this complex seven-player deal, the Yanks made it contingent on their being able to sign Rickey Henderson, its most important component. Henderson, a genuine superstar who'd been playing in relative anonymity, had been eligible to be a free agent after the 1985 season, but the Yanks got him to sign a five-year, $8.6 million contract.

As Henderson's agent, Rich Bry said: "This is an excellent opportunity for Rickey to be with the Yankees, to have more fame and fortune than he's had before."

George Steinbrenner called Henderson "one of today's premier players," although originally he had been reluctant to pay "a singles hitter" so much money. "He can dominate a

December 5, 1984: *Rickey Henderson.* To get Henderson, the Yanks "stripped our minor leagues bare."

game with his offense, his defense, and, of course, his base stealing," Steinbrenner added.

That was all true. In Henderson, still only 26, the Yanks were getting the best leadoff man in the game, and the greatest base stealer in history. Since Oakland brought him to the majors in June 1979, he'd stolen 493 bases, including 100 or more three times, topped by a record-shattering 130 in 1982. He had a lifetime .291 batting average, with 51 home runs, including a career-high 16 in 1984. Henderson also batted in a career-high 58 runs in '84, all to go with a .293 batting average and 66 stolen bases. The 66 stolen bases were four more than the entire Yankee *team* stole in 1984.

Rather than talk about the glory, tradition, and honor of playing for the Yankees, the reasons Henderson gave for signing were solely financial. "We analyzed what was going on," he said. "I could be a free agent next year, but I thought this was probably as good as I would get next year. It gives me security for life. We felt I would be better off playing in New York for my career."

Yet, as great a player as Henderson was, there were some downsides to this deal. Besides paying all that money to Henderson, the Yanks had included so many promising young players that vice president Woody Woodward said the deal "stripped our minor leagues bare."

The Yankees had another reason for thinking twice about this trade. They knew that once the A's had Jay Howell, they would feel free to trade their own relief ace, Bill Caudill, to the Toronto Blue Jays. The Yanks viewed Toronto as their chief competitor for the Eastern Division title in 1985.

Although 1984 was the first year Howell had spent an entire season with the Yankees, he was the only player going to Oakland who had more than a few games of big league experience. He'd been in 61 games in '84, mainly as a setup man for Dave Righetti, with nine wins, four losses, and seven saves.

Stan Javier and Jose Rijo were both 19 when they began the 1984 season as members of the Yankees. Javier was one for seven in seven games before batting .290 for Nashville of the Southern League. Rijo was 2-8 in 24 games with the Yanks but also spent time with Columbus of the International League.

Twenty-one-year-old Eric Plunk and 24-year-old Tim Birtsas both were at Class A Fort Lauderdale of the Florida State League in 1984 and didn't figure in the Yankees' immediate plans.

Pitcher Bert Bradley, a throw-in with Henderson, was 10-2 in 1984 for Tacoma of the Pacific Coast League. The year before, he was in six games for Oakland, without a decision, but that would be his only time in the big leagues.

As the Yankees feared, the A's did trade Caudill to Toronto (for outfielder Dave Collins and shortstop Alfredo Griffin), and Toronto would win the division title in 1985 with Caudill leading the team in saves.

December 5, 1984: Traded Catcher Rick Cerone to the Atlanta Braves for Minor League Righthanded Pitcher Brian Fisher

Needing catching help after the August 1979 death of Thurman Munson, the Yanks traded for Rick Cerone in November of '79. In 1980, Cerone won the job as Munson's successor and had his finest offensive season. Playing in 147 games, he batted .277 with 14 home runs and 85 runs batted in. But since then he'd never played in more than 89 games (1982) or batted higher than .244 (1981).

Cerone, now 30, lost his spot as first-string catcher to Butch Wynegar in 1983, and then had his worst season in 1984. He played in only 38 games, batted .208, and spent two months on the disabled list. When the Yanks acquired catcher Ron Hassey in a trade with the Cubs the day before, everyone expected they would trade Cerone.

Despite Cerone's recent problems, John Mullen, Atlanta's general manager, thought he would bounce back. "I think if he gets out of New York and comes to Atlanta, he'll do a good job for us," Mullen said.

Mullen's counterpart, Yankee GM Clyde King, was equally hopeful about Brian Fisher, his new addition. Fisher had not had a very good season with the Braves' Richmond team in the International League in 1984—a 9-11 record and 4.28 earned run average—but King said the reports on him had been "good."

December 20, 1984: Traded Outfielder Steve Kemp, Shortstop Tim Foli, and Cash to the Pittsburgh Pirates for Shortstop Dale Berra, Lefthanded Pitcher Alfonso Pulido, and Minor League Outfielder Jay Buhner

This was the Yankees' third multiplayer deal of the month, and one they had to reconfigure before Commissioner Peter Ueberroth would agree to it. As originally designed, the Yankees were going to give the Pirates Steve Kemp and Tim Foli, while also giving them a substantial amount of money to help cover the cost of Kemp's salary. (The Yanks had given Kemp a five-year contract two years earlier when they signed him as a free agent.) When Ueberroth questioned the money aspect of the deal, a second part was added. The money was reduced (probably to $800,000) and the Yanks would also get pitcher Alfonso Pulido.

Had he not had such a large contract, the Yanks probably would have kept Kemp. But manager Yogi Berra did not anticipate him being any more than a pinch hitter or occasional designated hitter in 1985, roles not commensurate with the amount of money they would have had to pay him. Kemp had been a part-time outfielder, playing in 203 games in his two Yankee seasons. He'd been a big disappointment when he hit just .241 in 1983, his first season, but brought that up sharply to .291 in 1984.

While not thrilled about going to Pittsburgh, Kemp felt that he would at least get more playing time. He anticipated being the starting left fielder in an outfield that was expected to have Marvell Wynne in center field and newly-acquired George Hendrick in right.

Tim Foli, who'd asked the Yanks to trade him because of his lack of playing time, also had hopes of being a starter in Pittsburgh. He'd been the Pirates shortstop in the early 1980s, and though he was now 34, thought he could be again.

"I'll get a chance to play maybe," he said. "I had some fun when I was there before. The fans liked me." Foli played at all four infield positions in his one Yankee season, but got into just 61 games and batted .252.

By playing for manager Yogi Berra, who was also his dad, Dale Berra would become the first man to play for his father since Earle Mack played for Connie on the 1914 Athletics. Nevertheless, both Berras played down the family angle of their relationship.

"Could I sit him down?" Yogi asked. "Hell, yeah." Dale agreed. "He'd be the first to sit me down if I was playing bad," he said. "He'd be harder on me than other guys. He's not going to play favorites."

The 28-year-old Berra had been a mediocre player in his eight years with Pittsburgh. He had a .238 batting average and had led National League shortstops with 30 errors in 1984. He'd also made 30 errors in each of the two preceding seasons. However, the Yanks had no plans to play Berra at shortstop. They'd gotten him with third base in mind, with Yogi hinting that he'd likely platoon Dale with Mike Pagliarulo.

Questions of favoritism or discipline between father and son never got much of a chance to be answered. Sixteen games into the 1985 season, George Steinbrenner fired Yogi and replaced him with Billy Martin. Dale batted .229 in 48 games and was batting .231 in June of 1986 when the Yankees released him.

Pulido, the last-minute throw-in, had spent most of his career in the Mexican League, but was coming off an outstanding season at Hawaii. He won 18 games with only six losses and led the Pacific Coast League with 216 innings pitched. Pulido had gotten into one game for the Pirates in each of the last two seasons, and after spending 1985 at Columbus would go 1-1 for the Yanks in 1986.

Twenty-year-old Jay Buhner had played only one season as a professional, but it was a very impressive one. Playing for Watertown of the Class A New York–Pennsylvania League, he'd batted .323, with nine home runs and a league-leading 58 RBIs, all in just 233 at-bats. Still, he obviously needed more seasoning, and the Yanks would send him to Fort Lauderdale of the Florida State League.

December 27, 1984: Signed Free-Agent Righthanded Pitcher Ed Whitson from the San Diego Padres

Ed Whitson had pitched for four clubs in eight seasons, with a lackluster 53-56 won-lost

record and a 3.59 earned run average. However, he was coming off a 14-8 season for the
pennant-winning Padres, and to get him, the
Yankees had to outbid both San Diego and the
Atlanta Braves.

They anticipated Whitson would join
Ron Guidry, Phil Niekro, Dennis Rasmussen,
and John Montefusco to give them a solid 1985
starting rotation. Also in the mix was Joe
Cowley, who was both a starter and a reliever.
"This gives us a lot of versatility," said manager Yogi Berra. "I've got to sit down now and
look at our roster. It seems to keep changing
all the time. I could try Cowley in the bullpen."

The Yanks had entered the off-season
looking to add two pitchers, but GM Clyde
King said there were no other deals or free-
agent signings pending.

"Considering our division, we have to ask
is what we've done good enough," King said.
"The pitching has improved by getting Whitson, but I'm not satisfied."

This had been a busy month for the Yankees and evidently owner George Steinbrenner was satisfied with just providing one
pitcher, Whitson, for manager Berra.

"Yogi's had his Christmas," Steinbrenner
said. "He's finished."

January 8, 1985: Purchased Catcher Juan Espino from the Cleveland Indians

Nine months after they'd purchased him,
the Indians were selling Juan Espino back to
the Yankees. Actually, it was the Maine Guides
of the International League, where Espino
spent the entire 1984 season batting .251, selling him to that league's Columbus Clippers.

Espino eventually made it back to the
Yankees in 1985 and 1986, but spent most of
those two seasons, and all of 1987, with the
Clippers. Playing in parts of four seasons in
New York (1982, 1983, 1986, and 1987), Espino
batted .219 with one home run in 49 games.
The Yankees granted him free agency after the
1987 season.

February 27, 1985: Traded Third Base-man Toby Harrah to the Texas Rangers

for Outfielder Billy Sample and a Player to Be Named

Toby Harrah had spent one unsatisfying
season in New York and was elated to be leaving. Going back to Texas, the team he'd started
his career with when they were still the Washington Senators, made the move even more appealing. The Yanks had platooned Harrah at
third base in 1984, so he played in only 88 games,
hit just one home run, and batted a disappointing .217. It was the fewest games and lowest batting average for the 36-year-old Harrah since he
first became a regular with the 1971 Senators. "I
really don't apologize. I did the best I could,"
Harrah said of his disappointing season.

On the other hand, Billy Sample seemed
as happy to be leaving Texas as Harrah was to
be returning there. Sample had spent his whole
career with the Rangers, batting .270 in 675
games, but despite being a regular the past two
seasons, he too was disgruntled at his status.

"I wasn't progressing. I was regressing,"
Sample claimed. "My role this year probably
would have been pinch running and pinch hitting. Even if I'm in the same position with another club, it would be more advantageous for
me."

With the Yankees, Sample would compete with youngsters Henry Cotto and Vic
Mata to be the righthanded complement to
Ken Griffey in left field. When asked about
his reputation as a poor defensive player, Sample suggested that it was an unfair assessment.

"When you get a reputation it's hard to
get rid of it. I'm not as bad as the rep. I think
the last two years I've played left field as well
as anyone, even Rickey Henderson. There
should be a lot of ground covered between
Henderson, Winfield, and me."

On July 14, Texas sent righthander Eric
Dersin from their Daytona Beach club in the
Florida State League to the Yankees as the
player to be named. The Yanks assigned Der-
sin to Fort Lauderdale, their club in the Florida
State League.

July 17, 1985: Traded a Player to Be Named to the St. Louis Cardinals for Righthanded Pitcher Neil Allen

He'd once been a top-flight reliever, but
Neil Allen's reputation as a "stopper" had taken

a downturn since leaving the Mets in 1983. Still, manager Billy Martin thought he might help solve a problem in the Yankee bullpen. Locked in a battle with the Toronto Blue Jays for the Eastern Division title, Martin felt he had to have a reliable righthanded short reliever. He'd gotten 16 saves from lefthander Dave Righetti, but only five from the Yanks' righthanded short relievers: rookie Brian Fisher had four, and veteran Rich Bordi had the other one. The Yankees made room for Allen by sending pitcher Mike Armstrong to Columbus of the International League.

Allen had racked up 67 saves with the Mets from 1979 to 1982, but he was pitching poorly in 1983 and the Mets traded him to St. Louis for first baseman Keith Hernandez. However, the Cardinals already had a stopper, Bruce Sutter (who was the league's best), and so manager Whitey Herzog used Allen as a starter. He won ten and lost six in that role, but was back in the bullpen in 1984, going 9-6 in long relief. With Sutter now pitching for Atlanta, Allen picked up two saves in the first two weeks of the season, but he'd been struggling since. Appearing in 23 games, he had a 1-4 record with a 5.59 ERA, and still had just the two saves.

Martin said he was unsure how long it would take for Allen to regain his former effectiveness. "I'm going to talk to him and see how he feels and use him now in long relief," he said. "Maybe I'll use him in short relief too, but it depends on the ballclub. I want to get his confidence back."

The Yanks eventually settled the trade by sending the Cardinals cash, rather than a player.

September 13, 1985: Purchased Lefthanded Pitcher Rod Scurry from the Pittsburgh Pirates

Still chasing the first-place Blue Jays, Yankee manager Billy Martin was desperate for a lefthanded reliever, one who could come in and retire a lefthanded batter in an important situation. In a loss to Toronto the night before, he'd been forced to use lefty Dave Righetti in such a spot in the sixth inning. That was unusually early for Righetti, the ace of the Yankee bullpen who seldom pitched before the eighth.

Getting Rod Scurry, a 29-year-old lefty with a history of cocaine addiction, was an indication of just how desperate the Yankees were. A member of the Pirates since 1980, Scurry had appeared in 257 games with 34 saves. He'd had his best season in 1982—a 1.74 earned run average and 14 saves in 76 games. Thus far in 1985, Scurry had two saves in 30 games for the Pirates.

Aware of the potential for relapse with cocaine users, general manager Clyde King said that the Yankees would closely monitor their new acquisition.

"Scurry has agreed to be tested, as he has been in Pittsburgh, as often as three times a week if the Yankees so desire," King said. "We have been assured by the Pirates that he has agreed to undergo regular testing, the results of which, by the way, have been consistently negative, and he will continue to do so with the Yankees."

Scurry would earn a win and a save in the last few weeks of the 1985 season, and then pitch in 31 games for the Yanks in 1986 (1-2 with two saves). They released him in late March 1987.

September 15, 1985: Traded Lefthanded Pitcher Jim Deshaies and Two Players to Be Named to the Houston Astros for Righthanded Pitcher Joe Niekro

Phil Niekro knew the Yankees were seeking another starting pitcher for the stretch run, but didn't know the pitcher they were after was his brother. "I haven't talked to him in a few weeks," Phil said, "but he didn't know anything."

Joe "was at the top of our list," said owner George Steinbrenner, despite the fact that the Yanks had first gone after Tom Seaver of the White Sox and Don Sutton of the Athletics. They backed off from each deal when those clubs asked for rookie outfielder Dan Pasqua in return.

The Niekros, who'd played together on the 1973-74 Atlanta Braves, had a combined 501 wins between them, just 28 short of the record for most major league wins by brothers held by Gaylord and Jim Perry. Phil had 299 wins, and Joe had 202.

Joe, who at 41 was six years younger than Phil, had been pitching in the big leagues since 1967. He'd been with the Cubs, Padres, Tigers, Braves, and for the past 11 years, the Astros. He was a two-time 20-game winner who was 9-12 with a 3.72 ERA this season. Joe was expected to replace the struggling Marty Bystrom in the rotation.

Twenty-five-year-old Jim Deshaies was currently 8-6 with Columbus of the International League. He'd pitched in two games for the Yanks in 1984, losing his only decision.

Neither infielder Neder Horta, who went to Houston on September 24, nor pitcher Dody Rather, whom the Astros received in January 1986, ever reached the major leagues.

December 6, 1985: Traded Outfielder Billy Sample to the Atlanta Braves for Minor League Infielder Miguel Sosa

In 1985, his one year as a Yankee, Billy Sample hit .288 in 59 games as a reserve outfielder and pinch hitter. His 1986 season with Atlanta would be his final one in the big leagues, though he was just 30 years old when it ended.

Miguel Sosa had 123 home runs in seven years playing for various teams in Atlanta's minor league system. He had ten in a three week period for the International League Richmond Braves during the 1985 season, but finished with just 14. He also hit a career-low .192. Sosa never made it to the major leagues.

December 11, 1985: Traded a Player to Be Named to the Cleveland Indians for Infielder Mike Fischlin

A .222 batter in eight big league seasons, Mike Fischlin spent three years as a part-time shortstop for Houston, and the last five as a utility infielder with the Indians. General manager Clyde King said that the Yankees intended to use him as a utility player, which they did.

Fischlin, who'd come up through the Yankee farm system before they traded him to the Astros, would play 71 games at short and second in 1986, batting .206 in 102 at-bats. The Yanks made him a free agent after the season.

On April 11, 1986, the Yanks sent minor league pitcher Kevin Trudeau (8-3 at Oneonta of the Class A New York–Pennsylvania League in 1985) to the Cleveland organization as the player to be named.

December 11, 1985: Traded Right-handed Pitcher Rich Bordi and Infielder Rex Hudler to the Baltimore Orioles for Outfielder Gary Roenicke and a Player to Be Named

This transaction, the Yanks' second of the day, ended an almost nine-year trade hiatus between them and their division rivals from Baltimore. In that last one, on January 20, 1977, they'd sent outfielders Elliott Maddox and Rick Bladt to the Orioles in exchange for outfielder Paul Blair.

In 31-year-old Gary Roenicke, the Yanks were getting another excellent defensive outfielder, although not of the same caliber as Blair. Primarily a platoon player under Earl Weaver in Baltimore, Roenicke had hit 108 home runs in nine seasons, eight of which were spent with the Orioles. He would play the same role in 1986, batting .265, but with only 136 at-bats. The Yankees made Roenicke a free agent at the end of the season, and he signed with Atlanta.

Rex Hudler had been the Yanks' first pick in the 1979 amateur draft, but he had yet to justify that honor. Now 25, he'd spent almost all his career in the minor leagues, with the exception of nine games with the Yanks in 1984, and 20 in 1985. Although Hudler would last only one season with the Orioles, he would have a long major league career.

In 1985, Rich Bordi had a 6-8 record with two saves in 51 games for the Yanks, 48 of which were in relief. He would go 6-4 for the Orioles in 1986, then get released, whereupon the Yankees signed him and sent him to Columbus in the International League. In 1987, after 25 games with the Clippers, Bordi would return to New York and have a 3-1 record in 16 games. The Yanks released him after the 1987 season.

On December 16, 1985, the Orioles sent the Yankees third baseman Leo Hernandez to complete the trade. Hernandez would play just seven games for the Yanks in 1986, his final seven as a big leaguer, and was released in October.

December 12, 1985: Traded Right-handed Pitcher Joe Cowley and Catcher Ron Hassey to the Chicago White Sox for Lefthanded Pitcher Britt Burns, Minor League Shortstop Mike Soper, and Minor League Outfielder Glen Braxton

The Yanks made their third deal in two days, but to the surprise of many it did not include Don Baylor. Not that the Yanks hadn't tried to include Baylor, but because the White Sox would not meet some of his money demands, Baylor wouldn't waive the no-trade clause in his contract. Nevertheless, in Britt Burns, a 26-year-old lefty with a 70-60 lifetime record, the Yanks got the man they were after. Burns was coming off an 18-11 season, his best ever, and was enthused about the trade. "I'm excited about the possibility of wearing a World Series ring at this time next year," he said.

Burns also claimed that the reports about the extent of injury to his right hip were exaggerated. "It would be more accurate to describe it as an aggravation type of thing rather than a problem," he said. "I've had it ever since high school. At no time does it keep me from going out to the mound. Medication controls it. It's not something that's going to haunt me or the Yankees for any period of time."

But, unfortunately, Burns was a better pitcher than he was a prophet, as his hip problem *would* haunt both him and the Yankees. He would re-injure the hip in spring training, an injury that doctors diagnosed as degenerative. Although he would attempt to come back several times, Burns would never pitch in another major league game. Nor would shortstop Mike Soper or outfielder Glen Braxton, the two minor leaguers the Yanks received in this deal, ever play in a major league game.

Meanwhile, Joe Cowley would win 11 and lose 11 for the White Sox in 1986, and then end his career with an 0-4 season for the 1987 Phillies. A longtime minor league in the Atlanta organization, Cowley had signed with the

December 12, 1985: *Ron Hassey.* **Two months after trading him, the Yanks would get Hassey back.**

Yanks as a free agent following the 1983 season. He had a 10-3 record at Columbus of the International League when the Yanks brought him up in mid 1984. Cowley won his first eight decisions before finishing 9-2. He followed that with a 12-6 mark in 1985.

Ron Hassey batted .296 in 92 games in 1985, his first season as a Yankee, while sharing the catching chores with Butch Wynegar. Wynegar was now a free agent; however, the trade of Hassey seemed to suggest that the Yanks were planning to re-sign him. There also remained the possibility that the White Sox and Baylor would agree to financial terms. If they did, according to Ken Harrelson, Chicago's vice president for baseball operations, the White Sox would trade veteran catcher Carlton Fisk to the Yankees even up for Baylor.

Baylor didn't come to terms with Chicago, and on March 28, 1986, the Yanks would trade him to the Boston Red Sox for Mike Easler.

February 6, 1986: Signed Free-Agent Lefthanded Pitcher Al Holland from the California Angels

By adding Al Holland to a staff that already had Dave Righetti, Bob Shirley, and Rod Scurry, the Yankees now possessed four lefthanded relievers. Nevertheless, new manager Lou Piniella insisted that Righetti would remain his number one reliever and not be converted back to a starting role.

Holland had himself once been his team's number one reliever. After three years as a setup man with the Giants, he went to the Phillies and led them in saves in 1983 (25) and 1984 (29). But following the '84 season, Holland gained a great deal of weight and lost speed on his fastball. He had only five saves in 1985, while moving during the season from the Phillies to the Pirates to the Angels.

With that in mind, the Yanks put a weight clause in his contract, and also a stipulation that Holland, who'd had drug problems in the past, undergo periodic drug testing.

Holland would appear in 25 games in 1986, and though he didn't get any saves, he did win his only decision. In 1987, he pitched his final three major league games for the Yanks.

February 13, 1986: Traded Righthanded Pitcher Neil Allen, Catcher Scott Bradley, Minor League Outfielder Glen Braxton, and Cash to the Chicago White Sox for Catcher Ron Hassey, Minor League Righthanded Pitcher Eric Schmidt, Minor League Catcher Chris Alvarez, and Minor League Outfielder Matt Winters

Two months earlier the Yanks had traded catcher Ron Hassey to Chicago believing that another trade, one in which they would send the Sox Don Baylor for Carlton Fisk, was imminent. That trade never happened, and now the Yanks wanted Hassey back to be their number two catcher behind Butch Wynegar.

Manager Lou Piniella felt that Hassey, who batted .296 in 1985, was "ideal as his backup." Otherwise that job would have fallen to the now traded 25-year-old Scott Bradley,

who over the last two seasons had played in only 28 major league games. "It's rare for a team to have a backup catcher who can swing the bat as well as he can," Piniella said of Hassey. "We're very happy to get him back."

Hassey said that he too was pleased at returning to New York. "I was disappointed when I got traded the first time because I wanted to come back where I had a good year," he said. His wife was unruffled about the turn of events. "We said this is crazy. But I guess with the Yankees, you have to expect anything," said Jennifer Hassey.

The White Sox made the trade because they were short of relief pitching. Impressed by Neil Allen's 2.76 earned run average in his half season in New York, they were counting on Allen to help solve that deficiency. Meanwhile, Allen's departure from the Yankees left Brian Fisher as the only experienced righthander in their bullpen. Piniella shrugged that off, pointing out that what was critical in Yankee Stadium was having lefthanded relievers, not righthanders; nevertheless, he didn't dismiss the possibility of trading for a righthanded reliever. Piniella even suggested he might use a minor league prospect like Brad Arnsberg or Bob Tewksbury in that role.

Like Hassey, Matt Winters had also been Yankee property before; in fact, he'd spent eight years in the Yankee farm system. Winters batted .308 for the International League Columbus Clippers in 1985, but in December, the Yanks had released him. He signed with Chicago as a minor league free agent, and now, two months later, he was back with the Yankees and likely headed back to Columbus.

Neither Eric Schmidt (11-12 with Glens Falls of the Eastern League in 1985) nor Chris Alvarez (.276 for the Sox entry in the Gulf Coast League) had any big league experience. Nor did Glen Braxton, who had been part of the December trade that sent Hassey to Chicago. The Yanks were returning him to the White Sox because he had an injured knee that they hadn't known about at the time of the trade.

On that same December 1985 day that the Yanks released Winters, they also released righthander Don Cooper. Obtained in a minor league trade for outfielder Derwin McNealy before the start of the 1984 season, Cooper had no decisions in seven games for the Yanks in 1985.

March 28, 1986: Traded Designated Hitter Don Baylor to the Boston Red Sox for Designated Hitter Mike Easler

Don Baylor had informed the Yankees that he was dissatisfied with being a part-time player and wanted out of New York. The club had tried to accommodate him three months earlier, in December 1985, attempting to trade him to the Chicago White Sox for pitcher Britt Burns. But Baylor had a no-trade clause in his contract, and when the White Sox failed to agree to some of his financial demands, he refused to waive that clause. (The Yanks got Burns anyway, in a trade that month for pitcher Joe Cowley and catcher Ron Hassey.) The Red Sox, on the other hand, were on a list of teams that Baylor had agreed to be traded to. It was the first deal the Yanks had made with Boston since they sent Danny Cater to the Red Sox for Sparky Lyle back in March 1972. (The 14-year trade interval was the longest the Yanks then had with any major league club.)

The Red Sox planned for Baylor to be their designated hitter in 1986, the same role he'd played in his three years with the Yankees. He had 71 home runs and 265 RBIs in those three years, and in 1983 had led the club in batting with a .303 mark, the first, and ultimately only, .300-season of his career. While Baylor's home runs and RBIs remained high for all three years in New York, his batting average dropped to .262 in 1984 and just .231 in 1985.

Baylor first became unhappy during the last two months of the '85 season when manager Billy Martin platooned him at DH with left-hand hitting Dan Pasqua. His displeasure continued when he learned that Lou Piniella, Martin's successor, planned a similar role for him this year, this time platooning with Ken Griffey.

But with the arrival of Mike Easler, Piniella said that he now expected Easler to be his lefthanded designated hitter, with newly acquired Gary Roenicke filling Baylor's former role on the right side. "That opens a spot in left for Cotto," Piniella added, referring to Henry Cotto who was batting .368 in spring training games.

At 35, Easler was one year younger than Baylor. He was a .293-hitter in 12 major league seasons, but hit only .262 as Boston's DH in 1985. Piniella said he expected that average to improve with the Yankees. "We can give him a little more lefthanded protection in the lineup," Piniella said. "He'll be productive for us."

May 1, 1986: Signed Free-Agent Shortstop Ivan DeJesus from the St. Louis Cardinals

Ivan DeJesus had played his entire, often controversial, career in the National League. He made his debut with the 1974 Dodgers and then played for the Cubs, the Phillies, and in 1985 with the Cardinals. DeJesus's .252 batting average in 59 games for St. Louis, brought his lifetime average to .254.

Signed by the Yanks' International League team in Columbus, he hit .262 in 25 games for the Clippers before being called up on June 15. Bobby Meacham's performance at shortstop had not satisfied the Yankees, and manager Lou Piniella was sending Meacham back to Columbus.

DeJesus's Yankee career lasted just nine days. Used mainly as a defensive replacement, he was hitless in four at-bats when the Yanks released him on June 24.

May 2, 1986: Signed Lefthanded Pitcher Tommy John as a Free Agent

The Yanks summoned Tommy John from Florida, where the veteran lefthander had been working out after having gone to spring training with the club as a non-roster player. His opportunity came because the Yanks had to put two of their pitchers, Ed Whitson and John Montefusco, on the disabled list. Also getting another opportunity was righthander Mike Armstrong, whom the Yanks recalled from the International League Columbus Clippers.

This would be John's second go-around in New York. After the Yanks traded him to California on August 31, 1982, he pitched for the Angels until June 1985 when they released him. Modesto, Oakland's affiliate in the California League, signed him, but John also saw duty with the A's before they released him at the end of the season.

Shortly after rejoining the Yankees, manager Lou Piniella brought him in to relieve starter Bob Shirley in the seventh inning of a 7-0 loss to Texas. The Yankee Stadium fans greeted his entry into the game with their loudest roar of the day.

"The crowd response was outstanding; it made an old-timer feel welcome," said John, who was just three weeks short of his 43rd birthday. "It's something no one would have thought possible this spring when I ventured forth. It was probably the biggest upset since Truman beat Dewey."

John would go 5-3 in 1986, although a two-month stay on the disabled list marred his season. Yet, he bounced back to lead the club in games started in 1987 and 1988, winning 22 and losing 14 over that two-year span. John was 2-7 in 1989 when the end finally came. On May 30, the Yanks gave him his final release. John finished his career 12 wins short of 300 (288-231), and with a 91-60 mark for his two tours of duty with the Yankees.

June 29, 1986: Traded Outfielder Ken Griffey to the Atlanta Braves for Outfielder Claudell Washington and Shortstop Paul Zuvella

Claudell Washington joined pitchers Rod Scurry and Al Holland as members of that list of 21 players that commissioner Peter Ueberroth had imposed punishment on for their involvement with drugs to have since become Yankees (shortstop Dale Berra was already a team member).

At 31, Washington was six years younger than Ken Griffey, and would become a competitor for Griffey's spot in the outfield with the recently recalled Dan Pasqua. A 13-year veteran, who'd played for five teams in his career, Washington had a lifetime .279 average with 124 home runs. He'd spent a month on the disabled list this season and was batting .270 in 40 games for Atlanta.

Manager Lou Piniella announced that "Claudell will play in the outfield, and Zuvella will play shortstop." Later, Piniella took more of a wait-and-see attitude in assessing Washington's role. "We just got this guy. Let me think about it," he said.

Pasqua assumed the job would go to Washington. "They're not going to bring in a guy like Claudell just to sit him when he gets, here," he said. Pasqua was right. Before he left after the 1988 season to sign with California, Washington batted .287 and hit 26 home runs in 282 games with the Yanks.

Griffey, dissatisfied with the way the Yanks had used him, had requested they trade him as early as 1983, his second year with the team. He'd hit well in New York, a .285 average in 551 games, including a .303 mark this season. Still, he was glad the trade had finally come and was particularly pleased that it was to a National League team. "It's home," said Griffey who'd played nine years for the Cincinnati Reds before his trade to the Yankees in November 1981.

Paul Zuvella was with Atlanta in 1985, batting .253 as a utility infielder. But Andres Thomas won that job this spring, and the Braves sent Zuvella to Richmond of the International League, where he was hitting .317. The shortstop position, recently occupied by Dale Berra and Mike Fischlin, had been a problem for the Yankees all season. Erratic fielding had cost the opening-day starter, Bobby Meacham, the job, and now Piniella hoped Zuvella could fill the role. "Our scouts say Zuvella can play," he said. "A couple of our coaches have seen him and like him."

However, Zuvella failed to hit, getting just four hits in 48 at-bats. A month later, when Wayne Tolleson joined the team, the Yanks shipped Zuvella back to the International League, sending him to Columbus. He came back to spend part of the 1987 season with the Yanks, but they chose not to re-sign him after he batted .176 in 14 games.

To reach the 24-man limit after this one-for-two trade, the Yanks put pitcher Joe Niekro on the disabled list. They did so despite Niekro's claim that his bruised index finger did not affect his pitching.

July 2, 1986: Purchased Infielder Bryan Little from the Chicago White Sox

A week earlier, the Yanks had traded outfielder Ken Griffey to the Atlanta Braves for outfielder Claudell Washington and shortstop Paul Zuvella. Perhaps as an adjunct to that trade, they now sent shortstop Andre Robertson from their International League team in Columbus to the Braves' Richmond team in the same league. Robertson had been with the Yankees from 1981 to 1985, but was never again the player he had been before a serious automobile accident in 1983. Overall, he batted .251 in 254 games for New York, but never played another major league game after leaving the Yankee organization.

Robertson's departure from Columbus left the Clippers with just two middle infielders, Mike Soper and Bobby Meacham. To rectify the situation, the Yanks bought Bryan Little from Chicago's Buffalo team of the American Association, where he was batting .284, and sent him to Columbus.

Little had spent time with Montreal from 1982 to 1984, and the White Sox the past two seasons. Later in the '86 season he joined the Yankees and batted .195 in 14 games. The Yank released him in October, ending his big league career.

July 9, 1986: Traded Righthanded Pitcher Ed Whitson to the San Diego Padres for Righthanded Pitcher Tim Stoddard

When Ed Whitson lost six of his first seven games in 1985, the pattern of his year and a half as a Yankee was set. He quickly earned the enmity of the fans, who began greeting his every appearance with boos. Whitson had clashed with manager Billy Martin in '85, and this season Lou Piniella, Martin's successor, had used him mostly as a mop-up man. Over the previous two and a half weeks, he'd pitched just one-third of an inning. Whitson's overall record in New York was a respectable 15-10, but a better gauge of his performance was his high 5.38 earned run average.

Not surprisingly, Whitson was thrilled to be leaving New York; still, he left with conciliatory words. "It's not like all people in New York are bad," he graciously conceded. "They've got some outstanding fans there, that's for sure, and I wish them all the best of luck, the Yankees and George Steinbrenner. I've got to thank him because he really did what he said

he would do with the contract and getting me out of there if I didn't like it. He fulfilled it. I can't say enough about him. He never ripped me and he had plenty of chances, I guess. Until the day I die, I'll respect him."

Piniella said of Whitson's departure: "It should make Eddie happy. He's been accommodated. Good luck to him." First baseman Don Mattingly was one of many Yankees who saw the trade as desirable for both Whitson and the team. "You feel bad about Eddie, and you get tired of hearing about Eddie," he said. "I'm glad we got somebody who hopefully wants to play for us. I hated to see the guy suffer, but to me he was kind of messing things up. He wasn't pitching, so what was he doing here? He didn't want to be here. He wanted to prove something this year, but it didn't work out. Everybody moves on."

Tim Stoddard had chalked up 65 saves in his nine prior seasons, including 26 with the 1980 Baltimore Orioles. He had a 1-3 record for the Padres this season, with no saves, but Piniella thought Stoddard's experience made him a valuable addition.

"Stoddard pitched in pennant situations with Baltimore," Piniella said. "He's an experienced pitcher and his strikeouts per inning indicate he's throwing the ball well. We're happy to have him here."

Before they released him on August 14, 1988, just over two years after acquiring him, Stoddard pitched in 109 games for the Yanks, mostly in middle relief. He won ten, lost six, and had 11 saves.

July 29, 1986: Traded Catcher Ron Hassey, Minor League Shortstop Carlos Martinez, and a Player to Be Named to the Chicago White Sox for Outfielder Ron Kittle, Catcher Joel Skinner, and Infielder Wayne Tolleson

After Ron Hassey pinch hit a ninth inning single in the Yanks' 6-4 loss at Milwaukee, he returned to the clubhouse where Rickey Henderson notified him that he'd been traded back to the Chicago White Sox. The Yanks had first traded Hassey to Chicago in December 1985 and then reacquired him two months later, in February of 1986.

Hassey wasn't being traded because he was playing poorly—he was batting .298 with 29 runs batted in. His drawback was that he batted lefthanded, and the Yanks, four games behind the first-place Red Sox, were looking to add righthanded hitters.

Hassey couldn't quite understand the trade. Like many others around the Yankees, he felt that it wasn't righthanded hitting, but a lack of pitching that was holding the team back. "Our biggest need is not hitting. Everyone knows that," he said.

Evidently the Yankee front office felt differently. Having traded Don Baylor, and having recently lost switch-hitting Butch Wynegar to the disabled list, they believed that the lack of righthanded hitting was the club's major weakness.

Joel Skinner, a 25-year-old righthanded hitter, had played parts of the last four seasons with Chicago, and though he was batting just .201, he would take over as the Yanks' first-string catcher. Meanwhile, the Yanks were counting on Ron Kittle to supply righthanded power from the designated hitter slot, where they planned to platoon him with left-hand hitting Mike Easler. Kittle, the American League Rookie of the Year in 1983, had slugged 35, 32, and 26 homers in his first three full seasons and had 17 home runs and 48 RBIs for Chicago this season. His last home run, a two-run shot the night before, had helped the White Sox beat Boston, 4-1.

The trade would also allow the Yankees to replace the weak-hitting Paul Zuvella at shortstop with Wayne Tolleson, a veteran who'd spent five of his six major league seasons with Texas. (Zuvella, with four hits in 48 at-bats, went to the International League Columbus Clippers several days later.)

"Finally we have some complementary parts," Piniella said. "We needed a righty with power. We got it. We needed a shortstop. We got it."

Carlos Martinez went from the Yanks' Albany team of the Eastern League to the White Sox Buffalo club in the American Association. He reached the majors with Chicago in 1988 and had a six-year stay in the American League.

On December 24, 1986, Chicago received minor league catcher Bill Lindsey, a .261 batter for Albany, as the player to be named. Lind-

sey's stay in the big leagues would consist of the nine games he played for the White Sox in 1987.

Kittle would hit only four home runs for the Yanks over the last two months of the 1986 season. In 1987, he batted .277 and hit 12 homers in 59 games, but the Yanks released him in December.

Tolleson would play with the Yankees though 1990, batting .223 in 355 games. The Yankees released him in October 1990, ending his major league career.

November 26, 1986: Traded Right-handed Pitchers Doug Drabek and Brian Fisher, and Minor League Righthanded Pitcher Logan Easley to the Pittsburgh Pirates for Righthanded Pitchers Rick Rhoden and Cecilio Guante, and Lefthanded Pitcher Pat Clements

The Yanks had been after Rick Rhoden even before the 1986 season began. Now, in the

November 26, 1986: *Rick Rhoden.* **His durability made Rhoden appealing to the Yankees.**

first trade made by Woody Woodward, the team's new general manager, they had him. Negotiations had almost broken down twice, once with Rhoden's agent Tony Attanasio over the terms of the contract, and once with Pittsburgh GM Syd Thrift over the players involved. The rebuilding Pirates had asked the Yankees for position players, specifically highly rated outfield prospect Jay Buhner and third baseman Mike Pagliarulo. They "settled" for the three young pitchers, including minor leaguer Logan Easley, whom the Yanks also classified as a major league prospect.

The 33-year-old Rhoden had compiled a 121-97 record since breaking in with the Dodgers in 1974. Traded to Pittsburgh in April 1979, he'd won at least ten games in eight different seasons, including the last five. Rhoden was also extremely durable. In 1986, he'd pitched 253.2 innings, completed 12 of his 34 starts, and won 15 games. Rhoden had worked more than 200 innings in each of the last five seasons, an achievement that made him especially tempting to the Yankees.

He was happy to be with the Yanks, Rhoden said, adding that the accusation that he cheated by "scuffing" baseballs was untrue. "If players are worried about it that puts something else in their mind and that helps me," he said. "I've never been found guilty of doing anything to the ball."

Cecilio Guante had pitched in 201 games in five years with Pittsburgh, all in relief. He had a record of 13-17 with 20 saves, and had gone 5-2 with four saves in 1986. Guante had earned a reputation as an excellent setup man, but one who didn't react well to the increased pressure of save situations.

Thrift had offered the Yanks a choice of Pat Clements, a lefthander, or Lee Tunnell a righthander. They chose Clements on the recommendation of manager Lou Piniella, who liked what he'd seen of him when Clements pitched for the Angels in 1984. Clements, a rookie, was 5-0 that year, but he'd almost reversed that record in two seasons with the Pirates, losing all six of his decisions.

Brian Fisher had also had an impressive rookie year. Pitching in 55 games for the 1985 Yankees, all in relief, he went 4-4 with 14 saves. He appeared in 62 games in 1986, again all in relief, and had a 9-5 mark with six saves. In both seasons, Dave Righetti got the over-

whelming number of saves on the team, but in both years, Fisher had the next highest total.

Like Fisher, Doug Drabek was 24 years old with a promising future. He'd started 21 games in 1986, his rookie season, winning seven and losing eight.

At 25, Easley was the oldest of the three pitchers going to Pittsburgh, but the only one who had yet to reach the majors. In the Yankee system since 1981, he'd been with Albany of the Eastern League in 1987, where he won eight and lost seven.

December 11, 1986: Traded Designated Hitter Mike Easler and Minor League Infielder Tom Barrett to the Philadelphia Phillies for Righthanded Pitcher Charles Hudson and Minor League Righthanded Pitcher Jeff Knox

Mike Easler could have become a free agent in March 1987, but instead had demanded that the Yankees trade him. That demand so irritated owner George Steinbrenner, that despite Easler's solid 1986 season—a .302 batting average, 14 home runs, and 78 RBIs—he was determined to get rid of him. And while no one in the Yankees' front office objected to trading Easler, all but Steinbrenner had opposed trading him for Charles Hudson. The Yanks had tried to trade him to Minnesota for righthanded pitcher Mike Smithson, but the Twins didn't want Easler, they wanted one of the Yankee pitchers.

The 27-year-old Hudson had a 32-42 record in four seasons with Philadelphia, and was coming off a mediocre 7-10 season, with a 4.94 ERA and numerous blown late-inning leads. Nevertheless, manager Lou Piniella said that Hudson would get a fresh start in New York.

"He's going to get an opportunity in spring training to make our staff. We're impressed with his arm. He's been a little inconsistent and he's had problems getting behind hitters, but hopefully a change of scenery will do him good."

Piniella added that the Yankees would continue to look for pitching help. However, should none be available, Hudson would likely compete with second-year man Bob Tewksbury for the fifth spot in the rotation.

Supposedly, Detroit's Jack Morris, who was a free agent, was number one on the club's list of desirable pitchers. But strangely, neither the Yankees nor any other club went after Morris or any of the season's other high-priced free agents. (Eventually, the Players Association filed and won a collusion suit against the owners over this issue.)

Although Easler had played very few games in the outfield over the past three seasons, Phillies manager John Felske said the club "was going to gamble" that he could play left field on the fast artificial turf of Veterans Stadium.

Of the two minor league throw-ins, Tom Barrett (the brother of Boston second baseman Marty Barrett) would play briefly for the Phillies and Red Sox, but Jeff Knox would not reach the big leagues.

December 19, 1986: *Butch Wynegar*. **Playing in New York proved unhealthy for Wynegar.**

December 15, 1986: Signed Free-Agent Infielder Lenn Sakata from the Oakland Athletics

Although he'd played several different positions in his career, Lenn Sakata was mainly a second baseman. In signing him, the Yanks were protecting against the possibility that they'd be unable to re-sign their own second baseman, free agent Willie Randolph. (They did re-sign Randolph.)

Sakata had played briefly with Milwaukee in the late 1970s and then spent six seasons in Baltimore. He signed as a free agent with Oakland in 1986, but played only 17 games for the A's, batting .353 in 34 at-bats. He spent most of the season with Tacoma of the Pacific Coast League, where he batted .313 in 119 games.

Sakata would bat .267 in 19 games for the 1987 Yankees, who then released him after the season, ending his career.

December 19, 1986: Traded Catcher Butch Wynegar to the California Angels for Righthanded Pitcher Ron Romanick and a Player to Be Named

In four and a half seasons with the Yankees, Wynegar batted a combined .259, but just .223 and .206 the past two seasons. He'd also

grown increasingly discontented in New York; a condition resulting from his self-description as a low-keyed player playing for high-keyed managers like Billy Martin and Lou Piniella. Convinced he could no longer function under these conditions, Wynegar left the team on July 31, 1985. The Yankees put him on the restricted list and stopped paying him. After being treated by a psychiatrist, Wynegar sued the club to get his money, contending that a mental disability should be treated the same as a physical disability. Because of this dispute, any trade involving Wynegar had to wait until he and the club worked out an agreement, which they now had done.

Ron Romanick was 12-12 as an Angels rookie in 1984 and then 14-9 in 1985. He split the 1986 season between California, where he was 5-8, and the Edmonton Trappers of the Pacific Coast League, where he won two and lost three. Following the trade, Romanick never again pitched in the major leagues.

The deal was not completed until June 22, 1987, when the Yankees received minor league righthander Alan Mills from California. The Yanks assigned the 20-year-old Mills to their Prince William affiliate in the Carolina League.

December 24, 1986: Signed Free-Agent Outfielder Gary Ward from the Texas Rangers

After eight seasons in the minors, and brief appearances with Minnesota in 1979 and 1980, the Twins brought Gary Ward up to stay in 1981. He hit 28 and 19 home runs the next two seasons and then was traded to Texas in December 1983. Ward was a regular for the Rangers in 1984 and 1985, batting .284 and .287 with a total of 36 home runs. He raised his average to .316 in 1986, but a combination of family problems and stomach troubles limited him to just 105 games. His absences made playing time for rookie outfielders Pete Incaviglia and Ruben Sierra, and both did so well that despite Ward's .289 lifetime batting average, the Rangers felt no need to re-sign him.

The Yankees, with no such riches, had made the acquisition of a righthanded power hitter their primary off-season goal. They'd batted just .254 against lefthanders in 1986 (.271 overall), and had a 24-29 record against lefthanded starters, while going 66-43 against righthanded starters. Manager Lou Piniella said he would probably platoon Ward in left field with either Claudell Washington or Dan Pasqua, and also use him as a designated hitter. He expected to bat Ward in the fifth or sixth slot in the batting order, but said: "We'll let spring training answer all those questions."

The 33-year-old Ward thought differently about Piniella's plan to platoon him. "It might start out that way," he said, "but I doubt if it will finish like that." Primarily an opposite field hitter, he said he looked forward to playing in Yankee Stadium with its short distance to the right field fence. "That's where my power is," Ward said. "If I'm going to play 81 games there, I have to be able to take advantage of that short porch."

Because Ward was a Type-A free agent, the Yanks had to give Texas their first choice in the spring 1987 amateur draft.

Ward played 146 games for the 1987 Yankees. He had 16 home runs and 78 runs batted in, but after a strong first half he finished with a .248 batting average. In 1988, he batted just .225 in 91 games and in mid–April of 1989 the Yankees released him.

January 5, 1987: Traded Righthanded Pitcher Scott Nielsen and Minor League Infielder Mike Soper to the Chicago White Sox for Lefthanded Pitcher Pete Filson and Minor League Infielder Randy Velarde

This was the fourth trade in the last 13 months between George Steinbrenner's Yankees and Eddie Einhorn and Jerry Reinsdorf's White Sox. In the first one, the one that sent Britt Burns to the Yankees, Mike Soper came with him. Now Soper was going back to Chicago, although he still trailed Ron Hassey who had been in three of those trades. When told about Soper's round trip, Larry Himes, Chicago's new general manager, said he "didn't realize that we've been trading some of the same players back and forth. We're going to have to try to do something different."

Soper had hit very poorly in 1986—.214 with Albany of the Eastern League and .195 with Columbus of the International League. Nevertheless, the Yanks thought enough of him to keep him on their 40-man roster.

Scott Nielsen had gone 11-7 at Columbus in '86, and also split eight decisions with the Yankees. Two of his four wins were shutouts (the only Yankee pitcher to have two shutouts in 1986), including one against the pennant-winning Red Sox.

Himes predicted that Nielsen would help fill the middle relief role that the now departed Gene Nelson, Bill Dawley, and Dave Schmidt had occupied in 1986. "He's a command pitcher," Himes said. "He spots his fastball and slider. He gives us security with our middle relief."

Nielsen, who was leaving the Yankees, and Pete Filson, who was coming, were both 28 years old. Filson began his big league career with Minnesota in 1982 and was traded to the White Sox in 1986. They sent him to Buffalo, where he led the league in wins (14) and ERA (2.27), and was the 1986 American Association's Pitcher of the Year. Nevertheless, he had failed to impress in a late season call-up by Chicago.

The Yanks would send Filson back to Triple-A in 1987, where he would have another excellent season, going 12-4 for the International League Columbus Clippers. He also pitched in seven games for the Yanks, winning his only decision, but failed to make the club in 1988 and was released in late March.

Randy Velarde, who'd been in the White Sox low minors for two seasons, would make his Yankee debut in late August 1987. He would go on to be a valuable utility player (.264 in 658 games) for the Yanks until he left to sign with the California Angels in November 1995.

February 13, 1987: Signed Free-Agent Catcher Rick Cerone from the Milwaukee Brewers

The Brewers had gotten Rick Cerone in a trade with Atlanta for Ted Simmons in March of 1986. He hit .259 in 68 games, but when they chose not to re-sign him, Cerone asked George Steinbrenner for a tryout. Instead, Steinbrenner, saying a tryout wasn't necessary, signed him to a contract. Cerone, who'd upset the Yankee owner by asking for arbitration during his first Yankee tour, was very appreciative of Steinbrenner's gesture and happy to be back in New York. At 32, he believed he still had many years of playing time left.

"I felt like last year shouldn't be the end of the line, that I had a pretty good year in Milwaukee," Cerone said. "But my biggest fear was that if I wasn't with somebody by the spring, that I would be out of sight and out of mind. I've been around 11 years, but I'm not old yet. I'm not ready to give it up."

Cerone was a Class B free agent and so Milwaukee would get New York's second choice in the amateur draft. (The Yanks had already lost their first by signing free-agent Gary Ward.)

Joel Skinner, obtained in a trade with the White Sox the previous July, would be going into the 1987 season as the Yankees' number one catcher. With Butch Wynegar traded to California, Cerone would have only minor leaguers Phil Lombardi, Juan Espino, and Mitch Lyden too compete with for a reserve position.

However, after Skinner failed to hit, Cerone became the club's number one catcher in 1987. He batted .243 in 113 games, but after the season the Yanks acquired Don Slaught from Texas and released Cerone the day before the 1988 opener.

June 6, 1987: Traded Righthanded Pitcher Joe Niekro and Cash to the Minnesota Twins for Catcher Mark Salas

After batting .300 as a Twins rookie in 1985, Mark Salas fell off to .233 in 1986. But he was back up at a lofty .378 after 22 games this season, and he was a lefthanded hitter. With Don Mattingly sidelined by an injured back, and with his other key lefthanded hitters struggling, a hot-hitting lefthanded batter was something manager Lou Piniella sorely needed. To get Salas, the Twins said, the Yanks would have to part with pitcher Joe Niekro. Reluctantly, the Yanks agreed. "We hated to lose Niekro," Piniella said, "but that's the only way we could make the trade."

Niekro had a 3-4 record this season, bringing his totals as a Yankee to 14-15. Now 42 years old, Niekro seemed uncertain of his future after learning the club had traded him. "All I can say is that it was a real surprise, I can't say anything now. I can't say what I'm going to do."

Niekro reported to the Twins, where he would end his career the next season.

June 10, 1987: Traded Outfielder Keith Hughes and Minor League Infielder Shane Turner to the Philadelphia Phillies for Outfielder Mike Easler

Six months after trading Mike Easler to Philadelphia for pitcher Charles Hudson, the Yankees, short of lefthanded hitters, got him back. Easler was batting .282 in 33 games for the Phillies, but hadn't shown much power—one home run and ten runs batted in.

Saying "it was like starting over again," Easler was glad to be coming back. The Yanks, and the Red Sox before them, had used Easler almost exclusively as a designated hitter, but with no such position in the National League, the Phillies had him playing left field.

The club made room for Easler by sending catcher Joel Skinner to Columbus of the International League. Skinner was batting just .137, and had lost his job to Rick Cerone. Also, the Yanks had traded for catcher Mark Salas four days earlier. "I had a 100 at-bats and played well, but didn't get any hits," Skinner said. "When you do that, you can't expect to keep playing."

Writers covering the Yankees had voted Keith Hughes the club's top rookie in spring training; nevertheless, after four hitless at-bats, the Yanks sent him back to Columbus. Philadelphia kept Hughes in the International League, sending him to Maine, while assigning infielder Shane Turner to their Class AA team at Reading in the Eastern League.

Although, Easler batted .281 in 65 games for the Yanks, they released him at the close of the season, ending his career. "I never should have left the American League," he said.

July 13, 1987: Traded Righthanded Pitcher Bob Tewksbury, Minor League Righthanded Pitcher Dean Wilkins, and Minor League Lefthanded Pitcher Rich Scheid to the Chicago Cubs for Lefthanded Pitcher Steve Trout

After trading Steve Trout to the Yankees, Cubs GM Dallas Green said that Trout could put the division-leading Yanks into the World Series. Certainly his addition gave the Yanks a most formidable five-man rotation, as he joined fellow lefthanders Ron Guidry, Tommy John, Dennis Rasmussen, and the lone righthander, Rick Rhoden. The Yankees had pursued Trout throughout spring training, but the Cubs had been reluctant to let go of one of their better pitchers. In recent weeks the Yanks had turned their attention to other lefthanders, specifically San Francisco's Dave Dravecky and San Diego's Mark Davis. That ended when those two were involved in a seven-player trade between the Giants and Padres.

Trout, who would turn 30 at the end of July, had a 80-78 career record while pitching for the White Sox and Cubs. He was 6-3 this season, but in his last two starts had thrown consecutive shutouts against San Diego and Los Angeles.

Cubs manager Gene Michael was both surprised and sorry about losing Trout. "I know nothing about it," Michael said. "They told me in the dugout in the ninth inning." Nor was Trout pleased. "I've got nothing to say," he said, looking visibly upset.

Bob Tewksbury had been back and forth between the Yankees and the International League Columbus Clippers this year. He'd had a fine rookie season in 1986, winning nine and losing five, with a 3.31 earned run average. But after beginning this season with the Yanks, they sent him to Columbus in mid–April. Tewksbury went 6-1 for the Clippers, so the Yanks recalled him. Then, after a win and four losses and a 6.75 ERA, they sent him back.

The two minor league pitchers, Rich Scheid and Dean Wilkins, had been high picks in the 1986 free-agent draft. Both began the 1987 season at Fort Lauderdale of the Florida State League and then were promoted to Albany-Colonie of the Eastern League. (Wilkins had since been sent back to Fort Lauderdale.)

The Cubs brought Tewksbury to Chicago, but Scheid stayed in the Eastern League, with the Pittsfield Cubs, and Wilkins went to the Winston-Salem Spirits of the Carolina League.

August 26, 1987: Traded Lefthanded Pitcher Dennis Rasmussen to the Cincinnati Reds for Righthanded Pitcher Bill Gullickson

Reds general manager Bill Bergesch said this trade of veteran pitchers (both Dennis Rasmussen and Bill Gullickson were 28) was the result of some casual discussions he'd had with Woody Woodward, his Yankee counterpart. "It started off in a conversation about what we could do to help each other, and it evolved from there," Bergesch, a former Yankee vice president, said. "They could use a righthander, we could use a lefthander." Gullickson [97-84 lifetime] is in a slump, and Rasmussen [39-24 lifetime] hasn't done as well as last year. Maybe a change of scenery could help them both."

Woodward endorsed the righty-lefty aspect of the deal. "We made the trade mainly to get a little better balance of righthanders and lefthanders on the staff." (Rick Rhoden had been the Yanks' only righthanded starter.) "Dennis had an outstanding year last year. It's just a shame he didn't pick up where he left off last season. His inconsistency bothered us."

After a combined 12 wins and 11 losses in

1984-85, Rasmussen went 18-6 in 1986, a season in which no other Yankee pitcher exceeded nine wins. He'd won nine this season, with seven losses, but had a 4.75 ERA, and as Woodward said, he'd been inconsistent.

Gullickson, meanwhile, had throughout his career been one of baseball's most consistent pitchers. He was one of only five active pitchers who had won at least 12 games in each of the past five seasons. (Charlie Hough, Jack Morris, John Tudor, and Fernando Valenzuela were the others.)

Gullickson's slump, which Bergesch referred to, consisted of an 0-5 record and a 6.17 earned run average in his last six starts. His recent bad outings had dropped his season totals to 10-11, with a 4.85 ERA. Still, Woodward confessed that the Yanks had liked Gullickson "for some time." In fact, two years earlier, before Montreal traded him to Cincinnati, the Yanks and Expos had discussed a trade for him. It would have brought Gullickson and star outfielder Andre Dawson to New York for Rasmussen, pitchers Joe Cowley and Rich Bordi, and outfielder Henry Cotto.

Gullickson went 4-2 the last month of the 1987 season, but was a free agent and signed to play with the Yomiuri Giants in 1988.

August 26, 1987: Traded Minor League Lefthanded Pitcher Ken Patterson and a Player to Be Named to the Chicago White Sox for Infielder Jerry Royster and Minor League Infielder Mike Soper

While still only 22 years old, Mike Soper had now been a minor figure in three Yankee–White Sox trades. The White Sox included him in the December 1985 trade that brought Britt Burns to New York. Later, the Yanks sent him back to Chicago with Scott Nielsen in the trade for Pete Filson and Randy Velarde. Despite all that movement, Soper would never play in a big league game. Neither would pitcher Jeff Pries, whom the Yanks sent to Chicago on September 19 as the player to be named. But Ken Patterson would. Patterson, who had a 12-10 in three minor league seasons, would make his major league debut for the White Sox in 1988.

Jerry Royster was in his first American League season, after having been a National Leaguer since 1973. He'd played nine years for Atlanta, but also with Los Angeles and San Diego. A regular for the Braves between 1976 and 1980, he'd spent most of his career as a part-time player and entered the 1987 season with a career .250 batting average.

Royster had become a free agent following the 1986 season, and the Yanks were interested in signing him then. Instead, he signed with the White Sox, for whom he was batting .240 with seven home runs and 23 RBIs. His arrival in New York ended the big league career of infielder Juan Bonilla, who'd also played briefly for the Yanks in 1985. The club let Bonilla go to make roster room for Royster.

Although Royster would bat a rousing .357 in 18 games for the Yanks, they would release him the day before the 1988 opener.

September 4, 1987: Signed Righthanded Pitcher Neil Allen as a Free Agent

Chicago had used Neil Allen mostly as a starter after getting him from the Yankees prior to the 1986 season. He won seven of nine decisions in '86, but also spent a month on the disabled list with a sore arm. Allen's arm problems were back this season, and after he'd compiled an 0-7 record, and made two more trips to the disabled list, the White Sox released him. That was on August 29, and now, six days later, he was back with the Yankees.

Allen would pitch in eight September games for the Yanks, including one start. He lost his only decision, and so finished the season at 0-8. He was much better in 1988, winning five and losing three in 41 appearances. After the season, he signed with Cleveland, but his career ended after three 1989 games.

November 2, 1987: Traded a Player to Be Named to the Texas Rangers for Catcher Don Slaught

The Yankees had been so confident that Joel Skinner would be their first-string catcher in 1987, they'd even bypassed free-agent Rich Gedman. However, Skinner had difficulty getting base hits and lost his job to veteran Rick Cerone. But the Yanks viewed Cerone as a short-term solution (they would release him before the 1988 opener), and Don Slaught, they hoped, would be the number one catcher in 1988.

Slaught had a .270 career batting average in six seasons, three with Kansas City and three with Texas. But he too had lost his first-string job during the 1987 season, after the Rangers called up rookie Mike Stanley. In all, '87 was Slaught's poorest year; he batted only 237 times with a career-low .224 average.

Although Slaught's acquisition was new general manager Lou Piniella's first deal, Piniella seemed nonchalant about it. "I haven't given it that much thought," he said. "All I'm trying to accomplish is to get players I think can help us win. I felt we needed a catcher, and we acquired one that will help us."

Actually, after giving up on Skinner last summer, the Yanks had tried to get Slaught, but were unable to work out the details. "I had heard rumors about going to the Yankees even before Stanley came up," Slaught said. "I'm happy about the trade. I've heard about all the fuss there, but I'm going in there with a positive attitude. I'm going into it with the idea that I'll be the number one catcher and get an opportunity to play every day."

The identity of the player to be named was withheld until the deal became final, which would not be until Slaught passed a physical exam. Everyone suspected it would be 24-year-old righthander Brad Arnsberg, and on November 10, the Yanks announced that indeed it was Arnsberg. Once a highly-rated prospect, Arnsberg had a 1-3 record in eight games as a Yankee over the past two seasons.

November 11, 1987: Signed Right-handed Pitcher Steve Shields as a Free Agent

As an Atlanta rookie in 1985, Steve Shields had started six of his 23 games, but had been strictly a relief pitcher since. He was 1-2 that season, had no record in brief appearances with the Braves and Royals in 1986, and was 2-0 with Seattle in 1987.

The Yanks signed the 30-year-old Shields, who was officially classified as a minor league free agent, to a split contract between the major league club and their Columbus team in the International League.

November 13, 1987: Traded Outfielder Dan Pasqua, Catcher Mark Salas, and Minor League Lefthanded Pitcher Steve Rosenberg to the Chicago White Sox for Righthanded Pitchers Richard Dotson and Scott Nielsen

Several weeks of discussion preceded this deal, the sixth between the Yanks and White Sox in 23 months. The Yanks wanted Chicago lefthander Floyd Bannister, a pitcher they'd long coveted, but when the Sox asked for third baseman Mike Pagliarulo in exchange, GM Lou Piniella refused and accepted righthander Richard Dotson instead.

"I like his style of play," Piniella said of Dotson. "He's a bulldog on the mound."

At 28, Dotson was also four years younger than Bannister. He had a 94-88 career record, but due in part to an injury, had never been able to duplicate his outstanding 1983 season. Since going 22-7 to lead the league with a .759 winning percentage in '83, Dotson had won 38 and lost 48, including an 11-12 mark in 1987.

As to any possible problem related to pitching in New York, Dotson said he wasn't worried. "The last two years in Chicago weren't normal either," he said. "I've learned not to worry about things you can't control. The circumstances there probably won't affect me."

Dotson would win 12 and lose nine for the 1988 Yankees, but his earned average was an unimpressive 5.00. His record was 2-5 and his ERA 5.57 when the Yanks released him in June 1989. A month later he re-signed with the White Sox.

In three seasons with the Yankees, Dan Pasqua had a .251 average, with 42 home runs and 112 runs batted in. He'd asked to be traded, and the Yanks, who had expected much more offense from him, were glad to oblige.

In 1987, a year when their catching was unsettled, the Yanks traded Joe Niekro to Minnesota in June to get Mark Salas. A lefthanded hitter, Salas batted .200 in 50 games.

Twenty-three-year-old Steve Rosenberg split the 1987 season between Albany of the

Eastern League, where he was 4-4, and Columbus of the International League, where he won four and lost one.

Scott Nielsen, a returning former Yankee, also split his '87 season: 3-4 for Hawaii of the Pacific Coast League and 3-5 for the White Sox.

December 11, 1987: Traded Catcher Phil Lombardi, Minor League Outfielder Darren Reed, and Minor League Lefthanded Pitcher Steve Frey to the New York Mets for Shortstop Rafael Santana and Minor League Lefthanded Pitcher Victor Garcia

Wayne Tolleson was the Yanks' number one shortstop in 1987, backed up by Bobby Meacham. But Tolleson had undergone rotator cuff surgery a few days earlier, and owner George Steinbrenner had never cared much for Meacham. Getting a shortstop for 1988 was a high priority, and general manager Lou Piniella had talked to Oakland about Alfredo Griffin and to Cleveland about Julio Franco. Unable to get either, he and his counterpart on the Mets, Joe McIlvaine, put together a deal for Rafael Santana.

"What I like," Piniella said of his new shortstop, "is he's played on a world championship team. As general manager, I hope to make more trades with teams that have won." (Santana was the shortstop for the Mets when they won the 1986 World Series.)

Santana, now nearing 30, had originally been Yankee property. He'd gone to St. Louis in 1981 as the player to be named in the trade that brought pitcher George Frazier to New York. He'd been the Mets' starting shortstop since 1985 and this past season batted .255, with five home runs and 44 runs batted in. Still, with the Mets grooming rookie Kevin Elster to replace him, Santana's future with the club appeared uncertain.

"I wanted to stay with the Mets," Santana said. "But on the Mets I wasn't going to play every day. Now at least I have a chance. If I had to be traded, I'd rather go to the Yankees. I'm glad to stay in New York." Santana added that he foresaw no problem in playing for manager Billy Martin. "I think everything

will be all right," he said. "I don't know him, but I'm not worried. I do my job."

After he batted .240 as the Yankees' everyday shortstop in 1988, Santana had elbow surgery that made him miss all of 1989, and the Yanks released him late that year.

Among the four other players in the deal, catcher Phil Lombardi was the only one with big league experience. Lombardi had played in 20 games for the Yanks in 1986 and five in 1987, and had 11 hits in 44 at-bats.

The Yankees were reluctant to part with outfielder Darren Reed, whom they considered a definite big league prospect. In 1987 he'd hit better than .300 at both Albany of the Eastern League (.319 in 107 games) and Columbus of the International League (.329 in 21 games).

Reed would have a brief major league career, as would pitcher Steve Frey, but pitcher Victor Garcia, the Mets fourteenth-round pick in the 1985 amateur draft, would never rise that high.

December 22, 1987: Traded Lefthanded Pitcher Steve Trout and Outfielder Henry Cotto to the Seattle Mariners for Righthanded Pitcher Clay Parker, Lefthanded Pitcher Lee Guetterman, and Minor League Righthanded Pitcher Wade Taylor

When the Yanks got Steve Trout from the Chicago Cubs in July 1987, he had just thrown two consecutive shutouts. However, he'd never had that kind of success in New York, going 0-4 in 14 games (nine starts) with a 6.60 earned run average. Consistently wild, he walked 37 men in 46.1 innings and threw nine wild pitches.

Several former teammates had claimed that because Trout did not pitch well under pressure, New York had not been a good place for him. They expected the 30-year-old lefthander to return to form in Seattle, where, ironically, the Yanks would be paying a large portion of his salary. Yankee general manager Lou Piniella also thought that Seattle was a good spot for Trout because he would be reunited with Billy Connors, his pitching coach with the Cubs.

For each of the past three seasons, Henry

Cotto had shuttled between the Yanks and their International League team at Columbus, including four different stays with the Clippers in 1987 alone. While in New York, Cotto played in 137 games and batted .242.

As with Trout, going to Seattle appeared to also be a good career move for Cotto. The Mariners had failed to offer center fielder John Moses a contract for 1988, which would give Cotto, a good defensive outfielder, his opportunity to become a regular.

After going 0-4 in relief in 1986, his rookie season, Lee Guetterman was mostly a starter in 1987, winning 11 of 15 decisions. Ten of his wins (and all four losses) were as a starter. Aware that the 6-foot-8 Guetterman could do both, Piniella said: "He'll get a chance to be a fifth starter. If not, he'll pitch out of the bullpen."

Clay Parker had started the 1987 season with Chattanooga of the Southern League. After going 7-5 for the Lookouts, Seattle moved him up to their Triple-A Calgary team in the Pacific Coast League. Parker won eight and lost one at Calgary, which earned him a late-season call-up by the Mariners. He got into three games without a decision.

Twenty-two-year-old Wade Taylor pitched for the Mariners' Bellingham club in the rookie Northwest League in 1987. He didn't do well: a 2-5 record and a 4.47 earned run average. Nevertheless, Piniella said that Taylor had impressed the Yankees when he was pitching for the University of Miami, and they assigned him to Fort Lauderdale of the Florida State League for 1988. In 1991 Taylor made it to New York, winning seven and losing 12, but he was hurt for much of 1992 and never returned.

January 6, 1988: Signed Free-Agent First Baseman Jack Clark from the St. Louis Cardinals

Although Jack Clark was among the premier righthanded sluggers in the game, repeated trips to the disabled list had adversely affected his career. This past season, torn ligaments in his right ankle limited him to just two at-bats after September 9; still, he hit 35 home runs and batted in 106 runs for the pennant-winning Cardinals.

Clark reached the majors to stay with the 1977 San Francisco Giants. Traded to St. Louis in 1985, he was a lifetime .276-batter, with 229 career home runs and 811 runs batted in.

Clark's injured ankle had kept him out of the 1987 National League Championship Series and World Series, but he was confident about 1988.

"I'm going to be healthy," he said. "I can hit, and as long as I can hit, there should be a place for me."

Because the Yanks had Don Mattingly at first base, that place figured to be as the team's designated hitter. "It's too early to say where he'll be batting in our lineup," said manager Billy Martin. "And I don't know what position he'll be playing. It won't be too much at first base. But he certainly helps our righthanded power, which we really need."

Clark seemed resigned to being primarily a designated hitter. "I'm expecting to do a lot of DH-ing here," he said. "But I'll play first base, the outfield, whatever." He also voiced his displeasure with the Cardinals, accusing them of holding his injury against him and calling him a one-dimensional player. "They really told me to take a walk."

Clark revealed that when St. Louis learned that the Yanks were after him they offered him an even better deal. "But that was too late. I'd already given my word to the Yankees."

The Yanks had not only helped themselves, they'd also helped their intracity rivals, the Mets. The Mets had finished just three games behind the Cardinals in the NL East in 1987. Now with Clark gone, they became the favorites to win the division in 1988. (They did, by 15 games over Pittsburgh. St. Louis dropped to fifth, 25 games behind the Mets.)

January 18, 1988: Signed Free-Agent Lefthanded Pitcher John Candelaria from the New York Mets

He signed with the Yankees, John Candelaria said, because they were more likely than the Mets to use him as a starting pitcher. The Mets had traded for him in the final weeks of the 1987 season, ending his three-year stay with the California Angels. Candelaria pitched in three games for the Mets, winning two, and the club assumed he'd re-sign with them for 1988.

"The money had nothing to do with turning down the Mets offer," Candelaria said. "The Mets were offering me a role as a spot starter and long relief. I felt I was still capable of pitching well and effectively as a starter."

Yankee general manager Lou Piniella agreed. "Candy is going to be one of our starters," he predicted. "After talking to a few of our scouts and our manager, we feel he can step right into our rotation and do a good job. This makes up in a large part for the loss of Gullickson." (Starter Bill Gullickson had signed to play in Japan.)

Others in the Yankee hierarchy were not so sure that Candelaria was ready to assume the role of a full-time member of the rotation. He'd had elbow surgery in 1986 and was twice placed on the disabled list in 1987 for a drinking problem.

Candelaria spoke frankly about his battle with alcohol. "I was in a rehabilitation program for alcohol abuse," he said. "That's no copout. I had certain things happen in my life, and I was under a lot of strain. I just broke down. I feel that's over with and I can go on. I hope it's behind me; no, I know it's behind me."

Now 34, Candelaria had begun his career with Pittsburgh in 1975. Two years later he had his finest season, going 20-5, and leading the National League in winning percentage (.800) and earned run average (2.34). In 13 seasons, he'd won 151 games (151-95), pitched more than 2,000 innings, and had an ERA of 3.22.

February 25, 1988: Signed Free-Agent Outfielder Jose Cruz from the Houston Astros

Because of his age (he was 40), and his poor 1987 season, the Yanks signed Jose Cruz to a non-guaranteed contract. An 18-year National League veteran, the last 13 with Houston, Cruz had accumulated more than 2,200 hits and had batted .300 or better six times. (One year he finished at .299.) But after he slipped to .241 in 126 games in 1987, the Astros chose not to resign him.

"If they played me every day, I would've hit better than .240," Cruz said. "They tell you to be ready to play, then they don't play you."

Cruz would make the club in 1988, but

after batting just .200 in 80 at-bats, the Yanks released him on July 22.

March 30, 1988: Traded Outfielder Orestes Destrade to the Pittsburgh Pirates for Lefthanded Pitcher Hipolito Pena

Orestes Destrade was still two months short of his 25th birthday, but since 1981 he had played for seven different teams in the Yankee farm system. He finally made it to New York in 1987, going five for 19 in nine games. But with Don Mattingly firmly established at first base, Destrade knew that he would likely spend 1988 where he'd spent 1986 and 1987—with the International League Columbus Clippers. He asked the Yankees to trade him, and they obliged.

Hipolito Pena pitched for Vancouver of the Pacific Coast League in 1987, winning five and losing six. He also spent part of the season in Pittsburgh, as he had done in 1986. Pena was in ten games for the Pirates in 1986 and 16 in 1987, and had identical records both years—no wins and three defeats.

The Yankees sent the 34-year-old Pena to Columbus, but called him up later in the season. He got into 16 games for the Yanks, finally winning one (he also had a loss) to end his major league career with one win and seven losses.

July 15, 1988: Traded Minor League Righthanded Pitcher Amalio Carreno to the Philadelphia Phillies for Infielder Luis Aguayo

A utility infielder for nine years with Philadelphia, Luis Aguayo could play second base, third base, and shortstop. With Mike Pagliarulo bothered by a strained hamstring, Aguayo figured to get some immediate action at third base. A lifetime .240-hitter, he was batting .247 in 97 at-bats this season.

To make room for Aguayo, the Yanks sent rookie infielder Randy Velarde to Columbus of the International League. Aguayo batted .250 in 140 at-bats, but after the season the Yanks let him go, and Cleveland signed him as a free agent.

Philadelphia kept Amalio Carreno in the Eastern League, transferring him from Albany to Reading. His major league career would consist of three games without a decision for the 1991 Phillies.

July 21, 1988: Traded Outfielder Jay Buhner, Minor League Righthanded Pitcher Rich Balabon, and a Player to Be Named to the Seattle Mariners for Designated Hitter Ken Phelps

The Yanks had been looking for a left-handed power hitter since the winter, and if nothing else, Ken Phelps was that. Since 1983 he'd hit 105 home runs for Seattle, including 14 this season, and was the Mariners' all-time leader in that department. But Phelps, a month shy of his 34th birthday, presented one problem—he had no position. Nominally a first baseman, he could really be used only as the designated hitter. Nevertheless, manager Lou Piniella was glad to have him and speculated on how to get his bat into the lineup.

"What we'll do," he said, "is rest [Dave] Winfield a day a week, [Rickey] Henderson a day a week and [Jack] Clark a day a week. Another option is to put Phelps at first and move [Don] Mattingly to the outfield."

A most productive minor leaguer, Jay Buhner played seven games for the Yanks in 1987, getting five hits in 22 at-bats. This season, he'd been back and forth between New York and the International League Columbus Clippers. In his three stays with the Yankees, he was a combined 13 for 69 with three home runs, but also 25 strikeouts.

After leaving New York, Buhner would go on to hit more home runs than any other player the Yanks had ever traded away. He would also become a symbol of an era when the Yanks exchanged a slew of promising youngsters for faded veterans.

However, righthanded pitchers Rich Balabon and Troy Evers were not in that category. Neither Balabon, who was 1-1 at Fort Lauderdale of the Florida State League, nor Evers, who won nine and lost ten for Albany of the Eastern League and was assigned to the Mariners in October, ever made it to the major leagues.

August 30, 1988: Traded Righthanded Pitcher Cecilio Guante to the Texas Rangers for Righthanded Pitcher Dale Mohorcic

Looking to bolster their beleaguered bullpen following a sixth straight loss, the Yanks exchanged one righthanded reliever for another. After going 3-2 in 1987, and spending a good part of the season on the disabled list, Guante was 5-6 with 11 saves in 56 games this season. He'd also brought his earned run average down from 5.73 in 1987 to just 2.88 this season. Despite that, Guante had never ranked high with Lou Piniella, his manager in '87. Billy Martin had replaced Piniella this season, only to be replaced by Piniella again in late June.

Dale Mohorcic relieved in 58 games as a 30-year-old rookie in 1986, and in 74 in 1987, saving a total of 23. He was on the disabled list in August 1987, and then again early this season after having shoulder surgery in March. Mohorcic was 2-6 with five saves in 43 games in 1988, but had lost the closer's job to Mitch Williams. Nevertheless, the Yankees were still in the race, and saw him as someone who could give them a lot of innings in September.

Mohorcic appeared in 13 games in September 1988, winning two, losing two, and saving one. The Yanks released him following the 1989 season, after he'd gone 2-1 with two saves.

October 24, 1988: Traded Outfielder Jack Clark and Lefthanded Pitcher Pat Clements to the San Diego Padres for Righthanded Pitchers Jimmy Jones and Lance McCullers, and Outfielder Stan Jefferson

Serving mainly as the designated hitter, Jack Clark batted just .242 in 1988, his one season in New York. Still, he was a major source of Yankee power, leading the club with 27 home runs, and driving in 93 runs. Clark, a month short of his 33rd birthday, said he'd enjoyed playing in New York, but also expressed a desire to play on the West Coast. "I would have gladly come back," he said, "but I'm glad to be going closer to home. That's important to me."

While they hated to lose Clark's bat, the

Yanks knew that they would have to lose one of their big hitters to get the pitching help they so desperately needed.

"We're going to do everything we can to strengthen our pitching staff," said GM Bob Quinn. "This is only the start. [Lance] McCullers is one of the bright young relief pitchers in the game. [Jimmy] Jones hasn't reached his full potential, but he would have been second on our staff in innings pitched."

Quinn was correct. Rick Rhoden was the only Yankee to pitch more innings in 1988 than the 179 Jones worked while compiling a 9-14 record and a 4.12 earned run average. It was Jones's second full season with the Padres and brought his lifetime record to 20 wins and 21 losses.

Jones would spend a good part of the next two seasons with Columbus in the International League. He pitched in a combined 28 games for the Yankees in 1989-90, winning three and losing three.

McCullers, like Jones, was 24. He had a 21-28 record with 36 saves in four seasons with San Diego. Reporters asked Quinn if getting McCullers would allow the Yankee to return bullpen ace Dave Righetti to the starting rotation.

"This one deal doesn't necessarily mean that Righetti's role has changed," Quinn said. "This is something Dallas Green [the new manager] and I can discuss now that we've made the trade. It'll be Dallas's decision, but it's a decision we should make as soon as possible so Righetti will know what his role will be."

Stan Jefferson, a 26-year-old former Met, played a full season with the Padres in 1987, but batted just .230. He'd split 1988 between San Diego and the Class AAA Las Vegas Stars of the Pacific Coast League.

In 1987 Pat Clements won three and lost three, with seven saves for the Yanks, but he pitched in only six games in 1988 while spending most of the season at Columbus.

November 17, 1988: Traded Minor League Righthanded Pitcher Eric Schmidt to the California Angels for Catcher Brian Dorsett

Brian Dorsett made his major league debut in 1987 playing in five late-season games

with Cleveland. He was with Edmonton of the Pacific Coast League in 1988, batting .264, with 11 home runs, and had one hit in 11 at-bats for the Angels. The Yanks assigned him to Columbus of the International League, the same club for which Eric Schmidt had gone 2-10 in 1988.

Dorsett would spend the 1989 and 1990 seasons at Columbus, with brief appearances in each season for the Yankees (a total of 22 games). After his release in November 1990, he signed with San Diego.

November 17, 1988: Signed Right-handed Pitcher Don Schulze as a Free Agent

Don Schulze had gone 10-13 in 1988 for the Toledo Mud Hens, the Tigers Triple-A club in the International League. The year before, he'd gone 11-1 for Tidewater, the Mets affiliate in that league. The 26-year-old Schulze had also pitched in the majors in parts of five seasons with the Cubs, Indians, and Mets and had a lifetime 12-23 record as a big leaguer. The Yanks signed him as a minor league free agent.

November 23, 1988: Signed Free-Agent Second Baseman Steve Sax from the Los Angeles Dodgers

Steve Sax was one of the game's better offensive second baseman. He had a .282 career-average in his seven-plus seasons in Los Angeles, and a high of .332 in 1986. Sax, who'd batted .277 in 1988, had been expected to re-sign with the world champion Dodgers, but became disenchanted at their reaction to his contract demands. He cited the differences in the way the general managers of the two clubs treated him as the major factor in his decision to leave Los Angeles.

"There was a great difference in the tone of negotiations between Bob Quinn [Yankees] and Fred Claire [Dodgers]," Sax said. "The attitude was completely different. The Yankees treated me as someone they greatly respected. I felt it wasn't the same with the Dodgers. I felt Claire was really aloof. The tone of voice he spoke to me in and the way he looked at me really turned me off."

By signing Sax the Yankees signaled that they would pass on re-signing Willie Randolph, their own longtime second baseman. Injuries had slowed Randolph the past two seasons, and new manager Dallas Green had informed George Steinbrenner that he preferred Sax. At 29, Sax was five years younger than Randolph, although not his equal defensively.

Ironically, two-and-a-half weeks after the Yankees signed Sax, Randolph signed as a free agent with the Dodgers.

December 3, 1988: Signed Free-Agent Lefthanded Pitcher Dave LaPoint from the Pittsburgh Pirates

"I'm a New York kid," was Dave LaPoint's response when asked why he chose to sign with the Yankees. "It was when I was driving home from New York," he continued. "I was thinking here you got a kid from the best state in the nation [he was a native of Glens Falls, NY] going to the best city in the nation, to play for the best team in the nation."

Coming home obviously appealed to La-Point after all the traveling he'd done in his major league career. He'd broken in with the Milwaukee Brewers in 1980, but then moved to the Cardinals, to the Giants, to the Tigers, to the Padres, back to the Cardinals, then to the White Sox, and last August to the Pirates.

Asked why he had been traded six times, released once, and was a free agent twice, La-Point explained the reason behind each move, while adding that Detroit's Sparky Anderson was the only manager he hadn't "gotten along" with. "I didn't hit it off with Sparky from the start," he said.

General manager Bob Quinn predicted that LaPoint (67-66 lifetime, with a 3.81 ERA) would compete for a place in the Yankees' 1989 starting rotation with John Candelaria, Richard Dotson, Jimmy Jones, Al Leiter, and Rick Rhoden.

Quinn also hoped to add another name in that competition, as the Yanks were actively seeking to trade for yet another starting pitcher. "We hope we'll be able to pull off a trade between tomorrow and Thursday," Quinn said. Among those pitchers the club supposedly was

seeking were Don Carman of the Phillies, Storm Davis of the Athletics, Bob Knepper of the Astros, Dave Steib of the Blue Jays, and Rick Sutcliffe of the Cubs.

A shoulder injury would severely curtail LaPoint's 1989 season. He made 20 starts, with no complete games, and had a record of six wins and nine losses. Then, after going 7-10 in 1990, the Yanks released him in February 1991.

December 5, 1988: Traded Shortstop Bobby Meacham to the Texas Rangers for Outfielder Bob Brower

The trade ended Bobby Meacham's mostly unhappy six year stay in New York. A series of injuries and his often erratic play had hindered him throughout those six seasons. In only one, 1985, was Meacham the Yanks' full-time shortstop, and then he hit only .218. Despite his weak offense, he retained his position for the first six weeks of the 1986 season, but then lost it after a run of sloppy play.

The 28-year-old Meacham recalled his demotion. "But two weeks and five errors later, I was on the bench," he said. "And two weeks after that I was in Columbus sitting on the bench and coaching first base. That still blows me away." In all, Meacham played in 457 games for the Yankees and batted .236.

Because Texas had sent Curtis Wilkerson, their 1988 second baseman, to the Cubs earlier in the day, Meacham was expected to compete with Jerry Browne for the job in 1989. However, a day later they traded Browne to Cleveland for Julio Franco and it was Franco who would be the Rangers' second baseman in '89. Meacham, meanwhile, never again played in the major leagues.

Bob Brower had a .244 average in 230 games for Texas over the past three seasons. He would have a .232 average in 26 games for the Yanks in 1989, his final big league season.

December 8, 1988: Signed Free-Agent Righthanded Pitcher Andy Hawkins from the San Diego Padres

Andy Hawkins said he chose the Yankees over San Diego, Philadelphia, and Minnesota because they were the only team to give him a three-year guarantee; the others offered just two. Hawkins joined second baseman Steve Sax and pitcher Dave LaPoint, signed earlier this off-season, in making up the Yankees' most expensive free-agent splurge since 1982. Outfielders Don Baylor and Steve Kemp, and pitcher Bob Shirley were the prizes that year.

Hawkins, 14-11 in 1988, had been a good if unspectacular pitcher for the Padres. His only outstanding season was in 1985, when he won his first eleven decisions and finished 18-8 with a 3.15 earned run average. In seven big league seasons, Hawkins had a 60-58 record with a 3.84 ERA. Manager Dallas Green said his new acquisition would likely be the ace of his staff, an indication of how poor Green expected his pitching to be in 1989.

Hawkins did prove to be the Yanks' best pitcher in '89, leading the club in wins (15), games started (34), innings pitched (208.1), and strikeouts (98). He also had the most complete games (5) and the most shutouts (2). He was much less effective in 1990, winning five and losing 12. Hawkins lost his first two decisions in 1991, and had a 9.95 ERA after four games when the Yanks released him on May 9.

December 20, 1988: Signed Free-Agent Catcher Jamie Quirk from the Kansas City Royals

Jamie Quirk had spent 11 of his 14-season career with the Kansas City Royals. He had only a .240 lifetime batting average, but he was a good defensive catcher and could also play other positions. The Yanks had Don Slaught as their number one catcher for 1989, but expected Quirk would battle Joel Skinner for the number two spot.

As it turned out, the Yanks traded Skinner to Cleveland during spring training, and midway through the season rookie Bob Geren replaced Slaught as the first-string catcher. Earlier, on May 16, the Yanks had released Quirk after he went 2 for 24 in 13 games.

January 10, 1989: Traded Righthanded Pitcher Rick Rhoden to the Houston Astros for Outfielder John Fishel, Minor

League Righthanded Pitcher Pedro Deleon, and Minor League Lefthanded Pitcher Mike Hook

The turnover in the Yankee mound staff continued as Rick Rhoden became the fourth pitcher from the 1988 club to depart since the close of the season. Ron Guidry had retired after a brilliant 14-year career; they'd released Tommy John, and Neil Allen had left as a free agent. (The Yanks would re-sign John in February.)

Just a few weeks before trading him, new manager Dallas Green had said that Rhoden would be in his starting rotation, joining John Candelaria, newly signed free-agents Andy Hawkins and Dave LaPoint, and a fifth member to be chosen from among Al Leiter, Jimmy Jones, and Richard Dotson.

Now, however, the Yanks had decided that one high-priced veteran pitcher, Rhoden or Dotson, had to go. Rhoden had led the team with 16 wins in 1987, and also in strikeouts, with 107. But he was only 12-12 in 1988, and he was six years older than Dotson. Age was the reason GM Bob Quinn gave when explaining why the Yanks chose to trade Rhoden and keep Dotson.

"We were in a position to trade one of our pitchers, and with Rhoden pitching at age 36 next season, he was the most likely to be traded."

In return for Rhoden, the Yanks were getting three minor leaguers, only one of whom, outfielder John Fishel, had previous big league experience. Fishel had spent most of the 1988 season with Tucson in the Pacific Coast League, where he batted .261 with 18 home runs. He did, however, have six hits in 26 at-bats, with one home run for the Astros in '88, but they would be his only big league at-bats.

Pedro DeLeon was 14-5 for Osceola in 1988, with a Florida State League–leading five shutouts. Promoted to Columbus of the Southern League later in the season, he won two and lost two. Twenty-year-old Mike Hook had gone 7-6 for Asheville of the South Atlantic League in '88.

For 1989, the Yanks assigned Fishel to Columbus of the International League and both Hook and DeLeon to Albany of the Eastern League.

January 26, 1989: Signed Lefthanded Pitcher Chuck Cary as a Free Agent

Chuck Cary had compiled a 2-4 record while pitching for Detroit in 1985-86 and Atlanta in 1987-88. But he'd spent much of the '88 season on the disabled list, and the Braves had released him in December.

After his release Cary went to play winter ball and learned to throw the screwball from former Yankee Luis Arroyo, whereupon the Yanks signed him as a six-year minor league free agent. They did so on the recommendation of personnel chief George Bradley, who'd been Detroit's coordinator of scouting when Cary signed originally with the Tigers.

The 29-year-old Cary began the 1989 season with Columbus of the International League, but was called up in May. Often injured, he compiled an 11-22 mark over the 1989–91 seasons, before the Yanks released him in October 1991.

March 19, 1989: Traded Catcher Joel Skinner and Minor League Outfielder Turner Ward to the Cleveland Indians for Outfielder Mel Hall

The Yanks acquired Mel Hall because the likelihood was growing that Dave Winfield's back problems would prevent him from being ready to play on Opening Day. (They didn't yet know that Winfield would miss the entire 1989 season.)

"Look at his record," said Yankee manager Dallas Green, speaking of Hall. "He's a .280 guy, a 75 RBI guy, and we're looking to strengthen the production we need out of our outfield."

Hall, a onetime Cub who'd been with Cleveland since June 1984, was pleased to be going to New York. "It's definitely a career move for me," he said. "I'm moving right to a front-line contender. I couldn't be a happier man."

Hall was a most consistent hitter. He'd batted .280 each of the last two seasons and had a .281 lifetime batting average in more than 700 big league games. Defensively, he wasn't quite as good. He had a mediocre throwing arm and was at best an average

fielder. Hall had played left field with the Indians, but Green said he planned to shift him to right field, perhaps to platoon him with Gary Ward. Pat Corrales, a Yankee coach and Hall's onetime manager at Cleveland, said of Hall's arm, "It's adequate if he works at it. There may be better arms, but he's fundamentally sound."

Hall was confident that he could play right field, which he had done regularly when he was with the Cubs. "I've played there a bit," he said. "I've been around long enough that I feel like I can make the adjustment. I can play any outfield position adequately."

Hall would play four full seasons in New York, batting .273 with 63 home runs and 265 RBIs in 519 games. In November 1992, he would sign to play with the Lotte Marines of the Japanese Pacific League.

Joel Skinner had batted a disappointing .137 in 1987, and just .227 in 88 games in 1988. The Yanks now had Don Slaught as their number one catcher, and with veteran Jamie Quirk and rookie Bob Geren available if needed, they no longer had any need for Skinner.

Turner Ward had been in the Yankees' minor league system for three seasons. He was at Columbus of the International League in 1988, where he batted .251 with seven home runs and 28 stolen bases.

March 20, 1989: Traded Righthanded Pitcher Steve Shields to the Minnesota Twins for Righthanded Pitcher Balvino Galvez

The Yankees and Twins completed this trade before their spring training game at Fort Lauderdale. The Yanks had signed Steve Shields as a minor league free agent in October 1987. He was with them for most of the 1988 season, winning five and losing five in 39 relief appearances.

In 1986, Balvino Galvez had an 0-1 record in ten games for the Dodgers. He'd been in the minors the past two seasons, and despite his wildness Minnesota had considered him a good prospect.

Shields would pitch in 11 games for Minnesota in 1989, his final season, while Galvez never returned to the majors.

March 23, 1989: Traded Righthanded Pitcher Charles Hudson to the Detroit Tigers for Third Baseman Tom Brookens

With Rafael Santana, the Yanks' regular shortstop, set to undergo elbow surgery, replacing him had become a top priority. Tom Brookens had played some shortstop in his ten years in Detroit, but he'd been primarily a third basemen. His role in New York figured to be as relief for Mike Pagliarulo at third base against certain lefthanders. Meanwhile, the Yanks were continuing discussions with several teams for the purpose of obtaining a full-time shortstop, with Atlanta Braves rookie Jeff Blauser seeming the most likely choice.

Syd Thrift, the Yankees' new senior vice president for baseball operations, said that "having Brookens is a plus factor whether we obtain Blauser or not. It was a necessary move due to the condition of our players." (This trade, the third the Yanks had made this week, was the first under Thrift.)

Brookens had played in 136 games for the Tigers in 1988, batting .243, three points below his lifetime average. He would bat .226 in 66 games for the Yanks in 1989, who then released him at the end of the season.

Charles Hudson got off to a great start with the Yanks in 1987, winning his first six decisions. Yet, he finished that season with an 11-7 record, and had a 6-6 mark in 1988. This exhibition season, Hudson had been consistently unimpressive. In ten innings pitched, he'd given up nine runs and 15 hits, and had an 0-2 record.

With the Yanks still carrying 14 pitchers so close to Opening Day, getting rid of Hudson was not a difficult decision. Nevertheless, Hudson hadn't anticipated the Yanks trading him. "I was surprised. I expected something was going to happen, but I didn't think about it," he said. "I was just hoping it wouldn't happen to me."

March 27, 1989: Traded Minor League Righthanded Pitcher Dana Ridenour to the Seattle Mariners for Designated Hitter Steve Balboni

Aware that Dave Winfield's back surgery would likely keep him out for a minimum of two months, the Yanks found themselves suddenly short of righthanded power. (Winfield would actually miss the entire 1989 season.) Steve Balboni, they hoped, would supply that righthanded power. In the five seasons since he left the Yankees, Balboni had hit 140 home runs. He'd beaten the Mariners in an arbitration dispute this past winter, so Balboni wasn't surprised that they'd traded him, although he hadn't expected to be going back to New York.

Yankee manager Dallas Green announced immediately that Balboni would be his righthanded DH and that he would bat fourth, behind Don Mattingly.

"I'm glad to see him," Green said. "We've been looking at the righthanded hitters we've got, and they weren't going to scare a lot of pitchers. It will make pitchers think twice about pitching around Mattingly."

Balboni would play in 226 games for the Yanks over the 1989 and 1990 seasons, hitting 17 home runs each season and batting a combined .216. The Yanks released him just prior to the opening of the 1991 season.

Dana Ridenour had split 1988 between Albany of the Eastern League, where he was 5-4, and Columbus of the International League, where he was 1-2. He never reached the major leagues.

April 30, 1989: Traded Lefthanded Pitcher Al Leiter to the Toronto Blue Jays for Outfielder Jesse Barfield

Toronto GM Pat Gillick hadn't made a trade in 20 months, or since he'd gotten veteran lefthander Mike Flanagan from Baltimore on August 31, 1987. However, unlike Flanagan, the lefthander he was getting in this deal was no veteran; instead, he was one of the most promising young pitchers in the Yankee organization. Al Leiter, now 23, had pitched parts of the 1987 and 1988 seasons for the Yanks, winning six and losing six. Leiter was off to a 1-2 start this season, and the Yanks hated losing him, but with Dave Winfield out indefinitely, they dearly needed a righthanded power hitter.

Dave Righetti was a close friend of Leiter's, yet he agreed that it was a worthwhile trade. "Our needs are desperate," Righetti said.

It would certainly prove to be worthwhile for the Yanks in 1989. Leiter, who'd spent five weeks on the disabled list in 1988, went on it again shortly after joining the Blue Jays. He would appear in only one game for them the entire year.

Jesse Barfield, who broke in with Toronto in 1981, had peaked in 1986 when his 40 home runs led the American League. Barfield also had 108 RBIs that year, with a .289 batting average. He hadn't approached those numbers since, and currently was batting .200, although he'd already hit five home runs in the season's first month. That gave the 29-year-old Barfield a lifetime total of 179 home runs, and he would hit 62 more for the Yankees over the next four years.

Among the best-throwing outfielders ever, Barfield would be the Yanks regular right fielder in 1989 and 1990. Injured for much of 1991 and 1992, he signed to play in Japan following the '92 season.

June 21, 1989: Traded Outfielder Rickey Henderson to the Oakland Athletics for Lefthanded Pitcher Greg Cadaret, Righthanded Pitcher Eric Plunk, and Outfielder Luis Polonia

Though Rickey Henderson was only 30 years old, many in the Yankee organization felt his abilities were starting to decline. So when Henderson, who was eligible for free agency after this season, asked for a three-year contract, the Yanks decided to move him. When the A's specifically asked for Henderson, and offered much-needed pitching help in return, the Yanks gladly made the trade.

Actually, a week earlier the Yanks had worked out a deal to trade Henderson to San Francisco, but Henderson had the right to approve the trade and vetoed it. However, he was quite willing to go across the bay to Oakland, the city where he'd begun his big league career.

Despite the feeling in the Yankee organization, Henderson had given no indication that he was going downhill. In his four-plus seasons in New York, he batted .288, with 513 runs scored, 406 walks, and 326 stolen bases. His best season as a Yankee came in 1985, his first year with the club. He batted .314, scored a league-leading 146 runs, and broke the club record with 80 stolen bases. He then broke that record with 87 stolen bases in 1986 and 93 in 1988. If Henderson had started slowly this season, he was batting just .247, it was likely due to the distraction caused by the contract negotiations.

"I felt it was time," Henderson said upon hearing of the trade. "There were rumors that I'd be traded and then they came to me and asked if I would take a trade. Oakland was the only place I knew I'd like to go." Yet, Henderson wasn't departing without some regrets. "I'm in between," he said. "I'm a little sad because I'm leaving New York, but I'm happy to be going back home. Oakland is a great organization."

Yankee manager Dallas Green said he was surprised that the Athletics wanted Henderson. "Not because he's not a great player," Green said, "but because of his high contract and the fact he hadn't gotten untracked this year." Some of Henderson's teammates also expressed surprise at his departure, also disappointment.

"It's tough losing Rickey," remarked first baseman Don Mattingly. "It kind of makes you remember that anyone can go, but I guess I knew that anyway."

"I'm very disappointed," added outfielder Jesse Barfield. "Not only because we're friends, but because I think he's an outstanding player and a catalyst to the ballclub."

While Syd Thrift, the Yanks' senior vice president, would have preferred a starting pitcher in return for Henderson, the A's would not agree to part with one. However, Thrift did point out that both righthander Eric Plunk and lefty Greg Cadaret had occasionally started games in the past and could become starters again.

Plunk was a minor leaguer when the Yanks included him in the December 1984 trade that first brought Henderson to New York. He had an overall 16-16 mark with the A's, including a 1-1 record and one save in 23 games this season. Plunk would pitch in 117 games for the Yanks, winning 15 and losing 13, before they released him (in retrospect, prematurely) following the 1991 season.

Cadaret had gone a combined 11-4 in his first two big league seasons, with no record and a 2.28 ERA in 26 games in 1989.

Luis Polonia, a 24-year-old singles hitter, batted .287 as a rookie in 1987 and .292 the next year. He was at .286 this season and had stolen 13 bases to give him a career total of 66.

July 10, 1989: Traded Righthanded Pitcher Scott Nielsen to the New York Mets for Minor League Outfielder Marcus Lawton

Most of Scott Nielsen's second stay with the Yankees was spent pitching for Columbus in the International League. He was 13-7 for the Clippers in 1988 and 4-8 this season. In seven 1988 games with the Yankees, he had a win and two losses, and this season had a relief win against Boston in June. That win would be Nielsen's final big league decision. The Mets sent him back to the International League, to Tidewater, and he never returned to the majors.

Marcus Lawton was a 23-year-old speedster who had stolen 319 bases in his minor league career. He was at Tidewater this season, batting .240 with eight stolen bases. The Yanks sent him to Columbus, but called him up later in the season. Lawton went 3-for-14 in ten games, which would be the sum of his big league career.

July 20, 1989: Traded Outfielder Stan Jefferson to the Baltimore Orioles for Righthanded Pitcher John Habyan

Stan Jefferson became a Yankee as part of the October 1988 deal that brought pitchers Jimmy Jones and Lance McCullers to New York. After he'd gotten just one hit in 12 at-bats this season, the Yanks sent him down to Columbus. The Orioles kept Jefferson in the International League, assigning him to Rochester, but would bring him to Baltimore later in the season.

John Habyan had a 9-10 record in parts of four seasons (1985–88) with the Orioles, both as a starter and a reliever. After being on the disabled list for much of this spring, he was currently 1-2 with a 2.17 earned run average for Rochester. Habyan exchanged places with Jefferson, going from the Red Wings to the Clippers.

July 22, 1989: Traded Third Baseman Mike Pagliarulo and Righthanded Pitcher Don Schulze to the San Diego Padres for Righthanded Pitcher Walt Terrell and a Player to Be Named

The fact that Mike Pagliarulo was a popular player with both his teammates and the fans wasn't enough for deal-maker Syd Thrift to overlook the 29-year-old third baseman's two-year-long slump. After hitting 28 and 32 home runs in 1986 and 1987, Pagliarulo had only 15 in 1988 and just four so far in 1989. Currently in a 2 for 23 slump, his average had fallen to .197, convincing the Yanks he was just another player who'd failed to live up to his potential.

Nevertheless, both pitcher Dave Righetti, the senior Yankee in point of service, and first baseman Don Mattingly, who was Pagliarulo's closest friend on the club, expressed their concern about the many changes the roster had undergone this season.

"He's just another friend who's gone again," said Righetti. "It seems like he didn't fit in their plans from the beginning. They were taking him out of games in spring training for defense and that hurt his pride. They trade the guys who want to be here, and the guys who moan about it, they keep," Righetti added.

"It bothers me because I'm a friend of Mike's and I like the way he played, but I'm hoping it works out for him," Mattingly said. "It's hard to build anything when you keep changing. We need some type of foundation, a base." (Walt Terrell would be the 15th man on the Yankee team this season who had not been with them a year ago.)

Both Thrift and manager Dallas Green had kind words for the departing Pagliarulo. "He was dedicated to hard work in the five and a half years of service he put in with the Yankees," Thrift said. "But we're pleased to acquire a proven veteran pitcher who is capable of giving us 200 innings a season."

Green added that "as much as we loved Pags for his work habits, team spirit and dedication, we just felt he was becoming stagnant here. I think the last two weeks he had become … near a basket case."

With Pagliarulo gone, the Yanks planned to use veteran Tom Brookens at third base for the remainder of the season.

Of Terrell, his new pitcher, Green said: "He's a bulldog. He can give us a lot of innings. If he pitches the way he has the last few years, it should help our rotation and get our bullpen back to where it was."

This was the third time in his career that the 31-year-old Terrell had been traded for a third basemen. The Mets, his first team, traded him to Detroit in 1985 for Howard Johnson, and the Tigers traded him to San Diego following the 1988 season for Chris Brown.

After double-figure win seasons between 1984 and 1987, Terrell was 7-16 for Detroit in 1988 and 5-13 for San Diego this season. Still, the Yanks were in the midst of a five-game losing streak and in great need of pitching help. They'd already used 14 different starters this season, including Greg Cadaret, who Green now intended to return to the bullpen.

Terrell made 13 starts for the Yanks in the second half of '89. He won six and lost five, and then signed as a free agent to pitch for Pittsburgh in 1980.

Don Schulze was currently with Columbus of the International League, where he'd won eight and lost four, but earlier in the season even he had made a couple of starts for the Yanks, winning one and losing one.

On September 27, the Yanks received righthander Fred Toliver as the player to be named. Toliver was, of course, the same man they'd sent to the Cincinnati Reds as the player to be named when they acquired Ken Griffey in 1981. The Yanks would release Toliver on April 2, 1990, without his ever pitching a game for them.

August 10, 1989: Claimed Righthanded Pitcher Goose Gossage on Waivers from the San Francisco Giants

With 306 career saves, Goose Gossage was second on the all-time list, trailing only Rollie Fingers who had 341. But at 38, he was no longer the intimidating pitcher he'd been in his first tour with the Yankees. Earlier in the week manager Dallas Green had questioned whether he could really help the club. "The Giants let him go and they're in a pennant race; that doesn't speak well for him," Green said.

Gossage had left the Yankees to sign with San Diego in January 1984 and spent the next four years with the Padres. He won 25 and lost 20 with 83 saves, before San Diego traded him to the Cubs in 1988. He went 4-4 with 13 saves for Chicago, but they released him just prior to the 1989 season. Signed by the Giants, he'd been in 31 games this year, with two wins, a loss, and four saves.

Jerry Kapstein, Gossage's agent, quickly dismissed the suggestion that there might be repercussions from his client's less than amicable 1984 departure from New York; Gossage had not left under friendly terms with owner George Steinbrenner. "The past is history," Kapstein said. "It's all water over the dam. Goose is very happy to be coming back to the Yankees."

Gossage would pitch in 11 games for the '89 Yanks. He got a win and a save, but the Yanks didn't re-sign him. Although he continued to pitch for four more years, he accumulated only three more saves to end his career with a total of 310.

August 29, 1989: Traded Lefthanded Pitcher John Candelaria to the Montreal Expos for a Player to Be Named

The Yankees were a team in turmoil. On their way to a fifth place finish, they had recently replaced manager Dallas Green with Bucky Dent, and the John Candelaria trade would be the last engineered by Syd Thrift. The Yankees' senior vice president for baseball operations had resigned after just five months as the club's chief trader, with that duty reverting back to general manager Bob Quinn.

The 35-year-old Candelaria had been the Yanks' best pitcher in 1988, compiling a 13-7 won-lost mark and a 3.38 earned run average. He did so despite an injury to his right knee that limited him to just 25 starts. But Candelaria was just 3-3 this season; moreover, he had undergone arthroscopic knee surgery that put him on the disabled list earlier this month. After a two-game rehabilitation assignment with Sarasota of the Gulf Coast League, he'd pitched 8.2 innings for the Yankees, allowing eight runs and 11 hits.

Two days later, on August 31, the Yanks received 24-year-old third baseman Mike

Blowers as the player to be named. Blowers was with Indianapolis of the American Association, where he'd batted .267 with 14 home runs. The Yanks brought him up immediately and he made his major league debut the next day.

August 30, 1989: Traded Designated Hitter Ken Phelps to the Oakland Athletics for Minor League Lefthanded Pitcher Scott Holcomb

With the Yankees now out of the race, they were in the process of "dumping" their high-priced older players for minor leaguers. The day before it had been John Candelaria, and today it was Ken Phelps. Since coming to New York in July 1988 (in what would become an infamous trade for Jay Buhner), Phelps had appeared in 131 games, batting .240 with 17 home runs. He was at .249 this season, but was the team leader in pinch hits, with ten.

The 35-year-old Phelps, unhappy at the way he was being used, welcomed the trade. He was especially pleased that it was to the Western Division–leading Athletics.

"I'm still kind of stunned," he said. "I've been hearing rumors since May and now it finally came true. It's an opportunity to finally play in a World Series."

The Yankees assigned Scott Holcomb, who had an 0-3 record with Tacoma of the Pacific Coast League, to Columbus of the International League.

November 21, 1989: Signed Free-Agent Righthanded Pitcher Pascual Perez from the Montreal Expos

The Yankees were willing to take a chance on Pascual Perez because they were short of starting pitchers for 1990. Despite his ongoing battle with cocaine and alcohol addictions, the 32-year-old Perez had been a first-rate pitcher at times. Always flamboyant, and often controversial, he'd put together 15-8 and 14-8 seasons with the Atlanta Braves in 1983-84, but followed with a 1-13 mark in 1985. After being out of baseball in 1986, Perez had spent the last three seasons with the Expos, winning 28 and losing 21.

According to George Bradley, the Yankees' vice president of player personnel, the club had no illusions about Perez. "We are very aware of his past problems," Bradley said. "However he has been involved in a program with the Expos that has kept him clean and we will help him remain with that program."

Expos GM Dave Dombrowski wasn't so sure. "I hope the Yankees take good care of him," he said. "He's a very fragile individual. He has a problem." Dombrowski thought Perez would have been better off remaining with the Expos. "I understand this is a big business. But for the good of the individual, I thought he'd stay with Montreal. I don't know how well he'd react to booing in New York."

Perez would win a total of just three games and lose six in 1990 and 1991, his two seasons with the Yankees. An injured shoulder kept him on the disabled list for large portions of both seasons and ended his career.

December 4, 1989: Traded Catcher Don Slaught to the Pittsburgh Pirates for Righthanded Pitcher Jeff Robinson and Minor League Righthanded Pitcher Willie Smith

While Jeff Robinson was a solid middle-reliever, and Willie Smith a highly-rated prospect, neither was the quality starting pitcher the Yanks were seeking. Nor, for that matter, was Pascual Perez, whom they'd signed a few weeks earlier. George Bradley, the team's director of player personnel, left no doubt that the search continued. "We're definitely looking for another excellent starting pitcher," he said.

Robinson had gone 7-13 for Pittsburgh in 1989, and 19 of his 50 games were as a starter. But aside from 1984, his rookie year with the Giants, he'd been primarily a reliever. In 312 games Robinson had a 39-45 mark with 35 saves. He would spend one season in New York, winning three and losing six, and then sign with the California Angels.

The 22-year-old Smith was a hard-throwing reliever who'd been compared to Red Sox relief ace Lee Smith. He'd split the 1989 season between Class A Salem of the Carolina League and Class AA Harrisburg of the

Eastern League. Along with a combined 7-5 record, Smith struck out 79 batters in 82 innings. The Yankees would release Smith after a couple of years in their farm system, but he would eventually reach the majors with the 1994 St. Louis Cardinals.

Don Slaught batted .266 in two seasons with the Yankees, serving as the number one catcher for most of that time. He'd spent part of 1988 on the disabled list with a groin injury, and the club considered him expendable after rookie Bob Geren took over the number one slot in mid–1989.

December 12, 1989: Traded First Baseman Hal Morris and Minor League Righthanded Pitcher Rodney Imes to the Cincinnati Reds for Righthanded Pitcher Tim Leary and Outfielder Van Snider

In trading for Tim Leary, who had a 45-56 career record, the Yanks were hoping they'd found the additional starting pitcher they'd been seeking, one that would allow them to

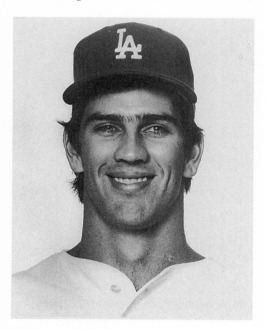

December 12, 1989: *Tim Leary.* Leary recognized that it was tougher to pitch in New York than in Los Angeles.

keep Dave Righetti in the bullpen rather than returning him to the rotation. Leary first reached the majors with the Mets in 1981 and, along with the Reds, had also pitched for the Milwaukee Brewers and Los Angeles Dodgers. He was a 17-game winner with the Dodgers in 1988, and the Yanks were hoping he'd be that kind of pitcher for them. He hadn't been in 1989, which led the Dodgers to trade him to Cincinnati in mid–July. The victim of poor offensive support in many of his starts, Leary finished the season with a combined 8-14 mark, but did have a respectable 3.52 earned run average.

Despite Leary's reputation for being sensitive, the former Met assured everyone that he had no problems about pitching in New York again. "I like New York, but I know the fans can really get on you and boo," he said. "It's a tougher town than Los Angeles. But I'm not that fragile."

Overall, Leary seemed delighted at the trade. "I'm pretty happy. I mean I'm excited," he said. "The Yankees have a good lineup and a good ball park to pitch in, and they can score runs. Most of all, they told me they need starting pitching."

The two youngsters the Yanks were losing had both had outstanding seasons in 1989. Hal Morris won the International League batting championship with a .326 mark for Columbus, while Rodney Imes was the Eastern League's Pitcher of the Year after compiling a 17-6 record at Albany. Morris had played in 38 games (with a .184 batting average) for the Yanks during the '88 and '89 seasons, but Imes never had reached the majors, or ever would.

While Van Snider had put together some good minor league seasons for the Royals and Reds, he'd batted only .222 for Nashville of the American Association in 1989. He had very limited big league experience, going 7 for 35 in 19 games for the Reds in 1988 and 1989. They would be the only big league games he would play.

December 21, 1989: Signed Catcher Rick Cerone as a Free Agent

Having traded catcher Don Slaught to Pittsburgh earlier in the month, the Yanks added Rick Cerone to play behind first-stringer

Bob Geren. For the 34-year-old Cerone, it would be his third tour of duty in New York; his second ended when the Yankees released him the day before the 1988 opener. He went to Boston, where he batted .269 and .243 the past two seasons, but the Red Sox declined to offer him a contract for 1990.

Cerone batted .302 for the 1990 Yankees; however, a knee injury limited him to just 49 games and after the season the club released him once again.

X. The Nineties

April 28, 1990: Traded Outfielder Luis Polonia to the California Angels for Outfielder Claudell Washington and Righthanded Pitcher Rich Monteleone

At 25, Luis Polonia was ten years younger than Claudell Washington, but he lacked the power the older man could provide. Polonia had batted .313 in 66 games for the Yanks in 1989 after coming in the June deal that sent Rickey Henderson back to Oakland. In 11 games this season, Polonia, who not only lacked power but was also a poor outfielder, had seven singles in 22 at-bats.

"Claudell does more for us," said George Bradley, the Yanks' vice president for player personnel. "He gives us power and defense. The only thing Luis does better is run."

Don Mattingly agreed. "Physically, the things he does will help us," said the Yankee first baseman. "He's an excellent outfielder; he runs well; he has pop in his bat, and he's a positive influence in the clubhouse. He's a good guy to have around."

Polonia was going to a team that planned to use him as their lead-off hitter and to play him every day. He said that while he was happy to be going someplace where he would get more playing time, he was sorry to be leaving New York.

"I'm just hoping I can come back here one day," Polonia said. "I love this city. I love the Yankees." However, he'd been convicted in an incident involving a 15-year-old girl in August 1989, and it was probably in his best interests to leave New York.

Washington, who was doing what Polonia wished to do—return to the Yankees—also expressed his joy about coming back to New York. "I like the Big Apple," he said. "I have a lot of fond memories here." He'd left to sign as a free agent with California following the 1988 season, but his first choice had been to stay with the Yankees. Washington batted .273 with 13 home runs for the Angels in 1989 but had only six hits in 34 at-bats this season.

Washington reminisced about his first stay in New York. "We had a lot of fun there. I learned a lot from Donnie [Mattingly]. Hopefully, he can help me get out of the slump I'm in." But Washington never did get out of that slump. He injured a finger and batted just .162 while playing his final 33 major league games. In his two stays with the Yankees, Washington batted a combined .277 in 315 games.

As a rookie, Rich Monteleone was 2-2 in 24 games for the Angels in 1989. He was currently with Edmonton of the Pacific Coast League, but the Yanks assigned him to the Columbus Clippers of the International League.

May 11, 1990: Traded Outfielder Dave Winfield to the California Angels for Righthanded Pitcher Mike Witt

Despite his stellar record with the Yankees, Dave Winfield had never been a favorite of owner George Steinbrenner. In just the last three years, the Yanks had talked about trading Winfield to Detroit for Kirk Gibson, to Toronto for George Bell, to Houston for Kevin Bass, and to Minnesota for several minor league prospects. But Winfield, who was now 38, had ten years of major league service and five years as a Yankee, which gave him the right to approve any trade. As he had with the other proposed deals, he balked at this one too when he heard of it.

"They say they've traded me, but I'm not going anywhere. I'm not packing for California. But I can't put on a Yankee uniform either. I'm in limbo," Winfield said. "My refusal to report to the Angels has nothing to do with them. They're nice people. But," he later added, "I'll say when, where, and how I go."

Mike Port, the Angels' general manager, was philosophical about Winfield's refusal to report: "This being the country it is, you can't make a player play," Port reasoned.

Meanwhile, Yankee GM Harding Peterson felt the trade was a done deal. "Mike Witt will join the Yankees, whether or not Dave Winfield reports to the Angels," Peterson said. "With this announcement Winfield is off our 40-man roster and off our active roster."

Winfield had missed all of the 1989 season while recovering from back surgery, and he'd gotten off to a slow start in 1990. He had a .213 average with just two home runs, and with the recent acquisition of Claudell Washington, manager Bucky Dent had reduced his playing time. But while some acrimony accompanied Winfield's departure, it couldn't detract from his excellent Yankee career. Since joining the team in 1981, he had a .290 batting average, 205 home runs, and 818 runs batted in. In six of his eight full seasons as a Yankee, Winfield hit at least 24 home runs, with a high of 37 in 1982, and in 1984, he batted a career-high .340 to finish second to teammate Don Mattingly in the batting race.

Mike Witt was in his tenth big league season, all with California, and had a career record of 109-107. A former mainstay of the Angels' rotation, he'd fallen out of favor with manager Doug Rader, who'd used him only in relief this season. Witt had been in ten games, but despite a 1.77 earned run average had an 0-3 record.

That Witt was now a Yankee was a surprise to those who'd heard Steinbrenner talk about him during spring training. Steinbrenner had claimed that Witt did not have the personality to be a successful pitcher in New York. Witt, he said, "would never be a member of the New York Yankees as long as I own the team." Steinbrenner still owned the team, but had obviously changed his mind.

Witt would have a very frustrating career

with the Yankees. He was 5-6 in 1990, but over the next three seasons suffered injuries to both his shoulder and his elbow. He was 0-1 in 1991, missed all of 1992, and was 3-2 in 1993, his final big league season.

After Winfield and Steinbrenner finished exchanging charges, a deal was finally worked out on May 16. Winfield received additional money from both the Yankees and the Angels and agreed to report.

June 4, 1990: Traded Righthanded Pitchers Lance McCullers and Clay Parker to the Detroit Tigers for Catcher Matt Nokes

The Yanks already had two catchers, so bringing in the lefthanded hitting Matt Nokes led to speculation that either Bob Geren or Rick Cerone would be traded. When manager Bucky Dent said that Nokes would platoon with Cerone, rumors began that the Yanks would deal Geren to the Mets for pitcher Ron Darling. "I'm not saying that Geren won't get an opportunity to catch," said Dent. "But Cerone has been swinging the bat well and Nokes gives us another lefthanded bat, which we needed."

As for a Geren-Darling trade, Yankee general manager Harding Peterson said he was never through dealing. "We still need some more offense," Peterson said. "But if we're talking to somebody and pitching comes up, we'll look in that direction."

The Yankees acquired the 26-year-old Nokes specifically to improve on their dismal 10-21 record against righthanded pitching. Nokes had hit 32 home runs for Detroit in 1987, but only half that amount in 1988, and just nine in 1989, when he was on the disabled list for nearly two months. He had only three this season, and the Tigers were very willing to trade him.

Dent, on the other hand, was glad to have Nokes in New York, both as a catcher and as a pinch hitter. "Right now, Claudell Washington is the only lefthanded batter on the bench," Dent said. "I usually have to pick my spots to use him. With Nokes, I have a chance to do something early."

Nokes would regain his home run stroke

with the Yankees, hitting 24 in 1991 and 22 in 1992. He was the Yanks' number one catcher in both seasons, but lost that job to Mike Stanley in 1993. Nokes spent two months on the disabled list in 1994, and after the season signed as a free agent with Baltimore.

In 1989, Lance McCullers first season in New York, he was 4-3 with a 4.57 ERA in 52 games. He'd had a brief stay on the disabled list earlier this season, but had come back to make 11 relief appearances and win his only decision.

McCullers wasn't surprised to learn the Yanks had traded him. "I heard about being traded ever since spring training," he said. "When Bucky came in last year [to replace Dallas Green as manager] I felt I did a good job for him. But then the rumors started. Whether Bucky didn't like the way I pitched, I don't know. I enjoyed being here, but maybe this is a chance to pitch regularly."

But although McCullers was only 26, his career was about over. After winning a game for the Tigers, he went back on the disabled list in July and missed the rest of the season. Out of organized baseball in 1991, McCullers pitched his final five games for Texas in 1992.

Injuries had also been Clay Parker's problem. He was on the disabled list three times in 1988 and once in 1989. Parker did make 17 starts for the Yanks in '89, with a 4-5 record, and he was 1-1 in five games this season. Like McCullers, he too would pitch his final games in 1992.

November 26, 1990: Signed Free-Agent Righthanded Pitcher Steve Farr from the Kansas City Royals

The Royals wanted to re-sign Steve Farr and the Cubs and Twins had also made offers, but in Farr's words all "were millions away" from what the Yanks offered. "It was a good solid offer," Gene Michael, the general manager of the Yankees, said. "We didn't negotiate on it."

Michael explained that the Yanks wanted Farr, who would turn 34 in December, as bullpen insurance in case they couldn't re-sign free-agent Dave Righetti. "We don't know if we can sign Righetti," he said. "I don't know if we're in danger of losing him. I can't tell."

After a rookie season with Cleveland, Farr had been with Kansas City since 1985. He had a 37-35 record and a total of 50 saves for his seven major league seasons. But after saving 20 in 1988 and 18 in 1989, he had only one in 1990. On the positive side, Farr had an outstanding 1.98 earned run average in '90, and his 13 wins were by far a career high.

The Yanks did lose Righetti. He signed with the San Francisco Giants, and Farr took over as the Yankee closer for the next three seasons. Although Farr had only a 9-9 won-lost record over that span, he led the team in saves in each season with 23, 30, and 25. Farr was a free agent after the '93 season and signed with the Cleveland Indians.

December 3, 1990: Traded Outfielder Oscar Azocar to the San Diego Padres for a Player to Be Named

General manager Gene Michael had designated outfielder Oscar Azocar for assignment after the previous week's addition of free-agent pitcher Steve Farr put the Yankees one over the 40-player limit. The 25-year-old Azocar was batting .291 for the International League Columbus Clippers when the Yanks called him up in July 1990. He batted .248 with five home runs, but drew just two walks in 214 at-bats.

On February 7, 1991, the Yanks received Mike Humphreys, an outfielder, as the player to be named. Humphreys batted .276 for Wichita in 1990 and led the Texas League in runs scored with 92. He finished the '90 season playing 12 games for Las Vegas in the Pacific Coast League and would now spend the next three seasons at Columbus. In each of those seasons Humphreys would play a few games for the Yankees, getting a total of 15 hits in 85 at-bats. In November 1994, he signed with the Cleveland Indians, but never played another major league game.

December 31, 1990: Purchased Righthanded Pitcher Scott Sanderson from the Oakland Athletics

In 13 big league seasons, six with the Montreal Expos, six with the Chicago Cubs, and one with Oakland, Scott Sanderson had won 115 games, lost 100, and had a 3.57 earned run average. He had a 17-11 record for the American League champion Athletics in 1990, but had engaged in a bitter salary dispute with management before signing his 1991 contract. Because he'd re-signed with Oakland, the A's had to get Sanderson's permission to trade him.

Actually, the 34-year-old Sanderson would have preferred to stay in Oakland. "I had a very positive experience there last year," he said. "It was a lot of fun playing for a winning team and I enjoyed it very much. I would have liked it better if the Athletics had said we want you," he added. "But the Yankees said we want you, and now I'm with them."

Dick Moss, Sanderson's agent, blamed A's GM Sandy Alderson for his client's departure. "Sandy Alderson has this theory that the team's so good anybody can come in and win 17 games, and do it for much less," Moss said. "We'll find out if he's right or wrong."

After winning three consecutive pennants, Oakland would drop to fourth in the AL West in 1991, while Sanderson would become the staff ace for the fifth-place Yankees. He won 16 games, double the amount of the team's next highest winner, Greg Cadaret. Then, after winning 12 games in 1992, second on the club in wins to Melido Perez's 13, Sanderson signed to pitch for the California Angels in 1993.

January 24, 1991: Signed Outfielder Pat Sheridan as a Free Agent

Before his midseason trade to San Francisco in 1989, Pat Sheridan had been an American Leaguer for eight seasons, split evenly between Kansas City and Detroit. After the Giants released him at the end of the '89 season, he signed with the Cubs' Iowa team in the American Association, but left after 23 games saying he wasn't getting enough playing time. Sheridan appealed to the Yankees because he was a lefthanded hitter, a commodity the Yanks were always seeking, even though he'd hit only 47 home runs in 814 major league games.

As a Yankee, Sheridan batted .204 with four home runs in 62 games in 1991, but failed to make the team in 1992, ending his career.

February 21, 1991: Signed Lefthanded Pitcher Steve Howe as a Free Agent

The departure of Dave Righetti, who'd signed as a free agent with the San Francisco Giants, left the Yanks unsure of their bullpen stopper for 1991. They'd signed righthander Steve Farr and still had lefthander Lee Guetterman; nevertheless, they chose to give Steve Howe another chance to right his career and his life.

Between 1980, when he was the National League's Rookie of the Year, and 1983, Howe accumulated 56 saves for the Los Angeles Dodgers. Then drugs took over his life. Since 1983, he'd pitched briefly for Minnesota and Texas, but had been suspended six times for substance abuse and had been out of the major leagues the past three seasons.

"He's getting a chance because he's good," said Yankee GM Gene Michael. "There's always a need for more lefthanded pitching."

Although the 33-year-old Howe said he was no longer addicted to drugs, he would still have to undergo periodic tests to prove he was truly drug-free. Michael was confident that Howe would pass those tests.

"He's been clean for two years. I asked a

February 21, 1991: *Steve Howe.* "There's always a need for more lefthanded pitching."

lot of people a lot of questions about him, his makeup, the type of person he is. I feel there's been a lot worse things done in baseball than bringing Steve Howe back. If it was my son or your son, you'd want to give him another chance."

Despite a seventh suspension for drug abuse in 1992, Howe remained a Yankee until they released him in June 1996. He appeared in 229 games, winning 18 and losing 10, with 31 saves.

March 19, 1991: Traded Lefthanded Pitcher Mark Leiter to the Detroit Tigers for Infielder Tory Lovullo

Switch-hitting Tory Lovullo had played briefly for the Tigers in 1988 and 1989, appearing in 41 games, with a .167 average. He'd then spent the entire 1990 season with the Toledo Mud Hens, batting .270 and leading the International League with 38 doubles. Lovullo, who could play several infield positions, had been playing third for Detroit during the exhibition season, which is where the Yankees intended to use him, possibly to platoon with Mike Blowers and Randy Velarde.

"There aren't many good lefty-hitting third basemen available," said Gene Michael, the Yankees GM. "We aren't going to stop looking, but we think Lovullo can help us. Our reports on him are good."

Lovullo, however, would spend most of the season with Columbus back in the International League. He played in only 22 games at third base for New York, batted .176, and after the season signed as a free agent with the California Angels.

Mark Leiter was the younger brother of Al Leiter, another young pitcher the Yanks had traded away. Mark had been the property of the Baltimore Orioles before having shoulder surgery that caused him to miss three seasons (1986–88). After Baltimore released him, the Yanks signed him and Leiter made his big league debut in 1990, pitching in eight games and splitting two decisions.

April 5, 1991: Claimed Outfielder Scott Lusader on Waivers from the Detroit Tigers

After finishing with a league-low .241 batting average in 1990, the Yanks were looking to add at least one proven hitter. They had hoped to get one of Pittsburgh's two sluggers, either Barry Bonds or Bobby Bonilla, but that now seemed highly unlikely. Scott Lusader was, of course, nowhere near the level of a Bonds or a Bonilla, still, the Yanks were expecting him to compete for their fifth outfield spot. They'd already told Pat Sheridan, who had hoped to fill that role, to report to Columbus in the International League or find another team.

Lusader had been with Detroit since 1987, but had never spent a full season with them. His four year Tiger totals were 124 games played and a .249 batting average. As he had with Detroit, Lusader would split the 1991 season between the minors and the majors. He batted .282 in 76 games at Columbus and was 1 for 7 in 11 games for the Yankees. They were his final major league games.

May 17, 1991: Traded Third Baseman Mike Blowers to the Seattle Mariners for Cash and a Player to Be Named

Just before Seattle's Randy Johnson and Bill Swift combined to shut them out, 1-0, the Yanks traded Mike Blowers to the Mariners who immediately shipped him to Calgary of the Pacific Coast League. Blowers was batting .200 with one home run in 15 games, bringing his three year totals as a Yankee to .203 and six home runs in 76 games.

To replace Blowers, the Yanks called up third baseman Tory Lovullo from the International League Columbus Clippers. They also recalled righthander Alan Mills from Columbus and sent utility player Jim Leyritz to the Clippers.

On June 22, Seattle sent the Yanks righthander Jim Blueberg, who was 3-5 with Jacksonville of the Southern League, as the player to be named. The Yanks kept Blueberg at the Class AA level, sending him to Albany of the Eastern League.

June 26, 1991: Traded Lefthanded Pitcher Steve Adkins to the Chicago Cubs for Minor League Lefthanded Pitcher David Rosario

Steve Adkins was a member of the 1989 Albany/Colonie Yankees team that won the Eastern League pennant by 19 games. Adkins was a major contributor, with a 12-1 record and a league-leading 2.07 earned run average. Promoted to the International League in 1990, he was 15-7 at Columbus, earning himself a promotion to New York.

Adkins went 1-2 in five games with the Yankees in late 1990; however, he was back in Columbus this season, where he had a 4-5 record with 57 batters walked in 80.1 innings. Wildness had always been a problem for the 26-year-old Adkins. Even the fine year he had with the Clippers in '90 was marred by his league-leading 98 walks.

David Rosario, a relief pitcher, was 3-1 with one save for Iowa of the American Association in 1991. He and Adkins switched teams: Rosario went to Columbus and Adkins went to Iowa, but neither ever advanced any higher.

January 6, 1992: Signed Free-Agent Outfielder Danny Tartabull from the Kansas City Royals

The Yanks hadn't made any moves this off-season, until now. Daniel McCarthy, named the club's interim managing general partner a week earlier, had given GM Gene Michael the go-ahead to sign Danny Tartabull, the American League's slugging leader in 1991. McCarthy was replacing George Steinbrenner, who had been banished from that role a year and a half earlier, though hardly anyone believed Steinbrenner had not had a say in this signing.

Tartabull had just completed a terrific 1991 season. Besides leading the league with a .593 slugging average, he had a .316 batting average, 31 home runs, and 100 runs batted in. In his career, first with Seattle and then with Kansas City, the 29-year-old Tartabull had a .287 batting average and 152 home runs. And because he'd always hit particularly well at Yankee Stadium (a .312 average), the Yanks

were counting on him to be the best all-around hitter in their 1992 lineup.

No one questioned Tartabull's ability; there were, however, whispers around the league concerning his attitude. Some thought Tartabull was more interested in his personal success than that of his team, while others questioned his reputation for not playing with the "little hurts" that all players sustain over a season.

"The best way to respond to that," Tartabull said, "is that anyone who says they have a problem with my attitude doesn't know Danny Tartabull."

Yet, in speaking of his new club, Tartabull, seemed to confirm his image as a glory-seeker. "I want to bring something back that hasn't been there in a while. I want to bring a championship back to New York. I want to be a leader and keep everything loose."

Despite Tartabull's "reputation," his new manager, Buck Showalter, seemed pleased to have him on his side. "You know you always had to be careful when Tartabull was up," Showalter said. "You felt lucky when you got him out."

The addition of Tartabull gave the Yankees a surplus of outfielders and led to speculation that Jesse Barfield would be the most likely to go. However, Barfield remained with the Yanks in '92, although he was injured and played in only 30 games. After the season, he signed to play in Japan.

January 7, 1992: Signed Free-Agent Infielder Mike Gallego from the Oakland Athletics

After the previous day's signing of free-agent outfielder Danny Tartabull, the Yanks still had two major weaknesses: starting pitching and an everyday third baseman. Mike Gallego would not be the answer at either of those problem areas, but he was a good man to have on a ballclub. He was a fine second baseman and shortstop, who in a pinch could fill in at third. A member of the Athletics since 1985, Gallego was only a .232 lifetime batter, but 1991 had been his finest season as he reached career highs in home runs, with 12 (one more than he had in his first six seasons), and runs batted in, with 49.

"We know Mike can solve problems for us in the infield," said general manager Gene Michael, who back when he was a Yankee player had filled the same utility role that Gallego was expected to have in 1992.

"Gene couldn't guarantee me a starting position at second, short, or third," Gallego said, "but he could guarantee that I'll be playing. That's all I need."

Gallego cited the Tartabull signing as having influenced his decision to sign with the Yanks. "What it did for me," he said, "is to prove the Yankees are looking to be a winning team." Another factor may have been the money he would be receiving. For a player of Gallego's limited abilities, he'd signed a very rewarding contract.

After missing much of the 1992 season on the disabled list, Gallego played a lot at shortstop in 1993 and 1994, batting a combined .262 in 261 games. He was a free agent in 1995 and signed to play again with Oakland.

January 8, 1992: Traded Righthanded Pitcher Darrin Chapin to the Philadelphia Phillies for a Player to Be Named

Eight different men had played third base for the Yankees in 1991. The eight batted a combined .225, had just 38 runs batted in, and committed 37 errors. Because third base had been such a problem for the Yanks, everyone assumed the player to be named in this trade would be Charlie Hayes, a third baseman. They were right, although the Yanks couldn't announce it until they'd made room on the 40-man roster. Hayes didn't officially become a Yankee until February 19.

At first glance, the 26-year-old Hayes didn't appear to be much of an improvement. He'd batted .230 with 53 RBIs in '91, and had fallen behind two other third basemen, Dave Hollins and Dale Sveum, on the Phillies' depth chart.

Nevertheless, Hayes would become the Yanks' full-time third baseman in 1992, hitting a respectable .257 with 18 homers and 66 runs batted in. But, the club failed to protect him in the expansion draft, and the Colorado Rockies made Hayes the overall third pick.

Darrin Chapin was 10-3 in 55 relief appearances with Columbus of the International League in 1991. The Yankees called him up in September and he was 0-1 in three games. Chapin would pitch in one last major league game with Philadelphia in 1992.

January 10, 1992: Traded Second Baseman Steve Sax to the Chicago White Sox for Righthanded Pitcher Melido Perez and Minor League Righthanded Pitchers Bob Wickman and Domingo Jean

General manager Gene Michael felt that despite infielder Pat Kelly's .242 average in 96 games in 1991, the rookie had shown enough promise to allow the Yankees to trade second baseman Steve Sax. Although Kelly had played mostly at third in '91, he was really a second baseman, and the Yanks were anxious to play him there.

"We wouldn't have traded Sax if we didn't have that kid sitting there," Michael said. "It helped us in a lot of ways. We got pitching, we got money, and we had a replacement."

Sax had been an excellent successor to Willie Randolph in his three years in New York, batting better than .300 twice (at .304, he was the only Yankee regular to hit above .300 in 1991) and stealing a combined 117 bases. He was also among baseball's best leadoff men, which left Buck Showalter, recently chosen to manage the club in 1992, the task of finding a replacement at that spot. Outfielder Roberto Kelly and second-year outfielder Bernie Williams seemed the likely candidates.

"Giving up Sax is certainly a loss," Showalter said. "We gave up a good player." Still, Sax was 33 years old, while Kelly was only 24. In trading him, the Yanks could use the savings from Sax's large salary (they did agree to pay part of it) to pursue other players.

Sax said he understood why the Yanks made the deal, although he wasn't happy about it. "I didn't want to be traded. I didn't want to jump ship now. I thought the Yankees were turning the corner. I knew Pat or me had to go."

Although Melido Perez expected to be joining his older brother Pascual on the Yankee staff, they would never truly became teammates

January 10, 1992: *Steve Sax*. With young Pat Kelly ready to take over at second base, the Yanks traded Sax for pitching help.

because Pascual's shoulder problems would prevent him from ever again pitching at the major league level. That kept the Perezes from joining Homer and Tommy Thompson (1912), Bobby and Wilmer Shantz (1960), Matty and Felipe Alou (1973), and Phil and Joe Niekro (1985) as brothers who played together with the Yankees.

Less colorful, and less trouble-prone than Pascual, Melido had a 45-46 lifetime record, including an 8-7 mark in 1991, his first full season that he'd failed to win at least 11 games. He would win 13 games (with 16 losses) in 1992, but only 20 over the following three seasons. Often on the disabled list, Perez ended his Yankee, and major league, career following the 1995 season. His overall record as a Yankee was 33 wins and 39 defeats.

Both 22-year-old Bob Wickman and 23-year-old Domingo Jean had begun the 1991 season in Class A, but the Yanks believed both had major league potential, particularly Wickman. Brian Sabean, the Yanks' vice president for player development said: "We considered Wickman one of their top arms, and I think

they did too."

Ed Ford, a former White Sox scout, said that Chicago had traded "two of their best pitching prospects." Ford speculated that "both kids could be big league pitchers and that's what you measure pitchers on. I think it's a real good trade for the Yankees," he added.

January 21, 1992: Signed Free-Agent Catcher Mike Stanley from the Texas Rangers

In six years with Texas, Mike Stanley had a .251 average, 16 home runs, and 120 runs batted in. The Yankees had signed Stanley to a minor league contract, but invited him to spring training where they would give him an opportunity to win the backup catcher's job. Bob Geren had filled that role in 1991, but Geren, who'd been with the club since 1988, had gone on waivers to Cincinnati a month earlier.

John Ramos, who batted .308 for Columbus of the International League in 1991, would be Stanley's main competitor for the number two spot behind Matt Nokes. Ramos had the same average in ten late season games with the Yankees; however, those ten games would be the only ones of his major league career.

Meanwhile, Stanley, after backing up Nokes in 1992, would become the Yanks' number one catcher for the next three seasons, batting a combined .285, with 69 home runs and 251 runs batted in. When Bob Watson and Joe Torre took over as general manager and manager following the 1995 season, they chose not to retain Stanley. They traded for Joe Girardi to replace him, and Stanley then signed as a free agent with the Boston Red Sox.

February 29, 1992: Traded Right-handed Pitcher Alan Mills to the Baltimore Orioles for Two Minor League Players to Be Named

The Yanks had designated pitcher Alan Mills for assignment on February 19 following the announcement that third baseman Charlie Hayes had officially joined the team. Hayes, as everyone suspected, was the player to be named in the January trade of minor league pitcher Darrin Chapin to the Phillies, and his addition had put the Yanks one man over the 40-player roster limit. Now the Yanks were getting what they could for the 25-year-old Mills, which was two players to be named.

Mills had a 1-5 record in 36 relief appearances with the Yanks in 1990 and split two decisions with them in 1991. He'd spent most of '91 with Columbus of the International League, where he was 7-5 while working as both a starter and a reliever.

The Orioles gave the Yankees a list of minor leaguers from which they could choose the two players they would receive. The Yanks immediately selected righthander Francisco de la Rosa, who had two games of big league experience with the Orioles in 1991. They picked the second one on June 8, righthander Mark Carper, whom they immediately assigned to Albany/Colonie of the Eastern League.

April 2, 1992: Signed Outfielder Dion James as a Free Agent

Primarily a singles hitter, Dion James had compiled a .284 batting average in his seven big league seasons with Milwaukee, Atlanta, and Cleveland. The Indians had released James following the 1990 season, and he'd spent the 1991 season out of organized baseball.

James would spend two seasons with the Yankees, batting .262 in 67 games in 1992, and then .332 in 113 games in 1993. A free agent in 1994, James signed to play with the Chunichi Dragons of the Japanese Central League.

April 9, 1992: Signed Righthanded Pitcher Shawn Hillegas as a Free Agent

It was actually Fort Lauderdale, the Yankees affiliate in the Class A Florida State League that signed pitcher Shawn Hillegas after Cleveland released him just prior to Opening Day. Hillegas, who'd also pitched for the Dodgers and White Sox, had gone 3-4 with seven saves for the Indians in 1991, but he'd been hit hard in the exhibition season this spring, allowing five earned runs in 10.1 innings.

Hillegas would make one start, a win, for Fort Lauderdale, and four starts (2-0) for Columbus of the International League, before the Yankees called him up. When they did, his performance was most unsatisfactory. After 26 games, he had a 1-8 record with a 5.51 ERA, and the Yanks released him on August 22.

June 9, 1992: Traded Lefthanded Pitcher Lee Guetterman to the New York Mets for Righthanded Pitcher Tim Burke

"The story of two pitchers trying to find their sinkerballs" was how Mets manager Jeff Torborg assessed this trade, only the second ever between the Yanks and the Mets that involved major leaguers from both sides. Each of these 33-year-old relievers had been successful in the past, but as Torborg suggested, both were struggling this season. Lee Guetterman was 1-1 with a 9.53 earned run average for the Yankees, while Tim Burke was 1-2 with a 5.74 ERA for the Mets, and neither one had a save.

"I hope the change of scenery will help both pitchers," said Yankee manager Buck Showalter. "I especially hope it helps the pitcher we are getting."

Showalter had been a teammate of Burke's at Nashville of the Southern League and Columbus of the International League back in 1983 when both were Yankee minor leaguers. Following the '83 season, the Yanks sent Burke to Montreal in a minor league deal for outfielder Pat Rooney. He reached the Expos in 1985 and won 43 games with 101 saves before they traded him to the Mets in July 1991.

Since coming to the Yankees from Seattle in 1988, Guetterman had appeared in 233 games, all but two in relief. He had a 21-19 record with 21 saves, with his best years coming in 1989, when he had 13 saves, and in 1990 when he had 11 wins.

Guetterman had complained that Showalter hadn't pitched him enough this year; however, when Showalter did use him, he'd been wild and generally ineffective. Both Guetterman and Burke had expected their clubs to trade them, and both welcomed their new opportunity.

"There is a lot of sadness," Guetterman said, "but under the circumstances there is hope."

Burke's hope was to regain his best pitch, the sinker. "When you are a sinkerball pitcher and your sinker is not sinking, then you are in trouble," he said.

Burke would win two and lose two in 23 games for the '92 Yanks, then sign as a free agent with Cincinnati but never again pitch in the major leagues.

June 17, 1992: Signed Lefthanded Pitcher Curt Young as a Free Agent

Curt Young pitched for the Oakland Athletics from 1983 to 1991, winning 64 games and losing 50. He'd signed with Kansas City for the 1992 season, but after compiling a 1-2 record and a 5.18 ERA in ten games, the Royals let him go on June 10. A week later the Yankees signed the 32-year-old lefthander and sent him to their Columbus team in the International League.

Young would make three starts for the Clippers and win them all. Promoted to New York, he would also win all three of his decisions with the Yankees, but leave after the 1992 season to again sign with Oakland.

August 22, 1992: Traded Righthanded Pitcher Tim Leary to the Seattle Mariners for Minor League Outfielder Sean Twitty

By trading Tim Leary (5-6 with a 5.57 ERA) and releasing Shawn Hillegas (1-8 with a 5.51 ERA), the Yanks parted with their two least effective starting pitchers.

"Both of them failed because they did not pitch well enough to stay here," said Yankee GM Gene Michael, stating the obvious. "Heaven knows, we need pitching. It was a trial and it didn't work." The Yanks were so anxious to get rid of Leary, they agreed to pay part of his salary both this season and next.

The 33-year-old Leary had been in his third season with the Yanks. In his first, 1990, he'd led the American League in losses with a 9-19 record, and in his second, 1991, he was 4-10 with a 6.49 earned run average, the highest ERA in Yankee history.

While Hillegas left in tears after getting the word from manager Buck Showalter, Leary was philosophical. "I'm frustrated I didn't do better here," he said. "I apologize to the Yankees and their fans." Nevertheless, he said he looked forward to joining the Mariners, whose manager, Bill Plummer, announced that he'd start Leary the next night in Boston against Roger Clemens.

"I looked at it as those guys served a purpose while we were waiting for the Sam Militellos and Russ Springers to get ready," Showalter said of the two departed pitchers. "In order to wait for them, you have to have people up here." Evidently believing Springer was now ready, Showalter called him up from Columbus of the International League.

The Yanks assigned Sean Twitty, who had a .232 average in 222 minor league games, to Fort Lauderdale of the Florida State League.

November 3, 1992: Traded Outfielder Roberto Kelly to the Cincinnati Reds for Outfielder Paul O'Neill and Minor League First Baseman Joe DeBerry

Nineteen ninety-two had been a typical year for 28-year-old Roberto Kelly, a player the Yankees had once considered "untouchable." He'd batted .272, with 66 RBIs and 28 stolen bases; however, the Yankees had hoped that '92 would be the year Kelly would combine his speed and power to finally establish himself as a "super star." He certainly hadn't done that. Nor had he endeared himself to management by his reaction to being moved from center field to left, allowing second-year-man Bernie Williams to take over in center.

Kelly's attitude didn't bother Cincinnati general manager Jim Bowden. "We are very pleased to acquire such a multitalented player," he said. "Roberto hits for both average and power, and he runs, fields, and throws very well. His style of play is well suited to Riverfront Stadium and the National League."

In Kelly's six years with the Yankees, the last four as a regular, he'd hit for a .280 average, with 258 runs batted in and 151 stolen bases. But while the Yanks were sacrificing speed, in Paul O'Neill they were gaining the dependable lefthanded hitter they'd been seeking.

"We were looking for lefthanded bats be-

November 6, 1992: Sold Lefthanded Pitcher Greg Cadaret to the Cincinnati Reds

Since coming from Oakland in June 1989, Greg Cadaret had been extremely versatile. He'd worked as a starter, a long reliever, and a short reliever, and compiled a 22-23 mark in 188 appearances. Nevertheless, the Yanks had been trying unsuccessfully to trade him for the past three months and had even been willing to take a minor leaguer in return.

Cadaret had begun the 1992 season as a starter, winning his first two games, but then lost five of the next six. He returned to the bullpen and finished with a 4-8 record and a 4.25 earned run average. In all, Cadaret appeared in 46 games in '92, allowing 104 hits and 74 walks in 103.2 innings.

November 3, 1992: *Paul O'Neill.* **"Hopefully, they have big plans for me. I want to go out and play and put up big numbers."**

cause I don't think we had enough," Gene Michael, the Yanks GM said. "I always said we were too righthanded. I feel this is a quality hitter and Yankee Stadium should be conducive to his hitting."

O'Neill, 29, had a .259 average and 96 home runs in 799 games with the Reds. He'd hit a career-high 28 homers in 1991, but hit only 14 in 1992, and had often had trouble hitting lefthanded pitchers. He batted just .201 against lefthanders in 1992, and the overwhelming majority of his home runs had come against righthanded pitchers.

Besides being an excellent outfielder, O'Neill was also a fiery competitor and a team player. He said he would gladly move from right field to left if the Yanks wanted to continue playing Danny Tartabull in right. "You come to spring training with your cleats and your glove and you do what you're told," he said. "Hopefully, they have big plans for me. I want to go out and play and put up big numbers."

Joe DeBerry, strictly a throw-in, had batted .240 with 15 home runs for Cedar Rapids of the Class A Midwest League in 1992.

December 4, 1992: Signed Free-Agent Shortstop Spike Owen from the Montreal Expos

Alvaro Espinoza had been the Yankee shortstop from 1989 to 1991, but the club had released him during the spring of 1992. Rookie Andy Stankiewicz and utility man Randy Velarde filled the position in '92, but neither man was considered a long range solution. The Yanks had gone into the off-season looking for a full-time shortstop, concentrating specifically on three that were free agents: Ozzie Smith of the Cardinals, Greg Gagne of the Twins, and Spike Owen of the Expos.

They chose to sign Owen, the Yanks claimed, because of his defense and leadership qualities. Actually, they were the only club that offered money to the 31-year-old Owen, a ten-year veteran who'd also played for the Mariners and the Red Sox. He was a lifetime .243 hitter, but had reached career highs in batting (.269) and home runs (seven) in 1992.

December 6, 1992: Traded First Baseman J. T. Snow, Righthanded Pitcher Russ Springer, and Lefthanded Pitcher

Jerry Nielsen to the California Angels for Lefthanded Pitcher Jim Abbott

In August 1992, after he'd turned down a long-term contract, the California Angels announced that lefthanded pitcher Jim Abbott was available. Since that time, Gene Michael, the general manager of the Yankees, and Whitey Herzog, his counterpart with the Angels, had been trying to package a trade that would bring Abbott to New York.

"Abbott's a very big attraction," Michael said, while Herzog jokingly suggested that he'd "talked to Gene Michael more than I had my wife the last couple of months."

The Yanks had agreed to give up J. T. Snow because they were set at first base with Don Mattingly, but they'd been reluctant to part with the two pitchers. They finally acceded to Herzog's demands for Russ Springer and Jerry Nielsen when the Expos, Twins, and White Sox joined in the chase for Abbott. "Those guys would have made our roster in 1993," said manager Buck Showalter.

All three youngsters had made their major league debuts with the Yanks in 1992. Snow, whose .313 average for Columbus led the International League, went 2 for 14 in seven games; Springer, 8-5 at Columbus, appeared in 14 games without a decision; and Nielsen, 3-5 at Albany/Colonie of the Eastern League, was 1-0 in 20 games.

At 25, Abbott was not only one of the league's best pitchers, but his having overcome a serious birth defect (he was born without a right hand) made him a fan favorite throughout baseball. His overall record was only 47-52, but in 1991, he'd won 18 games with a 2.89 earned run average for the last-place Angels and finished third in voting for the Cy Young Award. Abbot's win total dropped to seven in 1992, although his 2.77 ERA was the league's fifth best.

Determined to upgrade their pitching staff, the Yankees were also making a serious bid to sign free-agent Greg Maddux, the National League's Cy Young winner in 1992. Adding Abbott, they believed, might help them do so. "It shouldn't hurt making us more attractive to Maddux," reasoned Michael.

Abbott would have two so-so seasons in New York. He was 11-14 with a 4.37 ERA in 1993 (including a no-hitter against Cleveland), and 9-8 with a 4.55 ERA in 1994. In 1995, he signed with the Chicago White Sox.

December 10, 1992: Signed Free-Agent Lefthanded Pitcher Jimmy Key from the Toronto Blue Jays

One day after National League Cy Young winner Greg Maddux spurned them to sign with Atlanta, the Yanks signed veteran lefthander Jimmy Key. In all, it had been a frustrating off-season for the Yankees. Besides Maddux, they'd also been unsuccessful in their attempts to sign pitchers David Cone, Chris Bosio, Jose Guzman, Greg Swindell, and Doug Drabek, and outfielder Barry Bonds. Still, the 31-year-old Key was not exactly a booby prize. In nine years with Toronto, he'd won 116 games, had a 3.42 earned run average, and was one of only two pitchers who'd had 12 wins or more in each of the last eight seasons. Key had also been extremely effective pitching in Yankee Stadium. His record in what would be his new home park was a sparkling 8-1.

"You can't dwell on Bonds, or Maddux, or Cone," said Yankee manager Buck Showalter. "If one part of the equation doesn't work out, then you move onto the next part."

For Showalter that involved putting together his pitching rotation for 1993, which now had Key to go along with holdover Melido Perez, and Jim Abbott, whom the Yanks had gotten in a trade with California a week earlier.

Showalter was very pleased to have Key on his side. "I'm excited about getting a player of his background and with his track record coming to New York," Showalter said. "As important as that is, I'm excited that he wanted to come to play in New York."

Owner George Steinbrenner discounted his failures in luring other free agents to the Yankees. "I think Key is a guy I would have wanted as much as anybody," said the Yankee owner. "I like Jimmy Key. He would have been one of my first choices."

Key would prove a terrific addition in his first two Yankee seasons, going 18-6 in 1993 and 17-4 in 1994. He was on the disabled list for most of 1995, appearing in just five games, winning one and losing two, but came back to go 12-11 in 1996 as the Yanks won the World

Series. After the season Key signed as a free agent with the Baltimore Orioles.

December 15, 1992: Signed Free-Agent Third Baseman Wade Boggs from the Boston Red Sox

Wade Boggs was a former five-time American League batting champion and an eight-time member of the league's All-Star team. He'd batted above .300 in each of his first ten seasons in Boston and held the American League record for consecutive seasons with 200 or more hits, reaching that figure seven times. But in 1992, Boggs fell below the .300 mark for the first time in his big league career, dropping all the way to .259. He'd also missed several games because of back problems, which along with his sub-par season led to only one other team, the Los Angeles Dodgers, making a serious attempt to sign the 34-year-old Boggs.

Even with the Yankees, neither manager Buck Showalter nor general manager Gene Michael were in favor of the signing. Having lost Charlie Hayes to the Colorado Rockies in the expansion draft, the club needed a new third baseman; however, Boggs was not the one Showalter or Michael wanted. The Yankees signed Boggs for one reason; owner George Steinbrenner wanted him.

"If there were people who didn't think the signing was right, they will come around," Steinbrenner said. "Everyone pulls together once it is done. You're a company man. If you're not, you're in trouble."

The early thinking was that Boggs would bat second in the Yankee lineup, between lead-off man Bernie Williams and number three hitter Don Mattingly. Boggs and Mattingly had been less than friendly in the past, but both put that behind them.

"I'm excited to play with Don Mattingly," said Boggs. "I'm very enthusiastic about being a Yankee and playing for an organization so rich in tradition. The idea of being able to play in the American League East all factored into my decision."

Mattingly also assured everyone that their past differences would pose no problem. "Boggs is an excellent addition to our ballclub,

and I think we'll work real well together," the Yankee captain said.

Although he had a lifetime .338 average, Boggs had never hit particularly well at Yankee Stadium, only .276, compared to a lusty .369 at Boston's Fenway Park. Still, Steinbrenner wasn't dismayed. "I just got a hunch that maybe he is the best buy we've had in a long time," he said. "I think that he'll hit .300 next year. I'm not prepared to believe that Wade Boggs isn't still Wade Boggs."

Steinbrenner proved exactly right on this one. Boggs not only hit .302 in 1993, he followed it by batting .342 in 1994, .324 in 1995, and .311 in 1996. In each of those years he was a member of the American League All-Star team. He just missed the .300 mark in 1997 (.292), but his five-year average as a Yankee was .313. The Yanks made him a free agent after the '97 season, and he signed with the newly created Tampa Bay Devil Rays. During the 1999 season, Boggs joined the career 3,000-hit club, just a few days after San Diego's Tony Gwyn earned his place in that elite class.

February 2, 1993: Signed Lefthanded Pitcher Neal Heaton as a Free Agent

The Yanks signed Neal Heaton to a minor league contract after working him out for 20 minutes at Yankee Stadium. With Steve Howe as their only lefthanded relief pitcher, they invited Heaton to spring training, with the assurance he would be given an opportunity to make the club.

Heaton, who lived on Long Island, said he felt that signing with the Yankees was the best situation for him. "The bottom line is, I have to produce," he said. "The opportunity is there. I've got to show them I can still pitch, and I should be able to make the team."

Now nearing his 33rd birthday, Heaton had pitched for six clubs in his 11-year career, compiling a lifetime record of 79 wins and 96 losses. He'd been primarily a starter until 1991 when the Pittsburgh Pirates made him a reliever. Traded to Kansas City for Kirk Gibson in 1992, Heaton was 3-1 in 31 relief appearances for the Royals before they let him go on July 30. (Heaton claimed the Royals released him because he was getting close to where they would have to pay him some incentive bonuses.) After leaving the Royals, he pitched six games for Denver of the American Association and then an inning in one appearance for the Milwaukee Brewers.

Heaton did make the Yankees out of spring training, but with a 1-0 record and a 6.00 ERA in 18 games, the Yanks released him on June 27, ending his career.

June 18, 1993: Signed Lefthanded Pitcher Paul Gibson as a Free Agent

Both the Mets and the Tigers (who had him for four years before trading him to the Mets in 1992), had used Paul Gibson almost exclusively in relief. He'd started only 15 of his 265 big league games and 13 of those had come in his second season, 1989.

Gibson, whose overall record was 19-23, had a 1-1 record with a 5.19 earned run average for the Mets when they'd released him a week earlier. The Yanks signed him to a minor league contract and assigned him to the Class AAA Columbus Clippers of the International League.

July 30, 1993: Traded Righthanded Pitcher John Habyan to the Kansas City Royals in a Three-Way Deal and Received Lefthanded Pitcher Paul Assenmacher from the Chicago Cubs

Looking to strengthen a bullpen that currently had the highest ERA in the American League, the Yanks had been pursuing a trade for lefthander Paul Assenmacher for three weeks. The deal finally came together when they and the Cubs agreed on who would pay what part of Assenmacher's salary over the next two seasons. Even at that, the deal needed a third team, the Kansas City Royals, to make it work. The Yanks would send pitcher John Habyan to the Royals, who in turn would send outfielder Karl Rhodes from their American Association team at Omaha to the Cubs.

The 32-year-old Assenmacher had spent eight seasons in the National League with the Braves and Cubs, and had a 39-30 record with 47 saves in 505 games, all but one in relief. He had a 2-1 mark in 46 games with Chicago this

season; however, he had zero saves. Randy Myers had taken over the role of late-inning stopper, and the Cubs had used Assenmacher strictly as a lefthanded setup man, the same role the Yanks wanted him to fill with them.

Habyan had performed that same function very well in 1991 and in the first half of 1992, albeit from the right side. But in the second half of '92, he began having trouble with his best pitch, the slider, and his post–All-Star Game earned run average was a dreadful 8.22. Habyan was 2-1 this season, with a 4.04 ERA, but he'd lost his role as setup man to rookie Bobby Munoz.

August 31, 1993: Traded Minor League Righthanded Pitcher Rich Batchelor to the St. Louis Cardinals for Righthanded Pitcher Lee Smith

Still hoping that they could catch the first-place Toronto Blue Jays, the Yanks added veteran reliever Lee Smith just in time to beat the roster deadline for post-season eligibility. Smith was baseball's all-time saves leader, having accumulated 398 in his 14 big league seasons. But, he was now 35 years old, and along with his 43 successful saves for manager Joe Torre's Cardinals this season, had come 12 save opportunities that he'd squandered. Still, the 43 saves Smith did have were eight more than the entire Yankee staff combined. Yankee manager Buck Showalter was glad to have Smith, although he would have preferred to add a starting pitcher to his injury-riddled rotation had any been available.

Rich Batchelor, a 26-year-old relief pitcher, had begun the year at Albany/Colonie in the Eastern League, where he had 19 saves. Promoted to Columbus of the International League, his current team, he'd added six more. The Cardinals placed Batchelor on their roster, and three days later he made his major league debut.

After Smith pitched in eight games for the Yanks in the season's last month, registering three saves, he signed as a free agent with the Baltimore Orioles.

September 17, 1993: Traded Minor League Righthanded Pitcher Kenny

Greer to the New York Mets for Left-handed Pitcher Frank Tanana

In late July, the Yanks had contemplated a possible trade of rookie pitchers Mark Hutton and Domingo Jean to Seattle for Randy Johnson. Shortly after deciding not to pursue Johnson, two of their other pitchers, Scott Kamieniecki and Melido Perez, went down with injuries. To replace them, manager Buck Showalter had been forced to depend on Hutton and Jean, along with another rookie, Sterling Hitchcock, and it hadn't worked out well. Getting Frank Tanana was the second-place Yankees' last-gasp effort by to overtake the division-leading Toronto Blue Jays. Tanana figured to make three starts, and the club hoped to get at least five innings out of him in each.

The 40-year-old Tanana, now in his 21st and final big league season, had spent his entire career in the American League before joining the Mets this season. He had a lifetime record of 240 wins and 234 losses, including his 7-15 mark with the Mets. Tanana knew what the Yanks expected of him.

"If I lose, I'll be a bum. I understand that mentality. No problem," Tanana said. "I have nothing to show anyone," he added. "My record and career stand on their own merits. I've pitched in this atmosphere before. Hopefully, I'll win some games for this team and help get them into the World Series."

He didn't. Tanana went 0-2 in three starts for the Yankees, who eventually finished 7 games behind the Blue Jays.

Kenny Greer, a relief pitcher, had a 9-4 record and six saves for Columbus of the International League. He finished the season with the Mets, getting a win in his only appearance.

November 27, 1993: Traded Infielder Andy Stankiewicz and Righthanded Pitcher Domingo Jean to the Houston Astros for Righthanded Pitcher Xavier Hernandez

Steve Farr, the Yanks' 1993 saves leader with 25, had filed for free agency. Farr's departure created a righthanded vacancy in the Yankee bullpen they were hoping to fill with Xavier Hernandez. In Houston the past two seasons, Hernandez had been the number two man behind Doug Jones. As the number one man, Jones got most of the saves; nevertheless, Hernandez had been a most effective reliever. He'd gone 9-1 with a 2.11 earned run average and seven saves in 1992, and 4-5 with a 2.61 ERA and nine saves in 1993.

General manager Gene Michael suggested that there were two ways the Yanks could use Hernandez. "He can be the stopper or he can be the lead-in to the stopper," Michael said. "He's a quality reliever and has success at both. He can handle some of the closer's role or the bulk of it from the right side, and Steve Howe and Paul Assenmacher can handle the bulk of it from the left side." (Michael was counting on this new arrangement to be an improvement over 1993, when the Yanks blew 15 of 53 save opportunities.)

After six years in their farm system, Andy Stankiewicz joined the Yanks in 1992. Playing mostly at shortstop, he batted .268 in 116 games and was the first Yankee rookie to have more than 100 hits since Willie Randolph in 1976. Stankiewicz's hit total was 107, including 22 doubles, but the Yanks gave Spike Owen the shortstop job in 1993. Stankiewicz spent the season with Columbus of the International League, getting just nine hitless at-bats with the Yanks. He would move on to the Montreal Expos in 1996 and then the Arizona Diamondbacks in 1998. The Diamondbacks released Stankiewicz during spring training 1999, and the Yanks signed him to a Triple-A contract.

The once-promising Domingo Jean had also spent most of '93 in the minors, first at Albany/Colonie in the Eastern League (5-3 with a 2.51 ERA), and then at Columbus (2-2 with a 2.82 ERA). The Yanks called him up in August, and he appeared in ten games, winning one and losing one.

Houston GM Bob Watson said the addition of Stankiewicz would help the Astros' infield, while Jean would be given a chance to make the club's starting rotation. He also admitted that Hernandez's eligibility for salary arbitration was a contributing factor to the club's trading him.

When the players went on strike in August 1994, the 29-year-old Hernandez had a 4-4 record, with six saves and a very unimpressive

5.85 earned run average. In November, the Yanks made him a free agent and he signed with Cincinnati.

December 9, 1993: Traded Shortstop Spike Owen and Cash to the California Angels for Minor League Righthanded Pitcher Jose Musset

Free-agent shortstops Ozzie Smith of the Cardinals and Greg Gagne of the Twins had also been available when the Yankees signed Spike Owen in December 1992. In fact, the Yanks were the only club that had seriously pursued Owen, and they'd signed him, they claimed, for his defense and his leadership. Now, by trading him to California, it appeared the club was acknowledging that signing him had been an error. Also, getting rid of the 32-year-old Owen would be a step in lowering a far too high payroll, and would allow them to pursue some of this season's crop of free agents.

"If we can move two or three contracts," general manager Gene Michael said, "I think it would be possible a lot of things could happen." As it was, they likely had to agree to pay part of Owen's contract before the Angels would agree to take him.

In his one season in New York, Owen batted .234 in 103 games. He was the regular shortstop for the first half of the season, but mostly sat on the bench in the second half as Mike Gallego took over the position. With Owen gone, Gallego and Randy Velarde became the leading candidates to be the Yankee shortstop in 1994, although Michael did not rule out the possibility of rookie Dave Silvestri winning the job.

"Spike Owen was a true professional and did a nice job for us last year," Michael said in assessing Owen's contribution. "Moving him gives us a chance to move along some of our young players, and Dave Silvestri is one of the young players who should be given the opportunity now."

Jose Musset, a 25-year-old career minor league relief pitcher, had a 13-16 record, 29 saves, and a 4.43 earned run average in four seasons. He'd been at Midland in the Texas League in 1993, where he was 2-6 with a 5.49 ERA, but had 21 saves.

December 20, 1993: Signed Free-Agent Outfielder Luis Polonia from the California Angels

On leaving New York after his trade to California in 1990, Luis Polonia said, "I'm just hoping I can come back here one day. I love this city. I love the Yankees."

Polonia became a Yankee the first time when Oakland included him in the trade that brought them Rickey Henderson. He was becoming a Yankee a second time mainly because the Yanks were unable to induce Henderson to return to them as their left fielder and lead-off man.

A lifetime .294 hitter, Polonia batted just .271 for the Angels in 1993, although he did steal a career-high 55 bases, 16 more than the entire Yankee team stole in '93. While Polonia's caught stealing percentage was much poorer than Henderson's, and he seldom walked, he still considered himself the league's second-best lead-off man.

"Right now, if you compare all the lead-off hitters in the American League, I believe that Rickey is the only one above me," Polonia said. "You have to go after the best. If you go after someone other than Rickey, there is no one better than me."

January 13, 1994: Signed Free-Agent Outfielder Daryl Boston from the Colorado Rockies

Daryl Boston, a ten-year veteran with a .251 lifetime average, had played 500 games as an American Leaguer (with Chicago), and 506 games as a National Leaguer (with New York and Colorado). Now, after three years with the Mets and one with the expansion Rockies, he was headed back to the American League, if he could make the team.

Signed to a minor league contract, Boston did make the 1994 Yankees. After he batted a disappointing .182 in 52 games, the Yanks made him a free agent, but no other team signed him.

January 15, 1994: Signed Free Agent Righthanded Pitcher Donn Pall from the Philadelphia Phillies

Two days after signing free-agent outfielder Daryl Boston, the Yanks signed free-agent pitcher Don Pall. The 32-year-old Pall had been with the White Sox from 1988 until they traded him to the Phillies on September 1, 1993. Used mostly in middle relief, he'd appeared in 263 games and had a 21-19 record.

Pall would go 1-2 in 26 games for the 1994 Yankees before they released him on July 29. After finishing the season with the Cubs, Pall spent 1995 with Nashville of the American Association. In 1996, he joined the Florida Marlins and on September 1, 1998, gave up Mark McGwire's 57th home run, the one that broke Hack Wilson's National League single-season record.

January 28, 1994: Signed Free-Agent Lefthanded Pitcher Bob Ojeda from the Cleveland Indians

After being seriously injured in the March 1993 boating accident that killed fellow Cleveland Indians pitchers Tim Crews and Steve Olin, Bob Ojeda underwent a long rehabilitation period before returning. He made it back to the Indians in August, and appeared in nine games, winning two and losing one with a 4.40 earned run average.

Before coming to Cleveland, the 36-year-old Ojeda had pitched six years for the Red Sox, five for the Mets, and two for the Dodgers, accruing a lifetime 115-98 record. He had his best season when he went 18-5 for the world champion Mets in 1986 and led the National League with a .783 winning percentage.

The Yanks signed Ojeda to a minor league contract, but indicated that they would give him a chance to compete for the fifth starting position on their pitching staff with youngsters Sterling Hitchcock and Mark Hutton. "Sometimes these things work out better," said Gene Michael, the Yankees general manager. "At Yankee Stadium he's the type of pitcher you want. I know the guy still knows how to pitch."

Ojeda would make two starts as a Yankee, pitching a combined total of three innings. He had no decisions, but allowed eight earned runs and 11 hits in the three innings, leading the club to release him on May 5, ending his major league career.

February 9, 1994: Traded Righthanded Pitcher Bobby Munoz, Minor League Lefthanded Pitcher Ryan Karp, and Minor League Second Baseman Kevin Jordan to the Philadelphia Phillies for Lefthanded Pitcher Terry Mulholland and a Player to Be Named

The Yanks had identified three starters for their projected 1994 rotation: Jimmy Key, Melido Perez, and Jim Abbott, and had been looking to trade for at least one more ever since the 1993 season ended. Before this trade for Terry Mulholland, they'd also pursued San Diego's Andy Benes and Houston's Pete Harnisch. Now, as spring training was set to begin, they had Mulholland as a fourth starter and would seek a fifth from a group that included youngsters Scott Kamieniecki, Sam Militello, Mark Hutton, and Sterling Hitchcock, and newly acquired veteran, Bob Ojeda.

"The way I look at it, it improves us," said Gene Michael, the Yankees general manager. "If you improved yourself, you've closed the gap." (The gap Michael was referring to was with the Toronto Blue Jays, who'd won the last two Eastern Division titles and World Series.)

Mulholland, who was nearing 31, came up with the San Francisco Giants in 1986, but had been with Philadelphia since early in the 1989 season. Relying more on control than power, and possessor of the game's best pickoff move, he'd won 41 games for the Phillies over the past three seasons, including a career high 16 wins in 1991.

Phillies GM Lee Thomas said he'd traded Mulholland because he feared he'd be a free agent at the end of the season and would leave anyway. The Yanks were hoping to negate that by signing him to a long-term contract, but Mulholland wasn't so sure.

"Being this is my first three hours with the Yankees," he said, "it's hard to say I'm looking forward to finishing my playing career as a Yankee."

Bobby Munoz had been a starter during

his minor league days, but the 38 games he'd pitched as a Yankee rookie in 1993 were all in relief. After a strong start, he'd faltered in the second half, a failing management attributed to his being overweight. Munoz ended the season with a 3-3 record and a 5.32 earned run average.

Thomas had asked the Yanks for Hutton, Hitchcock, or Bob Wickman in addition to Munoz, but Michael refused. Instead they sent 24-year-old lefthander Ryan Karp, who had a combined 16-3 record in 1993 while pitching for Class A teams at Greensboro in the South Atlantic League and Prince William in the Carolina League. Despite those impressive numbers, Karp did not throw hard, and the Yanks didn't believe he had major league potential.

Second baseman Kevin Jordan had also had a fine minor league season in '93, batting .283 for Albany/Colonie, while leading the Eastern League with 33 doubles. However, the Yanks were set with Pat Kelly at second, making the 24-year-old Jordan expendable.

It wasn't until after the 1994 season ended that this deal would be completed. On November 8, the Phillies sent the Yankees Jeff Patterson a minor league righthanded pitcher. By that time Mulholland had already left as a free agent. He hadn't signed a long-term contract with the Yanks, as they'd hoped, nor had he had great success in the strike-shortened 1994 season. In his one partial year in New York, Mulholland went 6-7 and had a 6.49 earned run average. He would eventually sign with his original team, the Giants.

February 15, 1994: Signed Free-Agent Righthanded Pitcher Jeff Reardon from the Cincinnati Reds

Throughout the 1980s Jeff Reardon had been among the game's outstanding relief pitchers. His won-lost record was just 72-77, but he'd compiled 365 saves, good for second place on the all-time list behind only Lee Smith. Reardon reached the big leagues with the 1979 New York Mets, though he had his best years with the Expos, Twins, and Red Sox. But he was now 38, and after having saved only eight games for the Cincinnati Reds in 1993, his career seemed to be over. Reardon didn't

think so, and signed with the Yanks, he said, because they had shown the most interest in him.

"I look at it as a way of showing people I can still pitch," Reardon said. "I thought I proved it last year, but I guess not. People ask why don't I just retire. I think I can still pitch."

The four righthanders who had worked in the Yankee bullpen in 1993, Smith, Steve Farr, Rich Monteleone, and Bobby Munoz, were all gone. So, although Reardon had signed a minor league contract, general manager Gene Michael said that he would be given an opportunity to make the club out of spring training.

The 38-year-old Reardon did make the team, but after winning one and saving two, the Yanks released him on May 6, ending his career.

March 21, 1994: Traded Lefthanded Pitcher Paul Assenmacher to the Chicago White Sox for Minor League Righthanded Pitcher Brian Boehringer

The Yanks had agreed to pay a part of Paul Assenmacher's salary, an offer that certainly made the 33-year-old middle reliever more appealing to the White Sox. Assenmacher had spent two months with the Yanks in 1993, appearing in 26 games, winning two and losing two. His departure left manager Buck Showalter with just two lefthanders in the bullpen, Steve Howe and Paul Gibson, and increased the likelihood that another lefthander, rookie Sterling Hitchcock or veteran Bob Ojeda, would make the club. Both had pitched very well during spring training, although neither one had much experience as a reliever.

Twenty-five-year-old Brian Boehringer had begun the 1993 season with Sarasota of the Florida State League. But after winning ten and losing four, with a 2.80 ERA, the White Sox promoted him to Class AA Birmingham of the Southern League, where he went 2-1.

Boehringer would pitch for Albany/Colonie of the Eastern League in 1994, and then shuttle between the Yankees and teams in their farm system the following three seasons.

In all, Boehringer would appear in 56 games for the Yanks between 1995 and 1997, with five wins and nine losses, and a 5.54 earned run average.

The Yankees made Boehringer available in the expansion draft that followed the 1997 season. The Tampa Bay Devil Rays selected him and then traded him to the San Diego Padres.

April 26, 1994: Signed Catcher Bob Melvin as a Free Agent

The Red Sox, catcher Bob Melvin's fifth major league team, had released him two weeks earlier. Melvin had a .234 career average for his ten major league seasons, including a .222 mark for the Sox in 1993.

Signed to a minor league contract, the 32-year-old Melvin would get into nine games for the Yankees in 1994, getting four hits in 14 at-bats. After coming off the disabled list on July 22, the Angels claimed him off the waiver list, and then traded him to the White Sox.

May 1, 1994: Signed Shortstop Kevin Elster as a Free Agent

Kevin Elster had played all or part of seven seasons with the Mets before becoming a free agent in 1993. During the '93 season, both the Dodgers and the Marlins signed and released him, and he ended up playing just ten games all year, and they were for San Antonio of the Texas League.

San Diego signed Elster and took him to spring training in 1994, but released him when arm troubles kept him from performing adequately. While he continued to work out on his own, his brother convinced Yankee general manager Gene Michael that the 29-year-old Elster was injury free. Michael signed him to a minor league contract; however, Elster's injury problems continued, and he spent most of the 1994 season in the minors or on the disabled list. As a Yankee, Elster batted 20 times without getting a hit. Then, after getting into ten games in 1995, with just two hits in 17 at-bats, the Yanks released him on June 8.

July 3, 1994: Signed Righthanded Pitcher Greg Harris as a Free Agent

Released by the Red Sox a week earlier, Greg Harris would now be joining his eighth team since reaching the major leagues in 1981. The 38-year-old Harris, who was 3-4 with an 8.28 ERA in 35 games, said he had spurned offers from Cleveland and Texas to sign with the Yanks.

To make room for Harris, who had a 72-86 career record, the Yankees sent lefthander Sterling Hitchcock to Columbus of the International League and released righthander Sam Militello. The release ended the career of Militello, a "can't miss" prospect who finished with four wins and four losses in 12 games spread over the 1992 and 1993 seasons.

After three relief appearances, and a loss in his only decision, the Yankees released Harris ten days after signing him.

August 3, 1994: Claimed Lefthanded Pitcher Rob Murphy on Waivers from the St. Louis Cardinals

The first-place Yankees added veteran Rob Murphy on the assumption that the upcoming players' strike could be averted, or be a short one if it took place. They claimed Murphy, a 34-year-old lefty with a 3-4 record and a 3.79 ERA for St. Louis, to augment their lefthanded relief corps. Before joining the Cardinals in 1993, Murphy had pitched for the Reds, Red Sox, Mariners, and Astros. He had a 31-36 record and 30 saves in 580 games, all in relief.

"He's not the best pitcher on earth," said Yankee GM Gene Michael, "but he's a good pitcher. We think he can help us."

Murphy appeared in three games, pitching 1.2 innings without a decision, before the strike came on August 12 and ended the season and Murphy's Yankee career.

August 31, 1994: Traded Lefthanded Pitcher Paul Gibson to the Milwaukee Brewers for a Player to Be Named

The baseball strike had been on since August 12, but hope remained that an agreement could still save some part of the remaining season. The division-leading Yanks made this deal to beat the deadline for postseason eligibility with that hope in mind. Their acquisition of lefty Rob Murphy at the beginning of August, and the need to add a righthanded reliever made veteran lefthander Paul Gibson expendable. (Later in the day, the Yanks would get a righthanded reliever by trading a player to be named to the Red Sox for Scott Bankhead.)

The Yanks had signed Gibson as a free agent in June 1993 and sent him to Columbus of the International League. After three games with the Clippers, they brought him up and he made 20 relief appearances, winning two and losing none. This season, he'd been in 30 games, splitting two decisions.

The 34-year-old Gibson, who was also the club's player representative, felt the Yanks had not given him enough opportunities to pitch and was very disappointed at leaving.

"To be traded in the middle of all this [the strike], it hurts, it really does," he said. "This is a great group of guys, with the best talent in baseball. To have the rug pulled out from under you and told to go to Milwaukee or any other place, it feels bad."

Yanks GM Gene Michael reacted less emotionally, suggesting that if the Brewers had not taken Gibson, he would have gone to the minors instead. "They said they would take him," Michael said. "It wasn't the kind of thing that was a big deal."

Instead of sending a player to the Yankees, the Brewers sent a cash payment. Meanwhile, Gibson never pitched for the Brewers, and after spending the 1995 season in the minors, the Yanks signed him as a free agent. He pitched in four games in 1996 without a decision before they released him in May.

August 31, 1994: Traded Cash and a Player to Be Named to the Boston Red Sox for Righthanded Pitcher Scott Bankhead

The Yanks had traded lefthander Paul Gibson earlier in the day to make room for righthander Scott Bankhead on what they hoped would be their postseason roster. Gene

Michael, the Yanks' general manager, said that because the team had three lefthanded starters, having another righthanded reliever like Bankhead ready to come out of the bullpen was important.

A onetime starter with the Royals and Mariners, the 30-year-old Bankhead had been on the disabled list with shoulder problems five times in his career. Now a full-time middle-innings reliever, he was 3-2 in 27 appearances for Boston this season.

Because of a failure by players and management to settle the strike, Bankhead didn't get a chance to pitch for the Yanks in 1994. Nor did the Yanks send Boston a player in exchange for him, just money. Bankhead did pitch in 20 games in 1995, splitting two decisions before the Yanks released him in July.

December 14, 1994: Traded Minor League Lefthanded Pitcher Keith Heberling and a Player to Be Named to the Chicago White Sox for Righthanded Pitcher Jack McDowell

The months lost from the 1994 strike had prevented Jack McDowell from completing his six years of service time, and thus becoming an unrestricted free agent. Therefore, it remained uncertain if this deal would stand, or whether the Yanks would have to try to sign him as a free agent.

Yankee general manager Gene Michael was aware of the risk, but was optimistic. "We hope we can sign him," he said. "You have to take chances in this game. We think he's a good one to take a chance on."

McDowell, who had an overall 91-58 record with Chicago, was certainly worth taking a "chance on." He'd been a 20- and 22-game winner in the two seasons preceding the strike, and in both years led the league in games-started and complete games.

"The first thing that jumps out at you is his competitiveness," said Yankee manager Buck Showalter. "He likes to get out there and finish what he started."

There were, however, some cautioning notes. McDowell had won the Cy Young Award for his splendid 1993 season, but he'd pitched poorly against Toronto in the League

Championship Series (0-2 with a 10.00 ERA) and then had a mediocre 1994 season. When the strike came in August, he had a 10-9 record and a 3.73 earned run average.

Lefthander Keith Heberling won 11 lost seven, and had a 2.92 earned run average with the Yankees' Class A Tampa club in the Florida State League in 1994. He seemed to be inequitable compensation for someone like McDowell, leading to speculation that the player to be named would be Danny Tartabull, an outfielder the Yanks had been trying to trade. But Tartabull would remain a Yankee, at least temporarily, and on April 23, 1995, the Yanks sent 26-year-old outfielder Lyle Mouton to Chicago to complete the deal.

McDowell would go 15-10 in 1995, while leading the Yanks in most pitching categories, but left after the season to sign as a free agent with Cleveland.

December 15, 1994: Signed Free-Agent Infielder Tony Fernandez from the Cincinnati Reds

Although he'd played third base at Cincinnati in 1994, the Yanks planned to return Tony Fernandez to his more familiar shortstop position in 1995. It would be a stopgap measure, someone to hold the position for a year or so until 20-year-old Derek Jeter, the Yankees' shortstop of the future, was ready for the big leagues.

The 32-year-old Fernandez, a 12-year veteran, had spent all of his career at short, most of it with the Toronto Blue Jays, but also for two years with the Padres, and for one each with the Mets and Reds. A multiple Gold Glove winner with a .285 lifetime batting average, he had a .279 mark for the '94 Reds, while playing in 104 games in that strike-shortened season.

Limited by injury, Fernandez would play in 108 games in 1995, and while he fielded well, he batted just .245. Jeter took over at shortstop in 1996, and Fernandez, after spending the entire season on the disabled list, signed to play with Cleveland in 1997.

April 5, 1995: Traded Minor League Outfielder Fernando Seguignol, a

Player to Be Named, and Cash to the Montreal Expos for Righthanded Pitcher John Wetteland

Under normal circumstances the regular season would have been underway by April 5, but in recent years nothing had been normal in baseball. The most recent, and most damaging, disruption was a player's strike that had wiped out a major portion of the 1994 season, including the World Series; so instead of playing regular-season games, those Yankee players who chose to attend were in Fort Lauderdale conducting their first voluntary workout.

One of the major unsettled issues in that strike concerned the increasing disparity between the wealthy "big market" teams and the poorer "small market" teams, a disparity clearly evident in this deal. Montreal, perhaps the poorest of all the small market teams, had decided that they couldn't afford to go to arbitration with a player like John Wetteland, who would likely command a huge salary. Kevin Malone, the Expos' director of player personnel, justified the trade strictly in terms of salary.

"With the payroll we must have we had to let some players go," Malone said. "Unfortunately, John Wetteland was one of them. He's the best closer in the business. People on the team and in the city will fall in love with him. I've never seen a guy with more intensity. He intimidates the opposition. The Yankees will feel they've won the game when he comes in."

The Yankees had offered Montreal highly-rated minor league third baseman Russ Davis for Wetteland. However, Malone said he preferred 20-year-old outfielder Fernando Seguignol, a switch hitter who'd batted .289 for Class A Oneonta, while leading the New York–Pennsylvania League with nine triples.

Yankee owner George Steinbrenner, desperate to bring a world championship to New York, was unapologetic about the seeming inequity of the transaction. "Nothing in the world is perfect," Steinbrenner said. "We all understand which teams we were buying when we bought in, and which markets we were buying into."

The 28-year-old Wetteland had the perfect equipment and makeup for a closer: an overpowering fastball, a great curve, and an aggressive style. He'd spent six years in the National League, the first three with the Los Angeles Dodgers, but it was after coming to Montreal in 1992 that he'd established himself among baseball's top relievers. Over the last three seasons Wetteland had appeared in 189 games for the Expos, with save totals of 37, 43, and 25.

When the strike ended the 1994 season, the Yankees had been comfortably ahead in the American League East race. Now, with the addition of Wetteland and Jack McDowell, acquired from the White Sox during the winter, they believed that they were headed to their first World Series since 1981. However, despite Wetteland's 31 saves, they didn't get there in 1995, but did in 1996 when he had a league-leading 43 saves.

Wetteland added three more saves in the World Series win over Atlanta and won the Series MVP award. But even George Steinbrenner had a limit to his payroll. Convinced that third-year man Mariano Rivera was ready to assume the closer's role, the Yanks chose not to retain Wetteland, who then signed with the Texas Rangers for 1997.

April 7, 1995: Signed Outfielder Dion James as a Free Agent

Three years earlier, almost to the day, the Yankees had first signed Dion James as a free agent. He was with them in 1992 and 1993, but after a very successful '93 season—he hit .332 in 113 games—James left in 1994 to play with the Chunichi Dragons of the Japanese Central League.

James would bat .287 in 85 games as a reserve outfielder in 1995, but he had little power—he hit just two home runs—and the Yanks elected not to re-sign him for 1996. However, on April 5 of '96, after Montreal's Ottawa farm team released him during spring training, the Yanks signed James for a third time, but released him on May 1 after he'd gone 2 for 12 in six games.

June 5, 1995: Claimed Righthanded Pitcher Josias Manzanillo on Waivers from the New York Mets

A marginally skilled relief pitcher, with a 5-5 career record, Josias Manzanillo was 1-2 with a bloated 7.88 earned run average for the Mets this season. To make room for Manzanillo, the Yanks sent righthander Joe Ausanio (2-0, 5.73) back to Columbus of the International League, ending his two-year Yankee career.

Manzanillo appeared in 11 games for the Yanks over the next month, with no decisions but a much improved 2.08 earned run average. On July 6, he went on the disabled list, missed the rest of the season, and the Yankees granted him free agency when it ended.

June 19, 1995: Signed Outfielder Darryl Strawberry as a Free Agent

While cynics claimed that the Yankees had signed Darryl Strawberry as a gimmick to hype their poor attendance, George Steinbrenner said the signing had been strictly a baseball decision. The Yankee owner believed that despite Strawberry's recent troubles, the onetime Mets slugger could help his club.

"We're supportive of Darryl and we shall do everything possible to help him meet the challenge ahead," Steinbrenner said. "At the same time, we feel confident Darryl will do his absolute best for us."

Strawberry, now 33, had been in trouble with the law several times in the recent past, having been charged with alcohol abuse, drug abuse, domestic abuse, and income tax evasion. He was currently under a 60-day suspension for the all-encompassing substance abuse. Nevertheless, Strawberry claimed he was now a changed man, and following the end of his suspension (it would end in a few days), he would head to the Yankees' training complex in Florida to begin the process of getting in shape.

"I am proud and honored to have the opportunity to play in New York and to be part of the Yankee organization," he said. "The fans in New York are the best in baseball."

The Yankee players were generally receptive to having Strawberry join them. "I welcome it," said team captain Don Mattingly. "I'm glad he's here."

But pitcher Steve Howe, who'd had his own problems with drug abuse, wasn't so sure. "If he's a distraction in the clubhouse, it'll show," he said. "If he doesn't make it to a game, you'll know about it. My hope is that he gets to concentrate on what he has to do. Coming to New York is going to be difficult enough."

Strawberry, the National League Rookie of the Year in 1983, had been among the game's top power hitters for the Mets between 1984 and 1990. He continued to be productive after his trade to the Dodgers in 1991, but that had been his last good year. After amassing 280 home runs in the eight seasons between 1984 and 1991, Strawberry hit just 14 while playing in a combined 104 games for the Dodgers in 1992 and 1993, and the Giants in 1994.

July 16, 1995: Traded Shortstop Dave Silvestri to the Montreal Expos for Minor League Outfielder Tyrone Horne

The Yankees had designated shortstop Dave Silvestri for assignment nine days earlier, so they were delighted to receive any player for him, especially one playing at the Class AA level.

The Expos had made Tyrone Horne the 44th pick in the 1989 draft, but he had never fulfilled his promise and was currently in his seventh season as a minor leaguer. Horne was with the Harrisburg Senators, where he had a .299 batting average, 14 home runs, 47 runs batted in, and 14 stolen bases. The Yankees kept the lefthanded hitting Horne in the Eastern League, sending him to the Norwich Navigators.

While Silvestri could play several infield positions, he had never shown an ability to hit major league pitching. In 43 games over the past four seasons, he'd managed only 14 hits in 73 at-bats for a .192 average. In 17 games this season, Silvestri was 2 for 21, with one home run and four runs batted in.

July 28, 1995: Traded Minor League Righthanded Pitchers Marty Janzen, Jason Jarvis, and Mike Gordon to the

Toronto Blue Jays for Righthanded Pitcher David Cone

The Yankees were bringing David Cone in to help them reach the playoffs, something that was now possible for them to do even if they failed to overtake the Eastern Division–leading Boston Red Sox. Baseball had arranged for a "wild-card" team to enter the postseason, and the Yanks were in contention for that spot.

Being acquired in midseason to help a team win a pennant was familiar territory for the 32-year-old Cone. In the summer of 1992, Toronto had gotten him from the Mets, and he helped the Blue Jays win the World Series that year. But after spending just half a season with the Blue Jays, he signed to play in 1993 with the Kansas City Royals, the team that first brought him to the big leagues back in 1986. Cone won the Cy Young Award by going 16-4 for the Royals in the strike-shortened 1994 season, but was traded back to Toronto in April.

Cone had a lifetime 120-76 record,

July 28, 1995: *David Cone.* "He was on the top of everyone's Christmas list."

including a 9-6 mark with a 3.38 earned run average for the Blue Jays this season. But in addition to his pitching abilities, the Yanks also liked the fact that Cone had spent five seasons with the Mets, which to them meant that the increased pressure of pitching in New York would not bother him. His new teammates appeared extremely thankful to have him for the stretch drive.

"What's not to like?" said captain Don Mattingly. "It's kind of like with John Wetteland. We got him for nothing. I don't even know the three other guys," Mattingly added in referring to the three minor leaguers headed to Toronto.

"This is large," third baseman Wade Boggs said. "He was on the top of everyone's Christmas list."

After assuring everyone that Cone had been the best pitcher available, general manager Gene Michael remained cautiously optimistic.

"I wouldn't say this makes us the favorites because I don't forecast," Michael said, "but it's nice and I like it. I think it increases our chances." (Later in the day, Michael would take another step he hoped would increase the Yankees' chances. He would trade disgruntled outfielder Danny Tartabull to Oakland for disgruntled outfielder Ruben Sierra.)

Toronto GM Gord Ash had asked Michael for pitchers Bob Wickman, Mariano Rivera, and Matt Drews in return for Cone, but with the trading deadline nearing, and Toronto hopelessly out of the race, Ash settled for the three minor leaguers. "We feel these are three premier pitching prospects," he said.

Of the three, all righthanders, Marty Janzen was considered the best. He'd been 10-3 at Tampa of the Florida State League before a recent promotion to Norwich of the Eastern League. Mike Gordon and Jason Jarvis were both in Class A: Gordon at Tampa, and Jarvis at Greensboro in the South Atlantic League.

July 28, 1995: Traded Outfielder Danny Tartabull to the Oakland Athletics for Outfielder Ruben Sierra and Minor League Righthanded Pitcher Jason Beverlin

Having already secured pitcher David Cone from Toronto, in a trade for three minor

league pitchers, the Yanks now added Ruben Sierra, a talented but troublesome switch-hitting outfielder. The club felt that the addition of Cone and Sierra greatly enhanced their chances of winning the Eastern Division title, or at least gaining entry to the playoffs via the newly-created "wild-card" formulation.

In trading Danny Tartabull, at the time their highest-paid player ever, the Yankees were getting rid of someone much like Sierra, the player they were getting—talented, but unhappy to be where he was. Tartabull had fallen out of favor with the New York fans, with Yankee management, and particularly with owner George Steinbrenner. He'd shown some flashes of the ability the Yanks expected to see when they signed him—31 home runs and 102 RBIs in 1993—but he was often injured and had been an overall disappointment.

Tartabull left with a .252 batting average, 81 home runs and 282 RBIs in three-plus seasons as a Yankee. He was batting .224 with six home runs this season and had been asking the Yanks to trade him since June.

"It's been an ongoing thing," he said. "I'm just kind of glad it's all over. I just want to go to the ball park and think about baseball and play baseball."

At 29, Sierra was three years younger than Tartabull, but had worn out his welcome in Oakland with his "me first" attitude. He was unpopular with his teammates and with his manager, Tony LaRussa, who had referred to Sierra as "the village idiot."

Sierra, now in his fourth season with the A's, had previously spent seven years with the Texas Rangers. He had a .273 lifetime batting average with 213 home runs, and was currently hitting .265 with 12 home runs. In the eight seasons between 1987 and 1994, Sierra had driven 811 runs, second in the major leagues only to Toronto's Joe Carter's 875.

Jason Beverlin, a throw-in, was 3-9 with Oakland's West Michigan team in the Class A Midwest League.

August 11, 1995: Traded Outfielder Luis Polonia to the Atlanta Braves for Minor League Outfielder Troy Hughes

Luis Polonia batted .311 in strike-shortened 1994, his first year back in New York. He was at .261 in 67 games this season, but had become expendable after the Yanks signed outfielder–designated hitter Darryl Strawberry. Rather than release Polonia and be responsible for about half a million dollars of his salary, they Yanks simply got what they could for him.

What they got was outfielder Troy Hughes, who was batting .255 for Greenville of the Class AA Southern League. The Yanks sent Hughes to the Norwich Navigators of the Class AA Eastern League.

September 25, 1995: Purchased Left-handed Pitcher Rick Honeycutt from the Oakland Athletics

An injury to pitcher Jack McDowell had forced manager Buck Showalter to move Sterling Hitchcock out of the bullpen and into a starting role. Only one week remained in this shortened season and the Yanks were close to clinching the wild card spot; nevertheless, Showalter wanted another lefty in the bullpen to go with the two he had, Steve Howe and Bob MacDonald.

For 41-year-old Rick Honeycutt, the Yankees would be his sixth team in a 19-year career, the first half of which had been as a starter. He had a 107-142 career record, including a 5-1 mark and a 2.42 ERA in 49 games for the last-place Athletics this season.

While calling the Yankees a "special team," Honeycutt said he would have preferred to finish the season with Oakland, even though the A's would not be involved in any postseason activity. But then neither would Honeycutt, who by joining the Yankees this late in the season would be ineligible for the postseason should they get there.

To open a place on the roster for Honeycutt, rookie righthander Jeff Patterson (0-0 in three games) was designated for assignment, ending his very brief Yankee career.

October 16, 1995: Signed Righthanded Pitcher Dwight Gooden as a Free Agent

Pitcher Dwight Gooden had missed the last one and a half seasons while under suspension for drug violations. But just as he'd done with Darryl Strawberry four months earlier, George Steinbrenner rescued another one-time Mets star from encroaching oblivion. Steinbrenner said he had spoken with Gooden and was "very impressed with the sincerity of Dwight's commitment to restructuring his life." He added that the scouting reports he'd received on the 30-year-old Gooden had been "awesome."

In 1985, one year after winning the National League's Rookie of the Year Award, Gooden had his greatest season. He won a league-leading 24 games while losing only four, led the league in ERA (1.53), complete games (16), and innings pitched (276.2), and was the unanimous winner of the Cy Young Award. Overall, he had a splendid 157-85 won-lost record, but hadn't had a winning season since 1991.

Gooden was ecstatic at his good fortune. "Being a Yankee is a dream come true," he said. "A year ago I hit rock bottom. Now, I'm a Yankee."

Strawberry was also excited about having his once and future teammate on the Yankees. He appeared confident that like himself, Gooden would not return to his former ways. During the season, he had lobbied for his friend. "He knows I'm back and his desire is to get back," Strawberry said. "He really wants to play in New York. There's really no better place. Maybe people will see we've changed."

Gooden would go 11-7 for the world champion Yankees in 1996, and also throw his first no-hitter. But after a 9-5 season in 1997, he signed as a free agent with the Cleveland Indians.

November 20, 1995: Traded Minor League Righthanded Pitcher Mike DeJean and a Player to Be Named to the Colorado Rockies for Catcher Joe Girardi

Since the end of the 1995 season, Bob Watson had replaced Gene Michael as the Yankees' general manager and Joe Torre had replaced Buck Showalter as the manager. In their first moves, Watson and Torre decided they would sacrifice offense for defense by allowing catcher Mike Stanley to depart as a free agent (he would sign with Boston in December) and making the trade for Joe Girardi.

Torre, a former catcher, defended the switch from Stanley to Girardi. "It depends on what's important to you," he said. "My priority is a catcher. Hopefully, we'll have enough offense. We could make up elsewhere what we're going to lose behind the plate."

The 32-year-old Girardi played four years with the Cubs before the new Colorado team made him their first-round pick in the November 1992 expansion draft. He had a lifetime .269 average in 608 games for the Cubs and Rockies, but had just 18 home runs and only 190 runs batted in. Eight of those home runs and 55 of the RBIs had come in hitter-friendly Denver this past season, by far his best offensively as a big leaguer. Still, it was Girardi's throwing and defense that Torre stressed in appraising his new receiver.

"When a pitcher has confidence in a catcher, he pitches better," Torre said. "Joe Girardi is one of the best catchers in the game. I like the way he takes charge. He's a good physical catcher. He makes all the plays. He has a good arm. Putting fingers down is what it's all about. I feel comfortable having Joe behind the plate."

For his part, Girardi welcomed the trade, claiming that he and his wife were excited about coming to New York. "For two Italians, I don't think there's a better place," he said.

The two minor leaguers the Yanks gave up to get Girardi were both right-handed pitchers. One was Mike DeJean, who had a 5-5 record, with 20 saves in 59 games with Norwich of the Eastern League in 1995. The other was Steve Shoemaker, who went to Colorado on December 6, as the player to be named. Shoemaker had won four and lost five pitching at Class A in '95: 0-1 for Tampa of the Florida State League, and 4-4 for Greensboro of the South Atlantic League.

December 7, 1995: Traded Lefthanded Pitcher Sterling Hitchcock and Third Baseman Russ Davis to the Seattle Mariners for First Baseman Tino Martinez and Righthanded Pitchers Jeff Nelson and Jim Mecir

Even if Don Mattingly didn't retire, as he suggested he would, the Yankees knew they would need a new first baseman in 1996. Mattingly had occupied that position for 14 glorious years, but not since 1989 had he produced an offensive year like the one Seattle's Tino Martinez had this past season. Mattingly had just seven home runs and 49 RBIs for the Yanks in 1995, while Martinez had a .293 batting average, 31 home runs, and 111 runs batted in.

Before his breakthrough year in 1995, Martinez had put together three satisfactory seasons as Seattle's full-time first baseman. And while he was not the equal of Mattingly defensively, he was an adequate first baseman; however, what was perhaps even more important to the Yankees, Martinez's reputation among his peers was much like Mattingly's.

"When you talk to the inside people in baseball," said Joe Torre, the Yanks' new manager, "they talk about his desire and his work ethic. Those things spell leadership to me."

Martinez was thrilled with the prospect of playing for the Yankees. "I've always been a Yankee fan," he said. "It's a dream come true to play for them." Yet, he was aware that he would have to overcome some obstacles. After playing in low-key Seattle, he would have to adjust to the turmoil of playing in New York, while simultaneously attempting to replace the extremely popular Mattingly.

Nevertheless, Martinez called the events of this day "probably one of the greatest days of my life." Besides joining the Yankees, the team he'd rooted for as a child, he was also celebrating his 28th birthday, and the birth of a daughter.

In four seasons with the Mariners, Jeff Nelson had a 13-13 record with nine saves. Rated among the top setup men in the game, he had a 7-3 record with a 2.17 ERA in 1995, while holding the opposition scoreless in 50 of his 62 appearances. At six-foot-eight, and with a sidearm delivery, he was especially effective against righthanded batters, who had a skimpy .187 career batting average against him.

Jim Mecir had been Seattle's third round draft choice in 1991, but he was already 25, and his only big league experience was two games with the Mariners in 1995. He'd spent most of the '95 season with Tacoma of the Pacific Coast League, where in 40 relief appearances he was 1-4 with a 3.10 ERA and eight saves.

For the Mariners, who had been looking for another lefthanded starter to go with Randy Johnson, 24-year-old Sterling Hitchcock was the key player in the deal. After splitting ten major league decisions while bouncing back and forth between New York and the minors between 1992 and 1994, Hitchcock had his breakthrough season in 1995. In 27 games, all starts, he went 11-10 with a 4.70 earned run average and pitched four complete games, including one shutout. He'd also finished strong, winning five of his last six starts. Nevertheless, the Yanks were willing to trade Hitchcock because lefthander Andy Pettitte had looked even more impressive, going 12-9 in 1995, his rookie season.

Seattle planned to use Russ Davis as the replacement at third base for the recently traded Mike Blowers. The 26-year-old Davis had compiled impressive power numbers in the minors, but he was blocked in New York by the presence of Wade Boggs. Davis had gotten to play in 40 games for the Yanks in 1995, at third, first, and designated hitter, batting .276 with two home runs.

December 11, 1995: Signed Free-Agent Infielder Mariano Duncan from the Cincinnati Reds

In 1995, a season he'd split between the Phillies and the Reds, Mariano Duncan batted .287 in 81 games. More noted for his hitting than his fielding, the 31-year-old Duncan had compiled a .262 average in his ten seasons with Los Angeles, Philadelphia, and Cincinnati.

Newly-named manager Joe Torre, who was familiar with Duncan from his National League days, said he might use him as a designated hitter; however, Duncan's primary role figured to be as a reserve infielder, replacing Randy Velarde who'd signed a free-agent contract with the California Angels three weeks earlier.

December 21, 1995: Sold Lefthanded Pitcher Rick Honeycutt to the St. Louis Cardinals

Picked up by the Yankees in late September 1995, Rick Honeycutt made three appearances, pitching a total of just one inning and allowing three runs. Going to St. Louis would reunite him with Tony LaRussa, a manager he'd pitched for on three pennant-winners at Oakland, and who had signed recently to manage the Cardinals in 1996.

December 28, 1995: Traded a Player to Be Named to the Chicago White Sox for Outfielder Tim Raines

In Tim Raines, the Yanks were getting a veteran player, one who could supply speed and leadership to a team that new general manager Bob Watson said lacked both qualities.

"We needed some foot speed, some leadership," said Watson. "More than that, we had heard through various and reliable sources that Tim wanted to play in New York and also wanted to play for the Yankees."

That was true. Raines, who'd batted .285 in 1995, had expressed a desire to play with a contender, specifically the Yankees. Nevertheless, Yankee owner George Steinbrenner and White Sox owner Jerry Reinsdorf chose to delay the announcement of the deal, which probably had been completed more than a week ago.

The switch-hitting Raines had spent 17 seasons in the big leagues. He had a .296 lifetime average, and had accumulated 2,295 hits and 1,134 walks. Among current payers, Raines was generally rated behind only Ricky Henderson both as a base stealer and as a lead off man.

Raines also had 777 stolen bases in his career, fourth on the all-time list, but most had come in his 12 years with Montreal and in his first year in Chicago. Over the past three seasons he'd stolen a total of just 47, a decline he attributed to two factors. It was partly because he was hitting in front of slugger Frank Thomas, Raines claimed, and partly because the White Sox were no longer letting him run on his own.

Yankee manager Joe Torre, who had managed against speedy National League teams for 14 years, said that he would allow Raines to run almost whenever he wanted. Remembering those National League teams, Torre said: "They put so much pressure on the pitchers and the defense with the extra dimension of speed. That's the main reason we were looking for a Tim Raines."

There was another reason. Torre expected to have many young players on his first Yankee team, and he believed that the 36-year-old Raines would help provide leadership for them.

On February 6, 1996, the Yanks sent Chicago minor league third baseman Blaise Kozeniewski to complete the trade.

Raines would play three seasons for the Yankees, before signing with Oakland in January 1999. He batted a combined .299 and helped the Yanks win World Series titles in 1996 and 1998.

December 30, 1995: Signed Free-Agent Lefthanded Pitcher Kenny Rogers from the Texas Rangers

The signing of lefthander David Wells by division-rival Baltimore moved Yankee owner George Steinbrenner to try to sign a lefthanded starter of his own. The Yanks' "brain trust" deliberated between Texas' Kenny Rogers and the other available lefthanded starter, California's Chuck Finley, who likely would have been less expensive.

"I was flopping back and forth," admitted Joe Torre, the Yankees' new manager. "I had plus things on both sides. There was two years age-wise (Rogers was 31, Finley, 33), but leadership qualities on the other side. A guy like Rogers has a lot of weapons to go after you with. Chuck has been a mainstay on that staff, a grinder. It was a tough call."

Rogers, the winner in these deliberations, had been primarily a relief pitcher while in the minors and in his first four years with Texas. Between 1989 and 1992, he'd been in 286 games for the Rangers, with only 12 starts. But when Kevin Kennedy became the Rangers' manager in 1993, he moved Rogers into the starting rotation. Over the next three seasons (including the partial season in 1994), Rogers won 44 games and lost only 25. He was 17-7

in 1995, with a 3.88 earned run average, his lowest ERA since becoming a starter.

June 12, 1996: Traded Righthanded Pitcher Rich Monteleone to the California Angels for Outfielder Mike Aldrete

Rich Monteleone pitched for the Yankees from 1990 through 1993, winning 17 and losing nine, mainly as a long man out of the bullpen. Since becoming a free agent following the '93 season, he'd pitched for the San Francisco Giants, the Chunichi Dragons of the Japanese Central League, and the California Angels. The Angels made Monteleone a free agent after the '95 season, and the Yanks International League affiliate, the Columbus Clippers, signed him. Now, after a 4-3 record in 21 games for the Clippers, he was going back to the Angels.

Before being traded to the Angels in August 1995, 35-year-old Mike Aldrete had played for the Giants, the Expos, the Padres, the Indians, and the Athletics. He had a .264 batting average in ten major league seasons, and in addition to playing the outfield, could play first base, serve as a lefthanded designated hitter, or come off the bench to pinch hit. Aldrete's arrival allowed manger Joe Torre to send his prized young outfielder Ruben Rivera back to Columbus, where he would have the opportunity to play every day.

Although Aldrete missed almost a month on the disabled list, he played in 32 games in 1996, batting .250 with three home runs. He had one at-bat in the World Series win against Atlanta, but the Yanks did not re-sign him for 1997.

June 21, 1996: Traded Minor League Righthanded Pitcher Mike Judd to the Los Angeles Dodgers for Lefthanded Pitcher Billy Brewer

While pitching for the Kansas City Royals between 1993 and 1995, Billy Brewer had won eight and lost seven in 144 relief appearances. The Dodgers traded shortstop Jose Offerman to get Brewer in December 1995, but he'd been with LA's Albuquerque club of the

Pacific Coast League all season. He was currently 2-2 for the Dukes, with a 3.13 ERA and two saves.

A day after trading for Brewer, the Yankees made room for him by releasing Steve Howe. Since 1991, Howe had been in 229 games with the Yanks, all in relief; he'd won 18, lost ten, and had 31 saves. The Yanks also sent righthander Jim Mecir to the International League Columbus Clippers, while calling up Clippers lefthander Dale Polley. Polley would go 1-3 in 32 games, and then he too would be released.

Twenty-one-year-old Mike Judd was 2-2 with ten saves for Greensboro of the South Atlantic League. The Dodgers kept him in that league, moving him to their affiliate in Savannah.

Brewer would split the remainder of the 1996 season between New York, where he was 1-0 in four games, and Columbus. After the season, he signed as a free agent with Cincinnati.

July 31, 1996: Traded Outfielder Ruben Sierra and Minor League Righthanded Pitcher Matt Drews to the Detroit Tigers for First Baseman Cecil Fielder

The Yankees felt they needed another righthanded power hitter for the postseason, particularly if they should again have to face the Seattle Mariners in the American League Division or Championship Series. The Mariners had eliminated the Yanks in the Division Series in 1995, with all three Yankee losses coming against lefthanders, two to Randy Johnson and one to reliever Norm Charlton. Since then, Seattle's lefthanded pitching had become even more formidable with the addition earlier in the week of Terry Mulholland and Jamie Moyer. If the Yankees needed any reminders of their weakness against lefthanded pitchers, it had come earlier this evening. The Rangers' Darren Oliver had beaten them, 9-2, dropping the Yanks' season record against lefties to 15 and 16. Minutes after the final out, and less than two hours before the trading deadline, they completed this deal for Tiger slugger Cecil Fielder.

The 32-year-old Fielder was among the game's top long ball threats. He had hit 276

home runs in eight seasons with Toronto and Detroit, and at least 28 in each of the past six seasons, including a career-high 51 in 1990. In 107 games this season, Fielder had 26 home runs and 80 runs batted in to go with his .247 batting average. By contrast, the Yankees as a team had just 87 home runs this season, one of only three American League clubs with fewer than 100.

"I had some great years here," Fielder said of his time in Detroit, "but it's time to move on. I'm just happy to have the opportunity to go somewhere with someone in contention. I'll try to help the Yankees win the pennant and the World Series."

Manager Joe Torre said he planned to use Fielder as his designated hitter and return Darryl Strawberry to the outfield. That delighted Strawberry. "It's a big lift for me knowing I'm going back to the outfield," he said.

Strawberry also saw the addition of Fielder as a big lift for the team. "With the kind of power hitter he is, Cecil will be a big plus in our lineup. He'll fit right in here," Strawberry predicted. "A lot of guys are pretty excited about Cecil being here in the middle of our lineup. We needed an extra righthanded bat." Torre tentatively agreed. "Cecil will probably hit cleanup to separate the lefty hitters, but I'd like to play with that," he said.

Yankee general manager Bob Watson admitted that the Yankee lineup had been too lefthanded. "We needed to strengthen our right side and we felt in order to do that we had to give up something to get something."

Watson had been very reluctant to give up on pitcher Matt Drews, a player that both he and George Steinbrenner earlier had put a "no trade" label on. The Yanks had deemed the 21-year-old Drews their top pitching prospect ever since making him their first round pick in the 1993 draft. He'd had an outstanding 1995 season, winning 15 and losing seven with Tampa of the Florida State League, but had pitched very poorly this season. His combined 1996 record at Tampa, Norwich of the Eastern League, and Columbus of the International League was one win and ten losses, and he'd walked 72 batters in 84 innings. (The Tigers sent Drews to Jacksonville of the Southern League where he lost all four of his decisions and walked 19 in 31 innings.)

While the Yankee brass hated to see

Drews leave, neither they nor the Yankee players seemed sorry to see Ruben Sierra go. Sierra had come from Oakland in exchange for Danny Tartabull almost exactly one year earlier, and over the final two months batted .260 with seven home runs in 56 games.

He'd been in 96 games this season, with a .258 batting average, but had just 11 home runs and 52 runs batted in. Along with his struggles at the plate, the 30-year-old Sierra had antagonized many of his teammates with his surliness and moodiness. Trade rumors involving Sierra had been around for weeks, so his departure was expected.

"Nothing surprises me," Sierra said of the trade. "I've been in this league for ten years, so none of this surprises me. But this is hard man. This team could go to the World Series. This is hard."

Fielder would bat .260 and hit 13 home runs down the stretch to help the Yanks win the 1996 pennant and World Series. The following season, 1997, he again batted .260 with 13 home runs, while spending two months on the disabled list. In December '97, he signed as a free agent with the Anaheim Angels.

July 31, 1996: Traded Righthanded Pitcher Mark Hutton to the Florida Marlins for Righthanded Pitcher David Weathers

Thirty minutes before the August 1 trading deadline, the Yanks completed this swap of 26-year-old righthanders. It was their second deal of the night, coming less than an hour after they'd traded Ruben Sierra and minor league righthander Matt Drews to Detroit for Cecil Fielder.

Since signing with the Yankees in December 1988, native Australian Mark Hutton had made all the stops in their farm system. He'd appeared briefly in New York in 1993 (1-1 in seven games) and 1994 (0-0 in two games), but spent all of 1995 with Columbus in the International League. Hutton had a horrible year with the Clippers. He won two and lost six with an 8.43 earned run average, while spending most of the season on the disabled list. He'd continued on the disabled list for the first two months of this season and had been in 12 games for the Yanks with an 0-2 record since returning.

David Weathers had pitched briefly for Toronto in 1991 (1-0 in 15 games) and 1992 (0-0 in two games), before the Florida Marlins selected him in the November 1992 expansion draft. In three plus seasons with the Marlins, as a starter and reliever, he had a 16-22 record, including a 2-2 mark in 31 games this season.

August 22, 1996: Claimed Infielder Luis Sojo on Waivers from the Seattle Mariners

Yankee manager Joe Torre had two reasons for acquiring veteran infielder Luis Sojo. One was because Torre wanted to give rookie shortstop Derek Jeter an occasional day off down the stretch. And two was because he felt uncomfortable using either of his other utility infielders—the poor-fielding Mariano Duncan or the weak-hitting Andy Fox—at such a key position.

Sojo, on the other hand, was a reliable fielder with a .259 batting average over seven major league seasons with Toronto, California, and Seattle. He'd batted just .211 in 77 games this season, with one home run and 16 runs batted in.

August 23, 1996: Traded Outfielder Gerald Williams and Righthanded Pitcher Bob Wickman to the Milwaukee Brewers for Lefthanded Pitcher Graeme Lloyd and Outfielder Pat Listach

General manager Bob Watson denied that he'd made this deal because the Yankees' once healthy Eastern Division lead had now shrunk to five games. "This is not something new," he said. "This is something I was trying to do all summer. I've been working on this a long time."

Watson revealed that while he had been reluctant to meet other team's demands for a lefthander earlier in the season, both he and manager Joe Torre agreed that now was the right time to pay the necessary price to get someone like Graeme Lloyd.

Acknowledging that he'd also considered

going after Detroit's Mike Myers, Watson said: "There was no other quality lefthander out there and I didn't want to lose the opportunity to get this particular young man [Lloyd]. And we're running out of time."

Lloyd, a 29-year-old Australian, was 2-4 with a 2.82 ERA this season, his fourth in the big leagues. In 183 games, all with the Brewers and all in relief, he had a 7-16 record and just four saves.

John Wetteland, the ace of the Yankee bullpen, welcomed the addition of Lloyd. "It gives you a lot of flexibility," Wetteland said. "And Graeme is very, very difficult on lefties." Which was precisely the reason the Yanks had traded for him—to pitch to lefthanded hitters in specific situations.

They had originally proposed a one-for-one deal—Lloyd for Bob Wickman—but Milwaukee insisted on the inclusion of Gerald Williams.

"I didn't throw him in. They demanded Gerald," explained Watson. The 30-year-old Williams had spent five years with the Yankees, batting .254 in 313 games. He'd been a most valuable reserve outfielder, but in joining the Brewers he would now get a chance to be a starter.

Like Williams, Wickman had also been a Yankee since 1992. He'd been a part-time starter in 1993, when he won 14 and lost four, but the Yanks had used him almost exclusively in relief since. Wickman had a 4-1 record in 58 games in 1996, and a 31-14 mark in 223 games overall.

In 1992, Pat Listach was a 25-year-old shortstop who batted .290 and was the American League's Rookie of the Year. Listach had not come close to duplicating that season's performance since, nor was he a shortstop anymore. After suffering a knee injury in 1994, the Brewers had moved him, first to second base and now to the outfield. The Yanks saw Listach as Williams's replacement, that is, as a reserve outfielder; however, he reported to the club injured and they immediately placed him on the disabled list.

Six days later, on August 29, the Brewers sent the Yankees Ricky Bones, a 27-year-old righthanded pitcher, plus a player to be named to compensate for the loss of Listach. (Listach was returned to the Brewers after the season.)

Bones, 7-14 for the Brewers, made four decisionless appearances for the Yanks and then signed as a free agent with Cincinnati.

In November, the Yanks received shortstop Gabby Martinez as the player to be named. Martinez played in the Texas League in 1996, where he batted .251 for El Paso.

August 30, 1996: Traded a Player to Be Named to the Pittsburgh Pirates for Third Baseman Charlie Hayes

Since picking up Detroit's Cecil Fielder on July 31, specifically to help improve their record against lefthanded pitchers, the Yanks had gone just 2-9 against southpaws. And although they were still leading the Eastern Division, they'd now lost five in a row, which led some observers to interpret the acquisition of Charlie Hayes, a .248-hitter for Pittsburgh, as a sign of panic.

The situation grew worse when several Yankee players voiced their displeasure at the deal, particularly third baseman Wade Boggs. The lefthanded hitting Boggs knew that the arrival of Hayes, the eighth new player added to the Yankee roster in the past month, meant that they would now bench him against lefthanded pitching. Boggs was particularly upset with manager Joe Torre's explanation for getting Hayes. Torre had claimed that Boggs was "tired," and that his bat was "slow at times." Hayes "might help us win one or two games," Torre said in justifying the trade.

"You don't ask questions around here. You look at the lineup card and you go out and play," said Boggs. "I'll get 3,000 hits somewhere," he added, referring to what was perhaps the real reason for his unhappiness.

Utility man Jim Leyritz sided with Boggs in opposing the trade. "I think it's a slap in the face to Wade," Leyritz said. "I think it's a slap in the face to a lot of people. Me, [Mariano] Duncan and [Luis] Sojo can play third. We got three players who can play third if that's their reason. It's not a good reason."

Back in 1992, Hayes batted .257, with 18 homers and 66 runs batted in as the Yankees' full-time third baseman. But after the season the Yanks signed Boggs as a free agent and then left Hayes unprotected in the expansion draft. The new Colorado Rockies made him the overall third pick and Hayes played in Colorado for two seasons. His first, 1993, had been his career best in average (.305), home runs (25), and RBIs (98). He also had a career-high 45 doubles, the most in the National League that season. Hayes then moved on via free agency to the Phillies in 1995 and to the Pirates this season.

The Yankees completed the trade the next day by sending righthander Chris Corn to the Pirates. Corn was having a sensational season for Class A Tampa of the Florida State League. He had a 12-4 record, a 2.91 earned run average, and 109 strikeouts in 170.1 innings pitched.

December 5, 1996: Traded Catcher Jim Leyritz to the California Angels for Two Players to Be Named

At five years and 126 days, Jim Leyritz had been both the senior Yankee in point of service, and a hero of the 1996 World Series win over Atlanta. But Leyritz was a 32-year-old backup catcher with a high salary, and as Yankee GM Bob Watson explained, the Yanks had rookie Jorge Posada, who was seven years younger, ready to take his place.

"The guy made a big contribution," Watson said of Leyritz. "That hit he had in the World Series and the homer in the playoffs last year [against Seattle] were big. He's going to be missed, but we had to make a decision and we made it."

Leyritz had been the most versatile player on the Yankee team. In addition to serving as Andy Pettitte's personal catcher, he'd also played first base and the outfield, frequently served as the designated hitter, and in emergencies had even played at second and third base. He had a .266 average for his Yankee career, including a .264 mark in 1996.

Leyritz was philosophical about his departure. "I think it's easier to leave because we just won it," he said. "Ten years down the road I'm still part of Yankee history. I would have left with an empty feeling if we hadn't won." Still, he questioned the wisdom of trading him. "I think they left quite a hole," he said, "especially if Joe [Girardi] gets hurt."

Four days later the Yanks received third baseman Ryan Kane and righthander Jeremy Blevins from the Class A level of the Angels

December 5, 1996: *Jim Leyritz*. **The versatile Leyritz had been the senior Yankee in point of service.**

minor league system. Kane had spent 1996 with Cedar Rapids of the Midwest League, where he batted .258 with 14 home runs, while Blevins won two and lost three for Boise of the Northwest League.

December 11, 1996: Signed Free-Agent Lefthanded Pitcher Mike Stanton from the Texas Rangers

The Yankees were understandably concerned about their starting pitching. Jimmy Key had gone to Baltimore via free agency, and Kenny Rogers and Dwight Gooden had injuries to their pitching arms that could prevent them from being ready for the 1997 opener. Most of the off-season speculation centered around which big name starter the Yanks would sign, with free-agents Roger Clemens of the Red Sox and David Wells of the Orioles the prime targets. Additionally, the club knew they could also lose free-agent John Wetteland, their bullpen stopper of the past two seasons, although manager Joe Torre seemed to have a ready solution in Mariano Rivera, who'd served as Wetteland's setup man.

"With the closing situation, I think we

can use Rivera," Torre said. "I don't think there's any question, emotionally, he has the ability to close."

If Rivera became the closer, the Yanks would need a new setup man. That made their acquisition of 29-year-old lefthander Mike Stanton, in the words of his agent Sam Levinson, "a perfect match." The Rangers had wanted to keep Stanton, but the Yankees' offer of a three-year contract, as opposed to the two offered by Texas, and the chance to play for a championship team, led Stanton to sign with the Yanks.

Stanton had pitched for the Atlanta Braves from 1989 until July 1995, when he was traded to the Red Sox. A year later, in July 1996, Boston traded him to Texas and he was a combined 4-4 in 81 games with one save for the Red Sox and Rangers. A middle reliever for most of his career, Stanton had a total of 56 saves, including a career-high 27 with the 1992 Braves.

December 17, 1996: Signed Free-Agent Lefthanded Pitcher David Wells from the Baltimore Orioles

The Yankees had made it perfectly clear that Roger Clemens of the Red Sox was the free agent they most wanted to sign. But after Clemens signed with the Toronto Blue Jays, the Yanks turned to David Wells, a 33-year-old Babe Ruth enthusiast, who had made no secret of his desire to play for the Yankees.

"The opportunity to achieve a childhood dream is what this is about for me," Wells said. "I grew up as a Yankee fan in San Diego. They're always the team I followed in the American League. This is something I've always wanted."

Having lost Jimmy Key to the Orioles as a free agent, the signing of Wells from Baltimore as a free agent made it the equivalent of a trade of these two fine lefthanders. Key had gone 12-11 for the champion Yankees in 1996, while Wells was 11-14 for the second-place Orioles. However, Key was two years older, and though he would have preferred to remain in New York, the Yanks balked at signing him for more than one year.

Besides his one season in Baltimore, Wells had also pitched six years for Toronto, two and a half seasons for Detroit, and a half season for Cincinnati, winning 90 games and losing 75. He had his best season in 1995 when he won a combined 16 games for the Tigers and Reds. (He was 10-3 for the Tigers and 6-5 for the Reds.) Throughout his career, Wells had been particularly effective pitching at Yankee Stadium, where he had a 10-1 record and a 2.93 earned run average.

Although disappointed that the club wouldn't allow him to wear Ruth's number three, long since retired, Wells was generally ecstatic about coming to the Yankees. "I'm going to a stadium where I pitch well. I think I can continue that success. I kept saying this is what I wanted. Now I've got it."

January 3, 1997: Signed Righthanded Pitcher Willie Banks as a Free Agent

Between 1991 and 1995, Willie Banks had pitched for the Twins, the Cubs, the Dodgers, and the Marlins, and had a career 26-35 record. The Phillies claimed him on waivers following the '95 season, but released him during spring training, and Banks was out of baseball for the entire 1996 season.

January 9, 1997: Signed Free-Agent Outfielder Mark Whiten from the Seattle Mariners

Back on September 7, 1993, Mark Whiten had one of the greatest offensive days in baseball history. In the second game of a doubleheader at Cincinnati, he tied the major league single-game records for most home runs (four) and most runs batted in (12). He was playing for the St. Louis Cardinals then, one of seven teams Whiten had been with since reaching the majors with Toronto in 1990. His manager at St. Louis was Joe Torre, who would now be his manager with the Yankees.

Great days, or even good days, had been sporadic for the 30-year-old Whiten. He'd had his best year with those 1993 Cardinals; he batted just .253, but had 25 home runs and 99 RBIs. Whiten had moved around in 1996, playing for three teams: Philadelphia, Atlanta, and Seattle. He had a combined .262 average and 22 home runs, giving him an overall career average of .257 with 93 home runs.

Whiten would encounter personal problems in the summer of 1997, which contributed to the Yankees' August 15 decision to release him. He'd been in 69 games as an outfielder and designated hitter, and batted .265 with five home runs.

April 22, 1997: Traded Outfielder Ruben Rivera, Minor League Righthanded Pitcher Rafael Medina, and Cash to the San Diego Padres for the Rights to Righthanded Pitcher Hideki Irabu, Minor League Second Baseman Homer Bush, Minor League Outfielder Gordon Amerson, and a Player to Be Named

After several successful seasons with the Chiba Lotte Marines of Japan's Pacific League, Hideki Irabu, whose contract had expired, decided he wanted to pitch in the major leagues. Irabu had gone 12-6 for the Marines in 1996, with 167 strikeouts in 157.1 innings. His fastball had been clocked at 97 miles per hour, and Jim Fregosi, a former major leaguer who was now a scout, had compared Irabu to Roger Clemens.

While many teams coveted Irabu, the San Diego Padres had a working agreement with Chiba Lotte and therefore controlled his American rights. However, Irabu said he didn't want to play for the Padres; he wanted to play only for the Yankees. San Diego tried to arrange trades with the Orioles, the Indians, and the Mets, but when Irabu continued to insist he would not play for any team but the Yankees, the Padres finally acquiesced.

Yankee owner George Steinbrenner had been the driving force in making the trade, but it would be manager Joe Torre who would have to decide how to use the 27-year-old Irabu, should the Yanks be able to sign him. (Irabu would sign with the Yankees, but not until May 29.)

Torre, who had not taken part in the decision to obtain Irabu, speculated on where he might function on the Yankee pitching staff.

"The bullpen comes to mind for me right now only because by the time he is ready to get here—if this whole thing is true and taking place—we should have five starters. I can't see any one of my five starters, at this point, being in the bullpen." However, Torre added, "If what Jim Fregosi says about him is true, that's got to be pretty impressive."

Impressive enough to cost the Yankees two of their finest young players and a reported $3 million. Although Ruben Rivera was currently recuperating from shoulder surgery and hadn't played this season, he'd once been the Yanks' number one outfield prospect. He'd shown big league potential in 1996, batting .284 in 46 games, but because the club wanted to give him more at-bats, in June they sent him back to Columbus of the International League. Rivera, perhaps unhappy over the demotion, disappointed the Yankee brass by batting just .235 with ten home runs for the Clippers.

Like Rivera, Rafael Medina was a native of Panama, but at 22, he was a year younger and had no big league experience. He'd been at Norwich of the Eastern League in 1996, where he'd completed one of 19 starts, and had a 5-8 won-lost record with a 3.06 earned run average.

Twenty-four-year-old Homer Bush was the most promising of the Padres' minor leaguers accompanying Irabu to New York. Bush had gotten off to a great start with the Class AAA Las Vegas Stars of the Pacific Coast League in '96, batting .362 after 32 games before an injury caused him to miss the rest of the season. He was back with Las Vegas this season, and when the Yanks got him officially, they sent him to Columbus.

The other two players were outfielders: Gordon Amerson, who batted .203 for Clinton of the Class A Midwest League in 1996, and Vernon Maxwell, San Diego's number two pick in the 1996 draft, whom the Yanks received on June 9 as the player to be named.

June 9, 1997: Traded Righthanded Pitcher David Weathers to the Cleveland Indians for Outfielder Chad Curtis

David Weathers came to the Yankees in a July 31, 1996, trade for pitcher Mark Hutton. He was 0-2 with a 9.35 earned run average, but was more successful in the post-season, winning a game in both the Division and League Championship Series. After he'd started poorly this season—an 0-1 record and a 10.00 ERA in ten games—the Yanks sent Weathers to the International League Columbus Clippers, where he had spent the last three weeks.

"David was his own worst enemy," said Yankee manager Joe Torre. "He didn't have the confidence in himself that I had in him. He got off on the wrong foot and was never able to recover. It's unfortunate he had trouble getting the job done."

After three seasons with the Angels, Chad Curtis was traded to the Tigers in 1995, and then to the Dodgers in July 1996. He'd signed with Cleveland as a free agent this season, and had been in 22 games with a .207 average when he went on the disabled list after a May 14 clubhouse altercation with then teammate Kevin Mitchell. (Curtis was scheduled to be reactivated in a few days.) An excellent fielder and base runner, Curtis had a .264 lifetime average with 161 stolen bases.

July 25, 1997: Signed Outfielder Pete Incaviglia as a Free Agent

A week earlier, when Cecil Fielder went on the disabled list, the Yanks had begun seeking another righthanded slugger to add some punch to their lineup. After failed attempts to get Jose Canseco or Mike Stanley, they signed 33-year-old Pete Incaviglia to a minor league contract and sent him to the International League Columbus Clippers.

"We're going to give him some time to knock the rust off because he hasn't played for three weeks," said Yankee GM Bob Watson. (Incaviglia had a .246 average with five home runs in 138 at-bats for Baltimore this season, but it had been 11 days since the Orioles released him, and he hadn't played much before that.)

Incaviglia, who had signed with the Rangers out of college in 1986, spent five years in Texas. Since then, he'd played for Detroit, Houston, Philadelphia, Baltimore, and even one year in Japan, where he was a teammate of Hideki Irabu on the Chiba Lotte Marines. In all, Incaviglia had 206 major league home runs, but also 1,264 strikeouts.

The Yankees called Incaviglia up after he'd played just three games for the Clippers. "Anyone who had ever played this game had dreamed of wearing a Yankee uniform," he said. "It's exciting."

It was also short-lived. Incaviglia appeared in five games as a designated hitter, getting four singles in 16 at-bats. On August 13, the Yanks got Stanley in a trade with the Red Sox and two days later released Incaviglia.

July 29, 1997: Traded Infielder Mariano Duncan to the Toronto Blue Jays for Minor League Outfielder Angel Ramirez and Cash

Needing to make room for newly acquired Pete Incaviglia, the Yanks satisfied Mariano Duncan's season-long desire to be traded. Actually, they'd traded both Duncan and pitcher Kenny Rogers to San Diego a few weeks earlier in a deal for outfielder Greg Vaughn, but that fell through when Vaughn failed his physical.

The Yanks had signed Duncan as a free agent in 1995 to serve as a utility infielder for departed free-agent Randy Velarde. But by Opening Day 1996, Pat Kelly and Tony Fernandez were on the disabled list, which created an opening at second base. General manager Bob Watson tried to trade for a replacement second baseman, but eventually chose to give Duncan the job when the other clubs asked for either pitcher Scott Kamieniecki or pitcher Mariano Rivera in return.

Duncan rewarded the club's faith in him with an excellent season. He batted .340 with 56 runs batted in, and then hit .313 in the World Series victory over Atlanta. Nevertheless, he was 34, a notoriously weak fielder, and the Yankees preferred he not play second base in 1997. Duncan had been sharing the position with Kelly and Luis Sojo this season, appearing in 50 games, but batting just .244.

"Everybody knows what I went through this year," Duncan said. "This was the most difficult situation of my career. But I'm proud of the ring on my finger; no one can take that away."

Twenty-four-year-old outfielder Angel Ramirez was at Knoxville of the Southern

League, where he was batting .309 with five home runs in 85 games.

August 13, 1997: Traded Minor League Righthanded Pitcher Tony Armas and a Player to Be Named to the Boston Red Sox for First Baseman–Catcher Mike Stanley and Minor League Infielder Randy Brown

General manager Bob Watson's impetus for making this trade was the Yankees' mediocre 20-18 record against lefthanders this season. (They were 50-30 against righthanders.) Further hampered by the loss of Cecil Fielder to a thumb injury a month earlier, and with the likelihood of facing lefthanders Randy Johnson, Jeff Fassero, and Jamie Moyer of Seattle, Jimmy Key of Baltimore, and Chuck Finley of Anaheim down the stretch, Watson found it imperative to add a righthanded power hitter.

Mike Stanley had filled that role for the Yanks from 1992 through 1995, and Watson and manager Joe Torre were confident he could do it again. Stanley was also versatile. He could be the designated hitter; he could give Tino Martinez an occasional day off by playing first base; or, in an emergency, he could be the third-string catcher behind Joe Girardi and Jorge Posada. Stanley hit 24 home runs for the Red Sox in 1996, and he'd added 13 more this season.

"I felt adding another quality right-handed bat would give Joe Torre the weapons he needs to take a real, real serious run and send the message to the rest of the league, especially the people that we are chasing, the fans, and the media that the Yankees are in this to win the whole thing," Watson said.

Tony Armas, who was just 19, had been on the Yankees' list of "untouchables," according to Watson. "But this shows you what we are all about when we say we are committed to winning. My position is, if it makes good baseball sense and good economic sense, go ahead and do it."

Both Armas and Randy Brown, the minor leaguers in the deal, remained in their respective leagues, but switched teams. Armas went from Tampa in the Class A Florida State League to Sarasota, while Brown went from

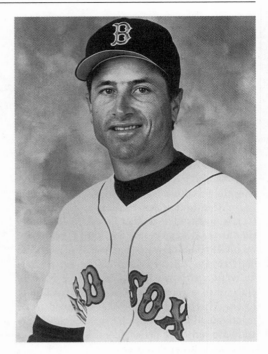

August 13, 1997: *Mike Stanley.* **Expecting to face tough lefthanders down the stretch, the Yanks wanted Stanley's righthanded bat.**

Trenton in the Class AA Eastern League to Norwich.

Watson had said he would try to sign Stanley for more than just the remaining six weeks of this season, but failed to do so. After batting .287 with three home runs in 28 games, Stanley signed to play with Toronto in 1998.

On September 29, the Yanks sent righthander Jim Mecir to Boston as the player to be named. Mecir had split the 1996 and 1997 seasons between New York and Columbus of the International League. In a total 51 relief appearances with the Yankees, he had a 1-5 record with no saves. After the season, the Red Sox left him unprotected and the Tampa Bay Devil Rays made him the 36th pick in the November expansion draft.

August 15, 1997: Traded Minor League Righthanded Pitcher Frisco Parotte to the Chicago Cubs for Second Baseman Rey Sanchez

Supposedly, the Yanks were getting Rey Sanchez to back up shortstop Derek Jeter and second baseman Pat Kelly. However, there was strong evidence that they'd really gotten him to be their starting second baseman, replacing Kelly who was in a 4 for 27 slump.

The need for another infielder had arisen after Luis Sojo broke his forearm. While general manager Bob Watson admitted that Sanchez had not been his first choice, he did say that he'd been "high on my list." Others possibly higher on Watson's list were Jeff Huson of Milwaukee and Craig Grebeck of Anaheim. The Yanks had even called up Homer Bush from Columbus of the International League in case of an emergency, but now after getting Sanchez, Bush, who'd played in two games, would be returning to Columbus. "I got a chance to come up, and I can say I played with the Yankees," Bush said as he departed.

The 29-year-old Sanchez had been with the Cubs for his entire seven-year major league career. He had a .262 lifetime batting average, including a .249 mark in 97 games this season. On joining the Yankees, Sanchez did take over at second base and batted .312 in 38 games, but left after the season to sign with San Francisco.

The Yanks had picked up righthander Frisco Parotte, now 21, on the 29th round of the 1993 draft. Currently at Greensboro of the South Atlantic League, he was 1-1 with two saves and a 4.19 earned run average.

November 7, 1997: Traded Lefthanded Pitcher Kenny Rogers to the Oakland Athletics for a Player to Be Named

While Kenny Rogers had pitched a few good games in his two years in New York, they were far too few for someone who'd signed a four-year, $20 million contract. He'd gone 12-8 in 1996, but only 6-7 in 1997 and even worse, had fallen out of favor with owner George Steinbrenner, manager Joe Torre, and the fans. Actually, the Yanks had tried to trade the 33-year-old Rogers, along with infielder Mariano Duncan, to San Diego the previous summer. Outfielder Greg Vaughn would have come to the Yankees in the deal, but the Yanks canceled it when Vaughn failed his physical.

"I have nothing against Kenny Rogers, but we just felt it was in our best interest and his to get him into a situation where he can be comfortable and start over," said Steinbrenner, who would be paying a portion of his salary for the next two seasons. "He can do that in Oakland. There's no New York pressure. Not everyone is a New York person," the owner concluded.

While the trade was constructed to read that Oakland would send the Yankees a player to be named, both clubs had already agreed that the player would be 31-year-old third baseman Scott Brosius. The Athletics would protect Brosius in the November 18 expansion draft and then formally turn him over to New York.

Brosius had missed 47 games with a broken arm in 1996, but still batted .304 with 22 home runs and 71 runs batted in. However, he'd followed that with an awful 1997 season: a meager .203 batting average, 11 home runs, and 41 RBIs. Overall, Brosius was a .248-hitter for his seven seasons in Oakland, but the Yanks were hoping that in 1998 he could approach the form he'd shown in 1996.

November 11, 1997: Traded Third Baseman Charlie Hayes to the San Francisco Giants for Minor League Lefthanded Pitcher Alberto Castillo and Minor League Outfielder Chris Singleton

From late August 1996, when the Yanks got him from Pittsburgh, and on through the 1997 season, Charlie Hayes had battled Wade Boggs for playing time at third base. Both were unhappy, and now one was gone and one would be going. (Boggs was a free agent who would sign in December to play for the new Tampa Bay Devil Rays.)

"George [Steinbrenner] wanted him gone, so he's gone," said Tommy Tanzer, Hayes's agent. "The conflict with Boggs wore everybody down and eventually it gobbled up Charlie. I'm not saying Charlie handled it well. I think we just knew it was time to move on. You can't fight city hall—or people higher."

Steinbrenner did indeed want Hayes gone, so much so that he agreed to pay his entire salary for the next two seasons. General manager Bob Watson confirmed that the Yanks had not intended to shelter Hayes, who'd batted .258 with 11 home runs and 53

RBIs in 1997, in the upcoming expansion draft.

"We were not planning to protect him, and if we lost him, we wanted to get something back for him. It's no secret he had fallen out of favor with certain individuals in this organization."

The departures of Hayes and Boggs left a hole at third base that the Yanks seemed unlikely to fill with either minor league prospect Mike Lowell or newly acquired Scott Brosius, a .203-batter for Oakland in 1997. Watson acknowledged that he would seek a trade for a third baseman, with John Valentin of the Red Sox and Robin Ventura of the White Sox seemingly the prime targets.

Chris Singleton batted .317 with 26 doubles, ten triples, and nine home runs for Shreveport of the Texas League in 1997, although at 25, he was old for a player to still be at the Class AA level. Singleton's statistics were far more impressive than those of pitcher Alberto Castillo, the other player the Yanks were getting for Hayes. Castillo had pitched for Class A San Jose of the California League in '97, winning two and losing two with a 5.61 ERA.

November 25, 1997: Signed Free-Agent Infielder Dale Sveum from the Pittsburgh Pirates

When the Yankees traded Charlie Hayes and allowed Wade Boggs to leave via free agency, they created an opening at third base for 1998. Seemingly not ready to turn the position over to rookie Mike Lowell, they had acquired Scott Brosius from Oakland in a trade for pitcher Kenny Rogers; however, Brosius, a righthanded batter, was coming off a .203 season for the Athletics, and the Yanks were unsure if he would hit enough to be a full-time player. In Dale Sveum, they were getting a 34-year-old lefthanded hitter who manager Joe Torre could use if he chose to platoon his third basemen.

A ten-year veteran, Sveum had played for the Brewers, Phillies, White Sox, Athletics, and Mariners before going to Pittsburgh in 1996. He was a lifetime .239 hitter, but in 1997 batted .261 in 126 games for the Pirates, with 12 home runs and 47 runs batted in.

Brosius would hit well enough to be the full-time third baseman in 1998, while Sveum would play in just 30 games. He was batting .155, with no extra-base hits when the Yank released him on August 3.

December 10, 1997: Signed Free-Agent Designated Hitter Chili Davis from the Kansas City Royals

After watching the underperforming Cecil Fielder and eight others fill the designated hitter role in 1997, owner George Steinbrenner made the acquisition of a new DH a number one priority for 1998. The man he wanted for the job was Chili Davis.

"We thought one of our problems last year was moving from DH to DH," Steinbrenner said. "You look at Davis and he's a professional DH. That's what we lacked last year." Davis truly had become a professional DH, having not played in the field since 1994.

"You want your DH to get homers and RBIs and he'll do that," predicted Yankee general manager Bob Watson. The switch-hitting Davis certainly had done so in the past. Over his 17-year major league career with the Giants, Twins, Angels, and Royals, he had 328 home runs and close to 1,300 runs batted in. In 1997, his one season in Kansas City, he hit 30 home runs and had 90 RBIs to go with a .279 average. Davis had driven in 90 or more runs in nine of the past 11 seasons, and for the past five had batted a combined .310 with runners in scoring position. His 30 home runs in 1997, which were a career-best, helped persuade Steinbrenner to go after him despite Davis's advanced baseball age.

"He's a well-conditioned athlete, so I'm not worried about him being 38," Steinbrenner said. "He's a warrior. He brings a lot of extras with him. We got a guy who fits the bill and got rid of a guy who didn't fit the bill," the owner said, taking a final swipe at Fielder.

December 22, 1997: Signed Free-Agent Righthanded Pitcher Darren Holmes from the Colorado Rockies

Darren Holmes wasn't the front-line starter the Yanks were seeking; nevertheless, he figured to be a valuable addition to their pitching staff. While six of his 42 appearances for the Rockies in 1997 had been as a starter, Holmes was primarily a relief pitcher. His record in '97 was 9-2, with three saves, though he did have an unimpressive 5.34 earned run average, poor even by Coors Field standards.

Speaking of his new acquisition, Yankee general manager Bob Watson stressed Holmes's adaptability. "When I talked with Joe Torre, he thought with that versatility he [Holmes] might fit in as a possible fifth starter. Or he can be worked out of the bullpen on the days [Mariano] Rivera is not available to close. He has closing in his background."

The 31-year-old Holmes had also pitched for the Brewers and briefly for the Dodgers before becoming an original member of the Rockies in 1993. He had a career record of 28-22 and, as Watson said, did have closing in his background, having compiled 55 saves.

February 6, 1998: Traded Minor League Lefthanded Pitcher Eric Milton, Minor League Righthanded Pitcher Danny Mota, Minor League Outfielder Brian Buchanan, Minor League Infielder Cristian Guzman, and Cash to the Minnesota Twins for Second Baseman Chuck Knoblauch

Seldom had a player seemed happier to be joining a new club than Chuck Knoblauch appeared to be at joining the Yankees. "I'm excited. I can't believe I'm a Yankee, and it feels great saying that," he said. "I can't wait to have a chance to win every night."

Knoblauch had gone from winning the American League Rookie of the Year Award in 1991, to currently ranking among the game's best second baseman. He had a .304 batting average for his seven years with Minnesota, and held the club career stolen bases record with 276. Knoblauch had also led the league in doubles, with 45 in 1994, and triples, with 14 in 1996. In 1997, he scored 117 runs and stole 62 bases for the Twins, while hitting .291, the first time in four seasons he'd failed to reach the .300 mark.

Minnesota had won the World Series in 1991, Knoblauch's rookie year, then finished

February 6, 1998: *Chuck Knoblauch.* **The Yanks added Knoblauch while managing to keep most of their best prospects.**

second in the Western Division in 1992. But the Twins had not been competitive since, and Knoblauch had asked them to trade him to a team with which he could return to the World Series, specifically the Yankees. Three months earlier, the Twins and Yanks had discussed a deal that would have brought Knoblauch to New York; however, the talks bogged down when Minnesota asked for any three of four young minor leaguers, all of whom the Yanks regarded as "untouchable." The four were pitcher Eric Milton, outfielder Ricky Ledee, third baseman Mike Lowell, and shortstop D'Angelo Jiminez.

Now, with the approval of Bud Selig, baseball's acting commissioner who had to okay the $3 million going from New York to Minnesota, the deal was completed. While the Yanks hated giving up Milton, they felt they couldn't pass on a 29-year-old All-Star, one whom they envisioned batting lead off and pairing with shortstop Derek Jeter to form baseball's best double play combination.

"He's going to help because the lineup is going to be more stable," said Yankee outfielder Paul O'Neill. "You can pencil in guys every day and it becomes more clearly defined what you're expected to do."

Brian Cashman, who'd replaced Bob Watson as the Yankees' general manager three days earlier, explained the club's thinking in making the trade. "The goal was to secure the player and do it while doing as little damage to the organization as you can have, and I think we've done that."

By "doing as little damage to the organization," Cashman meant that while Milton was gone, the Yanks retained several of their other prize minor leaguers, including Ledee, Lowell, and pitcher Luis de los Santos.

Milton, who'd starred at the University of Maryland, was the Yanks' number one pick in the 1996 amateur draft. They sent him to Tampa in the Florida State League to begin the 1997 season, and later to Norwich of the Eastern League. Making 14 starts in each league, Milton was 8-3 at Tampa and 6-3 with Norwich.

In 1995, Brian Buchanan had suffered a near career-ending compound leg fracture. He missed almost the entire season, but came back to have a decent year in 1996 and an even better one in 1997. Playing most of the '97 season with Norwich (he also played 18 games at Columbus of the International League), Buchanan batted a combined .305 with 14 home runs and 76 RBIs. Yet despite his excellent season, the Yanks had left him unprotected in the November 1997 expansion draft, moreover, no other team seemed interested.

Both 19-year-old Cristian Guzman and 22-year-old Danny Mota played at the Class A level in 1997: Guzman with Greensboro of the South Atlantic League, and Mota with Oneonta of the New York–Pennsylvania League. Guzman, a switch hitter, batted .273, while Mota pitched in 27 games, won his only decision, and had 17 saves and a 2.22 earned run average.

March 8, 1998: Traded Infielder Andy Fox to the Arizona Diamondbacks for Righthanded Pitchers Marty Janzen and Todd Erdos

Two days after putting pitcher Danny Rios on waivers (Kansas City would claim him) and signing Cuban defector Orlando Hernandez, the Yanks added two more right-handed pitchers. Both Marty Janzen and Todd

Erdos had pitched briefly at the major league level, but both figured to spend 1998 with Columbus in the International League. (They did, although Janzen also pitched for Norwich in the Eastern League, while Erdos did get into two games with the Yankees.)

Janzen had come up through the Yankee organization and was the highest rated of the three Class A pitchers the Yanks sent to Toronto in July 1995 for David Cone. He'd yet to live up to expectations, winning six and losing seven for the Blue Jays, while splitting the last two seasons between Toronto and the International League Syracuse Chiefs.

Erdos had a 2-0 record in 11 relief appearances for the San Diego Padres in 1997, after having registered 27 saves for Mobile of the Southern League earlier in the season. Both he and Janzen had been taken by the Diamondbacks four months earlier in the November 1997 expansion draft—Erdos in the second round and Janzen in the third.

After spending all of 1996 with the Yankees, batting .196 in 113 games, Andy Fox was at Columbus for most of 1997. He did play in 22 games with the Yanks, with a .226 average, but the recent addition of Chuck Knoblauch had made it unlikely that Fox could stick with the Yankees in 1998. Fox was out of minor league options, which meant if the Yanks didn't trade him they would lose him to waivers.

"There really was no fit here for Andy," said GM Brian Cashman. "And we're glad to be able to accommodate him and find him a chance to earn work in the major leagues."

Fox appeared sorry to leave, but said he was happy to be rejoining Buck Showalter, his former manager with the Yankees who would be leading the Diamondbacks.

"It worked out well for me," he said. "Winning a World Series ring here was great, but it's nice to go someplace where people know you and want you."

June 4, 1998: Traded Righthanded Pitcher Willie Banks to the Arizona Diamondbacks for Righthanded Pitcher Scott Brow and Minor League Right-handed Pitcher Joe Lisio

Willie Banks had been out of baseball in 1996; nevertheless, the Yanks signed him in

January 1997 and assigned him to Columbus of the International League. After Banks had compiled a 14-5 record with the Clippers, the Yanks called him up and he went 3-0 in five games. His record in nine games this season was 1-1, but Banks had a 10.05 earned run average and the Yanks had recently designated him for assignment.

Twenty-nine-year-old Scott Brow (the same age as Banks) had pitched briefly for the Toronto Blue Jays in 1993, 1994, and 1996. This season, he'd been in 17 games for the Diamondbacks, with a 1-0 record and a 7.17 ERA. The Yanks sent Brow to Columbus, while transferring Joe Lisio from High Desert in the California League, where he was 1-2, to Tampa of the Florida State League.

August 23, 1998: Traded Minor League Outfielder Shea Morenz and Minor League Righthanded Pitcher Ray Ricken to the San Diego Padres for Righthanded Pitcher Jim Bruske and Minor League Righthanded Pitcher Brad Kaufman

Although they were comfortably ahead in the Eastern Division race, recent injuries to Jeff Nelson and Darren Holmes had left the Yanks short of righthanded relievers. Available were minor leaguers Scott Brow and Marty Janzen, both of whom had major league experience, but neither one had been pitching well.

Meanwhile, Jim Bruske had compiled a 3-0 mark in 35 relief appearances for the Dodgers earlier this season. In late July, the Dodgers traded him to San Diego, and after four games, the Padres sent him to Las Vegas of the Pacific Coast League. Bruske had been in five games with the Stars, and had one decision, a loss, and a 6.00 ERA. Overall, the 33-year-old Bruske had spent two stints with both the Dodgers and the Padres, and had a 7-1 record in 87 games, all in relief.

The Yanks assigned Bruske to Columbus with the likelihood they would bring him up after September 1, when roster sizes expanded. They did, and Bruske went 1-0 in three games but was released during spring training, 1999. Also going to Columbus was Brad Kaufman,

who had a 9-9 record and a 6.39 earned run average for Las Vegas.

Going the other way, to Las Vegas, were Ray Ricken, who had a 5-4 record in 14 starts for the Norwich Navigators of the Eastern League, and outfielder Shea Morenz, a former first-round draft choice, who'd yet to live up to expectations. Morenz had been also been at Norwich, where in 116 games he'd batted .252, with 15 home runs and 52 runs batted in.

November 16, 1998: Traded Minor League Third Baseman Allen Butler to the Minnesota Twins for Righthanded Pitcher Dan Naulty

Dan Naulty had spent considerable portions of each of his three big league seasons with Minnesota on the disabled list. Yet, he'd managed to pitch a combined 97 games for the Twins, all in relief, and had a 4-5 record, five saves, and a 4.61 earned run average. Naulty had an 0-2 record and a 4.94 ERA in 19 games in 1998, but his season ended prematurely when he went on the disabled list on July 12.

Playing in the hitter-friendly South Atlantic League in 1998, Allen Butler batted .268 for the Greensboro Bats, with 19 home runs and 81 runs batted in.

February 1, 1999: Traded Third Baseman Mike Lowell to the Florida Marlins for Minor League Lefthanded Pitcher Ed Yarnall, and Minor League Righthanded Pitchers Mark Johnson and Todd Noel

Each of the key members of the pitching staff that led the Yanks to 125 victories in 1998 figured to be back in 1999; nevertheless, GM Brian Cashman believed the strength and depth of Yankee pitching talent at the minor league level needed improvement.

"You never have enough pitching. Pitching is the name of the game," Cashman said. "If a club steps up and satisfies us to the point we're comfortable moving a player of Mike Lowell's caliber, we'll move."

While the club was sorry to lose such a

highly rated prospect as Lowell, they believed that each of the three young pitchers they were getting possessed major league potential.

"If we could utilize Lowell by trading him and bringing three legitimate prospects into the organization, we were going to do it," Cashman explained. "Our goal for the winter, once all of our guys were signed, was to try to shore up our pitching at the minor league level. And we believe we've done that."

Coincidentally, all three of the Yanks' new pitchers had gone to Florida as a result of the Marlins' dispersal of their best players following their World Series victory in 1997.

Lefthander Ed Yarnall came from the Mets in the May 1998 trade for Mike Piazza. The Marlins kept Yarnall in the Eastern League, transferring him from the Mets' Binghamton team to their affiliate in Portland. After he went a combined 9-0, the Marlins promoted Yarnall to the International League Charlotte Knights, where he had a 4-5 record.

Mark Johnson, a former first-round draft pick by the Astros, went to Florida in December 1997 as the player to be named in the deal that had sent Moises Alou to Houston a month earlier. Like Yarnall, Johnson also pitched for Portland in '98, winning five and losing 14 in 26 starts.

Twenty-year-old Todd Noel, the youngest of the three, had also been a first round draft pick. The Chicago Cubs picked Noel number one in 1996, but then included him in the July 31, 1998, trade that brought them pitcher Felix Heredia. Noel had a combined 8-8 record in the Midwestern League, pitching first for Rockford and then for Kane County.

Cashman assessed the three this way: "Noel is a big power pitcher, Johnson has an above-average fastball, and Yarnall is a finesse lefthander."

Lowell had appeared to be the Yanks' third baseman of the future after he hit 30 home runs in 1997: 15 at Norwich in the Eastern League, and 15 at Columbus in the International League. The club had signed Scott Brosius to play third in 1998 with the expectation that Lowell would take over in 1999. Lowell went back to Columbus in '98 and had an even better season: a .304 average, 26 home runs and 99 RBIs. The Yanks called him up in September and he played in eight games, get-

ting four hits in 15 at-bats. However, Brosius had done so well in the team's record-breaking '98 season, the Yanks signed him to a three-year deal, making Lowell expendable.

Nevertheless, Yankee manager Joe Torre thought the trade would be in Lowell's best interests. "I'm happy for him," Torre said, "because he was going to have to wait a couple of years to play for us, and he's probably ready to play in the big leagues right now."

February 18, 1999: Traded Lefthanded Pitchers David Wells and Graeme Lloyd, and Second Baseman Homer Bush to the Toronto Blue Jays for Righthanded Pitcher Roger Clemens

After rolling through the American League and sweeping the San Diego Padres in the World Series, many people were calling the 1998 Yankees the best team in baseball history. They'd gone through the off-season without making any major personnel moves; nevertheless, when spring training began, the Yanks were the clear favorites to win another pennant. Therefore, this trade, which brought them Roger Clemens, winner of the last two Cy Young awards, stunned everyone.

In many ways, Clemens's trade to the Yankees highlighted the dangers to the game caused by the growing disparity between baseball's big market teams and its small ones. Clemens would actually have preferred that Toronto trade him to the Houston Astros, closer to his home. But, he didn't prefer it enough to play for the lesser amount of money the Astros offered. Clemens later told the Blue Jays he would be willing to stay in Toronto, but by that time Jays GM Gord Ash had decided he'd rather have a first-rate lefty on the staff.

Over the years, and especially when he pitched for the Red Sox, Clemens had often antagonized the Yankees with his aggressive style of pitching. Now he was a Yankee, and thrilled to be one.

"I know the tradition. I love it," he said. "I love pitching at Yankee Stadium, the monuments, all the stuff that goes with it."

The Red Sox had given up on Clemens two years earlier, and the parting had been

February 1, 1999: *Roger Clemens*. Clemens's unhappy exit from Boston figured to further fuel
the bitter Yankees–Red Sox rivalry.

bitter. His pitching against Boston in a Yankee uniform was sure to add another chapter
to the long and storied Yankees–Red Sox rivalry. On the other hand, no one could remember a player more sorry to leave the Yankees than David Wells. Nor were there many
Yankee players that their fans were more sorry
to see go. Furthermore, many observers believed that by exchanging Wells for Clemens,
the Yankees had actually weakened themselves.

Wells, who got the news in Tampa, had
become extremely popular in his two seasons
in New York. Besides being a very good
pitcher, he loved the city and the team, and
the fans loved his rebellious style.

"I'm a little emotional right now," he said
on learning he was going back to Toronto. "Just
give me a couple of days. It's a little tough to
take."

The Yankees had signed Wells as a free
agent in December 1996, doing so only because
they couldn't sign Clemens. While sometimes
erratic, Wells had gone 16-10 and 18-4 as a
Yankee, had pitched a perfect game in 1998,
and had an unblemished 5-0 record in post-
season play.

"He almost became a cult hero overnight
because of the perfect game," said David Cone,
Wells's friend and teammate, who would pitch
baseball's next perfect game, in 1999. "He made
his mark in Yankee history. He should be
proud of that. It won't be forgotten." Yet, Cone
was pleased that in return for Wells, the Yanks
were getting someone the caliber of Clemens.
"How can you not be pleased," he said, "when
you add the best pitcher in the game."

George Steinbrenner had also been fond
of Wells, but couldn't resist another chance to
get Clemens, a five-time Cy Young Award
winner and a pitcher he'd coveted for years.
"We're getting a man who makes it a notable
day in Yankee history," Steinbrenner said.

At age 36, Clemens was still at the top of
his form. His 20-6 record for the Blue Jays in
1998 marked his fifth 20-win season and raised
his lifetime record to 233-124. Besides leading
all active pitchers in games won, Clemens also
led in strikeouts (3,153), shutouts (44), and was
third in earned run average (2.95).

"Roger Clemens is a non-stop Hall of
Famer," said Yankee manager Joe Torre, stating the obvious. "The last two years, what he's
done, it's incredible." Torre also pointed out
the special circumstances under which all Yankee managers labored. "We need to get to the
World Series, because of who we are and what
we spend on players," he said.

Clemens's addition made the Yanks so
likely to return to postseason play that their
only weakness seemed to be finding a replacement for Graeme Lloyd. Lloyd had only four
wins and one save in his 109 games with the
Yankees, but he'd been a most valuable situa-
tional pitcher. Torre had used him as his middle-innings lefthander against tough lefthanded hitters. Lloyd had been extremely
effective in 1998, appearing in 50 games, with
a 3-0 record and a 1.67 earned run average.

Lloyd was surprised that the Yanks would
choose to alter a championship team. "I'm
shocked," he said. "To break up the team—it's
a shame."

Meanwhile, Homer Bush thought the
trade would help his career. Bush had a .378
batting average in his two seasons, but had batted only 82 times. With Chuck Knoblauch
ahead of him, he would likely see little playing time in New York.

"It's a great opportunity for me after

watching greatness in New York," Bush said. "Maybe here I can get more at-bats and have some fun."

March 30, 1999: Traded Righthanded Pitcher Darren Holmes to the Arizona Diamondbacks for Righthanded Pitcher Ben Ford and Catcher Izzy Molina

The Yankees had made an off-season trade for righthanded reliever Dan Naulty, believing that he could fill the same role that Darren Holmes had in 1998. They also believed Naulty could do it for a lot less money, even after agreeing to send the Diamondbacks about a million dollars to help cover Holmes's salary. The 33-year-old Holmes appeared in 34 games for the Yankees in 1998, but also spent five weeks on the disabled list with disk problems in his lower back. He had an 0-3 record, with two saves and a 3.33 earned run average.

Arizona GM Joe Garagiola, Jr., said Holmes and John Frascatore, whom he'd gotten in a trade with St. Louis earlier in the day, were "reliable, durable guys who deepen our bullpen."

Ben Ford, who would begin the season with the International League Columbus Clippers, was also a reliever. Since the Yankees drafted him out of high school in 1994, Ford had never started a game. He was working his way through the Yanks' minor league chain when Arizona selected him in the November 1997 expansion draft. The six-foot-seven-inch Ford had a 2-5 record and 13 saves for Tucson of the Pacific Coast league in 1998 and also appeared in eight games for the Diamondbacks.

Twenty-seven-year-old Izzy Molina had signed as a free agent with Arizona this past December. He'd spent parts of the last three seasons with Oakland, compiling a .203 batting average in 68 games.

July 3, 1999: Claimed Infielder Jeff Manto on Waivers from the Cleveland Indians

Just when it appeared that Shane Spencer had beaten out Chad Curtis and Rickey Ledee

as the Yanks' regular left fielder, an irregular heartbeat forced Spencer to go on the disabled list. The club filled his roster spot by claiming veteran infielder Jeff Manto from Cleveland. The 34-year-old Manto had been a 35th round draft choice of the Yanks in 1982, but chose not to sign with them. Three years later he signed with the Angels and had subsequently gone on to play for the Orioles, the Phillies, the Mariners, the Tigers, and the Red Sox. A .227 career-hitter, Manto had been in 12 games for Cleveland with five hits in 25 at-bats.

When the Yanks traded him for Jim Leyritz on July 31, they designated Manto for assignment. He'd been in six games with one hit in eight at-bats.

July 3, 1999: Signed Lefthanded Pitcher Allen Watson

Seeking possible future lefthanded bullpen help, the Yanks signed 28-year-old Allen Watson and sent him to their International League team in Columbus. To clear a spot on the 40-man roster, they moved injured minor league righthander Mike Jerzembeck to the 60-day disabled list.

Yankee manager Joe Torre was managing the Cardinals in 1991 when St. Louis drafted Watson in the 21st round. Watson reached St. Louis in 1993 and also had pitched for the Giants, the Angels, the Mets, and the Mariners. Seattle had gotten him after just three appearances. Often injured, Watson had done a lifetime record of 47-55, including a combined two wins and three losses in 17 games for the Mariners and the Mets this season.

July 31, 1999: Traded Minor League Righthanded Pitcher Gerald Padua to the San Diego Padres for Catcher Jim Leyritz

The trade for Jim Leyritz would be the only one the Yanks would make before the trading deadline as attempts to get relievers Arthur Rhodes from Baltimore or Roberto Hernandez from Tampa fell through. Leyritz, 35, had been one of the heroes of the Yanks' 1996 World Series win over Atlanta, but in December of that year the club traded him to the Angels. He'd been on the move ever since, having made stops in Texas and Boston before coming to San Diego. Just off the disabled list after breaking a hand on June 22, he was hitting .239 with eight home runs and 21 RBIs in 50 games.

Leyritz denied that he'd asked the Padres to trade him to New York; nevertheless, he was most appreciative of them having done so. "They could have traded me anywhere," he said, "but it shows the class of this organization to give me another opportunity back in New York."

Yankee manager Joe Torre, along with several of his players, were glad to have Leyritz back. "He's a good hitter and he loves the spotlight," Torre said. "He's a friend of all of ours," added Derek Jeter. "He was part of the '96 team. He's valuable."

Leyritz, in turn, explained why he was thrilled to be back. "Playing in New York for as many years as I did, it's almost like being in the World Series every day." To make room for Leyritz, the Yanks designated infielder Jeff Manto for assignment.

Gerald Padua, a 22-year-old righthander form the Dominican Republic, had compiled an impressive record with the Class A Greensboro Bats of the South Atlantic League. In a league that was geared towards hitters, he'd won nine and lost four, with a 2.86 earned run average. Padua had struck out 155 in 139.2 innings while walking just 35. The Padres kept him at Class A, assigning him to Rancho Cucamonga of the California League.

December 13, 1999: Traded Outfielder Chad Curtis to the Texas Rangers for Minor League Righthanded Pitchers Sam Marsonek and Brandon Knight

The highlight of Chad Curtis's two and a half seasons in New York were his two home runs (including the game winner) in game three of this past season's World Series sweep of Atlanta. During his tenure with the Yankees, the 31-year-old Curtis had clashed personally with several of his teammates, including Derek Jeter. Nevertheless, he'd been a reliable outfielder and designated hitter for the Yanks. Since coming from Cleveland in a June

1997 trade for pitcher David Weathers, he'd batted .263 in 340 games. Curtis's departure seemed to indicate that either Shane Spencer or Ricky Ledee would be the Yankees' left fielder in 2000.

Brandon Knight, 24, was with the Rangers Triple-A team at Oklahoma City in 1999, where he had a 9-8 record and a 4.91 earned run average. His five complete games were the most in the Pacific Coast League that season.

Twenty-one-year-old Sam Marsonek pitched for Charlotte of the Class A Florida State League in 1999. He won three, lost nine, and had a 5.54 ERA.

December 14, 1999: Traded Righthanded Pitcher Dan Naulty to the Los Angeles Dodgers for Minor League First Baseman Nick Leach

In his one season in New York, 29-year-old Dan Naulty had a 1-0 record and a 4.33 earned run average in 33 games. He's not been on the Yanks' post-season roster, and on December 8, the club had designated him for assignment; that meant they had ten days in which to trade him, send him outright to the minor leagues, or place him on unconditional waivers.

By trading him they acquired first baseman Nick Leach, 22, who had 20 home runs, 74 runs batted in, and a .283 average for the Vero Beach team of the Class A Florida State League.

December 22, 1999: Traded Righthanded Pitcher Hideki Irabu to the Montreal Expos for Minor League Righthanded Pitcher Jake Westbrook and Two Players to Be Named

Despite occasional outstanding performances, Hideki Irabu had not come close to being the pitcher the Yankees had expected him to be. The rights to the former star pitcher of the Japanese Pacific League's Chiba Lotte Marines were owned by the San Diego Padres, but Irabu insisted he would play only for the Yankees. After much negotiating, the Yanks arranged a trade for him in April 1997, sending the Padres two fine young prospects: outfielder Ruben Rivera and pitcher Rafael Medina, plus a bundle of money.

The 30-year-old Irabu's seeming disregard for staying in physical shape had frustrated manager Joe Torre and incensed owner George Steinbrenner. While Irabu had earned the American League Pitcher of the Month Award in both May 1998 and July 1999, overall, he had just a 29-20 record with 4.80 ERA for his three years as a Yankee (11-7 and 4.84 in 1999).

Yankee GM Brian Cashman, who engineered the trade, summarized Irabu's stay in New York. "We saw those flashes of brilliance that attracted us. But obviously there were times when there were inconsistencies. Maybe he gets a fresh start in a new country with a new team," said Cashman. "In New York it's a tough situation. It's not for everybody," he added. "I'm not saying it wasn't for Hideki. But playing elsewhere can be easier for some players. That might be the case with Hideki."

Irabu's departure opened a spot in the 2000 starting rotation that the Yanks hoped rookie lefthander Ed Yarnall would fill. In five 1999 appearances, two of which were starts, Yarnall won his only decision and had a 3.71 ERA.

Jake Westbrook, 22, had a 42-25 record in four minor league seasons. In 1999, he was 11-5 with a 3.92 earned run average for Harrisburg of the Eastern League.

Selected Bibliography

Books

Alexander, Charles C. *Our Game—An American Baseball History.* New York: Henry Holt, 1991.

_____. *Rogers Hornsby: A Biography.* New York: Henry Holt, 1995.

_____. *Ty Cobb.* New York: Oxford University Press, 1984.

Allen, Maury. *Where Have You Gone, Joe DiMaggio?* New York: E.P. Dutton, 1975.

Allen, Mel, and Ed Fitzgerald. *You Can't Beat the Hours.* New York: Harper & Row, 1964.

Anderson, Dave. *Pennant Races: Baseball at Its Best.* New York: Doubleday, 1994.

Barber, Red. *1947—When All Hell Broke Loose.* Garden City, New York: Doubleday, 1982.

Bjarkman, Peter, ed. *Encyclopedia of Major League Baseball Team Histories.* Westport, Connecticut: Meckler, 1991.

Broeg, Bob, and William J. Miller, Jr. *Baseball from a Different Angle.* South Bend, Indiana: Diamond Communications, 1988.

Charlton, James. *The Baseball Chronology.* New York: Macmillan, 1991.

Connor, Anthony J. *Baseball for the Love of It.* New York: Macmillan, 1982.

Creamer, Robert W. *Babe, the Legend Comes to Life.* New York: Simon & Schuster, 1974.

_____. *Baseball in '41.* New York: Viking Penguin, 1991.

_____. *Stengel, His Life and Times.* New York: Simon & Schuster, 1984.

DiMaggio, Dom, and Bill Gilbert. *Real Grass Real Heroes.* New York: Kensington, 1990.

Feller, Bob, with Bill Gilbert. *Now Pitching Bob Feller.* New York: Harper Perennial, 1991.

Frommer, Harvey. *New York City Baseball.* New York: Macmillan, 1980.

Gallagher, Mark. *The Yankee Encyclopedia, Volume 3.* Champaign, Illinois: Sagamore, 1997.

Goldstein, Richard. *Spartan Seasons.* New York: Macmillan, 1980.

Golenbock, Peter. *Dynasty: The New York Yankees 1949–1964.* New York: Berkley, 1975.

Graham, Frank Jr. *A Farewell to Heroes.* New York: Viking Press, 1981.

Halberstam, David. *October 1964.* New York: Villard Books, 1994.

_____. *Summer of '49.* New York: William Morrow, 1989.

Helyar, John. *Lords of the Realm.* New York: Ballantine Books, 1994.

Henrich, Tommy, and Bill Gilbert. *Five O'Clock Lightning.* New York: Birch Lane Press, 1992.

Honig, Donald. *Baseball America.* New York: Macmillan, 1985.

_____. *Baseball When the Grass Was Real.* New York: Coward, McCann & Geoghegan, 1975.

Hynd, Noel. *The Giants of the Polo Grounds.* New York: Doubleday, 1988.

James, Bill. *The Bill James Historical Baseball Abstract.* New York: Villard Books, 1986.

Jennison, Christopher. *Wait 'Til Next Year.* New York: W.W. Norton, 1974.

Johnson, Lloyd, and Miles Wolff, eds. *The Encyclopedia of Minor League Baseball.* Durham, North Carolina: Baseball America, 1997.

Jordan, David M. *A Tiger in His Time: Hal Newhouser and the Burden of Wartime Ball.* South Bend, Indiana: Diamond Communications, 1990.

Kavanagh, Jack. *Walter Johnson, A Life.* South Bend, Indiana: Diamond Communications, 1995.

Kelley, Brent P. *They Too Wore Pinstripes: Interviews with 20 Glory-Days New York Yankees.* Jefferson, North Carolina: McFarland, 1998.

Kubek, Tony, and Terry Pluto. *Sixty-One: The*

Team, the Record, the Men. New York: Macmillan, 1987.

Kuklick, Bruce. *To Everything a Season.* Princeton, New Jersey: Princeton University Press, 1991.

LeConte, Walter. *The Ultimate New York Yankee Record Book.* New York: Leisure Press, 1984.

Leib, Fred. *Baseball as I Have Known It.* New York: Coward, McCann & Geoghegan, 1977.

Linn, Ed. *The Great Rivalry: The Yankees and the Red Sox 1901–1990.* New York: Ticknor and Fields, 1991.

Lowenfish, Lee. *The Imperfect Diamond.* New York: Da Capo Press, 1991.

Mann, Jack. *The Decline and Fall of the New York Yankees.* New York: Simon & Schuster, 1967.

Mayer, Ronald A. *The 1937 Newark Bears.* East Hanover, New Jersey: Vintage Press, 1980.

Mead, William B. *Even the Browns.* Chicago: Contemporary Books, 1978.

Miller, James Edward. *The Baseball Business: Pursuing Pennants and Profits in Baltimore.* Chapel Hill: The University of North Carolina Press, 1990.

Moffi, Larry. *This Side of Cooperstown: An Oral History of Major League Baseball in the 1950's.* Iowa City: University of Iowa Press, 1996.

Moore, Jack B. *Joe DiMaggio, Baseball's Yankee Clipper.* New York: Praeger, 1986.

Mosedale, John. *The Greatest of All: The 1927 New York Yankees.* New York: The Dial Press, 1974.

Neft, David S., and Richard M. Cohen. *The Sports Encyclopedia: Baseball, 18th ed.* New York: St. Martin's, 1998.

Oakley, J. Ronald. *Baseball's Last Golden Age, 1946–1960: The National Pastime in a Time of Glory and Change.* Jefferson, North Carolina: McFarland, 1994.

Okrent, Daniel, and Harris Lewine, eds. *The Ultimate Baseball Book.* Boston: Houghton Mifflin, 1979.

Peary, Danny, ed. *Cult Baseball Players.* New York: Simon & Schuster, 1990.

Reichler, Joseph L. *The Baseball Trade Register.* New York: Collier Books, 1984.

Reidenbaugh, Lowell. *Take Me Out to the Ball Park.* St. Louis: The Sporting News, 1983.

Rice, Damon. *Seasons Past.* New York: Praeger, 1976.

Ritter, Lawrence S. *The Glory of Their Times.* New York: Macmillan, 1966.

Robinson, Ray. *Iron Horse: Lou Gehrig in His Time.* New York: W.W. Norton, 1990.

Rosenthal, Harold. *The 10 Best Years of Baseball.* Chicago: Contemporary Books, 1979.

Seidel, Michael. *Streak: Joe DiMaggio and the Summer of '41.* New York, McGraw-Hill, 1988.

Seymour, Harold. *Baseball: The Golden Age.* New York: Oxford University Press, 1971.

Shatzkin, Mike. *The Ballplayers.* New York: William Morrow, 1990.

Smith, Robert. *Baseball in the Afternoon.* New York: Simon & Schuster, 1993.

Sowell, Mike. *The Pitch That Killed.* New York: Macmillan, 1989.

Spatz, Lyle. *New York Yankee Openers: An Opening Day History of Baseball's Most Famous Team, 1903–1996.* Jefferson, North Carolina: McFarland, 1997.

Thorn, John, and Pete Palmer, eds. *Total Baseball.* New York: Total Sports, 1999.

Tygiel, Jules. *Baseball's Great Experiment.* New York: Vintage Books, 1984.

Whittingham, Richard, ed. *The DiMaggio Albums.* New York: G.P. Putnam's Sons, 1989.

Williams, Joe. *The Joe Williams Reader,* edited by Peter Williams. Chapel Hill, North Carolina: Algonquin Books of Chapel Hill, 1989.

Wolff, Rick, ed. dir. *The Baseball Encyclopedia, 9th Ed.* New York: Macmillan, 1993.

Newspapers

Arizona Republic
Atlanta Journal-Constitution
Baltimore News American
Baltimore Sun
Boston Globe
Boston Herald
Boston Post
Chicago Tribune
Cincinnati Enquirer
Cleveland Plain Dealer
Dallas Morning News
Detroit Free Press
Detroit News

Houston Post
Kansas City Star
Los Angeles Times
Miami Herald
Milwaukee Journal
Minneapolis Tribune
New York American
New York Daily News
New York Herald
New York Herald Tribune
New York Journal American
New York Post
New York Press

New York Sun
New York Times
New York Tribune
New York World
New York World Telegram
Newark Star Ledger
Philadelphia Bulletin
Philadelphia Inquirer
Philadelphia Press

Pittsburgh Post-Gazette
San Diego Union
Seattle Post Intelligencer
Sporting Life
Sporting News
Toronto Globe and Mail
Washington Evening Star
Washington Post

Index